EU Justice and Home Affairs Law

Volume II: EU Criminal Law, Policing, and Civil Law

Fourth Edition

STEVE PEERS

Professor of Law
University of Essex

OXFORD

UNIVERSITY PRESS

OXFORD

UNIVERSITY PRESS

Great Clarendon Street, Oxford, OX2 6DP,
United Kingdom

Oxford University Press is a department of the University of Oxford.
It furthers the University's objective of excellence in research, scholarship,
and education by publishing worldwide. Oxford is a registered trade mark of
Oxford University Press in the UK and in certain other countries

First Edition published in 1999
Second Edition published in 2006
Third Edition published in 2011
Fourth Edition published in 2016

Impression: 1

Published in the United States of America by Oxford University Press
198 Madison Avenue, New York, NY 10016, United States of America

British Library Cataloguing in Publication Data
Data available

Library of Congress Control Number: 2016934360

ISBN (Vol I) 978-0-19-877683-3
ISBN (Vol II) 978-0-19-877684-0
ISBN (Set) 978-0-19-877685-7

Printed and bound by
CPI Group (UK) Ltd, Croydon, CR0 4YY

Preface to the Fourth Edition

In the six years since the entry into force of the Treaty of Lisbon, the European Union has developed its legal framework in the areas of police, criminal law, and civil cooperation, in particular in the areas of suspects' and victims' rights, cross-border evidence transfer, substantive criminal law, the creation and development of EU agencies, and the exchange of personal data for law enforcement. Most recently, the terrorist attacks in Paris and elsewhere in the EU have raised public concerns about security. The tension in this field between ensuring security and protection of civil liberties and human rights grows ever-sharper.

In this light, the time was ripe for a fourth edition of this book, now divided into two volumes in light of the increase in case law and legislation. The focus of this book is on the analysis of the developments since the Treaty of Lisbon entered into force and the previous third edition (completed in 2010).

As before, the book begins with an overview of the main themes of Justice and Home Affairs Law (in the policing, criminal, and civil law fields) and then examines the institutional framework in these fields, followed by chapters on each of the substantive areas of law. The chapters have been restructured to create a distinct chapter devoted to EU legislation on domestic criminal procedure, in particular the legislation on suspects' and victims' rights. As in previous editions, the focus is on the primary sources of EU JHA law, rather than the secondary literature; and the discussion of human rights in each chapter is not intended to be exhaustive, but to provide general background.

I have provided more in-depth analysis on selected areas of law where there is case law already or which will likely be important in practice, namely the European Arrest Warrant, suspects' rights, victims' rights, cross-border double jeopardy rules, and data retention.

I am, as before, indebted to Tony Bunyan and Statewatch for continued advice and assistance. Thanks also to Ognjenka Manojlovic for help with the tables and indexes.

I have endeavoured to state the law as of 14 December 2015. Updates and analysis of later developments in this field, keyed to this book, are available on the 'EU Law Analysis' blog which I edit.

Summary Table of Contents

Table of Cases

Table of Legislation

Directives

Recommendations

Decisions

Table of Proposed Legislation

EU MEASURES

Framework Decisions

Table of Abbreviations

CA	Court of Appeal
CATS	Comite Article trente-six
CEPS	Centre for European Policy Studies
CETS	Council of Europe Treaty Series
CFR	Common Frame of Reference
CFSP	Common Foreign and Security Policy
CIS	Customs Information System
CJEU	Court of Justice of the European Union
CMLR	Common Market Law Reports
CMLRev	Common Market Law Review
Coreper	Committee of Permanent Representatives
COSI	Committee on Internal Security
CYELS	Cambridge Yearbook of European Legal Studies
DCFR	Draft Common Frame of Reference
EAW	European Arrest Warrant
EC	European Community
ECB	European Central Bank
ECHR	European Convention on Human Rights
ECJ	European Court of Justice
ECR	European Court Reports
ECRIS	European Criminal Records Information System
EDU	Europol Drugs Unit
EEC	European Economic Community
EEW	European Evidence Warrant
EFARev	European Foreign Affairs Review
EIO	European Investigation Order
EJLR	European Journal of Law Reform
EJN	European Justice Network
ELJ	European Law Journal
ELRev	European Law Review
EP	European Parliament
EPC	European Political Cooperation
EPO	European Protection Order
EPPO	European Public Prosecutor's Office
ETS	European Treaty Series
EU	European Union
EUCPN	European Crime Prevention Network
FIU	Financial intelligence unit
ICCPR	International Covenant on Civil and Political Rights
ICLQ	International and Comparative Law Quarterly
IJCCLCJ	International Journal of Crime, Criminal Law and Criminal Justice
JHA	Justice and Home Affairs
LIEI	Legal Issues of European/Economic Integration
MEP	Member of the European Parliament

OECD	Organization for Economic Cooperation and Development
OJ	Official Journal
OLAF	Office européen de lutte antifraud
OUP	Oxford University Press
PIF	Protection of Financial Interests
PNR	Passenger name records
QB	Queen's Bench
QMV	Qualified majority vote
SIS	Schengen Information System
TEU	Treaty on European Union
TFEU	Treaty on the Functioning of the European Union
UCLAF	Unité communautaire de lutte antifraud
UK	United Kingdom
UN	United Nations
UNTOC	United Nations Convention against Transnational Organized Crime
VAT	Value Added Tax
VIS	Visa Information System
WLR	Weekly Law Reports
YEL	Yearbook of European Law

1

Introduction

Policing and criminal law are among the topics of greatest public concern. Given the sensitivity of such issues, and the initial perception that they were 'internal' issues with limited relevance, it was not surprising that they were among the last topics to be addressed in the European Union's integration project. But due to increased public anxiety about migration and security issues in particular following the terrorist attacks of 11 September 2001 and subsequent attacks on Member States' territories, Justice and Home Affairs (JHA) matters have moved up the EU's agenda. Similarly, increasing economic integration in Europe has led to the adoption of a number of measures addressing civil law issues.

This book sets out and analyses both the institutional arrangements for cooperation and the substantive law which has been adopted (and to some extent, is under discussion) in the fields of policing, criminal law, and civil cooperation. These fields are united by a series of four common and closely connected themes which are discussed in each chapter.

First and foremost, a central issue in EU policing and criminal law is the balance between protection of human rights and civil liberties on the one hand and the State interests in public order and security on the other. This balance has become particularly difficult to maintain since 11 September 2001, and in light of later attacks within the EU. Although human rights issues arise in all areas of EU law, both the rights to be secured and the public interests to be protected are particularly fundamental in the area of policing and criminal law. Therefore the relationship between EU law in the relevant fields and human rights obligations is analysed throughout this book, in order to assess whether the EU is striking the right balance between the protection of rights and the interests of security and control.[1]

A second theme, now largely of historical importance following the entry into force of the Treaty of Lisbon, is the complex and often controversial interaction and overlap between the supranational European Community legal order and the intergovernmental legal order of the EU's third pillar (as those legal orders were known before the Treaty of Lisbon came into force). This interaction and overlap still applies to the issues addressed in this book, because of the distinct institutional rules which applied to these areas in the past, and which were in force when much of the relevant legislation was adopted. Furthermore, this theme is linked to the first, because a lack of adequate judicial and parliamentary accountability and control led to an increased risk that the EU JHA measures adopted in the past did not ensure sufficient standards of human rights protection, and because the maintenance of unanimous voting by Member States

---

[1] See s 3 of chs 2–8.

before most JHA measures could be approved arguably contributed to the lowering of standards in JHA legislation. So the relationship between EU policing, criminal, and civil cooperation law and other EU law rules, in particular concerning the free movement of persons, is analysed throughout this book, in order to define the borderline between the two and to compare the relevant substantive law.[2]

The third theme is the continued dispute over the scope of the powers granted to the EU in the areas of policing, criminal, and civil cooperation law, because the issues in question are considered to be central to the sovereignty of each State, and because there has often been a great reluctance to amend the details of particular national laws. This theme is connected with the other two, because Member States are in some cases reluctant to change their laws because they wish to maintain a particular approach to human rights protection, and because the prior requirement for unanimous voting in policing and criminal law (before the entry into force of the Treaty of Lisbon) allowed any one Member State to insist on the narrowest interpretation of EU competence. Therefore the extent of EU competence is analysed throughout this book, in order to suggest a coherent interpretation of the scope of that competence in light of the text and context of the Treaties.[3]

Finally, the fourth theme is the convoluted territorial scope of EU policing, criminal, and civil cooperation law, which has several elements. First of all, the underlying objections of some Member States to any EU obligations in these areas of law resulted in the creation of a complex series of 'opt-outs' for the UK, Ireland, and Denmark. Secondly, with the 2004, 2007, and 2013 enlargements of the EU, there was a delay before some areas of this law applied to the new Member States. A similar delay will apply to any future enlargements. Thirdly, Norway, Iceland, Switzerland, and Liechtenstein are very closely associated with parts of EU law in this area, but not at all associated with the other parts of that law. Therefore, the territorial scope of EU policing, criminal law, and civil cooperation measures is explained throughout this book, so that readers can, if they wish, determine which rules apply to a particular State (or States).[4]

The entry into force of the Treaty of Amsterdam in 1999 created hopes that EU decision-making in this field of law would be more open, that judicial control in this area would be improved, and that the substantive EU measures to be adopted would strike an acceptable balance between the protection of human rights and civil liberties and the interests of ensuring public security. Unfortunately, in practice, taken as a whole, there were widespread doubts about the adequacy of the substantive standards adopted by the EU from 1999 to 2009 in many areas of the law in this field, and the democratic and judicial controls over the adoption, interpretation, and legality of EU acts were by and large clearly deficient. Therefore there was a continued imbalance in both the substantive and institutional law of the European Union in this field, favouring prosecutorial and repressive values and principles over other values and principles long established in European societies, and in particular over the human rights which the European Union claims to respect.

---

[2] See s 4 of chs 2–8.   [3] See s 2.3 of chs 2–8.   [4] See s 2.4 of chs 2–8.

However, the entry into force of the Treaty of Lisbon brought the possibility of fundamental change in this area, in light of the improved rules on decision-making, judicial accountability, and human rights protection set out in the Treaty. Over five years have passed since then, and there are marked improvements in the post-Lisbon legislation compared to the pre-Lisbon laws. However, most of the pre-Lisbon laws remain in force unamended. This volume aims to assess the strengths and weaknesses of the law in this complex and controversial field.

2

Institutional Framework

2.1 Introduction

As noted in chapter 2 of the first volume, the central theme in the institutional development of EU Justice and Home Affairs (JHA) law has been the debate as to whether the law in this area should be adopted and applied on an 'intergovernmental' basis, reserving essentially all power to the national governments of the Member States, or instead on the basis of the supranational 'Community method', which gives much of the power instead to the more integration-minded EU institutions (the Commission, the European Parliament, and the EU's Court of Justice). Before the Treaty of Lisbon, the EU framework for the adoption of policing and criminal law measures largely took an intergovernmental approach, allowing national executives to agree on measures without the usual level of control exercised by national parliaments and national courts, and without sufficient controls exercised by the European Parliament or the EU courts by way of a substitute. The key reason for establishing an intergovernmental system—and maintaining it for longer than it was maintained for immigration and asylum law—was (some) Member States' view that policing and criminal law issues are so central to their sovereignty that the supranational Community method should not be applied. The intergovernmental approach impacted on the content of policy: unsurprisingly, the national ministries took this opportunity to focus on law enforcement objectives, arguably at the expense of a more balanced approach. But measures in this area also raise acute issues concerning human rights protection, legitimacy, and accountability, simply due to their subject-matter, and the practical effectiveness of an intergovernmental approach was also questioned.

The Treaty of Lisbon tried to address concerns, by simplifying and normalizing the framework for decision-making and the jurisdiction of the EU courts, creating a single legal framework for legal instruments and their legal effects, and increasing the level of human rights protection by making the EU's Charter of Fundamental Rights binding and requiring the EU to accede to the European Convention on Human Rights (ECHR). However, as with prior Treaty amendments in this field, the trade-off for the greater application of the traditional 'Community method' to this area of JHA law was the greater capacity for those Member States (the UK, Ireland, and Denmark) which were reluctant to see this method applied to JHA law to stand aside and not participate fully in the EU's policies.

Because of continuing disputes between Member States on JHA institutional issues and the resulting renegotiations of the basic legal framework concerning JHA as set out in the Treaties establishing the EU, the institutional framework for EU JHA law is historically complex, in particular due to its use of different rules over time regarding decision-making, jurisdiction of the EU courts, legal instruments and their legal effect, and territorial scope. This chapter examines first of all the historical development of the institutional framework in this area, while fully examining the interpretation of the current rules as set out in the Treaty of Lisbon. It next looks at issues of EC and EU competence, the rules concerning the non-participation of some Member States from aspects of JHA cooperation, and the inclusion of some non-Member States (Norway, Iceland, Switzerland, Liechtenstein) in aspects of those rules. The chapter then provides an overview of: the rules concerning human rights protection in EU law; the division and overlap between the rules concerning JHA cooperation and other areas of EU law; the use of the EU budget to fund JHA cooperation; and the external relations aspects of JHA cooperation. Each of Chapters 3–8 then follows the same structure, examining six particular topics from the same perspective, as well as analysing in detail (except for less detail as regards civil law) the particular EU measures in each field. This chapter also provides a specific overview of the issues of transparency and legitimacy in EU Justice and Home Affairs Law.

Due to the division of the book into two volumes, the institutional chapter in this volume focuses on the institutional issues of particular relevance to policing and criminal law. The general JHA institutional framework and the issues of particular relevance to civil law (which has traditionally been bracketed with immigration and asylum issues) are discussed in the institutional chapter in volume 1.

2.2 Overview of the Institutional Framework

The Treaties establishing the EU first made specific mention of policing and criminal law issues in the Treaty on European Union (TEU), or Maastricht Treaty, which entered into force 1 November 1993, which, inter alia, set up a special legal framework for the adoption of rules concerning Justice and Home Affairs.[1] Because of the different rules governing the adoption of measures concerning economic integration in the Community treaties, as compared to the rules concerning the Common Foreign and Security Policy (CFSP) and JHA, it was often suggested that the TEU created a sort of 'Greek temple' structure with 'three pillars', which comprised in turn the Community treaties (first pillar), CFSP (second pillar), and JHA (third pillar). This temple structure was held together by common core rules in the TEU concerning the foundations of the Union on the one hand,[2] and the final provisions of the TEU (addressing issues such as accession to the EU and amendment of the Treaties) on the other.[3]

Thirdly, the Treaty of Amsterdam, which entered into force 1 May 1999,[4] transferred part of the third pillar (dealing with immigration, asylum, and civil law) to the EC Treaty, subject to specific rules which differed considerably, at least initially, from the normal rules which applied to the first pillar.[5] This Treaty also significantly amended the rules applicable to the issues which remained in the TEU's third pillar, namely police

---

[1] Respectively Arts J–J.11 TEU and K–K.9 TEU, as originally introduced by the Maastricht Treaty.
[2] Arts A–F TEU, as originally introduced by the Maastricht Treaty.
[3] Arts L–S TEU, as originally introduced by the Maastricht Treaty.
[4] See further II:2.2.2 below.   [5] See further I:2.2.2.

and criminal law cooperation. Alongside these changes, this Treaty also integrated the substantive rules (the 'Schengen *acquis*') which had been developed by a core group of Member States outside the EU and EC legal framework, due to the absence of consensus among all Member States over whether all internal border checks between Member States should be abolished. The Schengen *acquis* mainly comprised rules on border control and visas, but also addressed some policing and criminal law issues.[6]

Next, the Treaty of Nice, which entered into force 1 February 2003, made modest changes to issues relating to JHA cooperation, as it mainly focused on other amendments to the Treaties which were believed to be necessary to prepare the EU for substantial enlargement, which took place subsequently in 2004 and 2007.

Finally, the Treaty of Lisbon, which entered into force on 1 December 2009, transferred the remaining third pillar to the first pillar and made a number of changes to all aspects of JHA cooperation.[7] The European Community and the European Union, previously legally distinct entities, were merged into a single entity called the European Union. As a consequence, the EC Treaty was renamed the Treaty on the Functioning of the European Union (TFEU), and the TEU was revised considerably, so that it now contains the basic rules on the institutional foundations of the Union along with (as before) the detailed rules (as amended) on the Union's Common Foreign and Security Policy.

Since the Articles of the TEU have been amended significantly twice, this book refers throughout to the Maastricht Treaty version as the 'original TEU', the Treaty of Amsterdam version as the 'previous TEU', and the Treaty of Lisbon version as the 'revised TEU'.

Although the Treaty of Lisbon transformed the institutional framework applicable to Justice and Home Affairs issues, it is still necessary to examine the previous institutional frameworks briefly, because many pre-Lisbon measures still remain in force, and the legal effect of those measures has been preserved pursuant to transitional rules set out in the Treaty of Lisbon.[8]

There were four key distinctions between the Community method and the intergovernmental system for adoption of EU law. The first distinction was the role of the EU's political institutions. Within the first pillar, the Commission, made up of persons appointed by the Council or the European Council (see below) and approved by the directly elected European Parliament, had a monopoly over proposals for measures in the vast majority of cases. The Council, made up of ministers from Member States, acted to adopt measures by a qualified majority vote (QMV) in a sizeable majority of cases. Although the job of implementing Community legislation was in principle left to the Member States, there were cases where implementing powers were conferred on the Commission, or, in exceptional cases, upon the Council.[9] Also, the European Parliament had a substantial role in the adoption of legislation, in particular by means of the so-called 'co-decision' procedure, which gave it an equal role with the Council in

---

[6] For the text of the Schengen *acquis*, see [2000] OJ L 239. On the process of integrating the Schengen *acquis* into the EC and EU legal order, see I:2.2.2.2.

[7] See II:2.2.3 below.   [8] On those rules, see II:2.2.3.3 below.

[9] See Art 202 EC (now Art 291 TFEU after the Treaty of Lisbon). See further I:2.2.2.1.

the procedure for agreeing a large proportion of legislation.[10] However, in the 'intergovernmental' process, the Commission had no power of initiative or at least had to share its monopoly with Member States. The Council almost invariably had to vote unanimously, giving each Member State's representative a veto. The EP was at best consulted.

Secondly, there were distinctions as regards the EU's Court of Justice. Within EC law, the Court had extensive jurisdiction, particularly over: actions to enforce EC law, where the Commission sued the Member States for a declaration that they have breached their EC obligations;[11] references for a preliminary ruling on the interpretation or validity of EC law, which could be sent by any national court or tribunal;[12] and annulment actions against acts of the EC institutions.[13] There was also a special procedure applicable in advance of the EC's conclusion of an international treaty, to determine whether conclusion of that treaty would be compatible with EC law.[14] In contrast, the third pillar provided for special rules which significantly restricted the Court's jurisdiction.

Thirdly, there were distinctions as regards the legal instruments used. EC law applies via means of Directives, Regulations, and Decisions.[15] In contrast, EU third pillar law used different instruments, although those instruments changed with the adoption of the Treaty of Amsterdam.[16]

Finally, there was a distinction as regard the effect of the law. EC law measures had 'direct effect', meaning that they are applicable in national courts and could be directly invoked as part of national law if they were clear, precise, and unconditional (although Directives did not have direct effect against private parties). National law also had to be interpreted to be consistent with Directives 'as far as possible'. Furthermore, there were detailed rules on the remedies which had to be adopted to give effect to EC law, including, in certain conditions, a right of damages against a Member State which breached EC law. Finally, EC law was supreme over Member States' national law, requiring that conflicting national provisions be set aside. As we shall see, these principles did not fully apply to third pillar measures.

In either the first or the third pillar, the EU institutions could only act where the relevant Treaties conferred a power upon them. Each legal base conferring power set out the limits of the relevant power and the applicable decision-making procedure.

With the entry into force of the Treaty of Lisbon, the previous 'first pillar' rules apply to all policing and criminal law measures adopted afterward. Since this Treaty also subsumed the Community into the Union, this book refers in most cases to 'EU' legislation and policy, except in special cases where it is necessary to distinguish between the Community and the Union for historical purposes.

---

[10] The rules of the co-decision procedure were set out in Art 251 EC (now the ordinary legislative procedure, as set out in Art 294 TFEU, after the Treaty of Lisbon).

[11] Art 226 EC; see also Art 227 EC (Member States suing Member States) and Art 228 EC (power to impose fines and penalties if Member States disobey an Art 226 ruling). See now Arts 258–60 TFEU after the Treaty of Lisbon, which has also amended these provisions to some extent.

[12] Art 234 EC, now Art 267 TFEU after the Treaty of Lisbon.

[13] Art 230 EC. See also Art 232 EC (actions for failure to act) and Art 235 EC (actions for damages against the EC institutions). These provisions are respectively now Arts 263, 265, and 268 TFEU after the Treaty of Lisbon.

[14] Art 300 EC (now Art 218(11) TFEU after the Treaty of Lisbon).

[15] See Art 249 EC (now Art 288 TFEU after the Treaty of Lisbon).   [16] II:2.2.2 below.

2.2.1 Framework prior to the Treaty of Amsterdam

2.2.1.1 Framework prior to the Maastricht Treaty

Informal cooperation on JHA matters began in the 1960s and 1970s, when various drafts of a Convention addressing fraud against the EEC budget were considered, although not agreed.[17] Member States also signed Conventions as far back as 1968 on the mutual recognition of companies and on the jurisdiction over and recognition of civil and commercial judgments, followed by a Convention in 1980 on choice of law in contractual disputes.[18] Such Conventions were partly foreseen by Article 220 EEC (later Article 293 EC, and then repealed by the Treaty of Lisbon), which called upon the Member States, 'insofar as is necessary', to negotiate treaties between themselves on certain specified matters which were likely to assist the Communities' initial objective of market integration.

Prior to the Maastricht Treaty, the formal role of the EC institutions in JHA cooperation was nil. All negotiations were treated as discussions between the Member States, and any resulting acts were classified as public international law, not EC law. All agreements had to be reached unanimously. The Commission was an observer in these talks and the EP was occasionally asked for its opinion. Nor was there any role for the EC institutions in the Schengen measures. As for the EU's Court of Justice, there was no interest in giving it jurisdiction to interpret intergovernmental measures, except for those dealing with civil cooperation.[19]

Furthermore, only a limited range of instruments were used during this 'informal' intergovernmental period. The only hard-law instruments adopted were Conventions, which are a standard form of international treaty. Although ten such Conventions were agreed before 1993 (excluding the Schengen Conventions, as they were not in principle agreed among all Member States), mostly within the framework of 'European Political Cooperation' (EPC), the original system for EU foreign policy cooperation, only the Rome and Dublin Conventions (dealing respectively with conflict of law in contractual disputes and allocation of responsibility over asylum applications) were ever ratified.[20] Also the Brussels Convention on jurisdiction over and recognition of civil and commercial judgments, linked to the EEC Treaty by Article 220 EEC, was ratified.[21]

Finally, the legal effect of the various measures adopted was up to national law to determine. So those Member States taking a 'dualist' view of the effect of public international law required changes to their national law before a Convention could take effect in their domestic legal order, and those taking a 'monist' view of public international law saw each Convention as an essential part of their legal system. Since the soft law measures were not binding, their effect in practice depended upon how many Member States wished to implement them.

---

[17] For further detail, see p 9 of the first edition of this book.   [18] See further ch 8 of this volume.
[19] See II:2.2.1.2 below.
[20] See ch 8 of volume 2 and ch 5 of volume 1 respectively; on the other Conventions see ch 3 of volume 1.
[21] See ch 8 of this volume.

2.2.1.2 *Framework in the Maastricht Treaty*

The intergovernmental approach was entrenched by the Maastricht Treaty, which effect-ively established a 'formal intergovernmental' system for JHA cooperation. While some Member States wished substantial amounts of this cooperation to take place within the framework of the supranational EC Treaty, other Member States wanted no application of the EC method whatsoever to JHA issues. All issues relating to civil law, criminal law, and policing were subject to this intergovernmental system.

As noted above, the Maastricht Treaty consisted of a single Treaty—the Treaty on European Union—ostensibly governing all aspects of integration among the EC's Member States, but this Treaty contained three separate approaches to integration, commonly referred to as 'pillars'.[22] The rules governing the bulk of JHA cooperation constituted the third pillar.

The specific provisions of the original version of the third pillar rules began with the original Article K TEU, which formally established JHA cooperation as part of the European Union process. Article K.1 then listed nine items which the Member States regarded as matters of 'common interest', '[f]or the purposes of achieving the objectives of the Union, in particular for the free movement of persons, and without prejudice to the powers of the European Community', which included: combating drug addiction; combating international fraud; civil judicial cooperation; criminal judicial cooper-ation; customs cooperation; and police cooperation.

Next, the original Article K.2 stated that JHA cooperation had to be 'dealt with in compliance with' the European Convention on Human Rights (ECHR), and asserted that the EU Treaty could not affect 'the exercise of the responsibilities incumbent upon Member States with regard to the maintenance of law and order and the safeguarding of internal security'.

The original Article K.3(2) TEU provided that the Council, not the Member States, was to adopt JHA measures, except for Conventions, which the Council was to draw up and recommend to Member States for adoption in accordance with each Member State's constitutional requirements. The Council had to adopt measures unanimously, except for procedural questions, measures implementing Joint Actions (see below) and measures implementing Conventions, which had to be adopted by a two-thirds vote of Member States unless the relevant Convention provided otherwise.

The Commission had a *shared* power along with the Member States to make propos-als in the first six areas of common interest, but only the Member States could make proposals in the other three (criminal judicial cooperation; customs cooperation; and police cooperation). The original Article K.6 TEU gave the EP only limited rights, in particular the right to be 'regularly inform[ed]' of discussions and 'consult[ed]' by the Member State holding the rotating Council Presidency on the 'principal aspects' of discussions.

---

[22] On the 'pillar structure', see R McMahon, 'Maastricht's Third Pillar: Load-Bearing or Purely Decorative?' (1995) 22 LIEI 1:51; P Muller-Graff, 'The Legal Bases of the Third Pillar and its Position in the Framework of the Union Treaty' (1994) 29 CMLRev 493; D Curtin, 'The Constitutional Structure of the Union: A Europe of Bits and Pieces' (1993) 30 CMLRev 17; and E Denza, *The Intergovernmental Pillars of the European Union* (OUP, 2002), ch 1.

Besides Conventions, the original Article K.3(2)(a) allowed the Council to adopt 'joint positions'; the original Article K.3(2)(b) allowed for the adoption of 'joint actions' where the Union's objectives could be better achieved by such action than by the Member States acting alone; and Article K.5 referred to 'common positions', which Member States were to defend 'within international organizations and at international conferences'.

In practice, ten Conventions were agreed during the Maastricht period,[23] along with five Protocols on the Court of Justice[24] and four other Protocols.[25] Two Conventions concerned civil law, and both were replaced by Community acts before Member States began ratifying them.[26] The remaining eight concerned criminal law, customs, and policing.

Five of these eight Conventions have entered into force, although two of those five Conventions were then subsequently replaced by measures adopted during the Amsterdam era of the third pillar (between 1999 and 2009).[27]

The first Convention to come into force was the Europol Convention on 1 October 1998, followed shortly by the Protocols to that Convention on jurisdiction for the Court of Justice (29 December 1998) and on immunities of Europol staff (1 July 1999), at which point Europol began operations.[28] The Convention and its Protocols were subsequently replaced by another third pillar act, adopted under the legal framework established by the Treaty of Amsterdam, as from 1 January 2010.[29] Secondly, the Convention on fraud against the EC budget entered into force on 17 October 2002, along with the first substantive Protocol to that Convention and the Protocol conferring jurisdiction on the Court of Justice. The Second Protocol to the Convention then came into force on 19 May 2009. Some of the newer Member States have not yet ratified the Convention and its Protocols.[30] Thirdly, the Convention on corruption came into force on 29 September 2005, following its ratification by the last of the first fifteen Member States on 30 June 2005. All except two of the newer Member States have ratified it.[31]

Fourthly, the Customs Information System (CIS) Convention, and the Protocol to this Convention on Court of Justice jurisdiction, entered into force on Christmas Day 2005. Previously, pursuant to an Agreement on provisional application of the Convention, the Convention had provisionally applied to eight of the first fifteen Member States

---

[23] The Conventions on Europol, the Customs Information System, fraud ([1995] OJ C 316/1, 33, and 48), service of documents ([1997] OJ C 261/1), parental responsibility ([1998] OJ C 221/1), customs cooperation ([1998] OJ C 24/1), driving disqualification ([1998] OJ C 216/1), corruption ([1997] OJ C 195/1), consented extradition ([1995] OJ C 78/1), and disputed extradition ([1996] OJ C 313/11).

[24] Protocols to the Europol, the Customs Information System, fraud, service of documents, and parental responsibility Conventions (respectively [1996] OJ C 299/1, [1997] OJ C 151/15, [1997] OJ C 151/1, [1997] OJ C 261/18, and [1998] OJ C 221/19).

[25] Protocol on Europol privileges and immunities ([1997] OJ C 221/1), First Protocol to fraud Convention ([1996] OJ C 313/1); Second Protocol to fraud Convention ([1997] OJ C 221/12), and Protocol to Customs Information System Convention ([1999] OJ C 91/1).

[26] These were the Conventions on service of documents and parental responsibility. See II:8.2.2.2 below.

[27] On this replacement process, see II:2.2.2 below.

[28] [1999] OJ C 185/1. The Convention and Protocols also entered into force for all of the Member States which joined the EU in 2004 and 2007. Further Protocols to the Convention were also adopted after the entry into force of the Treaty of Amsterdam: [2000] OJ C 358/1, [2002] OJ C 312/2, and [2004] OJ C 2/1.

[29] [2009] OJ L 121/37.   [30] See Appendix I.   [31] The exceptions are Croatia and Malta.

from 1 November 2000, and to a further six of the first fifteen Member States subsequently, so the CIS system became operational in March 2003.[32] A later Protocol to this Convention, adopted in 1999, came into force on 14 April 2008; it also applies to all Member States.[33] However, like the Europol Convention, the CIS Convention and the 1999 Protocol have been replaced by a Decision adopted in 2009.[34] Finally, the Naples II Convention on customs cooperation came into force on 25 June 2009, and has been ratified by all Member States.

Of the three criminal, customs, and policing Conventions that have not entered into force, all are subject to possible early application, permitting Member States which have ratified a Convention to declare that the Convention is applicable in the interim to relations with those other Member States which had also ratified it and made the same declaration. Taking the earliest Conventions first, fourteen of the first fifteen Member States and several of the new Member States have ratified the 1995 and 1996 extradition Conventions, and many of these Member States apply the Conventions in advance of ratification.[35] However, these two Conventions have been replaced by the Framework Decision on the European Arrest Warrant with effect from 1 January 2004, except for certain derogations allowing for the possible continued application of the Conventions in specified cases.[36] Finally, the driving disqualification Convention has only been ratified by a small number of Member States, although some of those states apply it in advance of its entry into force.[37]

In most cases, the Council adopted an explanatory report on interpretation of Conventions and Protocols, but the interpretation advocated by such reports is only persuasive, not mandatory.[38] It should be kept in mind that the Conventions did not apply automatically to the ten Member States that joined the EU in 2004 as from 1 May 2004. Instead, the newer Member States had to accede to the Conventions;[39] the ratification position has been set out above. On the other hand, the Conventions applied to Romania and Bulgaria (and will apply to Croatia) pursuant to Council Decisions adopted following their accession to the EU.[40]

Thirty-nine Joint Actions were adopted during the Maastricht period. They largely concerned criminal law and policing, with a few (ten) addressing asylum funding or aspects of visas or immigration law. None concerned civil cooperation. Only fourteen are still in force,[41] and the Commission has proposed to repeal a further seven, due to

---

[32] [1995] OJ C 316/58. For details of the CIS in practice, see II:7.6.1.2 below.

[33] A further Protocol was agreed after the entry into force of the Treaty of Amsterdam: [2003] OJ C 139/1.

[34] [2009] OJ L 323/20, replacing the Convention and its substantive Protocols from 27 May 2011 (Art 36).

[35] For ratification and application details, see Appendix I.

[36] [2002] OJ L 190/1. See II:3.5 below.

[37] For ratification and application details, see Appendix I.

[38] For instance, see Case 157/80 *Rinkau* [1980] ECR 1391 on the explanatory report to the Brussels Convention. The Court of Justice has taken into account the explanatory report to a third pillar Convention in one case: Case C-388/08 PPU *Leymann and Pustovarov* [2008] ECR I-8993, para 74. No reports were drawn up for the Europol and CIS Conventions or their Protocols, or the Court of Justice Protocol to the fraud Convention. For a list of these explanatory reports, see Appendix I.

[39] See further II:2.2.5.3 below.   [40] Ibid.

[41] For the list of Joint Actions still in force, see Appendix II. Another one will be repealed as from 4 Oct 2016: see Art 14(1) of Dir 2014/42 ([2014] OJ L 127/39).

obsolescence.[42] Twelve Joint Actions are no longer in force because they had lapsed once the funding programmes they established came to an end or were replaced,[43] and two others lapsed once Europol began operations.[44] The two Joint Actions regarding a uniform residence permit and airport transit visas were replaced by EC Regulations;[45] three other Joint Actions were replaced by Framework Decisions;[46] three were replaced by Decisions;[47] one was repealed by a Directive;[48] and the unpublished Joint Action on the 'Balkan Drug Route' is assumed to have lapsed.[49]

Joint Positions fell into desuetude, with only two ever adopted.[50] A further three were apparently adopted, but it was not clear whether these were instead 'Common Positions' as provided for by Article K.5.[51] The Council also adopted a number of Decisions and many soft-law Resolutions, Conclusions, and Recommendations during the Maastricht period.

What was the legal effect of these measures? As noted above, Conventions were an established instrument of public international law, so there was no doubt that they were binding on each Member State at international level once ratified. But in the absence of any indication that the EU Treaty aimed (at the time) to create a supranational legal system like the Community's, it was presumably still left up to each Member State to determine the legal effect of a Convention in its national law.

There was ongoing controversy over the legal effect of Joint Actions, with thirteen of the first fifteen Member States backing the Council legal service's view that all Joint Actions were 'obligatory in law and that the extent of the obligation on the Member States depends on the content and the terms of each Joint Action', and two (the UK and Portugal) arguing that Joint Actions 'were not automatically…legally binding…the whole question of whether [a Joint Action] was legally binding depended on its actual text'.[52] The Council legal service invited the Court of Justice to settle this point in a legal action brought by the Commission to annul a Joint Action, but the ECJ implicitly (and rightly) followed its Advocate-General's advice that the issue was irrelevant to the

---

[42] COM (2014) 715, 28 Nov 2014.

[43] II:2.6 below. Technically, one of these twelve (establishing the 'Sherlock' programme) did not lapse as such, but rather was repealed by the Joint Action establishing the 'Odysseus' programme (see ibid).

[44] See II:7.8 below.   [45] See further I:4.7 and I:6.9.

[46] The Joint Actions on trafficking in persons and sexual exploitation, private corruption, organized crime, and racism (respectively [1997] OJ L 63/2, [1998] OJ L 358/2, [1998] OJ L 351/1, and [1996] OJ L 185/5); for the replacement Framework Decisions, see [2002] OJ L 203/1, [2004] OJ L 13/44, [2003] OJ L 192/54, [2008] OJ L 300/42, and [2008] OJ L 328/55. On these measures, see II:5.5.1.2 below.

[47] The Decisions on liaison officers ([2003] OJ L 67/27; see II:7.6.3 below), synthetic drugs ([2005] OJ L 127/32; see II:5.5.1.2 below), and the European Judicial Network ([2008] OJ L 348/130; see II:3.8 below), replacing Joint Actions on the same topics (respectively [1996] OJ L 268/2, [1997] OJ L 167/1, and ([1998] OJ L 191/4).

[48] The Joint Action on money laundering ([1998] OJ L 333/1), repealed as from 4 Oct 2015: see Art 14(1) of Dir 2014/42 ([2014] OJ L 127/39). It had previously been amended by Art 5 of the Framework Decision on money laundering ([2001] OJ L 182/1). See II:3.6.2 and II:3.7.4 below.

[49] This Joint Action was unpublished; see the press release of the Fisheries Council, 19–20 Dec 1996.

[50] Joint Position on the definition of 'refugee' ([1996] OJ L 63/2) and on joint training of airline staff and joint assistance in non-EU airports ([1996] OJ L 281/1). These measures have not been repealed.

[51] [1997] OJ L 279/1; [1997] OJ L 320/1; and [1999] OJ L 87/1. The first two concerned planned OECD and Council of Europe Conventions on corruption, and the third concerned a planned UN Convention on organized crime. They have never been repealed, but are obsolete as the treaties in question have now been drawn up.

[52] Outcome of proceedings of K.4 Committee of 7 Apr 1995 (Council doc 6684/95, 4 May 1995).

case before it.[53] In practice, most Joint Actions appeared to use mandatory language, although not necessarily in every clause. As for Joint Positions, it is not clear what legal effect they had; the Joint Position on the definition of 'refugee' stated expressly that it would 'not bind the legislative authorities or affect decisions of the judicial authorities of the Member States'.[54] The Council appeared to believe that Common Positions could bind Member States.[55] In any event, the legal effect of these third pillar measures will change if they are amended after the entry into force of the Treaty of Lisbon, pursuant to the transitional rules established by that Treaty.[56]

As for the Court of Justice, during the Maastricht era, the Court had no *mandatory* jurisdiction over third pillar matters.[57] However, Article K.3(2)(c) EU provided that the Court *could* be given jurisdiction to interpret or settle disputes concerning Conventions, 'in accordance with such arrangements' as each Convention might (or might not) lay down. There was no provision for jurisdiction of the Court over any other third pillar measures. In practice, there were fierce disputes between the Member States on the role of the Court of Justice in third pillar Conventions not long after the Maastricht Treaty entered into force. Eventually this issue was settled by agreement in 1996 on standard rules to be used for criminal law and policing Conventions, beginning with the Europol, CIS, and fraud Conventions.[58] Three further Conventions on criminal and customs cooperation (concerning corruption, driving disqualifications, and customs operations) also ultimately contained a role for the Court in receiving preliminary rulings concerning each Convention.[59] On the other hand, the Court was not given jurisdiction to interpret the two extradition Conventions (which have not entered into force), although it nonetheless touched on their interpretation in the context of cases concerning the Framework Decision on the European Arrest Warrant, which replaced them for most purposes.[60] All of these specific rules have become moot, since the end of the transitional period on the Court's jurisdiction established by the Treaty of Lisbon on 1 December 2014. Since that point, the ordinary rules on the Court's jurisdiction apply.[61]

Two civil law Conventions agreed during the Maastricht period provided for *sui generis* jurisdiction for the Court of Justice.[62] However, these two Conventions were replaced before they ever entered into force by EC Regulations agreed shortly after the entry into force of the Treaty of Amsterdam,[63] and so their rules on the Court's

---

[53] Case C-170/96 *Commission v Council* [1998] ECR I-2763.   [54] N 50 above.

[55] For instance, see the text of the Common Position on the UN organized crime Convention, n 51 above.

[56] See II:2.2.3.3 below.

[57] For further details of the Court's jurisdiction during this period, see the first edition of this book, pp 27–9, and S Peers, 'Who's Judging the Watchmen?' The Judicial System of the Area of Freedom, Security and Justice' (2000) 18 YEL 337 at 343–50.

[58] See Protocols to these Conventions, n 24 above. The Court of Justice Protocol to the fraud Convention also applies to the substantive Protocols to that Convention, n 25 above.

[59] N 23 above.

[60] Cases C-296/08 *Santesteban Goicoechea* [2008] ECR I-6307 and *Leymann and Pustovarov*, n 38 above. On the substance of these cases, see II:3.5 below.

[61] See II:2.2.3.3 below.

[62] The Conventions and Protocols on the service of documents and matrimonial matters, nn 23 and 24 above.

[63] Regs 1347/2000 on jurisdiction over and enforcement of matrimonial and custody judgments ([2000] OJ L 160/19) and 1348/2000 on service of documents ([2000] OJ L 160/37). See further ch 8 of this volume.

jurisdiction are not further considered here as they were ultimately irrelevant. However, two earlier civil cooperation Conventions which did enter into force were subject to special rules on the jurisdiction of the Court of Justice, pursuant to separate Protocols: the Brussels Convention on civil jurisdiction and recognition of civil and commercial judgments and the Rome Convention on conflict of laws in contract.[64] These Conventions have both now been replaced by EC Regulations,[65] entailing eventually the application of the usual rules on the Court of Justice's jurisdiction (after the entry into force of the Treaty of Lisbon). However, it should be noted that the Brussels Convention still applies to litigation commenced before the replacement Regulation applied,[66] and the Rome Convention still applies to contracts concluded before the replacement Regulation applied,[67] as well as to Denmark.[68] In practice, over a hundred cases on the Brussels Convention were referred to the Court of Justice from national courts since the relevant Protocol to that Convention entered into force on 1 September 1975, and several cases have been referred to the Court of Justice regarding the Rome Convention.[69]

2.2.2 Treaty of Amsterdam

During negotiation of the Treaty of Amsterdam,[70] amendments to the JHA provisions of the TEU became a key issue, in particular on the grounds that: the objectives of JHA cooperation were not clear; the institutional roles were ill-defined and left in part for future negotiation; the legal effect of the new instruments was ambiguous; and aspects of the third pillar/first pillar borderline were controversial.

However, Member States were split on the issue of how decisively to introduce elements of the Community method to this area, and how much intergovernmentalism to retain. The result was a complex compromise, splitting up the JHA framework during this period between the rules governing the adoption of immigration, asylum, and civil law measures on the one hand, and the rules on the adoption of policing and criminal law measures, on the other. The former issues were transferred to the first pillar, where they were addressed by new rules inserted as Title IV of Part Three of the EC Treaty ('Title IV').[71] The latter issues were still addressed within the framework of the third pillar, but the relevant rules were comprehensively amended.[72] The Treaty of Nice subsequently made limited amendments to each set of rules.[73]

---

[64] See the consolidated texts of the Brussels Convention and Protocols ([1998] OJ C 27/1) and the Rome Convention and its Protocols ([2005] OJ C 334/1). The latter Convention and its Protocols have been extended to the Member States which joined the EU in 2004 and 2007: see [2005] C 169/1 and [2007] OJ L 347/1.

[65] Regs 44/2001 ([2001] OJ L 12/1) and 593/2008 ([2008] OJ L 177/6).

[66] The date of application of Reg 44/2001 was 1 Mar 2002 (Art 76). The Brussels Convention was replaced as regards Denmark only later, by a treaty between Denmark and the EC that applied from 1 July 2007 ([2005] OJ L 299/61; [2006] OJ L 120/22). See further II:2.2.5.2 below.

[67] Reg 593/2008 applied from 17 Dec 2009 (Art 28).

[68] Denmark is not covered by Reg 593/2008 due to its opt-out from EU civil law (see II:2.2.5.2 below).

[69] See II:8.5.3 below. The relevant Protocols concerning the Court's jurisdiction over the Rome Convention entered into force 1 Aug 2004, and Ireland opted out of them.

[70] [1997] OJ C 340; in force 1 May 1999.   [71] Arts 61–9 EC.

[72] Previous Arts 29–42 TEU (previous Title VI of the TEU).

[73] [2001] OJ C 80; in force 1 Feb 2003. Within the third pillar, the Treaty of Nice amended Art 29 TEU, added a new Art 31(2) TEU, and revised the rules relating to enhanced cooperation (Arts 40, 40a, and 40b replaced Art 40 TEU).

In general, the role of the 'supranational' EU institutions (the Commission, the EP, and the EU courts) increased with the entry into force of the Treaty of Amsterdam and increased further in practice after that, as evidenced in particular by the Commission's decision to create a Directorate-General for Justice and Home Affairs in 2000. Nevertheless, Member States still retained greater control over all aspects of JHA integration than they did over economic integration within the Community framework.

For the third pillar, the basic rules on decision-making and legal instruments were set out in the previous Article 34 TEU. The Council still had to act unanimously when adopting third pillar measures, but implementing measures had to be adopted by another form of vote (see below). The Commission increased its power, gaining a shared initiative with the Member States for the items in the remaining third pillar. In practice, it was active in using this initiative, proposing many of the most important criminal law measures adopted by the Council.[74] As before, Member States holding the rotating Council Presidency were active in making proposals; in several cases, there were joint proposals from several Member States, particularly from several Member States holding the Council Presidency in succession.

As for the EP, Article 39 EU retained its Maastricht-era powers, but the Treaty of Amsterdam also added the right to be consulted by the Council before adopting most third pillar legal acts (with the exception of Common Positions—see below), within a time-limit that the Council laid down, although this period had to be at least three months. However, as might be expected, the opinions of the EP had limited if any impact upon Council third pillar measures.

The Treaty required third pillar implementing measures to be adopted by the Council, by means of QMV for implementing Decisions and a two-thirds vote for implementing Conventions.[75] However, on several occasions the Council conferred implementing powers upon the Commission.[76]

In practice, the use of Conventions was phased out after the Treaty of Amsterdam provisions entered into force. Only one new Convention was adopted, shortly after the Amsterdam provisions took effect,[77] along with five new Protocols to pre-existing Conventions.[78]

All of the six Conventions and Protocols adopted after the Treaty of Amsterdam entered into force, since that Treaty required that Conventions entered into force once at least half of the Member States had ratified them, with respect to the ratifying Member States, 'unless they provide otherwise'.[79] The 2000 Convention on mutual assistance and its Protocol needed eight of the first fifteen Member States to ratify them

---

[74] See, for instance, the Framework Decisions on the European Arrest Warrant and on terrorism ([2002] OJ L 190/1 and [2002] OJ L 164/3; see II:3.5 and II:5.5.1.2 below).

[75] Art 34(2)(c) and (d) EU.

[76] For example, see the Decisions on management of the project to establish a second-generation Schengen Information System (SIS II: [2001] OJ L 328/1), and on implementation of the SIS II ([2007] OJ L 205/63).

[77] Convention on mutual assistance on criminal matters ([2000] OJ C 197/1). See further II:3.6.1 and II:7.9 below.

[78] See three Protocols amending the Europol Convention ([2000] C 358/1, [2002] OJ C 312/1, and [2004] OJ C 2/1); the Protocol to EU Mutual Assistance Convention ([2001] OJ C 326/1); and the Protocol to the CIS Convention, regarding customs files ([2003] C 139/1).

[79] Art 34(2)(d), previous TEU.

in order to enter into force,[80] and obtained the requisite number of ratifications in 2005, following which the Convention entered into force on 23 August 2005 and the Protocol entered into force on 6 October 2005.[81] However, several Member States have yet to ratify the Convention and/or the Protocol. Part of the mutual assistance Convention was implemented early by a Framework Decision, and a Directive adopted after the entry into force of the Treaty of Lisbon will, when applied after spring 2017, largely replace the Convention and Protocol.[82]

The three Protocols amending the Europol Convention entered into force in spring 2007, after they were ratified by all Member States, but they were later repealed, along with the main Europol Convention, by a third pillar Decision, with effect from 1 January 2010.[83] Finally, the Protocol to the CIS Convention entered into force ninety days after eight of the first fifteen Member States ratified it,[84] which took place on 15 October 2007.[85] This Protocol was also repealed, with effect from 27 May 2011, due to the replacement of the CIS Convention with a third pillar Decision.[86] It should be noted that the Court of Justice confirmed that the EU had the power to replace Conventions with Framework Decisions (and, by analogy, by Decisions as well).[87]

With Conventions phased out, the Council became attracted instead to the instrument of Framework Decisions, in particular since they were binding upon Member States and applied by a certain date (generally two years at the latest) without the need for national treaty ratification procedures. In practice, the Council adopted a total of thirty-four Framework Decisions;[88] although two of them were annulled by the Court of Justice for encroaching upon EC competence.[89]

In particular, Framework Decisions were used for the harmonization of substantive criminal law and for harmonization of both domestic criminal procedural law and for the adoption of rules on mutual recognition in criminal matters, with a few of them addressing police cooperation issues.

Decisions were frequently adopted during the Amsterdam era of the third pillar, with the adoption of fifty-seven formal Decisions as provided for in the Treaty.[90] In practice, Decisions set up EU-wide bodies or networks or EU funding programmes, or facilitate cross-border activity of national authorities.[91] In addition, the Council also adopted

---

[80] Art 27(3), 2000 Convention, n 77 above; Art 13(3), 2001 Protocol, n 78 above.

[81] For the ratification details, see Appendix I.

[82] See respectively the Framework Decision on joint investigation teams ([2002] OJ L 162/1); and Dir 2014/41 on a European investigation order ([2014] OJ L 130/1), which must be applied by 22 May 2017 (Art 36(1)). For details, see II:7.9 and II:3.6 below.

[83] The Decision establishing Europol, which repealed the three Protocols to the Europol Convention ([2009] OJ L 121/37).

[84] Art 2(3), CIS Protocol, n 78 above.   [85] Art 2(4), CIS Protocol, n 78 above.

[86] Art 35 of the Decision establishing the CIS ([2009] OJ L 323/20).

[87] See Case C-303/05 *Advocaten voor de Wereld* [2007] ECR I-3633.

[88] For a full list, see the Table of Legislation.

[89] These were the Framework Decisions on environmental crime and on shipping pollution (respectively [2003] OJ L 29/55 and [2005] OJ L 255/164), annulled respectively by Cases C-176/03 *Commission v Council* [2005] ECR I-7879 and C-440/05 *Commission v Council* [2007] ECR I-9097. Both measures were subsequently replaced by EC Directives: Dirs 2008/99 ([2008] OJ L 328/28) and 2009/123 ([2009] OJ L 280/52). See further II:2.4 and II:5.2.4 below.

[90] For a full list, see the Table of Legislation.

[91] For example, see the Decisions on Eurojust ([2002] OJ L 63/1), funding programmes (II:2.6 below), a network for protection of public figures ([2002] OJ L 333/1), and on the use of liaison officers ([2003] OJ L 76/27).

other types of Decisions, for instance to implement Conventions,[92] or to extend the scope of the Conventions on corruption and in order to sign or extend the scope of third pillar treaties.[93] At the time of entry into force of the Treaty of Lisbon, forty-three formal third pillar Decisions were still in force.[94] Thirteen Decisions had either been repealed and replaced by other measures, or had lapsed because they were concluded only for a limited period of time (because they related to funding programmes). Three more Decisions were repealed in 2013, when SIS II became operational.[95]

Common Positions were used in several cases for their pre-Amsterdam purpose, to establish EU negotiating positions at international conferences.[96] This then entailed the application of Article 37 EU (since repealed by the Treaty of Lisbon), which specified that Member States had to 'defend' those Common Positions at 'international organisations and at international conferences in which they take part.' Article 37 was also used to coordinate positions without the adoption of a formal Common Position.[97] The Council also adopted Common Positions on other international matters, comprising one measure on the transfer of data to Interpol,[98] and a series of controversial Common Positions on anti-terrorism measures, which had a joint legal base of the second pillar and the third pillar.[99] Only three of these Common Positions were still in force as of the entry into force of the Treaty of Lisbon.[100]

The legal effect of the types of third pillar instruments provided for in the Amsterdam version of the third pillar was, in two cases, expressly laid out.[101] Framework Decisions 'aim[ed] to approximat[e]...the laws and regulations of the Member States' and were 'binding on the Member States as to the result to be achieved but' left 'to the national authorities the choice of form and methods'. This second part of this definition was identical to the definition of Directives then set out in Article 249 EC (now Article 288 TFEU), except that it is also specified that Framework Decisions 'shall not entail direct

---

[92] On the measures implementing the Europol Convention, see II:7.8 below.

[93] See respectively [2003] OJ L 226/27 (extending Convention to Gibraltar) and (for instance) [2003] OJ L 181/25 (treaty with USA) and [2009] OJ L 325/4 (extension in scope of agreement with USA).

[94] See Appendix II.   [95] Art 69 of the 2007 Decision establishing SIS II, n 76 above.

[96] See the Common Positions on the proposed Council of Europe 'Cyber-crime' Convention ([1999] OJ L 142/1), on the proposed firearms Protocol to the UN Convention on organized crime ([2000] OJ L 37/1), and on the proposed UN Convention on corruption (Council docs 12837/2/01, 8897/4/02, and 12215/2/02, all dated 30 Oct 2003 (adopted 2001 and 2002), unpublished). The Council subsequently adopted a number of unpublished Common Positions setting out the EU position at conferences of parties to these Conventions. See Council docs: 15012/1/06 rev 1, 30 Nov 2006, concerning the corruption Convention, adopted by JHA Council, 4–5 Dec 2006; 11171/1/08, 22 Sep 2008, concerning the United Nations Convention against Transnational Organized Crime (UNTOC), adopted by the JHA Council, 25 Sep 2008; and 11452/2/09, 30 Sep 2009 adopted by the JHA Council on 23 Oct 2009, concerning the UN Convention against corruption. With the adoption of the relevant treaties, or following the relevant international meetings, these measures are all now redundant, although they have never been formally repealed.

[97] See II:2.7 below.   [98] Common Position on transfer of data to Interpol ([2005] OJ L 27/61).

[99] One concerns general policy in combating terrorism ([2001] OJ L 344/90) and transposes relevant Security Council resolutions into EU law. The other concerns the application of specific measures to combat terrorism ([2001] OJ L 344/93), and has been implemented by further measures listing individuals and groups considered to be 'terrorist' by the Council and taking certain action against them. See further II:7.4.5 and II:2.2.3.2 below.

[100] The Common Positions on combating terrorism (ibid) and on the transfer of data to Interpol, n 98 above. On the legal base for the subsequent amendments to the Common Position on the application of specific measures to combat terrorism, see II:2.2.3.2 below.

[101] Art 34(2)(b) and 34(2)(c) EU.

effect'. Decisions could be adopted 'for any other purpose consistent with the objectives of [the third pillar]', excluding 'any approximation of the laws and regulations of
the Member States'. These measures were also binding and did not entail direct effect. It
should be emphasized that the previous EU Treaty third pillar rules apparently did not
merely leave the legal effect of Decisions and Framework Decisions for each Member
State to determine according to its rules on the effect of public international law within
the domestic legal system, but rather appeared to harmonize the effect of those measures within national legal orders. In other words, even if a Member State is ordinarily
'monist', the rules appeared to preclude Framework Decisions and Decisions from having direct effect in its legal system. On the other hand, the rules were silent as to the
legal effect of Conventions and Common Positions, although the Treaty specified that
Common Positions shall 'define the approach of the Union to a particular matter'.

The Court of Justice has ruled on the legal effect of both Framework Decisions and
Common Positions. The leading case on Framework Decisions is the 2005 judgment
of the Court of Justice in *Pupino*, in which an Italian court asked the Court of Justice
whether the Framework Decision on the rights of crime victims in criminal procedure
had an 'indirect effect' equivalent to that of Directives.[102] The Court answered that
it did, because of: the comparison between the definitions of EC Directives and EU
Framework Decisions; the binding nature of Framework Decisions; the existence of the
Court's jurisdiction (albeit less extensive than for EC law), which 'would be deprived of
most of its useful effect if individuals were not entitled to invoke framework decisions
in order to obtain a conforming interpretation of national law before the courts of the
Member States'; and the principle of loyalty to the Union as set out in Article 10 EC,
which applied implicitly to the third pillar.[103]

However, the Court confirmed that, just like Directives, unimplemented Framework
Decisions could not impose criminal liability upon individuals or aggravate such liability, for this would breach the principle of the legality of criminal law.[104] For those
Framework Decisions that aim to harmonize substantive national criminal law,[105] this
distinction is crucial. But the Court then ruled in *Pupino* that such a limitation did not
apply to measures concerning criminal *procedure*: for such measures, national law must
be interpreted in light of a Framework Decision unless that would entail a breach of the
right to a fair trial.[106]

Subsequently, the Court elaborated on the nature of Framework Decisions as compared
to other third pillar legal instruments in the *Advocaaten voor de Wereld* judgment.[107]
In this case, the Court ruled that the Framework Decision on the European Arrest
Warrant took the correct legal form, given that this measure harmonized national laws

---

[102] Case C-105/03 [2005] ECR I-5285. On the principle as it applies to Directives, see the case law beginning with Cases 14/83 *Von Colson and Kamann* [1984] ECR 1891 and Case C-105/89 *Marleasing* [1990]
ECR I-4135.

[103] Paras 31–43 of the judgment (ibid). Following the entry into force of the Treaty of Lisbon, the application of the loyalty principle to all areas of EU activity is explicit (Art 4(3), second and third sub-paragraphs,
revised TEU).

[104] Paras 44 and 45 of the judgment (ibid).   [105] See II:5.5 below.

[106] Paras 43–48, 58, and 59 of the judgment, n 102 above.

[107] Case C-303/05, n 87 above, at paras 24–43.

as regards criminal law, and the Treaty did not confine the use of Framework Decisions to the issue of substantive criminal law. This measure could not have taken the form of a Decision, since Decisions cannot harmonize national law, or a Common Position, since such measures are limited to defining the Union's approach to a particular matter (see further below). It could have taken the form of a Convention, but since the Treaty did not establish any form of priority between third pillar instruments, the Council had a choice of whether to adopt a Framework Decision or a Convention, and could not be criticized for choosing to adopt a Framework Decision. Moreover, it was open to the Council to replace Conventions by means of Framework Decisions, as a more restrictive interpretation was not supported by the Treaty and would limit the effectiveness of the Council's power to adopt Framework Decisions.

As for Common Positions, the Court of Justice ruled on their legal effect in the case of *SEGI*,[108] which was an appeal from an order of the Court of First Instance which had rejected an action for damages from an organization which the EU had labelled as terrorist, by means of a Common Position. Since the organization was based inside the EU, the Union did not impose financial sanctions upon it, on the assumption that before the entry into force of the Treaty of Lisbon, it lacked competence to do this.[109] The Court of Justice ruled that:[110]

> …Article 34 EU provides that the Council may adopt acts varying in nature and scope.… A common position requires the compliance of the Member States by virtue of the principle of the duty to cooperate in good faith, which means in particular that Member States are to take all appropriate measures, whether general or particular, to ensure fulfilment of their obligations under European Union law (see *Pupino*, paragraph 42). Article 37 EU thus provides that the Member States are to defend the common positions '[w]ithin international organisations and at international conferences in which they take part'. However, a common position is not supposed to produce of itself legal effects in relation to third parties.

It may be presumed that Conventions, as an established instrument of public international law, are binding. *A contrario* reasoning from the Treaty provisions defining Framework Decisions and Decisions, and the Court's judgment in *Advocaten voor de Wereld*, suggests that Conventions could be used to approximate national laws *or* for any other purpose consistent with Title VI, or for a combination of these purposes.

Although the Court of Justice has not ruled directly on the legal status and effect of third pillar Decisions, it follows from the *Advocaten voor de Wereld* judgment that they could not be used to harmonize national law, but could (by analogy) replace previously adopted Conventions. In fact, the Council adopted Decisions to replace the Conventions establishing Europol and the Customs Information System, and their related Protocols.[111]

---

[108] Cases C-354/04 P *Gestoras pro Amnistia* [2007] ECR I-1579 and C-355/04 P *SEGI* [2007] ECR I-1657.

[109] More precisely, the organization was only subject to Art 4 of the Common Position on the application of specific measures to combat terrorism, n 99 above. The competence to adopt financial sanctions against such alleged terrorists is now arguably conferred by Art 75 TFEU: see further II:2.2.3.2 below.

[110] Para 52 of the *SEGI* judgment, n 108 above.

[111] [2009] OJ L 121/37 and [2009] OJ L 323/20.

Other 'first pillar' principles applicable to the third pillar include: the rule that provisions of legislation which do not refer to national law should be interpreted as having an autonomous Union-wide meaning;[112] the rule that statements by the EU institutions cannot normally be used to interpret binding acts;[113] and the principle that new procedural rules apply to procedures pending at the time when those new rules enter into force.[114]

The Court of Justice has also confirmed that the principle of supremacy applies to the third pillar.[115] In light of this judgment, it is strongly arguable that the principles of damages liability for Member States for breaches of EU law, and of equal and effective remedies for breach of EC law, apply also to some degree to third pillar measures, along with some principles relating to external competence.[116] Finally, in light of *Pupino*, it could be argued that Conventions confer direct effect (as the application of the principle to these measures has not been ruled out by the EU Treaty); the Court of Justice has not yet addressed this question either.[117]

As for the jurisdiction of the Court of Justice over the third pillar in the Amsterdam era,[118] the Court's role was expanded significantly as compared to the pre-Amsterdam rules. Article 46(b) of the previous TEU stated that the Court's first pillar jurisdiction only applied to the third pillar to the extent set out in Article 35 of the previous TEU. First of all, Article 35(1) to (4) of the previous TEU, along with Declaration 10 in the Final Act of the Treaty of Amsterdam, copied precisely the preliminary rulings jurisdiction which had already been awarded to the Court as regards several Conventions in 1996, and which was subsequently awarded in several other pre-Amsterdam Conventions: an option for Member States to award the Court jurisdiction over references from national courts; a further option to limit that jurisdiction to final courts only; and a final option as to whether to require final national courts to send references to the Court. But the scope of this jurisdiction was expanded by the Treaty of Amsterdam to include not only jurisdiction over Conventions and measures implementing them, but also 'on the validity and interpretation of framework decisions and decisions, on the interpretation of conventions established under this Title and on the validity and interpretation of measures implementing them'.

Nineteen Member States opted in to the Court's post-Amsterdam third pillar jurisdiction over preliminary rulings: twelve of the first fifteen Member States (all except the UK, Denmark, and Ireland), plus seven of the twelve Member States joining the EU in 2004 and 2007 (all except Estonia, Poland, Slovakia, Bulgaria, and Malta).[119] All

---

[112] Case C-66/08 *Koslowski* [2008] ECR I-6041, paras 42–3.

[113] *SEGI*, n 108 above, at paras 58–62.

[114] Case C-467/05 *Dell'Orto* [2007] ECR I-5557, paras 47–9.

[115] Case C-399/11 *Melloni*, ECLI:EU:C:2013:107. On this issue, see 'Salvation outside the Church? The Development of the EU's Third Pillar' (2007) 44 CMLRev 883 at 919–20 and K Lenaerts and T Corthaut, 'Of Birds and Hedges: The Role of Primacy in Invoking Norms of EU Law' (2006) 31 ELRev 287 at 289–91.

[116] On the damages liability and effective remedies principles, see 'Salvation', ibid, at 921–4. On external competence, see II:2.7.2 below.

[117] On the other hand, it cannot be argued that Common Positions have direct effect, given that (according to the *SEGI* case) they cannot affect the legal position of third parties.

[118] See E Denza, *The Intergovernmental Pillars of the European Union* (OUP, 2002), ch 9, and 'Salvation outside the Church', n 115 above, at 885–909.

[119] [2010] OJ L 56/14.

of these Member States except Spain permitted all national courts or tribunals to send questions. Eleven Member States reserved the right to require their final courts to refer (the exceptions were Greece, Cyprus, Latvia, Lithuania, Portugal, Finland, Sweden, and Hungary).

Next, Article 35(5) of the previous TEU set out another type of exclusion from jurisdiction: the Court of Justice could not 'review the validity or proportionality of operations carried out by the police or other law enforcement services of a Member State or the exercise of the responsibilities incumbent upon Member States with regard to the maintenance of law and order and the safeguarding of internal security'. This was expressly a restriction on the Court's ability to rule on certain acts committed by national authorities; it did not restrict the Court from ruling on the validity or interpretation of EU acts, and in any event, the final judgment in cases referred from national courts is given by the national courts.

Article 35(7) of the previous TEU, first sentence, followed the model of interstate dispute settlement already agreed for six pre-Amsterdam criminal, policing, or customs law Conventions, allowing Member States to sue each other after six months of attempting to reach a settlement in the Council. However, this provision widened the Court's dispute-settlement jurisdiction to cover all measures adopted under Article 34(2) of the previous TEU, namely Common Positions, Framework Decisions, Decisions, Conventions, and measures implementing Decisions and Conventions. The second sentence of Article 35(7) followed the model of Commission/Member State dispute settlement also seen (with more variety) in five pre-Amsterdam criminal and customs law Conventions. Here the Commission could only sue Member States where there was a dispute over a Convention.

Finally, Article 35(6) of the previous TEU gave the Court the power of direct judicial review, a wholly new power compared to its pre-Amsterdam jurisdiction. It could rule on the legality of Framework Decisions or Decisions on grounds of 'lack of competence, infringement of an essential procedural requirement, infringement of this Treaty or any rule of law relating to its application, or misuse of powers'. These grounds were taken from Article 230 EC (now Article 263 TFEU). Only the Commission and Member States had the power to bring such cases; other persons, including the EP, did not.

In practice, when the Treaty of Lisbon entered into force the Court had ruled on: ten references for interpretation of some of the third pillar provisions of the Schengen *acquis*;[120] three references for interpretation of the Framework Decision on crime victims' rights;[121] a reference on the validity of the Framework Decision on the European Arrest Warrant;[122] four references on the interpretation of the same Framework

---

[120] Cases: C-187/01 and C-385/01 *Gozutok and Brugge* [2003] ECR I-1345; C-469/03 *Miraglia* [2005] ECR I-2009; C-436/04 *Van Esbroek* [2006] ECR I-2333; C-467/04 *Gasparini* [2006] ECR I-9199; C-150/05 *Van Straaten* [2006] ECR I-9327; C-288/05 *Kretzinger* [2007] ECR I-6441; C-367/05 *Kraaijenbrink* [2007] ECR I-6619; C-297/07 *Bourquain* [2008] ECR I-9425; and C-491/07 *Turansky* [2008] ECR I-11039. All concerned the Schengen 'double jeopardy' rules. On the judgments, see II:6.8 below.

[121] *Pupino*, n 102 above; Case C-467/05 *Dell'Orto* [2007] ECR I-5557; and Case C-404/07 *Katz* [2008] ECR I-7607. On the substance of these cases, see II:4.7 below.

[122] Case C-303/05 *Advocaten voor de Wereld* [2007] ECR I-3633; for the Framework Decision see n 74 above. On the substance see II:3.5 below.

Decision;[123] a challenge against an act of Eurojust, the EU's prosecutors' agency;[124] and two annulment actions against Framework Decisions adopted by the Council.[125] Two of these cases were subject to the special JHA emergency ruling procedure, mentioned above.[126] No dispute settlement cases were brought.

These special rules on the Court's jurisdiction continued to apply to measures adopted before the entry into force of the Treaty of Lisbon for another five years after that Treaty entered into force, ie until 1 December 2014.[127] After that point they ceased to apply, so their interpretation is of historic interest only.[128]

2.2.3 Treaty of Lisbon

2.2.3.1 Overview

The institutional framework governing EU JHA law again changed significantly with the entry into force of the Treaty of Lisbon on 1 December 2009.[129] First of all, the basic rules governing JHA cooperation were 'reunited' in one Title (Title V of Part Three) of the EC Treaty, which was in turn renamed the Treaty on the Functioning of the European Union (TFEU), because pursuant to the Treaty of Lisbon, the EU replaced and succeeded the European Community.[130] In effect, the previous third pillar was transferred into what was formerly known as the Community legal order, and the TEU no longer contains any detailed provisions on JHA matters. However, the TEU still specifies that the development of JHA law as a whole remains an objective of the EU.[131]

The previous third pillar has a form of legal 'afterlife', in the form of transitional rules relating to the jurisdiction of the Court of Justice over third pillar measures adopted before the entry into force of the Treaty of Lisbon ('pre-existing measures') and the legal effect of those measures.[132] Although the Treaty of Lisbon contains most of the provisions of the rejected Constitutional Treaty,[133] it is not identical to that Treaty, in particular as regards the opt-outs applicable to JHA law.

Title V contains in turn general provisions,[134] rules on immigration and asylum,[135] an Article on civil law,[136] five Articles on criminal law,[137] and three articles on policing.[138]

---

[123] Cases: C-66/08 *Koslowski* [2008] ECR I-6041; C-296/08 PPU *Santesteban Goicoechea* [2008] ECR I-6307; C-388/08 PPU *Leymann and Pustovarov* [2008] ECR I-8993; and C-123/08 *Wolzenburg* [2009] ECR I-9621. On the substance, see ibid.

[124] Case C-160/03 *Spain v Eurojust* (on the language requirements of Eurojust staff) [2005] ECR I-2077.

[125] Case C-176/03 *Commission v Council* and C-440/05 *Commission v Council* (both n 89 above). On the substance of these cases, see II:2.4 and II:5.2.4 below.

[126] *Santesteban Goicoechea* and *Leymann and Pustovarov*, n 123 above.

[127] On the transitional rules, see II.2.2.3.3 below.

[128] For a detailed discussion of the historic case law, see the third edition of this book, pp 35–6.

[129] [2007] OJ C 306.   [130] Art 1, third paragraph, revised TEU.

[131] Art 3(2), revised TEU.   [132] See II:2.2.3.3 below.

[133] [2004] OJ C 310. On the JHA provisions of the Constitutional Treaty, see the second edition of this book, pp 85–90.

[134] Ch 1 of Title V (Arts 67–76 TFEU), discussed in I:2.2.3.2 and II:2.2.3.2.

[135] Ch 2 of Title V (Arts 77–80 TFEU), discussed in chs 3–7 of volume 1.

[136] Ch 3 of Title V (Art 81 TFEU), discussed in ch 8 below.

[137] Ch 4 of Title V (Arts 82–86 TFEU), discussed in chs 3–6 below.

[138] Ch 5 of Title V (Arts 87–89 TFEU), discussed in ch 7 below.

Because of the abolition of the third pillar, 'Community' legal instruments (Directives and Regulations) have had to be used to regulate policing and criminal law since the entry into force of the Treaty of Lisbon. It follows that the principles of direct effect and supremacy of 'Community' instruments apply to measures in this field adopted after that date as well.

As for decision-making rules, the Treaty of Lisbon extended QMV in the Council and co-decision with the EP (now known as the 'ordinary legislative procedure')[139] to most criminal law and policing issues.[140] However, unanimity in the Council was retained for some sensitive issues of criminal law, policing, and family law.[141] In most of these cases, the EP is only consulted, but it has a new power of consent in some cases.[142] These cases of decision-making are examples of 'special legislative procedures' that differ from the ordinary procedure.[143]

Unanimity in the Council (or European Council) also applies to possible extensions of competence, or changes to decision-making rules.[144] The revised TEU also provides for a general power to alter decision-making rules (known as a *passerelle*), which applies to Title V as well as most of the rest of the Treaties. This permits a decision, without Treaty amendment, to move from unanimity to QMV or from a special legislative procedure to the ordinary legislative procedure.[145] Finally, Title V provides for two different variations of decision-making rules—a special rule (widely known as the 'emergency brake') relating to some areas of criminal law, if a Member State considers that a proposal 'would affect fundamental aspects of its criminal justice system',[146] and a special rule (referred to in this book as the 'pseudo-veto') relating to some cases where unanimity applies in the Council.[147] In either case, a 'fast-track' to 'enhanced cooperation', ie authorization of some Member States to proceed without the others, is provided for.[148]

---

[139] The details of this procedure are set out in Art 294 TFEU, which does not differ in substance from the previous Art 251 EC.

[140] See s 2.3 of chs 6 and 9–12.

[141] Arts 86(1) (European Public Prosecutor), 87(3) (police operations), 89 (cross-border police operations), and 81(3) (family law).

[142] The EP has the power of consent as regards legislation concerning the European Public Prosecutor (Art 86(1) TFEU).

[143] On this concept, see Art 289(2) TFEU.

[144] This applies to any decision to extend criminal law competence (Arts 82(1)(d) and 83(1), third sub-paragraph TFEU), to alter decision-making rules relating to family law (Art 81(3), second sub-paragraph), or to extend the powers of the European Public Prosecutor (Art 86(4)). The latter measure would be adopted by the European Council, rather than the Council. The EP has the power of consent pursuant to Art 86(4), but need only be consulted in the other cases.

[145] Art 48(7), revised TEU. The *passerelle* procedure requires the unanimous support of the Member States and the consent of the EP, plus involvement by national parliaments. This procedure only applies to acts of the *Council*, so cannot apply to Art 86(4) TFEU, which provides for action by the European Council. There are several specific provisions in the Treaties which are not subject to this procedure (Art 353 TFEU), but none of these exemptions concern JHA matters. It should also be noted that in the context of enhanced cooperation, the Member States participating in that cooperation can agree that the decision-making rules will change *for them*: see Art 333 TFEU and further I:2.2.5.5.

[146] Arts 82(3) and 83(3) TFEU.

[147] These cases are Arts 86 (European Public Prosecutor) and 87(3) (operational police cooperation).

[148] On the enhanced cooperation rules following the entry into force of the Treaty of Lisbon, see II:2.2.5.5 below.

Next, as regards policing and criminal law, there is no longer any right for individual Member States to submit initiatives for legislation, but it is still open to a group of one-quarter of the Member States (meaning, at present, at least seven Member States) to submit a joint initiative.[149]

Moving on to the jurisdiction of the Court of Justice over JHA matters, the restrictions previously imposed relating to the former third pillar were removed,[150] save for the transitional rules for pre-existing third pillar measures (since expired),[151] and the retention of the previous exception, as set out in the former Article 35(5) TEU,[152] relating to jurisdiction over 'the validity or proportionality of operations carried out by the police or other law-enforcement services of a Member State or the exercise of the responsibilities incumbent upon Member States with regard to the maintenance of law and order and the safeguarding of internal security'.[153]

The special 'urgency' procedure for certain JHA cases before the Court of Justice, first created in 2008, remains in force.[154] In addition, the Treaty of Lisbon added a new paragraph to Article 267 TFEU (former Article 234 EC), concerning preliminary rulings from national courts to the Court of Justice, which provides that:

> If such a question [for a preliminary ruling] is raised in a case pending before a court or tribunal of a Member State with regard to a person in custody, the Court of Justice of the European Union shall act with the minimum of delay.

This provision has been applied as regards persons held in detention in connection with EU anti-terrorist sanctions legislation, the European Arrest Warrant, and child abduction.[155] It does not create a separate new procedure by itself, but rather requires the Court to invoke the procedures (the urgent JHA procedure or the more general accelerated procedures) already set out in the Court's Statute and Rules of Procedure.

In practice, the Court of Justice has continued to receive a modest number of cases on EU criminal law (about five a year) since the Treaty of Lisbon entered into force. There was no surge in numbers, at least initially, after the transitional period on the CJEU's jurisdiction over pre-Lisbon third pillar measures expired in December 2014.

The transfer of the third pillar to the first pillar also means that the 'Community' rules on external relations are applicable to policing and criminal law matters, in place of the rules on external relations which were applicable to the former third pillar.[156] Furthermore, the Treaty of Lisbon extended the scope of the JHA opt-out rules applicable to the UK, Ireland, and Denmark to policing and criminal law. These developments are considered further below.[157]

---

[149] Art 76 TFEU, discussed further below (II:2.2.3.2).

[150] For the basic rules on the Court's jurisdiction and functioning after the Treaty of Lisbon, see Art 19, revised TEU, and Arts 251–81 TFEU.

[151] On these transitional rules, see II:2.2.3.3 below.   [152] See II:2.2.2 above.

[153] Art 276 TFEU. For interpretation of the previous clause, see II:2.2.2 above.

[154] See I:2.2.2.1.   [155] See respectively II:7.4, II:3.5, and II:8.6 below.

[156] See further II:2.7 below. On the substance of the treaties which have been agreed or are being negotiated in this area, see II:3.9, II:7.11 below, and I:8.9.

[157] II:2.2.5.

Finally, a number of the more general amendments to the Treaties made by the Treaty of Lisbon have a particular impact on EU JHA law. The amendments relating to the legitimacy and accountability of the EU are discussed further separately,[158] as are the general amendments relating to the competence of the EU.[159] The integration of the previous third pillar into the EC Treaty (now the TFEU) means also that various general and final provisions of the TFEU apply to policing and criminal law. This could be relevant as regards provisions having general application,[160] data protection,[161] non-discrimination on grounds of nationality,[162] statistics,[163] EU liability,[164] dispute settlement,[165] national security exceptions,[166] pre-existing treaties with third states,[167] the EU's 'residual powers',[168] and the territorial scope of EU law.[169] The JHA provisions of the Treaties are included (as they were before) by the provision on Treaty amendment, including new provisions on simplified Treaty amendment.[170] There is still an obligation to ensure consistency between the various policies of the Union,[171] and the provisions concerning the relationship between the EU and its Member States, including the division of power between them, could be particularly relevant to JHA cooperation.[172] So could the revised rules on the protection of human rights within the EU legal order.[173]

---

[158] II:2.5 below.   [159] II:2.2.4 below.

[160] Arts 8–13 TFEU, requiring all EU policies to take account of (respectively) sex equality, social concerns, non-discrimination, the environment, consumer protection, and the welfare of animals.

[161] Art 16 TFEU. See further II:7.2.3 below.

[162] Art 18 TFEU (former Art 12 EC). It should be noted, however, that the previous Art 12 EC already applied to third pillar cooperation: see Case C-123/08 *Wolzenburg* [2009] ECR I-9621, and the discussion in II:3.4 below.

[163] Art 338 TFEU (former Art 285 EC). On crime statistics, see II:7.7 below.

[164] Art 340 TFEU (former Art 288 EC), which the Court of Justice has jurisdiction over pursuant to Art 268 TFEU (former Art 235 EC). As discussed above (II:2.2.2), the Court of Justice confirmed that it had no jurisdiction 'whatsoever' over this issue as regards the prior third pillar: Case C-355/04 P *SEGI* [2007] ECR I-1657.

[165] Art 344 TFEU (former Art 292 EC), which reserves exclusive jurisdiction for disputes between Member States concerning EU law upon the Court of Justice, to the extent that it has jurisdiction over the matter concerned: see Case C-459/03 *Commission v Ireland* [2006] ECR I-4635.

[166] Arts 346–8 TFEU (former Arts 296–8 EC). There is no reason to doubt that the jurisprudence on the interpretation of the previous Articles 296–8 EC continues to apply after the entry into force of the Treaty of Lisbon to Articles 346–8 TFEU, given the lack of substantive amendment to these provisions.

[167] Art 351 TFEU (former Art 307 EC). See further II:2.7 below.

[168] Art 352 TFEU (former Art 308 EC), which provides for the adoption of measures by means of unanimity in the Council and consent of the EP '[i]f action by the Union should prove necessary, within the framework of the policies defined in the Treaties, to attain one of the objectives set out in the Treaties, and the Treaties have not provided the necessary powers'. The predecessor clause did not apply to the previous third pillar: see by analogy, Joined Cases C-402/05 P and C-415/05 P *Kadi and Al Barakaat* [2008] ECR I-6351, paras 194–205, and the discussion of Art 75 TFEU below (II:2.2.3.2).

[169] Art 52 TEU and Art 355 TFEU. Although the previous TEU did not define its territorial scope, some third pillar measures had specific provisions on the subject: see, for instance, Art 8 of the Framework Decision on unauthorized entry and residence ([2002] OJ L 328/1), applying that measure to Gibraltar.

[170] The possible use of the *passerelle* clause (revised Art 48(7) TEU) has been discussed above, but the Treaty of Lisbon also created the possibility for a slightly simplified system for amending the Treaty provisions concerning EU internal policies (revised Art 48(6) TEU), which applies, inter alia, to Title V TFEU.

[171] Art 7 TFEU, replacing the prior Art 3 TEU.

[172] Arts 4 and 5 TEU. See respectively II:2.2.3.2 and II:2.5 below. On the general rules on EU competence (Arts 2–6 TFEU), see II:2.2.4 below.

[173] Arts 6 and 7 TEU; see I:2.3.

2.2.3.2 General provisions

The general provisions of Title V of Part Three of the TFEU concern in turn: general objectives (Article 67 TFEU); the role of the European Council (Article 68 TFEU); the role of national parliaments (Article 69 TFEU); evaluation of JHA policies (Article 70 TFEU); the creation of a standing committee on operational security (Article 71 TFEU); a general security restriction (Article 72 TFEU); coordination of national security agencies (Article 73 TFEU); competence to adopt measures concerning administrative cooperation (Article 74 TFEU); competence over anti-terrorism measures (Article 75 TFEU); and a rule reserving power for Member States to propose policing and criminal law initiatives collectively (Article 76 TFEU). Some of these provisions (Articles 71, 72, 73, 75, and 76) are particularly relevant to policing and criminal law matters, and so are discussed in this chapter. The more general provisions (Articles 67, 68, 69, 70, and 74) were considered in the parallel chapter in volume 1.

Firstly, Article 71 TFEU, inserted by the Treaty of Lisbon, provides for the creation of a standing committee on internal security:

> A standing committee shall be set up within the Council in order to ensure that operational cooperation on internal security is promoted and strengthened within the Union. Without prejudice to Article 240, it shall facilitate coordination of the action of Member States' competent authorities. Representatives of the Union bodies, offices and agencies concerned may be involved in the proceedings of this committee. The European Parliament and national Parliaments shall be kept informed of the proceedings.

This committee (known as 'COSI', based on the French acronym) was established by the Council shortly after the date of entry into force of the Treaty of Lisbon.[174] The Decision establishing COSI makes clear that the committee does not have the competence to adopt legislative measures, and does not conduct operations,[175] but rather 'shall facilitate, promote and strengthen coordination of operational actions of the authorities of the Member States competent in the field of internal security', and 'shall also evaluate the general direction and efficiency of operational cooperation; it shall identify possible shortcomings or failures and adopt appropriate concrete recommendations to address them.'[176] It includes representatives from JHA agencies involved in operations.[177] As a Council committee it is subject to the rules on access to documents.[178]

There is no longer any reference, following the entry into force of the Treaty of Lisbon, to the previous committees which assisted the Council's discussions as regards the legislative (and to some extent the operational) aspects of the previous third pillar.[179] However, the Council (or, more precisely, Coreper)[180] has chosen to retain the

---

[174] [2010] OJ L 52/50. The Council established the Committee as a procedural matter, pursuant to Art 240(3) TFEU, which meant that the Decision was adopted by a simple majority with no opt-out procedures possible. There was no role for the EP or the Commission.

[175] Art 4, COSI Decision.   [176] Arts 2 and 3(2), COSI Decision.

[177] Art 5, COSI Decision.   [178] See II:2.5 below.

[179] These were the Art K.4 Committee before the Treaty of Amsterdam, and the Art 36 Committee after the Treaty of Amsterdam, named after the relevant Treaty Arts.

[180] See Art 19 of the Council's rules of procedure ([2009] OJ L 325/35).

committee that previously assisted its work as regards the legislative aspects of policing and criminal law, along with the 'Strategic Committee on Immigration, Frontiers and Asylum' and a number of other JHA working parties.[181]

The next question is the extent of national competence as regards internal security. This issue arises most obviously in respect of Article 72 TFEU, which provides that '[t]his Title shall not affect the exercise of the responsibilities incumbent upon Member States with regard to the maintenance of law and order and the safeguarding of internal security.' In fact, this provision copies the wording of the previous Articles 64(1) EC and 33 TEU. But this issue also arises as regards Article 73 TFEU, which had no equivalent in the previous versions of the Treaties, and which provides that:

> It shall be open to Member States to organise between themselves and under their responsibility such forms of cooperation and coordination as they deem appropriate between the competent departments of their administrations responsible for safeguarding national security.

Furthermore, the revised Article 4(2) TEU provides that:

> The Union shall respect the equality of Member States before the Treaties as well as their national identities, inherent in their fundamental structures, political and constitutional, inclusive of regional and local self-government.
>
> It shall respect their essential State functions, including ensuring the territorial integrity of the State, maintaining law and order and safeguarding national security. In particular, national security remains the sole responsibility of each Member State.

Only the requirement to respect Member States' 'national identities' previously appeared expressly in the Treaties,[182] and the Court of Justice has only briefly touched upon the interpretation of this provision.[183] This may, however, be due to the exclusion of the Court's jurisdiction as regards this provision,[184] a restriction which was lifted by the Treaty of Lisbon. Furthermore, Articles 344–6 TFEU (previously Articles 296–8 EC) provide for specified exceptions relating to the arms trade and national security; those provisions were not substantively amended by the Treaty of Lisbon, and (as noted above) have applied to policing and criminal law matters as well after that Treaty entered into force.

To what extent do these provisions reserve competence to Member States? First, Article 72 TFEU should be interpreted the same way as the previous Treaty Articles with identical wording. Although these Articles have not yet been interpreted by the Court of Justice, the best interpretation is that they confirmed that the use of coercive measures in order to enforce measures adopted pursuant to the JHA provisions of the Treaties is left to the Member States' authorities, in particular as regards arrest, detention, and the use of force. EU agencies are therefore limited to supporting actions of national authorities, except (and only) to the extent that the Treaty confers express

---

[181] See Council docs 16070/09, 16 Nov 2009 and 17653/09, 16 Dec 2009. The Art 36 Committee is now called the 'Coordinating Committee in the area of police and judicial cooperation in criminal matters', but still uses its prior French acronym ('CATS'; see Council doc 17611/09, 15 Dec 2009).

[182] Previous Art 6(3) TEU.

[183] Case C-473/93 *Commission v Luxembourg* [1996] ECR I-3207.

[184] See the previous Art 46 TEU, and more generally II:2.2.2 above.

powers to act on such agencies.[185] This interpretation is also consistent with the limitation on the Court's jurisdiction pursuant to Article 276 TFEU.[186]

In particular, the express restriction upon Europol taking 'coercive measures' set out
in Article 88 TFEU should be understood as a specific application of this general rule.
However, Article 72 should not be understood to preclude the adoption of measures
pursuant to Article 86 TFEU which confer upon the European Public Prosecutor those
powers which the Treaty expressly provides for, or such further judicial or prosecutorial powers as would be clearly necessary to carry out the Prosecutor's functions.
Fundamentally, this exclusion should not be seen as a restriction on the *subject-matter*
which the EU is competent to address, but rather as a rule regarding the division of
powers between the EU and the Member States as regards the *execution* of operational
measures necessary to implement EU rules. Where the drafters of the Treaty of Lisbon
wished to restrict the Union's competence regarding specific JHA issues, they have
done so expressly,[187] and so further specific restrictions on competence over specific
subject-matter cannot be inferred from a general rule like Article 72.

Next, to what extent does Article 73 TFEU limit the EU's competence? This Article
does not as such exclude the EU from competence to adopt measures concerning cooperation regarding national security. This is particularly obvious when comparing it to
the Treaty Article which quite clearly reserves 'competence' to Member States, such as
Article 79(5) TFEU. Following the model of Article 79(5), if the drafters of Article 73
had wished to reserve national competence over security services unambiguously,
Article 73 could simply have provided that, '[t]his Title shall not affect the competence
of Member States to organise between themselves...'. In any event, Article 73 does not
impact upon the ability of the EU to regulate security services *to the extent that they
participate in law enforcement*. If the EU were precluded from regulating such matters, this would restrict the effectiveness of the EU to regulate law enforcement issues,
given the involvement of security agencies in law enforcement, and so such an exclusion would surely have to be provided for expressly. Furthermore, this interpretation
would significantly undermine the accountability of EU action in this area.

As for the adoption of EU measures regulating internal security cooperation per se,
Article 73 leaves it 'open' to Member States to cooperate on this matter, but does not
expressly rule out the adoption of EU measures on this issue. Nor does such cooperation fall outside the scope of the EU's JHA objectives of ensuring a 'high level of security'
by means of measures concerning police, judicial, 'and *other* competent authorities'.[188]

Nevertheless, EU competence over the regulation of internal security agencies
appears to be ruled out by one of the TEU's general clauses on the relationship between
the EU and the Member States. As we have seen above, Article 4(2) TEU states that a
'particular' rule regarding the EU's respect for 'essential state functions' is that 'national
security remains the sole responsibility of each Member State'. It is hard to see how an
EU power to regulate such matters could be exercised without encroaching upon this
'sole responsibility'. Nevertheless, the general rule in Article 4(2) TEU should not be

---

[185] See more specifically II:6.2.4 and II:7.2.4 below.
[186] On Art 276 TFEU, see further II:2.2.2 above.   [187] See Art 79(5) TFEU.
[188] See Art 67(3) TFEU.

understood, any more than the specific rule in Article 73 TFEU, to exempt security agencies entirely from the scope of EU law when they exercise law enforcement functions, as distinct from functions relating to national security.

Finally, how should the broader requirement in Article 4(2) TEU of 'respect' for essential state functions, 'including…maintaining law and order and safeguarding national security', be interpreted? Since the reference to 'maintaining law and order' is identical to Article 72 TFEU in this respect, this part of Article 4(2) adds no further limitation to the EU's powers.[189] As for the reference to 'safeguarding national security', it is only relevant to the extent that *national* security is at issue, rather than *internal* security. But even to the extent of the overlap between the two provisions, the obligation to *respect* State functions as regards national security as set out in Article 4(2) TEU is less far-reaching than the requirement of requirement not to *affect* internal security responsibilities as set out in Article 72 TFEU. It must therefore be concluded that the general rule in the first sentence of Article 4(2) TEU does not lay down any additional restriction on EU action besides those spelt out in Article 72 TFEU as regards responsibilities for law and order and internal security, and in the second sentence of Article 4(2) TEU as regards the sole responsibility for national security.

Next, Article 75 TFEU provides for the adoption of legislation on anti-terrorist sanctions. This is a new provision inserted by the Treaty of Lisbon, so the background first of all needs to be explained.[190] Before the entry into force of the Treaty of Lisbon, the EU adopted measures freezing the assets and income of persons and groups who were believed to be terrorists but whose alleged activities were primarily outside the EU. One category of such groups and persons were those who were allegedly linked to Al-Qaeda and the Taliban, and the EU established a legal framework by means of which it simply copied the lists of such persons and groups designated by a committee of the United Nations Security Council.[191] The second category (subject to separate legislation) consisted of those persons and groups which the EU institutions believed to be terrorists, but who were listed as terrorists on the basis that a 'competent authority' was investigating or prosecuting them for terrorist offences (the 'autonomous' list).[192]

In both cases, the legal bases for the adoption of the relevant measures were Articles 60, 301, and 308 of the previous EC Treaty. Article 301 provided for the adoption of economic sanctions against third countries by QMV in Council after a Commission proposal, with no involvement of the EP, following the adoption of a foreign policy measure pursuant to Title V of the previous TEU. Article 60 of the previous EC Treaty applied the same procedure as regards financial sanctions against third countries.[193]

---

[189] It might be objected that where a Treaty rule is repeated, there must be some additional legal meaning accorded to the second appearance of the rule. However, the drafters of the Treaty of Lisbon were apparently quite content to repeat several provisions of the Treaty purely for the sake of emphasis—as evidenced by Arts 4(1) TEU and the second sentence of Art 5(2) TEU, for instance.

[190] On the substance of EU anti-terrorist sanctions legislation and the litigation concerning its application, see II:7.4.5 below.

[191] Reg 881/2002, [2002] OJ L 139/9, as amended by Reg 561/2003, [2003] OJ L 82/1.

[192] Reg 2580/2001, [2001] OJ L 344/79, which applied alongside a foreign policy measure (Common Position 2001/931, [2001] OJ L 344/93).

[193] Art 60(2) EC set out a specific rule relating to financial sanctions by Member States, but there was no equivalent rule in the prior Art 301 EC.

Finally, Article 308 of the previous EC Treaty was used as an additional legal base so that the EU sanctions measures could be extended to persons and groups not connected with a third state's government; this provision was subject to unanimous voting in the Council and consultation of the EP, with no requirement of a prior foreign policy measure. No EU sanctions measures were adopted against persons or groups who were believed to be terrorists but whose activity was mainly *internal* to the EU, because it was believed (correctly or not) that the EC and EU had no power to adopt sanctions in that case. Following the entry into force of the Treaty of Lisbon, the correctness of that view is now moot. However, the EU nevertheless designated some such groups and persons as 'terrorists' on its autonomous list, for the (sole) purpose of cooperating as regards 'enquiries and proceedings' in respect of such persons within the scope of the third pillar (as it then was).[194] The legal bases used for these measures were upheld by the Court of Justice, which ruled that Articles 60 and 301 EC could be used as regards the material scope of sanctions against Al-Qaeda, but not as regards the personal scope of such sanctions, because those Treaty Articles only provided competence to adopt sanctions measures as regards entire countries or 'the rulers of such a country and also individuals and entities associated with or controlled, directly or indirectly, by them'. Article 308 EC gave the EC the power to extend the scope of those sanctions to persons not connected to a governing regime, because the failure to adopt uniform rules in this regard could impact upon the operation of the common market (which was at the time a requirement for the use of Article 308).[195]

The Treaty of Lisbon replaced Articles 60 and 301 EC with Article 215 TFEU, which applies to both economic and financial sanctions (without any special rule relating to national financial sanctions) and also permits the EU to apply such sanctions 'against natural or legal persons and groups or non-State entities'. The decision-making process remains the same as before, with the addition of a requirement that the EU's High Representative for foreign policy jointly propose the measure concerned.[196] Article 215 also requires the adoption of 'legal safeguards' relating to sanctions measures; measures based on this Article are not legislative acts.

But the Treaty of Lisbon also added Article 75 TFEU, which provides that:

> Where necessary to achieve the objectives set out in Article 67, as regards preventing and combating terrorism and related activities, the European Parliament and the Council, acting by means of regulations in accordance with the ordinary legislative procedure, shall define a framework for administrative measures with regard to capital movements and payments, such as the freezing of funds, financial assets or economic gains belonging to, or owned or held by, natural or legal persons, groups or non-State entities.
>
> The Council, on a proposal from the Commission, shall adopt measures to implement the framework referred to in the first paragraph.

---

[194] See Art 4 of Common Position 2001/931, n 192 above. The application of this provision was at issue in Case C-355/04 P *SEGI* [2007] ECR I-1657.

[195] Joined Cases C-402/05 P and C-415/05 P *Kadi and Al Barakaat* [2008] ECR I-6351, paras 163–78, 211–16, and 222–36.

[196] On this position, see Art 18, revised TEU.

The acts referred to in this Article shall include necessary provisions on legal safeguards.

As compared to Article 215 TFEU, the basic measures to be adopted pursuant to Article 75 TFEU are legislative acts which must be adopted by the use of the ordinary legislative procedure, with no requirement of the adoption of a prior foreign policy act or for a joint proposal by the High Representative. There is also an opt-out from Article 75 measures for the UK and Denmark (but not Ireland), although the UK intends to opt in to such measures.[197] No opt-out applies to Article 215 TFEU.

Which of these provisions applies to the adoption of anti-terrorist measures? Unsurprisingly the EP argued that Article 75 applies,[198] but the Council and Commission argued that Article 215 applies. Shortly after the entry into force of the Treaty of Lisbon, the Council adopted a measure amending the basic framework for sanctions against Al-Qaeda and the Taliban on the basis of Article 215 TFEU,[199] and the EP challenged this before the Court of Justice, primarily on the basis that this measure had the wrong legal base.[200] According to the CJEU, first of all the differences between Articles 75 and 215 TFEU meant that they were 'incompatible' as a dual legal base for the measure concerned. Next, the Court ruled that the previous Articles 60 and 301 EC, along with the relevant aspects of Article 308, had now been replaced by Article 215 TFEU. In contrast, Article 75 created a link to JHA matters, not the CFSP; and the CFSP applied to terrorist threats in the context of foreign policy. It must follow from this judgment that Article 75 can only apply to actions against terrorists where there are no foreign policy aspects, ie where the terrorist group carries out its actions entirely or largely within the EU.

Finally, Article 76 TFEU provides for a continued possibility for Member States to propose measures concerning policing and criminal law:

The acts referred to in Chapters 4 and 5, together with the measures referred to in Article 74 which ensure administrative cooperation in the areas covered by these Chapters, shall be adopted:
(a) on a proposal from the Commission, or
(b) on the initiative of a quarter of the Member States.

This retains a power enjoyed (and often exercised) by Member States before the Treaty of Lisbon.[201] However, as compared to the prior third pillar, Member States cannot propose measures individually, but can make initiatives only if (at least) a quarter of Member States propose them. So far, there have been four such initiatives.[202] The

---

[197] See II:2.2.5.1 and II:2.2.5.2 below.
[198] Use of Art 75 also entails scrutiny powers for national parliaments (see I:2.5), whereas Art 215 does not.
[199] Reg 1265/2009 ([2009] OJ L 346/42).
[200] Case C-130/10 *EP v Council*, ECLI:EU:C:2012:472.
[201] See the prior Art 34 TEU, discussed in II:2.2.2 above.
[202] These are initiatives for Directives on: the right to interpretation and translation in the framework of criminal proceedings ([2010] OJ C 69/1); a European protection order ([2010] OJ C 69/5); a European investigation order ([2010] OJ C 165/22); and changing the seat of the European Police College ([2013] OJ C 361/4).

question arises whether Member States can withdraw or amend such initiatives, either collectively or individually. The TFEU provides that the *Commission* can always amend its proposals, and that Member States must normally vote unanimously to amend *Commission* proposals.[203] The absence of a reference to Member State initiatives suggests that these rules do *not* apply to such initiatives. In other cases, the TFEU sets out special rules for Member State initiatives.[204] However, although Member States cannot withdraw or amend their initiatives, there is nothing in the Treaty to prevent (a) Member State(s) voting against initiatives that it (or they) have made, or, where relevant, pulling an emergency brake concerning those initiatives.[205] While it might seem odd that a Member State would vote against its own initiative, it is conceivable that a Member State might change its mind due to a change of government or in reaction to public discussion of the proposal, or because the proposal has been amended during the decision-making process and the Member State in question disagrees with such changes.

2.2.3.3 *Transitional rules*

The transitional rules in the Treaty of Lisbon[206] relating to the abolition of the former third pillar appear in a special transitional Protocol, which governs a number of issues concerning the transition from the previous rules in the Treaties to the new rules introduced by the Treaty of Lisbon. There are three different issues relating to the former third pillar addressed by the Protocol: the jurisdiction of the Court of Justice over third pillar measures adopted before the entry into force of the Treaty of Lisbon ('pre-existing third pillar measures') for a five-year transitional period (ending 1 December 2014); the legal effect of those same measures (*not* subject to a transitional period); and the possibility of the UK to opt out of those measures at the end of the five-year transitional period.[207] The first two issues are considered here, while the third issue is considered further below, along with the other relevant opt-outs for the UK on JHA matters.[208]

First of all, the transitional provision on the Court of Justice states that the powers of the EU institutions, namely the role of the Commission in infringement actions and the jurisdiction of the Court of Justice, remained the same for pre-existing third pillar measures as before the Treaty of Lisbon for the five-year transitional period, including

---

[203] Art 293 TFEU. It is assumed in practice, at least by the Commission, that the former rule gives full discretion to the Commission to *withdraw* its proposals. However, the CJEU has set some constraints on this: see Case C-409/13 *Commission v Council*, ECLI:EU:C:2015:217.

[204] See Arts 294(15) and 238(2) and (3)(b) TFEU, as regards the ordinary legislative procedure and Council voting rules respectively.

[205] Equally, there is nothing to stop (a) Member State(s) which proposed an initiative bringing an action to annul it after its adoption.

[206] For more detailed analysis of this issue, see S Peers, 'Finally "Fit for Purpose?" The Treaty of Lisbon and the End of the Third Pillar Legal Order' (2008) 27 YEL 47.

[207] A complete list of binding pre-existing third pillar acts which were in force at the date of entry into force of the Treaty of Lisbon, as well as subsequent amendments and proposed amendments to those acts, appears in Appendix II.

[208] II:2.2.5.1.

where a Member State accepted the jurisdiction of the Court of Justice over references for a preliminary ruling pursuant to the previous rules.[209] This rule is now entirely moot, since that transitional period expired on 1 December 2014, and so will not be further considered here.[210]

Secondly, there are special rules on the legal effect of pre-existing third pillar measures. The transitional protocol provides that the legal effect of acts adopted on the basis of the TEU before the Treaty of Lisbon entered into force 'shall be preserved until those acts are repealed, annulled or amended in implementation of the Treaties'; this also applies to 'agreements concluded between Member States on the basis of' the TEU.[211] The latter phrase covers third pillar Conventions. There is no time limit on the application of this provision, which at the very least preserves the lack of direct effect of pre-existing Framework Decisions and Decisions, and also preserves other restrictions which arguably exist as regards the legal effect of pre-existing third pillar measures as compared to other EU law.[212] According to the CJEU, this provision means that the Council can still continue adopt measures *implementing* pre-Lisbon third pillar acts on the conditions that applied prior to 2009 (ie a QMV vote in Council), on condition that it still consult the EP, pursuant to the previous Article 39 TEU.[213]

In practice, this transitional rule remains relevant, since only a modest number of pre-Lisbon measures have been amended or repealed since the Treaty of Lisbon entered into force, mainly a handful of Framework Decisions on substantive criminal law and mutual recognition.[214] However, a Regulation to replace the third pillar Decision establishing Europol will soon be adopted, and a proposal to replace the rules establishing Eurojust is also pending.[215] As for the definition of an 'amendment' to a pre-existing third pillar act,[216] there is no *de minimis* rule, so it would seem that even a minor amendment to a pre-existing third pillar act would trigger the application of the new rules on legal effect to all the measures concerned. It makes sense that where there are measures implementing a parent act, only an amendment to the parent act would trigger the new rules concerned, which would then apply to the entirety of the parent act and all implementing measures as an *ensemble*, because the implementing measures depend on the parent act for their validity.[217] In order to give the protocol its

---

[209] Art 10(1), transitional protocol. All references in this sub-section are to the transitional protocol, unless otherwise indicated. On the substance of the previous rules on the Court's jurisdiction, see II:2.2.2 above.

[210] For detailed comments, see the third edition of this book, pp 61–3.

[211] Art 9. This provision also applies to pre-existing CFSP acts.

[212] On the legal effect of pre-existing third pillar measures, see II:2.2.2 above.

[213] Joined Cases C-317/13 and C-679/13 *EP v Council*, ECLI:EU:C:2015:223; Case C-540/13 *EP v Council*, ECLI:EU:C:2015:224; and C-363/14 *EP v Council*, ECLI:EU:C:2015:579. See also pending Cases C-595/14 *EP v Council*, C-14/15 *EP v Council*, and C-116/15 *EP v Council*. The judgment in Case C-130/10 *EP v Council*, ECLI:EU:C:2012:472 also touched upon the interpretation of these rules (as regards pre-Lisbon CFSP measures).

[214] See II:3.6, II:3.7, and II:5.5 below.   [215] See II:6.9 and II:7.8 below.

[216] This question is also relevant as regards the opt-outs of the UK and Ireland from JHA matters, since special rules apply if they opt-out of an amendment of an act which they are already bound by. See II:2.2.5.1 and II:2.2.5.2 below.

[217] The 2015 judgments of the CJEU (n 213 above) implicitly confirm this interpretation.

full effect, the new rules on legal effect and Court jurisdiction should apply to a pre-existing third pillar measure as soon as an amending act enters into force, rather than the date of applicability or the deadline for Member States to apply the amending act. For the same reasons, the provisions of the Schengen *acquis* allocated to the previous third pillar should be treated as a single act for the purposes of the protocol; but these provisions must be severed from the provisions of that *acquis* which were allocated to the EC legal order in 1999 (ie immigration measures), since the latter provisions are outside the scope of the transitional protocol.

2.2.3.4 *Special decision-making rules*

As noted above, in order to assuage some Member States' concerns about the loss of sovereignty in vital areas relating to criminal law and policing, the JHA provisions in the Treaty of Lisbon contain two special decision-making rules, one known as the 'emergency brake' and the other referred to in this book as the 'pseudo-veto'. The emergency brake applies to decisions regarding domestic criminal procedure and substantive criminal law,[218] while the pseudo-veto applies to decisions regarding the European Public Prosecutor and operational police cooperation (except for measures building upon the Schengen *acquis*).[219] In each case it will be necessary to distinguish between the legal bases which are subject to these special rules, and those legal bases which are not.[220] Both of these special procedures could lead to a discussion of a draft proposal or initiative at the level of the European Council (the EU leaders) and in both cases, one possible outcome is a 'fast-track' approval for a group of Member States to adopt the relevant measure without the participation of other Member States (the concept of 'enhanced cooperation'), circumventing the substantive or procedural requirements which would normally apply before enhanced cooperation could be authorized.[221]

But there are differences between the two procedures, which will therefore be considered in turn. In particular, a veto is distinct from an emergency brake because there are no limitations of the grounds on which a Member State could exercise a veto, whereas an emergency brake can only be pulled on specified grounds; and even if a emergency brake could be challenged or overridden, a veto cannot. Moreover, the pseudo-veto would trigger enhanced cooperation in a *positive* way—ie, a group of Member States *wanting* the adoption of a proposal would refer the issue to the European Council—whereas the emergency brake would trigger enhanced cooperation in a *negative* way, because it would be invoked by a single Member State objecting to a measure. Also,

---

[218] Arts 82(3) and 83(3) TFEU, referring to Arts 82(2) and 83(1) and (2) TFEU. However, where the adoption of 'Community criminal law' measures pursuant to Art 83(2) TFEU requires unanimous voting (for instance, as regards tax or racism), the emergency brake procedure would implicitly not apply, since it can only be used to suspend the ordinary legislative procedure (Art 83(3) TFEU), which always entails QMV.

[219] Arts 86 and 87(3) TFEU.

[220] Notably Arts 82(1) (cross-border mutual recognition measures), 85 (Eurojust), 87(2) (other forms of police cooperation), 88 (Europol), and 89 (cross-border police operations). See further II:3.2.4, II:5.2.4, II:6.2.4, and II:7.2.4 below.

[221] On those rules, see II:2.2.5.5 below.

the Member States invoking the pseudo-veto process would have comparative 'safety in numbers'.

In either case, it should be recalled that as few as seven Member States could make a criminal law or policing proposal pursuant to the Treaty of Lisbon provisions, so in such a case those Member States would only have to find two more allies to ensure the adoption of the measure by means of enhanced cooperation.[222]

2.2.3.4.1 Emergency brake

The Treaty rule which provides for this procedure as regards criminal law proposals or initiatives reads as follows: [223]

> Where a member of the Council considers that a draft directive as referred to in [the relevant provision] would affect fundamental aspects of its criminal justice system, it may request that the draft directive be referred to the European Council. In that case, the ordinary legislative procedure shall be suspended. After discussion, and in case of a consensus, the European Council shall, within four months of this suspension, refer the draft back to the Council, which shall terminate the suspension of the ordinary legislative procedure.
>
> Within the same timeframe, in case of disagreement, and if at least nine Member States wish to establish enhanced cooperation on the basis of the draft directive concerned, they shall notify the European Parliament, the Council and the Commission accordingly. In such a case, the authorisation to proceed with enhanced cooperation referred to in Article 20(2) of the Treaty on European Union and Article 329(1) of this Treaty shall be deemed to be granted and the provisions on enhanced cooperation shall apply.

The following analysis sets out in turn: a comparison between the emergency brake rules and the rules on enhanced cooperation; an examination of the grounds for invoking the emergency brake, including the question of whether a decision to pull the brake is judicially reviewable; an analysis of the procedure in the European Council; and an assessment of the overall political context of the emergency brake.

First of all, the fast-track route to enhanced cooperation which would apply if the emergency brake were pulled would circumvent the usual requirements of a proposal from the Commission, the consent of the EP, and the support of a qualified majority of *all* Member States before enhanced cooperation is applied.[224] After enhanced cooperation is authorized, only the representatives of the participating Member States could vote on the legislation in the Council;[225] but in the EP, *all* MEPs would have a vote. It should also be pointed out that a Member State which did not originally participate in the adoption of the legislation could participate later if it were able to comply with the relevant conditions.[226] On the other hand, Member States joining the EU in future would not be obliged to participate in the relevant measure.[227]

---

[222] See Art 76 TFEU, discussed in II:2.2.3.2 above.

[223] This discussion is adapted from S Peers, 'EU Criminal Law and the Treaty of Lisbon' (2008) 33 ELRev 507 at 522–9.

[224] Art 329(1) TFEU.   [225] Art 330 TFEU.

[226] Art 331(1) TFEU. This also applies to the UK and Ireland, if they decide to opt-out of the legislation: see II:2.2.5.1 below.

[227] Revised Art 20(4) TEU.

The practical importance of circumventing the requirement for an approval of the enhanced cooperation by a qualified majority of *all* members of the Council can be demonstrated by the difficulties in adopting the Commission's original proposal on suspects' rights within the previous legal framework, where there was no fast-track route to enhanced cooperation.[228] Several Member States objected to the adoption of this proposal, preventing its adoption due to the previous requirement of unanimity for third pillar measures, but a qualified majority of Member States was in favour of the *proposal*. However, when the German Council Presidency in 2007 held an indicative vote as to whether there was enough support to authorize enhanced cooperation as regards this measure, there was *not* a qualified majority in favour of *authorizing enhanced cooperation*. It can be seen that the Treaty of Lisbon rules, by removing the requirement of QMV approval by all Member States (along with other requirements), therefore in principle make enhanced cooperation more likely. In fact, it is possible that the mere existence of the emergency brake process has encouraged Member States (and the Commission and EP) to authorize enhanced cooperation more readily (as regards criminal law) pursuant to the normal authorization rules, thereby avoiding the high-profile drama of a referral of draft legislation to the European Council.[229]

Some important *substantive* conditions being circumvented would be the requirements not to 'undermine the internal market', not to 'constitute a barrier to or a discrimination in trade between Member States' and not to 'distort competition between them'.[230] This could be particularly relevant where some Member States do not participate in measures adopted pursuant to the 'Community criminal law competence' in Art 83(2) TFEU,[231] or in measures which are otherwise likely to have a significant impact on private industry (such as legislation concerning money laundering or relating to bank account information). The Final Act of the Treaty of Lisbon includes a declaration concerning the possible use of a special rule regarding distortion of competition in the event that this happens.[232]

Emergency brakes can be found elsewhere in the Treaties,[233] although such brakes have never in fact been used to date. They are always linked to qualified majority voting. The criminal law emergency brakes are distinct in that they are the only emergency brakes which could trigger a fast-track authorization of enhanced cooperation.

The second issue is the grounds for pulling an emergency brake, including the question of the extent to which a Member State's power to pull the emergency brake would be

---

[228] COM (2004) 328, 28 Apr 2004. On the substance of this issue, see II:4.6 below.

[229] There is nothing in the Treaty to suggest that *only* the fast-track process, rather than the normal procedure, can be used to authorize enhanced cooperation as regards criminal law.

[230] Art 326 TFEU.   [231] On this competence, see further II:5.4.1.2 below.

[232] Declaration 26, referring to Art 116 TFEU. It is arguable, however, that this Declaration only applies to opt-outs, rather than enhanced cooperation, since it refers to cases where a Member State 'opts not to participate' in a measure. Then again, if Member States which do not participate in a measure due to an opt-out are sanctioned, but those Member States which have not participated in the same measure due to enhanced cooperation are *not* sanctioned, this would breach the principle of equality of Member States, as set out in the revised Art 4(2) TEU.

[233] The current provisions relate to foreign policy (Art 31(2), revised TEU) and social security coordination (Art 48 TFEU). The Treaty of Amsterdam initially provided for emergency brakes as regards authorization for enhanced cooperation (Arts 11(2) TEC and previous 40(2) TEU), but the Treaty of Nice abolished them.

reviewable. The decision to pull the emergency brake should not be directly reviewable as such before the EU courts, since it would be a step in the decision-making process, rather than a final legal act.[234] But if a Member State's attempt to pull the emergency brake were overruled by other Member States in the Council, the dissenting Member State could argue before the Court of Justice that it should have been allowed to pull the brake. Equally, if a Member State is allowed to pull the emergency brake and another Member State or the Commission argues that this should not have been allowed, there could be an annulment action before the Court of Justice raising this issue. In either case, the criteria for the use of the emergency brake would be justiciable.[235]

In considering the reviewability of an emergency brake, it will be necessary to strike a balance between the absolute right of a Member State to block a measure and the prospect that the majority of Member States might override one Member State's legitimate concerns about the integrity of its criminal justice system. So a Member State which wished to pull an emergency brake relating to criminal law would have to substantiate its argument that a draft measure would affect fundamental aspects of its criminal justice system. To do this, the dissenting Member State would have to demonstrate four things: its objections relate to a current draft proposal or initiative, not to a previous draft, or a hypothetical future draft; its concerns relate to its *criminal justice* system, not to another issue (such as world trade talks or the impact of the Second World War); the effect of the draft proposal or initiative on its criminal justice system, in order to prove that its national laws or principles would be required to change in some way; and why the relevant national rule is considered *fundamental*. In the latter two cases, any doubt would have to be resolved in favour of the Member State concerned, since that Member State is obviously the best judge (as it were) of its own criminal justice system, even if other Member States which have (or had) a similar or identical rule in their national legal system do not (or did not) consider that rule to be fundamental.

Implicitly it would be illegal for a *supporter* of the proposed legislation to use the emergency brake falsely, in order to trigger a fast-track authorization of enhanced cooperation, for the simple reason that such a Member State would not in fact have any genuine concerns about the impact of the proposal upon the fundamental aspects of its criminal justice system. Put another way, it has been pointed out by way of analogy that 'the abuse of emergency facilities is a crime in many Member States'.[236]

The third question is how the dispute settlement process in the European Council would work. The Treaty clearly specifies that a 'request' to the European Council would suspend the ordinary legislative procedure, presumably even 'stopping the clock' on the deadlines that apply to the second or third reading.[237] Although the Treaty only refers to a resumption of the legislative process, in the event of 'consensus', or a fast-track to enhanced

---

[234] See K Lenaerts, D Arts, and I Maselis, *Procedural Law of the European Union*, 2nd edn (Thomson, 2006), 215–16.
[235] The EP could not bring a legal challenge on this point, as it would have jointly adopted the legislation with the Council.
[236] S Carrera and F Geyer, *The Reform Treaty and Justice and Home Affairs: Implications for the Common Area of Freedom, Security and Justice* (CEPS Policy Brief No. 141, Aug 2007), 9.
[237] See Art 294 TFEU.

cooperation, in the event of a 'disagreement',[238] it is also possible that there would be a 'disagreement' without nine Member States in favour of enhanced cooperation, in which case the discussions on the draft proposal or initiative would be suspended indefinitely.

As for the EP, even though it would not be involved in the decision-making by the European Council, and would lose its normal veto power over authorization of enhanced cooperation, it would still retain its normal decision-making powers pursuant to the ordinary legislative procedure when it came to adopt the subsequent legislation, whether there was a deal among all Member States or whether the fast-track enhanced cooperation had been authorized.

Of course, if enough Member States really dislike a particular proposal, they could always try to assemble a blocking minority rather than use the emergency brake.[239] If the emergency brake were not pulled, this would preclude access to fast-track authorization of enhanced cooperation—and even access to enhanced cooperation under the ordinary procedure for authorizing it, as long as the Member States which constitute the blocking minority are also willing to block the authorization of enhanced cooperation by the Council in that case. This might lead the Member States in favour of the proposal to consider mechanisms to adopt it outside the EU legal framework.

As regards the political context of the emergency brake, given the high-profile awkwardness of pulling the brake, it is possible that in practice the mere threat of pulling it, or even the clear indication that pulling it might be contemplated, would be sufficient to induce a majority in Council to offer sufficient concessions to the dissenting Member State. Even before the Treaty of Lisbon entered into force, there was some EU legislation which deferred to the constitutional or fundamental criminal justice rules of Member States.[240] In light of this, it might be expected that an emergency brake would actually be pulled only when the two sides in a dispute held intractably opposed and irreconcilable positions of principle, and/or when a Member State's relationship with the EU had generally broken down.

Finally, it seems likely that the existence of the emergency brake will reduce the likelihood that Member States will litigate against controversial criminal law legislation before the Court of Justice. Where Member States are able to protect their interests by means of a political process, they should have less need of recourse to the courts.

2.2.3.4.2 'Pseudo-veto'

The Treaty rule which provides for this procedure reads as follows:[241]

> In the absence of unanimity in the Council, a group of at least nine Member States may request that the draft [regulation/measures] be referred to the European Council.

---

[238] Although a 'consensus' is not defined in the Treaty (see Art 15(4), revised TEU), presumably in this context at least it is implicitly defined by reference to a 'disagreement', and must therefore mean the consent of all Member States. It appears the UK, Ireland, and Denmark could also participate in the discussions in the European Council even if they have opted out of the original proposal, because the Protocol on their opt-out from JHA measures only refers to non-participation in discussions within the *Council* (Art 1, Title V Protocol; Art 1, Danish Protocol; and Art 1, Annex to Danish Protocol).

[239] For the definition of a blocking minority, see Art 16(4) and (5), revised TEU, and Art 3 of the transitional protocol.

[240] Art 9e of the Eurojust Decision, as amended ([2009] OJ L 138/14).

[241] Arts 86(1) and 87(3) TFEU.

In that case, the procedure in the Council shall be suspended. After discussion, and in case of a consensus, the European Council shall, within four months of this suspension, refer the draft back to the Council for adoption.

Within the same timeframe, in case of disagreement, and if at least nine Member States wish to establish enhanced cooperation on the basis of the draft [regulation/ measures] concerned, they shall notify the European Parliament, the Council and the Commission accordingly. In such a case, the authorisation to proceed with enhanced cooperation referred to in Article 20(2) of the Treaty on European Union and Article 329(1) of this Treaty shall be deemed to be granted and the provisions on enhanced cooperation shall apply.

It can be seen that this process is identical to the emergency brake rules, except that in this case the trigger for the process is the request by a group of Member States, rather than an objection by a single Member State, and the underlying decision-making process is different (unanimity in Council, rather than the ordinary legislative procedure). Much of the above analysis of the emergency brake is therefore equally applicable to the pseudo-veto process. But there are two distinct issues which call for further comment.

First of all, as with the enhanced cooperation procedure, the Treaty rules on the pseudo-veto procedure do not provide for the possibility of *failure* to adopt the proposal at all, in the event that it is blocked in the European Council and there are not enough Member States wishing to adopt it by means of enhanced cooperation. However, as regards the pseudo-veto, it is very likely that the nine Member States which refer the issue to the European Council would be willing to adopt that measure by such means, and would be taking that consideration into account when they refer the issue, so the prospect of failure would be unlikely. It should be noted, though, that the Treaty does not *require* that the same nine Member States who refer the issue to the European Council would then have to embark upon enhanced cooperation in the event of a continued disagreement.

Secondly, it should be noted that participants in the enhanced cooperation would be able to change the decision-making rules to shift unanimity to qualified majority voting and to shift a special legislative procedure to an ordinary legislative procedure.[242]

Although the two sets of special procedures are complex, overall they should generally be welcomed. The emergency brake procedure strikes a reasonable balance between the need to ensure the effectiveness and democratic legitimacy of EU policy on the one hand, by extending QMV and the role of the EP, and ensuring on the other hand that Member States can, if necessary, protect the fundamental elements of their criminal justice system. As for the pseudo-veto procedure, it also strikes a fair balance between the legitimate interests of Member States in protecting their sovereignty by means of a veto in the sensitive areas of police operations and the creation of a European Public Prosecutor and the desirability of facilitating enhanced cooperation within the EU framework for those Member States which are particularly committed to

---

[242] Art 333 TFEU; see further I:2.2.5.5.

particular proposals. While these special procedures, if ever used, would fragment EU law to some extent, the alternative to this would not be no fragmentation at all—rather it would be fragmentation *outside* the EU framework, where the problems of legitimacy are even more acute than those which exist within the EU legal system.[243]

2.2.4 Competence issues

The continuing controversy about the distinction between the EU's criminal, civil, or policing law competence and its non-JHA competence is discussed further below.[244] The remaining issues have concerned the scope and intensity of EU competence over these issues, in particular the extent of any 'cross-border' requirement for the EC or EU to adopt criminal or civil law measures and the intensity of EU powers over criminal procedure. These issues are addressed in detail in various chapters of this book.[245] The extension of majority voting to the adoption of EU law in these areas raises the prospect that outvoted Member States will raise competence issues in the Court of Justice, where there was no relevant or emergency brake.

The horizontal rules concerning EU competence, discussed further in the parallel chapter in volume 1, describe JHA matters a 'shared competence' between the EU and its Member States.[246] This still leaves it open for the EU to 'occupy the field' by fully harmonizing the issue concerned.[247] However, Article 2(6) TFEU also points out that the precise 'scope' of the EU's competence is set out in the specific Treaty provisions related to each area, and in this field, the Treaty expressly states that EU rules relating to substantive criminal law and domestic criminal procedure set 'minimum' standards only.[248] Furthermore, harmonization of national law is ruled out as regards crime prevention.[249] There are also horizontal reserves of national competence in the general provisions of the JHA Title and in the TEU, discussed in detail above.[250] On the other hand, the references to a common policy in the areas of immigration and asylum do not mean *a contrario* that full harmonization of the law is *excluded* in other areas (in particular, civil law, mutual recognition measures in criminal law, and policing law), since the possibility of full harmonization in areas of shared competence still applies to those parts of Title V as well.

Finally, it should be noted that the exercise of the EU's JHA competences is subject to the principles of subsidiary and proportionality.[251]

2.2.5 Territorial scope

Distinctions in the territorial scope of JHA measures have to some extent been created outside the EU legal framework, most prominently as regards the development of

---

[243] I:2.5.   [244] II:2.4.   [245] See s 2.4 of chs 3–8.   [246] Art 4(2)(j) TFEU.

[247] On the related question of external competence, see Art 3(2) TFEU and the discussion in II:2.7 below.

[248] Arts 82(2), 83(1), and 83(2) TFEU.

[249] Art 84 TFEU. The EU instead is limited to providing incentives, promoting, and supporting *Member States'* actions in this area: see Art 2(5) TFEU.

[250] Arts 72 and 73 TFEU and Art 4(2), revised TEU, discussed in II:2.2.3.2 above.

[251] See Art 5, revised TEU, and I:2.5.

the Schengen *acquis* from 1985 onward, and also as regards the negotiation of a later treaty largely concerning police cooperation, the 'Prum Convention', among a group of Member States in 2005.[252]

Since the Treaty of Lisbon abolished the third pillar and applied normal EU rules on decision-making, legal instruments, and judicial control to all JHA matters, the territorial scope of JHA measures remains the only issue that clearly differentiates JHA issues from most of the rest of EU law. The following discussion looks in turn at the legal position of: the UK and Ireland; Denmark; the Member States which joined the EU in 2004, 2007, and 2013; and Norway, Iceland, Switzerland, and Liechtenstein. Finally, it examines the general rules in the Treaties concerning 'enhanced cooperation', which in principle allow for the adoption of measures across most areas of EU law, including JHA law, without the full participation of all Member States. The general legal framework in each case was described in the parallel chapter in volume 1: the discussion here focuses on the rules as they affect civil, criminal, and policing law.

2.2.5.1 United Kingdom and Ireland

The UK and Ireland are both covered by a specific protocol on border controls, a specific protocol on the possibility of opting in to any JHA measure, and to specific rules as regards the Schengen *acquis*. Since the Treaty of Lisbon, the UK alone had an option to opt out of all third pillar measures adopted before the entry into force of the Treaty of Lisbon as of the end of a five-year transitional period in 2014. It decided to exercise this option, but it then opted back in to some of these measures. These various opt-outs will be considered in turn (except for the border control opt-out, which was discussed in volume 1).

The general JHA opt-out Protocol for these States applied (as from the Treaty of Amsterdam) to civil law measures, then was extended to criminal law and policing measures by the Treaty of Lisbon, which also made other amendments to the text.[253] However, Ireland has no opt-out as regards anti-terrorist sanctions.[254] The separate Protocol on the Schengen *acquis* applies when a criminal law or policing measure builds upon Schengen rules.[255]

The default position under the Title V Protocol is that the UK and Ireland opt out of each individual proposal, unless they choose to 'opt in' to each individual measure, by giving notice within three months after the proposal is made. Even if they opt out initially, they can opt in later on, after the measure is adopted.

In practice,[256] the UK and Irish governments have opted in to a significant majority of civil cooperation measures and about half of the criminal law and policing proposals.

---

[252] On Schengen integration, see I:2.2.2.2. For the text of the Prum Convention, see Council doc 10900/05, 7 July 2005. On its integration into the EU legal framework, see II:7.6 below.
[253] This book refers to this Protocol as the 'Title V Protocol' throughout. All references in this subsection are to this Protocol, unless otherwise indicated.
[254] Art 9, as inserted by the Treaty of Lisbon. The UK made a unilateral declaration to the Treaty of Lisbon asserting that it 'intends to exercise its right' to opt in to such measures (Declaration 65 in the Final Act).
[255] See particularly Case C-482/08 *UK v Council* [2010] ECR I-10413, where the CJEU ruled that a policing measure (law enforcement access to the Visa Information System) built upon the Schengen visa rules.
[256] For further detail, see s 2.5 of chs 3–8.

The two governments have largely opted in to or out of the same measures, but not all of the time. It is possible that a measure can be adopted despite an opt-in, if the UK or Ireland is still blocking it (or part of a blocking minority), by excluding that Member State from voting if there is no agreement within a 'reasonable time'. In June 2010, the Spanish Council Presidency threatened to invoke this clause and exclude the UK from participation in the proposed Directive establishing a European protection order, in order to obtain agreement on the proposal. However, the UK's qualms about the legal base of the proposal (extending to civil law issues) were shared by the Commission and some other Member States, and ultimately the civil law aspects of the proposal were instead removed and included in a separate Regulation.[257]

On several occasions, the UK decided to opt out of a proposal in the areas of civil, criminal, or policing law initially due to concerns about it (or possible changes to the proposal during negotiations), but then decided to opt in after its adoption,[258] pursuant to the enhanced cooperation rules.[259] In each case, the UK from the outset indicated an intention to opt in if the final text of the legislation satisfied its concerns, and participated actively (albeit informally) in the negotiations to that end.

The Title V Protocol also specifies that the UK and Ireland are not bound by the general rules on data protection that may be adopted pursuant to Article 16 TFEU to the extent that they are not bound by the underlying policing or criminal law measure to which those general rules relate.[260]

As discussed in the parallel chapter in volume 1, it is possible that the UK or Ireland could be forced to end their participation in JHA measures they have already opted in to, if they do not participate in measures amending them. As regards criminal law in particular, this should mean that any Council of Europe Conventions which had been disapplied in relations between Member States by the prior EU measures would then re-apply in relations between the UK and/or Ireland, on the one hand, and the other Member States, on the other, since the legal basis for disapplying those measures as between those States would no longer be in force.[261]

As for the Schengen *acquis*, the 'Schengen Protocol' to the Treaties gave the UK and Ireland the possibility of applying to participate in only part of that *acquis*, subject to a decision in favour by the Council, acting with the unanimous approval of the Schengen States.[262] As discussed in detail in the parallel chapter in volume 1, the Council accepted

---

[257] See the press release of the JHA Council, 3–4 June 2010. The UK and the other dissenting Member States were objecting to this proposal due to (well-founded) concerns about its legal base: see II:3.2.4 below. On the substance of the Directive, see II:3.7.6 below; for the text, see [2010] OJ C 69/5. On the civil law Regulation, see II:8.5.1 below.

[258] Reg 593/2008 on conflict of law in contract (Rome I Reg), Reg 4/2009 on maintenance, and Dir 2011/36 on human trafficking (respectively [2008] OJ L 177/6 and [2009] OJ L 7/1, and [2011] OJ L 101/1). The Commission approved UK participation by means of Decisions ([2009] OJ L 10/22, [2009] OJ L 149/73, and [2011] OJ L 271/49). See also the Commission opinions on UK participation in COM (2008) 730, 7 Nov 2008 and COM (2009) 181, 21 Apr 2009.

[259] Art 11a EC (before Lisbon) and Art 331(1) TFEU (after Lisbon); see further II:2.2.5.5 below.

[260] Art 6a, inserted by the Treaty of Lisbon. See more generally II:7.2.4 and II:7.2.5 below.

[261] For example, the Council of Europe Convention on extradition and its Protocols would re-apply between those States if the Framework Decision on the European Arrest Warrant were disapplied between them.

[262] Art 4, Schengen Protocol. This provision has not been amended by the Treaty of Lisbon.

the UK's application for partial participation in Schengen in 2000, and the parallel Irish application in 2002.[263] The UK then took part in the Schengen rules in practice since 2005, apart from the Schengen Information System, which it has applied from 2015.[264] The opt-in means that these Member States participate (or will participate) in almost all of the criminal law and policing provisions of Schengen,[265] including SIS data relating to policing and judicial cooperation, but not immigration.

This means that the UK and Ireland also have to opt in to measures building upon the parts of the Schengen *acquis* which they have already opted in to, although they have the possibility to opt out of new measures subject to the risk that some of their existing participation will be rescinded as a result. However, they cannot opt in to measures building upon parts of the Schengen *acquis* which they have not opted in to, even where those measures concern police cooperation—if they are related to visas, as was the case for the rules on law enforcement access to the data in the Visa Information System.[266]

Next, the UK (but not Ireland) had the possibility (which it used) of invoking a 'block opt-out' from all pre-Lisbon EU criminal law and policing law, at the end of the transitional period of five years established by the transitional Protocol attached to the Treaties by the Treaty of Lisbon which expired on 1 December 2014. The opt-out only applied to acts which had not been amended during that transitional period.[267] Equally, it did not apply to acts adopted *after* the entry into force of the Treaty of Lisbon, which the UK had opted in to.

To invoke this opt-out, the UK had to notify the Council '[a]t the latest' six months before the end of the transitional period (so by 1 June 2014) that it objected to the powers of the EU institutions (ie the Court of Justice and the Commission, as regards infringement proceedings) becoming applicable to those measures. The UK's notification triggered the non-application of the acts concerned.

However, the UK could 'at any time afterwards' notify the Council that it wished to participate in pre-existing third pillar measures which it has opted out of.[268] In practice, the UK decided that there were about thirty-five pre-Lisbon measures which it still wished to participate in, so it invoked this provision so that there was no gap in application of those measures.[269] In effect, then, the UK only opted out of *part* of its pre-existing third pillar commitments. It is still possible for the UK to opt back in to further pre-Lisbon measures in future, as the wording of this provision makes clear ('at any time'). Indeed, it may do this in practice, as discussed below. The Protocol

---

[263] Decisions 2000/365/EC ([2000] OJ L 131/43) and 2002/192/EC ([2002] OJ L 64/20).

[264] See [2004] OJ L 395/70 and [2015] OJ L 36/8.

[265] Art 1 of each Decision. The exceptions are cross-border hot pursuit by police (for the UK) and cross-border police hot pursuit and surveillance (for Ireland).

[266] Case C-482/08 *UK v Council* [2010] ECR I-10413.

[267] Art 10(4), first sub-paragraph, transitional protocol. For a list of the acts which were amended up until the end of the period, see [2014] OJ C 430/23.

[268] Art 10(5), transitional protocol.

[269] See the Council and Commission decisions authorizing the UK to opt back in to these measures ([2014] OJ L 345/1 and 6). For the details of the measures which the UK opted back into, see s 2.5 of each of chs 3, 5, 6, and 7 of this volume. The Council amended the Decisions on the UK's opt-in to the Schengen rules: for a consolidated version, see [2014] OJ C 430/1 and 6. For a list of the measures which the UK opted out of, see [2014] OJ C 430/17.

explicitly confirms that when the UK opted back in to these measures, the jurisdiction of the Court of Justice and the Commission's powers over infringement actions became applicable.

The transitional protocol gives the Council the power, by QMV on a Commission proposal without UK participation, to 'determine the necessary consequential and transitional arrangements'.[270] The Council adopted a decision to this end, covering the UK's participation for a 'crossover' week in December 2014, but also requiring the UK to consider whether it wished to opt back in to the 'Prum' decisions on information exchange by autumn 2015.[271] Also, the Council, acting by QMV on a Commission proposal *with* UK participation, 'may also adopt a decision determining that the United Kingdom shall bear the direct financial consequences, if any, necessarily and unavoidably incurred' by its ceased participation.[272] Again, the Council exercised this power, requiring the UK to pay back €1.5 million it had received to prepare for participation in the Prum Decisions, if in fact it decides not to participate.[273]

Finally, given that some pre-Lisbon measures in the area of criminal law or policing have been replaced by post-Lisbon measures in which the UK and/or Ireland do not participate, it is possible that those Member States have 'opted out by repeal' from the previous measures. But for the reasons detailed in the parallel chapter in volume 1, this interpretation is not correct, and the previous measures remain binding on the Member States concerned.[274]

2.2.5.2 Denmark

As noted in the parallel chapter in volume 1, Denmark gained an opt-out from EU civil law measures (along with immigration and asylum measures) in 1999, which was extended to policing and criminal law measures in 2009.[275] According to the relevant Protocol, third pillar acts adopted *before* the entry into force of the Treaty of Lisbon 'which are amended shall continue to be binding upon and applicable to Denmark unchanged'.[276] Denmark does, however, participate in the Schengen *acquis* and measures building upon it, and in a few civil law measures by way of treaties with the EU.

Furthermore, Denmark either has an option to denounce its opt-out entirely, or to move to an opt-out system essentially identical to that of the UK and Ireland (leaving aside Danish participation in Schengen). It held a referendum asking the Danish public to approve the latter option in December 2015, but the suggestion was rejected.[277]

---

[270] Art 10(4), second sub-paragraph, transitional protocol.
[271] [2014] OJ L 343/11. The UK government stated in autumn 2015 that it indeed wished to opt back in to the Prum Decisions.
[272] Art 10(4), third sub-paragraph, transitional protocol.   [273] [2014] OJ L 343/17.
[274] I:2.2.5.1.4.
[275] Protocol on Denmark. The Treaty of Lisbon added a new Art 2a concerning data protection, which is equivalent to a clause inserted into the Title V Protocol for the UK and Ireland (see II:2.2.5.1 above).
[276] Art 2, final sentence. Presumably the word 'amended' means amendments which are adopted after the Treaty of Lisbon entered into force, and also has the same meaning as it does in the Title V Protocol relating to the UK and Ireland (I:2.2.5.1) and in the transitional Protocol to the Treaty of Lisbon (II:2.2.3.3 above).
[277] For further details, see s 2.5 of each of chs 3 to 8.

2.2.5.3 Accession states

As discussed in more detail in the parallel chapter in volume 1,[278] the 2003 Accession Treaty which provided for ten new Member States to join the EU in 2004 requires them to be bound by the entire Schengen *acquis*, with certain parts (including most of the criminal law and policing provisions) applicable from the date of accession. The remainder of the *acquis* (in this context, hot pursuit, cross-border surveillance, and the Schengen Information System) only applied from a later date set by the Council, although in practice the newer Member States usually began to apply the SIS even before this point.

There are also two features of the accession process which are particularly relevant to civil, criminal, and policing law. First of all, the Act of Accession also provided that the new Member States had to accede to JHA Conventions or instruments 'which are inseparable from the attainment of the objectives of' the EU Treaty,[279] whether those measures were opened for signature by the old Member States or drawn up by the Council in accordance with Title VI of the EU Treaty (ie, the old third pillar); the new Member States also had to take the administrative and other measures necessary to facilitate JHA cooperation. Similarly, the new Member States had to accede to Conventions drawn up on the basis of Article 293 EC (since repealed by the Treaty of Lisbon) and those inseparable from the objectives of the EC Treaty.[280] They also had to accede to treaties established on the basis of Article 38 EU (external third pillar treaties).[281] In practice, the new Member States quickly ratified a significant number of Conventions and Protocols, although this ratification process is not yet complete.[282]

Secondly, a specific JHA safeguard in the Act provided that for three years after the date of accession (so up until 1 May 2007), the Commission could have taken 'appropriate measures' if there had been insufficient application of a measure concerning mutual recognition in civil law or criminal law by a new Member State.[283] In practice, this safeguard clause was not applied. There are also specific issues relating to northern Cyprus as regards the territorial scope of the EU's civil law legislation.[284]

The model set out in the 2003 Treaty of Accession was largely copied in the 2005 Treaty of Accession with Romania and Bulgaria, in force from 1 January 2007, except that this time most JHA Conventions applied to the new Member States from a date decided by the Council, acting unanimously.[285] Again the special JHA safeguard was not applied within its three-year period of applicability.[286] That revised model was copied in turn for the Treaty of Accession with Croatia.[287]

---

[278] I:2.2.5.3. [279] Art 3(4), Act of Accession. [280] Art 5(2), Act of Accession.
[281] For details on these treaties, see II:2.7.2. [282] For ratification details, see Appendix I.
[283] Art 39, Act of Accession.
[284] Case C-420/07 *Apostolides* [2009] ECR I-3571; see further I:8.2.5.
[285] Art 3 and Annex I to Act of Accession ([2005] OJ L 157/203). In practice, the Council extended the application of all relevant Conventions to Romania and Bulgaria by the end of 2007: [2007] OJ L 200/47 (Europol); [2007] OJ L 307/20 (CIS); [2008] OJ L 9/23 (anti-fraud Convention); [2007] OJ L 304/34 (corruption); [2008] OJ L 9/21 (Naples II); [2007] OJ L 307/18 (mutual assistance); [2007] OJ L 307/22 (driving disqualification); and [2007] OJ L 347/1 (Rome Convention).
[286] Art 38 of the Act of Accession (ibid). There were regular reports from the Commission on the application by Romania and Bulgaria of, inter alia, standards regarding judicial reform. See, for instance, COM (2010) 112 and 113, 23 Mar 2010.
[287] [2011] OJ L 112. The Commission has proposed Council decisions on Croatian participation in the Conventions on corruption (COM (2014) 681, 28 Oct 2014), mutual assistance (COM (2014) 685, 28 Oct 2014), fraud (COM (2015) 458, 16 Sep 2015), and customs cooperation (COM (2015) 556, 9 Nov 2015).

2.2.5.4 *Norway, Iceland, Switzerland, and Liechtenstein*

As noted in the parallel chapter in volume 1, Norway and Iceland participate in the Schengen rules, including the criminal law and policing provisions. Also, Norway and Iceland have agreed to treaties associating them with the EU's mutual assistance Convention and Protocol,[288] the surrender of fugitives (a version of the EU's European Arrest Warrant),[289] and the 'Prum Decision' relating to police cooperation.[290]

On the other hand, Switzerland and Liechtenstein, who are also associated with the Schengen *acquis* (as from 2008 and 2011), are not obliged to apply a particular Schengen rule relating to mutual criminal assistance,[291] and have not agreed any further treaties relating to mutual assistance, the surrender procedure, or the Prum Decision on police cooperation with the EU.

2.2.5.5 *General rules on enhanced cooperation*

As discussed in more detail in the parallel chapter in volume 1,[292] general provisions on 'enhanced cooperation', ie the process of some Member States participating in EU measures without some other Member States, were first introduced in the Treaty of Amsterdam, and these provisions were amended by the Treaty of Nice. These rules were never in fact used, except in the context of the UK and Ireland opting in to immigration, asylum, and civil law measures after those measures had already been adopted.[293] However, it is striking to note that there were two attempts to use these provisions in civil and criminal law: as regards a proposal on criminal suspects' rights, where enhanced cooperation failed because there were insufficient votes in the Council to support authorization of enhanced cooperation when the issue was raised informally;[294] and as regards the 'Rome III' proposal for choice of law on divorce, because the Commission did not respond, before the Treaty of Lisbon entered into force, to a group of Member States which requested authorization for enhanced cooperation.[295]

The Treaty of Lisbon subsequently amended the enhanced cooperation rules again, inter alia, in order to merge the separate rules governing the former first and third pillars.[296] Interestingly, one of the three examples of uses of enhanced cooperation to date is in the area of civil law (the Rome III Regulation on choice of law in divorce, after the Commission replied to the request on this issue). The possible relevance of enhanced cooperation in these fields is confirmed by the fast-track rules which could lead to enhanced cooperation as regards many criminal or policing law issues, which were discussed above.[297] As noted in chapter 8 of this volume, they could also be

---

[288] [2004] OJ L 26/1. The treaty entered into force on 1 Jan 2013: [2012] OJ L 322/1.

[289] [2006] OJ L 292/1. The treaty has been concluded by the EU ([2014] OJ L 343/1) and Norway, but is not yet in force pending Icelandic ratification. See further II:3.2.5 below.

[290] [2009] OJ L 353/1. The treaty has been signed and applies provisionally, but has not yet entered into force. The Commission proposed its conclusion after the entry into force of the Treaty of Lisbon (COM (2009) 707, 17 Dec 2009). See further II:7.2.5 below.

[291] On the specific legislation which these States apply, see s 2.5 of chs 3, 5, 6, and 7.

[292] I:2.2.5.5.   [293] See I:2.2.5.1 and II:2.2.5.1.   [294] See II:2.2.3.4.1 above.

[295] See II:8.6 below.   [296] Art 20, revised TEU and Arts 326–34 TFEU, discussed in I:2.2.5.5.

[297] See II:2.2.3.4 above.

relevant in the area of family law again, as with the Rome III Regulation, given that unanimity applies in this area. In that case, after authorization of enhanced cooperation,
unanimity of the participating States would have to be necessary to adopt the legislation. After enhanced cooperation is authorized, it is possible for the participating States
to agree to change the voting rules as regards an issue among themselves (Article 333
TFEU). This could be a route for those Member States to shift to QMV and/or the
ordinary legislative procedure as regards family law, the European Public Prosecutor,
operational police cooperation, or decisions to extend EU criminal law competence.

2.3 Human Rights

The details of the EU's human rights framework—consisting of general principles of
law, the EU Charter of Fundamental Rights, and the planned accession to the ECHR—
were discussed in detail in the parallel chapter in volume 1.[298] These provisions are
relevant to the subject-matter of this volume particularly as regards controls on detention, the right to a fair trial and effective remedy, rights of the defence, limits on criminalization, and double jeopardy rules.[299] The CJEU has also clarified the scope of the
EU rules and the limitations on these rights in the field of EU civil and criminal law.[300]
These issues are discussed in further detail in section 3 of Chapters 3–8 of this volume.

2.4 Impact of Other EU Law

It remains important in practice to distinguish between JHA rules (in their various
forms) and the rules governing other areas of EU law ('non-JHA law'), because the latter, but not the former, usually entails full application of the law to all Member States.[301]
The details of this distinction in general are discussed in the parallel institutional chapter in volume 1,[302] but this section supplements that analysis by looking in more detail
at issues specific to civil, criminal, and policing law.

During the Treaty of Amsterdam period, there were particular disputes about the
scope of EC powers over criminal law and policing-related issues. These arguments
culminated in two judgments of the Court of Justice supporting the Commission's view
that the EC, not the EU, had power during this period to adopt legislation concerning
the enforcement of environmental law, or law relating to the environment, by means of
imposing criminal liability.[303] The approach of the Court to the first/third pillar dividing
line in these judgments was to apply the previous Article 47 TEU (which provided that
the TEU did not affect the Community treaties) to assess whether the subject-matter of

---

[298] See I:2.3.   [299] Arts 6 and 47–50 of the Charter.   [300] Arts 51 and 52 of the Charter.
[301] For the detailed rules governing the territorial scope of JHA measures, see II:2.2.5 above.
[302] I:2.4. For more detailed comments regarding each field, see also section 2.4 in each of chs 3–8.
[303] Cases C-176/03 *Commission v Council* [2005] ECR I-7879 and C-440/05 *Commission v Council*
[2007] ECR I-9097. This led to the adoption of EC legislation providing for criminal penalties: Dirs 2008/
99 ([2008] OJ L 328/28), 2009/123 ([2009] OJ L 280/52), and 2009/52 ([2009] OJ L 168/24). See also the
Commission communication on this issue (COM (2005) 583, 23 Nov 2005), and the detailed comments in
II:5.4 below.

the contested third pillar Framework Decisions fell within the scope of the first pillar. Since it did, there was implicitly no need to assess whether the Framework Decisions could have fallen within the scope of the third pillar. Therefore, once a measure fell within the scope of a first pillar power, that automatically precluded the application of any third pillar competence, without any need to compare the first and third pillar competence or any possibility that a third pillar *lex specialis* might prevail over a more general first pillar power. It was not necessary for the EC to have exercised its competence previously; the mere *existence* of such a competence was enough.

This approach was also applied to the first/third pillar dividing line as regards policing issues, where the Court ruled that measures solely regulating law enforcement bodies' *use* of data supplied by the private sector fell outside the scope of the first pillar (and so implicitly within the scope of the third pillar),[304] but measures solely regulating the private sector's *supply* of that data to the law enforcement authorities fell within the scope of Community law (as it was then).[305]

Also, Court judgments on the dividing line between the first pillar and the second pillar (foreign policy) were surely relevant by analogy to the first/third pillar dividing line. On this point, the Court ruled that where an issue fell within the scope of both the EC's development policy powers and the EU's foreign policy powers, as, for example, where EU funding was offered to assist developing states to destroy small arms, Article 47 EU required that the issue be addressed solely on the basis of the Community's powers, even though development policy was a shared parallel power (ie the Member States had the power to adopt their own development policy measures outside the EC legal order, even acting collectively).[306] Although the EP successfully challenged a Commission decision applying the EU's development policy legislation to fund Philippine anti-terrorist measures, this was because the legislation concerned did not extend in scope to such measures, not because the EC lacked the competence to address them.[307] Furthermore, the Court of Justice ruled that the previous Article 308 EC, which gave residual powers to the EC to act to achieve its objectives when no more specific clause did so, could not apply as regards foreign policy objectives. More broadly:[308]

> …the coexistence of the Union and the Community as integrated but separate legal orders, and the constitutional architecture of the pillars, as intended by the framers of the Treaties now in force…constitute considerations of an institutional kind militating against any extension of the bridge to articles of the EC Treaty other than those with which it explicitly creates a link.

The overlap between the various areas of EU policy subject to different rules on legal effect and territorial scope was reflected in the case law of the Court of Justice. For instance, in the field of civil law, the Court confirmed its interpretation of the Brussels

---

[304] Joined Cases C-317/04 and C-318/04 *EP v Council and Commission* [2006] ECR I-4721.
[305] Case C-301/06 *Ireland v Council and EP* [2009] ECR I-593.
[306] Case C-91/05 *Commission v Council* [2008] ECR I-3651.
[307] Case C-403/05 *EP v Commission* [2007] ECR I-9045. There is now EU development policy legislation addressing such issues: Reg 1717/2006 ([2006] OJ L 317/1).
[308] Joined Cases C-402/05 P and C-415/05 P *Kadi and Al Barakaat* [2008] ECR I-6351, para 202.

Convention by comparison with the Title IV Regulation later replacing that Convention (or another civil law Regulation).[309] There were also cases where third pillar issues overlapped with non-JHA issues.[310] The best approach to the overlap arising in these cases was discussed in the parallel chapter in volume 1.[311]

Since the entry into force of the Treaty of Lisbon, the CJEU has in particular clarified the relationship between Article 75 TFEU and the EU's foreign policy powers,[312] as well as the EU's criminal law powers as compared to its internal market powers.[313] Issues might also arise as regards the relationship between the non-JHA provision concerning data protection rules (Article 16 TFEU), and specific JHA legislation which addresses data protection issues.[314] It should be borne in mind that Article 47 of the previous TEU, which as interpreted by the Court of Justice, gave a strong priority to the first pillar over the second and third pillars, has been repealed by the Treaty of Lisbon.[315]

2.5 Legitimacy and Accountability

In addition to the general observations about legitimacy and accountability of JHA matters raised in the parallel chapter in volume 1,[316] there are some specific issues as regards criminal law and policing.

First of all, as regards the legislation on access to documents,[317] the Court has given a wide scope of application to the 'public security' exception, with the effect that the rules on public access to documents do not benefit persons whose income and assets are frozen because they are considered to be 'terrorists'.[318] However, the EU Courts have nonetheless developed specific procedural protections for such persons when ruling on more direct challenges to the EU's anti-terrorist legislation.[319]

Secondly, in this field the existence of 'emergency brakes' and vetoes in key areas of criminal law and policing should ensure that the concerns of the public and national parliaments will be addressed in some cases. Third, where groups of Member States exercise the right of initiative as set out in Article 76 TFEU, there is less accountability, since public consultation is still unknown.[320] Fourth, the Treaty of Lisbon includes

---

[309] Cases: C-167/00 *Henkel* [2002] ECR I-8111, para 49; C-111/01 *Gantner Electronics* [2003] ECR I-4207, para 28; C-104/03 *St. Paul Dairy Industries* [2005] ECR I-3481, para 23; C-112/03 *Societe financiere et industrielle du Peloux* [2005] ECR I-3707, para 41; and C-292/05 *Lechoritou* [2007] ECR I-1519, para 45. Also, the opinions in several other cases interpreted the Convention in light of Title IV civil law legislation: Cases C-256/00 *Besix* [2002] ECR I-1699; C-334/00 *Fonderie Officine Meccaniche Tacconi* [2002] ECR I-7357; C-271/00 *Baten* [2002] ECR I-10489; C-437/00 *Pugliese* [2003] ECR I-3573; C-18/02 *DFDS Torline* [2004] ECR I-1417; C-159/02 *Turner* [2004] ECR I-3565; C-281/02 *Owusu* [2005] ECR I-1383; C-3/05 *Verdoliva* [2006] ECR I-1579; and C-539/03 *Roche Netherlands* [2006] ECR I-6535.
[310] Cases: C-503/03 *Commission v Spain* [2006] ECR I-1097; C-467/04 *Gasparini* [2006] ECR I-9199; and C-123/08 *Wolzenburg* [2009] ECR I-9621.
[311] I:2.4.2.
[312] Case C-130/10 *EP v Council*, regarding the scope of Art 75 TFEU (anti-terrorist sanctions) as compared to Art 215 TFEU (foreign policy sanctions), discussed in II:2.2.3.2 above.
[313] See II:3.9 below.   [314] See II:7.2.4 below.
[315] See instead Art 40 of the revised TEU, which takes a more balanced approach to the distinction between foreign policy and other EU policies. There is no replacement clause concerning the distinction between policing and criminal law and other EU policies.
[316] I:2.5.   [317] Reg 1049/2001 ([2001] OJ L 145/43).
[318] Case C-266/05 P *Sison* [2007] ECR I-1233.   [319] See II:7.4.5 below.
[320] On Member States' right of initiative more generally, see II:2.2.3.2 above.

specific provisions on scrutiny of evaluation measures, of the Committee on internal security, and on Europol and Eurojust,[321] but the latter provisions have not yet been implemented.

2.6 EU Funding

The parallel institutional chapter in volume 1 sets out the general details of JHA spending as a whole. For policing and criminal law in particular, there were distinct rules during the Treaty of Amsterdam era, when spending on these issues was subject to the EC budget *unless* all Member States agreed otherwise.[322] With the entry into force of the Treaty of Lisbon, there is no longer any scope to charge JHA spending outside the EU budget.

During the Maastricht period, the measures in this area comprised: the 'Grotius' programme on incentives and exchanges for legal practitioners, established initially from 1996 until 2000;[323] the 'STOP' programme on combating sexual exploitation, also initially applicable from 1996 to 2000;[324] the 'Oisin' programme on support for law enforcement, applicable from 1997 to 2000;[325] and the 'Falcone' programme on combating international organized crime, applicable from 1998 to 2002.[326] On the other hand, the Europol Convention required that Europol be funded from Member States' budgets,[327] although this changed from 2010, when a new Decision replaced the Europol Convention (see further below).

After the Treaty of Amsterdam entered into force, in the sphere of civil law, the Community first extended the Grotius programme for a further year (2001) as regards civil law,[328] and then adopted a funding programme covering 2002–06.[329] As for the third pillar, the Grotius, Oisin, and STOP programmes were extended for 2001–02, joined at the time by a fourth programme concerning crime prevention (Hippocrates).[330] They were then replaced by a general third pillar funding programme, 'AGIS', running from 2003 to 2007.[331]

The third pillar aspects of SIS II funding had to be charged to the EC budget, as the necessary unanimity for charging the Member States' budgets did not exist.[332] As for EU agencies, the prosecutors' agency, Eurojust, was from the outset funded by the EC budget,[333] while the European Police College was initially funded by Member States,[334] but was later funded from the EC budget after an overhaul of its institutional framework in 2005.[335]

---

[321] Arts 70, 71, 85, and 88 TFEU.   [322] Previous Art 41(3) EU.   [323] [1996] OJ L 287/3.
[324] [1996] OJ L 322/7.   [325] [1997] OJ L 7/5.   [326] [1998] OJ L 99/8.
[327] Art 35, Europol Convention ([1995] OJ C 316/1).
[328] Reg 290/2001 ([2001] OJ L 43/1). The reference amount for spending was €650,000 for the year.
[329] Reg 743/2002 ([2002] OJ L 115/1). There is no reference amount for spending.
[330] [2001] OJ L 186/1, 4, 7, and 11. The reference amounts for spending were respectively €4, 8, 4, and 2 million over the two years.
[331] [2002] OJ L 203/5. The reference amount for spending was €65 million over the five years.
[332] See JHA Council conclusions, 28/29 May 2001.
[333] [2002] OJ L 63/1; see amendment to the financial rules in [2003] OJ L 245/44.
[334] [2000] OJ L 336/1.   [335] [2005] OJ L 256/63.

As detailed in the parallel chapter in volume 1, the EU's annual budgets began to fund Eurojust from 2002,[336] and the European Police College and EU crisis management from 2006.[337] The 2007–13 financial framework included EU programmes in this field: a revised civil justice programme;[338] programmes focused on criminal justice and law enforcement;[339] and programmes outside the scope of JHA law as such, including on anti-terrorist crisis management.[340] The annual budget for 2010 subsequently fully integrated Europol funding into the EU budget.[341] Most recently, the EU's funding arrangements for 2014–20 include two relevant funds, on the civil and criminal issues, and security and policing issues respectively.[342]

2.7 External Relations

2.7.1 General rules on EU external relations

Before the Treaty of Lisbon entered into force, distinct rules applied to the external relations aspects of the former third pillar. Presumably these rules are still relevant to the third pillar treaties adopted during this period, and so they are considered further below.[343] This sub-section examines the impact of the EU's general external relations rules on civil, criminal, and policing law matters, supplementing the more detailed discussion in the parallel chapter in volume 1.[344] Since the Treaty of Lisbon, external relations concerning policing and criminal law are governed by the same rules as other JHA law.

The general EU external relations rules provide that the Union, which has legal personality enabling it to become party to treaties,[345] can enjoy external relations competence either expressly, by a provision such as Article 79(3) TFEU, which grants express power for the EU to adopt treaties concerning readmission,[346] or implicitly, 'where the Treaties so provide or where the conclusion of an agreement is necessary in order to achieve, within the framework of the Union's policies, one of the objectives referred to in the Treaties, or is provided for in a legally binding Union act or is likely to affect common rules or alter their scope' (ie as a corollary of the exercise of its internal powers).[347] Civil law, criminal law, and policing issues are governed by the implied powers principle.

EU external relations competence becomes *exclusive*, leaving no power for Member States, when EU powers over an issue are inherently exclusive,[348] or also where its powers are in principle shared but 'when [a treaty's] conclusion is provided for in a legislative act of the Union or is necessary to enable the Union to exercise its internal

---

[336] [2002] OJ L 29.   [337] [2006] OJ L 78.   [338] [2007] OJ L 257/16. See II:8.8 below.
[339] [2007] OJ L 58/7 and 13. See II:3.8 and II:7.10 below.
[340] [2007] L 257/23. See II:7.10 below.   [341] [2010] OJ L 64.
[342] Reg 1382/2013 establishing a Justice Programme ([2013] OJ L 354/73) and Reg 513/2014 establishing a policing fund, as part of the Internal Security Fund ([2014] OJ L 150/93).
[343] II:2.7.2.   [344] I:2.7.
[345] Art 47, revised TEU. Before the Treaty of Lisbon, the EC had legal personality (Art 210 EC), but the EU's legal personality was open to dispute (see II:2.7.2 below).
[346] On readmission treaties, see further I:7.9.1.   [347] Art 216(1) TFEU.
[348] See the list of exclusive EU powers in Art 3(1) TFEU.

competence, or in so far as its conclusion may affect common rules or alter their scope,[349] in particular where the EU has fully harmonized the issue internally.[350] The latter principle is relevant for civil, criminal, and policing law, given that all JHA matters are in principle issues of shared competence,[351] but where to some extent the EU is not precluded from fully harmonizing the relevant area. On the other hand, where the EU can only set minimum standards as regards internal rules, external competence is necessarily shared between the EU and its Member States.[352] Several declarations attempt to clarify the issue of external competence as regards aspects of civil, criminal, and policing issues; these are considered elsewhere in this volume.[353]

However, even where the EU has exclusive competence, it may still empower the Member States to adopt legally binding acts, including treaties.[354] In this area, the EU has authorized the Member States to sign treaties within the EC's (now the EU's) exclusive competence relating to civil law, subject to a specific control procedure.[355]

Otherwise, where the EU has only partially harmonized a field falling within the shared competence of the EU and its Member States, the EU and its Member States share external competence, which often leads to 'mixed agreements', ie treaties signed by both the EU and its Member State,[356] giving Member States a *de facto* veto over the negotiation of the agreement. Nevertheless, it is not unusual for Member States to leave it to the EU alone to sign treaties in this field.

The process for negotiating and concluding EU treaties is based on the Commission as negotiator, with signature and ratification (which the EU calls 'conclusion') by the Council. The Council follows the same voting rule as applies to the adoption of internal EU legislation concerning the same subject-matter. So, since 2003, the Council voted by QMV as regards civil law issues (except for family law); since December 2009, QMV has applied to most criminal law and policing issues with the entry into force of the Treaty of Lisbon.[357] The EP must consent to all treaties, inter alia, concerning issues which are subject to the ordinary legislative procedure or the consent procedure as regards internal legislation;[358] this applies to most civil, criminal, and policing matters.[359] It is possible, where EU involvement in particular treaty negotiations or ratification is impracticable, for the Council to authorize the Member States to act on the Union's behalf.[360]

---

[349] Art 3(2) TFEU.

[350] The possibility of full harmonization in areas of shared competence is implicitly provided for in the definition of shared competence in Art 2(2) TFEU.

[351] See Art 4(2)(j) TFEU.

[352] See Arts 82(2) and 83(1) and (2) TFEU, which constrain the EU to adopt 'minimum' rules only, and so the EU is unlikely to attain exclusive external competence as regards substantive criminal law or domestic criminal procedure.

[353] See II:3.9, II:8.9, II:7.12, and II:7.11 below (declarations as regards civil law, criminal law, and policing external competence).

[354] See the definition of exclusive EU competence in Art 2(1) TFEU.

[355] Regs 662/2009 and 664/2009 ([2009] OJ L 200/25 and 46). See further II:8.9 below.

[356] For a full analysis of these principles with detailed references, see P Eeckhout, *EU External Relations Law*, 2nd edn (OUP, 2011), chs 3 and 4.

[357] See II:2.2.2 and II:2.2.3 above.   [358] Art 218(6)(a) TFEU.

[359] The only exceptions relate to family law, 'Community criminal law' where the underlying subject-matter is subject to unanimous voting (eg tax issues), and operational police cooperation (Arts 81(3), 83(2), 87(3) and 89 TFEU).

[360] See the examples of civil law treaties, referred to in II:8.9 below.

Treaties concluded by the EC (now the EU) are binding on the Community (now the Union) institutions and the EU's Member States,[361] and take precedence over secondary EC (now EU) law; but the treaties and the general principles of EC (now EU) law take precedence over treaties concluded by the Community (now the Union).[362] To date, the EC (now the EU) has negotiated or concluded a considerable number of civil law treaties, and a more modest number of criminal law and policing treaties.[363]

The CJEU has its usual powers as regards treaties concluded by the EU, as well as a special jurisdiction as regards external relations, to give an opinion on whether a planned treaty would conflict with the treaties, including the division of competence between the EU and its Member States.[364] This special jurisdiction has been used twice in the field of civil law, and in a third case relating to policing is pending.[365]

A particular issue could arise if the EU wishes to negotiate further treaties concerning data protection as regards policing and criminal law with third states after the entry into force of the Treaty of Lisbon, given the existence of a specific power in the revised TEU concerning data protection within the scope of the CFSP.[366] However, this competence would be limited to matters concerning the common foreign and security policy of the EU, and could not 'affect the application of the procedures and the extent of the powers of the institutions laid down by the Treaties' as regards any other competences (including any JHA competences).[367]

2.7.2 External relations and the former third pillar

First of all, during the 'Maastricht era',[368] procedures were drawn up for applying Article K.5 EU, which required the defence of EU common positions at international conferences. Usually Member States' positions were coordinated informally, with only three formal Common Positions on the defence of an EU position at international conferences drawn up during this period.[369] There was also a developed programme of links with non-EU countries. In particular, the EU's enlargement was prepared for by a Joint Action concerning evaluation of applicant States' adoption of the EU third pillar *acquis*.[370]

After the Treaty of Amsterdam entered into force, external relations within the scope of the third pillar were subject to Articles 37 and 38 EU. Article 37 provided for the coordination of EU action in international conferences and the defence of relevant Common Positions in conferences. As noted above, it resulted in the adoption of Common Positions on several occasions.[371] Member States also coordinated their positions on certain proposed treaties without the adoption of formal Common Positions,

---

[361] Art 216(2) TFEU (ex Art 300(7) EC).   [362] See Eeckhout (n 356 above), ch 9.

[363] See: II:8.9, II:3.9, and II:7.11 below, and s 2.5 of chs 3 and 7 of this volume.

[364] Art 218(11) TFEU (ex-Art 300(6) EC).   [365] See II:8.9 and II:7.6 below.

[366] Art 39, revised TEU. The external competence related to this provision would flow from Art 37 TEU.

[367] Art 40, revised TEU, which is within the jurisdiction of the Court of Justice pursuant to Art 275 TFEU.

[368] For more on external relations and JHA during this period, see the first edition of this book, pp 33–4.

[369] [1997] OJ L 279, [1997] OJ L 320, and [1997] OJ L 87/1, on the OECD and Council of Europe corruption Conventions and the UN Convention on organized crime.

[370] [1998] OJ L 191/8.   [371] II:2.2.2 above.

for example when the Council of Europe's anti-terrorism Convention was under negotiation. This resulted in the adoption of 'disconnection' clauses in treaties, allowing for
the continued existence of separate third pillar measures applicable to the EU Member
States; this was a pre-existing Community practice which was extended to the third
pillar.[372]

The adoption of treaties within the scope of the third pillar was subject to Article
38 EU, now repealed by the Treaty of Lisbon. This provided that Article 24 EU (which
concerned CFSP international treaties) applied to the third pillar; this Article was also
repealed by the Treaty of Lisbon.[373] Article 24 EU, as amended by the Treaty of Nice,
stated that the Council Presidency, rather than the Commission, negotiated third pillar
treaties on a mandate from the Council, and proposed them to the Council for conclusion. A special rule (Article 24(5) EU) provided that:

> No agreement shall be binding on a Member State whose representative in the Council
> states that it has to comply with the requirements of its own constitutional procedure;
> the other members of the Council may agree that the agreement shall nevertheless
> apply provisionally.

In practice, the first treaty within the scope of the third pillar was the treaty associating Norway and Iceland with the Schengen *acquis*, negotiated in accordance with the
sui generis rules applicable to that issue set out in the Schengen Protocol. The EU also
negotiated third pillar treaties with Norway and Iceland and the United States regarding mutual assistance and extradition, with Japan regarding mutual assistance, with
the USA and Australia as regards passenger name data, with Norway and Iceland as
regards association with the 'Prum Decision' rules on police cooperation, and (alongside the Community) with Switzerland and Liechtenstein as regards association with
the Schengen *acquis*.[374] Member States repeatedly invoked their constitutional rules
as regards the conclusion of third pillar agreements, thereby delaying their entry into
force considerably.[375]

As a consequence, by the time of the entry into force of the Treaty of Lisbon, only
the Schengen association treaties with Norway, Iceland, and Switzerland (but not the
Protocol regarding Liechtenstein), along with the mutual assistance and extradition
treaties with the USA, were in force. The new procedural rules set out in the Treaty then
applied to those treaties which were not yet concluded. This meant that Member States

---

[372] See Art 26(3) of the Council of Europe Convention on prevention of terrorism (CETS 196), Art 40(3)
of the Council of Europe Convention on trafficking in persons (CETS 197), Art 52(4) of the Council of
Europe Convention on money laundering (CETS 198), and Art 43(3) of the Council of Europe Convention
on child protection (CETS 201).

[373] While Art 37, revised TEU, confers express power to conclude CFSP treaties, the detailed rules on
negotiation of those treaties are now set out along with the general EU treaty-making rules in Art 218
TFEU, which includes some special rules on CFSP treaties.

[374] On the third pillar treaties, see II:2.2.5.4 above and II:3.2.5, II:3.9, II:7.2.5, and II:7.11 below.

[375] On the Prum treaty decision, see Council doc 5554/1/09, 15 Sep 2009. On the mutual assistance
and surrender treaties with Norway and Iceland, see Council docs 7988/07, 2 Apr 2007 and 7097/1/07,
19 Mar 2007. On the PNR treaty with Australia, see Council doc 10439/2/08, 25 June 2008. On the PNR
treaty with the USA, see Council doc 5311/1/09, 19 Mar 2009. On the Schengen association agreement
with Liechtenstein, see Council doc 12428/1/08, 16 Sep 2008. On the Schengen association agreement with
Switzerland, see previously Council doc 14207/07, 23 Oct 2007.

could not invoke their constitutional procedures before the relevant treaties could be ratified, and in practice Member States did not insist upon becoming parties alongside the Union to those treaties in the form of 'mixed agreements' either.

Even though, as noted above, the EU Treaty did not expressly confer legal personality upon the Union until the entry into force of the Treaty of Lisbon, the pre-existing third pillar treaties all appear to be concluded with the Union, as a distinct entity with its own international legal personality, rather than with its Member States, thus apparently assuming that the Union had an implied legal personality during this period. A more controversial question is whether the Community rules (now the general EU rules) concerning external competence, including Article 351 TFEU (ex-Article 307 EC), or at least a variant of those principles, applied to the previous third pillar, including presumably the provisions of the Schengen *acquis* allocated to the third pillar. This question must be raised in particular in light of the Court of Justice ruling that the 'loyalty' principle of EC law (as it then was) implicitly applied to the previous third pillar,[376] given the relevance of that principle for EC external relations law, as noted above. If the EC rules were applicable, the impact would be that Member States were already restrained as regards their treaty-making concerning criminal law and policing due to the adoption of third pillar acts, even before the entry into force of the Treaty of Lisbon,[377] and therefore continue to be restrained as regards pre-existing third pillar acts even before those acts are amended.

Even if the EC external relations rules (as they then were) did not apply to the third pillar before the entry into force of the Treaty of Lisbon, at the very least, the rules of international law concerning conflicts among treaties presumably applied. Moreover, if Article 351 TFEU in particular only began to apply to Member States as regards policing and criminal law as from the entry into force of the Treaty of Lisbon, the question arises whether it only protects Member States' treaties in this area which were concluded before they joined the EU, or whether it protects all treaties concluded up until the entry into force of the Treaty of Lisbon, because that is the first point that Article 351 TFEU became applicable to this area of law.

2.8 Conclusions

As observed in the parallel chapter in volume 1, in light of the issues addressed by JHA measures, JHA cooperation at EU level should be subject to parliamentary and judicial control, and effective human rights protection, at least equivalent to the principles established by the best national traditions in this area. Until the Treaty of Lisbon, it was clearly not, in particular as regards criminal law and policing. The institutional framework for JHA law was unduly complex, insufficiently open and transparent, lacked sufficient democratic and legal legitimacy and accountability, raised serious human rights concerns, had a convoluted relationship with other areas of EU law, and in some areas

---

[376] See C-105/03 *Pupino* [2005] ECR I-5285 and discussion in II:2.2.2 above.

[377] Although the legal effect of pre-existing third pillar measures has been preserved until they are annulled, repealed, or amended (Art 9 of the transitional protocol; see II:2.2.3.3 above), this begs the question as to what the legal effect of these measures was as regards external competence.

provided for insufficient financial control. The Treaty of Lisbon has addressed most of these problems sufficiently in theory, although (as regards judicial control) not until after a five-year transitional period. But since many of the pre-Lisbon measures have not been amended, in particular controversial measures such as the European Arrest Warrant, the pre-Lisbon measures continue to have a problematic legacy in this area of law.

3

Criminal Law

Mutual Recognition

3.1 Introduction

The criminal law process is complicated enough to start with. But it is further complicated when there are cross-border elements, such as the presence of a suspect, witness,
or other evidence in another country. To address such issues, there is a considerable
body of international treaties, mostly emanating from the Council of Europe. But since
the operation of these treaties is often considered to be ineffective in light of a perceived
increase in cross-border crime, the EU has been active in adopting measures in this
area and planning further measures. In particular, since 1999, the EU has been implementing a principle of mutual recognition in criminal matters, according to which the
decisions of the judicial authorities of one Member State should as far as possible take
effect automatically in all other Member States.

There are objections to the detailed measures adopted to apply this principle, most
notably from national parliaments and courts, in light of doubts in particular about the
fairness of foreign criminal procedures due to the diversity of systems of criminal procedure between Member States and fears that criminal suspects facing trial in a foreign system will face *de facto* discrimination. The EU has tried to address these doubts by setting
standards for domestic criminal procedural law, as discussed in Chapter 4 of this volume.

This chapter surveys the issues arising from mutual recognition in criminal law in
detail, starting with the basic issues of the institutional framework, an overview of
measures adopted, legal competence, territorial scope, human rights, and overlaps
with other (non-JHA) EU law. It then examines the EU's mutual recognition measures,
starting with extradition and the 'flagship' European Arrest Warrant, moving to analyse
pre-trial measures addressing issues such as the movement of evidence and freezing
orders, and then post-trial measures such as the recognition of sentences and confiscation orders and the transfer of prisoners. Finally, it concludes by examining the issues
of administrative cooperation and EU funding and external relations, as they apply to
criminal procedure.

Issues related to jurisdiction (including cross-border double jeopardy) and prosecution, notably the development of Eurojust and the prospect of creating a European
Public Prosecutor, are addressed separately in Chapter 6 of this volume. The connected
issue of substantive criminal law is addressed in Chapter 5 of this volume, and the
closely related issue of policing is examined in Chapter 7 of this volume. As noted in the
latter chapter, this book observes the English distinction between the prosecution and
trial process before the courts (addressed in this chapter) and the *investigation* of crime
by the police or similar authorities (addressed in Chapter 7), even though in continental countries, investigations are more closely linked to the judicial process.

3.2 Institutional Framework and Overview

3.2.1 Cooperation before the Treaty of Amsterdam

Before the entry into force of the Treaty of Amsterdam in 1999, the main source of the law on international criminal procedure was Council of Europe Conventions, which addressed in turn: extradition;[1] mutual assistance in transferring evidence;[2] the international validity of criminal judgments (or transfer of sentences);[3] the transfer of sentenced persons (with a subsequent protocol);[4] and measures concerning the proceeds of crime.[5] Most of these Conventions have been universally ratified by Member States, but the Convention on the international validity of criminal judgments attracted much less interest.[6]

At first, the EU Member States focused on agreeing European Political Cooperation (EPC) Conventions that would enhance the application of the Council of Europe Conventions among themselves, and encourage cooperation between Member States in the areas where the Council of Europe Conventions had attracted little enthusiasm.[7] To this end, they agreed on Conventions concerning the application of a Council of Europe terrorism Convention (which contains further extradition and mutual assistance rules), the faxing of extradition requests, the international validity of criminal judgments, and the transfer of sentenced persons.[8] However, none of these Conventions entered into force, as they failed to attract much enthusiasm among Member States.[9]

Outside the framework of cooperation between the (then) EEC Member States, the 1990 Schengen Convention contained a number of detailed provisions on cross-border cooperation, addressing mutual assistance,[10] extradition,[11] and the transfer of sentenced persons.[12] The Schengen Executive Committee also adopted two relevant Decisions, concerning mutual assistance as regards drug trafficking and a separate agreement concerning cooperation regarding road traffic offences.[13] Furthermore, the Schengen Information System (SIS) contains data of use to prosecutions and judicial investigations, in particular as regards extradition, wanted persons, and objects which could be used as evidence.[14]

With the entry into force of the Treaty of Maastricht, the EU had a formal intergovernmental framework to address criminal procedural issues. The main development during the 'Maastricht era' was the signature of two extradition Conventions in 1995 and 1996, concerning in turn consented and disputed extradition.[15] These Conventions sought to reduce or eliminate a number of the main bars to extradition under the Council of Europe

---

[1] See II:3.5.1 below.   [2] See II:3.6.1.1 below.   [3] See II:3.7 below.   [4] See ibid.
[5] See II:3.6.2 and II:3.7.4 below.
[6] For ratification details of all of the Conventions and Protocols, see Appendix I.
[7] On the EPC process, see II:2.2.1.1 above.   [8] See II:3.5.1, II:3.6.1.1, and II:3.7 below.
[9] For ratification details of all of the Conventions and Protocols, see Appendix I.
[10] Arts 48–53 of the Convention (Chapter 2 of Title III), [2000] OJ L 239. See II:3.6.1 below.
[11] Arts 59–66 of the Convention (Chapter 4 of Title III). See II:3.5.1 below.
[12] Arts 67–9 of the Convention (Chapter 5 of Title III). See II:3.7.1.2 below.
[13] See respectively II:3.6.1 and II:3.7.1.1 below.
[14] See particularly Arts 95, 98, and 100 of the Convention. On the SIS, see II:7.6.1.1 below.
[15] See II:3.5.1 below.

Conventions. During this period, there were also lengthy attempts, starting in 1995, to agree a Convention on mutual assistance to supplement the Council of Europe measures, but these attempts did not bear fruit until after the Treaty of Amsterdam was in force. A Convention on recognition of driving disqualifications was signed in 1998, but it has attracted few ratifications.[16] There were also a handful of Joint Actions addressing criminal procedural issues. These measures concerned the exchange of liaison magistrates,[17] the 'Grotius' programme of incentives and exchanges for legal practitioners,[18] good practice in mutual legal assistance,[19] the creation of a European judicial network,[20] and money laundering and confiscation of proceeds.[21]

3.2.2 Treaty of Amsterdam

3.2.2.1 *Institutional framework*

The Treaty of Amsterdam inserted an Article 31 into the EU Treaty, which provided that:

Common action on judicial cooperation in criminal matters shall include:
(a) facilitating and accelerating cooperation between competent ministries and judicial or equivalent authorities of the Member States in relation to proceedings and the enforcement of decisions;
(b) facilitating extradition between Member States;
(c) ensuring compatibility in rules applicable in the Member States, as may be necessary to improve such cooperation;
(d) preventing conflicts of jurisdiction between Member States;
(e) progressively adopting measures establishing minimum rules relating to the constituent elements of criminal acts and to penalties in the fields of organised crime, terrorism and illicit drug trafficking.

The Treaty of Nice subsequently added a second paragraph to the previous Article 31 TEU, referring to the 'Eurojust' prosecutors' agency which EU leaders had agreed to create in the meantime. This issue, along with Article 31(1)(d) regarding conflicts of jurisdiction, is addressed further in Chapter 6 of this volume.

The measures adopted pursuant to Article 31 TEU were governed by the revised general third pillar rules on the jurisdiction of the Court of Justice, the role of the political institutions, and the use of specific instruments and their legal effect.[22] On the latter point, the Court's judgment in *Pupino*, finding that Framework Decisions had indirect effect,[23] was of great relevance to this area, since a number of Framework Decisions in the field of mutual recognition partly or wholly govern the legal position of individuals, whose legal position may be altered significantly by the ability to invoke the indirect effect of a Framework Decision.

Also, with the entry into force of the Treaty of Amsterdam, the various Schengen rules on criminal procedural matters were allocated to the third pillar of the EU.[24]

---

[16] See II:3.7.3 below.   [17] See II:3.8 below.   [18] See ibid.
[19] See II:3.6.1 below.   [20] See II:3.8 below.   [21] See II:3.6.2 and II:3.7.4 below.
[22] See II:2.2.2 above.   [23] Case C-105/03 [2005] ECR I-5285; see discussion in ibid.
[24] [1999] OJ L 176/17.

3.2.2.2 *Implementing the Treaty of Amsterdam*

As with other areas of Justice and Home Affairs (JHA) cooperation, some key basic principles for development of policy and legislation in this area were set out by the Tampere European Council in the autumn of 1999.[25] The relevant conclusions focused in particular on mutual recognition of judicial decisions, described as the 'cornerstone' of criminal (and civil) judicial cooperation; the principle of mutual recognition should apply not just to judgments but also to 'other decisions of judicial authorities'.

More specifically, the conclusions urged Member States to ratify the EU's two extradition Conventions, and stated that extradition as such should be abolished in the case of persons who fled after final sentencing. In other cases, there should be consideration of 'fast-track' extradition procedures, 'without prejudice to the principle of fair trial'. Furthermore, there should also be mutual recognition of 'pre-trial orders, in particular' measures on seizure of assets and evidence, and 'evidence lawfully gathered by one Member State's authorities should be admissible before the courts of other Member States, taking into account the standards that apply there'. Finally, the conclusions asked the Council and Commission to adopt a programme of measures to implement the principle of mutual recognition by the end of 2000.

Member States were called upon to provide full mutual legal assistance in the investigation and prosecution of serious economic crime (referring to taxes and duties), money laundering 'should be rooted out wherever it occurs', and the European Council was 'determined to ensure that concrete steps are taken to trace, freeze, seize and confiscate the proceeds of crime'. To that end, Member States were urged to implement various relevant EU and international measures.

To implement this agenda, the Council agreed upon the mutual recognition work programme, as requested, by the end of 2000.[26] The programme ultimately included a list of twenty-four measures, ranked by priority, but without dates for concluding the programme as a whole or agreeing individual measures.

According to its introduction, the mutual recognition programme was to be subject to a number of 'parameters': whether each measure should be general in scope or limited to specific crimes; whether the concept of double criminality (requiring the act in question to be a crime in both the requesting and the requested State) should be dropped; 'mechanisms for safeguarding the rights of third parties, victims and suspects'; the need to define 'common minimum standards' necessary to facilitate mutual recognition (eg the competence of courts); whether enforcement is direct or indirect;[27] the grounds for refusing recognition (such as public policy and double jeopardy, and exclusion of military, fiscal, or political offences); and the existence of 'liability arrangements in the event of acquittal'.

Before the entry into force of the Treaty of Lisbon, this programme was implemented by Framework Decisions on: a European Arrest Warrant (EAW), which replaces extradition

---

[25] Paras 32–52 of the conclusions.

[26] [2001] OJ C 12/10. See earlier Commission communication on the issue (COM (2000) 495, 26 July 2000) and discussion of the development of the principle in S Peers, 'Mutual Recognition and Criminal Law in the European Union: Has the Council Got it Wrong?' (2004) 41 CMLRev 5 at 7–10.

[27] Direct enforcement means application of the foreign decision without any intervening procedure in the executing Member State. Indirect enforcement means that some form of procedure (usually quite limited) by the executing State's authorities is necessary before the decision can be executed there.

between Member States; freezing orders; the mutual recognition of financial penalties; execution of confiscation orders (and related domestic law on confiscation); a European Evidence Warrant (following an earlier EU Convention and Protocol on mutual assistance in criminal matters); the transfer of sentenced persons; probation and parole orders; pre-trial supervision orders; recognition of convictions; the exchange of criminal records; and *in absentia* trials (trials held without the attendance of the accused).[28] However, the Commission decided against proposing EU legislation on witness protection.[29]

The development of EU policy in this area was clearly accelerated by the terrorist attacks of 11 September 2001, which were followed almost instantly by the proposal to establish the EAW and the agreement on the text. This Framework Decision became the 'flagship' of the EU's mutual recognition policy, but it was subsequently attacked on human rights grounds in the Court of Justice and national courts.[30] The adoption of further measures in this area was also encouraged by the Hague Programme of 2004, and its related Action Plan.[31]

Other relevant measures have included the development of the Schengen Information System (SIS), in particular as regards the inclusion of further data relevant to prosecutions, access to the SIS by judicial authorities, and the creation of a second-generation Schengen Information System, which will in particular include information on EAWs.[32] The Framework Decision on personal data protection, adopted in 2008, also applies to the judicial sector.[33]

There is also a link between measures on substantive criminal law and abolition of the dual criminality principle (the requirement that an (alleged) act must amount to a criminal offence in both States concerned) in the EU's mutual recognition measures, because the harmonization of substantive criminal law reduces the differences between national rules which underlie the principle of dual criminality.[34]

Finally, the Court of Justice had begun to play a significant role as regards interpretation of measures in this area even before the Treaty of Lisbon entered into force, receiving a reference on the validity of the Framework Decision on the EAW;[35] and six references on the interpretation of the same Framework Decision.[36]

3.2.2.3 *Basic principles of mutual recognition in criminal law*

Although the various EU measures setting out the details of the principle of mutual recognition in criminal law differ in the detail, they have certain common features which it is useful to summarize at the outset.[37]

---

[28] See II:3.5 to II:3.7 below.
[29] See the communication on this issue (COM (2007) 693, 13 Nov 2007).
[30] See further II:3.5.2 below.
[31] [2005] OJ C 53/1 and [2005] OJ C 198/1. See also the Commission communication on mutual recognition and harmonization of criminal law (COM (2005) 195, 19 May 2005; SEC (2005) 641, 20 May 2005).
[32] See II:7.6.1.1 below.   [33] [2008] OJ L 350/60. See II:7.6.4 below.
[34] See generally ch 5 of this volume.
[35] Case C-303/05 *Advocaten voor de Wereld* [2007] ECR I-3633. On the substance see II:3.5.2 below.
[36] Cases: C-66/08 *Koslowski* [2008] ECR I-6041; C-296/08 PPU *Santesteban Goicoechea* [2008] ECR I-6307; C-388/08 PPU *Leymann and Pustovarov* [2008] ECR I-8993; C-123/08 *Wolzenburg* [2009] ECR I-9621; C-261/09 *Mantello* [2010] ECR I-11477; and C-306/09 *I.B.* [2010] ECR I-10341. On the substance, see ibid.
[37] The Court of Justice has not yet been asked whether an identical clause must be interpreted the same way in different mutual recognition instruments. But it is willing to interpret one mutual recognition

A frequent feature of the mutual recognition measures is that they replace or supplement the Council of Europe measures referred to above, whether those measures have the full support of Member States or only limited support. It should be recalled that even those Council of Europe measures with wide support by Member States have restrictions on their scope and significant possibility for reservations, or provide only a general framework for cross-border criminal law cooperation. So there is a clear perceived 'added value' to the EU's involvement, which principle provides for a far more intensive degree of cooperation. In most cases, the EU mutual recognition measures 'replace' the 'corresponding' provisions of the relevant Council of Europe Conventions and prior EU measures as between Member States, without specifying exactly which provisions of the relevant Conventions are replaced. Most of the EU measures give a power to Member States to retain existing bilateral or multilateral treaties, or to conclude new bilateral or multilateral treaties, which expand or enlarge on the EU mutual recognition measures or simplify and facilitate the procedures for mutual recognition, subject to an obligation to inform the Council and/or Commission about such measures. This begs the question as to when such criteria are met.[38] A further underlying question is whether pursuant to such provisions, Member States can reduce protections regarding human rights in order to facilitate the movement of judgments and decisions between Member States.[39]

During the Amsterdam era, mutual recognition measures always took the form of Framework Decisions, while so far, all of the post-Lisbon measures have taken the form of Directives. Their application by Member States has been reviewed by the Commission several years after the implementation date. In a few cases, there have been time-limited derogations for a small number of Member States. Usually the mutual recognition measures apply regardless of when the underlying (alleged) criminal offence was committed, but in some cases Member States must or may limit the effect of the measures in time.

As for the substance, each of the mutual recognition measures sets out an obligation to recognize another Member State's judgment or decision, with limited grounds for a refusal to recognize such decisions. The measures refer to the 'issuing' State and the 'executing' State, rather than the 'requesting' and 'requested' State pursuant to Council of Europe measures—demonstrating the more binding degree of obligation as compared to the latter measures, and the more general difference between the principle of mutual recognition in criminal matters and traditional judicial cooperation rules. Although, in the sphere of judicial cooperation, the discretion of the requested State over *whether* to assist the requesting State has been limited by successive treaties, a fundamental degree of discretion over whether to assist the requesting State remains.[40] Conversely, in the system of mutual recognition, the decision of the issuing State (comparable to

---

measure 'by analogy' with others: Case C-60/12 *Baláž*, ECLI:EU:C:2013:733. It should follow that much of the case law on the EAW, discussed in I:3.5.2, is relevant to other mutual recognition measures that have similar provisions, particularly as regards issues like time limits, the overlap with free movement law, and the double jeopardy exception. But the CJEU case law on human rights as a (non) ground for refusal of an EAW should not be followed, for the reasons discussed there.

[38] See further II:3.9 below.   [39] See II:3.3.5 and II:3.5.2 below.

[40] See A Weyembergh, 'La reconnaissance mutuelle des decisions judiciaires en matiere penale entre les Etats Membres de l'Union europeenne: mise en perspective' in G de Kerchove and A Weyembergh, eds., *La reconnaissance mutuelle des decisions judiciaires penales dans l'Union europeenne* (Institut d'Etudes Europeennes, 2001), 25–63.

the 'home State' in free movement law) takes effect *as such* within the legal system of the executing State (comparable to the 'host State' in free movement law), subject to the remaining grounds for refusal to execute that decision. Therefore, the effect of a mutual recognition system is that the executing State has in principle lost some of its sovereign power over the full control of the enforcement of criminal decisions on its territory.

With some mutual recognition measures, there have been issues of material scope (ie defining the concept of criminal proceedings) as well as, to some extent, personal scope (ie limitations based on nationality and/or residence). The traditional ground of refusal as regards criminal cooperation, dual criminality has been abolished in most cases for a standard list of thirty-two crimes, as defined by the *issuing* State, subject to a three-year threshold of *possible* punishment (ie, the actual sentence which was imposed, or which is subsequently imposed in the event of a conviction, is not relevant for this purpose).[41] Other traditional grounds of refusal (political offences, military offences) have also been abolished, and the traditional 'fiscal offence' ground for refusal is now limited by the standard qualification that it cannot be applied merely because the two States in question levy different taxes or duties.

As for human rights, there are standard clauses in the main text and the preambles to the mutual recognition legislation,[42] but almost all of these measures beg the fundamental question as to whether Member States may or must refuse to recognize other Member States' judgments or decisions on human rights grounds—an issue discussed further below.[43] Other remaining grounds for refusal or other forms of restriction applying to most or all Framework Decisions (sometimes subject to further exceptions or special procedural obligations) include: territoriality (ie the possibility of refusing execution because the act concerned took place partly or wholly on the territory of the executing State);[44] *de minimis* rules (ie the amount of a financial penalty, the length of the sentence which was or could be imposed, or the amount of the time of custodial sentence or supervision period still left to serve); double jeopardy or *ne bis in idem*, which raises questions as to whether the general EU double jeopardy rules, including the provisions of the EU Charter of Rights, take precedence over the specific rules in the mutual recognition legislation;[45] the age of criminal responsibility; lapse of time (also known as statute-barring, ie the expiry of a time limit to begin and/or conclude a prosecution); *lis pendens* (ie proceedings for the same offence underway in the executing State);[46] immunity; amnesty or pardon—although sometimes this is a question of applicable law; *in absentia* trials, although the rules on this issue in the relevant legislation have been harmonized;[47] and the rule of specialty (ie the ban on prosecuting a person for an offence other than that which motivated the original mutual recognition decision).

---

[41] For this list of crimes, see Art 2(2) of the Framework Decision establishing the European Arrest Warrant ([2002] OJ L 190/1).

[42] See II:3.5 to II:3.7 below, in particular the discussion in II:3.5.2.   [43] II:3.3.5 and II:3.5.2.

[44] On criminal jurisdiction generally, see II:6.5 below.

[45] On the general double jeopardy rules, and the case for giving priority to those rules over mutual recognition measures, see II:6.8 below.

[46] On the coordination of multiple prosecutions, see II:6.6 below.

[47] On the standard *in absentia* exception, see II:3.3.5 and II:3.5.2 below.

The mutual recognition legislation also includes technical rules on processing applications, costs, and languages, as well as the use of standard forms. Decisions or judgments are issued through judges or prosecutors, not ministries as in Council of Europe measures. There are generally strict time limits to comply with (or refuse) the issuing State's decisions, as well as rules on applicable procedural law issues (ie determining when the power to take further decisions is transferred to the executing State, and when it is retained or transferred back to the issuing State).

Finally, an obvious distinction between the Council of Europe legal framework and the EU legal framework is the jurisdiction of the Court of Justice to interpret the relevant EU measures, and thereby to ensure a greater degree of uniform interpretation.

3.2.3 Treaty of Lisbon

The relevant provision of the Treaties following the entry into force of the Treaty of Lisbon is Article 82(1) of the Treaty on the Functioning of the European Union (TFEU):

1. Judicial cooperation in criminal matters in the Union shall be based on the principle of mutual recognition of judgments and judicial decisions and shall include the approximation of the laws and regulations of the Member States in the areas referred to in paragraph 2 and in Article 83.

    The European Parliament and the Council, acting in accordance with the ordinary legislative procedure, shall adopt measures to:
    (a) lay down rules and procedures for ensuring recognition throughout the Union of all forms of judgments and judicial decisions;
    (b) prevent and settle conflicts of jurisdiction between Member States;
    (c) support the training of the judiciary and judicial staff;
    (d) facilitate cooperation between judicial or equivalent authorities of the Member States in relation to proceedings in criminal matters and the enforcement of decisions.

The Treaty of Lisbon made a fundamental change to the decision-making in this area, applying the 'ordinary legislative procedure' (qualified majority voting in Council and joint powers for the European Parliament (EP)) in place of the prior rule of unanimity in Council with consultation of the EP. Nevertheless, there is a special procedure applicable to Article 82(2) TFEU, which concerns harmonization of criminal procedure; this is discussed in detail in Chapter 2 of this volume.[48] The application of this special rule to Article 82(2), but not to Article 82(1), makes it necessary to distinguish between these two legal bases.[49]

Compared to the previous Treaty provisions, Article 82(1) TFEU includes a reference to the principle of mutual recognition, which must include approximation of law. The Treaty retains a reference to facilitating (but not *accelerating*) cooperation between judicial or equivalent authorities (but not also ministries). However, the specific reference to facilitating extradition was dropped. There is a specific reference to ensuring mutual recognition instead, along with a further specific reference to

---

[48] See I:2.2.3.4.1.   [49] See II:3.2.4 below.

judicial training. Although the express reference to the basic principle of mutual recognition is new as compared to the previous Treaty rules, this principle had already been used as the basic principle governing the adoption of criminal law legislation within the previous third pillar legal framework.[50] The specific requirement that judicial cooperation 'shall include' approximation of procedural and substantive law indicates clearly that the European Union cannot limit itself to adopting mutual recognition measures.

Since the Treaty of Lisbon entered into force, the EU has adopted Directives on a European Investigation Order and protection orders, as well as on confiscation of criminal proceeds.[51] So far, the emergency brake has not been pulled. The Commission also suggested the conclusion of some treaties in this field that had been signed, but not concluded, before the entry into force of the Treaty of Lisbon.[52] The Court of Justice of the European Union's (CJEU's) jurisdiction was limited for a five-year transitional period (until 1 December 2014). It has continued to receive references regularly on the EAW, and it has also ruled on the rules on recognition of criminal sentences.[53]

The revised rules on opt-outs from JHA matters also apply to this area.[54] So do the general provisions of Title V of Part Three of the TFEU, in particular the provision that the Union JHA policy must have '…respect for fundamental rights and the different legal systems and traditions of the Member States',[55] and the power to adopt measures concerning cooperation between the administrations of Member States.[56]

3.2.4 Competence issues

The basic issues arising as regards Article 82(1) TFEU are the extent of the competence conferred by Article 82(1) as such, including the distinction between Article 82(1) and 82(2),[57] and the distinction between Article 82(1) and the rest of the JHA provisions. These issues will be examined in turn.

First of all, it is necessary to distinguish Article 82(1) and (2) TFEU, on the grounds that one paragraph is subject to the emergency brake and the other is not.[58] It would certainly be necessary to draw this distinction if a *dual* legal basis of these paragraphs would be considered incompatible due to this difference in decision-making.[59] However, since the emergency brake is not applicable every time that Article 82(2) TFEU is used to adopt measures, but will only apply in the exceptional cases where a Member State pulls the brake, then it should be possible to combine the two provisions. On the other hand, it is certainly necessary to distinguish between the two legal bases on the grounds that Article 82(2) is subject to a number of specific requirements ('necessary to facilitate', 'having a cross-border dimension', and 'tak[ing] into account'

---

[50] See II:3.2.2 above.   [51] See respectively II:3.6.1.3, II:3.7.6, and II:3.7.4 below.
[52] See II:3.9 below.   [53] See II:3.5 and II:3.7 below.   [54] See II:3.2.5 below.
[55] Art 67(1) TFEU.   [56] Art 74 TFEU. On the general provisions, see I:2.2.3.2.
[57] The discussion here on this point is adapted from S Peers, 'EU Criminal Law and the Treaty of Lisbon' (2008) 33 ELRev 507 at 510–14.
[58] Furthermore, Art 82(2) requires the use of Directives, whereas Art 82(1) does not.
[59] On the case law on dual legal bases, see I:3.2.4.

different national legal traditions) which do not apply to Article 82(1).[60] In the event of a dual legal base being used, an emergency brake could only be pulled as regards those aspects of a proposal that fall within the scope of Article 82(2), and so 'fast-track' enhanced cooperation could only apply to part of the relevant proposal. The remaining provisions could still be adopted separately, and would therefore apply to all Member States. But it is possible that many Member States (and/or the EP) would not want to adopt a mutual recognition measure, for example, unless all the Member States which would be bound by that measure were also bound by a parallel measure harmonizing procedural law (or substantive criminal law, where the emergency brake also applies).[61] A reasonable compromise would be to provide in the mutual recognition measure for broader grounds for refusal to execute decisions of the authorities of the Member State(s) which were not participating in the parallel measure.[62] The same compromise could also be used to address cases where the United Kingdom or Ireland opted in to a mutual recognition measure, but out of a parallel measure.

It is surprising to see that Member States were willing to accept the adoption of mutual recognition measures without a veto or at least an emergency brake, given the national constitutional disputes concerning the adoption of the EAW.[63] In light of those disputes, which reflected legitimate national concerns, it would have been preferable to allow for an emergency brake here as well. Moreover, applying an emergency brake to both paragraphs would have avoided the need to distinguish between them.

Having said that, how should Article 82(1) and (2) TFEU be distinguished? First of all, Article 82(1) concerns, inter alia, mutual recognition rules as such, whereas Article 82(2) concerns procedural harmonization in order to *facilitate*, inter alia, mutual recognition. Similarly, Article 82(2) cannot extend to rules concerning training, since Article 82(1) is a *lex specialis* for these issues. As for the power in Article 82(1)(d) to 'facilitate cooperation' as regards criminal proceedings and enforcement of decisions, it cannot extend to the *substance* of the national procedural laws which fall within the scope of Article 82(2), even though the latter appears to overlap with the former (since it also concerns 'facilitation' of, inter alia, 'judicial cooperation'). Otherwise the specific safeguards in Article 82(2) could be circumvented.

Applying these principles, Article 82(1) would be a sufficient legal base for adopting measures such as the Framework Decisions on the EAW, freezing orders, the mutual recognition of financial penalties and confiscation orders, the European Evidence Warrant (EEW), the transfer of prisoners, the mutual recognition of criminal sentences, prior convictions and probation/parole and pre-trial orders, mutual assistance and the transfer of information relating to criminal records, as long as the relevant proceedings take place in a judicial context. All of the legislation adopted on these issues before the entry into force of the Treaty of Lisbon was adopted on the basis of the previous

---

[60] The requirement to 'respect' different national legal systems (set out in Art 67(1)) also applies to Art 82(1), but this is arguably a subtly different obligation than the requirement to take those systems *into account*, as set out in Art 82(2). See the discussion of this point in II:4.2.4 below.

[61] Art 83 TFEU. See II:5.2.3 and II:5.2.4 below.

[62] See, by analogy, the special rules regarding recognition of UK judgments in Reg 4/2009 on maintenance proceedings ([2009] OJ L 7/1), discussed in II:8.2.5 below.

[63] See II:3.5.2 below.

Article 31(1)(a) TEU,[64] which was interpreted to encompass mutual recognition as a form of cooperation between administrations, although several measures were additionally adopted on the basis of other provisions of Article 31(1) TEU.[65] Article 82 TFEU provides for two separate powers for mutual recognition on the one hand, and cooperation between judicial authorities on the other.

In particular, it should be observed that the prior measures on the European Evidence Warrant and mutual assistance rules do not concern the *admissibility* of evidence (an issue which falls within the scope of Article 82(2)(a) TFEU), but rather the *transfer* of evidence between Member States, an issue within the scope of Article 82(1). Furthermore, a measure amending the Schengen double jeopardy rules would not concern the rights of suspects as such (Article 82(2)(b)), but rather fall within the scope of Article 82(1), since such a measure would concern mutual recognition (according to the Court of Justice),[66] and possibly also conflicts of jurisdiction.

The next key issue is the distinction between Article 82(1) TFEU and other JHA legal bases. As compared to other criminal law powers, Article 82(1) must be distinguished from the substantive criminal law powers set out in Article 83, because the latter Article is subject to the emergency brake procedure.[67] While rules concerning asserting jurisdiction can be regarded as ancillary to the definition of substantive offences, other procedural rules cannot, and the EU can only invoke such powers as the Treaty has conferred upon it. For example, it should be noted that the Directives on trafficking in persons and sexual exploitation of children include provisions on victim protection, which can be (and are) based on Article 82(2)(a) TFEU.[68]

The Treaty powers relating to the European Public Prosecutor (Article 86 TFEU) must be distinguished from Article 82 in that Article 86 requires unanimous voting. Any measure directly relating to the operation of the European Public Prosecutor, even if it concerns mutual recognition (ie national authorities' recognition of the Prosecutor's decisions and vice versa) must be based on Article 86.[69]

Next, there is also a need to distinguish between Article 82 and Article 87 TFEU, as regards policing powers, given that legislation on some aspects of police cooperation is not subject to an emergency brake (Article 87(2)), whereas measures on operational police cooperation are subject to unanimous voting (Article 87(3)).[70] On this point, it should be emphasized that Article 82 only extends to *judicial* proceedings, arguably as defined by Member States,[71] not to cooperation between police or other non-judicial

---

[64] On these measures, see II:3.2.2 above.

[65] The EAW Framework Decision also had a legal base of Art 31(1)(b) TEU, while the Framework Decisions on recognition of probation and parole orders and on recognition of pre-trial orders also had a legal base of Art 31(1)(c) TEU. Moreover, the Framework Decisions on the EEW, the recognition of convictions, and criminal records were based generally on Art 31.

[66] See, for instance, Cases C-187/01 and 385/01 *Gozutok and Brugge* [2003] ECR I-1345, para 33.

[67] Furthermore, Art 83(2) in some cases requires unanimous voting. See further II:5.2.4 below.

[68] See II:4.7.2 below.

[69] For instance, rules on the 'admissibility of evidence' referred to in Art 86(3). For more on Arts 85 and 86, see II:6.2.4 below.

[70] For further details on these provisions, including the distinction between Art 87(2) and (3), see II:7.2.4 below.

[71] This follows from the requirement of respect for national legal systems, as set out in Art 67(1) TFEU.

authorities. The policing legal bases would have to be used instead (or in addition) to adopt legislation on such issues. Although by way of exception, Article 82(1)(d) extends to authorities which are *equivalent* to judicial authorities, this extension is clearly limited in scope by the *ejusdem generis* rule of interpretation, considering also that the policing provisions of the Treaty are a *lex specialis*. Although Article 82(1)(d) is not expressly limited to judicial authorities, the whole of Article 82(1) is limited in scope to '[j]udicial cooperation' and Article 82(1)(d) is expressly limited in scope to criminal proceedings. Any other interpretation could render Article 87 redundant. In any case, it is hard to see how police officers are 'equivalent' to judges. Applying this rule, it may be doubted whether some of the provisions in the Directive on the European investigation order fall within the scope of Article 82.[72]

It is also necessary to distinguish between Article 82 and the civil law powers set out in Article 81 TFEU, given that civil law measures cannot be subject to an emergency brake, can only be proposed by the Commission, are subject to a stronger 'cross-border' requirement, and can potentially (and in fact usually) take the form of Regulations. The issue of distinguishing between these legal bases arose shortly after the entry into force of the Treaty of Lisbon, when the Commission queried the correct legal base for the proposed Directive on a European Protection Order,[73] since some Member States address such issues by means of civil or administrative law, not criminal law. It is understood that the Council legal service took the view that the proposal was correctly based on Article 82 TFEU, since the prevention of crime could fall within the scope of that Article.[74] Ultimately, the EU decided to adopt two separate legislative measures.[75]

On this point, while it is true that Article 67(3) TFEU refers to prevention of crime, more specific references to crime prevention are set out in Articles 84, 87(1), and 88(1) TFEU, not in Article 82.[76] The requirement to respect different legal systems, as set out in Article 67(1) TFEU, instead points towards the need to respect the different approaches that Member States have towards addressing this issue. So a measure based wholly on Article 82 can only address issues connected to criminal law proceedings. It would have been possible to adopt a measure based jointly on Articles 81 and 82 TFEU—but it would have to be proposed by the Commission. This interpretation is supported by the case law on the legal base for measures on the exchange of information on driving offences, discussed below.[77]

On the same issues, there are several criminal law measures that refer to issues which arguably fall within the scope of civil law, such as restitution of property,[78] compensation of victims by offenders, and return of property for crime victims.[79] Conversely, EU

---

[72] On the substance, see II:3.6.1.3 below.

[73] [2010] OJ C 69/5. On the substance, see II:3.7.6 below.

[74] See Council doc 6538/10, 17 Feb 2010.   [75] On the civil law Reg, see II:8.5.1.2 below.

[76] See also the analysis of the Commission legal service (Council doc 10005/10, 19 May 2010), which points out inter alia that the EU cannot harmonize national law on crime prevention pursuant to Art 84 TFEU.

[77] II:3.4.   [78] See the Convention on mutual assistance, discussed in II:3.6.1 below.

[79] See the Framework Decision and Directive on crime victims, discussed in II:4.7 below. Note also the exclusion of damages and restitution claims from the Framework Decision on financial penalties ([2005] OJ L 76/16, Art 1(b) of the Framework Decision).

civil law measures address issues such as civil claims related to criminal proceedings and representation in criminal trials for non-intentional offences.[80]

Finally, it is necessary to distinguish the whole of Article 82, and Article 82(1)(d) in particular, from Article 74 TFEU, which is a legal base for the adoption of measures concerning cooperation between national administrations, and between national administrations and the Commission. Such measures are non-legislative acts, adopted by QMV in the Council with *consultation* of the EP. The obvious distinction between Articles 74 and 82 TFEU is that the former concerns cooperation between *civil servants*, whereas the latter concerns cooperation between *judges*.[81]

3.2.5 Territorial scope

Prior to the entry into force of the Treaty of Lisbon, there were no opt-outs for Member States in this area, except for the delayed application of the relevant Schengen *acquis* to the UK and Ireland. The *acquis* applied to the UK from 1 January 2005,[82] and will also apply to Ireland at a date to be decided.[83] The EU rules and the Schengen *acquis* relating to criminal procedural law applied fully to the newer Member States from their dates of accession (1 May 2004 and 1 January 2007, and subsequently 1 July 2013 for Croatia),[84] and also applied fully to Denmark.[85]

The position changed with the entry into force of the Treaty of Lisbon, which extended the British and Irish opt-outs to new measures in the area of policing and criminal law, and provided for special rules if the UK and Ireland opted out of a measure which amends a measure which already applies to them.[86] In practice, the UK opted in to the Directives on the European Investigation Order and the European protection order, but Ireland opted out.[87] Conversely, Ireland opted in to the Directive on confiscation, but the UK opted out.[88] Both have opted in to the treaties in this area with Norway, Iceland, and Japan.[89]

On 1 December 2014, the UK invoked a block opt-out from JHA measures adopted before the Treaty of Lisbon, and simultaneously chose to opt back in to some of those measures. As regards mutual recognition, this entailed opting back in to most measures, namely: the relevant provisions of the Schengen *acquis*, Framework Decisions on the EAW, mutual recognition of financial penalties and confiscation orders, the consequences of convictions, transfer of prisoners, in absentia trials, criminal records, and

---

[80] See Cases C-7/98 *Krombach* [2000] ECR I-1935 and 157/80 *Rinkau* [1981] ECR 1391. On the *Krombach* case, see further II:3.3 and II:6.2.4 below.

[81] On Art 74 generally, see I:2.2.3.2.

[82] See decision on UK participation in Schengen ([2000] OJ L 131/43) and on the practical application of that decision ([2004] OJ L 395/70). However, the UK got access to the SIS (which supports the practical operation of mutual recognition measures) only in 2015. For more detail on UK participation, see II:2.2.5.1 above.

[83] See decision on Irish participation in Schengen ([2002] OJ L 64/20). For more detail on Irish participation, see II:2.2.5.1 above.

[84] For more detail on accession and the Schengen *acquis*, see II:2.2.5.3 above.

[85] On the substance of that *acquis*, see II:3.2.1 above.

[86] For the detail, see II:2.2.5.1 and II:2.2.5.1 above.

[87] On the substance of these measures, see II:4.6 and II:3.7.6 below.

[88] On the substance, see II:3.7.4 below.

[89] See Council docs 9262/10, 3 May 2010, and 7670/10, 7673/10, and 7676/10, 18 Mar 2010.

recognition of supervision orders.[90] However, it opted out of a number of measures,[91] namely the legislation on recognition of probation or parole orders and domestic confiscation orders, the EU Conventions on extradition and driving disqualification, and the EU's treaties with the USA. However, the block opt-out did not apply to acts adopted after the entry into force of the Treaty of Lisbon which the UK had opted in to (ie the Directives on the European Investigation Order, and Protection Order), or to pre-Lisbon acts amended since the Treaty of Lisbon, if the UK had opted in to the amended measure.[92] The UK can still opt back in to further pre-Lisbon measures in future.

On the other hand, Denmark is now excluded from measures in this area, unless those measures build upon the Schengen *acquis*.[93] But that country held a referendum in December 2015, to decide on whether to adopt a case-by-case system of opt-outs like the UK and Ireland. If so, a group of political parties had decided to opt in to the Directives on the European Investigation Order and the European Protection Order, but to opt out of the Directive on confiscation.[94]

As for non-Member States, pursuant to their association with the Schengen *acquis*, the relevant rules and measures building upon them (including aspects of the 2000 EU Convention on mutual assistance and its 2001 Protocol) also apply to Norway, Iceland, Switzerland, and Liechtenstein.[95] However, Switzerland and Liechtenstein have an exemption as regards any future measures building on the *acquis* which eliminate the 'double criminality' rule as regards search and seizure for offences relating to direct taxation.[96] It should be noted that the Court of Justice has implicitly assumed that it has jurisdiction to rule on the Schengen association treaty with Norway and Iceland.[97]

There is a treaty between the EU, Norway, and Iceland to implement all of the provisions of the EU mutual assistance Convention and its Protocol which do *not* fall within the scope of the Schengen *acquis*,[98] as well as a treaty establishing a surrender procedure between the EU Member States and Iceland and Norway.[99] The latter agreement is very similar to the Framework Decision on the EAW, but contains variations, particularly allowing for the continuation of a 'political offence' exception and the option to refuse to extradite States' own nationals, subject to some limitations.[100]

Finally, Switzerland and the EU (more precisely, the EC (as it was then) and the EU's Member States) have concluded a treaty which concerns the particular issue of

---

[90] See the Council and Commission decisions authorizing the UK to opt back in to these measures ([2014] OJ L 345/1 and 6).

[91] See the list of the measures which the UK opted out of: [2014] OJ C 430/17.

[92] In the field of mutual recognition, this is relevant to the EU Mutual Assistance Convention and its Protocol, freezing orders, and the European Evidence Warrant: see the list of such measures in [2014] OJ C 430/23.

[93] See I:2.2.5.2.   [94] The Danish public voted against.   [95] See I:2.2.5.4.

[96] Art 7(5) of the Schengen association treaty with Switzerland ([2008] OJ L 53/52) and Art 5(5) of the Protocol to that treaty concerning the association of Liechtenstein (COM (2006) 752, 1 Dec 2006). The Directive establishing the European Investigation Order (see II:3.6.1.3 below) falls within the scope of these exceptions.

[97] Case C-436/03 *Van Esbroek* [2006] ECR I-2623.

[98] [2004] OJ L 26/1. The treaty entered into force on 1 Jan 2013.

[99] [2006] OJ L 292/1. See also the earlier Decision defining the Schengen extradition *acquis* as regards Norway and Iceland ([2003] OJ L 76/25). The treaty is not yet in force.

[100] For details of the EAW, see II:3.5.2 below.

protection of the EU's financial interests. It contains a number of provisions relevant to mutual legal assistance.[101] The Commission has proposed the signature and conclusion of a parallel treaty with Liechtenstein.[102]

3.3 Human Rights

3.3.1 Right to a fair trial

Chapter 4 of this volume gives an overview of the right to a fair trial in criminal cases, but what about the particular issue of the application of Article 6 in cross-border cases?[103] In the well-known *Soering* judgment, which ruled that a State could not extradite a person to another country where there was a 'real risk' of treatment contrary to Article 3 of the European Convention on Human Rights (ECHR),[104] the Human Rights Court also ruled that such a removal could in principle violate Article 6 ECHR:

> The right to a fair trial in criminal proceedings, as embodied in Article 6 holds a prominent place in a democratic society. The Court does not exclude that an issue might exceptionally be raised under Article 6 by an extradition decision in circumstances where the fugitive has suffered or risks suffering a flagrant denial of a fair trial in the requesting country...[105]

There was no violation of Article 6 on the facts in *Soering*, or in the later judgment in *Mamatkulov and Abdurasulovic v Turkey*,[106] but in the subsequent *Bader* judgment, the Court found a violation of Article 6 due to a planned execution following an unfair trial in the requesting State.[107] The Human Rights Court subsequently found that any removal to face the death penalty in another State, regardless of the fairness of the trial, is a breach of Articles 2 and 3 ECHR in light of the Thirteenth Protocol to the ECHR, which rules out the death penalty in any circumstances.[108] In a number of cases, the Human Rights Court has decided that is unnecessary to rule on the Article 6 argument, where it had already found a breach of Article 3 if a person were to be extradited.[109]

A judgment on Article 5 ECHR (which concerns limits on detention) is relevant by analogy. In *Drozd and Janousek*,[110] the Human Rights Court considered whether France had responsibility under Article 5 for enforcing a criminal sentence which had

---

[101] Arts 25–38 of treaty ([2009] OJ L 46/6). The treaty entered into force as regards most Member States, the EC, and Switzerland on 8 Apr 2009 (see [2009] OJ L 177/7).

[102] COM (2009) 644, 23 Nov 2009.   [103] On the parallel asylum issues, see I:5.3.

[104] *Soering v UK* (A-161). On the question of whether life imprisonment falls within the scope of Art 3, see the admissibility decision in *Ahmad and others v UK*, 6 July 2010.

[105] Para 113 of the judgment, ibid.   [106] [2005] ECHR-I.

[107] *Bader v Sweden* [2005] ECHR-XI.

[108] *Kaboulov v Ukraine*, 19 Nov 2009 and *Al-Saadoon and Mufdhi v UK*, 2 Mar 2010, para 123; note that the latter judgment expressly rejected the argument that the trial in the requesting State would be or had been a 'flagrant denial of justice'. Ultimately, the Court ruled against the merits of the Art 2 issue in the first judgment, and did not find it necessary to rule on the merits of the Art 2 point in the second judgment, as it had found a violation of Art 3.

[109] For instance, see *Kaboulov* (ibid); *Baysakov and others v Ukraine*, 18 Feb 2010; *Ismoilov and Others v Russia*, 24 Apr 2008, and by analogy, *Saadi v Italy*, 28 Feb 2008.

[110] Judgment of 26 June 1992 (A-240).

been passed following a questionable procedure in the criminal courts of Andorra. Arguably, the detention breached Article 5(1)(a), which specifies that detention can be lawful only, inter alia, after conviction by a competent court. The argument was rejected by a narrow majority of the Court on the grounds that:[111]

> As the Convention does not require the Contracting Parties to impose its standards on third States or territories, France was not obliged to verify whether the proceedings which resulted in the conviction were compatible with all the requirements of Article 6 (art. 6) of the Convention. To require such a review of the manner in which a court not bound by the Convention had applied the principles enshrined in Article 6 (art. 6) would also thwart the current trend towards strengthening international cooperation in the administration of justice, a trend which is in principle in the interests of the persons concerned. The Contracting States are, however, obliged to refuse their cooperation if it emerges that the conviction is the result of a flagrant denial of justice [referring 'mutatis mutandis' to *Soering*].

The Court then went on to take note of a French declaration that it would refuse to cooperate with the Andorran government if it was 'manifestly contrary to the provisions of Article 6...or the principles embodied therein', and found confirmation in French case law refusing extradition unless there were a retrial following an *in absentia* judgment or in cases where a person faced the death penalty. So in the Court's view, it had 'not been shown that in the circumstances of the case France was required to refuse its cooperation in enforcing the sentences.'[112]

So there is a '*Soering* effect' to Article 6 ECHR, applicable not just to extradition but to the enforcement of foreign custodial sentences. Logically, the principle is also applicable to enforcement of financial penalties and other forms of cross-border cooperation in the same way; but unlike the '*Soering* effect' as it applies to Article 3 ECHR, the principle does not appear to require full application of Article 6 ECHR in the other State.[113] Rather it only applies where there is a 'flagrant denial' of justice. Moreover, the standard of proof for application of the principle appears to be higher than the 'real risk' threshold applicable to Article 3 ECHR. In fact, in *Drozd and Janousek* the majority of the Court did not examine the Andorran proceedings to see if such a flagrant denial had taken place, or even the French system for potentially refusing cooperation to see whether cooperation had been wrongly refused in this case. A concurring Opinion apparently suggested that the existence of the opportunity for a review in the requested State's legal system should always be sufficient to defeat any claim that the '*Soering* effect' applies to Article 6 in a particular case.[114]

Does Article 6 ECHR apply to the extradition proceedings *themselves*? The European Court of Human Rights (ECtHR) has ruled that it does not apply to extradition of

---

[111] Para 110 of the judgment.

[112] Para 111 of the judgment. For a detailed analysis, see *Ahmad and others v UK*, n 104 above.

[113] On both points, see further the concurring Opinion of Judge Matscher in the *Drozd and Janousek* judgment.

[114] See Judge Matscher's Opinion (ibid), arguing expressly that 'the requested State must, to be sure, carry out a review of some kind. Such a review is provided for in all legislative systems, the thoroughness of the review and the conditions of its exercise being left to the legislation of the requested State'. The evidence for his assertion about 'all' systems carrying out a review is not offered.

foreigners,[115] although the Court has not yet ruled in a judgment as to whether or not Article 6 covers proceedings for extradition of *nationals*. Similarly, in principle Article 6 does not apply to proceedings regarding the transfer of sentenced persons (and the transfer of sentences), because that Article does not apply to the execution of sentences.[116] However, the position is different when the transfer of persons is part of a plea bargain 'package', ie where the person concerned pleaded guilty in part in return for a promise that the sentencing State would request that the State administering the sentence would convert that sentence rather than administer it, with the result that the person concerned would spend less time in prison after the transfer. In such a case, Article 6 at least confers a right of access to court in order to challenge the sentencing State's decision to renege on its commitments.[117] It should also be noted that the right to the presumption of innocence *does* apply in the context of extradition proceedings, and so presumably applies to other cross-border criminal proceedings.[118]

What other Article 6 issues might arise as regards cross-border proceedings? As regards freezing orders, which are provisional measures pending a trial, it is arguable that since Article 6 ECHR guarantees a trial within a reasonable time, an executing State must ensure that once that reasonable time period is breached, the assets must be released.[119] As for confiscation orders following a criminal conviction, the right to a fair hearing (Article 6(1) ECHR) is applicable, but the presumption of innocence (Article 6(2)) is not, since the conviction has already been handed down.[120] Conversely, if the person concerned has been acquitted of the crime, any confiscation of assets on the basis that the person concerned can nevertheless be presumed to have committed that crime does violate Article 6(2).[121]

Since Article 6 applies throughout criminal proceedings, Article 6(1) should apply to freezing orders *mutatis mutandis* once a 'charge' is brought,[122] but in the absence of a conviction it is arguable that Article 6(2) will apply. Moreover, third parties have no standing under Article 6 ECHR when their property is seized or frozen in the context of proceedings against another person, and confiscation procedures in the absence of a criminal charge also fall outside the scope of Article 6.[123]

As for the compatibility of *in absentia* trials with the ECHR, it is clear from Strasbourg case law that the right to presence and representation at a criminal trial is breached not only where the trial goes ahead even when a defendant is not informed of the proceedings,[124] but also, in some cases where a defendant *is* informed and chooses not

---

[115] See, for instance, *Mamatkulov and Abdurasulovic* (n 106 above), paras 81–3.

[116] Decisions in *Veermae v Finland* (15 Mar 2005) and *Szabo v Sweden* (27 June 2006). See also II:3.3.2 and II:3.3.4 below.

[117] See *Buijen v Germany* and *Smith v Germany*, judgments of 1 Apr 2010.

[118] See *Ismoilov*, n 109 above.

[119] See *Patrikova v Bulgaria*, 4 Mar 2010, where there was a breach of Art 6 due to the unreasonable time period it took to decide on a damages action following an unlawful seizure of goods.

[120] *Phillips v UK* (Reports 2001-VII).   [121] *Geerings v Netherlands*, 1 Mar 2007.

[122] See P van Dijk and G van Hoof, *Theory and Practice of the European Convention on Human Rights*, 4th edn (Intersentia, 2006), 539–42.

[123] See respectively judgments of 24 Oct 1986 in *AGOSI v UK* (A 108) and of 5 May 1995 in *Air Canada v UK* (A316-A).

[124] Case law beginning with *Colozza v Italy* (Series A-89); see particularly the Grand Chamber judgment of 1 Mar 2006 in *Sedjovic v Italy*.

to attend, wishes to send a legal representative in his or her place, and the representative is not allowed to appear.[125] Furthermore, the Human Rights Court has expressly stated that a breach of Article 6 which is committed due to *in absentia* proceedings should in principle be remedied by holding a retrial.[126] The *in absentia* judgments of the Human Rights Court are also relevant to detention, because detention following a national *in absentia* judgment which breached Article 6 standards, in the absence of a retrial, will breach Article 5.[127]

Another Article 6 point is the admissibility of illegally obtained evidence. The Human Rights Court has ruled that it is not a breach of Article 6 to admit evidence obtained in breach of Article 8 ECHR (which protects the right to private and family life).[128] On the other hand, the use of evidence obtained in breach of Article 3 entails a breach of Article 6,[129] except where it is clear that the conviction was not based on the evidence obtained from the torture.[130] Even where the admission of evidence obtained illegally would not violate the ECHR, it might nonetheless be in breach of national law.

It is clear that the standards of Article 6 in relation to a fair trial must be upheld even where evidence, in particular the evidence of witnesses, is submitted from a foreign country pursuant to a mutual assistance treaty.[131]

Finally, an issue related to Article 6 is the protection of the right to property, pursuant to the First Protocol to the ECHR. It is clear from the case law of the ECtHR that the seizure or confiscation of property falls within Article 1 of that Protocol, which governs the deprivation of property or control of its use or enjoyment.[132] This Article requires the use, control, or deprivation of property to be a lawful measure in pursuit of a legitimate aim, subject to the requirement of proportionality, although the extent of the Strasbourg Court's supervision of State action is less stringent than it is under Articles 8–11 ECHR.[133] Applied to criminal proceedings, States can justify seizure or confiscation of property (presumably including seizure for its use as evidence) in light of the objectives underlying criminal law.[134] The rules on the right to property are also applicable to the payment of fines.[135]

---

[125] See *Poitrimol v France* (A 277-A), followed, inter alia, in *Lala v Netherlands* (A 297-A), *Pelladoah v Netherlands* (A 297-B), *Krombach v France* (Reports 2001-II), *Van Geyseghem v Belgium* (Reports 1999-I), and *Khalfaoui v France* (Reports 1999-IX). Compare with *Medenica v Switzerland* (Reports 2001-VI), where a trial in the absence of the accused did not violate Art 6, because his lawyers were able to attend and represent him, and *Eliazer v Netherlands* (Reports 2001-X), where the accused was not denied representation at his initial trial, but only an appeal right.

[126] See *Sedjovic*, n 124 above.

[127] *Stoichkov v Bulgaria*, 24 Mar 2005, where there was also a breach of Art 5(4) for lack of judicial review and Art 5(5) for lack of compensation for the illegal detention.

[128] See, for instance, *Khan v UK* (Reports 2000-V).

[129] See *Jalloh v Germany* (ECHR 2006-IX) and *Harutyunyan v Armenia* (ECHR 2007-XIII).

[130] *Gafgen v Germany*, Grand Chamber, 1 June 2010.   [131] See *A.M. v Italy* (Reports 1999-IX).

[132] See, for instance, *Phillips v UK* (n 120 above) and *Plakhteyev and Plakhteyeva v Ukraine*, 12 Mar 2009.

[133] See A Riza Coban, *Protection of Property Rights within the European Convention on Human Rights* (Ashgate, 2004).

[134] See particularly *Phillips* (n 120 above), along with *Air Canada* (n 123 above), where criminal law considerations were relevant even though no criminal charge was laid, and *AGOSI* (n 123 above) where the conduct of an innocent importer was relevant to whether the confiscation of property was proportionate.

[135] See *Mamikadis v Greece*, 11 Jan 2007.

3.3.2 Legality of criminal law

Article 7 ECHR provides for the legality, and particularly the non-retroactivity of criminal law. This Article is examined later as regards substantive criminal law and criminal jurisdiction,[136] but is it also relevant to criminal procedure?

Article 7 clearly applies to any judgment imposing criminal penalties, and the Strasbourg Court has ruled that it also applies to confiscation orders following a criminal conviction.[137] The 'starting point' for considering the applicability of Article 7 is whether a measure is imposed 'following conviction for a "criminal offence"',[138] which rules out its applicability to pre-trial measures. Indeed, the Human Rights Court has ruled out the applicability of Article 7 to pre-trial detention.[139]

As for applying Article 7 to criminal procedure, the Human Rights Court left the issue open in *Coeme and others v Belgium* as regards limitation periods for prosecution.[140] However, the Court did assume, without even considering the point that the removal of an immunity fell within the scope of Article 7.[141] Article 7 also applies to retroactive applications of extended detention and confiscation,[142] and requires clarity of the law (but not non-retroactivity) as regards changes of early release policies.[143]

It is not clear whether a 'Soering effect' requiring a refusal to assist with extradition or to execute other foreign criminal decisions applies to Article 7, with the consequence that there would be an obligation not to assist another State to enforce a criminal penalty that was retroactive or unclear, by means of extradition or the transfer of a sentence.[144] If so, the question would then arise whether the standard of review was the same as that applying to Article 6 (given the close links between Articles 6 and 7), or the same as that applying to Article 3 (given that Articles 3 and 7 are both non-derogable rights, pursuant to Article 15 ECHR). One such case reached the European human rights bodies, but was rejected on the merits.[145]

3.3.3 Search and seizure

Article 8(1) ECHR recognizes the right to respect for family life, private life, the home, and correspondence. This right is infringed in principle by searches of private property, whether a home or (in at least some cases) a business, and by seizures of items from such private premises. However, Article 8(2) permits interferences with Article 8 rights on grounds relating to public safety and public order. Such interferences must be

---

[136] II:5.3.1 and II:6.3.1 below.   [137] *Welch v UK* (A 307-A), particularly para 28.
[138] Ibid.   [139] *Stephens v Malta* (no 1), 21 Apr 2009.
[140] Reports 2000-VII.   [141] *S.W. v UK* and *C.R. v UK* (A335-B and A335-C).
[142] See respectively *M v Germany*, 17 Dec 2009 and *Nadtochiy v Ukraine*, 15 May 2008.
[143] *Kafkaris v Cyprus*, 12 Feb 2008. On recidivism and Art 7 EHCR, see *Achour v France*, 29 Mar 2006.
[144] Since Art 7 does not apply to pre-trial proceedings, any *Soering* effect could only apply as regards extradition or the transfer a prisoner to serve a sentence already handed down in breach of Art 7. The Human Rights Court has ruled that Art 7 does not apply to the transfer of a prisoner as such (*Szabo* decision, n 116 above), but that is a distinct question from the issue of whether there is an obligation to refuse assistance where the requesting State's judgment breached Art 7.
[145] *Bakhish v Germany* (Commission decision, 31 Oct 1997). On the position in EU law as regards the abolition of the dual criminality rule, see II:3.3.5 below.

'in accordance with law', which includes consideration of the quality and foreseeability of the law, as well as necessary and proportionate to the legitimate aim pursed by the interference. In a number of cases involving searches and seizure, the Human Rights Court has ruled that the 'prescribed by law' standard was not met.[146] As regards the principles of necessity and proportionality, in search and seizure cases the Human Rights Court takes into account the existence of 'adequate and effective safeguards against abuse', and 'the severity of the offence in connection with which the search and seizure was effected, the manner and circumstances in which the order had been issued, in particular further evidence available at that time, the content and scope of the order, having particular regard to the nature of the premises searched and the safeguards taken in order to confine the impact of the measure to reasonable bounds, and the extent of possible repercussions on the reputation of the person affected by the search'.[147]

3.3.4 Detention

Detention[148] for the purposes of extradition is authorized by Article 5 ECHR, provided that the detention is lawful (Article 5(1)(f)),[149] subject to the other provisions of Article 5 guaranteeing information for the detainee (Article 5(2)), judicial review (Article 5(4)), and compensation for wrongful detention (Article 5(5)).[150] As for enforcement of foreign sentences, detention to this end is not lawful without some legal basis in force, either with a basis in national law or based on the ratification by both states concerned of the relevant international treaty.[151] Neither is detention for the purpose of extradition if the person concerned is a national of the State concerned, if that State does not extradite its nationals.[152]

The ECtHR has ruled that if a person is detained for a very lengthy period purely because of a drawn-out extradition process, a State may be responsible for breaching Article 5.[153] Article 5 may also be breached if extradition is not pursued with due diligence,[154] and Article 3 may be breached if prison conditions which the detainee experiences pending extradition are sufficiently appalling.[155] But where the warrant itself is defective, the State which *issued* the warrant is liable for the wrongful detention in the executing State, until after the annulment of the warrant, when the executing State becomes liable.[156]

---

[146] For example, see *L.M. v Italy*, 8 Mar 2005 and *Sallinen and others v Finland*, 27 Sep 2005.

[147] See *Buck v Germany*, judgment of 28 Apr 2005, para 33.

[148] On the issue of detention in the context of immigration and asylum law, see I:7.3.2.

[149] Note that detention for extradition purposes is not subject to Art 5(1)(c) ECHR, which concerns pre-trial detention, with the consequence that Art 5(3) ECHR, which sets out rules on bail in such cases, is not applicable: see *Soldatenko v Ukraine*, 23 Oct 2008.

[150] For an application of all these provisions, see for instance, *Bordovskiy v Russia*, 8 Feb 2005. On the requirement of sufficiently precise rules governing detention for the purpose of extradition (ie 'lawful' detention), see, for example, *Koktysh v Ukraine*, 10 Dec 2009.

[151] See *Grori v Albania*, 7 July 2009 and more generally *Garkavyy v Ukraine*, 18 Feb 2010.

[152] See *Garabayev v Russia* (ECHR 2007-VII) and *Garkavyy*, ibid. See equally as regards refugees, if national law rules out their extradition, *Eminbeyli v Russia*, 26 Feb 2009.

[153] *Scott v Spain* (Reports 1996-VI). [154] For example, see *Quinn v France* (A 311).

[155] See, for instance, *Koktysh v Ukraine*, n 150 above. [156] *Stephens v Malta*, n 139 above.

As we have seen, Article 5 has limited application when a person is detained following a conviction in another State;[157] this was followed as regards Article 5(4) in the *Irirbarne Perez* judgment.[158] Equally, Article 5 is not breached by the transfer of a sentenced person who will serve a greater period in prison in practice as a result of the transfer (ie because the early release policies in the State which the prisoner was transferred to are less generous), as long as the actual criminal sentence initially imposed is not increased, unless there is a 'flagrant disproportionality' as regards the time which will actually be served.[159] However, a potential '*Soering* effect', which would prevent extradition or removal to face arbitrary detention, has been recognized in principle in the case law.[160] Finally, Article 3 ECHR precludes extradition or another form of transfer of a prisoner to another country if that removal would result in the person concerned facing prison conditions in *that* State which were so appalling as to breach Article 3 standards.[161]

3.3.5 Application to EU law

This sub-section will examine in turn: the sources and scope of the relevant human rights rules in EU law; the human rights implications of the principle of 'mutual trust' in other Member States, which forms a key part of the EU's mutual recognition principle in this area; and then two specific issues as regards EU mutual recognition legislation, namely the rules on *in absentia* trials in EU legislation and the application of the principle of the legality and non-retroactivity. Furthermore, the standard rules in EU mutual recognition legislation on human rights are discussed further below.[162] The adopted and proposed EU legislation on criminal suspects' rights is discussed in Chapter 4 of this volume.[163]

Although the EU Charter of Fundamental Rights and the general principles of EU law only apply to criminal proceedings which fall within the scope of EU law,[164] that will usually be the case for criminal proceedings with a cross-border dimension (within the EU), given that there are EU measures in place dealing with most aspects of this issue.[165] The Charter incorporates the right to a fair trial; the right to a defence; the principles of legality and non-retroactivity; and rules on detention; the right to private life; and a ban on removal to face torture or the death penalty.[166] The Court of Justice

---

[157] *Drozd* and *Janousek*, n 110 above.   [158] A325-C.

[159] *Veermae* and *Szabo*, n 116 above.

[160] See particularly decision in *Bankovic and others v U.K. and others*, 12 Dec 2001.

[161] See *Ryabikin v Russia*, judgment of 19 June 2008.   [162] See in particular II:3.5.2.

[163] I:4.7. See also II:5.3.2 and II:6.3.2 below, as regards the human rights aspects of EU law as regards substantive criminal law and criminal jurisdiction (including double jeopardy).

[164] See further I:2.3 and in the criminal law context, Case C-299/95 *Kremzov* [1997] ECR I-2629.

[165] See, for instance, C-303/05 *Advocaten voor de Wereld* [2007] ECR I-3633 and C-404/07 *Katz* [2008] ECR I-7607.

[166] Arts 6, 7, 19(2), 47, 48, and 49(1) and (2) of the Charter. The explanations to the Charter ([2007] OJ C 303/17) state that: Arts 6 and 7 correspond to Arts 5 and 8 ECHR, and have the same meaning, scope, and limitations (see Art 52(3) of the Charter); Art 19(2) is based on the ECtHR case law (mentioning *Soering* specifically); Art 47 has a wider scope than the ECHR (see below); Art 48 corresponds to Art 6(2) and (3) ECHR; and Art 49(1) and (2) corresponds to Art 7 ECHR. On the status of these explanations, see Art 52(7) of the Charter.

has made specific reference to the Charter provisions on a fair trial, non-retroactivity of criminal offences, the right to private life, and detention.[167]

Furthermore, given the non-application of Article 6 ECHR to extradition proceedings, it should again be reiterated that the right to a fair trial within the general principles of EU law and the EU Charter has a wider scope than Article 6 ECHR,[168] so the EU law principle and the Charter arguably govern the procedures relating to the European Arrest Warrant, to other extradition procedures within the scope of EU law, or to procedures governing other forms of cross-border cooperation that may fall outside the scope of Article 6 ECHR.[169] So the various rules on remedies in the EU's mutual recognition measures, as discussed below,[170] should therefore logically be interpreted consistently in line with the general principles of EU law and the Charter, not merely the ECHR.

Next, the key human rights issue underlying EU rules on mutual recognition in criminal matters is the extent of the principle that Member States must have mutual trust in each other's criminal justice systems, and in particular whether there is an exception to this principle on human rights grounds.[171] On this point, it is clear from the case law of the ECtHR that any potential responsibility in States that may arise from cross-border criminal cooperation cannot be wholly excluded solely because both States concerned have ratified the ECHR. The potential application of the ECHR to such cases (including cases involving two EU Member States) has been repeatedly presumed by the Court and Commission.[172] While the Commission's rulings in two cases suggested that both States' ratification of the ECHR was a factor to consider, and one case referred to a presumption of compliance with the ECHR in such 'internal' situations, the two decisions nevertheless went on to consider the merits of the human rights arguments.[173] So, to the extent that there is a presumption, it can clearly be rebutted. This is consistent with the position the European Human Rights Court has taken as regards EU asylum rules.[174]

In fact, if there were no possibility of human rights breaches in any Member State, then the European Convention on Human Rights and national constitutional protection for human rights would not be necessary. Although it could be argued that any

---

[167] See, for instance: *Katz*; *Advocaten voor de Wereld* (both n 165 above); Case C-105/03 *Pupino* [2005] ECR I-5285; C-237/15 PPU *Lanigan*, ECLI:EU:C:2015:474; and Case C-540/03 *EP v Council* [2006] ECR I-5769.

[168] See in particular I:6.3.4, and the explanations to Art 47 of the Charter (ibid).

[169] This argument is implicitly rejected in the Opinion in C-296/08 PPU *Santesteban Goicoechea* [2008] ECR I-6307, para 40. But with respect, this Opinion fails to take account of the wider scope of the general principles and the Charter as compared to Art 6 ECHR. Note also that EU mutual recognition legislation contains some specific rules on remedies (see II:3.5 to II:3.7 below) and that EU measures on suspects' rights apply also to EAW proceedings (II:4.6 below).

[170] See II:3.5 to II:3.7.

[171] This issue is arguably connected with the question of the extent of the EU's competence to adopt legislation pursuant to Art 82(2) TFEU: see II:3.2.4 above.

[172] *Koutsofotinos v Norway and Greece* (Commission decision, 10 Sep 1997); *Mills v UK and Germany* (Court decision, 5 Dec 2000). See also *Eminbeyli* and *Stephens*, nn 152 and 139 above.

[173] See *Lopez de Bergara v France*, 26 Oct 1998 and *Iruretagoyena v France*, 12 Jan 1998 (referring to a presumption).

[174] See I:5.3, particularly the decision in *T.I. v UK* (Reports 2000-III). However, see the admissibility decision in *Stapleton v Ireland*, 4 May 2010.

human rights problem in the issuing Member State could be addressed through its national courts and ultimately the Strasbourg system, the process of waiting to use the courts of the issuing State, and then the Strasbourg system, to remedy a breach of human rights is lengthy, during which time a person could be in detention, or face paying a hefty fine, frozen assets, or confiscated property. As the Strasbourg Court has repeatedly held, 'the Convention is intended to guarantee not theoretical or illusory rights, but rights that are practical and effective'.[175]

Moreover, the possibility of applying a human rights exception in order to block the recognition of another Member State's judgment due to that judgment's breach of the right to a fair trial in criminal proceedings has been recognized by the Court of Justice, albeit in the context of civil proceedings.[176] It would hardly be justifiable to refuse to recognize the same principle in the context of criminal proceedings per se, given the greater consequences for accused persons.

Moving on to specific substantive points, first of all, the application of the mutual recognition principle to *in absentia* trials has been an issue as regards several EU measures. The point is relevant because a number of the ECHR judgments mentioned above[177] concern cases where a person moved from one EU Member State to another Member State (or who already resided there)[178] or a non-Member State; but this did not alter the finding of a breach of Article 6 ECHR.[179] In one of these cases (*Krombach*), the criminal conviction (which could not be enforced because the convicted person was a German national resident in Germany, which did not then extradite its own nationals) was then followed by an attempt to claim civil damages against the convicted person. Since this issue fell within the scope of an EU civil law measure, there was a reference to the Court of Justice, which held (even before the Strasbourg Court ruled on the case) that the *in absentia* ruling was a breach of the right to a fair trial, requiring the German courts to exercise the mandatory 'public policy' ground in the EU civil jurisdiction rules for non-recognition of the French judgment.[180]

The relevant EU legislation, before its amendment in 2009, provided either for a possible request for a guarantee that a person 'will have the opportunity to apply for a retrial of the case in the issuing Member State' or an option of non-execution on the grounds that a person was convicted in an *in absentia* proceeding, if he or she had been given no summons or information about the hearing in the case.[181]

As compared to the Strasbourg case law, these provisions were problematic in that neither the scope of the definition of *in absentia* trials nor the purely optional nature of the guarantees and exceptions were sufficient. In particular, on the former point, there was no guarantee that the issuing State had to offer a retrial and that failing this, the executing State could not execute the issuing state's decision.[182] Moreover, the Strasbourg

---

[175] See, for example, judgment of 12 July 2001, *Prince Hans Adam II v Germany*, para 45.
[176] Case C-7/98 *Krombach* [2000] ECR I-1935. On the civil law implications, see II:8.3.2 below.
[177] II:3.3.1.   [178] See *Krombach* (ibid).
[179] For example, see *Poitrimol*, *Pelladoah*, and *Krombach*, n 125 above.
[180] *Krombach*, n 176 above.
[181] See II:3.5.2., II:3.7.1, II:3.7.4, and II:3.7.5 below. These measures were all amended by a later Framework Decision ([2009] OJ L 81/24), discussed in particular in II:3.5.2 below.
[182] See also the admissibility decision in *Einhorn v France* (Reports 2001-XI), para 33.

case law applies the *in absentia* guarantees not just to cases where the person concerned was unaware of the trial, but also to cases where the person knowingly avoided it, yet sought to send counsel on his or her behalf but the access by counsel was denied. While the 2009 amendments to the EU legislation brought the rules into line with Strasbourg case law, the fundamental problem remains that this ground for refusal to execute a decision remains optional.

The second specific issue as regards EU mutual recognition legislation is the application of the principle, set out in Article 7 ECHR, of non-retroactivity and legality of criminal law. First of all, the Court of Justice has taken the view that the principle does not apply to issues of criminal procedure,[183] but the Strasbourg case law has not definitively and fully settled this question.[184] Next, the Court has also ruled that the abolition of dual criminality in EU mutual recognition legislation does *not* violate the principle of legality set out in Article 7 ECHR as regards the European Arrest Warrant, even in the absence of identical or very similar substantive criminal law in the relevant Member States, because the principle need only be complied with in the issuing Member State.[185]

This leaves open the question whether there may be a power or an obligation to refuse to execute another Member State's decision where the substantive criminal law in the issuing Member State breaches the principle of non-retroactivity or legality of criminal law, including cases where the dual criminality safeguard has been removed retroactively, or where extraterritorial criminal jurisdiction has been imposed retroactively (or unclearly).[186]

3.4 Impact of Other EU Law

EU law other than JHA law overlaps with mutual recognition rules in several respects. This section examines in turn: the impact of the free movement of persons on mutual recognition in criminal matters; the converse impact of criminal law mutual recognition rules on the free movement of persons; and the impact of the criminal law mutual recognition rules on other non-JHA EU law.

First of all, the Court of Justice confirmed in the *Wolzenburg* case that EU third pillar measures are generally subject to the application of EU law on, inter alia, the free movement of persons: '...Member States cannot, in the context of the implementation of a framework decision, infringe Community law, in particular the provisions of the EC Treaty relating to the freedom accorded to every citizen of the Union to move and reside freely within the territory of the Member States'.[187] More specifically, while it is possible in principle to reserve the benefit of certain optional derogations set out in the Framework Decision establishing the European Arrest Warrant to

---

[183] See *Pupino*, n 167 above.   [184] See the discussion in II:3.3.2 above.
[185] *Advocaten voor de Wereld*, n 165 above.
[186] On the jurisdiction issue, see II:6.3.2 below. The Opinion in *Santesteban Goicoechea* (n 169 above), paras 42–6, states that Art 7 cannot apply to extradition proceedings, since it does not apply to procedural matters. With respect, this leaves aside the question as to whether Art 7 would apply if the issuing State's decision was based on *underlying substantive law* (or connected jurisdiction rules) which breached Art 7.
[187] Case C-123/08 [2009] ECR I-9621, para 45. See also C-42/11 *Lopes da Silva Jorge*, ECLI:EU:C:2012:517.

nationals of the executing State,[188] EU free movement law requires that such derogations also apply to citizens of other Member States who were sufficiently integrated into
that State, namely permanent residents as defined by free movement legislation.[189] The
Framework Decisions on pre-trial detention and probation and parole expressly confirm that they are subject to EU free movement law, without further clarification,[190]
while the Framework Decision on the transfer of sentenced persons sets out a special
rule (an option for Member States to waive the normal requirement of their consent)
for the return to the executing Member States of non-citizens who have a permanent
residence right under EU free movement law or immigration law.[191]

The latter Framework Decision also provides for the transfer of a prisoner to his or
her Member State of nationality where he or she does not normally live,[192] begging
the question as to whether this could only occur in the first place if the substantive
and procedural free movement rules governing that person's expulsion from the other
Member State which he or she has moved to were satisfied,[193] although the preamble
to the Framework Decision points to such a requirement.[194] The same issue arises as
regards other mutual recognition measures, most notably the issue of the European
Arrest Warrant,[195] where the assumption of the UK courts[195] that criminal proceedings
in general are unaffected by EC law (as it was then) is obviously wrong per se,[196] but
the Court of Justice has not yet been asked whether and if so, on what grounds, free
movement law could be raised as a barrier to the execution of an EAW, apart from the
question in *Wolzenburg* regarding equal treatment of permanent residents as regards
derogations from the rules. The better view is that the execution of an EAW does not
breach EU free movement law when free movement rights are not being exercised,[197]
and that where free movement rights (or rights to reside in a Member State pursuant to
EU immigration law) are being exercised, the execution of an EAW is a distinct issue
from the retention or loss of the underlying right to reside in the Member State executing the EAW following the conclusion of the criminal proceedings and the completion
of any custodial sentence that might be imposed in the event of conviction, or which
was already imposed.[198]

---

[188] See further II:3.5.2 below.

[189] On the definition of permanent residents under that legislation, see I:6.4.1. EU third pillar measures
do not address the position of persons who are dual citizens of two Member States, or of a Member State and
a third State. On these issues as regards immigration law, see I:6.4.1—but it is arguable that the immigration
rules might not be relevant by analogy to the issue of mutual recognition in criminal law, except where the
underlying free movement or immigration rule is anyway applicable.

[190] [2008] OJ L 337/102, recital 7 in the preamble, and [2009] OJ L 294/20, recital 18 in the preamble.
There was also a reference to the Court of Justice on the effect of free movement law on pre-trial detention
decisions (Case C-297/09 *X*, later withdrawn).

[191] Art 4(7)(a) of that Framework Decision ([2008] OJ L 327/27), which the Court of Justice moreover
referred to in the *Wolzenburg* judgment.

[192] Art 4(1)(b).   [193] On those rules, see I:7.4.1.   [194] Points 15 and 16 in the preamble.

[195] *Healey* [1984] 3 CMLR 575 (QB); *Bullong and Kember* [1980] 2 CMLR 125 (QB); *Virdee* [1980] 1
CMLR 709 (QB).

[196] See *Wolzenburg* as regards arrest warrants; as regards substantive criminal law, see the long-standing
case law discussed in II:5.4.2 below.

[197] For example, where an EAW is issued for a British national *residing in the UK* relating to criminal
offences which he or she allegedly committed during a *prior* visit to Spain.

[198] See paras 85 and 146 of the *Wolzenburg* Opinion, which suggest such an interpretation. On the separate issue of the relationship between extradition proceedings or EAWs and asylum proceedings, see I:5.7.

The Directive establishing a European Protection Order is also linked to free movement, since it only applies where a person seeks to move between Member States.[199] Similarly, the adoption of mutual recognition measures reduces Member States' justifications for limitations on equality rights of EU citizens in the context of imposing criminal penalties, because of the enhanced ease of enforcing national criminal law measures in other Member States.[200] The CJEU has been asked to decide whether EU *citizenship* law, as distinct from free movement law, imposes limits upon extradition to non-EU States.[201]

Secondly, criminal procedural law impacts on EU free movement law in several respects. As for free movement and access to employment, EU law probably does not give the right to apply for a job as a prison officer in another Member State, since such jobs involve powers of constraint.[202] However, private security employment and contracts must be opened to employees and businesses from other Member States.[203] Arguably, so should non-custodial jobs in prisons and work as a probation or parole officer, except perhaps where such persons control or work as officers in 'halfway houses' which can be considered similar to prisons. Although probation and parole officers often have the authority to terminate conditional release, arguably this is only an auxiliary power of constraint, comparable to powers enjoyed by private security guards, which does not bring them within the 'public employment' exception to free movement law.[204]

As for the free movement of victims, the Directive on a European Protection Order aims to encourage a person to move between Member States without any loss of security.[205] But what about the free movement of *offenders*? A Member State may wish to restrict an offender on probation or parole from leaving that Member State; this might be justified, subject to EU free movement law.[206] If a Member State wishes to restrict a parolee or probationer from *entering* its territory, it may rely on the same derogations, unless of course that person is one of its nationals. After a sentence is spent, it will be increasingly hard to justify restrictions on entry or exit, because a person must represent a severe *present* threat to a Member State to do so.[207] Subsequent lawful behaviour and expressions of remorse might even oblige a Member State to allow entry to a person who had committed terrorist offences some years before.[208] An ex-offender should also be able claim access to rehabilitation assistance in another Member State as a 'social advantage' available to workers, and to other EU citizens.[209] Arguably, it will

---

[199] See II:3.7.6 below.

[200] See II:5.4.2 below, and in particular the Opinion in Case C-224/00 *Commission v Italy* [2002] ECR I-2965, which makes a direct link between the lack of any measure (at the time) on mutual recognition of financial penalties (see now II:3.7.1.1 below) and Member States' justifications for unequal treatment as regards fines.

[201] Case C-182/15 *Petruhhin*, pending. It might be argued that removal to a third State by means of extradition deprives an EU citizen of the genuine enjoyment of citizenship rights, by analogy with the case law relating to citizenship and immigration: see I:6.4.1.

[202] See Case 149/79 *Commission v Belgium* [1980] ECR 3881.

[203] See the case law discussed in II:7.4.3.1 below.   [204] See the cases discussed ibid.

[205] Point 6 in the preamble, Dir 2011/99 ([2011] OJ L 338/2). On the substance, see II:3.7.6 below.

[206] For more detail on the relevant free movement rules, see I:7.4.1.

[207] Ibid.   [208] *Proll* [1988] 2 CMLR 387 (IAT).

[209] Art 7(2), Reg 1612/68 ([1968] OJ L 257/2); on 'social advantages' for other categories of EU citizens, see the case law beginning with Case C-85/96 *Martinez Sala* [1998] ECR I-2691, referred to in I:6.4.1.

now be harder to justify restrictions upon free movement of persons during probation or parole, now that the deadline to apply the Framework Decision on this subject has passed.[210] Similarly, it can be argued that detention of EU citizens pending trial in cases when nationals are not detained cannot be justified in light of the ease of issuing an EAW to ensure that the person concerned can be returned to the host Member State to face trial,[211] as well as the possibility of issuing a pre-trial supervision order that could be recognized in another Member State.[212]

According to the Court of Justice, EU citizens and their family members cannot count time in detention towards the period of residence necessary to obtain permanent residence or other forms of enhanced protection against expulsion in another Member State.[213] Furthermore, movement between Member States due to criminal proceedings could also affect acquisition of such enhanced protection against expulsion.[214] Finally, there is also a link between EU rules on social security and free movement and the transfer of sentenced persons.[215]

Thirdly, as for other areas of EU law, in the area of EU sex discrimination law, a Member State accepted during litigation that it could not discriminate between men and women in access to management, technical, and training jobs in prisons, but the Commission agreed that Member States could discriminate on grounds of sex for the job of warder and the Court agreed that they could discriminate for head warder posts.[216] A national court presumed, no doubt correctly, that women could not be banned from jobs as social workers in prisons, and they surely cannot be banned from probation and parole work.[217]

There is also a link between other non-JHA EU law and EU mutual recognition measures, for when non-JHA EU legislation prohibits something, and some or all Member States give effect to that obligation by creating a criminal offence, or alternatively when a non-JHA EU measure directly requires that Member States enforce a prohibition by criminal penalties,[218] then the double criminality rule restricting extradition, to the extent that it still exists following the application of EU mutual recognition measures,[219] is automatically weakened.

The protection of the EU's financial interests in a treaty with Switzerland entailed ratification of that treaty by both the Community (as it then was) and its Member States,[220] and the EU's measures on mutual assistance in criminal matters are paralleled by EU legislation which sets out rules for administrative assistance in tax matters.[221] It

---

[210] See II:3.7.5 below.   [211] See II:3.5.2 below.
[212] See the Framework Decision on mutual recognition of pre-trial supervision orders (II:3.6.3 below).
[213] Cases C-400/12 *G*, ECLI:EU:C:2014:9 and C-378/12 *Onuekwere*, ECLI:EU:C:2014:13.
[214] Case C-145/09 *Tsakouridis* [2010] ECR I-11979.
[215] Case C-302/02 *Effing* [2005] ECR I-552.
[216] Case 318/86 *Commission v France* [1988] ECR 3359.
[217] Case 14/83 *Von Colson and Kamann* [1984] ECR 1891.   [218] See II:5.4.1 below.
[219] See II:3.5 to II:3.7 below.
[220] A parallel treaty with Liechtenstein has also been proposed. See II:3.2.5 above.
[221] As regards tax recovery, see Dir 76/308 ([1976] OJ L 73/18), as codified following later amendments by Dir 2008/55 ([2008] OJ L 150/28), replaced by Dir 2010/24 ([2010] OJ L 84/1) as from 1 Jan 2012 (Art 28(1)). As regards administrative assistance, see, as regards direct taxation, Dir 77/799 ([1977] OJ L 336/15), as amended by Dirs 2003/93 ([2003] OJ L 264/23) and 2004/56 ([2004] OJ L 157/70), and replaced by Dir 2011/16 ([2011] OJ L 64/1). As regards VAT, see Reg 218/92 ([1992] OJ L 24/1), replaced by Reg 1798/2003

is striking that while mutual assistance or mutual recognition as regards the criminal law aspects of tax fraud is subject to the ordinary legislative procedure after the entry into force of the Treaty of Lisbon, administrative cooperation as regards taxation is still subject to unanimous voting.[222]

Non-JHA EU legislation also has implications for disqualifications, in particular as regards driving licences: Member States must refuse to issue a licence, or to recognize the validity of a licence, if that licence was restricted, suspended, or withdrawn in another Member State.[223] Also, it might be questioned whether measures concerning disqualifications which do not follow from a criminal conviction pronounced by a court would fall within the scope of the EU's criminal law competence.[224] This issue has been addressed by the CJEU, when it ruled that legislation on the exchange of information between Member States on infringements of traffic law should have been based on the legal base on transport (with no opt-outs), rather than police cooperation.[225]

3.5 Extradition and the European Arrest Warrant

3.5.1 Extradition

A basic element of cooperation between States regarding criminal matters is the concept of extradition, which entails an agreement between States to send a person who is absent from a State pending a criminal trial or following the imposition of a criminal sentence there to that State, in order to serve the sentence or to appear at the criminal trial. The basic international framework for extradition for European States is the 1957 Council of Europe Convention on Extradition, which all Member States have ratified, although only some Member States have ratified the four Protocols to the Convention.[226] In addition, all Member States have ratified the 1977 Council of Europe Convention on the Suppression of Terrorism, which affects both extradition and mutual assistance;[227] a 2003 Protocol to that Convention is not yet in force.[228]

To implement extradition, the 'requesting' State (the State of the prosecution, which wishes to assert jurisdiction over a fugitive to conduct a criminal prosecution, or to enforce a sentence or detention order) asks the 'requested' State (the 'host' State, which currently has the fugitive) to 'surrender' the fugitive to it, possibly after a provisional arrest to prevent flight. For this purpose, the requested State holds a special extradition proceeding, the details of which are left to national law.

Under the 1957 Council of Europe Convention, extradition must be granted wherever the fugitive has escaped from a custodial sentence of over four months' detention,

---

([2003] OJ L 264/1) and then Reg 904/2010 ([2010] OJ L 268/1). As regards excise duties, see Reg 2073/2004 ([2004] OJ L 359/1), replaced by Reg 389/2012 ([2012] OJ L 121/1).

[222] See Arts 113, 114(2), and 115 TFEU (former Arts 93, 95(2), and 94 EC), as interpreted in Cases C-338/01 *Commission v Council* [2004] ECR I-4829 and C-533/03 *Commission v Council* [2006] ECR I-1025.

[223] Art 11(4) of Dir 2006/126 ([2006] OJ L 403/18), applicable from 19 Jan 2009 (Art 18).

[224] See further II:3.7.3 below.

[225] Case C-43/12 *Commission v Council and EP*, ECLI:EU:C:2014:298, concerning Dir 2011/82 ([2011] OJ L 288/1). After that judgment, Dir 2015/413 ([2015] OJ L 68/9) was adopted to address this issue.

[226] ETS 24, 86, and 98 respectively. For details of ratification and signatures, see Appendix I.

[227] ETS 90.   [228] ETS 190. For details of ratification and signatures, see Appendix I.

or is accused of committing a crime which would be an offence resulting in at least one year's detention in both the requesting and requested States (the 'double criminality' rule). However, there are a number of important exceptions to this. A State may limit its extradition obligations to a selected list of crimes, or exclude a selected list from its obligations, and moreover no State has an obligation to extradite a person charged with a 'political offence' or where there would be prejudice, punishment, or prosecution 'on account of the fugitive's race, religion, nationality or political opinion'. Military offences are excluded and fiscal offences may be. Most important of all, States may choose to refuse extradition of their own nationals, and many EU Member States initially chose this option. Among other rules, lapse of time to bring criminal proceedings in the requesting or requested State prevents extradition.

A separate principle for the protection of the fugitive is the 'specialty' rule. This rule prevents the requesting State from bringing other proceedings against the fugitive for offences other than that for which he or she was extradited, except where the requested State gives its consent or the fugitive remains in or returns to the requested State. Furthermore, the fugitive cannot be sent to a *third* State ('re-extradited') by the requesting State without the requested State's consent. Requests under the Convention must be exchanged via embassies, but State parties can agree bilaterally on simpler rules for exchanges. In addition to the various options allowed in the text of the Convention, reservations to '*any* provision or provisions' are allowed.[229]

These extensive opt-outs and reservations led to four subsequent Protocols and to the Convention on the Suppression of Terrorism, which attempted to restrict their use. The first two Protocols, inter alia, narrow the 'political offence' and fiscal offences exceptions, and the Terrorism Convention lists six 'terrorist' offences which definitely shall not be classified as 'political offences' by signatory States, and allows States to exclude other crimes from the scope of the exception. However, parties may still refuse extradition if they suspect that the requesting State is persecuting the accused, and can enter a reservation if they consider that a particular offence falling within the list of 'terrorist offences' is indeed a political offence.[230] EEC Member States agreed an EPC Convention in 1979 attempting to restrict the use of such reservations between each other, but this Convention never entered into force and ratification attempts were abandoned.[231]

Because many EU Member States had not ratified one of the first two Protocols to the 1957 Convention and/or had chosen *à la carte* from the provisions of the 1957 Convention and its first two Protocols, extradition between them was deemed unsatisfactory. Therefore, the Schengen Convention and two EU Conventions of 1995 and 1996 aimed to restrict Member States' use of reservations and exceptions under the Council of Europe measures,[232] although the EU Conventions are not yet in force.[233] Also a 1989 EPC Convention tried to speed up existing mechanisms by allowing authorities to fax

---

[229] Art 26(1) (emphasis added).   [230] Art 13 of the Convention.
[231] UK government Command Paper, Cm 7823 (1980).
[232] Arts 59–66 (Schengen Convention); [1995] OJ C 78/1 (consented extradition); [1996] OJ C 313/11 (disputed extradition). See also the Schengen Executive Committee Declaration on extradition ([2000] OJ L 239/435).
[233] See Appendix I for ratification details.

extradition requests.[234] The Schengen provisions abolished the fiscal offences exception for VAT, customs duties, and excise duties; provided for requests to be sent to justice ministries; and allowed for speedy extradition with the fugitive's consent. Also, the inclusion of extradition requests in the SIS facilitated the practical application of the extradition rules.[235] The first EU extradition Convention provided for detailed rules governing such speedy consented extradition, and then the second Convention attempted to address a large number of barriers to extradition, in particular: lowering the threshold for extradition to a six months' custodial sentence in the requested State; weakening the double criminality rule as regards organized crime; abolishing the 'political offence' exception, although Member States could make a renewable reservation on this point; abolishing also the 'fiscal offences' exception, although Member States could provide that the exception was only abolished to the extent that the Schengen extradition required; requiring Member States to permit extradition of their nationals to other Member States, although Member States could make a renewable reservation on this point; limiting the Council of Europe restrictions relating to lapse of time, specialty, and re-extradition (to other Member States); and integrating the EPC Convention on faxing requests into the text.

Furthermore, there are specific extradition rules in a number of EU criminal law measures, in particular applying an 'extradite or prosecute' principle.[236] Also, the rules on sentencing in several EU measures specifically require that in at least some cases, the penalties should be stringent enough to give rise to possible extradition proceedings.[237]

3.5.2 European Arrest Warrant

Extradition between Member States has now largely been replaced by the Framework Decision establishing the European Arrest Warrant (EAW).[238] The Framework Decision was adopted in June 2002, and Member States were obliged to apply it by 31 December 2003.[239] It has attracted a significant amount of case law from the Court of Justice: a reference on its validity and over a dozen references on its interpretation.[240] First of all,

---

[234] For further details, see: <http://www.consilium.europa.eu/en/documents-publications/agreements-conventions/agreement/?aid=1989025>.

[235] On the SIS, see II:7.6.1.1 below.   [236] For details, see II:6.5 below.

[237] See the provisions discussed in II:5.6 below.

[238] The EU has also agreed some treaties on extradition to non-EU States (see II:3.9 below). The CJEU has been asked whether EU citizenship law limits extradition of EU citizens to third States: Case C-182/15 *Petruhhin*, pending.

[239] Art 34(1) ([2002] OJ L 190/1). All references in this section are to this Framework Decision unless otherwise indicated. On the EAW, see N Keijzer and E van Sliedregt, eds., *The European Arrest Warrant in practice* (Asser, 2009); E Guild and L Marin, *Still Not Resolved? Constitutional Issues of the European Arrest Warrant* (Wolf, 2009); R Blextoon, ed., *Handbook on the European Arrest Warrant* (Asser, 2005); S Alegre and M Leaf, *European Arrest Warrant: A Solution Ahead of its Time?* (Justice, 2003); and J Wouters and F Naert, 'Of Arrest Warrants, Terrorist Offences and Extradition Deals: An Appraisal of the EU's Main Criminal Law Measures Against Terrorism After "11 September"' (2004) 41 CMLRev 909.

[240] On validity, see Case C-303/05 *Advocaten voor de Wereld* [2007] ECR I-3633. On interpretation, see Cases: C-66/08 *Koslowski* [2008] ECR I-6041; C-296/08 PPU *Santesteban Goicoechea* [2008] ECR I-6307; C-388/08 PPU *Leymann and Pustovarov* [2008] ECR I-8993; C-123/08 *Wolzenburg* [2009] ECR I-9621; C-261/09 *Mantello* [2010] ECR I-11477; C-306/09 *I.B.* [2010] ECR I-10341; C-192/12 PPU *West*, ECLI:EU:C:2012:404; C-42/11 *Lopes da Silva Jorge*, ECLI:EU:C:2012:517; C-396/11 *Radu*, ECLI:EU:C:2013:39; C-399/11 *Melloni*, ECLI:EU:C:2013:107; C-168/13 PPU *F*, ECLI:EU:C:2013:358; C-237/15 PPU *Lanigan*, ECLI:EU:C:2015:474; and C-463/15 PPU *A*, ECLI:EU:C:2015:634. Two cases are pending: Case C-241/15 *Bob-Dogi* and C-404/15 *Aranyosi*.

as to the legal form of the Framework Decision, the Court of Justice confirmed that the Council could replace Conventions by means of a Framework Decision.[241]

As for the substance of the Framework Decision, it has replaced the corresponding provisions of the prior EU, EPC, and Council of Europe measures.[242] However Member States retained the option to apply earlier extradition rules as regards acts committed before a certain date.[243] In that case, the prior measures continue to apply in part as regards requests to those Member States which have limited the temporal application of the Framework Decision.[244] The Council of Europe Extradition Convention (and the Council of Europe's Terrorism Convention, when the 2003 Protocol to that Convention enters into force) permits States to replace the application of these Conventions between themselves if they agree a uniform law of extradition.[245] So the (EU) Council adopted conclusions urging Member States to declare officially the non-applicability of the Council of Europe measures between themselves.[246] More fundamentally, the Court of Justice has ruled that the purpose of the Framework Decision is to replace the traditional extradition system with a system of surrender on the basis of an EAW.[247]

The basic rule is that EAWs must be executed 'on the basis of the principle of mutual recognition and in accordance with the provisions of [the] Framework Decision'.[248] An EAW can be issued whether a person is wanted for trial or whether a person has already been convicted and escaped application of a custodial sentence or detention order.[249] It may be issued for any act punishable in the issuing State (the Member State issuing the arrest warrant) by a period of at least twelve months or, where a sentence has already been passed, for at least four months.[250] This threshold is in principle waived in the specific circumstances of the application of the Framework Decision on the recognition of pre-trial supervision orders, although Member States have the option of refusing to waive that threshold.[251] It should also be noted that the mere possibility of issuing an EAW in order to enforce a sentence against a person resident in another Member State

---

[241] *Advocaten voor de Wereld*, ibid. See II:2.2.2 above. This reasoning is presumably valid *mutatis mutandis* to a number of other mutual recognition measures which replace or repeal the corresponding provisions of Conventions: see II:3.6 and II:3.7 below.

[242] Art 31(1). Member States are free to retain or adopt treaties which further simplify the application of the Framework Decision (Art 31(2)). The Court of Justice has confirmed that this latter provision does not mean that Member States can keep applying the Council or Europe, EU, or EPC measures: judgment in *Santesteban Goicoechea*, n 240 above. This interpretation presumably applies *mutatis mutandis* to other mutual recognition measures with equivalent provisions.

[243] France, Italy, and Austria have applied this option (see declarations in [2002] OJ L 190/19). Also, Austria could refuse to extradite its own nationals until the end of 2008 unless dual criminality applied (Art 33(1)).

[244] Art 32. The Court of Justice has confirmed that in that case, Member States are still free to ratify the EU's extradition Conventions in order to simplify extradition somewhat as regards such persons: judgment in *Santesteban Goicoechea*, n 240 above.

[245] Art 28(3) of the former Convention; Art 9 of the latter Convention (as amended by the Protocol).

[246] Council doc 12413/03, 11 Sep 2003, adopted by the JHA Council, 3 Oct 2003.

[247] Judgments in: *Advocaten voor de Wereld*, para 28; *Koslowski*, para 31; *Leymann*, para 42; and *Wolzenburg*, para 56 (all n 240 above).

[248] Art 1(2).   [249] Art 1(1) and clause 5 of the preamble.

[250] Art 2(1). The (potential) sentence in the *executing* State is irrelevant, whether or not the (alleged) offence is on the list of thirty-two crimes discussed below: see the order in *A* (n 240 above).

[251] Art 21 of that Framework Decision ([2009] OJ L 294/20), which was applicable from 1 Dec 2012 (Art 27(1)). On the substance, see II:3.6.3 below.

does not extinguish the application of the 'enforcement condition' which applies to the Schengen double jeopardy rules, or mean that this condition is invalid.[252]

The central provision of the Framework Decision abolishes the principle of double criminality, where the warrant has been issued for one of the standard list of thirty-two offences 'as defined by the law of the issuing Member State', where such an offence could be subject to a sentence of at least three years.[253] In fact, the list contains more than thirty-two offences, since some points cover more than one offence. For acts not on the list, surrender of the person 'may' be subject to the condition of double criminality in the executing State (the State enforcing the arrest warrant),[254] with the consequence that there will still be an obligation to establish whether the act in question would be a crime in both States.

The validity of this partial abolition of dual criminality was challenged though the national courts, on the grounds that it breached the principle of the legality of criminal proceedings and the principles of equality and non-discrimination.[255] However, according to the Court of Justice, while these principles formed part of the general principles of EU law, and were moreover reaffirmed in the EU Charter of Fundamental Rights,[256] the principle of legality was not infringed because it was for the issuing Member State to comply with it when it defined the offences which it sought to punish or prosecute by means of executing an EAW.[257] As for the principles of equality and non-discrimination, the Court held that abolishing the dual criminality rule only as regards thirty-two specific offences was not a breach of those principles, since 'the Council was able to form the view, on the basis of the principle of mutual recognition and in the light of the high degree of trust and solidarity between the Member States, that, whether by reason of their inherent nature or by reason of the punishment incurred of a maximum of at least three years, the categories of offences in question feature among those the seriousness of which in terms of adversely affecting public order and public safety justifies dispensing with the verification of double criminality', and so any distinction between persons convicted or accused of those crimes and persons convicted or accused of other crimes was justified, even if those two groups of persons were comparable.[258] Also, the lack of precision in the definition of the offences was not problematic on this ground either, since the Framework Decision did not have the purpose of harmonizing substantive criminal law and the Treaty (as it then was) did not make application of the Framework Decision conditional on such harmonization.[259] This reasoning is presumably valid *mutatis mutandis* to the abolition of the dual criminality principle in a number of other mutual recognition measures.[260]

---

[252] Cases C-288/05 *Kretzinger* [2007] ECR I-6441 and C-129/14 PPU *Spasic*, ECLI:EU:C:2014:586. On the substance, see II:6.8 below.

[253] Art 2(2).   [254] Art 2(4).

[255] *Advocaten voor de Wereld*, n 240 above. See further II:3.3.5 above.

[256] Paras 45–7 of the judgment, ibid.   [257] Paras 48–54 of the judgment, ibid.

[258] Paras 57–8 of the judgment, ibid.

[259] Para 59 of the judgment, ibid. The Court referred to its case law on the double jeopardy rule, on which see II:6.8 below. Arguably the subsequent wording of the Treaty (Art 82 TFEU) entrenches the mutual recognition principle even more strongly (see II:3.2.3 above).

[260] See II:3.6 and II:3.7 below. However, note that the Framework Decision on mutual recognition of financial penalties abolishes dual criminality for a longer list of crimes (II:3.7.1.1 below). The *Advocaten voor de Wereld* judgment cannot automatically be applied by analogy to that measure.

There are three categories of grounds for which the execution of an EAW could be refused or delayed. The Court of Justice has ruled that these are the *only* grounds which could justify non-execution of an EAW.[261] First, there are three grounds for *mandatory* non-execution of the warrant: an amnesty in the executing State, if that State had jurisdiction to prosecute the offence under its national law; where the double jeopardy rule applies; and where the fugitive is below the age of criminal responsibility in the executing State.[262] The CJEU has interpreted the double jeopardy exception in its *Mantello* judgment.[263] According to the Court, the double jeopardy rule was a uniform concept of EU law that had to be interpreted autonomously of the law of the Member States. The basic elements of the rule ('same acts', and implicitly 'finally judged') had to be interpreted by analogy with the extensive case law on the Schengen double jeopardy rules.[264]

Second, there are seven grounds for *optional* non-execution:[265] residual application of the double criminality rule; a pending prosecution in the executing Member State for the same acts (*lis pendens*);[266] a decision not to prosecute, or a final sentence, in the executing State, which prevents further proceedings; time-barring of the action in the executing Member State, if it has jurisdiction; a prior judgment for the same acts in a third State, if that judgment has been enforced; the executing Member State's agreement to enforce the sentence itself, against one of its nationals or residents or a person staying there, where the EAW was issued for the purpose of enforcing a sentence; or where the executing Member State either regards the acts as taking place within its territory or would not exercise extraterritorial jurisdiction over acts which took place outside the issuing State's territory.

The Court of Justice has clarified that the exception concerning time-barring only applies where there was no final judgment; a final judgment dismissing a prosecution due to time-barring falls instead within the scope of the mandatory double jeopardy exception.[267] Furthermore, the exception relating to possible execution of a sentence against nationals, residents, or persons staying in the executing State has attracted a number of references to the Court of Justice.[268] It also interacts with the later Framework Decision on the recognition of custodial sentences.[269] First of all, in its *Koslowski* judgment, the Court of Justice interpreted the part of the exception relating to persons

---

[261] See, for instance, the judgments in: *Koslowski*, para 43; *Leymann*, para 51; *Wolzenburg*, para 57; and *Mantello*, para 37 (all n 240 above). In its judgment in *IB*, the CJEU stated that an asylum application does not fall within the scope of Arts 3 or 4 (para 43).

[262] Art 3. Note that this is the only mutual recognition measure which provides for mandatory grounds for non-execution.

[263] N 240 above.

[264] Arts 54–8 of the Schengen Convention ([2000] OJ L 239); see further II:6.8 below.

[265] Art 4.

[266] On this point, it should be noted that the traditional 'extradite or prosecute' rule found in many Framework Decisions on substantive criminal law (see II:6.5 below) is now irrelevant where an EAW is issued, since the EAW Framework Decision does not permit a refusal on the grounds that the executing State is *planning* to prosecute the person concerned. On the coordination of prosecutions in *lis pendens* cases, see II:6.6 below.

[267] Case C-467/04 *Gasparini* [2006] ECR I-9199, para 31.

[268] Art 4(6). See also the discussion of Art 5(3) below.

[269] See Art 25 of that Framework Decision ([2008] OJ L 327/27), applicable from 5 Dec 2011 (Art 29(1)). On the substance, see II:3.7.1.2 below.

'staying in' the executing State,[270] ruling that it could not apply to all persons temporarily located in the executing State, but equally could apply to a person staying there for a period of time who had established certain connections there. Moreover, the definitions of 'resident' and 'staying in' had an EU-wide autonomous meaning not dependent on the laws of the Member States. In order to apply any of the three categories of exception, Member States 'must assess whether there is a legitimate interest which would justify the sentence imposed in the issuing Member State being executed on the territory of the executing Member State', a condition which does not in fact appear in the Framework Decision. It followed that this exception 'has in particular the objective of enabling the executing judicial authority to give particular weight to the possibility of increasing the requested person's chances of reintegrating into society when the sentence imposed on him expires', and therefore that:

> ...the terms 'resident' and 'staying' cover, respectively, the situations in which the person who is the subject of a European arrest warrant has either established his actual place of residence in the executing Member State or has acquired, following a stable period of presence in that State, certain connections with that State which are of a similar degree to those resulting from residence.

In order to examine whether those 'certain connections' exist:

> ...it is necessary to make an overall assessment of various objective factors characterising the situation of that person, which include, in particular, the length, nature and conditions of his presence and the family and economic connections which he has with the executing Member State.

Applying these principles, the Court stated that interruptions of stay and noncompliance with immigration law (ie the immigration law aspects of the person's status) could not lead automatically to the conclusion that the person concerned was not 'staying in' the Member State, but could be 'of relevance' when deciding that issue. On the other hand, the commission of crimes in that State or the detention in that State following a conviction (ie the criminal law aspects of the person's status) were not relevant at all for deciding whether that person was 'staying' there—although they could be relevant for applying the second phase of the assessment, ie deciding whether there was a 'legitimate interest' in not executing the EAW in the particular case. The Court did not offer any indication of how to interpret the concept of the 'actual state of residence' (ie, the criteria to interpret the 'resident' requirement).[271] Nor did the Court address the question as to whether the person's *future* immigration status (ie whether the person had been, or could or would be, validly expelled as distinct from surrendered) was relevant to the application of the reintegration requirement.[272]

---

[270] N 240 above, paras 36–54.

[271] For further suggestions as to the interpretation of these concepts, see the *Wolzenburg* Opinion, paras 53–70.

[272] As the Opinion in *Koslowski* convincingly argues (paras 159–72), reintegration into the executing State's society is not feasible if the person will be expelled, but also any expulsion must comply with EU free movement or immigration law. See also the *Wolzenburg* Opinion, paras 84–6.

Subsequently, in the *Wolzenburg* judgment, the Court ruled that Member States retain a discretion to permit only *some* categories of nationals, residents, or persons staying on the territory to benefit from the possibility of refusing to execute a warrant,[273] on the grounds that allowing a choice for Member States to limit the scope of the exception would further the underlying objectives of the Framework Decision by bringing more people within its scope. However, this discretion was constrained by the principle of equal treatment of EU citizens who were nationals of other Member States, which meant that Member States at the very least had to treat EU citizens who had permanent residence status in that State the same as that State treated its own citizens.[274] EU citizens who had not yet obtained that status could be treated differently (ie not benefiting from the exception) because they were not in a similar position to nationals of the host State, as regards reintegration in the society of that State after serving their sentence, since they were not highly integrated into that State in the first place. Similarly, in its later judgment in *Lopes Da Silva Jorge*, the Court ruled that, in light of Article 18 TFEU, nationals of other Member States could not be automatically excluded from protection if Member States chose to implement this exception from the Framework Decision; rather Member States had to consider the family, economic, and social connections of citizens of other Member States.[275]

The Court did not address the question of whether EU free movement or immigration law might be a potential barrier as such to execution of an arrest warrant, ie because the offence that the person is charged with or convicted of is not serious enough substantively to justify removal from the territory.[276] Furthermore, the Court did not address the question of which third-country nationals, if any, could benefit from the same principle,[277] or the position of dual citizens.[278] Presumably the Court's ruling, by analogy, means that Member States are free to set other conditions restricting the scope of this ground for refusal of execution of an EAW, or the other optional grounds for refusal of execution in this Framework Decision or other mutual recognition measures, subject to the equality principle and also human rights obligations (on which, see the discussion further below).[279] On this point, it should be emphasized that the equality

---

[273] N 240 above.

[274] On the broader interaction between the mutual recognition principle and EU free movement law, see II:3.4 above. On the substance of the concept of permanent residence in EU free movement law, see I:6.4.1. The Court also made a link with an optional provision of the Framework Decision on recognition of custodial penalties, which applies the same five-year rule: see II:3.7.1.2 below.

[275] N 240 above.

[276] See II:3.4 above. EU legislation on asylum procedures contains an express provision on extradition law: see I:5.7.

[277] Logically the Court's approach in *Wolzenburg* should apply by analogy to EU citizens' third-country national family members who have obtained permanent residence status pursuant to EU free movement law (I:6.4.1), as well as those who obtain status identical or comparable to such permanent residence pursuant to the EEA or the EU/Turkey association agreement (see I:6.4.3). On the general question of equal treatment of third-country nationals, see I:3.4.3. On the immigration law links, see the Opinion in *Koslowski*, n 240 above.

[278] On the position of dual citizens, see II:3.4 above.

[279] *Contra* the Advocate-General's Opinions in *Koslowski* (para 74) and *Wolzenburg* (paras 60–3), the objective of reintegration into society is *not* the only basis for a limitation of the exception in Art 4(6), in light of the optional restrictions which the Court accepted on the scope of the Art 4(6) exception in the *Wolzenburg* judgment. So the Dutch rules limiting the Art 4(6) exception for non-Dutch citizens to cases where the person concerned could have been prosecuted in the Netherlands for the relevant offence and where the person concerned would not lose his or her residence right (see paras 80–6, *Wolzenburg* Opinion) are only objectionable to the extent that they infringe EU free movement or immigration law.

principle applies to the entirety of this (and other) Framework Decisions, not just to the specific clauses that mention nationals and residents of the executing State.[280]

Finally on this provision, the CJEU ruling in *IB* (see below) clarifies how to distinguish it from the separate but similar provision on possible guarantees where the EAW has been issued for the purpose of prosecution, where the trial was held *in absentia*.[281]

Next, there are three cases in which the executing judicial authority can (at its discretion) ask for certain guarantees in accordance with the executing Member State's law. First, where the sentence has been passed *in absentia*, if the person concerned had not been summoned in person or otherwise informed of the details of the hearing, the executing State may request the guarantee that he or she must have 'an opportunity to apply for a retrial' and be present at the judgment.[282] This provision was amended in 2009, by means of a Framework Decision that also inserted revised (uniform) rules relating to the *in absentia* exception in four other mutual recognition measures.[283] The new rule provides that an executing State may refuse to execute an EAW unless one of four conditions applies, as specified further: the person concerned was sufficiently aware of the trial; the person concerned was defended by a lawyer which he or she had instructed; the person concerned has waived his or her right to a retrial; or the person concerned has a right to a full retrial. These new rules reflect the case law of the ECtHR more accurately.[284]

According to the CJEU's ruling in *Melloni*,[285] it is not permissible for Member States to have more stringent rules (in other words, higher national human rights standards) as regards guarantees for EAWs following *in absentia* trials. That is because the EU legislature intended to adopt harmonized rules on this particular issue in 2009; those rules are compatible with the EU Charter of Fundamental Rights (since they reflect the Strasbourg Court case law); and Article 53 of the Charter, which states that the Charter does not restrict or adversely affect, inter alia, national human rights protection 'in their respective fields of application', does not allow Member States to apply higher national constitutional standards of human rights protection where the EU has fully harmonized rules which themselves are compliant with the Charter.

Second, where a life sentence could be imposed for the crime, the issuing State may be requested to guarantee that the sentence must be reviewable after twenty years at the latest.[286] Third, a judicial authority may insist, where an EAW is issued for the purpose of prosecution, that a national or resident of the executing State must be returned after the trial to serve their sentence in that State.[287] This provision also interacts with the Framework Decision on recognition of custodial sentences,[288] and furthermore it

---

[280] See paras 42–7 of the *Wolzenburg* judgment, n 240 above.   [281] Ibid.

[282] Art 5(1). Note that *in absentia* judgments trigger the application of the Schengen double jeopardy rules: see Case C-297/07 *Bourquain* [2008] ECR I-9425, and further II:6.8 below.

[283] [2009] OJ L 81/24, rescinding Art 5(1) and inserting a new Art 4a. This Framework Decision had to be applied from 6 Mar 2011, except as regards Italy, which had to apply it from 1 Jan 2014 (Art 8(1) and (2), 2009 Framework Decision, and declaration in [2009] OJ L 97/14). The other measures amended by the 2009 Framework Decision are the Framework Decisions on recognition of financial penalties, confiscation, custodial sentences, and probation and parole (see II:3.7.1, II:3.7.4, and II:3.7.5 below).

[284] See II:3.3.1 and II:3.3.5 above.   [285] N 240 above.   [286] Art 5(2).

[287] Art 5(3).   [288] N 269 above.

should obviously be interpreted consistently as far as possible with the nearly identical provision permitting refusal to execute an EAW, where the EAW was issued for the purpose of enforcing a sentence, if the executing Member State will take over the sentence. An entirely identical interpretation of the two provisions is not possible, however, since only one of the two provisions can apply to persons 'staying in' the territory.[289] According to the CJEU judgment in *IB*,[290] if a person was convicted in a trial held *in absentia*, any EAW issued to enforce the judgment must be considered as an EAW issued for the purpose of prosecution, not to enforce a sentence, because otherwise the fugitive would not be able to rely upon the safeguard of requesting a retrial.

As for other traditional restrictions on extradition obligations, Member States can no longer refuse to extradite their own nationals,[291] although there are some vestigial remnants of this principle.[292] There is no reference to a possible refusal to execute the warrant or guarantees on grounds of immunity, privilege, or pardon, although the Framework Decision provides that where a privilege or immunity exists, the time period to execute the warrant does not start until that privilege or immunity is waived.[293] Nor is there an exception for fiscal offences, military offences, or political offences as found in the Council of Europe's extradition Convention, although there is a provision in the preamble to the Framework Decision (discussed below) referring to the prohibition on execution of measures intended to persecute people on certain grounds, which corresponds to a part of the traditional 'political offence' exception. There is still a possible restriction on grounds of specialty (ie the principle that a person cannot be prosecuted for an 'offence other' than that named in the EAW), but Member States have the option to waive this protection.[294]

The Court of Justice has clarified aspects of the specialty rule, following a reference from a national court.[295] According to the Framework Decision, the rule does not apply, leaving aside cases where Member States have waived it, where: the person concerned has stayed in or returned to the State which wishes to bring the extra charges;

---

[289] Art 4(6), discussed above. The requirement of identical interpretation is bolstered by the reference to both provisions in the Framework Decision on custodial penalties (see n 269 above). The Court of Justice has also noted that the two provisions have the same objective (*Wolzenburg* judgment, para 62, n 240 above). See also the Opinion in *Koslowski* (para 73), n 240 above.

[290] N 240 above. In other words, Art 5(3) applies to such cases, rather than Art 4(6).

[291] See the clearly correct interpretation on this point in the Opinions in *Koslowski*, paras 40–112 and *Wolzenburg*, paras 121–44 (both n 240 above), in particular as regards the German rule that nationals cannot be subject to an EAW without their consent. Of course, the German rule is understandable in light of the constitutional problems implementing the Framework Decision there as regards extradition of nationals (see further below). In any event, the point has limited relevance given the Court's interpretation of Art 4(6) (see next footnote).

[292] Arts 4(6) and 5(3), discussed above. Since the *Wolzenburg* judgment (n 291 above) accepted the blanket application of Art 4(6) (and probably Art 5(3), by analogy) to nationals of the executing State, Member States with qualms about surrendering their own nationals have an obvious (and legitimate) option available to address their concerns. See also the specific derogation (now expired) for Austria and the temporal limitations which some Member States apply (n 243 above).

[293] Art 20, which also refers to a request for a waiver, but does not state what happens if the waiver is not granted. On this issue, see H Fox, *The Law of State Immunity* (OUP, 2002), 503–16.

[294] Art 27. An identical specialty provision appears in the Framework Decision on custodial penalties, except there is no possibility for Member States to waive its application (Art 18 of that measure, n 269 above; see II:3.7.1.2 below). It would be logical to interpret these provisions the same way.

[295] *Leymann and Pustovarov*, n 240 above.

the offence is not punishable by a custodial penalty or detention order; the criminal proceedings do not give rise to detention; the person concerned could be subject to a *restriction* on his or her liberty, as compared to a *deprivation* of it;[296] the person concerned has consented to surrender or to waiver of the specialty principle; or the executing State's authorities have consented to waiver of the principle.[297] The Court ruled that in order to determine what was an 'offence other' than that for which the person was surrendered:[298]

> ... it is necessary to ascertain whether the constituent elements of the offence, according to the legal description given by the issuing State, are those for which the person was surrendered and whether there is a sufficient correspondence between the information given in the arrest warrant and that contained in the later procedural document. Modifications concerning the time or place of the offence are allowed, in so far as they derive from evidence gathered in the course of the proceedings conducted in the issuing State concerning the conduct described in the arrest warrant, do not alter the nature of the offence and do not lead to grounds for non-execution under Articles 3 and 4 of the Framework Decision.

A modification of the description of the offence as regards the type of narcotics which were allegedly imported, without changing the legal description of the offence, does not amount to a charge for an 'offence other' than that for which the person concerned was surrendered, given that the offence concerned still fell within the same heading in the list of offences for which dual criminality is abolished.[299] Finally, the exception relating to cases where the criminal proceedings do not give rise to restrictions on liberty meant that such proceedings could go ahead, but that any pre-trial or post-trial detention which resulted could only be applied with the consent of the person concerned or the executing State's authorities pursuant to the rules in the Framework Decision. In the meantime, however, the person's liberty could still be restricted if that was lawful on the basis of the charges set out in the EAW.[300]

As for subsequent surrender to a third Member State on the basis of a second EAW, Member States can waive the traditional requirement that the original executing Member State has to consent to all such subsequent surrenders.[301] Even if a Member State does not waive this rule, subsequent surrender may be authorized without its consent if the fugitive consents, has not left the State where the first EAW was executed after an opportunity to do so, or is not subject to aspects of the specialty rule.[302] In such a case, the first issuing Member State must accept the surrender request from the second issuing Member State if the basic conditions set out in the Framework Decision are satisfied.[303] On the other hand, a fugitive who has already been surrendered to

---

[296] See the clarification of this point in n 240 above, para 70.

[297] Art 27(2) and (3). The last exception is subject to limits set out in Art 27(4): inter alia, consent must be refused where the mandatory exceptions in Art 3 apply, and otherwise may only be refused where Art 4 applies; the guarantees in Art 5 also apply.

[298] Para 57, *Leymann* judgment, n 240 above.   [299] Paras 60–3, ibid.

[300] Paras 72–6, ibid.   [301] Art 28(1).   [302] Art 28(2).

[303] Art 28(3), referring to Arts 3–5 and 8–9.

another Member State cannot be extradited to a *non*-EU State unless the executing State consents.[304]

The CJEU has clarified how the provisions on subsequent surrender apply when a *third* Member State requests surrender of the fugitive. In that case, in the interests of efficiency and mutual trust, it is not the *original* Member State which has to consent again to the surrender, but rather the *second* Member State.[305] With great respect, the Court's ruling on this point undermines the sovereignty of the original Member State, runs the risk that its power to decide on subsequent surrender could be circumvented by a chain of EAWs, and may deter the original Member State from agreeing to the initial or subsequent surrender (assuming it can find a valid ground to refuse).[306]

The procedural rules in the Framework Decision entail an obligation to take a final decision on the execution of an EAW request ten days after a person consents, or otherwise sixty days after the arrest. It if proves impossible to meet this deadline, the time limits can be extended by a further thirty days. If none of the time limits can be observed in 'exceptional' cases, Eurojust must be informed.[307] Where there is a request to prosecute the person for an additional offence or to authorize surrender to another Member State, there is a single deadline of thirty days after receipt of the request to make the decision.[308] The CJEU's judgment in *F* clarifies the application of these deadlines as regards the right to appeal.[309] According to the Court, the Framework Decision does not preclude Member States from allowing an appeal against execution of an EAW or the other decisions; it is not clear if it *requires* Member States to allow for an appeal.[310] But it neither requires nor precludes Member States from allowing for any appeal against any of these decisions to have suspensive effect. Furthermore, there is no obligation as a matter of EU law to have two levels of jurisdiction for any appeals regarding EAWs, even though there may be a national or international obligation to that effect. Also, any appeal with suspensive effect must observe the various time limits, unless there is a reference to the CJEU. In the event of an appeal against any decision to prosecute the person for an additional offence or to authorize surrender to another Member State, the thirty-day deadline does not apply to the appeal, but the main deadlines for executing an EAW apply.

What happens if the deadlines to execute an EAW are exceeded? The CJEU addressed this issue in its judgment in *Lanigan*. According to the Court, first of all the missed deadlines did not exempt the executing State from the underlying obligation to execute the warrant. Secondly, does this missed deadline have any impact on detaining the fugitive? The Framework Decision says that when executing an EAW, the national authorities must take a decision on whether to detain. A wanted person can be released

---

[304] Art 28(4).
[305] *West*, n 240 above. Furthermore, consent can only be refused on the grounds set out in the Framework Decision: Art 28(3), referring to Arts 3 to 5; see para 55 of the judgment.
[306] It is not clear after the *West* judgment whether the original executing State can refuse extradition to a third State pursuant to Art 28(4) after a second EAW has been executed, or whether that power also transfers to the second executing State.
[307] Art 17.   [308] Arts 27(4) and 28(3)(c).   [309] Judgment in *F*, n 240 above.
[310] It is hard to see how the absence of a right to an appeal could be compatible with Art 47 of the Charter. Moreover, it is hard to see why the Framework Decision refers to a right to counsel and a hearing (Arts 11 and 14), if there is no right to appeal. See also the rights for suspects in EAW cases discussed in I:4.6.

in accordance with national law, if the authorities take measures to prevent him or her from absconding.[311] In the Court's view, there was no general obligation to release the fugitive once the deadline to execute the EAW had passed.[312] Such an obligation would undercut the effectiveness of the Framework Decision. However, there was an obligation to count all the detention time served in the executing State towards against any custodial sentence imposed by the issuing State, even if that detention time was served after the deadline to execute an EAW.[313] Moreover, since the Framework Decision must be interpreted in light of the Charter, Article 6 of which limits detention consistently with Article 5 ECHR, the Strasbourg Court case law on detention pending extradition was applicable. This case law states for extradition detention to be justified, the extradition process has to be carried with due diligence.[314] The CJEU added that the executing State's court has to consider all relevant factors when deciding to consider detention, including a possible failure to act of the authorities; the fugitive's contribution to the duration of detention; the potential sentence; the risk of absconding; and detention which hugely exceed the time limits for a decision on execution of the EAW set out in the Framework Decision. Unfortunately the Court makes no reference to the possible issue of a European Supervision Order as an alternative means of limiting the risk of absconding without lengthy detention, perhaps because one of the Member States concerned in this case has not yet implemented it.[315]

On other procedural points, the CJEU has ruled that a fugitive does not have a right to a hearing before the issuing State issues an EAW, since that would undercut the entire EAW system.[316] Also, the Court has been asked to clarify what happens if the EAW was filled out defectively.[317]

The Framework Decision contains provisions on human rights which have to some extent been repeated in subsequent Framework Decisions.[318] In particular, the preamble specifies that:

> (12) This Framework Decision respects fundamental rights and observes the principles recognised by Article 6 of the Treaty on European Union and reflected in the Charter of Fundamental Rights of the European Union, in particular Chapter VI thereof. Nothing in this Framework Decision may be interpreted as prohibiting refusal to surrender a person for whom a European arrest warrant has been issued when there

---

[311] Art 12.

[312] As the Court noted, however, there is a specific obligation to release the fugitive from detention set out in Art 23(5), if the deadline to transfer him or her agreed between the issuing and executing authorities is missed.

[313] This rule appears in Art 26, as the Court noted.

[314] See I.3.3.4. The CJEU has now been asked to rule on whether a fugitive can still be surrendered on the basis of an EAW if the detention conditions in the issuing State breach ECHR standards (*Aranyosi*, n 240 above).

[315] On the supervision order, see I:3.6.3. Ireland has not implemented the relevant legislation, although the UK has.

[316] *Radu*, n 240 above.   [317] *Bob-Dogi*, n 240, pending.

[318] However, see the different wording of the Framework Decisions on the evidence warrant, mutual recognition of financial penalties, and recognition of confiscation orders (II:3.6.1.2, II:3.7.1.1, and II:3.7.4 below), as well as the Directive establishing the European Investigation Order (II:3.6.1.3 below). On human rights and mutual recognition in general, see II:3.3.5 above.

are reasons to believe, on the basis of objective elements, that the said arrest warrant has been issued for the purpose of prosecuting or punishing a person on the grounds of his or her sex, race, religion, ethnic origin, nationality, language, political opinions or sexual orientation, or that that person's position may be prejudiced for any of these reasons.

This Framework Decision does not prevent a Member State from applying its constitutional rules relating to due process, freedom of association, freedom of the press and freedom of expression in other media.

The main text of the Framework Decision then specifies that '[t]his Framework Decision shall not have the effect of modifying the obligation to respect fundamental rights and fundamental legal principles as enshrined in Article 6 of the Treaty on European Union'.[319] There are also provisions in the preamble, unique to this Framework Decision, concerning possible suspension of the Framework Decision if a Member State is suspended from EU membership due to human rights breaches, and protection against extradition in cases of torture or the death penalty.[320] Finally, Member States are required to establish remedies for fugitives as regards a right to information about the EAW, and (as noted above) the right to counsel and an interpreter, and the right to a hearing.[321] It should be noted that the subsequent proposed or adopted Directives on suspects' rights expressly apply to EAW proceedings.[322]

The Commission presented an initial assessment of the national implementation of the Framework Decision in 2005,[323] and subsequently updated this analysis in 2006, 2007, and 2011.[324] According to the first report, 2603 warrants were issued, 653 persons were arrested, and 104 persons were surrendered up until September 2004; the Commission estimated that the time to execute a warrant had fallen from nine months to forty-three days (thirteen days where the warrant was not contested). In the Commission's view, however, a number of Member States were not in full compliance with the Framework Decision, in particular by wrongly restricting its temporal scope, limiting the partial abolition of double criminality, granting decision-making powers to executive (rather than judicial) bodies, allowing their authorities to demand additional guarantees before surrender, providing for additional grounds for refusal (including an over-broad application of human rights grounds and the imposition of conditions concerning the surrender of nationals), insisting on additional procedural requirements for transmission of arrest warrants, failing to apply time limits, and setting out the procedural rights of the individual too vaguely.

This critical report on the EU's flagship mutual recognition measure resulted in an unprecedented debate in the JHA Council, which focused on the issues of the human rights ground for refusal, political grounds for refusal, the use of executive bodies instead of judicial bodies, and the limits on the temporal scope of the Framework Decision.[325]

---

[319] Art 1(3).
[320] Paras 10 and 13 of the preamble. On human rights protection against extradition, see II:3.3.1 above.
[321] Arts 11 and 14.   [322] See II:4.6 below.   [323] COM (2005) 63, 23 Feb 2005.
[324] Respectively COM (2006) 8, 24 Jan 2006; COM (2007) 407; and COM (2011) 175, 11 April 2011. The 2006 report merely took account of the late Italian implementation (Italy being the last Member State to implement the Framework Decision) in April 2005.
[325] See Council doc 8842/1/05, 19 May 2005.

The Council did not adopt any formal conclusions on these issues, but it asked the Commission to produce a further report by June 2006 and decided to conduct a practical evaluation of the application of the EAW.[326] Member States subsequently submitted detailed responses in writing objecting to the Commission's analysis.[327]

The second Commission report in 2007 concluded that there were still problems applying the Framework Decision in some Member States, inter alia, as regards transitional application of the EAW, surrender of own nationals, sentencing thresholds, double criminality checks, and incorrect or impermissible grounds for non-execution, including a large number relating to human rights.[328] Several Member States had amended national laws to bring them further into conformity with the Framework Decision. As for the Commission's previous report, half of the Member States' objections related to information which they should already have sent the Commission, a quarter were valid corrections, and the Commission did not agree with the other quarter of the objections. In practice, according to the report, in 2005, 6,900 warrants were issued in twenty-three Member States providing statistics, resulting in 1,770 arrests and 1,532 surrenders, with half consenting to surrenders and a fifth being nationals of the executing State, guarantees of return having been agreed in half of those cases. The time to execute the warrants was still forty-three days (eleven days in the case of consent), although in 5% of cases the relevant deadlines were not met. The Commission concluded that the Framework Decision was a 'success', and the remaining problems with its application were 'peripheral'.

Finally, in its third report on the law, issued in 2011, the Commission noted that between 2005 and 2009, 54,689 EAWs were issued and 11,630 EAWs were executed. Between 51% and 62% of fugitives consented to their surrender, and the average surrender time for those who did *not* consent was forty-eight days. However, the Commission conceded that in some cases the issue or execution of an EAW might breach fundamental rights, and called upon all Member States to introduce a proportionality test when issuing EAWs.

The latest statistics concerning the EAW, dating from 2013, show that in that year over 10,000 EAWs were issued by the Member States supplying statistics, although many Member States did not supply such statistics.[329] About 5,900 persons were arrested, and about 2,700 were surrendered. Clearly the EAW is frequently used in practice.

As for the Council's evaluation, it culminated in a series of draft recommendations, mostly concerning practical aspects of the application of the EAW but also touching on the sensitive issues of the grounds for non-recognition, including human rights grounds, and the possible abolition of the specialty rule.[330] Some recommendations were addressed to Member States, while another batch was addressed to the Council's working groups; the latter were then followed up by Council conclusions, which were

---

[326] Press release of JHA Council, 2–3 June 2005. The questionnaire for the evaluation, which began in 2006, can be found in Council doc 14272/05, 11 Nov 2005.

[327] Council doc 11528/05, 5 Sep 2005.

[328] See the responses of two Member States (Council docs 14308/07 and add 1, 12 and 13 Nov 2007).

[329] Council doc 8414/1/14, 15 May 2014.   [330] Council doc 8302/4/09, 28 May 2009.

adopted in June 2010.[331] It should also be noted that Eurojust, the EU prosecutors' agency, also has a role as regards EAWs.[332]

The implementation of the EAW has been equally controversial at national level in a number of Member States,[333] and three national constitutional courts struck down the national application of the Framework Decision, at least in principle. First of all, in spring 2005, the Polish Constitutional Court ruled that the national law implementing the EAW Framework Decision was unconstitutional as it permitted the extradition of Polish citizens, although that court delayed the application of its judgment for eighteen months so that the constitution could be modified; the constitutional amendment duly took effect in November 2006. Next, in July 2005, the German Constitutional Court ruled that the national implementing law was invalid, as regards German citizens; Spain and Hungary responded by disapplying the EAW as regards German warrants issued for German citizens, but the national law was amended by August 2006. Finally, in November 2005, the Cypriot Constitutional Court ruled that the EAW conflicted with the Cypriot constitution as regards the surrender of Cypriot nationals; so the constitution was amended as from July 2006. However, the Czech Constitutional Court in particular upheld the Framework Decision.

How should the EAW be assessed? The case law of the Court of Justice focuses overwhelmingly on the efficient application of the EAW. The Court's assumption in the *Wolzenburg* case that widening the application of the EAW as much as possible will necessarily assist to achieve its aims, along with the addition of a further requirement in order to apply some exceptions to the Framework Decision in the *Koslowski* case, is, with respect, misguided, as it overlooks the contrary objectives of free movement rules and fails to recognize that the enforcement of a sentence in the executing State still accomplishes the objectives of deterrence and punishment while increasing the chance of rehabilitation. The recommendation from the Council evaluation on the EAW to abolish the application of the specialty rule is profoundly unprincipled, since its abolition would allow unscrupulous prosecutors to circumvent all of the safeguards in the Framework Decision (for instance, by issuing an EAW and then proceeding with the 'real' prosecution for minor offences which fall below the punishment threshold in the Framework Decision or for offences which fall within the scope of the grounds for non-execution of an EAW). This would hardly improve the legitimacy of the EAW and could reduce the efficient application of the system by wasting executing States' time and resources chasing and processing fugitives whose alleged crime was quite trivial. This is already a problem to some extent, with some Member States issuing arrest warrants from crimes such as the 'theft of a piglet'.[334]

The most fundamental issue for the legitimacy of the EAW, other than the still-contested issue of the surrender of nationals, is the question of whether the EAW system is compatible with human rights, an issue which applies equally to all other mutual

---

[331] Council doc 8436/2/10, 28 May 2010.   [332] See II:6.9 below.

[333] See the summary with further references in the 2007 Commission report (n 328 above), and the analysis in Guild and Marin, n 239 above.

[334] Cf the inconclusive discussions on the proportionality of issuing EAWs (see the evaluation recommendations and conclusions, nn 330 and 331 above).

recognition measures.[335] Certainly it is problematic that the Commission has criticized Member States' attempts to protect the human rights of suspects who are the subject of EAWs: the 2007 report, for instance, objected to the Danish law which provides for refusal of surrender on grounds of 'torture, degrading treatment, violation of due process as well as if the surrender appears to be unreasonable on humanitarian grounds'. On the other hand, the 2011 report accepts that fugitives should not be surrendered if the detention conditions awaiting them in the issuing State breach ECHR standards.

The answer to this fundamental question depends in part on whether Member States' judicial authorities have an obligation, or at least the power, to refuse execution of other Member States' warrants on human rights grounds (in addition to the specific double jeopardy and *in absentia* provisions of the Framework Decision). The judgment in *Advocaten voor de Wereld* referred to a requirement to protect human rights within the context of the Framework Decision, but then ruled that the onus is on the issuing State to ensure the application of human rights as regards the dual criminality principle. However, this case did not address the issue of whether the executing State can examine the issuing Member State's request in order to consider non-execution on human rights grounds.

The express wording of the preamble of the Framework Decision suggests that a human rights ground for refusal must be possible: '[n]othing in this Framework Decision may be interpreted as prohibiting refusal to surrender a person' as regards discriminatory prosecution, and the Framework Decision 'does not prevent a Member State from applying its constitutional rules relating to due process' and other specified matters. Nevertheless, the Court of Justice case law on the grounds for non-execution has consistently concluded that the grounds for non-recognition in the Framework Decision are exhaustive,[336] implicitly denying the possibility of a general human rights ground for refusal.[337] In the *Radu* judgment, the Court avoided the questions on this issue squarely put by the national court and ignored the excellent analysis of its Advocate-General,[338] instead redrafting the national court's questions completely and addressing a 'straw man' argument that a fugitive ought to be told about a prospective EAW before it is even issued. In its *F* judgment, the Court explicitly said that the substantive merits of a case and procedural issues can be addressed in the State of origin,[339] although again this point had little or nothing to do with the proceedings in that case (the fugitive had consented to his surrender and had already returned to his State of nationality to face trial; the actual issue in that case was the procedure to challenge decisions on the specialty rule).

The Court's rulings do not answer the objection that human rights grounds for non-execution stem from the primary law of the EU (now including the EU Charter of Fundamental Rights), not secondary legislation. Indeed, that is the basis on which the

---

[335] See generally II:3.3.5 above.   [336] N 261 above.

[337] The double jeopardy and *in absentia* rules can be regarded as very specific grounds for refusal on human rights grounds.

[338] See also the earlier Opinions in *Wolzenburg*, *Koslowski*, and *Santesteban Goicoechea*.

[339] Para 50 of the judgment, n 240 above. The Court did not expressly say that as a consequence, there was no possible human rights ground for non-execution in the executing State.

Court has asserted an obligation to refuse to transfer asylum seekers to a Member State responsible under the EU's Dublin rules.[340] The Court appears to override even the very narrow obligations to refuse extradition as set out in the ECtHR's case law.[341] As for the argument that Member States must have mutual trust in each other's systems, as noted above, the inability to reject mutual recognition on human rights grounds, on the assumption that the problem will be fixed months later in the issuing State or years later in the ECtHR, would mean that human rights protection in this field would be theoretical and illusory, not real and effective.[342] Moreover, the clear signal from the EU legislature, in the later Directive on the European Investigation Order, is that there ought to be a genuine human rights exception from mutual recognition obligations.[343]

As for specific human rights issues, the mandatory non-execution of a warrant on double jeopardy grounds is welcome, but the merely *optional* non-execution for cases of final judgments and (in some cases) termination of prosecution is objectionable, in light of the Court of Justice's interpretation of the double jeopardy rules.[344] The *in absentia* exception (which appears in most other mutual recognition measures) does conform to ECtHR case law after its amendment in 2009,[345] but it is only optional, rather than mandatory. It is not clear yet if the Court's restriction of higher national constitutional standards of human rights protection has any relevance in the EAW context outside the *in absentia* issue; it could hardly be said that the entire Framework Decision has achieved as much harmonization overall as it did on this particular point. This point is crucial since it determines whether Member States have an *option* to refuse EAWs on human rights grounds, even if they have no *obligation* to do so.

On the issue of detention, as noted above, the Court's failure to promote the European Supervision Order as a solution is regrettable. Perhaps another national court should suggest to the Court that it was *per incuriam* in failing to mention this Framework Decision, which is designed precisely to deal with this problem. It seems objectionable that the executing State's failure to comply with its legal obligations to implement the other measure is not even a factor to be considered at a bail hearing. The Commission's laxness at ensuring that Member States comply with their obligation to apply that measure is even more alarming in this light.[346]

Finally, is the basic principle of mutual recognition acceptable? And if so, is the EU's approach to mutual recognition, as embodied in particular in the Framework Decision establishing the European Arrest Warrant, correct? Due to the broader implications of this debate, the answer is considered fully in the conclusions to this chapter.

3.6 Pre-Trial Measures

Further measures in addition to (or instead of) extradition proceedings are often necessary before a trial with cross-border aspects takes place. It is obviously necessary

---

[340] See I:5.3 and I:5.8.   [341] See II:3.3.4 above.
[342] II:3.3.5 above. See also the balance between the mutual trust principles and human rights protection in the *Wolzenburg* and *Koslowski* Opinions (ibid).
[343] See I:3.6.1.   [344] See II:6.8 below.   [345] On that case law, see II:3.3.1 above.
[346] See II:3.6.3 below.

to trace any relevant evidence or witnesses and ensure that the evidence can be used, or that the witnesses will testify, at the trial if possible. Sometimes it is necessary to issue freezing orders to ensure that property is available for evidence or for subsequent confiscation. Finally, an important issue for individuals is the length of any detention awaiting trial, which risks being longer where there are cross-border elements to a case. These three issues will be examined in turn.

3.6.1 Movement of evidence

In order to facilitate the movement of evidence in criminal cases,[347] the EU initially adopted specific and general measures on mutual judicial assistance, building on the existing international (Council of Europe) framework. Subsequently the EU has adopted mutual recognition measures in this area, starting with the Framework Decision on the European Evidence Warrant and culminating in the European Investigation Order.

3.6.1.1 Mutual assistance in criminal matters

The core texts on cross-border mutual assistance between judicial authorities in criminal law cases are the 1959 Council of Europe Convention ('the 1959 Convention') on Mutual Assistance and the first Protocol to that Convention (1978), which all Member States have ratified.[348] A Second Protocol to the Convention, which parallels the EU Convention of 2000 (see below) in several respects, was agreed in 2001, and a large majority of EU Member States have ratified it.[349]

The 1959 Convention applies to all offences except military offences, and there is no sentencing threshold or double criminality requirement for its use, as there is for extradition treaties, except for search and seizure measures.[350] A judge in the 'home State' of the prosecution, wanting to obtain evidence or other relevant material which another Member State is 'hosting', must send formal requests (called 'letters rogatory'), usually via his or her national ministry, to the relevant ministry of the host Member State, which forwards the request to a national judge. A judge in the prosecuting State can also request the attendance of a witness who is residing in another State, but any summons the prosecuting judge sends to such a witness is not enforceable unless the witness sets foot in the prosecuting Member State and then disobeys a second summons to appear. If a prosecuting judge would like to contact a potential witness in custody in another Member State, the would-be witness can refuse. There is an exception for political offences and fiscal offences; assistance may also be refused if a requested State considers that executing a request is 'likely to prejudice the sovereignty, security, *ordre public* or other essential interests of its country'.[351] In practice, reservations are also applied regarding double jeopardy.[352] The First Protocol to the Convention, inter alia,

---

[347] On the movement of evidence in civil cases, see II:8.5.4 below.
[348] ETS 30 and ETS 99. For ratification details, see Appendix I.
[349] ETS 182; for ratification details, see Appendix I.   [350] Art 5 of the Convention.
[351] Art 2 of the Convention.
[352] See the facts of the *Miraglia* case (C-469/03 [2005] ECR I-2009).

removes the exception for fiscal offences, although a State can still retain the exemption in part.

As for EU measures, the Schengen Convention contains rules on judicial assistance, which: require Member States to abolish the fiscal offence exception for excise duties, VAT, and customs duties (if they have not yet ratified the First Protocol to the Council of Europe Convention); widen the scope of proceedings for which assistance could be requested; allow direct contact between legal authorities without ministry intervention; and provide for posting procedural documents directly to persons in other Member States.[353]

Subsequently, to supplement the Council of Europe measures in order to facilitate the movement of evidence between Member States,[354] the EU adopted a Convention on Mutual Assistance in 2000 and a Protocol to the EU Convention in 2001; the Convention and Protocol are in force in a large majority of Member States.[355] The most important criminal law provisions of the Convention specify that:

a) the Schengen provisions on posting documents and contacting other judges directly have become the normal rule;[356]
b) the State where the evidence is located must normally comply with the formalities and procedures which the home State requests;[357]
c) the home State may request that a State with custody over a person transfer that person (possibly without his or her consent) to be a witness in the trial in the home State;[358] and
d) the home State may request a hearing by videoconference with a witness, an expert, or the suspect in the territory of the host State; a summons to such a conference will be mandatory for a witness or expert. Member States may opt of the provision for video hearings with the suspect.[359]

The 2001 Protocol is primarily concerned with financial crime. It provides in turn for assistance relating to requests for information on bank accounts, requests for information on bank transactions, and requests for monitoring of bank accounts,[360] although the first two types of assistance can be subjected to the conditions applicable to search and seizure,[361] and the first type can be limited to specific offences.[362] More generally, the Protocol contains provisions on: the obligation of requested authorities to inform the requesting authorities about their investigations; the forwarding of additional requests for mutual assistance; the waiver of banking secrecy in relation to mutual assistance; the

---

[353] Arts 48–53, Schengen Convention ([2000] OJ L 239).
[354] On the practice before the Convention, see the report in [2001] OJ C 216/14.
[355] [2000] OJ C 197/1 and [2001] OJ C 326/1. For ratification details, see Appendix I. On the Convention and Protocol generally, see E Denza, 'The 2000 Convention on Mutual Assistance in Criminal Matters' (2003) 40 CMLRev 1047; and D McClean, *International Cooperation in Civil and Criminal Matters*, 2nd edn (OUP, 2002), 224–37. On the policing issues arising from the Convention, see II:7.9 below.
[356] Arts 5 and 6.　　　[357] Art 4.
[358] Art 9. Consent is required by Cyprus, the Czech Republic, Denmark, Estonia, Finland, Germany, Latvia, Poland, and the UK.
[359] Art 10; Denmark, France, the Netherlands, Poland, and the UK have opted out of the provision. See also Art 11, on the hearing of witnesses and experts by telephone. On the human rights rules applicable in such cases, see *Viola v Italy*, judgment of 5 Oct 2006.
[360] Arts 1–3 of the Protocol; see also Art 4 (confidentiality of such requests).
[361] Arts 1(5) and 2(4).　　　[362] Art 1(3); but the Council can extend the scope (Art 1(6)).

abolition of the fiscal offence exception (copying the wording of the First Protocol to the Council of Europe Convention); abolishing the political offence exception (although Member States may limit this abolition to specific offences); and providing for dispute settlement in the Council or Eurojust in case requests are blocked on grounds of dual criminality or the remaining reservations under the mutual assistance Convention.[363]

These measures allow the prosecuting State to assert its authority *de facto* over persons and evidence in another Member State, albeit indirectly through the acts of the requested Member State's authorities. They also simplify the 'border controls' previously slowing down the processing of requests between Member States. However, the position of the defendant under these rules is problematic, as there is no reference to the right to cross-examine witnesses, and there are only limited minimum standards applicable to cross-border hearings (although the Council has the power to adopt a measure on this subject, which it has not yet used).[364] In fact, for suspects (as well as witnesses), there is no express right to counsel.

The EU has also adopted a number of measures on mutual assistance as regards specific crimes, in particular as regards drug trafficking,[365] and in conjunction with a number of Joint Actions harmonizing substantive criminal law.[366] More generally, a Joint Action on good practice on mutual assistance requires Member States to deposit statements with the Council Secretariat setting out in detail their intentions to respond to mutual assistance requests from other Member States swiftly and effectively,[367] and the SIS functions as a practical tool for listing persons who or objects which are connected with criminal proceedings.[368]

3.6.1.2 European Evidence Warrant

In order to apply the principle of mutual recognition to aspects of the movement of evidence between Member States, in 2008 the Council adopted a Framework Decision establishing a European Evidence Warrant (EEW), which Member States had to apply by 19 January 2011.[369] Since the Framework Decision was generally assumed to be unworkable by practitioners, it is not applied in practice, and the subsequent Directive establishing the European Investigation Order (EIO) has repealed it.[370] But its provisions are discussed here, in order to put the subsequent development of the EIO in context.

---

[363] Arts 5–10. Denmark, France, and Latvia have invoked a permitted reservation to limit the abolition of the political offence exception.

[364] Art 10(9) of the Convention.

[365] Executive Committee Decision SCH/Com-ex (93)14 ([2000] OJ L 239/427). The Commission has proposed to repeal this measure, on the grounds that it is obsolete: COM (2014) 714, 28 Nov 2014.

[366] For details of these measures, see the first edition of this book, pp 172–73. As regards identification and tracing of criminal proceeds, see also Art 4 of the Framework Decision on money laundering ([2001] OJ L 182/1).

[367] [1998] OJ L 191/1. The Commission has proposed to repeal this measure, on the grounds that it is obsolete: COM (2014) 715, 28 Nov 2014.

[368] See II:7.6.1.1 below.

[369] Art 23(1) of the Framework Decision ([2008] OJ L 350/72). All further references in this section are to this Framework Decision, unless otherwise noted.

[370] Art 34(2), Dir 2014/41 ([2014] OJ L 130/1), applicable from 22 May 2017 (Art 36(1)).

The Framework Decision does not apply to all movement of evidence; rather it was the first stage in a two-stage procedure (which culminated in the EIO) replacing mutual assistance measures with mutual recognition measures. So it does not apply to evidence which could only be obtained by: the holding of hearings, or similar measures; bodily examination or obtaining bodily material; gathering real-time information, for example by intercepting telecommunications or monitoring bank accounts; analysis of existing documents, objects, or data; or the furnishing of communications data by telecommunications companies.[371] The EEW can only be issued if the evidence sought is necessary and proportionate and if such evidence could be obtained according to the national law of the issuing State in similar cases; but it is up to the issuing State alone to judge these issues.[372] Detailed procedural safeguards proposed by the Commission, such as protections relating to privacy and self-incrimination, were dropped.[373]

Dual criminality is abolished for searches and seizures for evidence falling within the scope of the Framework Decision, for the standard list of thirty-two crimes.[374] The grounds for non-recognition (all optional) include a defective EEW, double jeopardy, immunity or privilege, territoriality, and national security.[375] As for remedies, they must be available in the executing State, at least as regards the exercise of coercive measures, although the substance of the EEW could only be challenged in the issuing State. The issuing State must grant remedies equivalent to those applicable to purely domestic proceedings, and both States have obligations as regards time limits and the facilitation of proceedings.[376] Next, the Framework Decision contains the standard human rights clauses, with the additional proviso that 'any obligations incumbent on judicial authorities in this respect shall remain unaffected'.[377] Finally, the EEW did not entirely replace traditional mutual assistance measures, but co-exists with them for a transitional period until the second stage of the EEW is in place and mutual assistance measures are fully replaced.[378]

From a human rights perspective, it is unfortunate that the exceptions to execution of foreign decisions are optional only, and that the Commission's proposed safeguards were dropped. The safeguards proposals reflected the jurisprudence of the European Court of Human Rights.[379]

3.6.1.3 European Investigation Order

The Directive establishing a European Investigation Order (EIO) was adopted, after long negotiations, in spring 2014.[380] Member States must apply the Directive by 22 May 2017.[381] The Directive replaces the Framework Decision on the European

---

[371] Art 4(2).   [372] Art 7.

[373] Art 12 of the Commission's proposal (COM (2003) 688, 14 Nov 2003).

[374] Art 14. There is a special rule for Germany, allowing it to maintain dual criminality for a further six crimes: see Art 23(4) and the German declaration published in [2008] OJ L 350/92. For the definition of 'search and seizure', see Art 2(e).

[375] Art 13.   [376] Art 18.

[377] Art 1(3); similar wording appears in the Framework Decision on the execution of confiscation orders (see II:3.7.4 below).

[378] Art 21 and recital 25 in the preamble.   [379] See II:3.3.4 above.

[380] Dir 2014/41 ([2014] OJ L 130/1). All references in this sub-section are to this Directive, unless otherwise noted.

[381] Art 36(1). The Directive does not apply to requests pending at that date: Art 35(1).

Evidence Warrant, as well as (as regards freezing of evidence) the Framework Decision on freezing orders.[382] It also replaces the 'corresponding' EU and Council of Europe Conventions and Protocols on mutual assistance (including the Schengen Convention provisions), as regards relations between participating Member States.[383] It is based on Article 82(1)(a) TFEU.[384]

The Directive follows the structure of the Framework Decision establishing the EEW with certain amendments, and with the inclusion of some of the specific rules on mutual assistance set out in the 2000 EU Mutual Assistance Convention and its Protocol. It will apply to all 'investigative measures' (this concept is not defined) with the exception of joint investigation teams.[385] It is not certain whether the Directive will apply to some issues dealt with in other EU measures, such as the criminal records legislation.[386] Otherwise the EIO will apply to most of the issues excluded from the EEW, ie hearings, bodily examinations, analysing data, and similar actions, along with obtaining banking data.

An EIO can only be issued if the issuing authority believes that it is necessary and proportionate, and could be issued in a similar domestic case. If the executing authority has doubts whether these principles were complied with, it can consult with the issuing authority.[387] If the requested investigative action is not available under the law of the requested State, that State can take a different action. However, this rule does not apply as regards a number of investigative measures, which must always be available under national law: obtaining evidence which the executing authority already possesses; obtaining information from police or judicial databases; hearing a person, such as a witness, expert, or suspected person; taking a non-coercive measure; or identifying a person's phone number or IP address.[388]

In addition to a general reference to human rights,[389] there are a number of optional grounds for non-execution of an EIO:[390] immunity or privilege, or limits on criminal liability as regards freedom of expression; harm to national security interests, sources of information, or use of classified information; where the EIO was issued by an administrative authority and would not be authorized in a similar domestic case; double jeopardy; territoriality (if the act is not criminal in the territory of the executing State); 'substantial grounds to believe' that there would be incompatibility with the EU Charter of Fundamental Rights or human rights as general principles of EU law; dual criminality, except for the usual list of offences, with a sentencing threshold of three years; or where the executing State only allows certain investigative measures for serious crimes. But the latter two exceptions cannot apply where the requested measure is one of the investigative measures which must always be available under national law.[391]

---

[382] Art 34(2). On the latter measure, see II:3.6.2 below.

[383] Art 34(1); there is no indication of which provisions are considered to 'correspond'. On the position of non-participating Member States and associated non-EU States, see generally II:3.2.5 above.

[384] On the competence issues, see II:3.2.4 above.   [385] Art 3.

[386] Recital 9 in the preamble states that the Directive does not apply to cross-border police surveillance, which is regulated by Art 40 of the Schengen Convention (see II:7.9.2 below).

[387] Art 6. If the EIO was not issued by a judicial authority or a prosecutor, it must be validated by one: Art 2(c)(ii).

[388] Art 10.   [389] Art 1(4).   [390] Art 11(1).   [391] Art 11(2), referring to Art 10(2).

The Directive also contains rules on time limits, the transfer of evidence, legal remedies, and the postponement of transfers.[392] There are also specific rules on various types of special investigative procedures, which in some cases amend the previous rules on these issues: the temporary transfer of persons in custody; hearings by telephone or videoconferences; obtaining banking information; gathering evidence in real time (including controlled deliveries, ie 'sting' operations by police or customs officers); covert operations; and telecommunications interception.[393]

Overall, the EIO Directive appears to be a serious attempt to provide the EU with a modern set of rules for the cross-border transfer of evidence, which is a key aspect of the day-to-day work of practitioners involved in crimes with an international dimension. It balances a streamlined process (such as the inclusion of time limits for replying to requests) with a number of important safeguards, as regards the grounds for refusal, the validation of requests from police officers, the proportionality requirement, and the broad list of grounds for refusal, including a comparatively strong human rights exception. In many respects, it is a model for other mutual recognition measures, and it is unfortunate that those measures (particularly the EAW) have not been reviewed in order to include similar safeguards.

3.6.1.4 Criminal records

One aspect of mutual assistance that has received special attention from the EU in recent years is the exchange of information concerning criminal records. This is due to a concerted attempt to increase the effectiveness of the rules concerning the exchange of this information. It should also be kept in mind that this issue is linked to other EU legislation concerning the taking account of prior convictions, the issue of disqualifications following a criminal conviction, and to the double jeopardy principle, and can also affect a person's position in other respects as set out in national law (the increased possibility of pre-trial detention and different rules on trial procedure and enforcement of a sentence).[394]

The Council of Europe's mutual assistance Convention provides that a requested State shall send extracts from its judicial records to a requesting State, to the same extent as it complies with requests from its own authorities. Otherwise, the request shall be complied with in accordance with the requested State's law.[395] This Convention also provides that all its Contracting Parties will inform the other Contracting Parties at least once a year of all criminal convictions and subsequent measures concerning the latter's nationals which are entered into the judicial record.[396] The First Protocol to

---

[392] Arts 12–15.

[393] Arts 22–31. In many of these cases, there are extra grounds for refusing a request besides those listed in Art 11.

[394] See respectively II:3.7.2, II:3.7.3, and II:6.8 below. EU free movement law also contains provisions on the exchange of police records (see I:7.4.1).

[395] Art 13 of the Convention. Five Member States have reservations on this clause.

[396] Art 22 of the Convention. Eight Member States have reservations on this clause.

the Convention supplements the latter point by providing that further information on these convictions must be provided on request.[397]

In order to speed up the transfer of information from criminal records, the EU Council adopted, as an interim measure, a Decision in 2005 which set out a standard form and detailed rules regarding sending requests for information on convictions and requires immediate transmission of information regarding convictions of nationals of other Member States.[398] Member States had to withdraw any reservations to the Council of Europe Convention on the first issue, but could retain them on the latter issue.

As both the mutual recognition programme and the Hague Programme called for broader measures to enhance the exchange of information on criminal convictions, the Commission had released in the meantime a White Paper on the issue in early 2005.[399] This White Paper pinpointed difficulties in rapidly identifying Member States where individuals have already been convicted, obtaining information quickly and by a simple procedure, and in understanding the information provided. To address these issues, the Commission suggested a two-stage process. In the first stage, a European index of offenders would be established, in order to make it easier to identify which Member States a person had been convicted in. In a second stage, a standard format would be used to exchange detailed information about the convictions.

In response to the White Paper, the JHA Council agreed in April 2005 that information on EU citizens would instead be exchanged bilaterally between Member States, with an index of offenders used only as regards non-EU nationals.[400] The Commission subsequently proposed a Framework Decision concerning the exchange of information on EU citizens' criminal records, which the Council adopted in 2009, alongside an implementing Decision.[401] Member States were obliged to apply these measures by 7 and 27 April 2012;[402] on the latter date, the prior EU Decision was repealed and the Framework Decision replaced some of the relevant Council of Europe measures in relations between Member States.[403]

This Framework Decision repeats the obligation in the 2005 Decision for each Member State to send to each other Member State information on the criminal convictions of nationals of those other States as soon as possible, extending this to cases where the person concerned is a dual national of the convicting Member State.[404] This information must be stored in the system established by the Framework Decision for possible further transmission,[405] and the Framework Decision elaborates upon the process

---

[397] Art 4 of the First Protocol. The UK and Ireland have reservations on this clause.
[398] [2005] OJ L 322/33. The Decision applied from 21 May 2006 (Art 7).
[399] COM (2005) 10, 25 Jan 2005.   [400] See press release of the 14 Apr 2005 JHA Council.
[401] [2009] OJ L 93/23 and 33.
[402] Art 13 of the Framework Decision and Art 8 of the 2009 Decision.
[403] Arts 12 of the Framework Decision. More precisely, Art 22 of the Council of Europe mutual assistance Convention and Art 4 of the First Protocol to the Convention are replaced, while Art 13 of that Convention remains in force, with a continued waiver of Member States' reservations.
[404] Art 4, Framework Decision; compare to Art 2 of the 2005 Decision. Art 4(4) of the Framework Decision incorporates Art 4 of the First Protocol to the Council of Europe Convention.
[405] Art 5, Framework Decision.

of sending and replying to requests for information on criminal convictions.[406] There are specific rules on personal data protection.[407] The criminal record information is to be exchanged using a standard format,[408] which was established by the Council in the parallel Decision establishing a European Criminal Records Information System (ECRIS).

ECRIS is not an EU-wide database; nor does it give any Member States' authorities access to the criminal records database of other Member States.[409] Instead, the 2009 Decision establishes the standard format for the supply of criminal records information which might be exchanged pursuant to the Framework Decision, by means of common codes indicating generally the type of offence and type of penalty imposed on the person concerned.[410]

A subsequent Directive contains a brief reference to criminal records as regards sexual offences against children.[411] The Commission also intends to propose legislation on the exchange of information on the criminal records of third-country nationals in 2016.[412]

3.6.2 Freezing orders

The enforcement of foreign freezing orders is governed first of all by the 1990 Council of Europe Convention on the proceeds of crime, ratified by all Member States, which requires States to enforce orders freezing the proceeds of crime issued by other signatory States.[413] However, the obligation is subject to many possible grounds for refusal.[414]

Initially, EU measures in this area were confined to an obligation to give freezing requests from other Member States equal priority with domestic requests.[415] But subsequently freezing orders were the subject of the EU's second Framework Decision concerning mutual recognition in criminal matters.[416] The Framework Decision applies to orders issued by 'judicial authorities' (as defined by the issuing State) in the framework of criminal proceedings,[417] not only to freeze criminal assets (the subject of the 1990 Council of Europe Convention), for the purpose of their subsequent confiscation,[418] but also to orders concerning the freezing of evidence, for the purpose of subsequent transfer to the issuing State pursuant to mutual assistance rules.[419] As regards the

---

[406] Arts 6–8, Framework Decision; compare to Art 3 of the 2005 Decision.

[407] Art 9, Framework Decision; compare to Art 4 of the 2005 Decision.

[408] Art 11, Framework Decision.

[409] Art 3 of the 2009 Decision. On such forms of information exchange, see II:7.6 below.

[410] Art 4 of the Decision.

[411] Dir 2011/93 ([2011] OJ L 335/1), Art 10. On the issue of disqualifications, see II:3.7.3 below.

[412] The proposal is planned by Jan 2016: see the JHA Council conclusions of 20 Nov 2015, point 10. See also the earlier discussion paper on this issue: COM (2006) 359, 4 July 2006.

[413] Arts 11 and 12 of the Convention (ETS 141). See now Arts 21 and 22 of the replacement 2005 Council of Europe Convention on the same issue (CETS 198), which a majority of Member States have ratified (see Appendix I for ratification details).

[414] Art 18 of the 1990 Convention and Art 28 of the 2005 Convention, both n 413 above.

[415] Art 4 of the 2001 Framework Decision on money laundering ([2001] OJ L 182/1); Art 3 of the 1998 Joint Action on this subject was identical ([1998] OJ L 333/1). See further II:3.7.4 below.

[416] [2003] OJ L 196/45. Member States had to comply by 2 Aug 2005 (Art 14(1)).

[417] Art 2(a).   [418] On this issue, see further II:3.7.4 below.

[419] Arts 3(1) and 10. On these rules, see II:3.6.1 above.

freezing of evidence, the Framework Decision will be replaced by the Directive establishing the European Investigation Order as from 22 May 2017.[420]

Member States must recognize and execute the freezing order of another Member State, subject only to the most limited list of grounds for non-recognition appearing in any EU measure to date.[421] In particular, dual criminality is abolished for the standard list of thirty-two crimes.[422] However, where a freezing order relates to subsequent confiscation (as distinct from securing evidence), a broader dual criminality condition can be applied, to require that an act constitute an offence *to which a freezing order could apply* in both States.[423] Other grounds (all optional) for non-execution are a defective freezing certificate, an immunity or privilege under the executing State's law, or where it is 'instantly clear' from the certificate that the subsequent rendering of judicial assistance would breach the double jeopardy principle.[424] An executing Member State may also set a time limit for freezing the property.[425]

The Framework Decision includes the same human rights provisions as the Framework Decision establishing the EAW,[426] so these provisions presumably must be interpreted the same way.[427] Also, this Framework Decision provides for remedies to be exercised in either the issuing or executing State. Although the substantive reasons for the freezing can only be challenged in the issuing State, both States are obliged to facilitate access to remedies and the issuing State is obliged to set time limits that guarantee access to an effective legal remedy.[428]

According to a Commission report on the application of this Framework Decision, eight Member States had not yet applied it by October 2008.[429] The Commission report claims, inter alia, that some Member States made errors as regards abolition of dual criminality, reimbursement, and contact between judicial authorities, and that fourteen Member States provide for forbidden grounds for non-execution (in particular concerning human rights). Overall, the Commission concluded that application of the Framework Decision was 'not satisfactory', due to the limited number of notifications and the 'numerous omissions and limitations' in the laws which had been notified.

This measure is subject to the same objections that apply to other EU mutual recognition measures, *a fortiori* because there are so few grounds for refusing execution (in particular, there are no grounds for refusing execution on grounds of *in absentia* judgments and extraterritoriality), and because they are all optional. Furthermore, the double jeopardy provision is weak, because it is highly unlikely that it will be evident from the certificate connected to the freezing order that the double jeopardy principle is infringed; this will only be evident following further communication between the issuing and executing authorities, and/or subsequent objections by the suspects. If freezing orders apply beyond the time period for a trial to take place within a 'reasonable time', as required by Article 6 ECHR, it is arguable that they should no longer be

---

[420] See Arts 34(2) and 36(1) of Dir 2014/41 ([2014] OJ L 130/1). On the EIO, see further II:3.6.1.3 above.
[421] Art 5(1).   [422] Art 3(2).   [423] Art 3(4).
[424] Art 7. There are also some limited grounds for postponement of execution (Art 8).
[425] Art 6(2).   [426] See clause 6 of the preamble and Art 1, second line.
[427] See II:3.5.2 above.   [428] Art 11.
[429] COM (2008) 885, 22 Dec 2008. According to a later update by the Council, 25 Member States had implemented this measure as of 5 June 2015 (Council doc 9638/15, 5 June 2015).

executed; it is unfortunate that the Framework Decision does not set out this principle expressly. The Commission's complaints regarding non-recognition on human rights grounds should be rejected for the reasons set out above.[430]

As noted above, this Framework Decision will be replaced from May 2017, as regards the freezing of evidence, by the Directive on the European Investigation Order, discussed above.[431] It remains to be seen whether it will ultimately be replaced as regards freezing of assets.

3.6.3 Recognition of pre-trial supervision orders

There is evidence that foreigners suspected of committing a crime are kept in detention while awaiting trial in cases where nationals suspected of committing the same crime would not be,[432] because of the greater difficulty in ensuring that foreigners will attend the trial and serve any criminal sentence which may be imposed. This difficulty was first of all reduced significantly with the application of the European Arrest Warrant,[433] and it is arguable that discriminatory detention of citizens of other Member States breaches EU free movement law.[434] The issue is now addressed by a Framework Decision adopted in 2009, which Member States had to implement by 1 December 2012.[435] Unusually, there is no previous international measure addressing the same issues as this Framework Decision. This measure overlaps in some cases with the Directive establishing a European Protection Order.[436]

The Framework Decision specifies that it does not confer a right to pre-trial release; this issue is left to national law.[437] Implicitly the Framework Decision does not harmonize national law as regards when a person can or must receive bail (for example in light of the seriousness of the particular offences alleged, the prior behaviour or criminal record of the person concerned, and the risk of absconding), or of any conditions that can or must be attached to bail.[438] It includes a standard human rights provision,[439] along with a novel provision specifying that it does not alter national responsibilities as regards 'the protection of victims, the general public and the safeguarding of internal security, in accordance with' Article 33 of the prior TEU (now Article 72 TFEU).[440] The Framework Decision applies to six specified types of supervision measure;[441] Member States may notify the Council of other types of supervision measure which they are willing to enforce.[442]

Member States are obliged to apply the Framework Decision where the person concerned is lawfully and ordinarily resident in their territory, subject also to that person's

---

[430] II:3.5.2. [431] II:3.6.1.3.

[432] See Annex 3 to the annex to the Commission Green Paper on pre-trial supervision orders (SEC (2004) 1046, 17 Aug 2004).

[433] See II:3.5.2 above. [434] See II:3.4 above and Case C-297/09 *X*, withdrawn.

[435] [2009] OJ L 294/20, Art 27(1). See also the earlier Commission Green Paper on this issue (COM (2004) 562, 17 Aug 2004). All subsequent references in this sub-section are to this Framework Decision, unless otherwise noted.

[436] See II:3.7.6 below. [437] Art 2(2). [438] See Art 5(3) ECHR.

[439] Art 5. See also points 16 and 17 in the preamble. [440] Art 3. [441] Art 8(1).

[442] Art 8(2), which contains a non-exhaustive list of five other types of supervision measure.

consent.[443] They may also, if the person concerned requests, apply the Framework Decision where that person is not lawfully and ordinarily resident, but in that case the application of the Framework Decision depends on the consent of the executing state.[444] The principle of dual criminality is abolished for the standard list of thirty-two crimes with a three-year punishment threshold, but Member States may insist, at the time of adoption of the Framework Decision, on applying that principle by way of derogation for 'some or all' of the offences on the list, for 'constitutional reasons'.[445] There are optional grounds for refusal of execution: a defective certificate; absence of consent by the person concerned or the executing State in the circumstances described above; double jeopardy; residual cases of dual criminality; statute-barring (if the alleged offence fell within the jurisdiction of the executing State); immunity (in accordance with the executing State's law); the age of criminal responsibility in the executing State; and where the executing State would have to refuse to execute an EAW that might be issued in the event of a breach of the order.[446] There is no ground for refusal on grounds of territoriality, or the executing State's existing prosecution of or intention to prosecute the person concerned, but arguably this issue is covered by the link to the grounds to refuse to execute an EAW.

There are detailed provisions governing which Member State has competence to take action relating to the supervision order,[447] and providing for coordination between Member States' authorities as regards later developments after the supervision order is issued.[448] There is no provision as such which grants the person concerned a remedy against the decision to approve a supervision order, but then again the Framework Decision grants the person concerned an explicit or implicit right of consent before the supervision order can be transferred in the first place.

If an EAW or similar measure is issued as regards the person concerned by the issuing Member State, the executing Member State must surrender that person in accordance with the Framework Decision establishing the EAW. In principle, the executing Member State cannot invoke the custody threshold in the latter Framework Decision (an actual sentence of more than four months, or a potential sentence of more than twelve months), except by way of derogation.[449] The preamble to this Framework Decision makes clear that otherwise the EAW Framework Decision fully applies in the event that an EAW is issued to ensure the return of the person concerned to face trial in the issuing State.

---

[443] Art 9(1). The concept of consent is not further defined.

[444] Art 9(2); see also Art 9(3) and (4).

[445] Art 14. Germany, Poland, Hungary, and Lithuania made declarations to this effect ([2009] OJ L 294/40).

[446] Art 15. It is not clear if the latter point refers only to the mandatory grounds for refusal to execute an EAW, or also to the optional grounds which the Member State concerned applies. For more on the EAW, see II:3.5.2 above.

[447] Arts 11, 16, and 18. See also Art 13, on the possible adaptation of the supervision measure in the executing Member State. The Framework Decision does not address the question of what happens if the executing Member State has a more severe regime relating to bail, ie if it would not have released the person concerned pending trial.

[448] Arts 17, 19, and 20.

[449] Art 21, referring to Art 2(1) of the Framework Decision establishing the EAW ([2002] OJ L 190/1).

According to the Commission's 2014 report on the application of the Framework Decision, sixteen Member States had not applied it by that point.[450] The latest information shows that thirteen Member States have still not applied it.[451] No Member States had yet used it in practice, at the time of the Commission report. In the Commission's view, one Member State breached the Framework Decision by failing to provide for all the mandatory measures referred to in it. Others had added extra grounds for refusal, or not transposed the rules on issuing an EAW in relation to the supervision order.

This Framework Decision may make a useful contribution to reducing unjustified pre-trial detention of EU citizens accused of crimes outside their country of nationality, a problem which the case law on the EAW does not fully resolve.[452] If it proves insufficient to this end, it may be necessary to adopt further measures addressing this issue. On this point, it should be noted that the Commission has issued a Green Paper on pre-trial detention.[453] As long as the Commission does not follow up the Green Paper or take any effective measures to ensure that all Member States implement the Framework Decision properly, pre-trial detention will continue to be a serious problem plaguing the cross-border application of criminal proceedings.

3.7 Post-Trial Measures

Following the conclusion of a trial, several cross-border issues may arise.[454] The most obvious possibility is the transfer of enforcement of a sentence, whether custodial or non-custodial. The next question is whether a criminal conviction in one Member State may or must be taken into account for the purpose of subsequent criminal proceedings in other Member States (in addition to the separate issue of the double jeopardy effect of the conviction).[455] There may also be a cross-border consequence to a criminal conviction as regards confiscation of criminal assets, or disqualification from carrying out a profession or activity. Finally, there are cross-border aspects to conditional release on probation or parole, as well as orders for the protection of persons.

3.7.1 Enforcement of sentences

An early Council of Europe Convention (from 1970) concerns the enforcement of both custodial and non-custodial sentences, but it has attracted few ratifications from EU Member States; a subsequent Council of Europe Convention on the transfer of sentenced persons was far more successful, attracting unanimous support of Member States.[456] The first EU measure concerning this issue was a Convention between the Member States in 1991, agreed in the framework of European Political Cooperation

---

[450] COM (2014) 57, 2 Feb 2014.

[451] Council doc 5859/3/15, 22 July 2015. The information was correct as of 22 July 2015.

[452] See Case C-237/15 PPU *Lanigan*, ECLI:EU:C:2015:474, discussed in II:3.5.2 above.

[453] See II:4.6 below.

[454] For a detailed analysis of post-trial mutual recognition issues, particularly as regards recognition of custodial sentences, see the Commission's Green Paper on criminal sanctions (COM (2004) 334, 30 Apr 2004), particularly at 23–5, 34–46, and 57–68.

[455] On double jeopardy, see II:6.8 below.

[456] ETS 70 and 112. For ratification details, see Appendix I.

(EPC), and also addressing both types of penalties, but it failed to attract enough ratifications to enter into force.[457] The EU has subsequently adopted mutual recognition
measures concerning both the enforcement of financial penalties and the transfer of
custodial sentences.

3.7.1.1 Financial penalties

Initially, within the framework of Schengen cooperation, Member States negotiated an
agreement on the specific issue of recognizing financial penalties imposed for road traffic offences.[458] This agreement appears not to have entered into force in practice, and
the issue has been subsumed within the context of a broader Framework Decision on
the mutual recognition of financial penalties, which was adopted in 2005 and had to
be applied by Member States by 22 March 2007.[459] That Framework Decision has been
interpreted in one judgment of the CJEU.[460]

The Framework Decision follows the template established by the Framework Decision
on the European Arrest Warrant, obliging Member States to recognize the judgments
of other Member States except where a ground for non-recognition exists.[461] Dual
criminality is abolished not only for the 'standard' list of thirty-two crimes (inevitably without any sentencing threshold, since the Framework Decision does not apply
to custodial sentences) and to a further seven crimes in addition: conduct infringing
'road traffic regulations, including' breaches of law on driving hours, rest periods, and
hazardous goods; 'smuggling of goods'; 'infringement of intellectual property rights';
'threats and acts of violence against persons, including violence during sports events';
'criminal damage'; 'theft'; and any acts constituting offences which the issuing Member
State has established to implement obligations arising from first or third pillar acts.[462]
Presumably these additional offences have been added because the impact of imposing financial penalties is less severe than imposing custodial penalties, and/or because
such less serious crimes are more frequently punished by fines rather than custodial
sentences.

Confiscation measures and orders in *civil* proceedings fall outside the scope of the
Framework Decision.[463] In certain cases, the Framework Decision applies to sentences
imposed against legal persons and sentences not imposed by courts, although Member
States had the right to opt to delay application of the Framework Decision to such cases
until 22 February 2010.[464] More precisely, the Framework Decision applies to decisions
made by an administrative authority relating to criminal matters or infringements of

---

[457] For details, see: <http://www.consilium.europa.eu/en/documents-publications/agreements-conventions/agreement/?aid=1987010>.

[458] [2000] OJ L 239/428.

[459] Art 20(1) of Framework Decision ([2005] OJ L 76/16). All references in this sub-section are to this
Framework Decision, except where otherwise noted.

[460] Case C-60/12 *Baláž*, ECLI:EU:C:2013:733.   [461] Art 6.   [462] Art 5.

[463] Art 1(b). The former are covered by the separate measure on that subject (see II:3.7.4 below) while
the latter are covered by civil law rules (see II:8.5.1 below). For instance, see Case C-7/98 *Krombach* [2000]
ECR I-1935.

[464] Art 20(2), read with Art 21.

the rule of law, if the person concerned could challenge those decisions before a court with criminal jurisdiction.[465]

The CJEU has interpreted the rules on this issue,[466] ruling that the concept of a 'court having jurisdiction in particular in criminal matters' was a uniform concept of EU law. According to the Court, the meaning of the phrase could not depend upon the classification of offences in national law, but rather indicated a body which 'satisfies the essential characteristics of criminal procedure', even if that body also dealt with non-criminal cases. There has to be an 'overall assessment of a number of objective factors'. In this case, the Austrian body concerned had the general characteristic of a 'court or tribunal' in EU law (independence, acting *inter partes*, etc.), and moreover applied criminal law safeguards such as the concept of criminal responsibility and the proportionality of penalties. As to whether the suspect had an opportunity to try the case before a court with criminal jurisdiction, Member States could require the suspect to comply with a prior administrative procedure first, before going directly to such a court, as long as access to that court was not 'impossible or excessively difficult'. The court in question 'must have full jurisdiction' on the legal assessment and factual circumstances, as well as the chance to examine the evidence and determine the responsibility of the suspect and the level of the penalty. If the suspect had not brought an appeal, that was irrelevant, since it was sufficient only that he or she had the 'opportunity' to bring one.

There are eight grounds for non-execution, comprising in particular double jeopardy (worded differently from the EAW exception), extraterritoriality, immunity, childhood, *in absentia* proceedings (as amended by the 2009 Framework Decision on this subject), and a financial threshold (penalties below the value of €70 need not be enforced).[467] In addition to the standard human rights provision, there is also an express human rights exception: a Member State *may*, 'where the certificate' describing the issuing State's judgment 'gives rise to an issue that fundamental rights or fundamental legal principles as described in Article 6 of the [EU] Treaty may have been infringed, oppose the recognition and the execution of decisions'.[468] Compared to the EU's other mutual recognition measures, this provision is unique, but if the provision is read literally, it will be impossible to apply in practice: there appears to be no way that the *certificate*, which is simply a standard form with boxes to be ticked and lines to be filled in with factual information in order to allow the prior judgment to be enforced, could *as such* give rise to concerns that human rights have been infringed by that prior judgment.[469]

According to the Commission's report on the application of the Framework Decision,[470] only a minority of Member States (eleven) had reported on their implementation of this measure by October 2008, making it impossible to draw conclusions

---

[465] Art 1(a)(ii) and (iii).   [466] *Baláž*, n 460 above.

[467] Art 7. For details of the new *in absentia* rule, see II:3.5.2 above. In *Baláž* (n 460 above), the CJEU said that the grounds for non-execution had to be interpreted strictly (para 29), although it did not expressly say that the list of such grounds was exhaustive. The Court also seemed to suggest that some of the grounds could only apply if there were a human rights complaint, but with respect this is clearly wrong (para 28).

[468] Art 20(3). Art 20(8) requires Member States to transmit information on the application of this provision to the Council and Commission, and Art 20(9) provides for a review of this exception by Feb 2012. It was not reviewed in practice.

[469] See the broader points on human rights and mutual recognition in II:3.3.5 and II:3.5.2 above.

[470] COM (2008) 888, 22 Dec 2008.

about the implementation of the Framework Decision in practice.[471] Of those Member States which had applied the measure, the Commission regretted that most had made the optional grounds for execution mandatory and that some had allegedly added extra grounds for refusal. However, in part the latter complaint begs the question as to whether there is an implied 'human rights' ground for refusal (broader than the express ground discussed above), since some Member States provide for a refusal to execute decisions due to a breach of due process or because of discrimination on grounds of race, political opinion, etc.

3.7.1.2 Custodial penalties

As regards the enforcement of custodial penalties, there are two parallel issues: the enforcement of the *sentence* alone (where the sentenced person is on the territory of the requested State, and, for example, cannot be extradited from that State to serve the sentence in the State which imposed it), and the transfer of a *sentenced person* (who is generally already imprisoned on the territory of the requesting State) which necessarily entails the transfer of enforcement of the sentence as a corollary measure. As noted above, the first issue has been the subject of both a Council of Europe Convention which has attracted limited ratifications and an EPC measure which has not entered into force at all. In comparison, the 1983 Council of Europe Convention on the transfer of sentenced persons has attracted ratification by every EU Member State (and many other States besides).[472] There is also a Protocol to the Convention, agreed in 1997, which a large majority of Member States have ratified.[473] The main Convention requires the consent of not only the requesting and requested State, but also the sentenced person, in order for the transfer to take place; the principle of dual criminality also applies.[474] The Protocol provides first of all that if a person escapes the sentencing Member State and flees to the Member State of his or her nationality in order to escape enforcement of the penalty, the sentencing Member State may ask the State of nationality to enforce the sentence; there is no obligation in such cases to obtain the consent of the sentenced person.[475] The sentenced person's consent is also waived in cases where he or she is to be expelled pursuant to a deportation or expulsion order, although: that person may still express an opinion on the transfer; there is a specialty rule comparable to the rule applicable in extradition law; and Contracting Parties can choose not to apply this provision of the Protocol.[476]

Within the EU, the issue of the transfer of sentenced persons was first addressed by an EPC Convention of 1987, which attracted only a few ratifications.[477] Subsequently,

---

[471] The latest information indicates that 25 Member States had implemented the Framework Decision by 4 June 2015 (Council doc 9667/15, 5 June 2015).

[472] ETS 112.   [473] ETS 167. For ratification details, see Appendix I.

[474] Art 3(1) of the Convention.   [475] Art 2 of the Protocol.

[476] Art 3 of the Protocol. On the specialty rule in extradition law, see II:3.5.1 above. Ireland does not apply this provision, and Belgium applies it subject to a condition of habitual residence.

[477] For details, see: <http://www.consilium.europa.eu/en/documents-publications/agreements-conventions/agreement/?aid=1987010>. For ratification details, see Appendix I.

the Schengen Convention supplemented the Council of Europe Convention by providing for the same waiver of the consent requirement for fugitives as set out in the
Protocol to the latter Convention.[478]

In 2008, the Council adopted a Framework Decision on the transfer of custodial
sentences, which applies the mutual recognition principle to the transfer of sentenced
persons.[479] Member States had to apply this Framework Decision by 5 December
2011,[480] although it only applies to requests received after that date.[481] As from that
date, the Framework Decision replaced the corresponding provisions of the two
Council of Europe Conventions and the Protocol to the Convention on sentenced persons, the relevant provisions of the Schengen Convention, and the EPC Convention
on this issue.[482] The CJEU has been asked to interpret the Framework Decision in
pending cases.[483]

As for the substance of the Framework Decision, it is subject to the standard human
rights provisions.[484] The Framework Decision applies either where the sentenced person lives in his or her State of nationality, or *will* live in his or her State of nationality
once an expulsion or deportation order is carried out, or where another Member State
consents to the transfer of the sentenced person.[485] For the latter category of cases,
Member States may declare that they waive the requirement of their consent, if the
person concerned has been a legal resident for at least five years and will continue to
reside there as a permanent resident, as defined by reference to EU free movement and
immigration law, and/or is a national of the executing State but is neither living there
nor due to be deported or expelled there.[486] The transfer process may be instigated by
the sentenced person, although there is no obligation for the States concerned to act on
his or her request.[487]

The traditional requirement for the consent of the sentenced person has also been
abolished by the Framework Decision, in the two cases covered by the Protocol to
the Council of Europe Convention as well as where the sentenced person lives in the

---

[478] Arts 67–9 of the Convention ([2000] OJ L 239). Note that the application of the Schengen Convention
predated the Council of Europe Protocol for some Member States; some Member States have not ratified the
Protocol yet (but conversely the Schengen Convention does not apply in Ireland yet, although the Protocol
does), and the Protocol also applies to a number of non-Member States, including all of the Schengen
associates. Also, the Protocol, but not the Schengen Convention, contains the additional rule waiving the
consent requirement in cases of deportation.

[479] [2008] OJ L 327/27.   [480] Art 29(1).

[481] Art 28(1). Requests received before that date remain subject to the previous legal instruments.

[482] Art 26(1).   [483] Cases C-554/14 *Ognyanov* and C-289/15 *Grundza*, pending.

[484] Art 3(4) and recitals 13 and 14 in the preamble.

[485] Art 4(1). Implicitly the requirement of consent by the executing State (required by the Council
of Europe Convention on sentenced persons and its Protocol) is waived in the former two cases. In all
cases, the sentenced person must be in either the issuing or the executing State (Art 3(2)). The expulsion
of the person concerned is subject to EU free movement law: see recitals 15 and 16 in the preamble and
II:3.4 above. Note that the Framework Decision has a wider personal scope than the Council of Europe
Convention on the transfer of sentenced persons, which only applies to nationals of the administering state
(Art 3(1)(a) of the Convention).

[486] Art 4(7). On the links with EU free movement law, see II:3.4 above. This provision is consistent
with the Court's interpretation of certain exceptions to the EAW Framework Decision: see Case C-123/08
Wolzenburg [2009] ECR I-9621, discussed in II:3.5.2 above. In fact, this judgment refers expressly to Art
4(7)(a) of the Framework Decision.

[487] Art 4(5).

Member State of his or her nationality.[488] Poland has a five-year derogation from the latter extension of the abolition of the consent requirement.[489] Where the consent requirement is waived and the sentenced person is still in the territory of the issuing State, he or she is still entitled to give an opinion on the transfer.[490]

Next, the Framework Decision abolishes the dual criminality requirement for the standard list of thirty-two offences and three-year punishability threshold, although by way of derogation, Member States can opt out of this obligation.[491] With the abolition of the three key traditional grounds for refusing a transfer, the remaining grounds for non-execution take on greater importance. Member States may refuse to execute a request, inter alia, if: the certificate is defective; the enforcement would violate the double jeopardy rule; the judgment is statute-barred in the executing Member State; there is an immunity in the executing Member State; the person concerned would not have been liable under the executing State's law on the age of criminal responsibility; the trial took place *in absentia* (as amended by the 2009 Framework Decision on this subject); there are fewer than six months of the sentence remaining; or on grounds of territoriality.[492] The principle of speciality also applies, in exactly the same way as for the European Arrest Warrant, except that for this Framework Decision Member States cannot agree to waive the principle.[493]

The executing State is obliged in principle to take over enforcement of the judgment,[494] and cannot aggravate the issuing State's sentence 'in terms of its nature or duration',[495] although this begs the question as to whether a more stringent regime on early release could be applied.[496] On the other hand, the executing State may reduce the duration of sentence imposed,[497] but only where that sentence is above the maximum that could be imposed in that State for the same offence.[498] Where the issuing State's sentence is incompatible with the executing State's sentence 'in terms of its nature', the latter State may 'adapt' the sentence, but this must 'correspond as closely as possible' to the original sentence, and cannot entail a conversion of a prison sentence into a fine.[499]

Finally, it is explicitly stated that this Framework Decision will apply where an EAW is not executed because the executing Member State has undertaken to enforce a prior sentence itself, or where the executing Member State has insisted on a guarantee that

---

[488] Art 6(2). The requirement otherwise applies (Art 6(1)).   [489] Art 6(5).

[490] Art 6(3).

[491] Art 7. On the interpretation of this clause, see *Grundza*, pending (n 483 above).

[492] Art 9. On the 2009 Framework Decision on *in absentia* trials, see II:3.5.2 above.

[493] Art 18; compare to Art 27 of the EAW Framework Decision ([2002] OJ L 190/1), discussed in II:3.5.2 above. As noted there, it would be logical to interpret these provisions the same way; on the EAW provision, see Case C-388/08 PPU *Leymann and Pustovarov* [2008] ECR I-8993. The rule is different from the speciality rule in Art 3(4) of the Protocol to the Convention on sentenced persons, and moreover applies to all sentenced persons, not just those within the scope of Art 3 of that Protocol.

[494] Art 8(1).   [495] Art 8(4).

[496] On early release, see Art 17(3) and (4). On the human rights aspects of this issue, see the decisions of the European Court of Human Rights in *Veermae v Finland* (15 Mar 2005) and *Szabo v Sweden* (27 June 2006), discussed in II:3.3 above.

[497] Art 8(2).

[498] The pending *Ognyanov* case (n 483 above) asks the CJEU to clarify the relationship between the rules on early release and reduction of sentences.

[499] Art 8(3).

the issuing Member State return the fugitive after trial to serve his or her sentence, if imposed, in the executing State.[500]

According to the Commission's report on the application of the Framework Decision in 2014,[501] ten Member States had not yet transposed the Framework Decision at all.[502] The safeguards for the waiver of the prisoner's consent were not fully applied in all cases, and the Commission criticized some executing Member States for trying to alter the issuing State's original sentence more than the legislation allows for. It also complained because some Member States added additional grounds for refusal, or made the optional grounds mandatory for authorities.

This Framework Decision usefully clarifies the position in cases where persons are tried or serve their sentences in the Member State which had been asked to execute an EAW concerning them. But it is dubious to abolish the dual criminality rule where this entails serving a sentence in the territory of a State which did not criminalize the acts concerned, and for the reasons set out above, this Framework Decision goes too far in abolishing the requirement of the consent of the person concerned, considering the principles of free movement law and the objective of social rehabilitation.[503]

3.7.2 Consequences of convictions

The first adopted EU measure concerning the consequences of convictions in subsequent criminal proceedings was a Framework Decision relating to counterfeiting currency, which requires Member States to recognize final sentences for the same crime handed out in another Member State 'for the purpose of establishing habitual criminality' in the same way as they would recognize a prior domestic conviction under their national law.[504] Subsequently, the Council adopted a broader Framework Decision in 2008,[505] which requires Member States to take account of prior convictions in other Member States concerning different facts relating to the same person 'to the extent previous national convictions are taken into account'; also 'equivalent legal effects' must be attached to such prior conventions 'as to previous national convictions, in accordance with national law'.[506] This rule shall apply as regards all stages of criminal proceedings and (implicitly) for any type of offence.[507] There are no grounds for non-recognition, but the Framework Decision leaves it open to Member States to apply a dual criminality rule.[508]

It is obvious that the practical application of this Framework Decision will be dependent on developing an effective mechanism to ensure the exchange of criminal records information between Member States.[509] The problem, as noted above, is that

---

[500] Art 25 of this Framework Decision, referring to Arts 4(6) and 5(3) of the EAW Framework Decision; see discussion of the latter provisions above (II:3.5.2).

[501] COM (2014) 57, 5 Feb 2014.

[502] The latest information shows that six Member States have still not transposed it as of 24 June 2015: Council doc 6069/2/15, 24 June 2015.

[503] See II:3.4.   [504] [2001] OJ L 329/3.

[505] [2008] OJ L 220/32. Member States had to apply this measure by 15 Aug 2010 (Art 5(1)). The 2001 Framework Decision (n 504 above) has not been repealed or amended.

[506] Art 3(1).   [507] Art 3(2).   [508] See recital 6 in the preamble.   [509] See II:3.6.1.4 above.

the information supplied pursuant to the EU measures on criminal record exchange may be inaccurate or insufficient for the second Member State's courts to use fully and fairly to decide whether to classify the (alleged) offender as a recidivist for the purposes of national criminal procedure.

According to a Commission report on application of this measure in 2014, six Member States had still not transposed the Framework Decision.[510] Three Member States refused to apply the measure in the event that the prior conviction was unfair. Several Member States did not limit their transposition to cases of 'final convictions', which the Commission rightly considered problematic. On the other hand, the Commission agreed with Member States that a dual criminality check was justifiable, since the concept was built in to the Framework Decision. Not all Member States had clearly transposed the principle of equivalence into national law.

3.7.3 Disqualification

The first EU measure adopted in this area was a Convention on the enforcement of driving disqualifications, agreed in 1998.[511] However, this Convention has attracted few ratifications,[512] and moreover is not a mutual recognition measure, providing instead for *conversion* of one Member State's decision into a decision taken within the framework of the legal system of another Member State. A Belgian initiative for a Framework Decision which sought to put into practice the recognition of disqualifications for working with children following a criminal conviction for sexual offences involving them,[513] as required by the EU's Framework Decision of 2003 concerning offences against children,[514] was not successful as such, mainly because of differences in national law regarding the existence of such prohibitions, the process for deciding upon them, and the storage and transmission of relevant criminal records information.[515] However, the initiative was integrated into the Framework Decision on the exchange of criminal records, adopted in 2009.[516] The subsequent Directive concerning offences against children also includes a rule on disqualification.[517] Member States are required to: prevent a person convicted of the relevant offences from exercising a professional activity involving 'direct and regular contacts' with children; ensure that employers in such cases can request information on relevant criminal convictions; and transmit the relevant information on convictions pursuant to EU rules on criminal records.

The difficulties encountered with the Belgian proposal explain why the Commission, in a 2006 Green Paper on recognition of disqualifications,[518] suggested a gradual piecemeal approach, applying the principle of mutual recognition to disqualifications only where a common basis between Member States existed, either on the basis of their national law (in the case of driving disqualifications) or as a result of EU measures (in

---

[510] COM (2014) 248, 3 June 2014.   [511] [1998] OJ C 216/1.
[512] For ratification details, see Appendix I.   [513] Council doc 14207/04, 5 Nov 2004.
[514] [2004] OJ L 13/44, Art 5(3).   [515] Council doc 7951/06, 31 Mar 2006.
[516] [2009] OJ L 93/23. See II:3.6.1.4 above.   [517] Art 10 of Dir 2011/93 ([2011] OJ L 335/1).
[518] COM (2006) 73, 21 Feb 2006.

the case of sexual offences or EU measures concerning procurement, for example). This view was backed by a majority of Member States.[519] Furthermore, the recast EU driving licence Directive contains some provisions on recognition of disqualification from driving, and EU legislation provides for the exchange of information on road traffic infractions.[520]

3.7.4 Confiscation orders

The starting point for any discussion of the rules on the confiscation of criminal assets is the 1990 Council of Europe Convention on the proceeds of crime, ratified by every EU Member State.[521] Chapter II of this Convention sets out requirements for the harmonization of domestic law on this issue, in order to facilitate the application of the Convention's rules on international cooperation. These requirements, inter alia, entail obligations to provide for the confiscation of the proceeds and instrumentalities of crime, or property which corresponds to the value of such proceeds (although States can enter a reservation limiting this obligation to specific offences), to adopt investigative measures to this end, and to set out legal remedies for interested parties.[522] Revised provisions appear in a 2005 Council of Europe Convention on the same subject, which a majority of Member States have ratified.[523] The 1990 and 2005 Conventions also require States to enforce confiscation orders relating to the proceeds of crime issued by other signatory States.[524] However, this obligation is subject to many possible grounds for refusal in the 1990 Convention, and most of these grounds are retained in the 2005 Convention.[525]

An initial EU Joint Action provided that Member States should not enter reservations to the 1990 Convention as regards the obligation to provide for confiscation of proceeds, as long as the offence in question can be punished by a sentence of more than one year, except as regards tax offences; Member States may also exempt 'minor crimes' from the obligation to confiscate property corresponding to the value of the proceeds of crime.[526] A Framework Decision adopted in 2001 reiterates these two obligations in a more binding form,[527] setting a more precise threshold of €4000 as a maximum exemption from the latter obligation.[528] Both the Joint Action and the 2001 Framework Decision specify that Member States must also give confiscation requests from other

---

[519] See Council doc 6682/05, 23 Feb 2005.   [520] See II:3.4 above.   [521] ETS 141.

[522] Arts 2–5 of the Convention; on the substantive criminal law obligations, see II:5.5.1.2 below.

[523] Arts 3–14 of the 2005 Convention (CETS 198), in force 1 May 2008. On the extent of signature or ratification by Member States, see Appendix I.

[524] Arts 13–17 of the 1990 Convention and Arts 23–7 of the 2005 Convention.

[525] Art 18 of the 1990 Convention and Art 28 of the 2005 Convention. For instance, the 2005 Convention does not permit the fiscal and political offence exceptions to be used in cases of terrorism, qualifies the dual criminality principle, and provides for wider cooperation in relation to non-criminal sanctions.

[526] Art 1 of Joint Action ([1998] OJ L 333/1).

[527] On the legal effect of Joint actions and Framework Decisions, see II:2.2.1.2 and II:2.2.2 above.

[528] Arts 1(a) and 3 of the Framework Decision ([2001] OJ L 182/1). Art 5 of the Framework Decision repealed some provisions of the Joint Action. Arts 1(b) and 2 of the Framework Decision set out substantive criminal law rules, on which see II:5.5.1.2 below.

Member States equal priority with domestic requests.[529] The Commission has twice reported on the national application of this Framework Decision, concluding that several Member States appear not to have implemented the first two obligations, and complaining that it had not received enough information to assess compliance with the latter obligation.[530]

Following the judgment of the Strasbourg Court in the *Phillips* case,[531] the Council adopted two further linked Framework Decisions. The first measure, adopted in 2005, harmonizes national law on the confiscation of criminal assets,[532] while the second measure, adopted in 2006, establishes mutual recognition as regards confiscation orders.[533] This issue is also addressed by the 2003 Framework Decision on freezing orders, discussed already above.[534]

The 2005 Framework Decision first obliges Member States to provide for normal powers of confiscation, enabling them to prosecute criminal proceeds from offences punishable by a deprivation of liberty of more than one year, or property of the same value.[535] Secondly, Member States must revise their laws to provide for powers of 'extended confiscation' in respect of seven crimes as defined by EU Framework Decisions: counterfeiting currency, money laundering, trafficking in persons, facilitation of irregular entry or residence, sexual exploitation, drug trafficking, or terrorism, provided that the offence is punishable by a specified minimum penalty threshold and could generate financial gain.[536] For this principle to apply, a national court must be 'fully convinced', based on 'specific facts', that the assets are derived from one of three situations (at the option of each Member State): the criminal activity of the person prior to conviction; *similar* criminal activity for a period prior to conviction; or from criminal activities, without assessing the issue over a prior time period, if it is established that the assets are disproportionate to that person's lawful income.[537] Member States *may* also consider adopting legislation to confiscate the assets of the closest relatives of the person concerned, or a legal person which the person concerned controls or derives most of the income from.[538] Also, Member States are obliged to provide for legal remedies for interested persons (as set out in the 1990 Council of Europe Convention), and the Framework Decision should not have the effect of altering the obligation to respect fundamental rights, including the presumption of innocence.[539] The Commission's report on the application of this Framework Decision indicates that a significant number of Member States did not apply it by the deadline date, and that in particular a number of Member States did not communicate the measures they had taken to ensure remedies for the persons concerned.[540]

---

[529] Art 3 of Joint Action, n 526 above, and Art 4 of the 2001 Framework Decision, n 528 above.
[530] COM (2004) 230, 5 Apr 2004, and COM (2006) 72, 21 Feb 2006.   [531] See II:3.3.1 above.
[532] [2005] OJ L 68/47, which Member States had to apply by 15 Mar 2007 (Art 6(1)).
[533] [2006] OJ L 328/59, which Member States had to apply by 24 Nov 2008 (Art 22(1)). See also the relevant police cooperation measures (II:7.7 below).
[534] II:3.6.2.   [535] Art 2, 2005 Framework Decision.
[536] Art 3(1), 2005 Framework Decision.   [537] Art 3(2), 2005 Framework Decision.
[538] Art 3(3), 2005 Framework Decision.
[539] Arts 4 and 5, 2005 Framework Decision. On the general issue of suspects and defendants' rights, see II:4.6 below.
[540] COM (2007) 805, 17 Dec 2007.

In 2008, the Commission released a communication on the proceeds of crime which called for recasting the existing legislation, including the possibility of adding new provisions on confiscation without a criminal conviction, creating a new criminal offence of owning 'unjustified' assets, strengthening mutual recognition obligations, extending the scope of mandatory confiscation, and enforcing the obligation to provide bank account information set out in the 2001 Protocol to the EU mutual assistance Convention.[541] This discussion eventually culminated in a Directive adopted in 2014, which amended the previous rules.

Directive 2014/42, which Member States have to apply by 4 October 2016,[542] fully repeals the 1998 Joint Action and partly repeals the 2001 and 2005 Framework Decisions.[543] Compared to the earlier measures, the 2014 Directive has a more precise definition of 'proceeds' of crime. The extended confiscation rule now applies to counterfeiting of non-cash payments, attacks on information systems, and corruption, but no longer applies to facilitation of irregular entry or residence; the minimum penalty thresholds and other qualifications have been amended.[544] Also, the three alternative tests for applying the extended confiscation rule have been replaced by a single test, with a lower standard of proof: a court need only be 'satisfied' that the property of a convicted person is 'derived from criminal conduct', based on the circumstances, specific facts, and available evidence, for instance the disproportionate value of property compared to the criminal's lawful income.[545] There is also a stronger and mandatory rule on confiscation from third parties,[546] and more detailed rules on safeguards for those affected by confiscation orders.[547] Finally, there are also rules on domestic freezing orders, management of frozen property, and compilation of statistics.[548]

As for recognition of confiscation orders, the 2006 Framework Decision applies to orders imposed by a court following criminal proceedings,[549] and obliges Member States to recognize and execute other Member State's decisions relating to confiscation, subject to reasons for non-execution or for suspension of execution set out within it.[550] It should be noted that an earlier Framework Decision provides for the provisional freezing of the assets concerned before a confiscation order can be issued.[551] Dual criminality is abolished as regards the standard list of thirty-two crimes. But here, by analogy with the Framework Decision on freezing orders, dual criminality continues to exist for all other acts not on the list that do not constitute offences that *could give rise to confiscation proceedings* in the executing Member State.[552]

---

[541] COM (2008) 766, 20 Nov 2008. On the 2001 Protocol, see II:3.6.1.1 above; and see now also the Directive on the European Investigation Order (II:3.6.1.3 above).

[542] [2014] OJ L 127/39, Art 12(1), as corrected ([2014] OJ L 138/114).

[543] Art 14(1), Dir 2014/42, which repeals Arts 1(a), 3, and 4 of the 2001 Framework Decision (the provisions on reservations from the 1990 Convention on confiscation orders, value confiscation, and mutual assistance) and Arts 1 (first four indents) and 3 of the 2005 Framework Decision (most of the definitions and the rule on extended confiscation).

[544] Arts 3 and 5(2), 2014 Directive.   [545] Art 5(1), 2014 Directive.

[546] Art 6, 2014 Directive; compare to Art 3(3), 2005 Framework Decision.

[547] Art 8, 2014 Directive; compare to Art 5, 2005 Framework Decision.

[548] Arts 7, 10, and 11, 2014 Directive.   [549] Art 2(c), 2006 Framework Decision.

[550] Art 7, 2006 Framework Decision.   [551] See II:3.6.2 above.

[552] Art 6, 2006 Framework Decision.

The grounds to refuse to execute a confiscation order are all optional. They consist of the same grounds applicable to freezing orders, along with several others, including a broader application of the double jeopardy principle, territoriality, *in absentia* trials (as amended by a separate Framework Decision in 2009), the rights of third parties, statute-barring under the executed State's law, and an extended confiscation order in the issuing State going beyond the provisions of the 2005 Framework Decision.[553] Even if the issuing State's order falls within the scope of the 2005 measure, an executing Member State may in effect 'convert' an issuing State's judgment if the two Member States have chosen different options for qualifying the burden and standard of proof as provided for in the 2005 measure.[554]

The 2006 Framework Decision includes the same human rights provisions as the Framework Decision establishing the EAW, with the addition of the proviso that 'any obligations incumbent on judicial authorities' in 'respect' of human rights 'shall remain unaffected'.[555] This wording confirms the interpretation of the human rights clauses in the EU's mutual recognition measures argued for above.[556]

Finally, this Framework Decision provides for remedies to be exercised in the executing State, and the substantive reasons for the confiscation order cannot be challenged there.[557] There is no reference to any procedural standards which must be applicable in the issuing State, although as noted above, the 2005 Framework Decision obliges Member State to provide for remedies to challenge any confiscation orders that are issued.[558]

The Commission reported on the application of this Framework Decision in 2010.[559] According to the Commission, only thirteen Member States had transposed the Framework Decision by that point.[560] Many of them had added additional grounds for refusing execution of a confiscation order (the Commission argues that the list of grounds is exhaustive), or insisted upon a hearing before recognizing any confiscation order. One Member State still fully insisted upon dual criminality in all cases, which was a breach of the Framework Decision. Another Member State added additional grounds for postponement of the execution of an order.

Assessing these measures, the 2006 Framework Decision is subject to the same objections that apply to other EU mutual recognition measures, although at least a separate measure requires the issuing Member State to establish remedies against confiscation orders. It is unfortunate that all the grounds for refusing recognition are optional, including the double jeopardy ground. The human rights provision could be clearer,

---

[553] Art 8, 2006 Framework Decision. On the amendments made to the *in absentia* trial exception in 2009, see II:3.5.2 above. The cross-reference to the extended compensation rules in the 2005 Framework Decision refers to the 2014 Directive instead, once Member States are obliged to apply the latter: see Art 14(2) of the Directive.

[554] Art 8(3), 2006 Framework Decision; see Art 3(2) of the 2005 Framework Decision. This proviso will arguably be redundant once the 2014 Directive is transposed by the Member State concerned, since the Directive applies a single test for extended confiscation.

[555] See paras 13 and 14 of the preamble and Art 1(2), 2006 Framework Decision.　　　[556] II:3.5.2.

[557] Art 9, 2006 Framework Decision.

[558] Art 4 of the 2005 Framework Decision, n 532 above; see now Art 8 of Dir 2014/42, n 543 above.

[559] COM (2010) 428, 23 Aug 2010.

[560] As of 3 June 2015, 23 Member States had notified transposition of the Directive: Council doc 7574/1/15, 3 June 2015.

but human rights would appear to be a ground for resisting recognition, and at least this provision is not so circumscribed as to lose its effectiveness.[561] The 2014 Directive takes a step in the right direction by including detailed rules on safeguards for persons subject to extended confiscation orders, setting a reasonable balance between protection of property rights and the need to take effective measures to combat economic crimes. It is odd that the Directive does not apply extended confiscation to smuggling of persons, offences against EU financial interests, or banking offences regulated by EU legislation.

3.7.5 Probation and parole

Responsibility for rehabilitation of offenders on early release or with probation or suspended sentences can be transferred to another State under a 1964 Council of Europe Convention on supervision of conditionally released and early released offenders, if the offender has his or her residence in a State other than the State of offence. Fewer than half of the Member States have ratified this Convention.[562] In 2008, the Council adopted a Framework Decision which replaced the corresponding provisions of this Convention as from 6 December 2011, the deadline for Member States to implement the Framework Decision.[563] It should be remembered that the detention of EU citizens from other Member States for longer periods than nationals of the host Member State is arguably a breach of EU free movement law, so this Framework Decision may facilitate full application of the principle of equal treatment.[564] This Framework Decision is linked in some cases to the application of the Directive on the European Protection Order.[565]

This Framework Decision is similar to the Framework Decision on the recognition of custodial sentences, which was adopted at the same time.[566] It applies to an exhaustive list of eleven types of probation or parole measures or alternative sanctions, for example restrictions on leaving the territory, instructions relating to behaviour, and reporting obligations.[567] However, Member States can choose to supervise other forms of alternative sanctions and probation measures if they wish.[568] The Framework Decision is subject to the standard human rights provisions.[569]

The mutual recognition obligation only applies to the Member State in which the person concerned is lawfully and ordinarily resident, if the sentenced person 'has returned or wants to return' to that State.[570] The nationality of the person concerned is implicitly irrelevant, although of course it may have been relevant in determining whether that person obtained residence status in the State concerned in the first place. This rule also implies that the sentenced person consents to the transfer, although there

---

[561] Compare with the relevant provision of the Framework Decision on mutual recognition of financial penalties (II:3.7.1.1 above).

[562] ETS 51. For ratification details, see Appendix I.   [563] [2008] OJ L 337/102, Art 25(1).

[564] See II:3.4 above.   [565] See II:3.7.6 below.   [566] See II:3.7.1.2 above.

[567] Art 4(1). It is implicit from the requirement to observe EU free movement law, referred to in the preamble (recital 7), that restrictions on leaving the territory can only be applied in accordance with that law (see II:3.4 above).

[568] Art 4(2).   [569] Art 1(4) and recital 5 in the preamble.   [570] Art 5(1).

is no provision in the Framework Decision which addresses the procedure for deter-mining the intent of the person concerned. As with the Framework Decision on the recognition of custodial sentences, the sentenced person may even request the convict-ing State to forward a request to recognize the probation decision to a Member State *other* than the Member State where the person concerned was previously lawfully or ordinarily resident, although there is no obligation on the latter Member State to accept such requests.[571] To the extent that the person concerned could not be refused entry to that Member State pursuant to EU free movement law,[572] this power of Member States to refuse to recognize the probation order is legally questionable.

The Framework Decision abolishes the dual criminality requirement for the stand-ard list of thirty-two crimes, with the standard three-year sentencing threshold, but for this particular Framework Decision it must particularly be emphasized that the threshold relates to *punishability*, not to the actual sentence received—so in at least some cases suspended sentences will still satisfy this threshold. As with the Framework Decisions on pre-trial orders and the recognition of custodial sentences, it is open to Member States to main dual criminality requirements by way of derogation.[573] The executing Member State may refuse to execute a decision on grounds of: inadequate certification; requests exceeding the scope of the Framework Decision; double jeop-ardy; residual (or retained) dual criminality; statute barring (if the executing Member State had jurisdiction over the offence); immunity under the executing State's law; the age of criminal responsibility; *in absentia* trials (this provision was amended by the 2009 Framework Decision on this subject); medical treatment that cannot be provided in the executing State; a probation period of under six months; or territoriality.[574] The Framework Decision provides for competence over supervision measures to transfer to the executing Member State,[575] with the possibility of transferring competence back to the issuing State in certain cases.[576]

Compared to the Council of Europe Convention on this issue, the Framework Decision contains more grounds for refusal of recognition, but these are more spe-cific than under the Convention, which includes grounds such as 'essential interests'; moreover, all of the grounds for refusal under the Framework Decision are optional, not mandatory.[577] Furthermore, the Framework Decision in principle waives the dual criminality rule, which is mandatory under the Convention,[578] and the underlying mutual recognition rule binds all Member States and is wider in scope.[579]

---

[571]   Art 5(2) to 5(4).

[572]   For a summary of the relevant substantive and procedural law, see I:7.4.1. Since in many cases per-sons covered by the Framework Decision will have been sentenced to a suspended sentence, it must follow that the crime they committed will often not be serious enough to justify refusal of entry pursuant to EU free movement law.

[573]   Art 10.   [574]   Art 11. On the revised *in absentia* trial exception, see II:3.5.2 above.

[575]   Art 7(1). See also Arts 13 and 14, but note the possible derogation in Art 14(3), and the consequential provisions in Arts 14(4) to (6) and 17. See also Art 19 on amnesty, pardon, and review, and Art 20, on end-ing jurisdiction of the executing State.

[576]   Art 7(2).   [577]   Compare to Art 7 of the Convention, n 562 above.

[578]   Art 4 of the Convention.

[579]   See Art 5 of the Convention, which gives signatory States the option to carry out supervision of the sentence only, not enforcement.

The Commission's report on the application of this measure states that only half of the Member States applied it by early 2014.[580] The latest indication is that only seventeen Member States apply it.[581] At the time of the Commission report, no transfers had actually taken place yet. According to the Commission, some Member States breached their obligations under the Framework Decision by adapting the sentence or not providing for all mandatory alternatives to detention. Also, some Member States added additional grounds for refusal, or did not respect time limits. On the whole, it seems that the potentially useful role which this measure might play in ensuring social rehabilitation and equal treatment of foreign prisoners or other convicted persons is being undercut by many Member States' failure to apply it, and the Commission's apparent indifference toward bringing infringement actions, since it gained the power to do so.

3.7.6 European Protection Order

In 2011, the EU adopted a Directive creating a 'European Protection Order' (EPO) in criminal matters, which Member States had to implement by 11 January 2015.[582] A parallel measure regulates protection orders issued pursuant to civil proceedings.[583]

The Directive defines an EPO as a decision taken by a judicial or equivalent authority concerning to a 'protection measure', which means a prohibition or restriction 'imposed on a person causing danger in order to protect a protected person against a criminal act which may endanger his [or her] life, physical or psychological integrity, dignity, personal liberty or sexual integrity'. A 'protected person' is the subject of the protection order, and the restrictions or prohibitions can constitute an order not to enter certain places where the protected person lives or visits, a prohibition or restriction of forms of contact with the protected person, or an obligation to keep a specified distance from that person.[584]

The EPO can be issued whenever the protected person stays or resides, or intends to stay or reside, in the executing Member State,[585] after a request by the protected person to the authorities of the issuing State.[586] The person causing danger has the right to be heard before the EPO is issued and to challenge it, unless he or she already had these rights in the earlier proceedings.[587] If the application for an EPO is refused, the person concerned must be informed about available remedies under national law.[588]

---

[580] COM (2014) 57, 3 Feb 2014.

[581] Council doc 5776/2/15, 22 July 2015. The information was correct as of 22 July 2015. It should be recalled that the UK has opted out in the meantime (see II:3.2.5 above).

[582] Dir 2011/99 ([2011] OJ L 338/2), Art 21(1). All references in this sub-section are to this Directive, except where mentioned.

[583] Reg 606/2013 ([2013] OJ L 181/4). On the competence issues concerning these measures, see II:3.2.4 above. On the substance of the Reg, see II:8.5.1.2 below.

[584] Arts 2 and 5. See also the other EU measures relating to crime victims, discussed in II:4.7 below. The measures applied to the 'person causing danger' might be linked to the Framework Decisions on pre-trial supervision or probation (Art 7(k): see II:3.6.3 and II:3.7.5 above). When the original national protection order is issued, the authority should inform the protected person about the possibility of applying for an EPO (Art 6(5)).

[585] Art 6(1).

[586] Art 6(2). The request can also be submitted via the authorities of the executing State (Art 6(3)).

[587] Art 6(4).   [588] Art 6(7).

The executing State's authority has an obligation to recognize the EPO and to take 'any measure that would be available under its national law in a similar case to ensure the protection of the protected person', unless there is a reason for non-recognition of the EPO.[589] It must inform the protected person and the person causing danger of this decision.[590] An executing State's authority can refuse to recognize an EPO if: the EPO is incomplete or delayed; the requirement of a prior relevant obligation or prohibition in the issuing State was not satisfied; the acts concerned do not constitute a criminal offence in that State (ie dual criminality); there was an amnesty in the executing State for the act concerned, and the act fell within its own competence; there was immunity in the executing State for the person causing danger; the act was statute-barred in that State; on grounds of double jeopardy; there is no criminal responsibility on grounds of age in the executing State; or on territoriality grounds.[591] In case of refusal, the executing State must inform the protected person and the person causing danger; the protected person must also be informed of any right to appeal under national law, or the right to apply for a national protection order in that State.[592]

The executing State is responsible for the enforcement of the EPO, in particular for bringing criminal or non-criminal proceedings in the event of breach of the EPO, and for taking any 'urgent and provisional measure' to put an end to the breach.[593] The issuing State retains jurisdiction to review, withdraw, or modify the protection measure.[594] However, the executing State may discontinue the enforcement of the EPO if it is clear that the protected person does not stay or reside or has left that State,[595] thereby drawing a strong link between this measure and the free movement rights of the victims and, implicitly, their abusers.[596] It may also discontinue enforcement if the maximum term of the order has been reached, the review by the issuing State has caused legal problems, or if a probation, parole, or supervision order has been transferred.[597]

In general, this is a useful initiative that should enhance the free movement of the victims of domestic violence in particular. However, it is problematic that they are not guaranteed a remedy against the refusal to recognize an EPO in the executing State, given the potential importance of that decision for their safety.

3.8 Administrative Cooperation and EU Funding

EU funds have made an increasingly significant contribution to the development of judicial cooperation. First of all, the EU budget funded the 'Grotius' programme on incentives and exchanges for legal practitioners, which was established initially from 1996 until 2000,[598] and then extended for 2001–02.[599] This programme was then subsumed within a general third pillar funding programme, 'AGIS', running from 2003–07.[600] This

---

[589] Art 9(1). This should correspond to the issuing State's measure as far as possible (Art 9(2)).
[590] Art 9(3).   [591] Art 10(1).   [592] Art 10(2).
[593] Art 11(1) and (2). The issuing State must be notified of breaches (Art 12).
[594] Art 13. Where a pre-trial supervision order or a probation order has been issued, the relevant provisions of the other EU measure apply (Art 13(3)).
[595] Art 14(1)(a).   [596] See generally II:3.4 above.   [597] Art 14(1)(b) to (d).
[598] [1996] OJ L 287/3.   [599] [2001] OJ L 186/1.   [600] [2002] OJ L 203/5.

was in turn replaced by criminal justice programmes for the periods 2007–13[601] and 2014–20.[602]

As for administrative cooperation, the Council has adopted a Joint Action on the exchange of liaison magistrates.[603] Like their police and customs counterparts,[604] liaison magistrates are in effect the 'ambassadors' of one legal system to another, attempting to facilitate cross-border cooperation in practice. The Council subsequently adopted a Joint Action establishing a European judicial network in criminal matters, which was replaced in 2008 by a Decision on the same subject.[605] The judicial network is a more formal structure consisting of contact points in each Member State, holding regular meetings, establishing directories of information and linked by a telecommunications network.

Finally, there are informal EU networks for legislative cooperation[606] and judicial training, the latter of which is the subject of EU funding programmes.[607] Measures to expand judicial training in the EU form part of the Stockholm Programme.[608]

3.9 External Relations

Apart from its special association with Norway, Iceland, Switzerland, and (in future) Liechtenstein,[609] and the particular process of evaluating States negotiating to join the EU,[610] the EU has also negotiated treaties with the USA concerning extradition and mutual assistance, and a treaty with Japan regarding mutual assistance. The treaties with the USA, which entered into force on 1 February 2010,[611] do not replace national bilateral treaties with the USA on these matters, but rather supplement those national treaties; the EU undertook to ensure, pursuant to the EU-USA treaties, that its Member States would reach separate agreements with the USA as regards their bilateral treaties. These bilateral agreements were all eventually finalized.

The EU-US extradition treaty has amended Member States' bilateral extradition treaties with the United States as regards widening the list of extradition offences, simplifying the transmission of documents, furnishing additional information, the temporary surrender of persons already in custody, competing requests for extradition, simplified procedures where the fugitive consents to extradition, the treatment of sensitive information, transit of fugitives, and the exclusion of the death penalty for fugitives. The mutual assistance treaty has amended bilateral treaties (where they exist) as regards

---

[601] [2007] OJ L 58/13.

[602] Reg 1382/2013 establishing a Justice Programme ([2013] OJ L 354/73).

[603] [1996] OJ L 105/1.   [604] See II:7.6.3 below.

[605] [1998] OJ L 191/4 and [2008] OJ L 348/130. See the website of the Network: <http://www.ejn-crimjust.europa.eu/>.

[606] See the Resolution establishing a network for legislative cooperation ([2008] OJ C 326/1).

[607] See the Commission communication on judicial training (COM (2006) 356, 29 June 2006), the Council conclusions in the press release of the JHA Council of 5–6 June 2003, and the Resolution of the Council and the Member States ([2008] OJ C 299/1).

[608] [2010] OJ C 115, point 1.2.6. Commission communications on this issue are due in 2011 (COM (2010) 171, 20 Apr 2010).

[609] See II:3.2.5 above.   [610] See II:7.11 below.

[611] [2003] OJ L 181/25. See the decision on conclusion of the treaties ([2009] OJ L 291/40). The extradition treaty has been extended to the Netherlands Antilles: [2009] OJ L 325/4.

the supply of banking information, joint investigation teams, video-conferencing of witnesses or experts, expedited transmission of documents, the extension of mutual assistance rules to administrative authorities, the protection of personal data, and confidentiality. However, the grounds for refusal of mutual assistance in existing treaties (or, in the absence of such treaties, in national law) are preserved.

These agreements were highly controversial, in particular for the secretive manner in which they were negotiated, but also for their content, especially as regards the prospect of joint investigation teams between officials of Member States and the USA and the weakness of the provisions on personal data protection.[612]

The EU/Japan mutual assistance treaty was signed in 2009, just before the Treaty of Lisbon entered into force.[613] It was then concluded and entered into force on 2 January 2011.[614]

Following the entry into force of the Treaty of Lisbon, the general EU rules on external relations apply to this area,[615] raising questions about the scope of EU external competence, as regards, for instance, the question of when agreements in this area must or may take the form of 'mixed' agreements, entailing the participation of both the EU and its Member States. However, the external competence deriving from EU measures in this area adopted before the entry into force of the Treaty of Lisbon will depend, until those measures are amended or replaced, upon the rules governing the EU external competence related to the former third pillar—which have not yet been clarified by the Court of Justice.[616] A fundamental question will be whether the Court will take an assertive approach to the extent of the EU's external competence as regards pre-Lisbon or post-Lisbon measures in this area, by analogy with the approach it has taken to external competence over civil jurisdiction treaties.[617] On this point, Declaration 36 in the Final Act of the Treaty of Lisbon states that Member States are still able to conclude treaties in this field 'insofar as such agreements comply with Union law'; this confirms that Member States have not lost all authority to sign treaties in this area, but does not limit the scope or intensity of the EU's competence.[618] It should be noted, however, that many EU criminal law mutual recognition measures contain detailed provisions governing Member States' obligations to disapply prior treaties (as regards relations between Member States), along with authorization to retain existing agreements or conclude new agreements that further simplify the application of the relevant mutual recognition rules.[619] It is arguable that the latter provisions refer only to agreements

---

[612] See V Mitsilegas, 'The New EU-USA Cooperation on Extradition, Mutual Legal Assistance and the Exchange of Police Data' (2003) 8 EFARev 515.

[613] For the text of the treaty, see [2010] OJ L 39/19.   [614] [2010] OJ L 343/1.

[615] See generally II:2.7.1 above.   [616] See II:2.7.2 above.

[617] See *Opinion 1/2003*, [2006] ECR I-1145, and generally II:8.9 below. It should be noted, however, that *Opinion 1/2003* focused on exclusive competence regarding civil *jurisdiction*, with exclusive competence over mutual recognition as a corollary. On external competence regarding criminal jurisdiction matters, see II:6.11 below.

[618] See equally II:8.9 below.

[619] For instance, see Art 31 of the EAW Framework Decision ([2002] OJ L 190/1). The Court of Justice has confirmed that these clauses do not authorize the Member States to retain in force the treaties that they are explicitly obliged not to apply any longer: Case C-296/08 PPU *Santesteban Goicoechea* [2008] ECR I-6307. On the power to retain or conclude special treaties, see by analogy the civil law judgment of the Court of Justice in C-533/08 *TNT-Express* [2010] ECR I-4107.

between Member States, not between Member States and third States.[620] A few EU measures also directly regulate some external aspects of the relevant issue.[621]

In the field of domestic criminal procedure, the EU's power to set minimum standards only necessarily means that the external competence in this area is shared. Also in this area, as noted already, a particular procedure for consultation of the Council of Europe has been established.[622] More generally, there are Council conclusions urging continued cooperation with the Council of Europe in the criminal law field.[623]

3.10 Conclusions

Mutual recognition is an attractive principle because the 'free movement of prosecutions' holds out the prospect of speedier and more effective prosecution, therefore bringing more criminals to justice and increasing public security across the European Union. But as noted at the outset, effective prosecutions are not the only objective which a criminal justice system must pursue.

Should mutual recognition proceed without substantive criminal law harmonization,[624] and a degree of harmonization of procedural law? On the first point, the abolition of dual criminality without a degree of harmonization of substantive law has provoked a hostile reaction from the public and national constitutional courts as regards the protection of a State's nationals, and defensive measures have therefore been invoked, including weakening the abolition of the principle of dual criminality in some later mutual recognition measures. The EU's model for mutual recognition in criminal law cannot be defended by reference to the internal market or civil law model, both of which require a degree of harmonization of substantive law or of conflict rules, contain human rights exceptions, and deal with matters which are much less sensitive from the perspective of national sovereignty and the protection of civil liberties.[625]

On the second point, as discussed further in Chapter 4, the EU has embarked upon the process of adopting rules on suspects' rights, but this process started years after most of the mutual recognition measures were adopted. In any event, the CJEU seems to be insisting on a strong degree of mutual trust in each Member State's judicial system, quite independently of the adoption of these measures.

As a result, the current state of mutual recognition in EU criminal law is problematic. The principle is justifiable, including the abolition of dual criminality, only if there

[620] This is explicit as regards the Framework Decisions on financial penalties ([2005] OJ L 76/16, Art 18) and on confiscation ([2006] OJ L 328/59, Art 21). There is no such provision in the Framework Decisions on freezing orders ([2003] OJ L 196/45) or on recognition of prior convictions ([2008] OJ L 220/32).

[621] See Arts 21 and 28(4) of the EAW Framework Decision, n 619 above.

[622] See II:3.3.5 above.   [623] [2009] OJ C 50/8.

[624] As discussed below (II:5.5), the EU has only harmonized the definitions of certain offences, frequently leaving options to Member States as regards these definitions. Similarly only a modest number of crimes are subjected to harmonized definitions as a result of UN or Council of Europe treaties. In EU mutual recognition measures, the principle of dual criminality has been abolished for a much longer list of crimes. See S Peers, 'Mutual Recognition and Criminal Law in the European Union: Has the Council Got it Wrong?' (2004) 41 CMLRev 5, at 26–34.

[625] See the comments in Peers, ibid, 23–6; for an alternative view, see J Wouters and F Naert, 'Of Arrest Warrants, Terrorist Offences and Extradition Deals: An Appraisal of the EU's Main Criminal Law Measures Against Terrorism after "11 September"' (2004) 41 CMLRev 909.

is a sufficient degree of harmonization of substantive and procedural standards in parallel, and the territoriality exception to mutual recognition is fully maintained. The strong version of the mutual trust rule assumes too easily the fairness of each Member State's proceedings, and many EU measures include an over-broad abolition of dual criminality, well beyond those crimes which Member States have harmonized *de jure* as a consequence of EU measures or international treaties or *de facto* as a result of spontaneous harmonization. Only a U-turn from the Court of Justice, taking more account of the adoption of Directives on suspects' rights (and their implementation in practice) could redress the balance.

4

Criminal Law

Criminal Procedure

4.1 Introduction

In order to ensure that substantive criminal law achieves its intended objectives, it is obviously necessary both to investigate alleged crimes and to prosecute the alleged offenders, and then to carry out any sentence imposed. But in democratic societies committed to human rights, ensuring effective prosecutions cannot be the sole object-ive. Since it is unacceptable to punish the innocent with the force of criminal sanctions such as imprisonment, the process of determining guilt or innocence needs to be fair. So the right to a fair trial carries a prominent place in any general international human rights treaty or national constitutional bill of rights, along with associated principles like the legality and non-retroactivity of criminal law.

As discussed in detail in Chapter 3 of this volume, the EU has tried to ensure mutual recognition in criminal matters, but there are doubts about the fairness of foreign crim-inal procedures. In order to address these doubts, the EU aims to set standards for domestic criminal procedural law. However, there have been objections in turn to such measures due to the limited legal powers of the EU as regards domestic criminal pro-cedure, qualms about harmonization of national law in such a sensitive and distinctive field, and doubts about the necessity of such measures in light of the fair trial provisions of the European Convention of Human Rights (ECHR) and the possibility of enforc-ing those rights in the European Court of Human Rights. But in the absence of har-monized procedural rights, the 'free movement of prosecutions and sentences' could arguably lead to the violation of the right to a fair trial. To address these concerns, the Treaty of Lisbon provides for a specific legal base for the adoption of measures regard-ing domestic criminal procedure, and the EU has begun to adopt an important body of legislation in this area.

This chapter examines that law in detail, starting with the basic issues of the insti-tutional framework, an overview of measures adopted, legal competence, territorial scope, human rights, and overlaps with other (non-JHA) EU law. It then examines the EU's harmonization of domestic criminal procedure, in the specific fields referred to in the Treaty of Lisbon in turn: evidence law, suspects' rights, and victims' rights.

4.2 Institutional Framework and Overview

4.2.1 Cooperation before the Treaty of Amsterdam

Before the Treaty of Amsterdam, cooperation on criminal procedural issues was non-existent between Member States, who were reliant on the ECHR to set minimum stand-ards on this issue.

4.2.2 Treaty of Amsterdam

The key relevant provision of the Treaties, following the Treaty of Amsterdam, was Article 31(c) of the TEU, inserted by that Treaty, which provided for powers to ensure 'compatibility in rules applicable in the Member States, as may be necessary to improve' cooperation on criminal matters.

From the outset, there was interest in harmonization of procedural law. While the Tampere conclusions referred to mutual recognition as the 'cornerstone' of EU criminal law, they also referred to the 'necessary approximation of legislation'. Approximation and mutual recognition together 'would facilitate co-operation between authorities and the judicial protection of individual rights'. More specifically, 'minimum standards should be drawn up on the protection of the victims of crime, in particular on crime victims' access to justice and on their rights to compensation for damages'. The subsequent work programme on mutual recognition referred also to 'mechanisms for safeguarding the rights of third parties, victims and suspects'.[1]

While the EU agreed on a number of mutual recognition measures before the entry into force of the Treaty of Lisbon, there was no real development as regards the law of evidence or suspects and defendants' rights.[2] However, victims' rights were addressed in particular by both a third pillar Framework Decision on their position in criminal procedure and by an EC law (as it then was) measure on compensation.[3]

Despite this modest legislative outcome and the limits on its jurisdiction, the Court of Justice received five references for interpretation of the Framework Decision on crime victims' rights.[4] This case law boosted the relevance of the Framework Decision, when the Court's judgment in *Pupino* ruled that the measure had indirect effect.[5]

4.2.3 Treaty of Lisbon

The relevant provision of the Treaties following the entry into force of the Treaty of Lisbon is Article 82(2) of the Treaty on the Functioning of the European Union (TFEU):

> 2. To the extent necessary to facilitate mutual recognition of judgments and judicial decisions and police and judicial cooperation in criminal matters having a cross-border dimension, the European Parliament and the Council may, by means of directives adopted in accordance with the ordinary legislative procedure, establish minimum rules. Such rules shall take into account the differences between the legal traditions and systems of the Member States.
>
>   They shall concern:
>
>   (a) mutual admissibility of evidence between Member States;
>
>   (b) the rights of individuals in criminal procedure;

---

[1] [2001] OJ C 12/10. See earlier Commission communication on the issue (COM (2000) 495, 26 July 2000).

[2] See II:4.5 and II: 4.6 below.   [3] See II:4.7 below.

[4] Cases: C-105/03 *Pupino* [2005] ECR I-5285; C-467/05 *Dell'Orto* [2007] ECR I-5557; C-404/07 *Katz* [2008] ECR I-7607; C-205/09 *Eredics* [2010] ECR I-10231; and C-483/09 *Gueye* [2011] ECR I-8263. On the substance of these cases, see II:4.7 below.

[5] Ibid.

(c) the rights of victims of crime;

(d) any other specific aspects of criminal procedure which the Council has identified in advance by a decision; for the adoption of such a decision, the Council shall act unanimously after obtaining the consent of the European Parliament.

Adoption of the minimum rules referred to in this paragraph shall not prevent Member States from maintaining or introducing a higher level of protection for individuals.

The detailed Article 82(2) TFEU replaced the previous vague power regarding ensuring compatibility of national law. Furthermore, the Treaty of Lisbon made a fundamental change to the decision-making in this area, applying the 'ordinary legislative procedure' (qualified majority voting in Council and joint powers for the EP) in place of the prior rule of unanimity in Council with consultation of the EP. However, Article 82(3) TFEU sets out a special emergency brake rule, allowing a Member State to halt discussions when a measure proposed pursuant to Article 82(2) 'would affect fundamental aspects of its criminal justice system'. This special procedure (which has never been used to date), which also applies to the adoption of substantive criminal law measures,[6] is discussed in detail in Chapter 2 of this volume.[7]

This special procedure applies to Article 82(2), but not to Article 82(1), so it is necessary to distinguish between these two legal bases.[8] The related power to adopt measures concerning the prevention and settlement of conflicts of jurisdiction (Article 82(1)(b)) is discussed in Chapter 6 of this volume.[9] Criminal procedure issues might also result from measures adopted regarding Eurojust and the European Public Prosecutor (Articles 85 and 86 TFEU); such issues are also discussed in Chapter 6.[10]

Since the entry into force of the Treaty of Lisbon, the EU's powers over criminal procedure have been implemented by three adopted Directives (and three further proposed Directives) dealing with suspects' rights, and by a general Directive on victims' rights, alongside some special rules on victims in substantive criminal law legislation.[11] The power to adopt EU measures in *other* areas of criminal procedure (Article 82(2)(d) TFEU) has not yet been invoked. Neither have there been any proposals to harmonize evidence law (Article 82(2)(a) TFEU).

4.2.4 Competence issues

Before the entry into force of the Treaty of Lisbon, there was a dispute as to whether the EU could harmonize domestic criminal procedural law, in particular because Article 31(1)(a) to (d) of the previous TEU referred essentially to cross-border matters, with only Article 31(1)(c) referring to powers to 'ensur[e] compatibility in rules applicable in the Member States, as may be necessary to improve such cooperation'. This issue

---

[6] Art 83(3) TFEU; see II:5.2.3 below.   [7] See II:2.2.3.4.1.   [8] See II:3.2.4 above.

[9] II:6.6 to II:6.8. On jurisdiction over offences as such, see II:6.5.

[10] II:6.9 and II:6.10. On the question of competing legal bases which might result, see II:6.2.4 below.

[11] See respectively II:4.6 and II:4.7 below. Dir 2014/41 on confiscation orders ([2014] OJ L 127/39) has the dual legal base of Arts 82(2) and 83(1) TFEU, although it does not concern any of the issues listed in Art 82(2). It should have been based on Art 82(1)(a) and/or (d), since it facilitates mutual recognition, along with Art 83(1) (since it harmonizes the penalty of confiscation orders for specified crimes).

remains relevant after the entry into force of the Treaty of Lisbon, as long as there are still pre-existing measures in force whose validity could still be called into question. On this point, the opening words of the previous Article 31(1) TEU provided that '[c]ommon action on judicial cooperation in criminal matters shall *include*' the following list of measures, indicating clearly that this list was non-exhaustive.[12] In any event, a broad interpretation of Article 31(1)(c) could be envisaged, in particular since the harmonization of law on procedural protection for suspects could in fact have facilitated national courts' willingness to cooperate with foreign courts.[13]

The distinction between Article 82(2) and Article 82(1) was discussed in Chapter 3 of this volume. As for Article 82(2) in particular, the adoption of measures on domestic criminal procedure has to be 'necessary' to 'facilitate mutual recognition and police and [criminal law] cooperation', which has to have a 'cross-border dimension'. Only 'minimum rules' can be adopted, and these rules have to 'take into account' national legal differences. In light of Article 82(2)(d), this list of powers (unlike the list of powers in the prior Article 31(1) TEU) must necessarily be exhaustive.

First of all, the concept of 'minimum' rules is implicitly further defined in the third sub-paragraph of Article 82(2), which provides that Member States are free to introduce or maintain higher standards for individuals. This proviso must mean that Member States are free to provide for higher standards of protection for suspects and victims than the EU measures provide for, but not lower standards.

Next, the requirement to take account of national legal traditions and systems is nearly identical to the general requirement set in Article 67(1) TFEU that the EU must 'respect' such systems and traditions. However, it is arguable that a requirement to 'take into account' is more of a positive obligation than an obligation to 'respect', perhaps entailing an obligation to reflect those differences in the adopted legislation, rather than merely to refrain from damaging national legal systems in that legislation.

This brings us to the most important limitation: the requirement that the measure must be necessary to facilitate mutual recognition and policing and criminal law cooperation with a cross-border dimension. It might be tempting, at first sight, to conclude that this power is be limited to matters which have a specific relationship with cross-border proceedings, like the EU's civil law powers.[14] But the wording of the criminal law power ('cross-border dimension') is broader than the wording of the civil law power ('cross-border implications'). Moreover, the phrase 'cross-border dimensions' also governs the scope of the European Union's substantive criminal law powers,[15] and it is hard to believe that the Union's power to harmonize substantive criminal law was intended to be limited to cases where an alleged offence has factual links to more than one Member State. Furthermore, the EU's specific criminal procedure powers would

---

[12] See similarly the discussion of competence in II:5.2.4 below.

[13] This interpretation is confirmed by the Opinions in Cases C-105/03 *Pupino* [2005] ECR I-5285 (paras 48–52) and C-303/05 *Advocaten voor de Wereld* [2007] ECR I-3633 (note 21). See also the Opinion in Case C-467/05 *Dell'Orto* [2007] ECR I-5557, paras 36–7. For a different view, see V Mitsilegas, 'Trust-Building Measures in the European Judicial Area in Criminal Matters: Issues of Competence, Legitimacy and Institutional Balance' in T Balzacq and S Carrera, eds., *Security versus Freedom? A Challenge for Europe's Future* (Ashgate, 2006), 282, who asserts that the previous TEU conferred no competence to adopt measures on criminal procedure.

[14] See II:8.2.4 below.   [15] See Art 83(1) TFEU, discussed in II:5.2.4 below.

be rendered meaningless if they could only be applied in cross-border proceedings, given that Article 82(1) already sets out a power to regulate criminal proceedings with a purely cross-border nature.

In particular, although rules on mutual admissibility of evidence must necessarily have a link to cross-border proceedings, it will be hard in practice to limit their impact to cross-border cases, given that some degree of harmonization of the laws of evidence is necessary in order to ensure mutual admissibility, and that such harmonization cannot easily be restricted to cases which have a specific cross-border element, given that the evidence might be collected before it was clear that such an element was present. The point applies equally to the European Union's powers as regards victims' and suspects' rights (which might also concern evidence issues),[16] *a fortiori* because the Treaty does not insist upon as strong a cross-border element in these matters as it requires as regards evidence law. The better approach to the limit on the European Union's criminal procedure is therefore to insist on a *degree of likelihood* that the rules in question will have a particular impact on cross-border proceedings. This will be the case in particular whenever there is (in effect) a 'free movement clause' in the legislation, which provides specifically that Member States could not refuse to recognize judgments and other decisions of judicial authorities on grounds falling within the scope of a measure adopted pursuant to Article 82(2) TFEU. This would parallel the limits which the Court has set as regards the comparable general power to harmonize law for the purposes of facilitating the internal market.[17] Of course, it also assumes that Member States would otherwise have the power or even the obligation to refuse to recognize other Member States' criminal law decisions on human rights grounds, an issue examined further below.[18] More generally, it must be kept in mind that measures adopted pursuant to Article 82(2) are expressly not limited to those necessary to facilitate *mutual recognition*, but can facilitate police and criminal law cooperation more generally.

Finally, there are questions regarding the scope of the individual provisions of Article 82(2). In the absence of any specific limit, the power to regulate suspects' rights conferred by Article 82(2)(b) applies to any aspect of the right to a fair trial (other than the double jeopardy rule, as noted above), provided that the general limits on the powers conferred by Article 82(2) are complied with. As for victims' rights, Article 82(2)(c) does not apply to the harmonization of rules concerning *state compensation* of crime victims, which was the subject of a Directive adopted pursuant to the previous 'residual powers' clause of the EC Treaty,[19] because Article 82 TFEU only applies to 'judicial cooperation'. In the absence of any other specific legal base addressing this issue, it remains within the scope of the Treaty's residual powers clause.[20]

The next key issue is the distinction between Article 82(2) TFEU and other Justice and Home Affairs (JHA) legal bases. The Treaty powers relating to Eurojust (Article 85

---

[16] See II:4.7 below (as regards victims' rights) and Art 6(2)(d) ECHR (as regards evidence).

[17] See particularly the tobacco advertising case law: Cases C-376/98 *Germany v EP and Council* [2000] ECR I-8419 and C-380/03 *Germany v EP and Council* [2006] ECR I-11573.

[18] II:3.3.5 and II:3.5.2.

[19] Dir 2004/80 ([2004] OJ L 261/15), based on the prior Art 308 EC. On the substance of this Directive, see II:4.7 below.

[20] Art 308 EC became Art 352 TFEU after the entry into force of the Treaty of Lisbon.

TFEU) must be distinguished from Article 82(2), since there is no emergency brake applicable to Article 85. It should follow that any harmonization of national criminal procedure directly related to the functioning of Eurojust, in particular (but not only) concerning the specific functions of Eurojust mentioned in Article 85(1)(a), (b), and (c), falls within the scope of Article 85. Similarly, any suspects' rights issues directly relating to the European Public Prosecutor fall within the scope of Article 86 TFEU.

4.2.5 Territorial scope

Prior to the entry into force of the Treaty of Lisbon, there were no opt-outs for Member States in this area, so all Member States are covered by the Framework Decision on crime victims. After the entry into force of the Treaty of Lisbon, which extended the British and Irish opt-outs to new measures in the area of policing and criminal law,[21] the UK and Ireland both opted in to the first two Directives on suspects' rights, but not the Directive on access to a lawyer or the subsequent three proposals on this issue. Both Member States opted in to the Directive on crime victims' rights.

   On the other hand, Denmark is now excluded from measures in this area although Denmark remains bound by the prior Framework Decision on crime victims, and all Member States are bound by the Directive on compensation for crime victims. None of the measures discussed in this chapter apply to the non-Member States associated with the Schengen *acquis*.

4.3 Human Rights

4.3.1 Right to a fair trial

As noted at the outset, the human rights principle of greatest relevance to criminal procedure is the right to a fair trial.[22] This right is set out in national constitutions, Article 6 ECHR, and Article 14 of the International Covenant on Civil and Political Rights (ICCPR). Article 6(2) ECHR expressly sets out a right to presumption of innocence in criminal cases, and Article 6(3) sets out minimum rights to be informed promptly of an accusation (Article 6(3)(a)), to have time and facilities for a defence (Article 6(3)(b)), to have access to a defence lawyer and free legal aid if 'the interests of justice' require (Article 6(3)(c)), to examine witnesses against and call witnesses for the defence (Article 6(3)(d)), and to 'to have the free assistance of an interpreter if he [or she] cannot understand or speak the language used in court' (Article 6(3)(e)). The Seventh Protocol to the ECHR, which has been ratified by a large majority of Member States, also includes the right to an appeal in criminal cases, the right to compensation for wrongful conviction, and freedom from double jeopardy; these rights also appear in the ICCPR.[23]

---

[21] For the detail, see II:2.2.5.1 above.

[22] For a detailed analysis, see S Trechsel and S Summers, *Human Rights in Criminal Proceedings* (OUP, 2005).

[23] Arts 2–4, Seventh Protocol. For ratification of the Protocol by Member States, see Appendix I. Double jeopardy is discussed in II:6.3.1 below.

As a case study in the relationship between the ECHR and EU law adopted in this field,[24] the case law on the right to an interpreter pursuant to Article 6(3)(e) ECHR should be examined in more detail. According to the European Court of Human Rights, the right applies 'not only to oral statements made at the trial hearing but also to documentary material and the pre-trial proceedings', and in particular to 'the translation or interpretation of all those documents or statements in the proceedings instituted against him which it is necessary for him to understand or to have rendered into the court's language in order to have the benefit of a fair trial'. However, the right 'does not go so far as to require a written translation of all items of written evidence or official documents in the procedure', but 'should be such as to enable the defendant to have knowledge of the case against him and to defend himself, notably by being able to put before the court his version of the events'. Moreover, 'the obligation of the competent authorities is not limited to the appointment of an interpreter but, if they are put on notice in the particular circumstances, may also extend to a degree of subsequent control over the adequacy of the interpretation provided.'[25] The Court has clarified that oral linguistic assistance (instead of translation) may be sufficient as regards documents; that the key issues are the 'linguistic knowledge' of the defendant, the nature of the offence with which the defendant is charged and any communications addressed to him by the domestic authorities; and that, even though the conduct of the defence is mainly a matter for the accused and his or her lawyer, the domestic courts are the 'ultimate guardians' of the right.[26] The right to 'free' assistance obviously means that the accused cannot be required to pay the relevant costs.[27] However, a waiver of the right is possible if the waiver can 'be established in an unequivocal manner and be attended by minimum safeguards commensurate with its importance' and if that waiver does 'not run counter to any important public interest'.[28]

4.3.2 Detention

Detention is authorized by Article 5 ECHR, provided that the detention is lawful (Article 5(1)), subject to the other provisions of Article 5 guaranteeing information for the detainee (Article 5(2)), judicial review (Article 5(4)), and compensation for wrongful detention (Article 5(5)). [29] The lawful grounds for detention include not only detention after a criminal conviction imposing a custodial sentence (Article 5(1)(a)), but also detention pending trial (Article 5(1)(c)) and detention pursuant to extradition proceedings (Article 5(1)(f)). Everyone subject to pre-trial detention is entitled to be brought 'promptly' before a judge or another judicial officer, and must receive a trial within a reasonable time, with the possibility of release pending trial (Article 5(3)).

---

[24] On the EU legislation, see I:4.6.1. Note also the obligations to inform a person of the reasons for any arrest or criminal charges, and of the nature and cause of any criminal accusation, 'in a language which he [or she] understands' (Arts 5(2) and 6(3)(a) ECHR).

[25] See, for instance, *Kamasinski v Austria*, (A-168), para 74, referring also to *Ludicke, Belkacem and Koç v Germany* (A-29), para 48.

[26] See paras 70–2 of *Hermi v Italy*, 18 Oct 2006.   [27] *Ozturk v Germany* (A-73).

[28] *Protopapa v Turkey*, 24 Feb 2009, para 82.

[29] On the issue of detention in the context of immigration and asylum law, see I:7.3.2.

4.3.3 Application to EU law

First of all, a criminal proceeding must first fall within the scope of EU law, in order for the EU Charter and the general principles of EU law to apply.[30] Clearly any dispute concerning the application of the Directives on criminal suspects' rights falls within the scope of EU law. The free movement issues discussed below are also within the scope of EU law.[31] But are there also other cases where EU law would apply to an issue of domestic criminal procedure?

The Court of Justice of the European Union (CJEU) has not yet fully answered this question, but it gave an indication in the *Fransson* judgment,[32] concerning the scope of the EU Charter ban on double jeopardy. The CJEU said that the Charter could apply to a criminal proceeding in relation to VAT, since the EU had harmonized the *substance* of VAT law, and there was a link with the financial interests of the Union (since EU revenues are partly derived from VAT), even though EU legislation did not harmonize the rules on collection or enforcement of VAT. Presumably this ruling applies by analogy to other Charter rights relevant to criminal proceedings. However, it is still open to debate whether EU law only applies where there is a link to the financial interests of the EU, or perhaps another important EU interest (such as counterfeiting the euro), or whether criminal proceedings which concern any enforcement of EU prohibitions, or the implementation of EU measures which criminalize acts,[33] would also fall within the scope of EU law, meaning that the defence rights in the Charter will apply.

As for the specific rights protected, the Court of Justice has recognized the right to a fair trial as part of the general principles on numerous occasions, in particular in the context of criminal proceedings, and has made references to ECHR jurisprudence in that context.[34] That right also appears in Article 47 of the Charter, along with Article 48 on the rights of the defence. The CJEU has also confirmed that Article 6 of the Charter incorporates ECHR standards on detention.[35] Furthermore, the Court has affirmed on many occasions that the right to private life, and the principle of non-retroactivity and legality of criminal law are recognized as general principles of EU law.[36]

4.4 Impact of Other EU Law

EU citizens facing criminal trials in another Member State have equal language rights as criminal defendants with citizens of the host Member State, even if the EU citizens in question are not workers but entered that country as tourists or were merely driving across it.[37] EU free movement law is also relevant to crime victims. EU citizens resident

---

[30] See Case C-27/11 *Vinkov*, ECLI:EU:C:2012:326.   [31] II:4.4.
[32] Case C-617/10 *Fransson*, ECLI:EU:C:2013:105. See further II:6.3 below.
[33] See further II:5.4 and II:5.5 below.
[34] See, for instance, Case C-105/03 *Pupino* [2005] ECR I-5285.
[35] Case C-237/15 PPU *Lanigan*, ECLI:EU:C:2015:474.
[36] On private life, see I:6.3.4 and II:7.3.2 below; on criminal law principles as regards substantive criminal law, see further II:5.3.1 below.
[37] Case C-274/06 *Bickel and Franz* [1998] ECR I-7637. See earlier, as regards workers, Case 137/84 *Mutsch* [1985] ECR 2681.

in, or even visiting, another Member State are entitled to equal treatment as regards state compensation schemes for crime victims as regards crimes committed against them in that State.[38] They are also entitled to equal treatment as regards victims' compensation for crimes committed outside the territory of the host State, at least in cases where the beneficiaries of the compensation are resident in that State on a long-term basis.[39] In fact, EC legislation (as it then was) has been adopted on state compensation of crime victims and on the immigration status of victims of trafficking in persons,[40] although the Court of Justice ruled that the EC legislation on compensation of crime victims was not relevant to the interpretation of an EU third pillar measure on the position of victims in criminal procedure.[41]

On the basis of the case law to date, it must be concluded that EU citizens involved in criminal proceedings in another Member State are generally entitled to equal treatment as regards all aspects of criminal procedure, subject only to exceptional cases where a residence (but not a nationality) requirement might be justified, due to the different position of non-residents as regards rehabilitation or as regards payments which amount to social benefits.[42]

4.5 Evidence Law

To date, there have been no EU measures adopted or proposed harmonizing national laws on the use of evidence in criminal investigations and trials.[43] As noted above,[44] Article 82(2) TFEU limits the EU's action in this area to measures concerning the 'mutual admissibility' of evidence, so more general harmonization of evidence law is precluded, except arguably in relation to suspects' rights, although it will be hard in practice to separate rules on the admissibility of evidence from evidence law in general. This area of law is also connected to EU measures regarding mutual recognition of decisions relating to evidence and the gathering of evidence in the context of police cooperation,[45] as well as crime victims' rights.[46]

The conceptual problem with the mutual admissibility of evidence is that the rules of evidence law are tailored closely to the specific, and widely varying, systems of criminal procedure in different Member States. Moreover, protection for the criminal suspect is built in at different stages of that procedure in different Member States. If any evidence secured in any one Member State is automatically admissible in any other, then such protection may be circumvented. As an example of the difficulties, can it be accepted that any evidence obtained illegally, in a Member State where such evidence

---

[38] Case 186/87 *Cowan* [1989] ECR 195.   [39] Case C-164/07 *Wood* [2008] ECR I-4143.
[40] See II:4.7 below.   [41] See Case C-467/05 *Dell'Orto* [2007] ECR I-5557.
[42] See the judgment in Case C-123/08 *Wolzenburg* [2009] ECR I-9621, the rules on sentenced persons discussed above, and the Opinion in *Wood*, n 39 above (paras 40–60), which suggests that some form of requirement of integration (ie residence period) might be imposed as regards victim compensation benefits where the crime was committed outside the territory of the host State.
[43] On civil law evidence issues, see II:8.5.4 below.   [44] II:4.2.4.
[45] Arts 82(1) and 87. On the competence issues, see ibid. On the substance of the law in these areas, see II:3.6.1 above and II:7.6 and II:7.7 below.
[46] See II:4.7 below.

could nonetheless be used in court, must also be admissible in Member States which do not accept the admissibility of illegally obtained evidence?[47]

The Stockholm Programme invited the Commission to 'explore whether there are other means [besides mutual recognition measures] to facilitate admissibility of evidence in this area'.[48] Just before the Programme was adopted, the Commission had already released a Green Paper on the mutual recognition and admissibility of evidence,[49] which, inter alia raised, the question of whether there should be common standards for gathering evidence in general and/or particular types of evidence. Ultimately the Commission decided against making proposals on mutual recognition and admissibility of evidence, because attention had become focused on the proposal for a Directive to establish a European Investigation Order, which was ultimately adopted in 2014.[50]

4.6 Suspects and Defendants

Even before the entry into force of the Treaty of Lisbon, there was a sustained effort to adopt EU legislation on this issue. An initial Commission Green Paper made the case for EU action in this area, referring to the decision to address such issues as part of the mutual recognition programme and arguing that Member States' mutual trust should be based on a greater degree of protection for individual rights than secured by ratification of the ECHR.[51] The Green Paper then examined several specific issues in detail: the right to legal assistance and representation; the right to interpretation and/or translation; special protection for vulnerable groups; and consular assistance.[52] It also addressed the issues of giving a standard Letter of Rights to criminal suspects across the EU, and of compliance with and monitoring of the rights to be examined at EU level.

Subsequently, the Commission proposed a Framework Decision addressing all of these issues.[53] Although the Hague Programme called for the adoption of this proposal by the end of 2005,[54] agreement on the substance was impossible to reach, as several Member States had legal and political objections to an EU measure on this issue.[55] There was a final attempt to agree on the text during the German Council Presidency in 2007, but agreement was still not possible, even on the basis of 'enhanced cooperation', since there was not a qualified majority of Member States in favour of authorizing it.[56]

In an attempt to revive discussions on this topic, the Commission and Council decided in 2009 to approach the issue on a case-by-case basis, instead of comprehensively. For its part, the Council adopted a Resolution just before the entry into force

---

[47] See II:3.3.1 above.   [48] [2010] OJ C 115, point 3.1.1.   [49] COM (2009) 624, 11 Nov 2009.
[50] See II:3.6.1.3 above.   [51] COM (2003) 75, 19 Feb 2003.
[52] Compare with the list of rights expressly set out in Art 6 ECHR (see II:3.3.1 above).
[53] COM (2004) 328, 28 Apr 2004. For comments, see R Loof, 'Shooting from the Hip: Proposed Minimum Rights in Criminal Proceedings throughout the EU' (2006) 12 ELJ 421.
[54] [2005] OJ C 53, point 3.3.1.
[55] See the report to the Dec 2005 JHA Council (Council doc 14248/1/05, 21 Nov 2005). On the competence issues, see II:4.2.4 above.
[56] See the conclusions of the June 2007 JHA Council. On enhanced cooperation generally, see I:2.2.5.5.

of the Treaty of Lisbon, setting out a 'roadmap' for strengthening the procedural rights of suspects and accused persons.[57] This Resolution sets out a political commitment to take EU action in this area, and endorses a list of specific measures to be addressed as a 'priority', although this list is expressly 'non-exhaustive'. The list comprises the following rights: interpretation and translation; information on rights and charges; legal advice and legal aid; communication with relatives, employers, and consular authorities; and special safeguards for vulnerable suspects or accused persons. These rights correspond to those listed in the Commission's 2004 proposal for a Framework Decision. The Resolution also invites the Commission to present a Green Paper on pre-trial detention.[58]

The Stockholm Programme then incorporated the roadmap on procedural rights, and also explicitly invited the Commission to examine whether the issue of presumption of innocence, along with other (unnamed) issues not mentioned in the roadmap, need to be addressed.[59] The Commission has presented six proposals to implement the Stockholm Programme, concerning: (a) interpretation and translation; (b) information about rights; (c) access to a lawyer; (d) safeguards for child suspects; (e) the presumption of innocence and in absentia trials; and (f) legal aid. The first three of these proposals have been adopted; the proposal on presumption of innocence was agreed in principle in October 2015; and the other two proposals are still under discussion. The Commission has also released its Green Paper on pre-trial detention, which is considered below as well.

Comparing the list of adopted, agreed, or proposed Directives to Article 6 ECHR, in principle these Directives incorporate the rules on presumption of innocence (Article 6(2) ECHR), information about charges (Article 6(3)(a) ECHR), facilities to prepare a defence (Article 6(3)(b) ECHR), aspects of legal aid and assistance (Article 6(3)(c) ECHR), and interpretation and translation (Article 6(3)(e) ECHR). However, the Directives do not as such incorporate the general aspects of the right to a fair trial (Article 6(1) ECHR), or the rights concerning witnesses (Article 6(3)(d) ECHR).[60]

When proposing the three latest measures, the Commission also adopted two Recommendations, on legal aid more broadly and on the rights of vulnerable persons.[61] It stated that further work on pre-trial detention was not a 'priority', and did not suggest any further plans for addressing other procedural rights in the EU framework, besides the possibility of consolidating legislation and identifying gaps.[62]

4.6.1 Translation and interpretation

Directive 2010/64 on interpretation and translation for criminal suspects, the first measure to be adopted on the 'roadmap' of suspects' rights, had to be implemented by Member States by 27 October 2013.[63] The CJEU has ruled once on the interpretation of the Directive, and another case is pending.[64]

---

[57] [2009] OJ C 295/1.   [58] On the mutual recognition aspects of this issue, see II:3.6.3 above.

[59] [2010] OJ C 115, point 2.4.   [60] On the substance of the various rights, see II:3.3.1 above.

[61] See respectively [2013] OJ C 378/11 and 8.

[62] Communication on procedural safeguards (COM (2013) 820, 27 Nov 2013).

[63] [2010] OJ L 280/1, Art 9(1). All the following references in this sub-section are to this Directive, unless otherwise mentioned.

[64] Cases C-260/14 *Covaci*, ECLI:EU:C:2015:686 and C-25/15 *Balogh*.

The Directive applies to 'criminal proceedings' (not defined) as well as 'proceedings for the execution of a European Arrest Warrant'.[65] The rights apply from the moment that a person is 'made aware' by the authorities, 'by official notification or otherwise', that he or she 'is suspected or accused' of 'having committed a criminal offence', until the 'conclusion' of those proceedings, 'which is understood to mean the final determination of the question whether the suspected or accused person has committed the offence, including, where applicable, sentencing and the resolution of any appeal'.[66] However, where sanctions for 'minor offences' may be imposed by an authority other than a criminal court, the Directive will only apply if those sanctions are appealed to a court having criminal jurisdiction.[67] The Directive does not affect national law on the presence of counsel during proceedings, or concerning the right of access to documents during criminal proceedings.[68]

The right to interpretation applies 'during criminal proceedings before investigative and judicial authorities, including during police questioning, all court hearings and any necessary interim hearings'.[69] It also applies to communications with legal counsel, where necessary to ensure fairness and in particular where there is a direct connection with 'any questioning or hearing during the proceedings or with the lodging of an appeal or other procedural applications'.[70] The right includes 'assistance' for a person with a hearing or speech impediment.[71] There must be a procedure to verify whether the person concerned understands the language of the criminal proceedings.[72] Technology such as video-conferencing, telephone, or Internet communication is permitted, unless the physical presence of an interpreter is necessary in the interests of fairness.[73]

As for the right to translation, the core of the right is the translation into a language the person understands of 'all documents which are essential to ensure that they are able to exercise their right of defence and to safeguard the fairness of the proceedings'; this does not amount to a right for a suspect to *submit* a document in a language other than the language of proceedings.[74] An 'essential' document includes decisions depriving the person of his or her liberty, the charge or indictment and any judgment.[75] In other cases, decisions on translation will be taken by the national competent authorities, but the Directive specifies that the person concerned, or his or her counsel, will have the right to 'submit a reasoned request' for further translations.[76] However, it is not necessary to translate passages of essential documents which are 'not relevant' for the suspected or accused person to have knowledge of in the case against him or

---

[65] Art 1(1). Note that the Framework Decision establishing the EAW already includes some procedural rights: see II:3.5.2 above.

[66] Art 1(2).

[67] Art 1(3). To interpret this clause, the case law on a similar definition in EU mutual recognition legislation might be relevant by analogy: Case C-60/12 *Baláž*, ECLI:EU:C:2013:733.

[68] Art 1(4). Both issues have since been addressed by later Directives: see II:4.6.2 and II:4.6.3 below.

[69] Art 2(1).   [70] Art 2(2).   [71] Art 2(3).   [72] Art 2(4).   [73] Art 2(6).

[74] Art 3(1), as interpreted in *Covaci* (n 64 above).

[75] Art 3(2). This provision overlaps with the later Directive on information about criminal charges. Also, it should be noted that this 'essential' information must already be given to persons pursuant to Arts 5(2) and 6(3)(a) ECHR.

[76] Art 3(3).

her.[77] As an 'exception', an 'oral translation or an oral summary of the essential docu-ments…may be provided instead of a written translation, on condition that such oral translation or oral summary does not affect the fairness of the proceedings'.[78]

Moreover, the person concerned may waive his or her translation (but not interpre-tation) rights, if he or she has 'received prior legal advice' or has 'otherwise obtained full knowledge of the consequences' of the waiver, as long as 'the waiver was unequivocal and given voluntarily'.[79]

For both rights, there is a right to challenge a decision that there is no need for inter-pretation or translation or the quality of that interpretation or translation.[80] Also, both rights apply to proceedings for the execution of a European Arrest Warrant (EAW).[81]

Next, the Directive obliges Member States to cover the costs of interpretation and translation, regardless of the outcome of the proceedings,[82] and Member States have to ensure that the interpretation and translation are of sufficient quality to safeguard the fairness of the proceedings, so that suspects 'have knowledge of the case against him and are able to exercise their right of defence'.[83] Member States have to endeavour to establish a register of qualified interpreters and translators, and ensure that interpret-ers and translators observe confidentiality requirements.[84] They also have to request that training of judges and prosecutors addresses the issues faced by suspects who need interpretation, and keep a record of cases where interpretation or translation was applied, or where translation rights were waived.[85] Finally, the Directive does not dero-gate from ECHR rules, the EU Charter of Rights, or international law or national law which provides a higher level of protection (a 'non-regression' clause).[86] It should be recalled in any event that the Treaties specify that the EU can only set minimum stand-ards in this area, with Member States always free to set higher standards for the person concerned.[87]

As compared to the case law on Article 6(3)(e) ECHR,[88] the Directive is clearer as regards the definition of an 'essential' document, adds a right to interpretation as regards communication with counsel, forbids waiver of the right to interpretation, clarifies the circumstances regarding waiver of the right to translation, and confirms that the right is free and applies to documents and to pre-trial proceedings. The excep-tions regarding translation of documents do not fall below the standards set by the Strasbourg case law. However, there are no provisions in the Directive dealing with courts' obligations to ensure effective translation, other than the useful (but vague) inclusion of provisions on judicial training. Also, the Directive goes beyond Article 6 ECHR in that it applies to proceedings for the execution of an EAW,[89] and moreover goes beyond the EAW Framework Decision in providing for specific interpretation and translation rights.[90]

---

[77] Art 3(4).   [78] Art 3(7).   [79] Art 3(8).   [80] Arts 2(4) and 3(5).
[81] Arts 2(7) and 3(6). The translation right only applies to the EAW as such, however.
[82] Art 4.   [83] Arts 2(8) and 3(9).   [84] Art 5(2) and (3).   [85] Arts 6 and 7.
[86] Art 8.   [87] Art 82(2), final sub-paragraph; see II:4.2.4 above.   [88] See II:4.3 above.
[89] On the scope of Art 6 ECHR, see II:3.3.1 above.
[90] The EAW Framework Decision ([2002] OJ L 190/1) refers only generally to the right to be assisted by an interpreter in accordance with national law (Art 11(2)), and to a right to information about the contents of the warrant (Art 11(1)), without expressly requiring a translation of the warrant.

The Council and Member States' governments had agreed to adopt a Resolution on the practical application of the Directive.[91] This Resolution would have addressed useful issues such as representation of professionals, qualification of interpreters and translators, training, registration, remote access to interpreters, and codes of conduct and best practice guidelines. Certain parts of the Resolution were inserted into the Directive, at the EP's behest.[92] Ultimately, the Resolution was not adopted because the Treaty prevents the Council and EP, while considering the adoption of a legislative act on a particular issue, from adopting other types of act on the same issue.[93] However, there seems no reason why the Resolution could not have been adopted *after* the adoption of the Directive; it was unfortunate that a pedantic approach to the interpretation of the Treaty prevented the adoption of such a useful practical measure. But in any event, unfortunately neither the draft Resolution nor the Directive itself addresses sufficiently the crucial issue of monitoring of the application of the rights,[94] or of remedies for their breach.

4.6.2 Letter of Rights

Directive 2012/13 on the right to information in criminal proceedings, the second measure to be adopted on the 'roadmap' of suspects' rights, had to be implemented by Member States by 2 June 2014.[95] The CJEU has ruled once on the interpretation of the Directive.[96] It is widely known as the Letter of Rights Directive.

The Letter of Rights Directive has the same scope as the Directive on interpretation and translation.[97] First of all, it confers a right to 'information about rights'. A suspect must be 'promptly' given information about the following procedural rights under national law, 'in order to allow for those rights to be exercised effectively': access to a lawyer; legal aid; information about the accusation; interpretation and translation; and the right to remain silent.[98] This information must be given 'orally or in writing, in simple and accessible language, taking into account any particular needs of vulnerable suspects or vulnerable accused persons'.[99]

To implement this objective concretely, all arrested or detained people facing criminal charges should promptly be given a written Letter of Rights, which they must be able to read and keep in their possession while detained.[100] In addition to the rights

---

[91] Council doc 14793/09, 23 Oct 2009.

[92] Compare points 10, 11, and 16 of the draft resolution to Arts 6, 5(2), and 2(6) of the Dir.

[93] Art 296 TFEU, third para.

[94] Compare Arts 15 and 16 of the Commission's 2004 proposal (n 53 above) with Art 7 of the Directive.

[95] [2012] OJ L 142/1, Art 11(1). All the following references in this sub-section are to this Directive, unless otherwise mentioned.

[96] *Covaci*, n 64 above.

[97] Arts 1 and 2. According to the *Covaci* judgment (n 64 above), the Directive applies to the issuing of a penalty order.

[98] Art 3(1). The rights to interpretation and translation and access to a lawyer will in large part constitute the national implementation of other Directives. This may be true in future of the rights to legal aid and to silence. As Art 3(1)(c) acknowledges, the right to information about the accusation is set out further in Art 6.

[99] See the Recommendation on this issue, n 61 above.   [100] Art 4(1).

referred to already, the Letter of Rights must give details on the following, according to national law: the right of access to the materials of the case; the right to have consular authorities and one person informed;[101] the right of access to urgent medical assistance; and the maximum number of hours or days suspects or accused persons may be deprived of liberty before being brought before a judicial authority.[102] Also, the Letter of Rights must include basic information about possible challenges to the lawfulness of the arrest, reviewing detention, or applying for bail.[103] The Letter must be written in 'simple and accessible language' (an Annex to the Directive gives a model),[104] in a language that the suspect understands.[105]

Persons arrested on the basis of an EAW are also entitled to a Letter of Rights that sets out the basic rights which they are entitled to.[106] However, the Directive does not apply otherwise to persons arrested pursuant to an EAW, although of course it will be (or was) applicable to them in the main criminal proceedings.

Next, there is a right to information about the accusation as such (implementing Article 6(1)(a) ECHR). This information must be given 'promptly', and 'in such detail as is necessary to safeguard the fairness of the proceedings and the effective exercise of the rights of the defence'.[107] Anyone arrested or detained must be told of the reasons for their arrest or detention, including the criminal act which they supposedly committed.[108] At least by the time when the charges are submitted to a court, there must be more 'detailed information' about the accusation, 'including the nature and legal classification of the criminal offence, as well as the nature of participation by the accused person'.[109] If there are any changes in this information, the suspect must be promptly informed.[110]

Also, there is a right of access to materials, reflecting in part the case law on Article 6(1)(b) ECHR. Any documents essential to an effective challenge of the 'lawfulness of the arrest or detention' must be 'made available' to suspects or their lawyers.[111] This must include access to 'all material evidence' which they possess, whether it implicates or exonerates the suspects, 'in order to safeguard the fairness of the proceedings and to prepare the defence'.[112] This access must be granted 'in due time to allow the effective exercise of the rights of the defence', and the very latest when the accusation is sent to a court. Any subsequent evidence shall also be transmitted.[113] But as a 'derogation', access to some materials 'may be refused if such access may lead to a serious threat to the life or the fundamental rights of another person or if such refusal is strictly necessary to safeguard an important public interest, such as in cases where access could prejudice an ongoing investigation or seriously harm the national security of the Member State

---

[101] See Dir 2013/48, discussed in II:4.6.3 below.   [102] Art 4(2).
[103] Art 4(3).   [104] Art 4(4). Member States can adopt their own version instead.
[105] Art 4(5).   [106] Art 5. Another Annex to the Directive contains a model Letter to this end.
[107] Art 6(1). According to the *Covaci* judgment (n 64 above), the Directive does not regulate the procedure of communicating the information, so a Member State may require a non-resident to appoint a legal representative upon whom to serve a document. But the suspect must have a sufficient time to consider that document.
[108] Art 6(2).   [109] Art 6(3).   [110] Art 6(4).
[111] Art 7(1). The translation of these documents is, of course, the subject of Dir 2010/64. Access must be free of charge: Art 7(5).
[112] Art 7(2).   [113] Art 7(3).

in which the criminal proceedings are instituted'—as long as 'this does not prejudice the right to a fair trial', and such a decision is 'taken by a judicial authority or is at least subject to judicial review'.[114]

Member States must keep records on the provision of information to suspects,[115] and permit challenges to any refusal to make information available.[116] There is no express provision on the waiver of any of the rights in the Directive. Finally, Member States must request that the training of judges and prosecutors addresses the issues in the Directive,[117] and there is a standard 'non-regression' clause.[118]

4.6.3 Access to a lawyer

Directive 2013/48 on access to a lawyer, the third measure to be adopted on the 'road-map' of suspects' rights, has to be implemented by Member States by 27 November 2016.[119] It also extends to a right to have a third party informed of the deprivation of liberty and to communicate with third persons and with consular authorities while deprived of liberty.[120] The Directive is subject to the usual rules on temporal scope in relation to proceedings,[121] and applies to persons subject to an EAW from the time of their arrest.[122] In the case of minor offences, the Directive might only apply to appeals.[123] Access to a lawyer must be granted from an early point in time in the proceedings,[124] and cover meetings with a lawyer and the lawyer's presence during questioning and key parts of the procedure.[125] Some of these rights can be limited in exceptional cases,[126] but there is an overarching right to confidentiality of lawyer/client communications.[127]

As noted already, the Directive also provides a right to inform one person of the arrest and to communicate with one person, although this is also subject to derogations.[128] There is also a right to contact consular authorities.[129] The various derogations are subject to a standard set of limitations,[130] and many of the rights in the Directive can also be waived.[131] Fugitives subject to an EAW can appoint a lawyer in the executing State to exercise most of the rights in the Directive as regards the EAW proceedings, as well as a lawyer in the *issuing* State to assist that other lawyer.[132]

Finally, national law on legal aid is unaffected by this Directive.[133] Member States must take particular account of vulnerable persons.[134] Also, there must be an 'effective remedy' if the rights in the Directive are breached, and Member States shall ensure that defence rights are protected if the suspect has made statements in breach of their right to a lawyer.[135] There is no provision on collecting data on the application of the Directive, but the usual non-regression clause applies.[136]

---

[114] Art 7(4).   [115] Art 8(1); this does not apply to the Art 7 right of access to materials.
[116] Art 8(2). It is not clear whether this applies to Art 7, but it should be, pursuant to Art 47 of the EU Charter. On the same basis, this should be a judicial remedy.
[117] Art 9.   [118] Art 10.
[119] [2013] OJ L 294/1, Art 15(1). All the following references in this sub-section are to this Directive, unless otherwise mentioned.
[120] Art 1.   [121] Art 2(1).
[122] Art 2(2). The Directive only applies to such persons as regards access to a lawyer (Art 10).
[123] Art 2(4).   [124] For details, see Art 3(2).   [125] Art 3(3).   [126] Art 3(5) and (6).
[127] Art 4.   [128] Arts 5 and 6.   [129] Art 7.   [130] Art 8.   [131] Art 9.
[132] Art 10.   [133] Art 11.   [134] Art 13.   [135] Art 12.   [136] Art 14.

4.6.4 Child suspects

The first of a package of three Directives on suspects' rights proposed in 2013 was a specific Directive on child suspects,[137] which is currently under discussion. This proposal has a simplified rule on its scope,[138] and it would also apply to children subject to EAW proceedings, from the time of their arrest.[139] A 'child' is anyone under the age of eighteen,[140] but the proposed Directive would continue to apply to anyone who turns eighteen during the course of the proceedings.[141]

Child suspects would have not only the general right to information, but also a right to be informed of nine more specific rights set out in this Directive.[142] The Letter of Rights they receive will also cover those additional rights.[143] The Directive then details those nine additional rights, namely: the right to have the holders of parental responsibility informed;[144] right to a lawyer;[145] right to an individual assessment;[146] right to a medical examination;[147] right to liberty and the right to specific treatment in detention;[148] right to protection of privacy;[149] right that the holders of parental responsibility have access to the court hearings;[150] right to appear in person at the trial,[151] and right to legal aid.[152]

Member States would also be obliged to record the questioning of child suspects,[153] to consider alternatives to detention for children where possible,[154] and to deal with cases concerning child suspects urgently.[155] Most of the rights in the proposal would apply equally to children arrested on the basis of an EAW, and Member States would be obliged to try to limit detention in such cases.[156] There would be more extensive rules on training and data collection, and the usual non-regression clause.[157] Member States would have to meet the costs of individual assessments, medical examinations, and recording of questioning.[158]

4.6.5 Presumption of innocence

The Commission already released a Green Paper on the presumption of innocence back in 2006.[159] This Green Paper asked questions concerning the burden of proof, the

---

[137] COM (2013) 822, 27 Nov 2013. All the following references in this sub-section are to this proposal, unless otherwise mentioned.

[138] Art 2(1).

[139] Art 2(2). Note that the execution of an EAW must be refused if the fugitive is below the age of criminal responsibility in the executing State: see I:3.5.2. The proposal does not affect the national rules on the age of criminal responsibility: Art 2(5).

[140] Art 3.   [141] Art 2(3).   [142] Art 4(1).   [143] Art 4(2).

[144] Art 5. Compare to the right to communication in Dir 2013/48 (II:4.6.3 above).

[145] Art 6. Dir 2013/48 applies, with no waiver possible.   [146] Art 7.   [147] Art 8.

[148] Arts 10 and 12.

[149] Art 14. This suggests a normal rule of holding hearings involving children in private; compare to the usual requirement for public hearings in Art 6 ECHR, which is however subject to possible limitations.

[150] Art 15.

[151] Art 16. Compare to the rules on *in absentia* trials, in the parallel proposal (II:4.6.5 below).

[152] Art 18. Compare to the parallel proposal on this issue (II:4.6.6 below).   [153] Art 9.

[154] Art 11.   [155] Art 13.   [156] Art 18.   [157] Arts 19, 20, and 22.

[158] Art 21, referring to Arts 7–9.   [159] COM (2006) 174, 26 Apr 2006.

right to silence, and the right against self-incrimination, and queried whether there are particular cross-border aspects of these issues. Ultimately, the Commission proposed a Directive on this topic as part of the 2013 'package' on procedural rights, and the EU's legislators agreed in principle on the proposal in October 2015.[160] The Directive will also include a basic rule on *in absentia* trials, an issue which the EU has previously regulated in the context of mutual recognition.[161]

The Directive will apply to 'natural persons who are suspected or accused in criminal proceedings' at 'all stages' of those proceedings.[162] There is a general right to a presumption of innocence,[163] as well as more specific prohibitions. Firstly, before a final conviction, 'public statements' and 'judicial decisions' cannot 'refer to suspects or accused persons as being guilty'.[164] Member States are obliged to take 'appropriate measures' if this rule is broken; and suspects should not be presented in public or court as if they are guilty.[165] Secondly, the burden of proof regarding guilt lies upon the prosecution, 'without prejudice to' any obligation upon the judge to seek evidence.[166] If any presumption shifts that burden to the suspect, it must be rebuttable and be 'confined within reasonable limits'.[167] If there is any doubt regarding the guilt of a suspect, it must benefit the accused.[168]

Thirdly, suspects have 'the right not to incriminate themselves'.[169] But this does not prevent gathering evidence by means of compulsory powers.[170] Fourthly, suspects have a right to silence, meaning 'the right to remain silent in relation to the offence that they are suspected or accused of having committed'.[171] As regards both the right to silence and the right not to incriminate oneself, Member States may allow judicial authorities to take account of cooperative behaviour when sentencing,[172] contrasting with the general rule that the exercise of these rights 'shall not be used against' a suspect or accused person or considered to be evidence of having committed the offence.[173] Furthermore, if any evidence obtained in breach of these rules is used in the proceedings, the rights of the defence must be respected.[174]

As regards *in absentia* trials, the Directive states first of all that suspects have a general right to be present at the trial.[175] Member States may allow a decision in the suspect's absence if either: (a) 'in due time', the suspect was informed of the trial and the consequences of non-attendance ; or (b) the suspect knew about the trial, and instructed a lawyer who in fact defended the suspect at that trial.[176] Even if these conditions are not

---

[160] COM (2013) 821, 27 Nov 2013 (proposal); Council doc 13471/15, 29 Oct 2015 (agreed text). All the following references in this sub-section are to the agreed text , unless otherwise mentioned.

[161] See particularly the discussion of the other legislation and the relevant case law on the EAW, in II:3.6.2 above.

[162] Art 2.   [163] Art 3.   [164] Art 4(1).

[165] Arts 4(2) and 4a; the latter will probably be Art 5 of the final Directive.

[166] Art 5(1), which will probably be Art 6(1) of the final Directive.

[167] Recital 14 (probably recital 22 of the final Directive).

[168] Art 5(1a), which will probably be Art 6(2) of the final Directive.

[169] Art 6(1a), which will probably be Art 7(2) of the final Directive.

[170] Art 6(2), which will probably be Art 7(3) of the final Directive.

[171] Art 6(1), which will probably be Art 7(1) of the final Directive.

[172] Art 6(2b), which will probably be Art 7(4) of the final Directive.

[173] Art 6(3), which will probably be Art 7(5) of the final Directive.   [174] Art 10(2).

[175] Art 8(1).   [176] Art 8(2).

satisfied, Member States can enforce an *in absentia* judgment if they have served the convicted person with the decision and informed the suspect of a right to retrial or to contest the previous conviction, where that remedy amounts to a fresh hearing of the charges.[177]

More generally, there is a general right to an effective remedy if the Directive is breached,[178] although it is not clear how this provision relates to the specific remedies referred to in the Directive. Perhaps the general right to a remedy would apply if the specific rights to a remedy were breached. But what if the general right to a remedy was breached in turn?

The agreed Directive also includes specific provisions on data collection (not on record-keeping though) and non-regression; there is no provision on training.[179] Overall, the Directive seems to be a vague but broadly faithful transposition of the main Strasbourg case law on these issues. However, there is an absence of rules on ensuring implementation.

4.6.6 Legal aid

The final agreed Directive on suspects' rights (at least for now) concerns aspects of legal aid.[180] This proposal would apply to anyone deprived of liberty (if they have the right of access to a lawyer under the prior Directive), or who was subject to an EAW request.[181] These groups of suspects would have a right to 'provisional legal aid'.[182] This aid must be 'granted without undue delay after deprivation of liberty and in any event before questioning'.[183] It must be granted until a final decision on legal aid has been decided, or where a lawyer is appointed after that point,[184] and 'provided to the extent necessary to effectively exercise the right of access to a lawyer' in the prior Directive on the right of access to a lawyer.[185] If it turns out that the suspect was not eligible for legal aid due to means testing, Member States can recover the money.[186]

For fugitives subject to an EAW, there would also be a right to ordinary legal aid, not just provisional legal aid. They would retain this right until they are either surrendered, or until the decision on surrender has become final.[187] Where the fugitive has lawyers in both the issuing and executing Member State pursuant to the prior Directive on access to a lawyer, he or she would have a right to legal aid in both States.[188] Finally, there is a short provision on the collection of data, and the usual non-regression clause.[189]

---

[177] Arts 8(3) and 9. Note that the Letter of Rights Directive does *not* require information on possible *in absentia* trials (cf Art 8(2)) or these retrial possibilities to be given to suspects. The process here can be compared to the service of documents rules applicable to civil proceedings: see II:8.5.2 below.

[178] Art 10(1).   [179] Arts 11–12.

[180] COM (2013) 824, 27 Nov 2013. All the following references in this sub-section are to this proposal, unless otherwise mentioned.

[181] Art 2.

[182] Art 4(1). The term 'provisional legal aid' means 'legal aid to a person deprived of liberty until the decision on legal aid has been taken' (Art 3(b)).

[183] Art 4(2).   [184] Art 4(3).   [185] Art 4(4).   [186] Art 4(5).   [187] Art 5(1).

[188] Art 5(2).   [189] Arts 6 and 7.

4.6.7 Detention rules

The Commission's 2011 Green Paper on pre-trial detention raised questions about the link between long periods of pre-trial detention as regards the EAW, and also detention issues in relation to the Framework Decisions on the transfer of prisoners and the European Supervision Order.[190] In fact, the Green Paper provided evidence that in some cases, poor detention conditions in another Member State have led to a refusal to execute an EAW, showing a clear need for EU measures in this area to facilitate mutual recognition. The Green Paper made a case for EU rules on a time-limit for pre-trial detention and for rules on judicial review. Subsequently, the lengthy pre-trial detention evidenced in the recent CJEU judgment in *Lanigan* makes the case for such rules again.[191]

So it is highly unfortunate that the Commission essentially shelved the issue in its 2013 Communication on procedural safeguards, not even considering the option of adopting a soft-law Recommendation on the issue, like the other two Recommendations it adopted at the same time. Arguably, excessive pre-trial detention in cross-border cases could be reduced in the meantime by the application of the European Supervision Order, but that hardly seems likely at present—given that only half the Member States have implemented the relevant law, the Commission shows no interest in enforcing that law, and in practice this law has never been used.[192]

4.6.8 Assessment

The development of EU legislation in this area is essential to ensure that suspects' rights are more effectively enforced and to guarantee a balance between the prosecution and defence interests in EU criminal law legislation. The first three Directives adopted in this area go some way toward adjusting that balance. Substantively, they only add a little to the relevant rights guaranteed in the ECHR (as interpreted by the Strasbourg Court), most notably the concept of a Letter of Rights. But they raise the possibility that the rights in question may be enforced more effectively—although this is probably unlikely in the absence of strong or clear provisions on remedies for breach of the Directives or on implementation, and in light of the Commission's traditional reluctance to bring infringement proceedings. The three further proposals for suspects' rights Directives will be useful additions to the legal framework, but the continued absence of a Directive regulating pre-trial detention is inexcusable.

4.7 Victims of Crime

EU measures concerning victims of crime constitute both general and specific measures. The first general measure was a Framework Decision on the status of victims in criminal proceedings, adopted in 2000, which was replaced by a Directive in 2012,[193]

---

[190] COM (2011) 327, 14 June 2011.   [191] N 35 above.   [192] See further I:3.6.3.
[193] Art 26(1); compare to Art 12, Framework Decision.

following a broad review of EU policy towards crime victims. The specific rules constitute rules on victims in other EU criminal law measures, Directives on the cross-border aspects of State compensation for victims and on the legal status of victims of human trafficking,[194] and an EU funding programme regarding victims of domestic violence.[195] It should also be recalled that EU citizens who travel between or reside in Member States have a right to equal treatment, if they (or their family members) become crime victims.[196] Furthermore, the Directive on a European Protection Order should also have the effect of assisting some crime victims.[197] Measures on crime victims also affect evidence law, as we shall see.[198] However, it is regrettable that the EU has not taken any steps to sign up to the Council of Europe's Istanbul Convention on violence against women and domestic violence, which concerns a number of issues within the scope of EU competence.[199]

4.7.1 General rules

4.7.1.1 Framework Decision

The Framework Decision on the status of victims of crime, adopted in 2001,[200] had to be applied in phases between March 2002 and March 2006.[201] The CJEU gave seven judgments interpreting the Framework Decision.[202]

The Framework Decision defined a 'victim' broadly, as meaning 'a natural person who has suffered harm, including physical or mental injury, emotional suffering or economic loss, directly caused by acts or omissions that are in violation of the criminal law of a Member State'.[203] According to the CJEU, in light of this definition, the Framework Decision did not apply to legal persons as victims.[204] It applied to 'criminal proceedings' defined in accordance with national law, and the Court of Justice confirmed that

---

[194] See the Commission communication on crime victims (COM (2011) 274, 18 May 2011) and Council conclusions of 2011: <https://www.consilium.europa.eu/uedocs/cms_data/docs/pressdata/en/jha/122529.pdf>.

[195] The 'Daphne' programme: see II:7.4.7 below.   [196] See II:4.4 above.

[197] See II:3.7.6 above.

[198] On EU competence to adopt measures on evidence law, see II:4.5 above.

[199] CETS 210; see Art 75(1) of the Convention, which provides for the EU to sign it. Several Member States have signed or ratified the Convention.

[200] [2001] OJ L 82/1. See earlier the Commission communication on crime victims (COM (1999) 349, 14 July 1999). On the Council's competence to adopt the Framework Decision at the time, see II:4.2.4 above. All references in this sub-section are to the Framework Decision, unless otherwise indicated.

[201] Art 17.

[202] Cases: C-105/03 *Pupino* [2005] ECR I-5285; C-467/05 *Dell'Orto* [2007] ECR I-5557; C-404/07 *Katz* [2008] ECR I-7607; C-205/09 *Eredics* [2010] ECR I-10231; C-483/09 *Gueye* and C-1/10 *Salmeron Sanchez* [2011] ECR I-8263; C-507/10 *X* [2011] ECR I-14241; and C-79/11 *Giovanardi*, ECLI:EU:C:2012:448.

[203] Art 1(a).

[204] *Dell'Orto* and *Eredics* (n 202 above), although the Court made clear in *Eredics* that it was open to Member States to extend the Framework Decision to legal persons as victims if they chose to. Nor did the Framework Decision entail an obligation to make legal persons criminally liable for their acts (*Giovanardi*). The Court did not address the issue of whether the Framework Decision applied when a legal person was the perpetrator of a crime, and *was* criminally liable under national law.

this includes private prosecutions.[205] But the Framework Decision did not harmonize substantive criminal law.[206]

As to the substance, the Framework Decision provided first of all generally for 'respect and recognition' for crime victims, requiring that each Member State ensure that victims have a 'real and appropriate role in its criminal legal system', that they were 'treated with due respect for the dignity of the individual during proceedings' and that they 'recognise the rights and legitimate interests of victims'.[207] In the case of 'particularly vulnerable victims', there was an obligation to provide 'specific treatment best suited to their circumstances'.[208] Member States also had to make provision for victims to supply evidence, but to refrain from questioning them any more than necessary.[209] Bringing these points together, the 'most vulnerable' victims had to be able to testify in a manner which protected them from the effects of giving evidence in open court, by means compatible with national legal principles.[210]

In the *Pupino* judgment, which concerned very young children who were allegedly abused in a nursery by their teacher, the Court of Justice unsurprisingly ruled that such victims had to be considered 'vulnerable' pursuant to the Framework Decision—leaving aside the bigger question of whether all minors had to be considered 'vulnerable'.[211] So these victims were entitled to the protection of a special procedure in which they did not have to give their testimony in court, as long as this was consistent with the right to a fair trial. But this did not entail an obligation to use those special procedures, where in effect the victim was asking for their use as a means to require the prosecutor to bring proceedings against an alleged perpetrator.[212]

Similarly, in the *Katz* case,[213] the Court ruled that a person bringing a private prosecution did not have the right to demand, in light of the generality of the Framework Decision, that he have the status of a witness; but nevertheless the Framework Decision required that he must be able to submit evidence in the proceedings in some form. The Court later clarified that this right to be heard in the proceedings entailed the possibility for the victim to describe what happened and to express an opinion, but not to insist on any particular penalty.[214]

Next, victims had the right to receive information on a number of issues, inter alia, on the conduct of the criminal proceedings following their complaint and on the release of the accused or convicted person, at least where there might be a danger to the victim.[215] If victims were parties or witnesses, Member States had to take necessary steps to reduce any communication difficulties they face (presumably by providing for translation and interpretation).[216] Member States also had to ensure legal and non-legal

---

[205] Art 1(c); see *Katz*, n 202 above. The Framework Decision was not confined to acts which took place on the territory of the State where proceedings are underway.

[206] *Gueye* and *Salmeron Sanchez*, n 202 above.   [207] Art 2(1).   [208] Art 2(2).

[209] Art 3.   [210] Art 8(4).

[211] N 202 above. The Advocate-General indeed argued that all child victims of crime had to be considered vulnerable (paras 53–9 of the Opinion). This judgment also addressed the legal effect of Framework Decisions: see II:2.2.2 above. The CJEU later ruled that child victims of sexual abuse were also 'vulnerable' (*X*, n 202 above).

[212] *X*, n 202 above.   [213] N 202 above.   [214] *Gueye* and *Salmeron Sanchez*, n 202 above.

[215] Art 4.

[216] Art 5. This right is not as fully-fledged as suspects' interpretation and translation rights (see II:4.6.1 above).

aid was provided to victims who were parties, and that victims who were witnesses or parties could receive reimbursement of their expenses.[217]

Victims' privacy and safety had to be protected, inter alia, from reprisals from the offender.[218] This could entail special methods of giving testimony, ensuring lack of contact with the offender in court proceedings, and limiting photography of victims in courtrooms. The CJEU clarified that these rules aimed 'to ensure that the ability of victims adequately to take part in the criminal proceedings is not jeopardised by the possibility that their safety and privacy is placed at risk'. But victims' right to a private life did not mean that they could influence the penalties which courts imposed upon offenders, such as a mandatory injunction in domestic violence cases, since these provisions in the Framework Decision did not aim to regulate any indirect consequences to the victims' private life stemming from the imposition of criminal penalties upon offenders.

Member States had to ensure that it was possible for the victim to receive a decision on compensation from the offender in criminal proceedings, unless in certain cases compensation was provided in another manner; and Member States had to return victims' property that was not needed for the purpose of criminal proceedings.[219] An Advocate-General argued that the former right had to include compensation for pecuniary losses, and that any exception from the possibility to obtain a decision on compensation had to be limited to certain cases only and take place usually within the framework of the same proceedings which resulted in a conviction of the offender. As for the return of property, the obligation to return it only applied where the ownership of the property was undisputed or had been established in criminal proceedings; otherwise the issue was a matter for civil law.[220]

The Framework Decision also required each Member State to 'seek to promote penal mediation' between victim and offender 'for offences which it considered appropriate'.[221] The CJEU clarified this obligation: Member States had discretion to decide which offences were covered by such proceedings. While their discretion could be affected by a need to use objective criteria to decide on which cases to cover, it was not a breach of the Framework Decision to confine penal mediation to cases involving offences against the person, transport safety, or offences against property.[222]

There were specific provisions for victims who are resident in another Member State, and for cooperation between Member States.[223] Finally, Member States also had to promote victim support organizations, train personnel in contact with victims (particularly police officers and legal practitioners), and ensure that intimidation of victims could not occur in venues such as courts and police stations.[224]

The Commission's first report on the national transposition of most provisions of the Framework Decision was quite critical regarding the lack of reported national measures which fully met the specific requirements of the Framework Decision.[225]

---

[217] Arts 6 and 7. Compare to the proposed measure on legal aid for suspects (II:4.6.6 above).
[218] Art 8.   [219] Art 9.   [220] Opinion in *Dell'Orto*, n 202 above, paras 73–96.
[221] Art 10(1). Art 10(2) states that Member States must ensure that any agreement between the offender and the victim in penal mediation proceedings 'shall be taken into account'.
[222] *Eredics*, n 202 above. Member States can equally exclude domestic violence cases from penal mediation: *Gueye* and *Salmeron Sanchez*, n 202 above.
[223] Arts 11–12.   [224] Arts 13–15.   [225] COM (2004) 54, 3 Feb 2004.

Its second report concluded that implementation of the Framework Decision was still 'not satisfactory', due to the continued variations and omissions in national law and the decision of some Member States to implement the Framework Decision by non-binding means.[226]

4.7.1.2 Directive

Member States had to comply with the crime victims' rights Directive by 16 November 2015,[227] when the Directive fully replaced the previous Framework Decision (except in Denmark).[228] Unlike the Framework Decision, the Directive confers directly effective rights on victims. Furthermore, the Directive made a number of substantive changes to the rules, which increased the overall standard of protection for victims' rights. The Commission released a detailed guidance document concerning implementation of the Directive.[229]

First of all, the Directive contains a new provision on its objectives, including a general requirement of decent treatment, including non-discrimination.[230] The definition of 'victim' now expressly includes family members in the event of a victim's death[231] There are wholly new rules on the victim's 'right to understand and to be understood',[232] followed by greatly expanded rules on the victim's right to receive information.[233] Victims have a 'right to interpretation and translation', which is much stronger than the rules on 'communication safeguards' in the Framework Decision.[234] They also have a 'right to access victim support services', which again is much stronger than the rules on 'specialist services and victim support organisations' in the Framework Decision.[235] On the other hand, the right to be heard for victims has not changed significantly.[236]

A potentially important new right for victims is the right to review a decision not to prosecute,[237] although this does not go so far as to require all Member States to ensure a prosecution following every complaint by a victim. While the 'procedural rules' for such reviews are determined by national law,[238] Member States do not have any discretion as regards the underlying obligation to provide for such reviews, or to limit the *substantive* grounds which might be pleaded in such challenges. For instance, it should

---

[226] COM (2009) 166, 20 Apr 2009.

[227] Art 27(1), Dir 2012/29 ([2012] OJ L 315/57). All references in this sub-section are to this Directive, unless otherwise indicated.

[228] Art 30.

[229] See: <http://ec.europa.eu/justice/criminal/files/victims/guidance_victims_rights_directive_en.pdf>.

[230] Art 1(2). There is a specific general rule on child victims (Art 1(2)).

[231] Art 2(1)(a); 'family members' are defined in Art 2(1)(b).   [232] Art 3.

[233] Arts 4–6; compare to Art 4, Framework Decision, and also to the Letter of Rights Directive on suspects (I:4.6.2 above). There is no Letter of Rights for victims.

[234] Art 7; compare to Art 5, Framework Decision. This provision is essentially a short version of suspects' rights to information and translation, set out in Dir 2010/64 (see II:4.6.1 above).

[235] Arts 8 and 9; compare to Art 13, Framework Decision.

[236] Art 10; compare to Art 3, first paragraph, Framework Decision. There is a specific provision on children, and a general proviso that the details of the right are left to national law (Art 3(2)). There is nothing to suggest any change in the previous case law regarding this right (on which, see I:4.7.1.1). A written statement or explanation by the victim is considered sufficient (recital 41 in the preamble), so this suggests there is no right to an oral hearing.

[237] Art 11.   [238] Art 11(1).

always be possible to argue that a decision not to prosecute was discriminatory, in light of the obligation to deal with victims and respond to victims' complaints in a non-discriminatory manner.[239] The preamble suggests that this right also applies 'where a prosecutor decides to withdraw charges or discontinue proceedings'.[240]

However, the Directive includes some special rules on this right. Where (under national law) the role of the victim is established only after a decision not to prosecute has been taken, only the victims of *serious* crime have such a right of review.[241] Also, the right of review does not apply to decisions taken by courts,[242] and it 'does not concern special procedures, such as proceedings against members of parliament or government, in relation to the exercise of their official position'.[243] Member States can also override the right to review in cases where a prosecutor decides not to prosecute following an out-of-court settlement.[244]

Procedurally, victims must be given sufficient information about their right to review 'without unnecessary delay'.[245] Normally the review must be carried out by a body independent of the body which decided not to prosecute,[246] but where the decision not to prosecute was taken by the highest prosecution authority and no review of that decision is possible under national law, the decision must be reviewed by the same authority.[247] The Directive is silent on what happens if the review is successful. Logically the principle of effectiveness of EU law requires that in this case, at the very least the prosecutors must reconsider their decision not to prosecute to the extent that it was flawed, and produce a fresh decision following that reconsideration.[248]

Next, the Directive provides for safeguards in restorative justice services, in place of the prior rules on 'penal mediation'.[249] But a series of rules have not been fundamentally altered: the right to legal aid;[250] the right to reimbursement of expenses;[251] the right to the return of property;[252] the right to a decision on compensation from the offender;[253] the rights of victims resident in another Member State;[254] the general right

---

[239] See Art 1(1), and recitals 61 and 63 in the preamble, as well as the general respect for the principle of non-discrimination in EU law (recital 66 in the preamble).

[240] Recital 44 in the preamble, which states that a 'decision ending criminal proceedings', which presumably includes a decision not to prosecute, 'should' include such situations.

[241] Art 11(2). 'Serious crime' is not defined, but see recitals 8 and 18 in the preamble.

[242] Recital 43 in the preamble. This means that victims have no right to review of a sentence, or to release of an offender on parole, although they do have the right to *information* about such developments (see Art 6).

[243] Recital 43.

[244] Art 11(5); according to recital 45 in the preamble, this exception applies only where the settlement 'imposes a warning or an obligation'.

[245] Art 11(3).   [246] Recital 43 in the preamble.

[247] Art 11(4). It seems implicit that the review need not necessarily be undertaken by a court, but that limitation is questionable in light of Art 47 of the EU Charter.

[248] Note that a decision not to prosecute will not normally constitute a final judgment for the purposes of double jeopardy rules, and so it would still be open to reopen the investigation or restart the prosecution without infringing the double jeopardy principle. See by analogy II:6.8 below.

[249] Art 12; compare to Art 10, Framework Decision. It follows that the case law on penal mediation under the earlier measure is no longer relevant.

[250] Art 13; compare to Art 6, Framework Decision.

[251] Art 14; compare to Art 7, Framework Decision.

[252] Art 15; compare to Art 9(3), Framework Decision.

[253] Art 16; compare to Art 9(1), Framework Decision.

[254] Art 17; compare to Art 11, Framework Decision.

to protection;[255] and the right to avoid contact with the offender.[256] Finally, there are a number of changes to other important rules: the rules on protection of victims during criminal investigations (interviews, legal assistance, medical examinations) have been expanded;[257] the right to privacy of victims has been elaborated further;[258] the provisions on victims with 'specific protection needs' have been hugely expanded;[259] there are expanded provisions on the training of practitioners;[260] the rules on cooperation between Member States' authorities have been expanded;[261] and there are new provisions requiring Member States to make victims more aware of their rights.[262]

4.7.2 Specific measures

As for the Framework Decisions with specific rules on crime victims, first of all the Framework Decision on terrorism provides that investigations and prosecutions shall not be dependent upon a complaint by a victim, at least where the offence takes place on the relevant Member State's territory; also Member States must provide support for victims' families.[263] Next, the Framework Decision on organized crime contains only the proviso that investigations and prosecutions shall not be dependent upon a complaint by a victim.[264]

Similar provisions appeared in the Framework Decisions on trafficking in persons and on sexual exploitation of persons, with the additional provisos that Member States must treat child victims of these crimes as 'particularly vulnerable' and that families of the victims must enjoy the right to receive information as set out in the general Framework Decision on victims' rights.[265] Subsequent Directives on the latter topics contain even more extensive provisions on victims' rights.[266]

The criminal law measures are supplemented by Directive 2004/80 on state compensation for victims, which Member States had to implement by 1 January 2006.[267] This Directive requires each Member State to establish a state compensation scheme for 'victims of violent intentional crimes committed in their respective territories, which guarantees fair and appropriate compensation to victims',[268] but the details of national

---

[255] Art 18; compare to Arts 2, 8(1), and 15, Framework Decision.

[256] Art 19; compare to Art 8(3), Framework Decision.

[257] Art 20; compare to Art 3, second paragraph, Framework Decision.

[258] Art 21; compare to Art 8(2), Framework Decision.

[259] Arts 22 to 24; compare to Art 2(2), Framework Decision.

[260] Art 25; compare to Art 14, Framework Decision.

[261] Art 26(1); compare to Art 12, Framework Decision.   [262] Art 26(2).

[263] Art 10 of Framework Decision ([2002] OJ L 164/3). The proposed Directive on terrorism also contains provisions on victims' rights (Arts 22 and 23, COM (2015) 625, 2 Dec 2015).

[264] Art 8 of the Framework Decision ([2008] OJ L 300/42).

[265] Art 7 of the Framework Decision on trafficking in persons ([2002] OJ L 203/1); Art 9 of the Framework Decision on sexual exploitation ([2004] OJ L 13/44). A 'child' is anyone under 18 years old (Arts 1(4) and 1(a) of the respective Framework Decisions).

[266] Arts 11–17 of Dir 2011/36 on trafficking in persons ([2011] OJ L 101/1); Arts 18–20 of Dir 2011/93 on sexual offences against children ([2011] OJ L 335/1).

[267] Art 18(1) of the Directive ([2004] OJ L 261/15). See the earlier Green Paper on this issue (COM (2001) 536, 28 Sep 2001). The Commission has adopted a Decision establishing standard forms relating to the implementation of the Dir ([2006] OJ L 125/25).

[268] Art 12(2) of the Directive.

schemes are not harmonized, due to concerns about lack of EC competence to do so. Instead, the Directive establishes a mechanism for persons who have suffered from a violent crime in a Member State other than the State of their habitual residence to claim compensation from the former State. However, a degree of harmonization has been established by a 1983 Council of Europe Convention on compensation of victims of violent crime, which the majority of Member States have ratified.[269]

The Court of Justice has ruled that this Directive does not affect the interpretation of the Framework Decision on victims, and moreover only applies to violent crime, not financial crime.[270] Also, the Court has ruled on the failure by several Member States to implement the Directive.[271] More problematically, the Court has ruled that the Directive only applies to cross-border cases, ignoring the requirement to set up a domestic compensation system for victims of violent intentional crime.[272]

According to the Commission report on the application of this Directive,[273] most Member States were compliant with the basic rule to establish national compensation systems, as well as the rules on cross-border compensation, although the view of claimants was more critical. The Commission therefore concluded that for now it was not necessary to amend the Directive, but rather to improve its implementation at national level.

4.7.3 Assessment

Compared to the international measures on the subject of protection of victims,[274] the EU's measures as regards the status of victims in criminal proceedings are less vague and are furthermore legally binding, bolstered by the principle of indirect effect. They will become even more binding and precise, when the Directive on victims is due for implementation. The EU could still have gone further on some points; for example, it should have been possible to agree that victims should have either a right to bring or attach themselves to criminal proceedings. In light of the free movement of legal persons guaranteed by EU internal market law, it would be appropriate to ensure that EU legislation applies, to the extent relevant, to crime victims who are legal persons. Furthermore, the EU has not addressed the social aspects of victimization,[275] except for State compensation, where due to legal arguments only the cross-border aspects of this

---

[269] ETS 116. For ratification details, see Appendix I.

[270] *Dell'Orto*, n 202 above. Nor does it apply to cases of criminal liability due to negligence, or where there is no cross-border element: Case C-79/11 *Giovanardi*, ECLI:EU:C:2012:448. The Court did not comment in the *Giovanardi* judgment on whether the Directive might apply where legal persons are the perpetrators, and on the dividing line between criminal or administrative liability in such a case (see further I:4.7.1.1).

[271] Cases C-112/07 *Commission v Italy*, judgment of 29 Nov 2007, and C-26/07 *Commission v Greece*, judgment of 18 July 2007, neither yet reported. The CJEU subsequently fined Greece pursuant to Art 260 TFEU (formerly Art 228 EC) for non-implementation of the latter judgment: Case C-407/09 *Commission v Greece* [2011] ECR I-2467. Also, the Commission has brought a separate proceeding against Italy for not setting up a domestic victim compensation scheme compliant with Art 12 of the Directive: C-601/14, pending. A recent reference raises the same issue: C-167/15 *X*, pending.

[272] Case C-122/13 *C*, ECLI:EU:C:2014:59.   [273] COM (2009) 170, 20 Apr 2009.

[274] See Council of Europe Committee of Ministers Recommendation (R (85) 11, 28 June 1985) and UN General Assembly Resolution 40/34 1985.

[275] See Council of Europe Committee of Ministers Recommendation (R (87) 21, 17 Sep 1987).

issue have been addressed. Here, it should have been possible nevertheless for Member States to agree informally that they would ratify the Council of Europe Convention on this issue.

4.8 Conclusions

As we saw in Chapter 3 of this volume, EU mutual recognition measures are based on a strong degree of mutual trust. But we should neither be so xenophobic as to assume that foreign criminal proceedings are always unjust, nor so naïve as to assume that such proceedings are always above reproach. The reality lies between the extremes of para- noia on the one hand, and Polyanna on the other. So the EU needs to strike a balance between blind faith in other Member States on the one hand, and undue interference with the valuable diversity of national criminal justice systems on the other.

The fair trials legislation adopted or proposed to date has certainly *not* undermined the diversity of national systems, as it closely hugs the security blanket of Strasbourg jurisprudence and offers only modest innovations as regards substantive rights, their implementation, or relevant remedies. Equally, the CJEU jurisprudence on the pre- Lisbon victims' rights legislation frequently expressly declined to affect the basic rules of national justice systems. Time will tell whether the case law of the Court of Justice on the post-Lisbon measures, or some new political will to address the problem of exces- sive pre-trial detention, will result in the EU adding more value in this area.

5

Substantive Criminal Law

5.1 Introduction

Substantive criminal law (the definition of criminal offences) is usually a matter for States, and often for regions within those States, to decide. But there is a history of international cooperation on this issue, because States are willing to agree treaties binding themselves to harmonize their domestic law in regard to a small number of specific (but usually serious) crimes which are perceived to pose particular cross-border issues. Furthermore, the harmonization of substantive criminal law removes or weakens a traditional barrier to judicial cooperation between States: the double criminality rule, which historically required an act to constitute a crime in both the State requesting assistance (such as extradition or the transfer of a prisoner) and the State which is being requested, before cooperation can go ahead.[1]

Although a number of substantive criminal law treaties have been adopted within other international frameworks, the EU has retained a distinct interest in adopting its own measures in this area, to deal with issues unique to the EU (like protection of the EU's financial interests), to address other issues not yet dealt with in other international fora (such as a harmonized definition of 'terrorism'), and to ensure a greater level of harmonization within the EU than provided for by international treaties (eg by removing Member States' reservations to those treaties or by harmonizing their interpretation).

EU measures have now been adopted in a number of areas, and have addressed not only the definition of offences, but also aspects of the general part of criminal law (eg attempts and complicity), the liability of legal persons, and harmonized sentencing rules.

This chapter starts with the basic issues of the institutional framework, an overview of measures adopted, legal competence, territorial scope, human rights, and overlaps with other areas of (non-JHA) EU law—a highly contested issue which the Treaty of Lisbon has attempted to resolve. It then examines offences harmonized by the EC/EU and the related general criminal law issues, followed by an analysis of EU harmonization of sentencing, and a summary of the EC/EU's external relations powers and practice in this field. The connected issues of mutual recognition, criminal procedure, and policing are addressed in Chapters 3, 4, and 7 of this volume respectively, and the issue of jurisdiction over criminal offences will be examined in Chapter 6,[2] because of the links between this issue, the cross-border double jeopardy rule, and the coordination of prosecutions by Eurojust.

---

[1] On the partial removal of the dual criminality rule by EU legislation, see II:3.5 to II:3.7 above.
[2] II:6.5 below.

5.2 Institutional Framework and Overview

5.2.1 Framework prior to the Treaty of Amsterdam

For some time, the Community and Union frameworks were not used to harmonize the substantive criminal law of the Member States. This issue was left in particular to the United Nations,[3] with a limited role for the Council of Europe, although the latter organization's role has expanded in recent years.[4] There were attempts by Member States in the 1960s and 1970s to agree measures on the specific issue of fraud against the EU budget, but these efforts were unsuccessful at the time.[5]

Efforts to harmonize substantive criminal law at EU level began to develop after the entry into force of the original Treaty on European Union (TEU) in 1993. In fact, initially the TEU's third pillar provisions did not explicitly grant the Council competence to adopt measures harmonizing substantive criminal law. Rather, Article K.1(7) EU referred to criminal judicial cooperation. However, it was soon felt necessary to agree 'combination' acts which set out both agreed substantive law principles and rules on judicial cooperation, because the harmonization of substantive law facilitated judicial cooperation by simplifying the application of the double criminality condition for judicial cooperation.

In addition, Article K.1(4) and (5) of the original TEU referred to 'combatting drug addiction' and 'fraud on an international scale' to the extent that this fell outside the scope of judicial, police, and customs cooperation, thus implying that there was competence to harmonize substantive criminal law in these areas independently of judicial cooperation.

In practice, the EU used the third pillar powers during the Maastricht era to adopt Conventions harmonizing substantive criminal law as regards fraud against the EU budget and corruption, as well as Joint Actions harmonizing law as regards drug trafficking, racism and xenophobia, organized crime, private corruption, trafficking in persons and sexual exploitation of children, and money laundering.[6] All of these Joint Actions only required Member States to present proposals to their national parliaments, without an explicit obligation upon the entire State to ensure that the national law was amended.

Also, *Community* powers were used, both before and after entry into force of the original TEU, to adopt legislation closely related to criminal law, although no EC legislation adopted before the entry into force of the Treaty of Amsterdam explicitly required Member States to impose criminal penalties.

Outside the EU framework, the Schengen Convention contained certain provisions relevant to harmonization of substantive criminal law, particularly regarding drugs and facilitation of unauthorized immigration.[7]

---

[3] From a huge literature, see (with further references), M Bassiouni, *International Criminal Law, Vol. I: Sources, Subjects and Contents*, 3rd edn (Martinus Nijhoff, 2008).

[4] In particular, there are Council of Europe Conventions in force addressing corruption (ETS 173) and cyber-crime (ETS 185). For Member States' ratification of these measures, see Appendix I.

[5] See II:2.2.1.1 above.   [6] For references to the relevant measures, see II:5.5.1.2 below.

[7] See Arts 27 and 71 of the Convention ([2000] OJ L 239).

5.2.2 Treaty of Amsterdam

The EU's objectives in the field of policing and criminal law were set out in Article 29 TEU, as revised by the Treaty of Amsterdam, which set out an objective of, inter alia, 'preventing and combating racism and xenophobia'. This was '[w]ithout prejudice to the powers of the European Community'. The objective was to be 'achieved by preventing and combating crime, organised or otherwise, in particular terrorism, trafficking in persons and offences against children, illicit drugs trafficking and illicit arms trafficking, corruption and fraud, through … [inter alia] approximation, where necessary, of rules on criminal matters in the Member States, in accordance with the provisions of Article 31(e)'.[8] Article 31 set out a list of measures which judicial cooperation 'shall include', and point (e) concerned 'progressively adopting measures establishing minimum rules relating to the constituent elements of criminal acts and to penalties in the fields of organised crime, terrorism and illicit drug trafficking'. So the EU did not set itself the aim of harmonizing all national substantive criminal law, but rather concerned itself with certain listed crimes, although the lists in Articles 29 and 31(e) were both expressly non-exhaustive ('in particular', 'shall include'). Also, the EU was limited by the previous Article 31 TEU to setting 'minimum' rules on offences and penalties, leaving Member States free to set higher penalties or to impose criminal sanctions on a wider range of activity than required by an EU measure.

The Treaty of Amsterdam also amended the EC Treaty to provide for legal bases for Community action closely related to criminal law matters. Article 280 EC, as amended by the Treaty of Amsterdam, had previously (as Article 209a EC) merely set out general principles concerning fraud against EC financial interests, but now also provided a legal base to adopt legislation using the co-decision procedure and qualified majority voting (QMV) in the Council on this issue, 'with a view to providing effective and equivalent protection in the Member States' for those interests. Although one would expect that such legislation would necessarily have to address criminal law issues, Article 280(4) EC specified that such measures 'shall not concern the application of national criminal law or the national administration of justice'. Also, Article 135 EC, a legal base for the adoption of measures concerning customs cooperation, was added to the EC Treaty by the Treaty of Amsterdam; it contained an identical proviso.[9]

As in other areas of Justice and Home Affairs (JHA) law and policy, the 1999 Tampere European Council (EU leaders' summit meeting) set out a political agenda concerning the exercise of the EU's powers in this area. The summit conclusions stated that 'with regard to national criminal law, efforts to agree on common definitions, incriminations and sanctions should be focused in the first instance on a limited number of sectors of particular relevance, such as financial crime (money laundering, corruption, Euro counterfeiting), drugs trafficking, trafficking in human beings, particularly exploitation of women, sexual exploitation of children, high tech crime and environmental

---

[8] The previous Art 31(e) TEU became Art 31(1)(e) after entry into force of the Treaty of Nice, which added a new Art 31(2) to the TEU, but its text was otherwise unchanged.
[9] Previous Arts 135 and 280 EC were renumbered Arts 33 and 325 TFEU respectively by the Treaty of Lisbon, and also amended; see II:5.2.3 below.

crime', and also called for 'the approximation of criminal law and procedures on money laundering'.[10]

In practice, during the Amsterdam era (1999–2009), the EU only used Framework Decisions, rather than Conventions or other measures, to harmonize substantive criminal law, except for a Decision on synthetic drugs.[11] This speeded up the harmonization process, because the Framework Decisions obliged a Member State to implement them within a relatively short period of about two years, without any form of ratification requirement in national parliaments, whereas Conventions are subject to national ratification, which usually takes over five years. Also, national courts must give 'indirect effect' to Framework Decisions (interpreting national law in light of them),[12] while it is not yet established whether EU law requires Conventions to have a particular legal effect in national legal orders. But in the area of substantive criminal law, the 'indirect effect' of Framework Decisions (and the direct and indirect effect of Directives) is apparently of limited relevance, because the Court of Justice has made clear that criminal sanctions cannot be imposed on individuals unless national law clearly provides for this.[13]

The areas covered by Framework Decisions comprise: counterfeiting of currency and of non-cash instruments (such as cheques, credit cards, and debit cards); money laundering; private corruption; terrorism; trafficking in persons; facilitation of illegal entry and residence; environmental crime, including pollution related to shipping; child pornography and prostitution; drug trafficking; attacks on information systems; organized crime; and racism and xenophobia.[14] Most of these measures replaced the pre-Amsterdam Joint Actions on the same topics. Like the prior Joint Actions, the Framework Decisions either address subjects outside the scope of current international criminal law conventions or aim to supplement those conventions by harmonizing the law in greater detail. However, compared to the Joint Actions, the Framework Decisions usually provide for specific penalties to be imposed against offenders and define the relevant offences in further detail. Furthermore, replacing Joint Actions with Framework Decisions had the automatic effect of extending the revised institutional rules of the Treaty of Amsterdam (clearer legal effect and jurisdiction of the Court of Justice) to these measures.[15]

There are several different aspects to each Framework Decision concerning substantive criminal law. The core of each act is the definition of the offence (often several offences). This definition is usually at a level of detail comparable to international criminal law Conventions. Next, each measure usually requires criminalization of related and inchoate offences, although the details are quite different and the principles underlying inchoate offences (such as whether an 'impossible attempt' should be criminalized or the extent of planning and preparation necessary to constitute an attempt) are

---

[10] Paras 48 and 55 of the European Council conclusions.
[11] On this Decision, see II:5.5.1.2 below.   [12] Case C-105/03 *Pupino* [2005] ECR I-5285.
[13] On the legal effect of third pillar measures, see further II:2.2.2 above; on the human rights background to the implementation of substantive EU criminal law by Member States, see II:5.3 below.
[14] For detailed references, see II:5.5.1.2 below.
[15] These issues have been revisited subsequently by the Treaty of Lisbon: see II:5.2.3 below.

not expressly harmonized. In some cases (private corruption, facilitation of illegal entry and residence, child pornography and prostitution, attacks on information systems, and drug trafficking), Member States have an option *not* to criminalize aspects of the relevant activity in certain circumstances.[16]

As for the extent of obligations, almost all measures require the Member States to impose criminal or non-criminal fines or other sanctions on legal persons who breach the relevant rules. For natural persons, as noted above, most of the Framework Decisions also contain provisions on sentencing, requiring Member States to impose a maximum possible sentence of at least 'x' years for those found guilty of the specified offence. In several of these cases, there are provisions for aggravated or reduced penalties where specified conditions are met. All measures contain rules on jurisdiction; as noted above, these rules are considered in detail in Chapter 6 of this volume.[17]

So far there has been no move to codify the measures which have been agreed, even in order to reduce or abolish divergences and inconsistencies on issues such as related offences, jurisdiction, and penalties.

Implementation of Framework Decisions by the Member States is overseen by the Commission, which compiles reports on implementation based on information supplied by the Member States; the Council then in principle reviews national implementation based on the Commission's reports, although the Council ceased to do this towards the end of the Amsterdam era.[18] Unlike first pillar obligations, third pillar obligations could not be enforced by means of the Commission bringing infringement actions against Member States pursuant to Article 226 EC (now Article 258 of the Treaty on the Functioning of the European Union (TFEU)), until the expiry of the five-year transitional period provided for by the Treaty of Lisbon relating to the Court's jurisdiction over third pillar acts adopted before the entry into force of that Treaty.[19] So until that point (1 December 2014), except for those Framework Decisions which were amended in the meantime,[20] the Commission reports and Council reviews were the main method of checking upon implementation by Member States.

As for the role of the Court of Justice, there were no references from national courts or dispute settlement cases to the Court relating to third pillar substantive criminal law measures, before the entry into force of the Treaty of Lisbon. There were, however, a large number of cases before the Court concerning Community law measures that had an impact upon criminal law.[21] Furthermore, the borderline between Community (first pillar) powers and Union (third pillar) powers over substantive criminal law was hotly disputed during the Amsterdam era. As a result, the Commission brought two annulment actions against the Council, alleging that two particular Framework Decisions fell within the scope of EC law, not the third pillar.[22] Both actions were successful, with the result that the Council and European Parliament (EP) began to adopt Community law

---

[16] On the relevance of this for EU criminal procedural measures, see II:3.10 above.
[17] II:6.5 below.   [18] For references to the reports, see II:5.5.1.2 below.
[19] See further II:2.2.3.3 above.
[20] For the initial proposals for such amendments, see II:5.2.3 below.
[21] On this issue generally, see II:5.4 below.
[22] Cases C-176/03 *Commission v Council* [2005] ECR I-7879 and C-440/05 *Commission v Council* [2007] ECR I-9097.

measures with provisions defining criminal offences.[23] Quite apart from these developments, there was a close relationship between a number of EC acts and third pillar measures in this area.

5.2.3 Treaty of Lisbon

Following the entry into force of the Treaty of Lisbon, the EU's competence to harmonize substantive criminal law is set out in the first two paragraphs of Article 83 TFEU:

1. The European Parliament and the Council may, by means of directives adopted in accordance with the ordinary legislative procedure, establish minimum rules concerning the definition of criminal offences and sanctions in the areas of particularly serious crime with a cross-border dimension resulting from the nature or impact of such offences or from a special need to combat them on a common basis.

   These areas of crime are the following: terrorism, trafficking in human beings and sexual exploitation of women and children, illicit drug trafficking, illicit arms trafficking, money laundering, corruption, counterfeiting of means of payment, computer crime and organised crime.

   On the basis of developments in crime, the Council may adopt a decision identifying other areas of crime that meet the criteria specified in this paragraph. It shall act unanimously after obtaining the consent of the European Parliament.

2. If the approximation of criminal laws and regulations of the Member States proves essential to ensure the effective implementation of a Union policy in an area which has been subject to harmonisation measures, directives may establish minimum rules with regard to the definition of criminal offences and sanctions in the area concerned. Such directives shall be adopted by the same ordinary or special legislative procedure as was followed for the adoption of the harmonisation measures in question, without prejudice to Article 76.

Article 83(3) TFEU then provides for a special emergency brake procedure in the event that a Member State believes that a proposed Directive in this area 'would affect fundamental aspects of its criminal justice system', entailing a dispute settlement procedure at the level of the European Council and a fast-track authorization of the 'enhanced cooperation' procedure if the dispute is not settled there.[24]

Compared to the previous rules, the main competence to harmonize substantive criminal law has become subject to qualified majority voting and co-decision—now known as the ordinary legislative procedure—instead of unanimity in the Council and consultation of the EP. However, in the case of the 'Community criminal law' competence provided for in Article 83(2), it is possible that unanimous voting will apply in the Council in some cases, for example if the EU wanted to adopt measures on tax fraud or further measures concerning racism, because those are cases where a special legislative procedure entailing unanimous voting applies to the underlying harmonization measures.[25]

---

[23] Dir 2008/99 on environmental crime ([2008] OJ L 328/28); Dir 2009/123 on shipping pollution ([2009] OJ L 280/52); and Dir 2009/52 on employer sanctions for hiring irregular migrants ([2009] OJ L 168/24).

[24] For detailed analysis of this process, see II:2.2.3.4.1 above. The procedure also applies to harmonization of domestic criminal procedural law, pursuant to Art 82(3) TFEU (see II:3.2.5 above).

[25] See respectively Arts 113 and 19(1) TFEU (ex-Arts 93 and 13(1) EC), which require unanimous voting in the Council.

As in other areas of policing and criminal law, the Commission has influence as regards Article 83(1) TFEU because individual Member States can no longer make legislative proposals on the listed areas of criminal law. But since both the first and second paragraphs are subject to the possibility that a group of at least one-quarter of the Member States may table a proposal, this is a reduction in the Commission's influence as regards Article 83(2), because previously only the Commission could table proposals relevant to criminal law pursuant to the relevant EC Treaty Articles. Moreover, if the Council were to adopt a decision extending the EU's criminal law competence pursuant to Article 83(1), the Council would not be required to act on the basis of a Commission proposal, because this would not be a legislative act.[26]

The Treaty of Lisbon also entailed application of the normal jurisdiction of the Court of Justice, subject to the relevant transitional rules (which expired on 1 December 2014, as noted above). However, there has been only one reference to the Court in this area since the Treaty of Lisbon entered into force.[27] Also, the instruments of 'Community' law, with their well-established legal effect, now apply to this field of law. However, it is notable that the EU is required to act by means of Directives in this area, and therefore cannot use Regulations.[28] Furthermore, the restrictions regarding criminal law that previously applied to the specific issues of fraud and customs cooperation were removed by the Treaty of Lisbon.[29]

On the eve of the entry into force of the Treaty of Lisbon, the Council adopted a Resolution on model provisions in legislation relating to criminal law, intended to guide the Council's future work.[30] It broadly endorsed the Council's prior practice in this area.[31] As for actual legislation, the EU has adopted Directives on trafficking in persons, sexual offences against children, attacks on information systems, counterfeiting the euro, and market abuse by bankers.[32] Further proposals on fraud against the EU budget and terrorism are under discussion. All except the Directive on bankers replace (or would replace) previous measures. The emergency brake has not been used to date.

5.2.4 Competence issues

One key question regarding substantive criminal law, as noted already, is the historic dispute regarding the division of powers between the EC and the EU (the first and third pillars) in this area, and the provisions of the Treaty of Lisbon which subsequently address this issue.[33] This point is examined in more detail below.[34]

---

[26] See revised Art 17(2) TEU. It would also be possible for the European Council to change the voting rule applicable to extensions of competence, pursuant to Art 48(7), revised TEU.

[27] Case C-158/14 *A*, pending.

[28] On the legal effect of the different EU instruments, see Art 288 TFEU.

[29] Compare Arts 33 and 325 TFEU to the previous Arts 135 and 280 EC.

[30] Council doc 16542/2/09, 27 Nov 2009.   [31] See II:5.5 and II:5.6 below.

[32] See n 31 above.

[33] The following discussion (and the discussion in II:5.4.1.2 below) is adapted from S Peers, 'EU Criminal Law and the Treaty of Lisbon' (2008) 33 ELRev 507 at 514–22.

[34] II:5.4.1.

The remaining issues concern the scope and intensity of the EU's competence as set out in Article 83(1) TFEU, as well as the relationship between the powers conferred by Article 83(1), as well as Article 83 as a whole, and the other provisions of the Treaties. Previously, as seen above, Article 31(1)(e) TEU stated that EU powers 'shall include' the adoption of measures harmonizing the definition of offences and relevant penalties in several specific areas; Article 29 TEU stated that the EU's third pillar objectives were to be achieved, inter alia, by approximating national law regarding a different list of crimes, 'in particular' certain listed offences; and the Tampere European Council conclusions referred to a third list of areas where the EU should focus its initial efforts to harmonize substantive law, 'such as', inter alia, financial crime. These provisions appeared to be non-exhaustive, but any ambiguity on this point has been resolved by the wording of Article 83(1) TFEU, which quite clearly gives the EU powers only as regards the ten crimes listed in the second sub-paragraph. If this list were not exhaustive, there would be no point to the third sub-paragraph of Article 83(1), which provides for the possibility of extending the EU's powers to further crime. The restriction of the EU's actions to specified crimes should be understood as a *quid pro quo* for the extension of QMV in this area.

Next, both Article 83(1) and (2) TFEU expressly limit the EU to adopting 'minimum rules' only, ie full harmonization of substantive criminal law is ruled out. This limitation also appeared in the previous Article 31(1)(e) TEU, but it did not apply to the exercise of Community criminal law competence per se.[35]

As for the relationship between Article 83(1) TFEU and other provisions of the Treaties, the first issue is the relationship between Article 83(1) and (2). It is necessary to distinguish between the two paragraphs because the decision-making procedure in each of them is potentially different—depending upon the other decision-making procedures in the rest of the Treaty, which, as noted above, would apply to the adoption of measures pursuant to paragraph 2. Furthermore, different substantive criteria would apply to the adoption of measures under the two paragraphs. Finally, it is arguable that the British, Danish, and Irish opt-outs from Title V do not apply to paragraph 2, whereas they undoubtedly apply to paragraph 1.[36]

So what is the relationship between the two paragraphs? In the absence of any express wording to the contrary (ie a phrase like 'without prejudice to'), each paragraph should logically be considered to be a *lex specialis* as regards the other paragraph. Therefore, the scope of paragraph 1 cannot be extended by the Council to cover offences within the scope of paragraph 2,[37] and paragraph 2 cannot be interpreted to

---

[35] This point was not relevant to the EC's environmental crime Directive (Dir 2008/99, [2008] OJ L 328/28), since the EC's environmental powers limited it to setting minimum standards only (previous Art 176 EC, now Art 193 TFEU, which has not changed this rule). On the other hand it was relevant to EC Directives setting out criminal law rules as regards shipping pollution and employer sanctions for hiring irregular migrants (respectively Dirs 2009/123 and 2009/52, [2009] OJ L 280/52 and [2009] OJ L 168/24). In the latter case, the Council and EP nevertheless restrained themselves to setting minimum standards regarding offences only (see the title of Dir 2009/52), but in the first case it appears that they did not.

[36] On this issue, see I:2.2.5.1, where it is argued that the opt-outs do apply.

[37] Such an extension could, for instance, lead to the application of QMV and the ordinary legislative procedure to criminal law measures concerning tax fraud (see Art 113 TFEU), and therefore would circumvent to some extent national parliaments' control of the *passerelle* clause that would otherwise apply to changing decision-making in that field (see revised Art 48(7) TEU).

cover items expressly listed *at the outset* as falling within the scope of paragraph 1. This is particularly relevant as regards trafficking in persons, arms trafficking, money laundering, counterfeiting means of payment, and computer crime.[38]

Next, what is the scope of Article 83 TFEU as compared to the Treaty's other policing and criminal law provisions? In particular, can Article 83 be used to adopt measures relating to jurisdiction, procedure, or investigations concerning the relevant crimes? Given that Article 83 refers only to criminal offences and penalties, while other provisions of Chapters 4 and 5 of Title V refer more specifically to conflicts of jurisdiction, procedure, and investigations,[39] it must follow, in the absence of any provisions in the Treaty regulating the relationships between the various legal bases, that the latter provisions have to be used to adopt measures concerning those aspects of criminal law and policing. This would entail the use of dual legal bases.[40] However, Article 83 TFEU must still be the correct legal base as regards rules requiring or permitting Member States to assert jurisdiction over crimes within the scope of that Article,[41] since such measures are ancillary to the definition of offences and do not fall within the scope of the power in Article 82(1) TFEU to *prevent and settle* such conflicts, except to the extent that they included rules on priority jurisdiction.[42]

On the other hand, it is surely beyond doubt that both paragraphs of Article 83 TFEU can be used to adopt rules harmonizing *penalties* for specific offences.[43] As for the first paragraph, the express reference to adopting minimum rules concerning offences and penalties is simply a continuation of the prior power set out in the previous Article 31(1)(e) TEU, as set out above. In the case of the second paragraph, the competence to define sanctions has gone beyond the EC's prior powers as defined by the Court,[44] but accepting a power to define sanctions following the entry into force of the Treaty of Lisbon respects the literal wording of this provision ('criminal offences *and* sanctions'). It should not be assumed that this provision must be subject to the same interpretation as the previous EC Treaty. After all, the drafters of the Treaty of Lisbon made the deliberate choice to amend substantially the substance of EC and EU competence as regards many aspects of JHA law. It can hardly be assumed that their only intention in doing so was merely to restate the existing law. Moreover, the interpretation of the

---

[38] The Commission argued that criminal law measures concerning the last three issues fell within the scope of the previous EC Treaty: see COM (2005) 583, 23 Nov 2005. As for trafficking in persons, following the entry into force of the Treaty of Lisbon there is now an express power on this subject in the immigration chapter of Title V (see I:7.2.4 above); and as for arms trafficking, the Commission later proposed an amendment to the EC firearms Directive which would have required Member States to criminalize certain acts, although the Council and EP did not agree to this proposal (see II:5.4.1.1 below).

[39] Moreover, these other provisions are not limited in scope to particular crimes.

[40] See the Directives on trafficking in persons and offences against children (Dir 2011/36, [2011] OJ L 101/1 and Dir 2011/93, [2011] OJ L 335/1), which contain the dual legal bases of Arts 83 and 82(2) (as regards the rights of victims). Note that there is no problem per se combining legal bases with and without an emergency brake rule: see II:3.2.4 above.

[41] EU measures on substantive criminal law have always contained such rules, but EC measures have not. For details see II:6.5 below.

[42] A small number of third pillar measures contain such priority jurisdiction rules: see II:6.5 below.

[43] The proposals tabled since the entry into force of the Treaty of Lisbon have contained such provisions (see II:5.5.1.2 below).

[44] See further the more detailed discussion of paragraph 2 in II:5.4.1.2 below.

second paragraph should be consistent with that of the first paragraph where the same wording is used; and the competence to adopt rules on sanctions to enforce other EU policies would enhance the effectiveness of those policies, which is the underlying purpose of paragraph 2.[45]

As for the relationship between Article 83 and Article 86 TFEU,[46] concerning the competence to establish the European Public Prosecutor, Article 86 is the correct legal basis for conferring specific procedural powers upon the Public Prosecutor,[47] and to that end it can be used to define the substantive crimes which the Prosecutor has jurisdiction over. However, it cannot be the source of rules harmonizing national law to this end, because Article 83 is a *lex specialis* on this issue. If the Prosecutor is ever established, presumably it will be necessary in the interests of coherence to ensure that the Prosecutor's jurisdiction matches the definition of crimes which the EU has already harmonized, or at least that the EU adopts parallel harmonization measures when the Prosecutor is established.

Two awkward issues could arise in this context. First of all, the power for the European Council to expand the powers of the Public Prosecutor is prima facie wider than the EU's powers to harmonize national criminal laws, since Article 86(4) refers, inter alia, to 'serious crime having a cross-border dimension' while Article 83(1) refers to '*particularly* serious crime with a cross-border dimension.'[48] So in theory, the European Public Prosecutor could be awarded jurisdiction to deal with crimes that have not been harmonized and even *could* not be harmonized by the EU (assuming that such crimes do not fall within the scope of Article 83(2) either). In this case, the measure conferring powers upon the Public Prosecutor to this end would have to define its jurisdiction without thereby harmonizing national law on this subject. In practice, the proposed Regulation on the Prosecutor (see Chapter 6 of this volume) is intended to be consistent with the proposed EU legislation on this issue.

Secondly, there could be complications because the EU can only harmonize national criminal law in order to establish minimum standards, whereas the Public Prosecutor would presumably have a uniform jurisdiction. This could be addressed by simply restricting the Public Prosecutor's activities to cases which fall within the scope of his or her uniform jurisdiction, while allocating competence to national authorities as regards cases falling outside the scope of that jurisdiction.

Next, what about the relationship between Article 83 TFEU and the other provisions of the treaties, besides the other criminal law and policing provisions? Is it still possible, for instance, to adopt 'Community criminal law' on the basis of the EU's environmental law powers (Article 192 TFEU, previously Article 175 EC), rather than Article 83(2) TFEU?[49] Similarly, could 'Community criminal law' relating to money laundering, for

---

[45] See further the discussion of the effectiveness/sanctions link in II:5.4.1 below.

[46] This point is particularly relevant since the Council must act unanimously pursuant to Art 86.

[47] See more precisely Art 86(3) TFEU. For more on Art 86, see II:3.2.4 above and II:6.2.4 and II:6.10 below.

[48] This gap could not be remedied by conferring extra powers upon the EU pursuant to the third subparagraph of Art 83(1), since any extension of powers pursuant to that provision would still be limited by the requirement that the other areas of crime concerned 'meet the criteria specified in this paragraph.'

[49] On the scope of such powers before the entry into force of the Treaty of Lisbon, see E Herlin-Karnell, 'Commission v Council: Some Reflections on Criminal Law in the First Pillar' (2007) 13 EPL 69; S White,

instance, be adopted on the basis of Article 114 TFEU (previous Article 95 TEC), rather than Article 83(1) TFEU?[50] The point is particularly important because there are no emergency brakes or opt-outs in most other provisions of the Treaties. To both questions, the answer is that Article 83 is a *lex specialis*, in the absence of any other provisions expressly conferring substantive criminal law competence in any other part of the treaties. It is irrelevant that the Court of Justice has ruled that at least some provisions of the EC Treaty, before its amendment by the Treaty of Lisbon, previously conferred criminal law competence on the Community, because the prior legal framework in this area was fundamentally altered by the Treaty of Lisbon in order to introduce a specific legal base dealing precisely with this issue. So it follows that the Commission's proposed use of Article 325 TFEU alone as the legal base for the proposed measure on fraud against the EU budget is incorrect.[51]

5.2.5 Territorial scope

First of all, as for measures adopted before the entry into force of the Treaty of Lisbon, EU measures on substantive criminal law applied to all Member States, because there was no opt-out as such from the previous third pillar. For the limited number of substantive criminal law measures within the scope of the Schengen *acquis*,[52] the UK and Ireland opted in,[53] and Norway, Iceland, Switzerland, and (in future) Liechtenstein apply the relevant rules.[54] The new Member States applied these Schengen rules, and all other relevant EU third pillar rules, from the date of their accession to the EU.[55] However, in the case of one *Community* measure imposing criminal law obligations relating to immigration law, three Member States are not bound by it pursuant to their opt-out from EC immigration law.[56]

Following the entry into force of the Treaty of Lisbon, the UK and Ireland can opt out of each legislative proposal in this area, but are also now subject to special rules if they opt out of measures amending acts by which they are already bound. However, it might be questioned whether the UK and Ireland are in fact able to opt out from 'Community criminal law' measures adopted on the basis of Article 83(2) TFEU if, as argued elsewhere in this book, their opt-out applies to these measures.[57] As for Denmark, it is excluded from all measures adopted after the entry into force of the Treaty of Lisbon, except those building upon the Schengen *acquis*, which are subject to special rules, until or unless it either renounces its JHA opt-out or chooses the British and Irish opt-out model.[58] To date, the UK or Ireland both opted in to the Directives on sexual offences and attacks on information systems, while Ireland opted in to the Directives

---

'Harmonisation of Criminal Law under the First Pillar' (2006) ELRev 81; and S Peers, 'The Community's Criminal Law Competence: The Plot Thickens' (2008) 33 ELRev 399.

[50] As noted above, the Commission argued that the previous Art 95 EC conferred criminal law competence in respect of money laundering, n 38 above.

[51] COM (2012) 363, 11 July 2012.   [52] See II:5.2.1 above.   [53] See further II:2.2.5.1 above.

[54] See further II:2.2.5.4 above   [55] See further II:2.2.5.3 above.

[56] Dir 2009/52 on the prohibition of the employment of irregular migrants ([2009] OJ L 168/24). The three Member States not bound by this Dir are the UK, Ireland, and Denmark: see I:7.2.5.

[57] See further II:2.2.5.1 above.   [58] See further II:2.2.5.2 above.

on trafficking in persons, counterfeiting the euro, and market abuse. The UK also opted in to the Directive on trafficking in persons after its adoption.[59] The UK opted out of the proposed Directive on the protection of the EU's financial interests, but Ireland opted in. Finally, the UK used the 'block opt-out' on pre-Lisbon JHA measures, with effect from 1 December 2014, to free itself from all of its prior EU obligations relating to substantive criminal law.[60] The UK therefore only has obligations as regards the three post-Lisbon Directives it opted in to.

5.3 Human Rights

5.3.1 International human rights law

Human rights measures do not generally impact directly upon substantive criminal law (as distinct from criminal procedure, where the right to a fair trial is a fundamental element of the law). However, in some cases the criminalization of certain acts breaches human rights obligations,[61] or the level of penalty amounts to an unlawful or disproportionate restriction on a protected right.[62] Conversely, sometimes it is necessary for States to criminalize certain acts and to carry out effective investigations and prosecutions in order to protect the human rights of the crime victims.[63]

The most significant human rights principle applicable to substantive criminal law generally is the principle of legality and non-retroactivity of criminal law, as set out in Article 7 of the European Convention on Human Rights (ECHR):

1. No one shall be held guilty of any criminal offence on account of any act or omission which did not constitute a criminal offence under national or international law at the time when it was committed. Nor shall a heavier penalty be imposed than the one that was applicable at the time the criminal offence was committed.
2. This article shall not prejudice the trial and punishment of any person for any act or omission which, at the time when it was committed, was criminal according to the general principles of law recognised by civilised nations.

Article 7 ECHR requires strict interpretation of criminal offences, which must be clearly provided for, with a foreseeable application.[64] The Human Rights Court has even followed the jurisprudence of the Court of Justice (see below) in applying the non-retroactivity principle also to require that subsequent more *lenient* treatment of

---

[59] The Commission approved UK participation by means of a Decision: [2011] OJ L 271/49.

[60] See the list of the measures which the UK opted out of: [2014] OJ C 430/17.

[61] For example, see the judgment of the European Court of Human Rights in *Dudgeon v UK* (A-45), where criminalization of homosexual acts violated the right to private life protected by Art 8 ECHR. Criminalization of controversial opinions (as long as they do not support violence directly) is a breach of Art 10 ECHR: see, for instance, *Jersild v Denmark* (A-298) and *Zana v Turkey* [1997] ECHR-VII, as regards racism and terrorism respectively.

[62] For example, see respectively *Sun v Russia*, judgment of 5 Feb 2009, and *Grifhorst v France*, judgment of 26 Feb 2009, as regards penalties for unauthorized declarations of cash when crossing borders.

[63] See generally A Mowbray, *The Development of Positive Obligations under the European Convention on Human Rights by the European Court of Human Rights* (Hart, 2004).

[64] For the principles, see *Kokkinakis v Greece* (A260-A); and see particularly their application in *Veeber (no 2) v Estonia* (Reports 2003-I) (altering conditions for liability retroactively) and *Baskaya and Okcuoglu v Turkey* (Reports 1999-IV) (no extension by analogy).

particular actions must apply to the benefit of those persons who committed the relevant behaviour before the law was liberalized.[65]

5.3.2 Application to EU law

The principle of the legality of criminal law and non-retroactive criminal liability is recognized as one of the general principles of Community law upheld by the Court of Justice. The principle has been applied by the Court to ban Member States' imposition of criminal liability for breach of an EC Directive or Regulation before Member States implement that measure in their national law.[66] The Court has applied this principle *mutatis mutandis* to the imposition of criminal liability for breach of EU Framework Decisions, as regards substantive criminal law (but not criminal procedure).[67] Similarly, the Court has ruled that Member States cannot apply criminal sanctions for breach of Community law for events which occurred before adoption of that EC legislation.[68] Notably, the European Court of Human Rights has emphasized that the principle fully applies even where national law is implementing Community obligations.[69]

Community law did not initially recognize the principle of many national legal systems that criminal defendants were entitled to the benefit of subsequent legislation if it is more favourable for them.[70] However, where Member States did apply such a principle, the Court of Justice was willing to interpret the EC legislation or EC Treaty Article at issue in order to determine whether the accused could benefit from the later rules.[71] The principle eventually governed any administrative law sanctions which enforce EC legislation.[72] Finally, the Court declared that the principle was a general principle of EC (now EU) law,[73] which means that it must be observed within the scope of application of EC and EU law, in particular whenever Member States are implementing EU or EC measures by imposing criminal penalties. As noted above, the European Court of Human Rights has now interpreted the ECHR to the same effect.

The EU's Charter of Rights contains the principles of legality and non-retroactivity of criminal liability, along with the principle of retroactive effect of more lenient penalties, and the principle that criminal penalties should be proportionate to the offence.[74]

---

[65] *Scoppola v Italy*, 17 Sep 2009. On the application of this principle to procedural law and to jurisdictional issues, see respectively II:3.3.2 above and II:6.3.1 below.
[66] Cases: 14/86 *Pretore di Salo* [1987] ECR 2545, 80/86 *Kolpinghuis Nijmegen* [1987] ECR 3969, C-168/95 *Arcaro* [1996] ECR I-4705; Joined Cases C-74/95 and C-129/95 *Criminal Proceedings v X* [1996] ECR I-6609; C-60/02 *X* [2004] ECR I-651; and C-387/02, C-391/02, and C-403/02 *Berlusconi* [2005] ECR I-3565.
[67] See Case C-105/03 *Pupino* [2005] ECR I-5285. [68] Case 63/83 *Kirk* [1984] ECR 2689.
[69] *Cantoni v France* (Reports 1996-V), para 30. [70] Case 234/83 *Duisberg* [1985] ECR 327.
[71] For example, see Joined Cases C-358/93 and C-416/93 *Bordessa* [1995] ECR I-361.
[72] Reg 2988/95 ([1995] OJ L 312/1); see Cases C-354/95 *NFU* [1997] ECR I-4559 and C-295/02 *Gerken* [2004] ECR I-6369.
[73] See the judgment in *Berlusconi*, n 66 above.
[74] Art 49 of the Charter ([2000] OJ C 364), amended in [2007] OJ C 303.

5.4 EU Criminal Law and Other Areas of EU Law

There are two types of intersection between other areas of EU law (outside the scope of EU criminal law per se) and substantive national criminal law. In some cases, national criminal law is often used to give effect to EU law rules and principles, besides those of criminal law proper. The broader question has been historically whether the Community had competence to *require* Member States to set out criminal law penalties. This question has been answered by Article 83(2) TFEU, as of the entry into force of the Treaty of Lisbon. Conversely, the imposition of criminal liability by national law is in some cases precluded because it prevents the exercise of Community law rights.

5.4.1 Community criminal law competence

5.4.1.1 Before the Treaty of Lisbon

Before the entry into force of the Treaty of Lisbon, the competence of the European Community to require Member States to impose criminal sanctions was much debated. As noted already,[75] Articles 135 and 280 EC, respectively inserted and amended by the Treaty of Amsterdam, specified that EC measures concerning customs law and the protection of EC financial interests 'shall not concern the application of national criminal law or the national administration of justice'.[76] On the other hand, Article 63(3)(b) EC, which was also inserted by the Treaty of Amsterdam, conferred a power for the Community to adopt measures on 'illegal immigration and illegal residence', without any proviso similar to those in Articles 135 or 280 EC.

During this period, the Commission and EP argued that some EC Treaty legal bases did confer the power upon the Community to require Member States to harmonize national criminal law in certain areas. However, due to the political and legal objections of Member States to the existence of EC competence over criminal law, the Council developed a practice of providing in EC legislation that the Community prohibits certain acts (in Regulations) or that the Member States must prohibit certain acts (in Directives).[77] In either case, human rights rules restrict the imposition or aggravation of criminal liability until a Member State has clearly provided for that liability in national law.[78]

But despite the Council's practice, the Court of Justice first of all developed general principles of EC law that required at least some degree of obligation upon Member States to enforce Community rules by criminal law, and then later confirmed that the Community indeed had some criminal law competence. On the first point, the leading case is *Commission v Greece* (*Greek maize*), in which the Court of Justice held that a Member State had an obligation to apply its substantive and procedural criminal law

---

[75] II:5.2.2 above.
[76] Also as noted above, these provisos were repealed by the Treaty of Lisbon (see now Arts 33 and 325 TFEU).
[77] On Regs in particular, see Case 50/76 *Amsterdam Bulb* [1977] ECR 137.
[78] See II:5.3.2 above.

to enforce EC law in the same way that it would apply its national criminal law to equivalent national offences.[79] Furthermore, such sanctions had to be 'effective, proportionate and dissuasive'. This 'equality of sanctions' principle was then inserted into the EC Treaty by the Maastricht Treaty as a principle governing fraud against the EC budget (Article 209a EC), and the Treaty of Amsterdam subsequently provided that national measures had to be 'effective' and a 'deterrent', and apply to 'other illegal activities' affecting the EC financial interests (Article 280 EC, now Article 325 TFEU). In several cases relating to EC fisheries conservation, the Court made it clear that there is an obligation to prosecute or take administrative action against individuals who breach EC law.[80]

Despite the Council's opposition, the Commission kept proposing Community measures including express obligations to criminalize certain activity. In particular, following the Treaty of Amsterdam, it proposed EC legislation, based on Article 280 EC, incorporating much of a pre-Amsterdam third pillar Convention (and Protocols) concerning fraud against the EU budget.[81] It also proposed a Directive on criminal law and the environment, and later a Directive accompanying a proposed Framework Decision on shipping pollution.[82] Within the internal market powers of the Community, the Commission proposed clauses in Directives on enforcement of intellectual property rights requiring Member States to criminalize serious infringements of such rights,[83] along with similar clauses in proposed Directives on money laundering and market abuse.[84] The Commission also argued that the Council lacked legal power under the third pillar to adopt some aspects of the Framework Decision on smuggling in persons or a Decision on counterfeit travel documents,[85] to address many 'cyber-crime' issues,[86] and to criminalize incitement to racism or xenophobia, on the grounds that such measures fell within the scope of the EC's anti-racism powers conferred by Article 13 EC.[87] There were also parallel disputes concerning competence related to customs issues.[88]

The Council's response was to reject any prospect of negotiating the proposed Directive on fraud against the EC budget or the Directive on environmental crime. Instead, Member States completed ratification of the Convention on the former subject and the Council adopted a Framework Decision on the latter.[89] The Council also moved

---

[79] Case 68/88 [1989] ECR 2685. See COM (95) 162, 3 May 1995 and Council Resolution ([1995] OJ C 188/1).

[80] Cases C-333/99 *Commission v France* [2001] ECR I-1025; C-418/00 and C-419/00 *Commission v France* [2002] ECR I-3969; C-454/99 *Commission v UK* [2002] ECR I-10323; and C-140/00 *Commission v UK* [2002] ECR I-10379.

[81] COM (2001) 272, 22 May 2001; revised after EP vote: COM (2002) 577, 16 Oct 2002.

[82] See respectively COM (2001) 139, 14 Mar 2001; revised after EP vote: COM (2002) 544, 30 Sep 2002 (environmental crime); Art 6 of COM (2003) 92, 5 Mar 2003 (shipping pollution Directive); COM (2003) 227, 2 May 2003 (shipping pollution Framework Decision).

[83] Art 20 of proposed Directive (COM (2003) 46, 30 Jan 2003).

[84] Respectively Art 1(1) of COM (2004) 448, 30 Jun 2004, and Art 14 of COM (2001) 281, 30 May 2001.

[85] See respectively Statement 154/02 in the Council summary of acts adopted in Nov 2002 (Council doc 15915/02, 16 Jan 2003) and Statement 22/00 in the Council summary of acts adopted in Mar 2000 (Council doc 8080/00, 28 Apr 2000).

[86] See the explanatory memorandum to the proposed Framework Decision on attacks on information systems (COM (2002) 173, 19 Apr 2004), p 8.

[87] See the Commission staff working paper on this point (Council doc 7880/02, 11 Apr 2002).

[88] See II:7.4.1 below.   [89] For details of these measures, see II:5.5.1.2 below.

the criminal law provisions of the proposed Directive on shipping pollution into the linked Framework Decision.[90] Finally, the Council removed the proposed criminal law provisions from the adopted Directives on intellectual property rights enforcement, money laundering, and market abuse.[91]

However, the Commission eventually decided to seize the Court of Justice with one of these disputes in an attempt to settle the issue. It brought a legal challenge pursuant to the previous Article 35 EU in 2003 against a Framework Decision on environmental crime, arguing that it usurped the EC's powers to adopt environmental legislation. The Court's judgment in September 2005 upheld the Commission's arguments and annulled the Framework Decision.[92] In its judgment, the Court started by referring to the previous Article 47 EU (later repealed by the Treaty of Lisbon), which provided that nothing in the TEU is to affect the EC Treaty; the rule was reiterated in the previous Article 29 EU. According to the Court's prior case law, this meant that Title VI measures could not 'encroach upon' Community powers.[93] Next, the Court set out the scope of the EC's environmental powers, beginning with the reference to the environment in the tasks and objectives of the EC, the horizontal requirement that EC policies must respect the environment, and the specific EC powers over the environment. According to consistent case law, the correct legal base of a measure must be interpreted in light of its aim and its content. In this case, the Framework Decision had the aim of environmental protection and its content essentially concerned harmonization of national criminal law.

The Court reiterated the 'general rule' that 'neither criminal law nor the rules of criminal procedure fall within the Community's competence'.[94] But (as in the case of national criminal law measures restricting free movement rights) this rule was a presumption that could be overturned: the rule 'does not prevent the Community legislature, when the application of effective, proportionate and dissuasive criminal penalties by the competent national authorities is an essential measure for combating serious environmental offences, from taking measures which relate to the criminal law of the Member States which it considers necessary in order to ensure that the rules which it lays down on environmental protection are fully effective'.[95] The Court then added that 'in this instance, although . . . the framework decision determine[s] that certain conduct which is particularly detrimental to the environment is to be criminal, [it] leave[s] to the Member States the choice of the criminal penalties to apply, although . . . the penalties must be effective, proportionate and dissuasive'.[96] Finally, the Court rejected a contrary argument based on the prior Articles 135 and 280 EC, the legal bases concerning customs cooperation and fraud against the EC's interests, which, as noted above,[97] then precluded the use of those particular EC powers to affect 'the application

---

[90] On the adopted measures, see ibid.

[91] See respectively Dirs 2004/48 ([2004] OJ L 157/45), 2005/60 ([2005] OJ L 309/15), and 2003/6 ([2003] OJ L 96/16).

[92] Case C-176/03 *Commission v Council* [2005] ECR I-7879.

[93] Case C-170/96 *Commission v Council* [1998] ECR I-2763. On the first/third pillar dividing line in general, see II:2.4 above.

[94] Para 47 of judgment, ibid.   [95] Para 48 of judgment, ibid.

[96] Para 49 of judgment, ibid.   [97] II:5.2.2.

of national criminal law and the administration of justice', on the grounds that it could not be inferred from those provisions that the EC lacked the power to impose criminal law sanctions in order to ensure the effectiveness of EC environmental law.[98] So the Court found that Articles 1–7 of the Framework Decision, which set out obligations for the Member States to impose criminal liability for natural persons and criminal or administrative liability for legal persons for specified offences, encroached upon EC law. Although the Commission had not challenged the remaining provisions of the Framework Decision, in particular accepting that Articles 8 and 9 concerning jurisdiction and prosecution did not fall within the scope of EC powers,[99] the Court annulled the entire measure as its provisions were indivisible.

This was a potentially far-reaching judgment, but the obvious question was its scope. Did the judgment apply only to issues within the scope of EC environmental law, or did it apply to other areas of EC law as well? Did it apply only to the definition of offences, or did it also apply to other aspects of criminal law as well? The Commission issued a communication not long after the judgment giving its interpretation of the judgment's implications.[100] In the Commission's view, the 2005 judgment applied 'to the other common policies and to the four [internal market] freedoms'.[101] Furthermore, the EC's power in such cases applied not just to the definition of offences, but also to the obligation to impose criminal penalties, and to 'the nature and level of criminal penalties applicable, or other aspects related to criminal law'.[102] It followed that a number of EU measures listed by the Commission were 'entirely or partly incorrect, since all or some of their provisions were adopted on the wrong legal basis'.[103]

The Commission therefore decided to bring proceedings for annulment of one of these measures, a Framework Decision on shipping pollution, before the Court of Justice (see below), but it was out of time to challenge any other adopted measures. Pending the judgment in that case, the Commission proposed a Directive on environmental crime, following the annulment of the relevant Framework Decision,[104] and withdrew a proposed Framework Decision on counterfeiting intellectual property, instead integrating all of its criminal law provisions (except the provision on criminal jurisdiction) into a proposed Directive on this issue.[105] The Commission also subsequently proposed a Directive which defined a criminal offence as regards the employment of irregular migrants.[106] Discussion of these proposals was placed on hold pending the Court's judgment on the validity of the Framework Decision on shipping pollution.

The judgment in that case definitively answered one of the two key questions regarding Community criminal law competence, but did not clearly answer the other key question.[107] First of all, the Court ruled that the EC had no competence to define

---

[98] Para 52 of judgment, n 93 above.   [99] See para 23 of the judgment, n 93 above.
[100] COM(2005)583, 23 Nov 2005.   [101] Para 8 of the communication.
[102] Para 10 of the communication (footnote omitted).   [103] Para 14 of the communication.
[104] COM (2007) 51, 9 Feb 2008.
[105] COM (2005) 276, 12 July 2005 (proposed Framework Decision); COM (2006) 168, 26 Apr 2006 (proposed Directive). The latter proposal was later withdrawn (see II:5.2.3 above).
[106] COM (2007) 249, 15 May 2007.
[107] Case C-440/05 *Commission v Council* [2007] ECR I-9097. For further analysis of the judgment, see S Peers, 'The Community's Criminal Law Competence: The Plot Thickens' (2008) 33 ELRev 399.

sanctions in relation to criminal offences: 'the determination of the type and level of the criminal penalties to be applied does not fall within the Community's sphere of competence'.[108] The Court did not rule, however, on Community competence to adopt measures as regards other aspects of criminal law (such as jurisdiction). More fundamentally, the Court failed to give a clear ruling on whether the EC had competence to define criminal offences in all areas of EC competence, deciding only that the definition of criminal offences with a view to protecting the environment could be integrated into a transport law measure, as in this case.[109] This meant that the provisions on criminal offences in the Framework Decision were invalid, and since the rest of the Framework Decision was indivisible from these provisions, it was annulled.[110]

The consequence of the judgment was that the Council and EP soon afterward adopted the proposed Directive on environmental crime, without the detailed provisions on offences as originally proposed by the Commission.[111] They also adopted a Directive amending the initial Directive on shipping pollution in order to add definitions of relevant criminal offences.[112] Most significantly, they agreed to exercise the EC's criminal law competence in an area *not* related to environmental protection, by adopting the proposed Directive on prohibition of employment of irregular migrants, including criminal law offences.[113] Nevertheless, they still rejected the suggestion of introducing criminal law provisions in an EC Directive relating to firearms,[114] and the Council gave up discussions on the proposed Directive on criminal sanctions for breaches of intellectual property law.

5.4.1.2 *After the Treaty of Lisbon*

As from the entry into force of the Treaty of Lisbon, the existence of 'Community criminal law competence' is confirmed and clarified in Article 83(2) TFEU.[115] Nevertheless, this provision raises a number of questions.

First of all, it should be reiterated that, as argued above:[116] Article 83(1) and (2) TFEU are *lex specialis* as regards each other; the other policing and criminal law provisions of the Treaties have to be used to adopt measures concerning *conflicts* of jurisdiction, procedure, and investigations; Article 83(2) can be used to adopt measures *asserting* jurisdiction in relation to specific offences, and not only to define offences, but also to prescribe sanctions in respect of those offences; Article 83(2) applies rather than Article 86 as regards the harmonization of the national criminal law which the European Public Prosecutor, if established, would have jurisdiction to enforce; and Article 83 (1) and (2) are each a *lex specialis* as compared to the rest of the Treaty as

---

[108] Para 70 of the judgment.   [109] Para 60 of the judgment.
[110] Para 73 of the judgment.   [111] Dir 2008/99 ([2008] OJ L 328/28).
[112] Dir 2009/123 ([2009] OJ L 280/52).   [113] Dir 2009/52 ([2009] OJ L 168/24).
[114] The Commission had proposed an amendment to the EC firearms Directive (Dir 91/477 [1991] OJ L 256/51) which would have required Member States to criminalize certain acts (Art 1(3), COM (2006) 93, 2 Mar 2006). The final amendments to the firearms Dir do not include this provision (Dir 2008/51, ([2008] OJ L 179/5).
[115] This book continues to use this anachronistic phrase to describe this form of competence, in the absence of any obvious alternative.
[116] II:5.2.4.

regards respectively the adoption of criminal law measures concerning specific listed crimes (Article 83(1)) and ensuring effective harmonization (Article 83(2)).

Next, given that the previous EC criminal competence arguably only applied to issues related to environmental protection,[117] does Article 83(2) TFEU apply to other areas as well? On this point, it could not seriously be asserted that Article 83(2) applies only to environmental protection. There is no limit on its subject-matter (other than the scope of the Treaties), but instead an abstract test of a requirement of a need for the effective implementation of a Union policy which has been subject to harmonization measures. Also, the wording of the second sentence of Article 83(2) refers generally to the rest of the Treaties, without any distinction. Finally, the exhaustive list of crimes in Article 83(1) TFEU suggests by *a contrario* reasoning that Article 83(2) is not limited in subject-matter.

So how should the conditions for the application of Article 83(2) TFEU be interpreted? First, the criminal law measures have to be 'essential' for implementation of an EU policy. According to the Court's case law, this condition previously applied to the prior Community criminal law competence, and there is no reason to imagine that the condition should apply differently under the Treaty of Lisbon provision. However, it is not easy in practice to assess whether this condition is satisfied.[118]

The second condition is that the area concerned must have been 'subject to harmonisation measures', which was also already required pursuant to the case law on the previous competence,[119] but is more explicit pursuant to Article 83(2) TFEU. So, for example, the EU could only adopt measures on intellectual property crime to the extent that the EU has harmonized intellectual property law.[120] It could not be said that there is a 'Union policy' that needs implementing effectively in the absence of harmonization in specific areas of law. On the other hand, there is nothing in the current legal framework or the Treaty of Lisbon that requires *full* harmonization as a pre-condition. In fact, such a requirement implicitly never applied as regards the previous legal framework, given that, as noted above, the Community could not fully harmonize environmental law.[121]

While misgivings were raised about the appropriateness of harmonization of sanctions by the Community,[122] these concerns are addressed in the Treaty of Lisbon by the existence of the emergency brake, which also applies to the definition of offences, and the requirement that the EU can only establish 'minimum rules' when exercising its powers pursuant to Article 83(2) TFEU.[123] Moreover, such concerns were previously

---

[117] The validity of Dir 2009/52 on employer sanctions, which defines a criminal offence in an area not linked to environmental protection, might conceivably be questioned.

[118] See the Opinion in the 2007 *Commission v Council* judgment and the analysis in Peers, n 107 above.

[119] See para 66 in the 2007 *Commission v Council* judgment, n 118 above: 'the Community legislature may require the Member States to introduce such penalties in order to ensure that *the rules which it lays down...are fully effective*'.

[120] Compare with the Commission's proposal on this issue (COM (2006) 168, 28 Apr 2006, since withdrawn), which would have provided for criminal offences and penalties regardless of whether the intellectual property right in question had been subject to harmonization by Community law or not.

[121] Art 176 EC, now Art 193 TFEU.

[122] See further the Opinion in Case C-440/05, and the discussion in Peers, n 107 above.

[123] As noted above (II:5.2.3), the latter rule was not expressly applicable in the previous legal framework.

addressed in practice as regards the harmonization of sanctions related to criminal law within the scope of the previous third pillar, by means of great flexibility accorded to Member States as regards the levels of sanctions.[124]

Article 83(2) TFEU also requires that the adoption of the criminal law measures must not precede the harmonization measures in other areas of EU policy ('...in an area which *has been subject* to harmonisation measures...' and the use of the 'same' decision-making procedure '*as was followed* for the adoption of the harmonization measures...').[125] In fact, strictly speaking, the English version of this Treaty provision would seem to rule out even the *simultaneous* adoption of criminal law measures and harmonization measures.[126] This strict interpretation should be doubted in light of the wording of the rest of the new provision and the underlying purpose of that new provision, because the 'effective implementation' of a Union policy could obviously be jeopardized in the meantime if criminal law measures could only be adopted *after* the harmonization measure. However, there would be no scope to interpret the new provision in light of the effectiveness principle to permit the adoption of the criminal law measures *before* the harmonization measures—because again, there would be no Union policy to implement effectively by criminal law measures if no harmonization measures had yet been adopted. In any event, even if the strict interpretation of the temporal scope of this clause is correct, Article 83(2) does not set out any minimum waiting period before the adoption of the criminal law legislation. So the procedural requirement of a later adoption of the criminal law measure could still be satisfied if the criminal law act were adopted *immediately* after the adoption of the harmonization legislation, both measures having possibly been negotiated in parallel.

Next, do criminal law measures adopted on this basis have to form a part of the original legislation on the issue, or do they have to be adopted as separate measures? The answer is that separate measures have to be adopted. First of all, the requirement to adopt the criminal legislation after the adoption of the harmonization measures points strongly to a legal requirement to adopt separate measures, particularly the requirement to apply the 'same' decision-making procedure '*as was followed* for the adoption of the harmonisation measures...'. Moreover, it should be recalled that as noted above, Article 83(2) TFEU is subject to the emergency brake procedure and possibly also the British, Irish, and Danish opt-outs. If legislation were adopted covering both the substantive and criminal law aspects of a policy, the application of the emergency brake or opt-out would mean that the same legislation would apply in part to all Member States, and in part only to some.

Admittedly, the Community has already adopted rules concerning the definition of criminal offences related to the ship-source pollution directive in the form of an amendment to that Directive,[127] rather than a separate act. However, it must be

---

[124] On the details of the penalty levels in third pillar criminal law measures, see further II:5.6 below.

[125] The case law on this point as regards the previous 'Community criminal law' competence is not clear: see comments in Peers, n 107 above.

[126] So would the French version: '...dans un domaine *ayant fait* l'objet de mesures d'harmonisation...' and '...à celle *utilisée* pour l'adoption des mesures d'harmonisation...'.

[127] Dir 2009/123, n 112 above.

remembered that this measure was adopted within the previous legal framework, not the post-Lisbon framework, which has changed the rules as regards the adoption of 'Community criminal law'.

Even if there is no *legal* obligation to adopt the criminal law measures in separate acts, it is still presumably open to the EU legislator to choose to use separate acts. Although it could be argued that a single legislative act combining both the harmonization measure and the related criminal law rules would be more transparent, on the other hand adopting a single piece of legislation which only applied in part to some Member States would hardly be transparent, and such an approach would run the risk that Member States would invoke opt-outs and emergency brakes even though their real objection was to the main subject-matter of the proposed legislation, rather than the criminal law aspects of it. Having said that, there would usually likely be a link between the argument that a particular proposal would cause fundamental problems for a national criminal justice system and an objection to the substance of the underlying harmonization being proposed. This point is particularly relevant to the Protocol on the UK and Irish opt-out from JHA policies, which includes specific rules on the ability of those Member States to opt out of a measure *amending* an act by which they are already bound.[128]

It may be useful to point to some cases where Article 83(2) TFEU could apply. The prior EC legislation on criminal offences as regards environmental crime, ship-source pollution, and employers of irregular migrants all lack provisions on the specific sanctions to be applied and on jurisdiction, so Article 83(2) could be used to adopt such rules. Previous third pillar measures on the issues of protection of the EU's financial interests, racism and xenophobia, and the facilitation of irregular migration also fall within the scope of Article 83(2); most of these acts already provide for rules on penalties and jurisdiction.[129] If it were desired to adopt criminal law measures for the enforcement of EU competition law, these would have to be carefully distinguished from the competence in Article 83(1) TFEU regarding the adoption of measures concerning (private) corruption.[130] This point is relevant since the decision-making rules are different (consultation of the EP for competition law measures,[131] as distinct from the ordinary legislative procedure for measures concerning corruption).

Finally, the Commission has tried to circumvent some of the restrictive elements of using the criminal law legal bases by suggesting that a measure regulating designer drugs (and replacing a pre-Lisbon third pillar measure) ought to be based on the internal market powers of the EU, with the criminal law aspects addressed by means of a cross-reference from the main EU drug trafficking legislation.[132]

---

[128] For details, see II:2.2.5.1 above.   [129] See II:5.6 and II:6.5 below.

[130] Previous third pillar measures apply to private corruption, as well as public corruption: see II:5.2.2 above.

[131] See Art 103 TFEU (ex-Art 83 EC).

[132] COM (2013) 619, 17 Sep 2013 (designer drugs proposal); COM (2013) 618, 17 Sep 2013 (criminal law proposal).

5.4.2 Criminal law as a restriction on free movement rights

When an accused person argues that a Member State is precluded from criminalizing particular activities at all because the criminalization directly prevents the exercise of free movement rights, he or she is not really claiming a Community (now Union) law 'defence'. Rather, he or she is claiming the invalidity of the underlying national legislation, or at least its inapplicability to his or her case. Such cases most usually arise when a Member State criminalizes the sale of a good originating from another Member State or the offer of a service by another Member State's service provider, but have also arisen in cases concerning free movement of capital, free movement of workers, and freedom of establishment. In such cases, the directly effective Articles 34, 45, 49, 56, and 63 TFEU (previously Articles 28, 39, 43, 49, and 56 EC respectively) confer a right to carry out the activity in question, and so no criminal conviction can possibly be imposed.[133] In particular, it is all but impossible for Member States to criminalize EU citizens for 'immigration offences', since their right to reside in a Member State flows directly from the Treaties.[134] Similarly, where secondary Community legislation grants free movement or other rights, Member States are precluded from imposing criminal sanctions.[135] Although the TFEU (previously the EC Treaty) and much secondary legislation allows for public policy and public security exceptions to free movement rights, the Court of Justice has consistently added that a Member State's decision to impose its criminal law to curtail free movement does not automatically mean that these exceptions are applicable. The test is whether the Member State is allowed to restrict the free movement in the first place, and while there is a presumption that criminal law is a matter for the Member States, that presumption can be overturned where its operation affects free movement.[136] However, the Court of Justice of the European Union (CJEU) has ruled that a Member State can restrict the free movement of capital in order to combat money laundering, if the EU third pillar measure on cooperation between national administrations is not sufficiently effective to address that Member State's legitimate concerns.[137] EU criminal law is also relevant to justifying Member States' restrictions on the free movement of persons.[138]

Furthermore, a criminal conviction pursuant to the law of a Member State may also infringe free movement law in two other ways. First, EU free movement law or immigration and asylum law may preclude acts taken as a *consequence* of sentences, when Member States expel or refuse to allow entry to an EU citizen or third-country nationals following a criminal conviction.[139] Second, the Court of Justice has found that a

---

[133] For examples, not all of which were successful attempts to resist the criminal conviction, see Cases 8/74 *Dassonville* [1975] ECR 837; 136/78 *Auer I* [1979] ECR 437; 222/86 *Heylens* [1987] ECR 4097; 279/80 *Webb* [1981] ECR 3305; and Joined Cases C-163/94, 165/94, and 250/94 *Sanz de Lera* [1995] ECR I-4821.

[134] Case 48/75 *Royer* [1976] ECR 497. The same applies to at least some third-country nationals who have a residence right as a result of EU law. See I:7.4.2.

[135] For example, see Joined Cases C-358/93 and C-416/93 *Bordessa* [1995] ECR I-361; Case 148/78 *Ratti* [1979] ECR 1629.

[136] Case 203/80 *Casati* [1981] ECR 2595.

[137] Case C-212/11 *Jyske Bank*, ECLI:EU:C:2013:270.

[138] Case C-348/09 *I*, ECLI:EU:C:2012:300.

[139] See I:7.4.1 (free movement law) and the immigration and asylum measures discussed in detail in chs 5 and 6 of volume 1.

particular sentence might violate the proportionality principle of free movement law, because the host Member State could have imposed a lesser civil penalty which would have preserved its right to combat certain behaviour with less damage to the free movement rights of EU citizens.[140] This principle also applies to the free movement of goods, where the Court has accepted that Member States can treat infringements of Value Added Tax (VAT) rules on import or export differently from internal infringements, because the latter are more easy to detect; but the difference cannot lead to a vastly more onerous penalty imposed upon importers and exporters in comparison with internal traders, because of the deterrent effect on free movement.[141]

A Member State prima facie breaches the principle of non-discrimination on grounds of nationality set out in Article 12 EC (now Article 18 TFEU) by applying harsher provisional penalties to non-residents, who are more likely to be nationals of other EU Member States, than it applies to residents.[142] Although such discrimination may be justified if there is no measure on the mutual recognition of criminal sentences between the relevant Member States, the difference in the provisional penalties applied to residents and non-residents must still be proportionate. Of course, it should be recalled that a number of EU measures on the mutual recognition of sentences have been adopted.[143]

5.4.3 Scope of the relationship

Not all impositions of criminal law by the Member States fall within the scope of Community (now Union) law, even where a particular case raises issues of non-JHA EU and criminal law simultaneously. For example, the Court of Justice has ruled that a person could not challenge national criminal penalties imposed upon breach of possession of illegally purchased cigarettes as a breach of Community law, because the possessor had not tried to exercise free movement rights directly.[144] An even clearer example of this distinction can be seen in the cases of *CIA Security* and *Lemmens*.[145] A Directive imposes obligations on Member States to notify their new technical standards to other Member States and to the Commission.[146] The Court of Justice ruled that while a company exercising free movement rights could use this Directive to resist application of a national technical standard which a Member State had failed to notify, a criminal defendant could not use the same Directive to object to the use of breathalyser evidence in a drunk-driving trial, even though the Member State in question had not notified the technical standards for that breathalyser. Similarly, a person cannot bring the validity of criminal sanctions imposed against him within the scope of free movement law merely by arguing that he might have exercised free movement rights had he not been imprisoned; there must be a more definite link to the Treaties or secondary legislation.[147]

---

[140] Cases 118/75 *Watson and Bellman* [1976] ECR 1185 and C-193/94 *Skanavi* [1996] ECR I-929.
[141] Cases 299/86 *Drexl* [1988] ECR 1213 and C-276/91 *Commission v France* [1993] ECR I-4413.
[142] Cases C-29/95 *Pastoors* [1997] ECR I-285 and C-224/00 *Commission v Italy* [2002] ECR I-2965.
[143] See II:3.7.1 above.   [144] Case C-387/93 *Banchero* [1995] ECR I-4663.
[145] Respectively Cases C-194/94 [1996] ECR I-2201 and C-226/97 [1998] ECR I-3711.
[146] Dir 83/189 as amended, consolidated in Dir 98/34 ([1998] OJ L 204/37).
[147] Case C-299/95 *Kremzov* [1997] ECR I-2629; see similarly Case C-328/04 *Vajnai* [2005] ECR I-8577.

In other cases, the Court of Justice has ruled that VAT and customs duties rules apply to illegal activities as a general rule, on the grounds that such activities (eg the sale of counterfeit perfume and gambling services, or the export of strategic goods) compete with legitimate trade, and so there would be a distortion of the principles of competition and fiscal neutrality if the transactions, imports, or exports were exempt from Community (now Union) law rules.[148] However, an exception exists for such matters as counterfeit currency and narcotic drugs (where not imported under strict controls for medical or scientific reasons), which are deemed to fall entirely outside the scope of legitimate trade. But what about cases where a product such as narcotic drugs is officially banned, but formally tolerated according to an official national policy, as is the case in the Netherlands? In the case of *Siberie*, the Court side-stepped the issue by ruling that such cases concerned the rental of a table, not the supply of drugs, and so VAT should be charged.[149] The Court subsequently accepted that the Netherlands is justified in discriminating indirectly against citizens of other Member States when applying this policy, in order to address drugs tourism and the related public nuisance.[150]

Finally, the Court of Justice has shown itself reluctant to give a definition of 'national criminal law', where a customs Regulation sets a common time limit for national authorities to begin administrative proceedings, but leaves time limits to bring criminal proceedings up to the Member States.[151] However, the Court defined 'criminal law' for the purposes of the former Brussels Convention, which governed jurisdiction over and enforcement of criminal law issues ancillary to civil law judgments in certain cases.[152]

5.5 Offences

5.5.1 Range of offences

The range of criminal offences relating to EC and EU law fall into three categories: the national criminal offences established pursuant to EC obligations (as they then were) to prohibit (but not necessarily criminalize) certain acts; EU obligations to criminalize acts pursuant to the former third pillar, and now Article 83(1) TFEU; and obligations to criminalize acts pursuant to 'Community criminal law competence' before the Treaty of Lisbon, and now Article 83(2) TFEU. These three categories will be considered separately in turn.

---

[148] See Cases C-3/97 *Goodwin* [1998] ECR I-3257 and C-283/95 *Fischer* [1998] ECR I-3369, and earlier cases cited therein, and subsequently: Case C-455/98 *Salumet* [2000] ECR I-4993; Joined Cases C-354/03, C-355/03, and C-484/03 *Optigen* [2006] ECR I-483; and Joined Cases C-439/04 and C-440/04 *Kittel* [2006] ECR I-6161. On the link between the theft of goods and VAT rules, see Case C-435/03 *BAT* [2005] ECR I-7077. Of course the imposition or exclusion of VAT or customs duties does not mean that the trader will escape criminal prosecution for such activities.

[149] Case C-158/98 [1999] ECR I-3971.   [150] Case C-137/09 *Josemans* [2010] ECR I-13019.

[151] Case C-273/90 *Meico-Fell* [1991] ECR I-5569; see subsequently Case C-62/06 *Zefeser* [2007] ECR I-11995 and Case C-75/09 *Agra* [2010] ECR I-5595.

[152] Case 157/80 *Rinkau* [1981] ECR 3181.

5.5.1.1 EC law prohibitions

The 'prohibitions' which appear in EC legislation have usually involved 'economic', or 'white-collar' crime, because these issues are most directly relevant to the functioning of the internal market. Usually, legislation has been adopted because of a fear that, without common rules governing the issue in each Member State, at least at the level of minimum standards, law-breakers would concentrate their energies on the Member States with the weakest commitment to combating the relevant crimes: a classic 'race to the bottom' argument concerning the prospect that individuals in a common market will locate their activities in the most favourable jurisdiction within that market, undermining the regulatory measures taken by the other jurisdictions.

The best-known EC law prohibition is that contained in the money laundering Directive, which obliges Member States to prohibit money-laundering as defined in the Directive: the conversion, transfer, concealment, disguise, acquisition, possession, or use of property derived from criminal activity.[153] The scope of the Directive and its detailed provisions were amended in 2001,[154] 2005,[155] and 2015.[156] The Commission sued Austria for continuing to allow its nationals to open anonymous accounts, arguing that this breached the Directive, although the case was subsequently withdrawn.[157] The Court of Justice has also ruled on the validity of the 'tip-off' provisions of the Directive.[158] Furthermore, the Court has ruled that Member States cannot simply ban the export of large amounts of currency on the grounds that this currency might be used for money laundering, since that would defeat the very purpose of free movement of capital.[159] However, Member States can impose a reporting requirement on such movements. As noted above, they can also restrict free movement of capital on money laundering grounds if there are no effective methods in place to address their concerns.[160] But conversely, the vague risk of money laundering could not justify a discriminatory system of taxation of gambling.[161]

The Community has also adopted legislation banning insider dealing,[162] later amended to ban 'market abuse' more broadly,[163] along with legislation restricting lorry-drivers' driving hours,[164] requiring workplace health and safety protection,[165]

---

[153] Dir 91/308 ([1991] OJ L 166/77), Arts 1 and 2.   [154] Dir 2001/97 ([2001] OJ L 344/76).

[155] Dir 2005/60 ([2005] OJ L 309/15). See implementing Commission Dir 2006/70 ([2006] OJ L 214/29).

[156] Dir 2015/849 ([2015] OJ L 141/73). Member States have to implement this Dir by 26 June 2017 (Art 67(1)).

[157] Case C-290/98 [2000] ECR I-7835.

[158] Case C-305/05 *Ordre des barreaux francophones et germanophone and Others* [2007] ECR I-5305.

[159] Joined Cases C-358/93 and C-416/93 *Bordessa* [1995] ECR I-361 and Joined Cases C-163/94, 165/94, and 250/94 *Sanz de Lera* [1995] ECR I-4821. See also EC legislation on cash movements across external borders (II:7.4.1 below).

[160] Case C-212/11 *Jyske Bank*, ECLI:E:C:2013:270.

[161] Joined Cases C-344/13 and C-367/13 *Blanco and Fabretti*, ECLI:EU:C:2014:2311.

[162] Dir 89/592 ([1989] OJ L 334/30). See judgments in Cases C-28/99 *Verdonck* [2001] ECR I-3399, C-384/02 *Grøngaard and Bang* [2005] ECR I-9939, and C-391/04 *Georgakis* [2007] ECR I-3741.

[163] Dir 2003/6 ([2003] OJ L 96/16), replaced by Reg 596/2014 ([2014] OJ L 173/1). The CJEU has interpreted this Directive several times, in Cases: C-628/13 *Lafonta*, ECLI:EU:C:2015:162; C-19/11 *Geltl*, ECLI:EU:C:2012:397; C-248/11 *Nilas*, ECLI:EU:C:2012:166; C-445/09 *IMC Securities* [2011] ECR I-5917; and C-45/08 *Spector* [2009] ECR I-12073.

[164] Initially by Reg 543/69 (OJ English Special Edition, 1969 (I) 170); subsequently by Reg 3280/85 ([1985] OJ L 370/1) and presently by Reg 561/2006 ([2006] OJ L 102/1), as amended by Reg 165/2014 ([2014] OJ L 60/1).

[165] For example, Dir 90/270 on workplace health and safety equipment ([1990] OJ L 156/14).

imposing economic and financial sanctions against third States,[166] banning unauthorized 'descrambling' of subscription-only broadcasting or Internet services,[167] restricting acquisition and possession of firearms,[168] and prohibiting various acts which affect the environment.[169]

There is another spate of Community measures which do not prohibit things, but which give effect to national, international, and EU measures which do prohibit them. The Community has competence in such areas because aspects of such trade are legal and so the operation of the common commercial policy and the internal market is inevitably affected. The most important of these regimes is the EC's drugs legislation, which comprises measures setting out procedures to monitor national production and marketing of prohibited precursor substances in the internal market and measures monitoring trade in precursors with third States.[170] Also, the Community has concluded an increasing number of treaties with third States regulating trade in precursors,[171] and has incorporated anti-drugs measures in its development policy legislation and treaties.[172]

Legislation with similar objectives exists to address the civil law aspects of both internal and external trade in cultural goods, in an attempt to prevent the illicit trade in such goods.[173] The Community has adopted legislation which both facilitates the internal free movement of strategic dual-use goods and establishes a common system for controlling exports, which is integrated with EU foreign policy measures.[174] Legislation also sets out the procedures governing lawful trade in explosives.[175] A customs Regulation requires Member States to prohibit the entry of goods infringing intellectual property

[166] For example, see Reg 990/93 ([1993] OJ L 102/14) imposing sanctions against the former Yugoslavia, subsequently amended and later repealed.

[167] Dir 98/84 ([1998] OJ L 320/54).

[168] Dir 91/477 ([1991] OJ L 256/51), amended by Dir 2008/51 ([2008] OJ L 179/5). On EC firearms laws, see further II:7.4.7 below.

[169] For example, Reg 259/93 ([1993] OJ L 30/1) on waste, later replaced by Reg 1013/2006 ([2006] OJ L 190/1) as amended by Reg 660/2014 ([2014] OJ L 189/135). See now the EC legislation on environmental crime (Dir 2008/99 [2008] OJ L 328/28), discussed further in II:5.5.1.3 below.

[170] As regards internal EC trade, Reg 273/2004 ([2004] OJ L 47/1), which replaced Dir 92/109 ([1992] OJ L 370/76), as amended by Reg 1258/2013 ([2013] OJ L 330/21). As regards external trade, Reg 111/2005 ([2005] OJ L 22/1), which replaced Reg 3677/92 ([1992] OJ L 357/1), as amended by Reg 1259/2013 ([2013] OJ L 330/30). See also the substantive criminal law measures and the policing and other measures concerning drugs (respectively II:5.5.1.2 and II:7.7.4 below).

[171] These comprise treaties with: Bolivia, Colombia, Ecuador, Peru, and Venezuela ([1995] OJ L 324/1, 10, 18, 26, and 34); Chile ([1998] OJ L 336/46); the USA ([1997] OJ L 164/22); Mexico ([1997] OJ L 77/23); Turkey ([2003] OJ L 64/28); China ([2009] OJ L 56/6); and Russia ([2014] OJ L 165/7).

[172] Reg 2046/97 ([1997] OJ L 287/1), replaced by Reg 1717/2006 on stability for development ([2006] OJ L 327/1; see Art 4(1)(a)), and in turn by Reg 230/2014 ([2014] OJ L 77/1); the inclusion of drugs policy clauses in EC development treaties was approved by the Court of Justice in Case C-268/94 *Portugal v Council* [1996] ECR I-6177.

[173] On internal trade, see Dir 93/7 ([1993] OJ L 74/74); replaced by Dir 2014/60 ([2014] OJ L 159/1). On external trade, see Reg 3911/92 ([1992] OJ L 395/1), replaced by Reg 116/2009 ([2009] OJ L 39/1).

[174] Reg 3381/94 ([1994] OJ L 367/1), replaced by Reg 1334/2000 ([2000] OJ L 159/1), in turn replaced by Reg 428/2009 ([2009] OJ L 134/1), as amended by Regs 1232/2011 ([2011] OJ L 326/26) and 599/2014 ([2014] OJ L 173/79).

[175] Dir 93/15 ([1993] OJ L 121/28). See further II:7.4.7 below.

rights onto the EC internal market from third countries,[176] and the Commission has proposed a Directive (since withdrawn) which would have required Member States to criminalize infringements of intellectual property rights.[177] Finally, the Community has adopted a number of measures relating to terrorism (in particular concerning asset freezing) and counterfeiting of the euro.[178]

5.5.1.2 EU law offences

The EU has adopted measures regarding nine of the ten crimes listed in Article 83(1) TFEU:

a) terrorism;[179]

b) trafficking in persons;[180]

c) child pornography and prostitution;[181]

d) drug trafficking;[182]

e) money laundering;[183]

f) corruption;[184]

---

[176] Reg 608/2013 ([2013] OJ L 181/15), which replaced Reg 1383/2003 ([2003] OJ L 196/7), which replaced Reg 3295/94 ([1994] OJ L 341/8), as amended by Reg 241/99 ([1999] OJ L 27/1).

[177] See II:5.2.3 above.   [178] See II:7.4.5 and II:7.7.4 below.

[179] Framework Decision ([2002] OJ L 164/3). Member States had to implement this by 31 Dec 2002. The Commission has released two reports on implementation: COM (2004) 409, 8 June 2004 and COM (2007) 681, 6 Nov 2007. The Framework Decision was amended in 2008: ([2008] OJ L 330/21); Member States had to implement the amending measure by 9 Dec 2010 (Art 3(1)). The Commission has reported on implementation of the amendment: COM (2014) 554, 5 Sep 2014. A proposal to amend and replace the Framework Decision by a Directive is under discussion (COM (2015) 625, 2 Dec 2015).

[180] Dir 2011/36 [2011] OJ L 101/1, replacing a prior Framework Decision: [2002] L 203/1; see earlier Joint Action ([1997] OJ L 63/2). Member States had to implement the Directive by 6 Apr 2013. The Commission released a report on implementation of the Framework Decision: COM (2006) 187, 2 May 2006.

[181] Dir 2011/93 [2011] OJ L 335/1, which Member States had to implement by 18 Dec 2013, replacing a prior Framework Decision ([2004] OJ L 13/44), which Member States had to implement by 20 Jan 2006. See the earlier Joint Action (ibid). The Commission released a report on implementation of the Framework Decision: COM (2007) 716, 16 Nov 2007.

[182] Framework Decision ([2004] OJ L 335/8), which Member States had to implement by 12 May 2006. The Commission has released a report on implementation (COM (2009) 669, 10 Dec 2009). It has also proposed an amendment: COM (2013) 618, 17 Sep 2013. See also earlier the Joint Action on this subject ([1996] L 342/6); due to its broad scope, this measure was *not* repealed by the Framework Decision. However, the Commission has subsequently proposed to repeal the Joint Action, on the grounds that it is obsolete: COM (2014) 715, 28 Nov 2014.

[183] Joint Action ([1998] OJ L 333/1); Framework Decision ([2001] OJ L 182/1). Member States had to implement the latter measure by 31 Dec 2002. The Commission has released two reports on implementation: COM (2004) 230, 5 Apr 2004 and COM (2006) 72, 21 Feb 2006. The Joint Action has been repealed, and the Framework Decision has been partly repealed, by Dir 2014/42 on confiscation measures (Art 14(1) of Directive, [2014] OJ L 127/39).

[184] Convention ([1997] OJ C 195/1), in force Sep 2005; Joint Action on private corruption ([1998] OJ L 358/2); Framework Decision on private corruption ([2003] OJ L 192/54). Member States had to implement the latter by 22 July 2005 (Art 9(1)). The Commission has released a report on implementation: COM (2007) 328, 18 June 2007, and two later general anti-corruption reports: COM (2011) 308, 6 June 2011 and COM (2014) 38, 3 Feb 2014.

g) counterfeiting of means of payment, which concerns both currency[185] and non-cash instruments;[186]

h) attacks on information systems;[187] and

i) organized crime.[188]

The fifth crime on the list, arms trafficking, was not addressed by a third pillar measure before the entry into force of the Treaty of Lisbon, and it remains to be seen whether will be addressed by an EU measure pursuant to Article 83(1) TFEU. It should be noted that although there are some EC law and foreign policy measures addressing aspects of arms trafficking,[189] Article 83(1) is a *lex specialis* as regards any substantive criminal law rules relating to arms trafficking, and it does not differentiate between internal and external aspects of the issue.

Taking these crimes in turn, first of all the EU adopted a Framework Decision on terrorism in 2002, and then amended it in 2008.[190] This measure requires Member States to criminalize terrorism as defined in a three-part test, involving the context of the acts, their aims, and the specific acts being committed.[191] The context is that the acts, 'given their nature or context, may seriously damage a country or international organization'. There must be an aim of either 'seriously intimidating a population' or 'unduly compelling a Government or international organisation' to act, or 'seriously destabilizing or destroying the fundamental political, economic, or social structures of a country or an international organization'. Thirdly, there must be a specific act from a list of eight types of specific acts, including acts such as attacks which may cause death, kidnapping or hostage-taking, hijacking, or 'causing extensive destruction' to specified public property or any private property 'likely to endanger human life or result in major economic loss'. The 2008 amendment to the Framework Decision supplements the list of 'linked offences' (aggravated theft, extortion, and drawing up false administrative documents) with three more: provocation, recruitment, and providing training for terrorism, based upon a 2005 Council of Europe Convention on this issue.[192]

---

[185] Dir 2014/62 ([2014] OJ L 151/1), replacing a prior Framework Decision: [2000] OJ L 140/1. Member States have to implement the Directive by 23 May 2016 (Art 14(1)); they had to implement part of the Framework Decision by 31 Dec 2000 and the rest by 29 May 2001. An amendment to this Framework Decision concerns procedural matters and so is considered in II:3.7.2 above. The Commission has released three reports on implementation of the Framework Decision: COM (2001) 771, 13 Dec 2001; COM (2003) 532, 3 Sep 2003; and COM (2007) 524, 17 Sep 2007.

[186] Framework Decision ([2001] OJ L 149/1), which Member States had to implement by 2 June 2003. The Commission has released two reports on implementation: COM (2004) 346, 30 Apr 2004 and COM (2006) 65, 20 Feb 2006.

[187] Dir 2013/40 ([2013] OJ L 218/8), which Member States had to implement by 4 Sep 2015, replacing a prior Framework Decision: ([2005] OJ L 69/67), which Member States had to implement by 16 Mar 2007. The Commission has released a report on implementation: COM (2008) 448, 14 July 2008.

[188] Joint Action ([1998] OJ L 351/1), replaced by a Framework Decision ([2008] OJ L 300/42), which Member States had to implement by 11 May 2010.

[189] See: the firearms legislation mentioned above, n 168; Dir 93/15 on explosives for civil use ([1993] OJ L 121/28); Reg 428/2009 on dual-use goods ([2009] OJ L 134/1); and the CFSP measures concerning arms exports (Common Position, [2008] OJ L 335/99), small arms and light weapons ([2002] OJ L 191/1), and arms brokering ([2003] OJ L 156/79; see Art 6 as regards criminal sanctions). On the legal base of the CFSP measures, see Case C-91/05 *Commission v Council* [2008] ECR I-3651.

[190] N 179 above.　　　　　[191] Art 1 of 2002 Framework Decision, n 179 above.

[192] CETS 196. For ratification details, see Appendix I. The 2015 proposal (n 179 above) would add criminal offences relating to travelling for terrorism and receiving training in terrorism.

A particular concern regarding this Framework Decision is its human rights implications.[193] At first sight, there are no grounds for concern, since the European Court of Human Rights has consistently rejected the idea that political violence committed within the territory of signatory States to the ECHR attracts human rights protection.[194] Moreover, the preamble to the Framework Decision states expressly that the Union is 'based on the principle of democracy and on the principle of the rule of law' and that the Framework Decision 'respects fundamental rights' as guaranteed by the ECHR and national constitutions and 'observes the principles recognized by' the EU's Charter of Rights. The preamble also states that the Framework Decision cannot be interpreted to 'reduce or restrict fundamental rights or freedoms such as the right to strike, freedom of assembly, of association and of expression, including the right of everyone to form and join trade unions...and the related right to demonstrate'. The Council also adopted a Statement connected to the Framework Decision,[195] asserting that the Framework Decision:

> ...covers acts which are considered by all Member States...as serious infringements of their criminal laws committed by individuals whose objectives constitute a threat to their democratic societies respecting the rule of law and the civilisation upon which the societies are founded. It has to be understood in this sense and cannot be construed so as to argue that the conduct of those who have acted in the interest of preserving or restoring those values, as was notably the case in some Member States during the Second World War, could now be considered as 'terrorist' acts. Nor can it be construed so as to incriminate on terrorist grounds persons exercising their fundamental right to manifest their opinions, even if in the course of the exercise of such right they commit criminal offences.

The main text of the Framework Decision also states that it 'shall not have the effect of altering the obligation to respect fundamental rights' as set out in Article 6 of the EU Treaty,[196] and the 2008 amendment states that it shall not require Member States 'to take measures in contradiction of fundamental principles relating to freedom of expression,' as further defined therein.[197]

Firstly, given its potential application to acts committed in *non*-democratic states,[198] does the Framework Decision sufficiently distinguish between an absolute prohibition on political violence in democratic societies and a more qualified prohibition relating to non-democratic states (ideally referring instead in the latter case to international humanitarian law)? Although the statement attached to the Framework Decision accepts the legitimacy of actions taken against invading forces, the legal effect of the statement is uncertain, because it is not set out in the text.[199] Also, its scope is

---

[193] On these issues, see S Peers, 'EU Responses to Terrorism' (2003) 52 ICLQ 227 at 235–37.

[194] See, for instance, *Zana v Turkey* [1997] ECHR-VII.

[195] Statement 109/2002 in the summary of Council acts for June 2002 (Council doc 11532/02, 22 Aug 2002).

[196] Art 1(2) of the Framework Decision, n 179 above. Such provisions also appear in EU measures concerning criminal procedure: see II:3.3.5 and II:3.5.2 above.

[197] Art 2, 2008 amendments, n 179 above.

[198] On jurisdiction pursuant to the Framework Decision, see II:6.5 below.

[199] On this point, see Case C-292/89 *Antonissen* [1991] ECR I-745, which is applicable equally to third pillar measures: Case C-355/04 P *SEGI* [2007] ECR I-1657.

uncertain: is it limited to historical events, or to activities within the EU, or to invasions as distinct from activities against undemocratic regimes? It appears that the statement is not limited temporally or geographically, and due to its broad wording, applies also to actions against undemocratic regimes. Moreover, it is unfortunate that the statement does not suggest any limitation on the nature of the violence that might be justified on the basis of a 'just war' principle, for example (as already noted) by reference to international humanitarian law. The statement could therefore be misused by those who practice political violence in modern democracies to justify their behaviour.

Secondly, in the absence of such circumstances of justified political violence, does the Framework Decision (as amended) otherwise give rise to human rights concerns, in particular as it applies to property damage and injury to police during a demonstration, or to the strong criticism of particular States or policies, in light of the broad wording of the criminalization of 'participation' in terrorist activities, and 'public provocation' to terrorism? While the express human rights protections in the preamble, the main text, and the attached statement appear to suggest that there is no cause for concern, the application of the Framework Decision in the context of subsequent EU policing measures suggests that there might be cause for concern in practice.[200]

The second crime on the list in Article 83(1) TFEU is trafficking in persons, which was addressed most recently by a Directive adopted in 2011, replacing a Framework Decision adopted in 2002.[201] These measures are considered in more detail in Chapter 7 of volume 1, along with the relevant international measures on the same topic.[202]

Next, the third crime listed in Article 83(1) TFEU is child pornography and prostitution, which was originally addressed by a 1997 Joint Action, later replaced by a Framework Decision in 2003.[203] The Framework Decision required Member States to criminalize sexual exploitation of children (defined as the coercion of a child into prostitution or pornography or the recruitment into, profiting from, or exploitation of child prostitution or pornography, or unlawful sex with a child in the context of coercion, the payment or money, or abuse of trust) and child pornography (defined as the production, distribution, supply, acquisition or possession of this material, as defined in the Framework Decision). However, Member States had an option to exempt from criminal liability pornographic material involving adults who appear to be children, or comprising only computer-generated images, with a view to focusing on cases where actual children were abused.[204] This Framework Decision covers some of the offences lifted in the Council of Europe's Convention on cyber-crime, as well as the subsequent Convention on child protection.[205] The subsequent Directive on this issue requires Member States also to criminalize sexual abuse of children more broadly, as well as 'grooming' children for sexual offences, while retaining possible exemptions relating to some consensual activity.[206]

---

[200] See II:7.6.3 and II:7.7.4 below.   [201] N 180 above.   [202] I:7.5.4 above.
[203] N 181 above.   [204] Arts 2 and 3 of the Framework Decision.
[205] Respectively ETS 185 and CETS 201. For ratification of these Conventions by the Member States, see Appendix I.
[206] Arts 3–6, Dir 2011/93, n 181 above.

Drug trafficking,[207] the fourth crime listed in Article 83(1) TFEU, has been the subject of a continuing dispute between some Member States favouring a very strict enforcement on sale and possession of drugs, and others favouring instead, at least in some cases, a 'health-oriented' approach of controlled *de facto* criminalization. The merits of formal decriminalization, at least for 'soft' drugs, have never been considered by the Commission or Council. As a result of the difference in views, the 1990 Schengen Convention contained an awkward compromise, requiring 'prevention and punishment' of the sale and possession for sale or export and administrative and penal sanctions against illegal export and sale, possession, and handling of drugs, including cannabis; but 'illegal' was not defined except by reference to existing UN Conventions.[208] The Maastricht Treaty contained references to both approaches, with a first pillar goal of 'preventing drug dependence' in former Article 129 EC and a third pillar objective of 'combatting drug addiction' in Article K.1(4) EU.

The initial key measure implementing the latter objective was the 1996 drugs Joint Action, a framework to be implemented by more specific measures, which reiterated Member States' obligations under UN Conventions; Member States also undertook to criminalize the incitement or inducement of others to commit certain drugs offences.[209] Although Member States only had to 'take the most appropriate steps' to combat illicit drugs cultivation, that principle was implemented in more detail by a separate Resolution, inviting Member States to make the sale of cannabis seeds an offence and to ban cultivation of cannabis under glass or indoors.[210] The Council also adopted a Resolution on 'drugs tourism' in an attempt to counter any 'race to the bottom' of drug users visiting the Member States with the least stringent drug laws, but the Resolution only established operational contacts, rather than harmonize national law or practice.[211]

A 1997 Joint Action on synthetic drugs established a procedure for the Council to consider adopting an EU-wide ban on 'designer drugs' after assessing their risk.[212] This procedure was implemented on six occasions, resulting in three bans.[213] In 2005, the Council replaced the Joint Action with a post-Amsterdam third-pillar Decision, which revised the risk assessment process and provides for the possible adoption of control measures by a qualified majority.[214] This Decision has been applied on several occasions.[215]

---

[207] For details of EC and EU anti-drug measures outside the scope of substantive criminal law, see II:7.7.4 below.

[208] Art 71, 1990 Schengen Convention ([2000] OJ L 239). On the implications of this provision for the double jeopardy rules in the Schengen Convention, see II:6.8 below.

[209] Arts 7 and 9 of the Joint Action, n 182 above.

[210] [1996] OJ C 389/1; see Art 8 of the 1996 Joint Action.

[211] [1996] OJ C 375/3. The measures did influence the CJEU to accept limits on the sale of cannabis to 'drug tourists' as a legitimate restriction on free movement: see Case C-137/09 *Josemans* [2010] ECR I-13019.

[212] [1997] OJ L 167/1.

[213] See Decisions concerning 4-MTA ([1999] OJ L 244/1), PMMA ([2002] OJ L 63/14), and 2C-I, 2C-T-2, 2C-T-7, and TMA-2 ([2003] OJ L 321/64), and Council conclusions concerning Ketamine and GHB (press release of JHA Council, 15–16 Mar 2001). The Council failed to agree on whether to subject MBDB to control measures (Council doc 6072/00, 11 Feb 2000).

[214] [2005] OJ L 127/32.

[215] [2008] OJ L 63/45; [2010] OJ L 322/44; [2013] OJ L 72/12; [2013] OJ L 272/44; and [2014] OJ L 287/22. The Commission proposed the replacement of this measure in 2013 (COM (2013) 619, 17 Sep 2013). See

Finally, the Council adopted a Framework Decision on drug trafficking, which requires Member States to criminalize: the production, sale, or distribution of 'drugs' as defined by the Framework Decision; the possession or purchase of such drugs to this end; the cultivation of cannabis, coca bush, and opium poppy plants; and the production, etc. of precursor drugs with the knowledge that they will be used for the manufacture or production of drugs. But this conduct falls outside the scope of the Framework Decision when carried out by individuals for their own personal use, as defined by national law.[216]

The sixth offence listed in Article 83(1) TFEU is money laundering. A 1998 Joint Action, amended by a 2001 Framework Decision,[217] requires Member States to criminalize money laundering related to *all* offences which are punishable by at least a maximum sentence of more than a year or a minimum sentence of six months, by withdrawing the relevant reservations to the 1990 Strasbourg Convention on the laundering, search, seizure, and confiscation of the proceeds of crime.[218]

Next, still on the issue of financial crime, the seventh crime listed in Article 83(1) TFEU is corruption, which is the subject of a Convention on corruption by Community *or* national officials, which applies to any acts of corruption, whether or not such acts affect the EU budget.[219] This Convention defines 'active corruption' and 'passive corruption' (in lay terms, 'giving bribes' and 'taking bribes')[220] as regards a 'Community official' or 'national official'.[221] 'Corruption' is to request or receive, or promise or give, an advantage 'to act or refrain from acting in accordance with his [or her] duty or in the exercise of his [or her] functions in breach of his [or her] official duties'.

The Joint Action on private corruption, replaced by the Framework Decision on the same issue, adjusted the definitions from the Convention to define active or passive corruption as a person acting or omitting to act 'in breach of his [or her] duties' for the benefit of a person 'acting in the course of his [or her] business activities', which entail working for or directing a private-sector entity in any capacity.[222] A breach of duty is to be defined by national law, but covers any 'disloyal behaviour' constituting

---

also the Commission report on the functioning of the Decision (COM (2011) 430, 11 July 2011). The CJEU has confirmed that the Council can still adopt implementing measures based on the Decision after the entry into force of the Treaty of Lisbon, but it has to consult the EP first: Joined Cases C-317/13 and C-679/13 *EP v Council*, ECLI:EU:C:2015:223.

[216] Art 2 of the Framework Decision, n 182 above.

[217] N 183 above. The subsequent amendments do not affect substantive criminal law.

[218] Art 1(1)(b) of the Joint Action and Art 1(b) of the Framework Decision (n 183 above), referring to Art 6 of the Convention (ETS 141), which sets out an obligation to make money laundering as defined in the Convention an offence, although States could (until the prohibition imposed by the EU measures) enter a reservation limiting this obligation to specific offences. The Convention has the same definition of 'money laundering' as the 1991, 2001, 2005, and 2015 EC money laundering Directives, nn 153–56 above. All Member States have ratified the Convention, which will ultimately be replaced by a later Convention agreed in 2005 (CETS 198), which entered into force on 1 May 2008 (for ratification details, see Appendix I). It contains the same definition of money laundering as the prior Convention (Art 9(1)), and the permitted reservations to the obligation to criminalize money laundering are now in line with the EU's Framework Decision (Art 9(4), together with the Appendix to the Convention).

[219] N 184 above.   [220] Arts 2(1) and 3(1) of the Convention.

[221] See the definitions in Art 1 of the Convention.

[222] Arts 2(1) and 3(1) of Joint Action, in conjunction with the definition of 'person' in Art 1; Art 2(1) of Framework Decision (both n 184 above).

a 'breach of statutory duty' or a 'breach of professional regulations or instructions'.[223] The Framework Decision specifies that the ban also applies to non-profit entities which participate in business activities.[224] According to the Joint Action, Member States had to at least criminalize all conduct which distorted or might distort competition, at least within the common market, and which could have resulted in economic damage to others by improper awards or execution of a contract.[225] The Framework Decision replaced this provision with a similar option to limit the offence to 'conduct which involves, or could involve, a distortion of competition in relation to the purchase of goods or commercial services'.[226] In order to invoke this option, Member States must make a declaration to this effect, valid for five years from 22 July 2005 (the implementation deadline for the Framework Decision);[227] the Council was to examine the question of whether such declarations could be renewed before 22 July 2010,[228] but did not do so. Only a small number of Member States made this declaration.[229]

National law implementing the Joint Action or subsequently the Framework Decision could overlap with EU competition laws and national competition laws (most of which are now similar to EU law rules). However, direct conflict between those rules may be limited, because the EU's Court of Justice has expressly ruled that Member States are free to enforce their competition laws by means of criminal sanctions in addition to EU administrative penalties.[230] It should also be noted that there are UN, OECD, and Council of Europe Conventions on corruption.[231]

Moving on to the eighth crime listed in Article 83(1) TFEU, the Framework Decision (now Directive) on counterfeiting currency specifies that the production and use, inter alia, of counterfeit currency (most importantly, but not only, the euro), shall constitute a criminal offence.[232] These laws aim to supplement a 1929 Geneva Convention on counterfeiting currency. Euro currency is defined by reference to EC monetary legislation, and the legislation forms part of a complex package of EC measures and other third pillar measures that contribute to combating euro counterfeiting.[233]

On the same topic, a Framework Decision of 2001 requires Member States to create a number of offences concerning the counterfeiting of non-cash instruments (in practice, credit and debit cards).[234] Member States are required to criminalize the theft, counterfeiting, or falsification of such items, as well as the receiving or fraudulently using such items, the use of computers to cause economic loss, or the production, sale, or use of instruments or programmes designed to facilitate such offences.

---

[223] Art 1 of Joint Action and Art 1 of Framework Decision.
[224] Art 2(2), Framework Decision. [225] Arts 2(2) and 3(2), Joint Action.
[226] Art 2(3), Framework Decision. [227] Art 2(4), Framework Decision.
[228] Art 2(5), Framework Decision.
[229] According to the Commission report on the application of the Framework Decision, Poland, Germany, and Italy have made valid declarations, while Austria made an invalid declaration. On the Polish declaration, see also Council doc 12400/05, 21 Sep 2005.
[230] Case 14/68 *Wilhelm* [1969] ECR 1. See further II:6.4 below.
[231] The EC has concluded the UN Convention (see II:5.8 below). For ratification details of the Conventions by Member States, see Appendix I
[232] N 185 above. [233] For a full summary and further references, see II:7.7.4 below.
[234] N 185 above.

As for the ninth specific EU offence, computer crime, Member States are obliged by the 2005 Framework Decision on attacks on information systems (now the 2013 Directive) to establish offences in relation to illegal access to information systems, ('where the offence is committed by infringing a security measure'), as well as illegal system interference and illegal data interference ('at least for cases which are not minor').[235] The Directive adds a requirement to criminalize illegal interception and tools to commit these crimes. This measure concerns some of the same issues addressed by the Council of Europe's cyber-crime Convention.[236]

Finally, the tenth crime on the list of specific EU powers is organized crime. This issue is addressed by a Framework Decision adopted in 2008, which replaced a Joint Action adopted in 1998.[237] The Framework Decision defines a 'criminal organisation' as 'a structured association, established over a period of time, of more than two persons acting in concert with a view to committing' crimes punishable by at least four years in prison, in order 'to obtain, directly or indirectly, a financial or other material benefit'.[238] Member States are obliged to criminalize participation in such an organization in one (or both) of two ways: either by 'actively tak[ing] part in' an organization's criminal activities or other activities (the 'association' version) or agreeing with other persons to pursue activities that would amount to the commission of the serious offences which criminal organizations commit, 'even if that person does not take part in the actual execution of the activity' (the 'conspiracy' version).[239] Most Member States and the Community are also parties to the UN Convention on transnational organized crime, which also has a definition of organized crime.[240]

5.5.1.3 EC criminal law measures

Before the entry into force of the Treaty of Lisbon, the Community adopted three Directives pursuant to its criminal law competence, and the Union adopted a number of third pillar acts which now fall within the scope of Article 83(2) TFEU.[241] These measures concern the following:

a) racism and xenophobia;[242]
b) facilitation of illegal entry and residence;[243]

---

[235] Arts 2–4 of the Framework Decision, n 186 above.
[236] CETS 185; for ratification details, see Appendix I.   [237] N 187 above.
[238] Art 1(1), Framework Decision. A 'structured association' is defined in Art 1(2).
[239] Art 2, Framework Decision.
[240] As regards EC accession, see II:5.8 below. As regards ratification by Member States, see Appendix I.
[241] Whether these measures (other than the environmental crime or shipping pollution Directives) *should* have been adopted as EC or EU acts instead is now a moot point, unless their validity is challenged on a reference from a national court.
[242] Framework Decision ([2008] OJ L 328/55), which Member States had to implement by 28 Nov 2010 (Art 10(1)); see earlier Joint Action ([1996] OJ L 185/5). The Commission has reported on implementation of this measure (COM (2014) 27, 27 Jan 2014).
[243] Framework Decision ([2002] OJ L 328/1). Member States had to implement this measure by 5 Dec 2004. There is a parallel Directive addressing immigration law aspects of this issue (Dir 2002/90, [2002] OJ L 328/17). The Commission has reported on national application of the Framework Decision (COM (2006) 770, 6 Dec 2006).

c) employment of irregular migrants;[244]
d) environmental crime, including pollution related to shipping;[245]
e) protection of the EU's financial interests;[246] and
f) market abuse.[247]

Again, taking these measures in turn, racism and xenophobia is the subject of a Framework Decision adopted in 2008, which replaced a Joint Action adopted in 1996.[248] The Framework Decision requires Member States to criminalize: public incitement to 'violence or hatred directed against a group of persons or a member of such a group defined by reference to race, colour, religion, descent or national or ethnic origin'; the commission of such an act 'by public dissemination or distribution of tracts, pictures or other material;' and 'publicly condoning, denying or grossly trivialising crimes of genocide, crimes against humanity and war crimes' or the Holocaust, as defined in the relevant legal instruments, 'directed against a group of persons or a member of such a group defined by reference to race, colour, religion, descent or national or ethnic origin when the conduct is carried out in a manner likely to incite to violence or hatred against such a group or a member of such a group'.[249] However, these obligations are potentially limited, first of all because 'Member States may choose to punish only conduct which is either carried out in a manner likely to disturb public order or which is threatening, abusive or insulting',[250] and secondly because each Member State may make a statement that it will criminalize denial of the Holocaust and war crimes, etc. 'only if the crimes referred to in these paragraphs have been established by a final decision of a national court of this Member State and/or an international court, or by a final decision of an international court only'.[251] Also, the reference to religion is intended to cover primarily acts which serve as a 'pretext for directing acts against a group of persons or a member of such a group defined by reference to race, colour, descent, or national or ethnic origin'.[252] Furthermore, for other offences, Member States must ensure that 'racist and xenophobic motivation is considered an aggravating

---

[244] Dir 2009/52 ([2009] OJ L 168/24), which Member States had to implement by 20 July 2011 (Art 17(1)). The Commission has reported on implementation of this Directive (COM (2014) 286, 22 May 2014).

[245] Dirs 2008/99 ([2009] OJ L 328/28) and 2009/123 ([2009] OJ L 280/52, amending Dir 2005/35, [2005] OJ L 255/11). Dir 2008/99 had to be implemented by 26 Dec 2010 (Art 8(1)), while Dir 2009/123 had to be implemented by 16 Nov 2010 (Art 2). These measures replaced Framework Decisions ([2003] OJ L 29/55 and [2005] OJ L 225/164), which had each been annulled by the Court of Justice: Cases C-176/03 *Commission v Council* [2005] ECR I-7879 and C-440/05 *Commission v Council* [2007] ECR I-9097, both discussed further in II:5.4.1.1 above.

[246] Convention ([1995] OJ C 316/48) and First Protocol ([1996] OJ C 313/1), which entered into force on 17 Oct 2002. The Second Protocol ([1997] OJ C 221/12) entered into force on 19 May 2009. For ratification details, see Appendix I. On implementation by Member States, see the Commission reports (COM (2004) 709, 25 Oct 2004 and COM (2008) 77, 14 Feb 2008). The Commission has tabled a proposal for a Directive, which would replace the Convention and Protocols (COM (2012) 363, 11 July 2012).

[247] Dir 2014/57 ([2014] OJ L 173/179). Member States have to comply with this Directive by 3 July 2016 (Art 13(1)).

[248] N 242 above. See also the Protocol to the Council of Europe cyber-crime Convention (ETS 189; for ratification details, see Appendix I).

[249] Art 1(1), Framework Decision.　　[250] Art 1(2), Framework Decision.
[251] Art 1(4), Framework Decision.　　[252] Art 1(3), Framework Decision.

circumstance, or, alternatively that such motivation may be taken into consideration by the courts in the determination of the penalties'.[253]

The entire Framework Decision is subject to the safeguard that it does not affect the obligation to ensure human rights protection in accordance with the previous Article 6 TEU, including the protection of freedom of association and expression. Also, it does not require Member States to override fundamental constitutional principles or rules relating to the liability of the press.[254] Assuming that these safeguards are properly respected, the Framework Decision should not in principle conflict with the rights of freedom of expression and association. In light of these safeguards, the limitation of the obligation to criminalize acts to those which incite violence or hatred, and the possibility for Member States to place further reasonable limitations on their obligations, the Framework Decision therefore strikes the right balance between the need to combat racism and xenophobia and the right to express unpopular and even obnoxious or outrageous opinions.[255]

The second measure within the scope of Article 83(2) TFEU is the facilitation of illegal entry and residence, as set out in the Directive and Framework Decision of 2002 on this subject and previously in Article 27 of the Schengen Convention.[256] This issue concerns irregular migration, so is considered in more detail in Chapter 7 of volume 1, along with relevant international measures on the same topic.[257] For the same reason, the third measure, concerning the employment of irregular migrants, is also considered in detail in Chapter 7 of volume 1.[258]

Next, following the annulment of the Framework Decisions on environmental crime, and ship-source pollution, EC criminal law Directives were adopted on both of these issues.[259] The environmental crime Directive requires Member States to impose criminal sanctions for: pollution (as defined) of the air, soil, or water, where this results in death or serious injury to persons, or 'substantial damage' to the air, soil, or water, or to animals or plants; waste management or transport, the unlawful operation of a plant in which a dangerous activity is carried out, and the unlawful production and use of radioactive materials in the same circumstances; the shipment of waste; the unlawful killing, trading, or possession of protected wild flora or fauna; the deterioration of habitats; and the unlawful trade in ozone-depleting substances.[260]

The Directive on shipping pollution obviously has a narrower scope, confining itself to requiring Member States to criminalize the discharge of pollution from ships into Member States' waters (as broadly defined) and the high seas.[261]

As for the Convention and Protocols on protection of the EU's financial interests, they are intertwined with the Community law principles and the substantive Community law discussed above.[262] Despite the *Greek maize* obligation to impose equivalent, effective, dissuasive, and proportionate penalties, detailed study showed that the remaining

---

[253] Art 4, Framework Decision.   [254] Art 7, Framework Decision.
[255] On the general human rights issues, see II:5.3.1 above.   [256] N 243 above.
[257] I:7.5.3.   [258] I:7.6.1.
[259] Dirs 2008/99 and 2009/123, n 245 above.   [260] Art 3 of Dir 2008/99, n 245 above.
[261] Arts 3–5 and 5a of Dir 2005/35, as amended by Dir 2009/123 (both n 245 above). On the validity of the underlying Dir 2005/35, see Case C-308/06 *Intertanko* [2008] ECR I-4057.
[262] II:5.4.1.1.

differences between substantive and procedural national laws hindered prosecutions against fraud affecting the EU's financial interests.[263] The Protection of Financial Interests (PIF) Convention and its Protocols were the subsequent response.[264]

The PIF Convention defines fraud against the EU's financial interests as 'any intentional act or omission relating to' the 'use or preparation of false, incorrect or incomplete statements or documents, which has as its effect' either the 'misappropriation or wrongful retention' of EU expenditure or the 'illegal diminution' of EU revenue.[265] The definition also includes 'non-disclosure of information in violation of a specific obligation with the same effect' and the 'misapplication of funds' for purposes other those originally granted. Member States must criminalize such action, except where frauds are less than €4,000.[266] The First PIF Protocol, addressing corruption against the EU's financial interests, defines 'corruption' consistently with the EU's general corruption Convention.[267] EU officials must be 'assimilated' to national officials and EU Commissioners, parliamentarians, judges, and auditors must be 'assimilated' to their national equivalents for the purpose of applying the criminal law obligations.[268] The Second PIF Protocol requires Member States to criminalize money laundering 'related to' the proceeds of fraud and corruption as defined in the PIF Convention and First Protocol.[269] Member States may enter a five-year reservation from the date of ratification of the Protocol providing that they need only criminalize the laundering of money from 'serious cases' of active and passive corruption, and this reservation can be renewed once for a further period of five years.[270]

Finally, the Directive on market abuse sets out three different offences: insider dealing, disclosure of inside information, and market manipulation.[271] These offences are defined by reference to EU banking legislation.[272] Since the Community prohibition on insider trading resulted in many cases before the CJEU, this Directive may also attract litigation in turn.[273]

5.5.2 Scope of offences

5.5.2.1 Liability of legal persons

There are wide differences among national laws regarding the issue of corporate criminal liability. Unsurprisingly, therefore, EC legislation imposing prohibitions does not usually specify whether Member States must implement it by imposing

---

[263] SEC (93) 1172, 16 July 1993; see later COM (95) 556, 14 Nov 1995.

[264] N 246 above.

[265] Art 1(1), PIF Convention. This definition covers fraud relating to VAT: Case C-105/14 *Taricco*, ECLI:EU:C:2015:555. The same judgment also ruled that Member States could not set out rules in national law which made it too difficult to conclude effective prosecutions due to lapse of time.

[266] Arts 1(2) and 2(2), PIF Convention.   [267] See II:5.5.1.2 above.

[268] Art 4, First Protocol.

[269] Art 2, Second Protocol. 'Money laundering' is defined by reference to the EC Directive, which now entails a reference to Dir 2015/849 (Art 66 of that Directive, [2015] OJ L 141/73).

[270] Art 18(1), Second Protocol. There is no definition of 'serious cases'. Of the Member States which have ratified the Protocol to date, only Spain has made a reservation. It expired on 19 May 2014.

[271] Arts 3–5, Dir 2014/57, n 247 above.   [272] Art 6, Dir 2014/57, n 247 above.

[273] See II:5.4 above.

sanctions upon legal persons or not. The Court of Justice has recognized this discretion by holding that, when enforcing EC legislation on drivers' hours, Member States are free to choose whether or not they impose criminal liability on legal persons (the usual legal form of the drivers' employers), as long as some effective, proportionate, and dissuasive penalty is applied.[274] But in one case EC law does specify an approach to the issue: Member States must 'pierce the veil' and prohibit a natural person from using inside information even when a legal person is the *de jure* possessor of the information.[275]

Member States were less reticent when agreeing EU third pillar measures and when exercising the Community's criminal law competence. The PIF Convention requires Member States to impose criminal liability on 'heads of businesses or any persons having power to take decisions or exercise control within a business', without further defining any of those terms.[276] This obligation was transposed to the anti-corruption obligations in the first PIF Protocol,[277] along with the Convention on national corruption law.[278]

Subsequently, Member States agreed on standard EU rules on the liability of legal persons, as first set out in the Second Protocol to the EU financial interests Convention. The Protocol defines a 'legal person' as: 'any entity having such status under the applicable national law, except for States or other public bodies in the exercise of State authority and for public international organizations'.[279] Liability must be imposed where a legal person can be held liable for specified crimes 'committed for their benefit by any person, acting either individually or as part of an organ of the legal person, who has a leading position within the legal person', based on representation of that legal person, power to take decisions on behalf of the legal person, or authority to exercise control within it. This liability extends to specified inchoate offences.[280] There is also a form of liability based on negligence, where the legal person 'can be held liable where the lack of supervision or control by' a legal person as previously defined has made commission of a specified criminal act possible 'for the benefit of that legal person by a person under its authority'.[281] It is expressly stated that corporate liability does not exclude criminal proceedings against natural persons.[282]

The Protocol then specifies the form that sanctions must take in the cases which it has set out: 'effective, proportionate and dissuasive sanctions, which shall include criminal or non-criminal fines and may include other sanctions such as:' exclusion from public benefits or aid; temporary or permanent disqualification from the practice of commercial activities; judicial supervision; or a winding-up order.[283] As for negligence liability, in such cases legal persons must be punishable by 'effective, proportionate and dissuasive sanctions or measures'.[284]

---

[274] Case C-7/90 *Vandevenne* [1991] ECR I-4371.

[275] Art 2(2), market abuse Directive (Dir 2003/6, [2003] OJ L 96/16); now Art 3(3) of Dir 2014/57, n 247 above.

[276] Art 3, PIF Convention ([1995] OJ C 316/48).

[277] Art 7(1), First Protocol ([1996] OJ C 313/1).

[278] Art 6 of Convention ([1997] OJ C 195/2).   [279] Art 1(d) ([1997] OJ C 221/12).

[280] Art 3(1) (ibid).   [281] Art 3(2) (ibid).   [282] Art 3(3) (ibid).   [283] Art 4(1) (ibid).

[284] Art 4(2) (ibid).

The rules in this Protocol then became a template for all future EU measures (and, to a limited extent, EC measures). The subsequent substantive criminal law measures which are still in force can be divided into those which have simply set out the Second Protocol rules without amendment and those which have made some amendments. The first category comprises: the Framework Decision on counterfeiting currency;[285] the Framework Decision on private corruption;[286] the Framework Decision on attacks against information systems;[287] and the Framework Decision on racism and xenophobia.[288]

The second category comprises:

a) the Framework Decision on counterfeiting payment cards, which does not oblige Member States to extend liability to legal persons as regards one of the offences defined in the Framework Decision (the theft of payment cards);[289]

b) the Framework Decision on terrorism, which does *not* define 'legal person', although a preambular clause states that 'actions by the armed forces of a state in the exercise of their official duties are not governed by this Framework Decision'. The specified sanctions apply regardless of whether a legal person has acted deliberately or negligently, and a fifth possible sanction is listed: 'temporary or permanent closure of establishments which have been used for committing the offence';[290]

c) the Framework Decision on facilitation of the illegal entry and residence of third-country nationals, which does not define 'legal person';[291]

d) the Directives on environmental crimes[292] and ship-source pollution,[293] which contain the standard rule on liability for legal persons but have no rules on sanctions for legal persons, besides an obligation to impose 'effective, proportionate and dissuasive penalties'; the Directive on the employment of irregular migrants is identical, except for an extra provision permitting Member States to publish a list of legal persons held liable for the relevant offence;[294]

e) the Framework Decisions and/or Directives on trafficking in humans,[295] combating sexual exploitation and child pornography,[296] and organized crime,[297] and the Directives on counterfeiting currency, attacks on information systems, and

---

[285] [2000] OJ L 140/1, Arts 1 (third indent), 8, and 9.

[286] [2003] OJ L 192/54, Arts 1 (first indent), 5, and 6.

[287] Arts 1(c), 8, and 9 ([2005] OJ L 69/67).   [288] Arts 5 and 6 ([2008] OJ L 328/55).

[289] Arts 1(b), 7, and 8 of the Framework Decision ([2001] OJ L 149/1).

[290] Arts 7 and 8 ([2002] OJ L 164/3). The 2008 amendment to this Framework Decision ([2008] OJ L 330/21) did not amend the rules on corporate liability.

[291] [2002] OJ L 328/1; however, the rules on liability and penalties in Arts 2 and 3 follow the template.

[292] Arts 1(d), 6, and 7 (Dir 2008/99, [2008] OJ L 328/28).

[293] Arts 8b and 8c of Dir 2005/35 ([2005] OJ L 255/11), as inserted by Dir 2009/123 ([2009] OJ L 280/52).

[294] Arts 2(g), 11, and 12 of Dir 2009/52 ([2009] OJ L 168/24).

[295] Arts 4 and 5, Framework Decision ([2002] OJ L 203/1); Arts 5 and 6, Dir 2011/36 ([2011] OJ L 101/1).

[296] Arts 6 and 7, Framework Decision ([2004] OJ L 13/44); Arts 12 and 13, Dir 2011/93 ([2011] OJ L 335/1).

[297] Arts 5 and 6 of the Framework Decision ([2008] OJ L 300/42).

market abuse,[298] which list a fifth possible sanction: 'temporary or permanent closure of establishments which have been used for committing the offence'; and

f) the Framework Decision on combating drug trafficking, which includes two extra sanctions: 'temporary or permanent closure of establishments which have been used for committing the offence' and the confiscation of proceeds, substances, and instrumentalities connected with the offences; it is also refers to exclusion from 'tax benefits or other benefits' instead of exclusion from 'public benefits'.[299]

5.5.2.2 *Inchoate offences*

The classic common law offences of attempt, conspiracy, and incitement find an echo in one form or another in other national legal systems. They are also explicitly or implicitly provided for in EC or EU legislation. The definition of money laundering includes 'participation in, association to commit, attempts to commit and...counselling' the measures prohibited by the Directive.[300]

The Court of Justice seems willing to find an obligation for Member States to ban attempts even when EC legislation does not expressly provide for it. In *Ebony Maritime*, the Court ruled that to ensure the '[e]ffective prevention' of breaches of EC sanctions against Yugoslavia, the legislation should apply not only to actual entries, but also to attempted entries into Yugoslav territorial waters.[301] This interpretation was bolstered by the legislation's ban on 'any activity the object or effect of which is, directly or indirectly, to promote' prohibited transactions.[302] It is clear that the primary reason for the Court's finding was not the wording of the legislation but the goal of ensuring the effectiveness of Community law, and the result of the ruling is that penalizing attempts to breach the Regulation was not an option but an obligation for Member States. If this is a general principle that applies to the interpretation of all EC legislation, its effect could be quite broad.

Inchoate offences are often explicitly provided for within EU measures. As seen above, the definition of fraud against the EU budget in the PIF Convention includes the 'presentation' of false, incorrect, or incomplete documents, as well as their 'use'. This criminalizes 'complete attempts', and the Convention also criminalizes 'incomplete attempts': Member States must criminalize the 'intentional preparation or supply' of such documents if such action is not already criminalized as a principal offence or an attempt.[303] The Convention also expressly requires Member States to criminalize 'participation in' or 'instigation of' the intentional preparation or supply of false, incorrect, or incomplete documents, although there is no further definition of 'participation'

---

[298] Arts 6 and 7, Dir 2014/62 ([2014] OJ L 151/1); Arts 10 and 11, Dir 2013/40 ([2013] OJ L 218/8); Arts 8 and 9, Dir 2014/57 ([2014] OJ L 173/179).

[299] Arts 1(3), 6, and 7 of the Framework Decision ([2004] OJ L 335/8).

[300] Art 1(3)(d), Dir 2015/849, n 269 above. See also Art 3(6) of the market abuse Directive (n 298 above), on 'recommending or inducing'.

[301] Case C-177/95 [1997] ECR I-1111, para 25.

[302] Art 1(1)(d) of Reg 990/93 ([1993] OJ L 102/14).   [303] Art 1(3) of Convention, n 276 above.

or 'instigation'.[304] Furthermore, Member States have broader obligations to apply criminal penalties to attempts to commit, participation in, or instigation of any of the main offences in the Convention (the use or presentation of documents, non-disclosure of information, or misapplication of funds).[305]

Attempts are also implicitly covered in the First PIF Protocol and in the Convention and Framework Decision on corruption, since, of seen above, these measures cover requesting and promising as well as giving and receiving advantages. The definition of the offences in the EU measures suggests that an offence of active or passive corruption is fully committed when a person agrees to act (or to omit to act) in return for an advantage. If, however, he, she, or it subsequently fails or is prevented from completing the act or omission, he, she, or it has nonetheless committed the full offence, not merely an attempt. The 'penalties' clauses of the PIF Protocol and the corruption Convention also require criminal liability for instigation or participation.[306]

According to the Second PIF Protocol, Member States must also criminalize inchoate offences related to laundering the proceeds of fraud and corruption against the EC budget.[307]

As for the EU's Framework Decisions and Directives, they establish the following:

a) the Framework Decision on terrorism applies to attempts and incitement to commit most offences;[308]

b) the Framework Decision on trafficking in persons applies to attempts and instigation,[309] and the replacement Directive applies to inciting and attempts;[310]

c) the Framework Decision on child pornography and prostitution applies to attempts to commit most offences (not to attempts to acquire or possess child pornography), and instigation;[311] the replacement Directive applies to inciting and attempts to commit most offences;[312]

d) the Framework Decision on drug trafficking applies to attempts (with a possible exemption) and incitement;[313]

e) the Framework Decision on corruption applies to instigation;[314]

f) the Framework Decision on counterfeiting currency (and the replacement Directive) applies to attempts to commit most offences, and to participation and instigation;[315] the Framework Decision on counterfeiting non-cash instruments applies to attempts to commit most offences, and to participation and instigation;[316]

---

[304] N 276 above.   [305] Art 2(1) of Convention.
[306] Art 5(1) of the Protocol and Convention; Art 2 of the Framework Decision, nn 276, 278, and 286 above.
[307] Arts 1(3) and 2 of the Protocol.
[308] Art 4 of Framework Decision, as amended in 2008, n 290 above.
[309] Art 2 of Framework Decision, n 295 above.   [310] Art 3, Dir 2011/36, n 295 above.
[311] Art 4 of Framework Decision, n 296 above.   [312] Art 7, Dir 2011/93, n 296 above.
[313] Art 3 of Framework Decision, n 299 above.
[314] Art 3 of Framework Decision, n 286 above.
[315] Art 3(2) of Framework Decision; Art 5 of Directive, n 285 above.
[316] Art 5 of Framework Decision, n 284 above.

g) the Framework Decision (and the replacement Directive) on attacks on information systems applies to attempts to commit most offences (with a possible exception) and to instigation/incitement;[317]

h) the Framework Decision on organized crime contains no provisions;[318] and

i) the Framework Decision on racism and xenophobia applies to instigation to deny the Holocaust and war crimes, etc. but *not* to instigation to commit the other offences referred to, or to attempts;[319]

j) the Directive on facilitation of irregular entry and residence applies to attempts and instigation;[320] and

k) the Directive on market abuse requires most attempts and incitements to be criminalized.[321]

The EC's criminal law measures each apply to incitement, but not to attempts or conspiracy.[322]

5.5.2.3 Complicity

There are several references to complicity in EC or EU legislation. The money laundering Directive refers expressly to 'aiding, abetting [and] facilitating' the offences described in the Directive, as well as 'assisting' a person involved in converting or transferring property derived from criminal activity as defined in the Directive.[323]

The PIF Convention and its First Protocol make no reference to criminal liability for complicity per se, although the Convention does refer to complicity in its jurisdiction rules.[324] However, this does not exclude the imposition of liability, but rather leaves it up to each Member State, as the second PIF Protocol makes explicit.[325] Corporate liability for complicity must be imposed under the Second Protocol, where the legal person can be liable on a *mens rea* basis; and the Second Protocol also has the effect of requiring Member States to make legal and natural persons alike criminally liable for complicity in laundering the proceeds of fraud and corruption against the EU budget.

As for the EU's Framework Decisions and Directives, the measures on corruption, terrorism (as amended), trafficking in persons, shipping pollution, child pornography and prostitution, drug trafficking, attacks on information systems, counterfeiting the euro, market abuse (with exceptions) and racism and xenophobia require Member States to criminalize aiding and abetting, while the Framework Decision on facilitation of illegal entry and residence requires them to criminalize accomplices.

---

[317] Art 5 of Framework Decision; Art 8, Dir 2013/40, n 298 above.   [318] N 297 above.
[319] Art 2(1) of Framework Decision, n 288 above.
[320] Art 2(a) and (c) of Directive, n 291 above.   [321] Art 6, Dir 2014/57, n 298 above.
[322] Art 10(2), Dir 2009/52; Art 4, Dir 2008/99; and Art 5b of Dir 2005/35, as inserted by Dir 2009/123, nn 292 and 294 above. In the latter two cases, the obligation to criminalize incitement only applies where the action is intentional.
[323] Definition of 'money laundering', n 269 above.   [324] Art 4(1).
[325] Art 3(3) of Protocol.

All EC criminal law Directives require Member States to establish liability for aiding and abetting the relevant offences.[326]

5.5.2.4 *Possession*

The money laundering Directive expressly requires Member States to prohibit the 'possession' of laundered money. The firearms Directive, as amended, also requires Member States to ban possession of some weapons altogether, and to ban possession of others without prior authorization.[327] It is rare to find such explicit bans in EC legislation, but the Court is content to allow Member States to criminalize possession of an object when enforcing that legislation, even where the legislation does not provide for it. For example, Member States are free to criminalize the possession of animals treated with hormones which the EC has prohibited, although the legislation only requires them to prohibit giving the hormones to animals and the slaughter or marketing of animals treated with the hormones and the sale of their meat.[328]

Within the former third pillar, the second PIF Protocol, by its *renvoi* to the money laundering Directive, has the effect of requiring Member States to criminalize all possession of the proceeds of fraud and corruption against the EU budget.[329] The Framework Decisions or Directives on drug trafficking, child pornography, attacks on information systems, counterfeiting currency, and counterfeiting non-cash instruments also require criminalization of possession of relevant items.[330]

5.5.2.5 *Omissions*

There are different views on the extent to which omissions, as distinct from acts, should be criminalized, and inevitable difficulties in determining the difference between acts and omissions. No EC or EU measures rule out the criminalization of omissions in principle, and it seems likely from the Court of Justice's 'hands-off' approach on most other criminal law issues that when interpreting Community law, the Court will leave it to the discretion of Member States to determine whether to criminalize and how to define omissions.

Obligations in the former third pillar measures are slightly more definite. Under the PIF Convention, omissions must explicitly be criminalized, while the First PIF Protocol, the corruption Convention, and the Framework Decision on private corruption criminalize omissions by implication, because they cover persons who refrain from acting in accordance with their duties or functions. Under the Second PIF Protocol, legal persons may be criminally liable if their omissions to supervise or control certain natural persons have made possible acts by those natural persons. The market abuse Directive also necessarily criminalizes omissions of information.

---

[326] Art 10(2), Dir 2009/52; Art 4, Dir 2008/99; and Art 5b of Dir 2005/35, as inserted by Dir 2009/123, nn 292–4 above. In the latter two cases, the obligation to criminalize incitement only applies where the action is intentional.

[327] Note 168 above.   [328] Case C-143/91 *Van der Tas* [1992] ECR I-5045.

[329] N 269 above.   [330] Nn 289, 295, 296, and 298 above.

5.5.3 Conditions of criminal liability

When should persons be criminally liable for their acts and omissions? Should they be liable when their conduct was intentional, or reckless (intentional liability), when it was negligent (negligence liability), or merely when they have caused a proscribed result to occur (strict liability)? EC legislation has not usually addressed this important issue directly, in large part because Member States have developed different principles on the dividing line between criminal and administrative law and retain the option of enforcing EC legislation by either. Moreover, Member States take different views on what type of liability to apply to different offences.

Unusually, the money laundering Directive makes it clear that Member States must only prohibit the named offences 'when committed intentionally', providing further that the conversion, transfer, concealment, disguise, acquisition, possession, or use of illicit property must be done with *knowledge* that the property derives from criminal activity. However, such knowledge or intent (for the purpose of the conversion or transfer) 'may be inferred from objective factual circumstances', and since Member States may expressly adopt 'stricter provisions' than the Directive, the imposition of negligence liability or strict liability is not precluded.[331] Equally, the Directive on employment of irregular migrants requires liability only for intentional acts, but sets just a minimum standard (see further discussion below).[332]

It is more usual for EC law to remain silent on the issues of criminal liability. In its silence, can individuals claim that a Member State's decision to enforce the EC rule by imposing strict criminal liability (requiring only proof of a criminal act, not intention to commit a crime) breaches Community law? The Court has ruled that they cannot. In *Hansen*, it ruled that a Member State was free to impose strict criminal liability on employers breaching EC legislation, as long as it met the *Greek maize* principles of imposing equal, effective, proportionate, and dissuasive sanctions.[333] Denmark's imposition of strict liability to enforce EC drivers' hours legislation met that test because it applied such liability for other breaches of national law, the imposition appeared to be effective and dissuasive, and the proportionality of the fine had not been challenged. But conversely, the Court made clear in *Vandevenne* that strict liability was entirely an option; Member States could certainly impose a different form of liability, or administrative penalties, if they wished, as long as the *Greek maize* principles were satisfied.[334]

Later, in *Ebony Maritime*,[335] the Court left it to the national court to find whether strict liability for breach of EC sanctions legislation was permissible in light of the *Greek maize* principles. However, it urged the national court to take account of the legislation's aim of ending massive breaches of international human rights and humanitarian law. With respect, it is inappropriate to focus solely on the impact of the offence when deciding whether criminal liability is appropriate, without considering the nature of the offence, the rights of the accused, or the severity of the penalty. In certain cases, it would conversely be appropriate to consider the overall impact of strict liability on human rights and/or on other EU objectives. For example, it is submitted that the

---

[331] Art 5, Dir 2015/849, n 269 above.   [332] Art 9(1), Dir 2009/52, n 294 above.
[333] Case C-326/88 [1990] ECR I-2611.   [334] N 274 above.   [335] N 301 above.

Court should preclude Member States from implementing the Directive on unauthorized employment of irregular migrants by imposing strict criminal or administrative liability on employers who hire irregular migrants,[336] because of the severe effects such liability would have on employment of minorities. In fact, subsequent economic sanctions legislation states expressly that acts must be intentional to attract a prohibition.[337]

EU measures have usually expressly or by strong implication required liability for intentions. For example, the PIF Convention covers only intentional acts or omissions, although such conduct (like money laundering) 'may be inferred from objective factual circumstances', and the Convention is only a minimum standard.[338] However, the EC Directive on environmental crime applies when the relevant acts are committed 'with serious negligence',[339] and the Directive on shipping pollution requires liability to be imposed if the impugned acts are committed 'with intent, recklessly or with serious negligence'.[340]

5.5.4 Defences

Normally, EU and EC laws do not make any mention at all of the defences to the offences which they have created (although a number of measures contain exclusions from the substantive scope of criminal liability). It must be presumed that the existence and application of defences is left to national law—although it would be interesting to see what the Court of Justice would make of a 'mistake of law' defence.[341] There are two exceptions to this rule. First of all, the first PIF Protocol and the corruption Convention preserve the immunities enjoyed by the staff of the EC institutions, although those immunities must be waived in certain circumstances.[342] Moreover, both texts preserve special legislation that Member States may have established to govern the status of government ministers.[343] Members of the Commission may not claim entitlement to be governed by such status. Secondly the Directive on e-commerce exempts firms which host, cache, or serve as a conduit for illegal Internet material from liability (presumably including civil liability) unless they were aware of the existence of the material. In effect, this amounts to a defence of automatism.[344] The ability of Member States to retain legislation relating to the liability of the press in the context of the Framework Decision on racism and xenophobia and the amended Framework Decision on terrorism may also amount to a defence in practice.[345] Finally, the Directives on trafficking in persons and sexual offences against children require Member States to provide for the possibility of exempting victims from criminal liability if they have been 'compelled

---

[336] N 294 above.

[337] See, for instance, Art 3(1) of Reg 2580/2001 ([2001] OJ L 344/70).

[338] Arts 1(4) and 9, PIF Convention, n 276 above.   [339] Art 4, Dir 2008/99, n 292 above.

[340] Art 4 of Dir 2005/35, as amended by Dir 2009/123; but note the mandatory exceptions set out in Art 5, again as amended by Dir 2009/123, n 293 above. These provisions (before amendment) were one of the grounds for the (unsuccessful) challenge to the validity of Dir 2005/35: Case C-308/06 *Intertanko* [2008] ECR I-4057.

[341] Causation issues are also presumably left to national law.

[342] Art 4(5) of Protocol and 4(4) of Convention.

[343] Art 4(3) of Protocol and 4(2) of Convention.

[344] Arts 12–14 of Dir 2000/31, [2000] OJ L 178/1.   [345] Nn 288 and 290 above.

to commit' crimes as a 'direct consequence' of the trafficking or abusive acts (ie the defence of duress).[346]

5.6 Penalties

As noted at the outset of this chapter,[347] most EU measures on substantive criminal law adopted after the Treaty of Amsterdam, including measures proposed or agreed after the entry into force of the Treaty of Lisbon, contain minimum sentencing rules. For the first three years after the Treaty of Amsterdam entered into force, the length of these sentences was agreed on an ad hoc basis by the Council, without any underlying plan as to when such rules would be imposed or what standards should apply to setting such sentences. In fact, the negotiation of a number of measures was delayed by disputes as to whether penalty levels should be set at all and if so, at what level. Eventually the JHA Council of April 2002 agreed standard rules, as guidelines for sentencing rules in all later measures.[348] In the view of a Commission Green Paper, national law on criminal penalties should be approximated further,[349] but the Commission has not followed this initiative up.

The measures adopted or proposed before the standard rules were agreed contain the following rules on sanctions:

a) the Framework Decision on counterfeiting currency requires Member States to impose a maximum sentence of at least eight years for counterfeiting currency;[350]

b) the Framework Decision on money laundering requires Member States to impose a maximum sentence of at least four years;[351]

c) the Framework Decision on terrorism requires Member States to impose a heavier sentence than normal for those committing the offences in the Framework Decision with a terrorist intent, a maximum sentence of at least fifteen years for directing a terrorist group in most cases, and eight years for participation in a terrorist group, with possible reductions for those who assist the authorities;[352]

d) the Framework Decision on trafficking in persons requires Member States to impose a maximum sentence of at least eight years in four special circumstances: where the crime endangered the victim's life, caused serious physical harm or involved serious violence, was committed against a vulnerable person (as defined), or was committed in the framework of the 1998 organized crime Joint Action (apart from its penalty level);[353] and

e) the Framework Decision on facilitation of illegal entry and residence requires Member States to provide for an aggravated sentence of at least eight years,

---

[346] Art 8, Dir 2011/36, n 295 above; Art 14, Dir 2011/93, n 296 above.

[347] II:5.2.2 and II:5.2.3 above.   [348] See press release of JHA Council, 25–26 Apr 2002.

[349] See the Green Paper on criminal sanctions (COM (2004) 334, 30 Apr 2004).

[350] Art 6 of Framework Decision ([2000] OJ L 140/1).

[351] Art 2 of Framework Decision ([2001] OJ L 182/1).

[352] Arts 5 and 6 of Framework Decision ([2002] OJ L 164/3). The 2008 amendment to the Framework Decision ([2008] OJ L 330/21) makes no change to these rules.

[353] Art 3 of Framework Decision ([2002] OJ L 203/1).

where the offence was committed for financial gain and was within the framework of the 1998 Joint Action on organized crime, or when endangering the lives of the persons subject to the offence. Member States may reduce this period to six years to retain the coherence of their national penalty system.[354]

The various references to the 1998 Joint Action on organized crime in these and other measures (see below) are now considered to be references to the Framework Decision replacing that Joint Action.[355]

All subsequent Framework Decisions agreed after April 2002 followed the template set out by the JHA Council at that time. This template sets out four levels of sanction: maximum levels of between at least one to three years, two to five years, five to ten years, and over ten years. The Council agreed that it is not necessary to set out sentencing rules in each measure or to use this sentencing template in all cases, although in fact it used the template for every Framework Decision. The template was applied as follows:

a) the Framework Decision on sexual exploitation required Member States to provide for a normal maximum sentence of at least one to three years,[356] increased to five to ten years in certain circumstances, in particular (for most offences) where the child was under the age of sexual consent and the child's life was endangered, the child suffered serious violence or harm, or where the acts were committed in the framework of a criminal organization as defined by the 1998 Joint Action.[357] There was also an obligation to ban convicted persons from 'if appropriate' from exercising professional activities related to the supervision of children, and an option to impose other criminal or non-criminal sanctions;[358]

b) the Framework Decision on private corruption requires Member States to provide for a normal maximum sentence of at least one to three years, with possible prohibition from business activity;[359]

c) the Framework Decision on attacks on information systems required Member States to impose a maximum sentence of at least one to three years for illegal system interference or illegal data interference (but not illegal system access, which was only subject to the general obligation to criminalize), with sentences extended to two to five years for the same offences and for illegal access in breach of a security measure, when those offences are committed in the framework of the 1998 organized crime Joint Action (apart from its penalty level);[360]

---

[354] Art 1 of Framework Decision ([2002] OJ L 328/1).

[355] The deadline to apply the Framework Decision was 11 May 2010 (Art 10 of the Framework Decision, [2008] OJ L 300/42).

[356] Art 5(1) of Framework Decision ([2004] OJ L 13/44).

[357] Art 5(2) of Framework Decision (ibid).

[358] Art 5(3) and (4) of Framework Decision (ibid). On recognition of these disqualifications in other Member States, see further II:3.7.3 above.

[359] Art 4 of Framework Decision ([2003] OJ L 192/54).

[360] Arts 6 and 7 of Framework Decision ([2005] OJ L 69/67). Member States *may* also apply the aggravated penalty when the conduct has 'caused serious damages or has affected essential interests'.

d) the Framework Decision on drug trafficking requires Member States to impose a maximum sentence of at least one to three years as a general rule, increased to five to ten years where the crime involved large quantities of drugs or the most unhealthy drugs, with at least a ten year maximum sentence if the crime was committed in the framework of the 1998 organized crime Joint Action; lesser penalties apply to precursors. Member States may reduce penalties if persons renounce drugs and assist the authorities, and must also provide for confiscation of relevant substances, instrumentalities, and proceeds;[361]

e) the Framework Decision on organized crime provides for a maximum penalty of between two and five years, with a reduction in penalties (optional for Member States) for those who 'squeal' on their criminal associates;[362] and

f) the Framework Decision on racism and xenophobia provides for a maximum penalty of between one and three years, as regards the main offences (but not as regards incitement and aiding and abetting).[363]

As for post-Lisbon Directives:

a) the Directive on trafficking in persons requires a maximum sentence of at least ten years, rather than eight years, in the same four special circumstances as before, with 'vulnerable' victims now defined to include all children, and at least five years in ordinary cases;[364]

b) the Directive on sexual offences against children requires maximum sentences of one, two, three, five, eight, or ten years for various crimes;[365]

c) the Directive on attacks on information systems provides for penalties of two, three, or five years for various acts;[366]

d) the Directive on counterfeiting the euro has maximum terms of five or eight years for certain offences;[367] and

e) the Directive on market abuse requires a maximum term of four years for insider dealing or market manipulation, or two years for unlawful disclosure of information.[368]

In each case, inchoate offences are subject only to the 'effective penalties' rule. None of these measures follow the agreed pre-Lisbon template.

Overall, the attempt to systematize the EU's sentencing rules proved to be short-lived, with a return to unsystematic rules on sentencing rules as soon as the Treaty of Lisbon entered into force. There has been no move to set minimum sentences. At least

---

[361] Arts 4 and 5 of Framework Decision ([2004] OJ L 335/8).

[362] Arts 3 and 4 of Framework Decision ([2008] OJ L 300/42).

[363] Art 3 of Framework Decision ([2008] OJ L 328/55).

[364] Art 4, Dir 2011/36 ([2011] OJ L 101/1). Penalties must be aggravated when the perpetrator was a public official.

[365] Arts 3–6, Dir 2011/93 ([2011] OJ L 335/1). There are also rules on aggravated circumstances and disqualifications (Arts 9 and 10).

[366] Art 9, Dir 2013/40 ([2013] OJ L 218/8). Identity theft is an aggravating circumstance (Art 9(5)).

[367] Art 5, Dir 2014/62 ([2014] OJ L 141/1).   [368] Art 7, Dir 2014/57 ([2014] OJ L 173/179).

the EU has been consistently including sentencing rules in its criminal law legislation for many years, excepting only the annulled Framework Decision on environmental crime,[369] and the Framework Decision on the counterfeiting of non-cash items.[370]

5.7 Administrative Cooperation

The main type of administrative cooperation as regards substantive criminal law has been the move toward developing comparable EU-wide crime statistics. The adoption of any measures would be subject to Article 338 TFEU, which now applies to the former third pillar since the entry into force of the Treaty of Lisbon. In the meantime, the Commission adopted an action plan on this issue for 2006–10,[371] which, inter alia, set out the objective of ultimately gathering comparable statistics on specific cross-border crimes (corruption, fraud, counterfeiting of goods, trafficking in cultural goods, and sexual offences against children), as well as money laundering and terrorist financing, trafficking in persons, juvenile crime, drug-related crime, violence against women, domestic violence, and environmental crime. However, the Commission's subsequent proposal for legislation on this issue was rejected and withdrawn.[372]

5.8 External Relations

The adoption of internal EU legislation gives rise to external EU competence over international treaties. Broadly speaking, depending on the extent of the internal harmonization, the EU's external competence is either shared with the Member States or exclusive, which means that the Member States are precluded from adopting treaties on the relevant issue.[373]

In light of EC legislation (as it then was) requiring Member States to prohibit acts such as money laundering,[374] the EC concluded or signed a number of international criminal law Conventions before the entry into force of the Treaty of Lisbon, although in all cases EC competence over these treaties was shared with Member States,[375] and indeed the EC's competence related to only a handful of provisions of these treaties, ie those provisions which did *not* deal expressly with substantive criminal law. The EC's external competence in this area grew in light of the Court of Justice's confirmation of EC competence to adopt internal legislation defining substantive criminal law offences, and the subsequent adoption of EC Directives imposing criminal law obligations,[376] although before the entry into force of the Treaty of Lisbon, the EC never exercised its external competence as regards criminal law obligations as such.

In practice, the EC concluded the UN's Vienna Convention on drugs, the main UN Convention on organized crime, the three Protocols to the latter Convention (concerning smuggling of persons, trafficking in persons, and firearms), and the UN Convention

---

[369] [2003] OJ L 29/55.   [370] [2001] OJ L 149/1.   [371] COM (2006) 437, 7 Aug 2006.
[372] COM (2011) 335, 8 June 2011 (proposal); [2014] OJ C 153/3 (withdrawal).
[373] On EU external competence generally, see II:2.7.1 above.   [374] See II:5.5.1 above.
[375] For details of ratification of all these Conventions by the Member States, see Appendix I.
[376] See II:5.4.1.1 above.

on corruption.[377] The Council has also adopted conclusions encouraging cooperation with the Council of Europe as regards criminal law.[378]

As for the previous third pillar,[379] it is not clear whether any external competence for the Union at all exists as a consequence of the adoption of internal EU measures, and the Union as such never signed or ratified any international criminal law Conventions before the entry into force of the Treaty of Lisbon. However, prior to this point, the Union's power to sign criminal law treaties was exercised to negotiate association treaties with the Schengen *acquis* for Switzerland and Liechtenstein, as well as treaties concerning extradition and mutual assistance with the US, Norway, Iceland, and Japan.[380] Moreover, the Union used its capacity to adopt Common Positions or Joint Positions on international negotiations on criminal law issues, as well as less formal means, to coordinate the negotiating position of Member States as regards a number of international criminal law treaties.[381]

The adoption of substantive criminal law measures subsequent to the entry into force of the Treaty of Lisbon falls squarely within the established legal framework regarding EC (now EU) external competence,[382] whether the measures are adopted pursuant to Article 83(1) or (2) TFEU. However, the requirement that EU measures in this area set only minimum standards means that the Union cannot in principle fully harmonize the field, and so must share competence with its Member States as regards international treaties concerning substantive criminal law. But the position may be different as regards provisions concerning criminal law jurisdiction.[383] So the declaration in the Final Act of the Treaty of Lisbon which attempts to limit the EU's external competence over, inter alia, criminal law simply confirms the obvious.[384]

In practice, the Commission separated the criminal sanctions from its proposal for the EU to conclude the Anti-Counterfeiting Trade Agreement, but ultimately the EP rejected the conclusion of this treaty.[385] It has also proposed that the EU conclude the Protocol to the UN tobacco control treaty,[386] and the EU has signed the 'foreign fighters' Protocol to the Council of Europe treaty on terrorism.[387] The Commission has also proposed that the EU sign a treaty on manipulation of sports results.[388] For its part, the CJEU has clarified that the inclusion of a brief reference to criminal law in a treaty does

---

[377] See respectively [1990] OJ L 326/56, [2004] OJ L 261/69, [2006] OJ L 262/34, [2006] OJ L 262/51, [2014] OJ L 89/7, and [2008] OJ L 287/1. Member States have also signed or ratified these treaties. For ratification details, see Appendix I.

[378] [2009] OJ C 50/8.

[379] On external competence in relation to the prior third pillar, see generally II:2.7.2 above.

[380] See II:3.2.5 and II:3.9 above.   [381] For the details, see II:2.2.2.2 and II:2.7.2 above.

[382] On the specific Treaty provisions inserted by the Treaty of Lisbon regarding EU external competence generally, see II:2.7.1 above.

[383] See II:6.12 below.   [384] On this declaration, see also II:3.9 above.

[385] COM (2011) 380, 24 June 2011.

[386] COM (2015) 194 and 195, 4 May 2015. There are separate proposals for the policing and criminal law aspects and the non-JHA aspects. The Decisions to sign the treaty on behalf of the EU were also split ([2013] OJ L 333/73 and [2013] OJ L 333/73 and 75).

[387] [2015] OJ L 280/24. The EU has also signed the main Convention, since it could not sign the Protocol unless it had signed that Convention too: [2015] OJ L 280/22.

[388] COM (2015) 84 and 86, 2 Mar 2015. Again, there are two separate proposals to sign the treaty, as regards the policing and criminal law aspects and the non-JHA aspects. There were separate decisions authorizing negotiations ([2013] OJ L 170/62 and Council doc 10180/13).

not mean that the EU's (or Member States') criminal law competence applies, if the criminal law provisions are purely ancillary to the main point of the treaty.[389]

5.9 Conclusions

Given the different social and cultural traditions of Member States, the close connection between criminal law and the sovereignty of States, and the democratic right of citizens within each State to decide what actions should or should not be criminalized, prima facie the idea of extensive harmonization of substantive criminal law in the European Union cannot be justified. But certain crimes have long been regarded by the international community as sufficiently important to address collectively, and certain other crimes should similarly be addressed collectively by the European Union.

A balance needs to be struck between the national sovereignty of States as regards deciding what actions to criminalize, and the possible impact of such national decisions upon the interests of other Member States or the European Union as a whole, given the possibility of a type of 'race to the bottom' (ie the movement of persons to commit offences in the most lenient Member States) if there are sufficiently wide divergences in criminal law as regards acts which have a significant cross-border impact. The provisions of the Treaty of Lisbon broadly strike that balance, specifying that the EU can only harmonize certain clearly specified crimes, or take action linked to harmonization in other areas,[390] and subject to the emergency brake which States can invoke in order to protect their distinctive criminal law traditions and (in practice) the pre-eminence of national parliaments in this area. In practice, the fairly modest use of these powers has continued to secure that balance.

In the longer term, the prospect of substantive criminal law harmonization without the emergency brake could only be justified, if at all, in exceptional cases where the EU interest heavily outweighs the national interest (only the protection of EU finances and counterfeiting of the euro qualify) or where there is an inextricable link to an area which has been very extensively harmonized by EU law, and where furthermore it is demonstrably necessary to enforce the harmonized rules by criminal law sanctions.

---

[389] Case C-137/12 *Commission v Council*, ECLI:EU:C:2013:675.

[390] It would be appropriate to limit the abolition of double criminality in principle only to the offences which the EU has thereby harmonized, or which are subject to spontaneous harmonization of national laws: see II:3.10 above.

6

Criminal Law

Jurisdiction, Coordination, and Prosecution

6.1 Introduction

The adoption of legislation defining certain acts as a crime is not, of course, sufficient in itself to deter or punish many of the persons who wish to commit such crimes. It is also necessary to establish effective mechanisms to ensure that those rules are enforced. While the policing aspects of enforcement are discussed in Chapter 7, this chapter focuses on the criminal law aspects of enforcement, beginning with the preliminary issue of the allocation of criminal jurisdiction between Member States. The chapter then considers the connected issues of resolving conflicts of jurisdiction and transferring proceedings between Member States, followed by the rules, stemming from the Schengen Convention, preventing cross-border 'double jeopardy', ie a prosecution in a second Member State after a trial of the same person for the same acts has been finally disposed of in a first Member State.

The EU also plays a more operational role in the criminal law aspects of the enforcement of criminal offences, by means of Eurojust, an EU agency to facilitate and coordinate the work of prosecutors in cross-border cases, established in 2002 and given further powers in 2008; its role will likely be changed again in the near future. Eurojust will also likely be supplemented soon by a new European Public Prosecutor.

The rules discussed in this chapter obviously supplement the rules on definition of crimes (see Chapter 5 of this volume) and also complement the rules on mutual recognition (Chapter 3 of this volume), in particular because the latter rules contain important exceptions relating to jurisdiction and double jeopardy. The cross-border double jeopardy rules also constitute another set of EU rules for the protection of suspects.[1] Furthermore, the rules in this chapter can be compared to the EU rules on civil jurisdiction (Chapter 8 of this volume) but, as will be seen, the EU's framework relating to criminal jurisdiction is far less developed than as regards civil jurisdiction, and seems likely to remain so for the foreseeable future. An essential safeguard against abuse of this flexibility is the rules preventing double jeopardy, which have become a source of conflict between the objectives of free movement and crime prevention.[2]

6.2 Institutional Framework and Overview

6.2.1 Cooperation before the Treaty of Amsterdam

As noted already in Chapter 3 of this volume, before the entry into force of the Treaty of Amsterdam in 1999, the main source of the law on international criminal

---

[1] See II:4.6 above.   [2] See Art 3(2) TEU.

procedure in EU countries was Council of Europe Conventions. In this area, the main Convention concerned was a Convention on transfer of proceedings,[3] which included rules on cross-border double jeopardy and avoiding conflicts of jurisdiction, along with rules on the transfer of proceedings as such. An earlier Convention on the international validity of criminal judgments had also contained double jeopardy rules.[4] However, these two Conventions have attracted limited interest from Member States.[5] A number of Council of Europe and UN Conventions dealing with particular crimes included provisions on criminal jurisdiction related to those crimes.[6]

These two areas were subsequently the subject of Conventions agreed by EU Member States, within the framework of European Political Cooperation (EPC) before the entry into force of the original TEU (known as the Maastricht Treaty). So Conventions on both the transfer of proceedings and the international validity of criminal judgments were drawn up, along with a Convention on cross-border double jeopardy, an issue not addressed separately by the prior Council of Europe Conventions.[7] However, none of these Conventions attracted sufficient ratifications from Member States to enter into force.[8]

Outside the framework of cooperation between the (then) EEC Member States, the 1990 Schengen Convention contained a number of detailed provisions on cross-border cooperation, including rules on double jeopardy (reproducing the provisions of the failed EPC Convention),[9] but not on transfer of proceedings or the international validity of judgments.

Although the entry into force of the Treaty of Maastricht gave the EU a formal intergovernmental framework to address criminal procedural issues, the EU did not use this framework to address jurisdiction issues before the entry into force of the Treaty of Amsterdam, except to adopt Conventions and Joint Actions on particular crimes which included jurisdiction rules in relation to those specific crimes, and (in two cases) rules on double jeopardy.[10]

6.2.2 Treaty of Amsterdam

EU powers concerning conflicts of jurisdiction were set out expressly in the previous Article 31(d) TEU, which provided that the EU can adopt measures concerning 'preventing conflicts of jurisdiction between Member States'.

The Treaty of Nice subsequently added a second paragraph to the previous Article 31 TEU,[11] referring to Eurojust, the prosecutors' body which EU leaders had agreed to create in the meantime (see below):

---

[3] ETS 73.   [4] ETS 70.   [5] For ratification details, see Appendix I.
[6] On those Conventions, see further II:5.5 above.   [7] See II:6.6, II:6.7, and II:6.8 below.
[8] For ratification details, see Appendix I.
[9] Arts 54–8 of the Convention ([2000] OJ L 239). See II:6.8 below.
[10] See II:6.6 and II:6.8 below.
[11] The previous Art 31(d) TEU was therefore renumbered Art 31(1)(d) TEU from that point on.

The Council shall encourage cooperation through Eurojust by:

(a) enabling Eurojust to facilitate proper coordination between Member States' national prosecuting authorities;

(b) promoting support by Eurojust for criminal investigations in cases of serious cross-border crime, particularly in the case of organised crime, taking account, in particular, of analyses carried out by Europol;

(c) facilitating close cooperation between Eurojust and the European Judicial network, particularly, in order to facilitate the execution of letters rogatory and the implementation of extradition requests.

The provisions of the revised TEU were governed by the revised general third pillar rules on the jurisdiction of the Court of Justice, the role of the political institutions, and the use of specific instruments and their legal effect.[12] On the latter point, the Court's judgment in *Pupino*, finding that Framework Decisions had indirect effect,[13] could be relevant to this area, assuming that the principle of indirect effect also applies to the Schengen Convention rules on double jeopardy.

In practice, the Tampere European Council conclusions of 1999 called for the creation of Eurojust, to be established by a measure to be adopted by the end of 2001. The Tampere conclusions also called for the adoption of a mutual recognition work programme by the end of 2000, and this work programme included the objective of adopting revised rules on double jeopardy, to replace the Schengen rules, as well as rules to facilitate the settlement of conflicts of jurisdiction.[14]

To give effect to these objectives, Eurojust was set up early in 2002, and its powers were later extended significantly in 2008.[15] A Framework Decision replacing the Schengen Convention rules on double jeopardy was proposed in 2003, but was not successful; instead, the double rules in the Schengen Convention became a major focus of the third pillar case law of the Court of Justice, following references from a large number of national courts.[16] In 2009, the Council adopted a Framework Decision on the issue of conflicts of jurisdiction,[17] and also discussed a Framework Decision on transfer of proceedings,[18] but was unable to agree upon the latter measure before the Treaty of Lisbon entered into force. Finally, the EU adopted a number of measures concerning substantive criminal law which contained provisions on jurisdiction.[19]

6.2.3 Treaty of Lisbon

Following the entry into force of the Treaty of Lisbon on 1 December 2009, EU powers concerning conflicts of jurisdiction are set out in Article 82(2)(b) of the Treaty of the Functioning of the European Union (TFEU), which specifically provides that the EU may adopt measures to 'prevent and settle conflicts of jurisdiction between Member States'. As compared to the previous Treaty, the powers include the *settlement* of conflicts instead of merely their prevention.

---

[12] See II:2.2.2 above.   [13] Case C-105/03 [2005] ECR I-5285; see discussion in ibid.
[14] [2001] OJ C 12/10. See further II:3.2.2.1 above.   [15] See II:6.9 below.
[16] See II:6.8 below.   [17] See II:6.6 below.   [18] See II:6.7 below.   [19] See II:6.5 below.

The role of Eurojust is now set out in Article 85 TFEU, which reads as follows:

1. Eurojust's mission shall be to support and strengthen coordination and cooperation between national investigating and prosecuting authorities in relation to serious crime affecting two or more Member States or requiring a prosecution on common bases, on the basis of operations conducted and information supplied by the Member States' authorities and by Europol.

     In this context, the European Parliament and the Council, by means of regulations adopted in accordance with the ordinary legislative procedure, shall determine Eurojust's structure, operation, field of action and tasks. These tasks may include:
   (a) the initiation of criminal investigations, as well as proposing the initiation of prosecutions conducted by competent national authorities, particularly those relating to offences against the financial interests of the Union;
   (b) the coordination of investigations and prosecutions referred to in point (a);
   (c) the strengthening of judicial cooperation, including by resolution of conflicts of jurisdiction and by close cooperation with the European Judicial Network.

     These regulations shall also determine arrangements for involving the European Parliament and national Parliaments in the evaluation of Eurojust's activities.
2. In the prosecutions referred to in paragraph 1, and without prejudice to Article 86, formal acts of judicial procedure shall be carried out by the competent national officials.

As compared to the previous Article 31(2) TEU, Article 85 TFEU refers to the initiation of investigations and the proposal for initiation of prosecutions, as well as the resolution of conflicts of jurisdiction. It also refers specifically to the role of the European Parliament (EP) and national parliaments, and provides for a reservation of national competence as regards 'formal acts of judicial procedure'. Furthermore, it is clear that the three tasks for Eurojust listed in Article 85(1) are not an exhaustive list of such tasks (see the words 'shall include').

There is also a new clause concerning the possible creation of a European Public Prosecutor (Article 86 TFEU):

1. In order to combat crimes affecting the financial interests of the Union, the Council, by means of regulations adopted in accordance with a special legislative procedure, may establish a European Public Prosecutor's Office from Eurojust. The Council shall act unanimously after obtaining the consent of the European Parliament.

     In the absence of unanimity in the Council, a group of at least nine Member States may request that the draft regulation be referred to the European Council. In that case, the procedure in the Council shall be suspended. After discussion, and in case of a consensus, the European Council shall, within four months of this suspension, refer the draft back to the Council for adoption.

     Within the same timeframe, in case of disagreement, and if at least nine Member States wish to establish enhanced cooperation on the basis of the draft regulation concerned, they shall notify the European Parliament, the Council and the Commission accordingly. In such a case, the authorisation to proceed with enhanced cooperation referred to in Article 20(2) of the Treaty on European Union and Article 329(1) of this Treaty shall be deemed to be granted and the provisions on enhanced cooperation shall apply.

2. The European Public Prosecutor's Office shall be responsible for investigating, prosecuting and bringing to judgment, where appropriate in liaison with Europol, the perpetrators of, and accomplices in, offences against the Union's financial interests, as determined by the regulation provided for in paragraph 1. It shall exercise the functions of prosecutor in the competent courts of the Member States in relation to such offences.

3. The regulations referred to in paragraph 1 shall determine the general rules applicable to the European Public Prosecutor's Office, the conditions governing the performance of its functions, the rules of procedure applicable to its activities, as well as those governing the admissibility of evidence, and the rules applicable to the judicial review of procedural measures taken by it in the performance of its functions.

4. The European Council may, at the same time or subsequently, adopt a decision amending paragraph 1 in order to extend the powers of the European Public Prosecutor's Office to include serious crime having a cross-border dimension and amending accordingly paragraph 2 as regards the perpetrators of, and accomplices in, serious crimes affecting more than one Member State. The European Council shall act unanimously after obtaining the consent of the European Parliament and after consulting the Commission.

As for decision-making, measures concerning conflicts of jurisdiction and Eurojust have, since the entry into force of the Treaty of Lisbon, been subject to qualified majority voting and co-decision (ie the ordinary legislative procedure) as compared to unanimity in the Council and consultation of the EP previously. There is no special feature applying to decision-making here (ie an emergency brake), as compared to the rules on substantive criminal law or domestic criminal procedure. It is possible that a joint proposal may be made by at least one-quarter of Member States.[20]

The rules are obviously different for the adoption of measures concerning the European Public Prosecutor's Office (EPPO). Such measures are subject to unanimous voting in Council with the consent of the EP. This is the only example of a 'special legislative procedure' as regards EU criminal law. An extension of the mandate of the Prosecutor would be subject to unanimity in the European Council (ie EU leaders) with the consent of the EP.[21] A change to the former, but not the latter, decision-making rules could be made by means of the general *passerelle* clause in the Treaties, subject to unanimity in the European Council, consent of the EP, and control by national parliaments.[22] Another particular feature of Article 86 TFEU is the possibility of a fast-track authorization of enhanced cooperation in the event of a veto; this rule also applies to measures on operational police cooperation.[23] It may also be relevant that the general provisions applying to Title V specify that Justice and

---

[20] Art 76 TFEU.

[21] This compares to unanimity in the Council to extend the scope of the EU's powers over substantive criminal law or national criminal procedure (Arts 82 and 83 TFEU): see II:4.2.3 and II:5.2.3 above.

[22] Art 48(7), revised TEU, which only applies to Art 86(1), but not Art 86(4), because it can only be used as regards decision-making by the *Council*, not the European Council.

[23] Art 87(3) TFEU; see II:7.2.3 below. For a detailed analysis of this special rule, referred to as a 'pseudo-veto' in this book, see II:2.2.3.4.2 above.

Home Affairs (JHA) measures must respect 'the different legal systems and traditions' of Member States.[24]

As with other aspects of criminal law and policing, the Treaty of Lisbon also applied the normal rules applying to the jurisdiction of the EU's Court of Justice to measures adopted after the entry into force of that Treaty, as well as to measures adopted before that Treaty either after a five-year transitional period (ending on 1 December 2014) or if those measures were amended in the meantime. The standard rules on the legal effect of EU law (formerly Community law) have also applied to measures adopted after the entry into force of the Treaty of Lisbon, and to measures adopted beforehand once they are amended.

As for the practical impact of the Treaty of Lisbon, so far there have been only a modest number of references to the Court of Justice relating to the issues addressed in this chapter. The transfer of proceedings proposal, which was under discussion before the Treaty of Lisbon entered into force, lapsed at that time, and has not been tabled again. However, several substantive criminal law measures with specific provisions on jurisdiction have been adopted or proposed.[25] Furthermore, legislation to revise the status of Eurojust and to create the office of a European Public Prosecutor has been proposed.[26]

6.2.4 Competence issues

First of all, it is necessary to distinguish the Treaty provisions concerning conflict of jurisdiction, Eurojust, and the European Public Prosecutor from other Treaty provisions. Then it is necessary to examine the extent of the Treaty powers as regards Eurojust and the EPPO.

Starting with EU powers over criminal procedure, double jeopardy rules fall within the scope of either the power to adopt rules on mutual recognition in Article 82(1)(a) TFEU (in light of the relevant case law of the Court of Justice),[27] and/or the power to adopt rules on preventing and settling conflicts of jurisdiction (Article 82(1)(b)). This is relevant since the power to adopt rules on suspects' rights (Article 82(2)(b)) is subject to an emergency brake rule, whereas Article 82(1) is not.[28] Since the Treaty provisions on Eurojust and the European Public Prosecutor are each a *lex specialis*, any rules on domestic criminal procedure linked to either entity must be adopted on the basis of the more specific legal bases. This is particularly relevant in light of the requirement for unanimous voting as regards Article 86 TFEU, and the lack of an emergency brake rule in Article 85 (as compared to Article 82(2)). A measure concerning Eurojust's role regarding conflicts of jurisdiction should have the dual legal base of Articles 82(1)(b) and 85 TFEU—keeping in mind that any measure with the latter legal base must take the form of a Regulation. However, a measure concerning conflicts of jurisdiction as

---

[24] Art 67(1) TFEU. See further II:2.2.3.2 and II:3.2.4 above.   [25] See II:6.5 below.

[26] See II:6.9 and II:6.10 below.   [27] See II:6.8 below.

[28] Note that the combination of legal bases which do and do not allow for an emergency brake is not per se a problem: see II:3.2.4 above.

regards the EPPO must be based on Article 86 TFEU, given its connection to the functioning of that office.

Next, as regards EU powers over substantive criminal law, rules concerning the assertion of jurisdiction over a particular crime fall within the scope of the EU's substantive criminal law powers set out in Article 83 TFEU, because such provisions are ancillary to the substantive criminal law powers and do nothing to prevent or settle conflicts of jurisdiction.[29] In fact, those rules often exacerbate such conflicts by requiring or encouraging Member States to take extraterritorial jurisdiction.[30] Also, rules concerning assertion of jurisdiction by the European Public Prosecutor must fall within the scope of Article 86, since they affect the functioning of that body.[31] However, while Article 86 is the correct legal base for defining *which* offences the EPPO will have the competence to prosecute, the definition of those offences as such falls within the legal base of Article 83.[32] Certainly Article 86 is a *lex specialis* as compared to the more general provision on fraud against the EU budget (Article 325 TFEU).

As compared to the EU's policing powers, rules relating to jurisdiction over investigations must fall within the scope of Article 87 TFEU, but rules concerning the involvement of Eurojust or the European Public Prosecutor in investigations relate to the operations of the bodies concerned, and are therefore within the scope of Articles 85 and 86. There is nothing in the policing provisions of the Treaty that restricts the scope of the latter Articles as regards investigations.

Finally, it should be noted that where issues relating to civil jurisdiction and criminal jurisdiction overlap, the Court of Justice has ruled that Member States' courts could not refuse recognition of other Member States' courts' civil judgments purely because the latter were founded on an assertion of extraterritorial criminal jurisdiction.[33]

As for the powers of Eurojust, the restriction on giving that body the power to take 'formal acts of judicial procedure' means that it cannot itself bring prosecutions against individuals, because at the very least, that exception refers to the bringing of criminal charges against individuals, in whatever form that process takes in the national legal framework. The concept of a 'formal act of judicial procedure' should also be understood as referring to other acts of coercion and constraint, for instance a decision to search property or to freeze assets. Furthermore, it is arguable that Eurojust cannot be given the power to *require* national authorities to begin prosecutions (as distinct from 'proposing' that they do so), or to take other 'formal acts of judicial procedure', because that would render the reserve of national competence set out in Article 85(2)

---

[29] The underlying substantive rules are discussed in ch 5 of this volume.

[30] See the rules discussed in II:6.5 below. The exception would be the few cases where the legislation also sets out rules on priority jurisdiction (see II:6.7 below), which requires the addition of Art 82(1)(b) as a legal base after the entry into force of the Treaty of Lisbon.

[31] On the limits to the territorial scope of the EPPO's jurisdiction, see II:6.2.5 below.

[32] For further discussion, see II:5.2.4 above. The proposed legislation on these issues correctly respects this distinction.

[33] Case C-7/98 *Krombach* [2000] ECR I-1935. Note that in this case, Mr Krombach was later detained in Austria because he was the subject of an alert for extradition purposes on the Schengen Information System, but that ultimately the Austrian courts released Mr Krombach due to their interpretation of the Schengen double jeopardy rules (on which see II:6.8 below). See the judgment of the European Court of Human Rights in *Krombach v France* (Reports 2001-II).

TFEU ineffective. On the other hand, Article 85(2) does not rule out giving Eurojust the power to require national authorities to begin *investigations*, as long as this falls short of requiring them to take formal acts of judicial procedure.

As for Eurojust's power to resolve conflicts of jurisdiction, certainly Eurojust could retain the power it already has to *suggest* a resolution to conflicts of jurisdiction.[34] But could the Treaty power potentially extend further, as far as the power to require one Member State not to prosecute, in favour of another? If that power went as far as the compulsion to withdraw charges that had already been laid, it would probably (depending on the national legal framework) amount to a 'formal act of judicial procedure'. However, a power to compel a national authority to *refrain* from bringing proceedings, which would probably amount to a requirement to *omit* to take a 'formal act of judicial procedure', should be considered to fall within the scope of Eurojust's (potential) powers, since otherwise its power to 'resolve' conflicts of jurisdiction would be robbed of all effectiveness. In that case, the right to a fair trial necessarily implies that the binding decision taken by Eurojust would have to be reviewable in the courts by the authorities concerned and by the criminal suspect.

As for the EPPO, the requirement to create the office 'from Eurojust' means that there would have to be a link between the two bodies, although in the absence of more precise Treaty rules there is a degree of discretion as to how close the link would have to be. It is clear from Article 86(2) TFEU that proceedings by the EPPO would have to be brought before the national courts, not before the current EU courts or any other EU judicial body that might be established. The issue of whether the EPPO (and thereby also the defence) would be subject to the relevant national judicial procedure, its own *sui generis* procedural rules, or some combination of the two, is left to be determined by the legislation establishing the Prosecutor, which is currently under discussion.[35] As noted above, the question of whether the EPPO or national prosecutors would have jurisdiction in a particular case, and which national court the EPPO would bring proceedings before in a particular case (and which would review the EPPO's procedural measures, pursuant to Article 86(3)), is a matter to be decided by that legislation also. There is no restriction set out in the Treaty as regards the powers which can be given to the EPPO except for the requirement to bring cases before the national courts,[36] so it would be possible to give the EPPO power to issue search or arrest warrants, for instance. But it would also be possible to leave such powers with the national authorities—perhaps giving the EPPO the power to require those authorities to act to support it, subject to limited exceptions.

6.2.5 Territorial scope

The measures in this chapter adopted prior to the entry into force of the Treaty of Lisbon (the jurisdictional rules in third pillar acts, the Framework Decision on conflicts of jurisdiction, and the Schengen double jeopardy rules) apply to all Member States, except that Ireland is not yet subject to the criminal law rules in the Schengen

---

[34] See II:6.9 below.   [35] See II:6.10 below.
[36] This is, moreover, necessarily implied by the reference in the Treaty to the adoption of rules on the judicial review of the EPPO's procedural actions.

Convention,[37] and the UK used its block opt-out to remove itself from the scope of the Framework Decision on conflicts of jurisdiction and pre-Lisbon measures on substantive criminal law. However, the UK remains bound by the Schengen double jeopardy rules and the pre-Lisbon Decision establishing Eurojust.[38]

Any measures in this area adopted or proposed after the entry into force of the Treaty of Lisbon are subject to possible opt-outs by the UK and Ireland, with special rules applicable if the measures amend (or, as regards the Schengen *acquis*, 'build on') measures which the UK and Ireland are already bound by. In practice, both Ireland and the UK have opted out of the proposals on Eurojust and the EPPO, while opting in to some of the substantive criminal law measures with jurisdiction rules.[39]

Also, measures adopted after the Treaty of Lisbon entered into force do not apply to Denmark at all, unless and until that Member State decides either to relinquish its JHA opt-out altogether or to adopt an alternative version of that opt-out, comparable to the UK and Irish opt-outs.[40] In December 2015, the Danish public voted against a partial opt in to JHA measures in a referendum, rejecting in particular their government's proposal to opt in to the post-Lisbon measures on substantive criminal law adopted to date, as well as the proposed Regulation on Eurojust (once adopted). Also, a 'yes' vote would have meant that Denmark would have applied the Schengen double jeopardy rules as a matter of EU law, not international law.

Furthermore, the Schengen double jeopardy rules (but not the other measures discussed in this chapter) also apply to the Schengen associates (Norway, Iceland, Switzerland, and Liechtenstein).

Arguably the opt-out rules (including the possibility of enhanced cooperation as regards the EPPO) imply a restriction on the territorial scope of the EPPO's jurisdiction. The Council cannot confer power to bring prosecutions upon the EPPO except as regards acts committed on the territory of the States participating in the legislation to establish the EPPO, otherwise the rules on opt-outs and enhanced cooperation would be circumvented. Of course, it would remain possible for those participating Member States to apply their own criminal law on this point extraterritorially if they wished. However, the Commission's proposal to establish the EPPO would give that Office some extraterritorial jurisdiction: it could prosecute acts committed on the territory of the participating Member States, or by their nationals, or by EU officials.[41]

6.3 Human Rights

6.3.1 International human rights law

Issues within the scope of this chapter arise as regards two issues: jurisdiction over offences and double jeopardy.

---

[37] Note, however, that Ireland provisionally applies the prior EPC treaty on this issue with several other Member States: see II:6.8 below.

[38] See the Council and Commission Decisions on the opt back in to third pillar measures ([2014] OJ L 345), and the list of third pillar measures which no longer apply to the UK ([2014] OJ C 430).

[39] For the details of the latter decisions, see II:5.2.5 above.

[40] See generally II:2.2.5.1 and I:2.2.5.2.

[41] Art 14, proposed Reg establishing EPPO (COM (2013) 534, 17 July 2013).

First of all, as regards jurisdiction, presumably the principle of the legality and the non-retroactivity of criminal law, as set out in Article 7 of the European Convention on Human Rights (ECHR), applies.[42] So, for instance, the rules on extraterritorial jurisdiction have to be sufficiently clear and foreseeable, and extensions of extraterritorial jurisdiction cannot be retroactive. This is true *a fortiori* to the extent that the principle of dual criminality is abolished as regards cross-border criminal cooperation, as it has been in many EU mutual recognition measures.[43] After all, the residents of foreign countries cannot generally be expected to have knowledge of an issuing State's criminal law, or even to have knowledge of its application to them.[44]

In one case, the Strasbourg Court has applied a requirement that the jurisdictional aspects of criminal law must be of sufficient quality, in the context of justifying lawful detention in a requested state pursuant to an extradition warrant. This analysis is surely applicable by analogy to Article 7 ECHR, although the Court ruled that Article 7 did not apply to pre-trial detention.[45]

Secondly, as regards double jeopardy, Article 4(1) of the Seventh Protocol to the ECHR, which several Member States have not ratified,[46] sets out a rule against double jeopardy in a single State: '[n]o one shall be liable to be tried or punished again in criminal proceedings under the jurisdiction of the same State for an offence for which he has already been finally acquitted or convicted in accordance with the law and penal procedure of that State'. Article 4(2) permits proceedings to be reopened 'if there is evidence of new or newly discovered facts, or if there has been a fundamental defect in the previous proceedings, which could affect the outcome of the case'. Derogation from the right in national emergencies is not permitted.[47] A similar provision appears in Article 14 of the International Covenant on Civil and Political Rights (ICCPR), which unlike the ECHR Protocol, has been ratified by every EU Member State. The ICCPR provision does not explicitly limit the application of the principle to one State, but the Human Rights Committee has assumed that such a territorial limitation is implicit.[48] Moreover, the ICCPR rule does not provide for a derogation, but rather can be suspended in emergency situations. It should be noted that some Member States have reservations on the Seventh Protocol provision, on the one hand, and the ICCPR, on the other.[49]

In the case law of the Strasbourg Court, the ECHR rule applies to prevent multiple criminal penalties being applied in respect of the same act, regardless of whether a

---

[42] On Art 7 ECHR, see also II:3.3.2 and II:5.3.1 above. Note that the European Court of Human Rights has ruled that 'jurisdiction is not a collateral issue since it forms the basis of any criminal proceedings', with the obvious implication that jurisdictional issues fall within the scope of Art 7 ECHR: *Stephens v Malta* (no 2), 21 Apr 2009, para 59.

[43] See II:3.5 to II:3.7 above.

[44] The extraterritorial application of an issuing State's law to its own residents (ie who have allegedly breached that law on a visit to another State) is a different matter, as they can be expected to have knowledge of that State's law and its scope of application.

[45] *Stephens v Malta* (no 1), 21 Apr 2009.

[46] On the ratification status of the Seventh Protocol, see Appendix I.

[47] Art 4(3) of the Seventh Protocol.

[48] Decision of 19 July 1986 in *A.P. v Italy* (Communication 204/1986, CCPR/C/31/D/204/1986, para 7.3).

[49] For details, see S Peers, 'Double Jeopardy and EU Law: Time for a Change?' (2006) 8 EJLR 199.

person has formerly been acquitted or prosecuted; the concept of a 'criminal' offence has the same broad autonomous meaning which the Court has applied to Article 6 ECHR; and the definition of the same 'acts' includes all criminal charges that are related to the same set of circumstances.[50] The case law on the latter element of the rule was confusing, and in 2009 the European Court of Human Rights revised its case law, following, inter alia, the jurisprudence of the EU's Court of Justice on this issue, and deciding that the rule applied to 'the prosecution or trial of a second "offence" in so far as it arises from identical facts or facts which are substantially the same'.[51] Moreover, '[t]he guarantee...becomes relevant on commencement of a new prosecution, where a prior acquittal or conviction has already acquired the force of *res judicata*', because it was a 'safeguard against being tried or being liable to be tried again in new proceedings rather than a prohibition on a second conviction or acquittal'.[52] The underlying test was therefore whether there was a 'set of concrete factual circumstances involving the same defendant and inextricably linked together in time and space, the existence of which must be demonstrated in order to secure a conviction or institute criminal proceedings'.[53] The rule applies as soon as there is a 'final judgment', ie it does not apply as long as an ordinary appeal is possible, but does apply even if there is still a possibility of 'extraordinary remedies such as a request for reopening of the proceedings or an application for extension of the expired time-limit'.[54] Once there is a final sentence, any pending criminal proceedings must be terminated.[55]

Finally, it should be noted that the Strasbourg Court has ruled that the transfer of a sentence does not amount to a second set of proceedings.[56]

6.3.2 Application to EU law

As regards jurisdictional issues, any obligations in this area deriving from Article 5 or 7 ECHR must apply to EU law, given that the relevant rights are included within the EU's Charter of Fundamental Rights and the general principles of EU law.[57]

As for double jeopardy, the EU's Charter of Rights contains a ban on both domestic and cross-border double jeopardy (within the EU) in Article 50, which provides that:

> No one shall be liable to be tried or punished again in criminal proceedings for an offence for which he or she has already been finally acquitted or convicted within the Union in accordance with the law.

The wording of the Charter clause is based on the ECHR, with extended territorial scope. This right is subject, within a single Member State, to the same limitations as the

---

[50] See particularly *Gradinger v Austria*, 23 Oct 1995 (A328-C) and *Fischer v Austria*, 29 May 2001, which distinguished on the third point between *Gradinger* and the apparently contradictory judgment in *Oliveira v Switzerland*, 30 July 1998 (Reports 1998-V). *Fischer* was followed in *W.F. v Austria*, 30 May 2002, and *Sailer v Austria*, 6 June 2002.

[51] *Zolotukhin v Russia*, 10 Feb 2009, para 82. On the EU rules, see II:6.8 below. See subsequently *Tsonyo Tsonev v Bulgaria (no 2)*, 14 Jan 2010.

[52] Para 83, ibid.   [53] Para 84, ibid.

[54] Para 108, ibid; see also *Nikitin v Russia* [2004] ECHR-VIII.

[55] *Muslija v Bosnia-Herzegovina*, judgment of 14 Jan 2014, para 37.

[56] Decision in *Veermae v Finland* (15 Mar 2005).   [57] See II:3.3.5 above.

ECHR right; the Charter's general limitations rule governs the application of the right in cross-border situations.[58] Since the Charter provision does not refer only to national proceedings, it would apply equally to the European Public Prosecutor, if that post were established.

Despite the provisions of the Charter, the ECHR rules, and the general principles of EU law, Court of Justice case law initially emphasized the distinction between the ECHR rules and the provisions of the Schengen *acquis* which extend the double jeopardy principle to relations between Member States (and Schengen associates), on the grounds that the Schengen rules applied to the same 'acts', while the ECHR and ICCPR rules applied to the same 'offence'.[59] However, as we have seen, the interpretation of the ECHR rules by the European Court of Human Rights was subsequently aligned to the Court of Justice's interpretation of the Schengen rules, making it unnecessary to maintain such a distinction. The CJEU therefore reversed its original approach, aligning in turn its interpretation of the Schengen rules and Article 50 of the Charter with the Strasbourg jurisprudence.[60] Nevertheless, the *ne bis in idem* rule has its limits: in the view of one Advocate-General, a repeat extradition request does not amount to a violation of the protection against double jeopardy.[61]

Furthermore, the general principles of EU law contain a rule against double jeopardy in *administrative* proceedings,[62] which does not generally extend to acts committed in third States.[63] The CJEU has clarified the link between this rule and the ban on double jeopardy in the Charter: the Charter rule only applies where both penalties are criminal in nature, applying the *Engel* criteria of the Strasbourg Court (the legal classification of the offence under national law; the nature of the offence; and the nature and severity of the penalty) to determine whether they are.[64]

6.4 Impact of Other EU Law

The protection of EU financial interests, or the enforcement of other EU obligations by imposing criminal penalties, can be linked to the interpretation of the EU cross-border double jeopardy rules, as seen in the *Gasparini* judgment, where the question of

---

[58] Arts 52(3) and 52(1) of the Charter ([2007] OJ C 303) respectively. See the CJEU ruling in Case C-129/14 PPU *Spasic*, ECLI:EU:C:2014:586, discussed in I:6.8.

[59] Case C-436/04 *van Esbroek* [2006] ECR I-2333, para 28. For detailed interpretation of these rules, see II:6.8 below.

[60] See *Spasic*, n 58 above, and the discussion in I:6.8.

[61] Opinion in Case C-296/08 PPU *Santesteban Goicoechea* [2008] ECR I-6307.

[62] See, for example, the *PVC II* judgments (Joined Cases C-238/99 P, C-244/99 P, C-245/99 P, C-247/99 P, C-250/99 P to C-252/99 P, and C-254/99 P, *LVM and others v Commission* [2002] ECR I-8375). On overlapping EU and national administrative proceedings, see Case C-17/10 *Toshiba*, ECLI:EU:C:2012:72.

[63] For example, see Cases T-223/00 *Kyowo Hakko* [2003] ECR II-2553 and T-224/00 *Archer Daniels Midland* [2003] ECR II-2597 (the latter judgment was upheld on appeal in Case C-397/03 P [2006] ECR I-4429); C-308/04 P, *SGL Carbon v Commission* [2006] ECR I-5977, para 26.

[64] See in particular Case C-489/10 *Bonda*, ECLI:EU:C:2012:319 (which applies the criteria in detail) and Case C-617/10 *Fransson*, ECLI:EU:C:2013:105.

whether prosecutions by different Member States related to the same acts required an interpretation of EU customs law.[65] Furthermore, as noted already,[66] EU law also establishes a double jeopardy principle in administrative proceedings, in particular competition proceedings. The standard test is that there must be a 'threefold condition of identity of the facts, unity of offender and unity of the legal interest protected. Under that principle, therefore, the same person cannot be sanctioned more than once for a single unlawful course of conduct designed to protect the same legal asset.'[67] As we shall see later on,[68] the third of these criteria does not apply to the EU law rules governing double jeopardy in criminal cases.

The exact scope of the EU ban on double jeopardy was clarified in the *Fransson* judgment,[69] where the CJEU said that it potentially applied to two proceedings in relation to VAT (if both proceedings were criminal), given that the EU had harmonized the substance of VAT law. Even though EU legislation did not harmonize the rules on collection of VAT, the CJEU said that there was a link with the financial interests of the Union. This judgment leaves the question open whether such a wide application of the EU rules only applies where there is such a link, or whether a link to the criminal enforcement of EU prohibitions and/or to EU measures which criminalize acts,[70] would also be subject to the EU double jeopardy rule.

6.5 Asserting Jurisdiction

There is no standard set of agreed rules, within the UN, the Council of Europe, or the EU, to determine which State's courts have jurisdiction over a crime. This contrasts with the great willingness of EU Member States, particularly (but not only) in the EU context, to agree rules on civil jurisdiction and conflict of law in civil cases.[71] As a result, different national jurisdictional principles overlap, possibly resulting in double criminal liability,[72] or conversely a vacuum of jurisdiction. All states agree on the 'territoriality' principle: crimes committed wholly or partly within their territory fall within their jurisdiction. Although this principle may appear simple, it can be difficult to apply when only certain elements of the crime took place in one Member State, or where the full offence occurred in one Member State but inchoate offences in another.

In addition, many states, most Member States among them, apply some form of 'extraterritorial' jurisdiction for acts committed abroad, at least for certain crimes.[73] This can take the form of: the 'active personality' principle (jurisdiction over acts committed by nationals of a state outside that state); the 'passive personality' principle

---

[65] Case C-467/04, [2006] ECR I-9199.   [66] II:6.3.2 above.

[67] See, for instance, Joined Cases C-204/00P, 205/00P, 211/00P, 213/00P, 217/00P, and 219/00P, *Aalborg Portland and others v Commission* [2004] ECR I-123, para 338.

[68] See II:6.8 below.   [69] N 64 above.   [70] See further II:5.4 above.

[71] See generally ch 8 of this volume. Note that in international criminal law, unlike civil law, the choice of law automatically determines the choice of court, because few if any courts are willing to apply foreign criminal law.

[72] Some crimes, particularly if committed over the Internet, could even give rise to liability in more than two states.

[73] See G Gilbert, 'Crimes *Sans Frontieres*: Jurisdictional Problems in English Law' (1992) BYIL 415.

(jurisdiction over acts committed *against* nationals of a state outside that state); the 'protective' principle (jurisdiction over acts committed against the essential interests of a state outside that state); the 'representational' principle (where a state agrees to assume the jurisdiction which in principle belongs to another state); and the 'universal jurisdiction' principle (where a crime is considered so heinous that all states have jurisdiction in principle to try a person accused of it).

EU measures have required Member States to adopt certain forms of the above principles in order to prohibit or criminalize certain acts effectively. The money laundering Directive requires Member States to prohibit laundering even if the activities which gave rise to the laundered money were perpetrated in another Member State or a third country.[74] In *Ebony Maritime*, the Court of Justice effectively treated breaches of EU economic sanctions rules as offences with universal jurisdiction, because the offence of entering Yugoslav waters imposed to implement to EC legislation could only be committed outside Member States' territory.[75] Therefore, all it took for a sanctions-breaker to fall within the criminal jurisdiction of a Member State was entry into a Member State's territory after an alleged breach of the sanctions, even when the alleged sanctions-breaker had only entered a Member State's waters after being boarded, commandeered, and then towed to a Member State's port. The nationality of the flag State, the vessel owner, the cargo owner, and presumably the crew, was irrelevant. However, the Court of Justice did not suggest that all EU legislation should receive such wide interpretation; instead, it appears that its interpretation was based upon the Security Council Resolution which the EU was implementing. Indeed, the UK Divisional Court is surely correct to conclude that, as a general principle, Community law (as it was then) does not alter national rules on criminal jurisdiction.[76]

Although there are no general EU rules on criminal jurisdiction, most EU measures concerning substantive criminal law have set out specific rules requiring or permitting Member States to assert their jurisdiction over criminal matters. The adopted measures within the scope of Article 83(1) TFEU (the current legal base concerning substantive criminal law not linked to 'Community' law, as it was previously known) which include provisions on jurisdiction comprise the following:[77]

a) a Framework Decision on terrorism;[78]

b) a Directive on trafficking in persons;[79]

c) a Directive on child pornography and prostitution;[80]

---

[74] Art 1(3) of Dir 2005/60 ([2005] OJ L 309/15); see now Art 1(4) of the replacement Dir 2015/849 ([2015] OJ L 141/73).

[75] Case C-177/95 [1997] ECR I-1111.

[76] *Ken Lane Transport Limited* [1995] 3 CMLR 140 (Div Ct).

[77] This list follows the order of crimes listed in Art 83(1) TFEU. On the ratification status of the Conventions and Protocols (including those listed below), see Appendix I. On the implementation deadlines for the Framework Decisions and Directives (again including those listed below), see II:5.5.1.2 above. On Art 83(1) itself, see II:5.2.3 and II:5.2.4 above.

[78] [2002] OJ L 164/3. This Framework Decision was amended in 2008 ([2008] OJ L 330/21), but the amendment only concerns the definition of criminal offences, not the related rules on jurisdiction.

[79] Dir 2011/36 ([2011] OJ L 101/1), replacing a prior Framework Decision: [2002] OJ L 203/1.

[80] Dir 2011/93 ([2011] OJ L 335/1), replacing a prior Framework Decision: [2004] OJ L 13/44.

    d) a Framework Decision on drug trafficking;[81]

    e) a Convention and a Framework Decision on corruption;[82]

    f) a Directive on counterfeiting currency;[83]

    g) a Framework Decision on counterfeiting non-cash instruments;[84]

    h) a Directive on attacks on information systems;[85] and

    i) a Framework Decision on organized crime.[86]

As regards issues within the scope of Article 83(2) TFEU (which concerns criminal law within the scope of Community law, as it was previously known), the following adopted measures include rules on jurisdiction:

    a) a Framework Decision on racism and xenophobia;[87]

    b) a Framework Decision on facilitation of illegal entry and residence;[88]

    c) a Convention on protection of the EU's financial interests (PIF Convention), with two Protocols;[89] and

    d) a Directive on criminal sanctions for insider dealing and market manipulation.[90]

The Framework Decisions on environmental crime and on ship-source pollution contained provisions relating to jurisdiction, but these rules are not considered further here, since both measures were annulled by the Court of Justice and the Directives which replaced them do not contain jurisdictional rules.[91] Also, the Directive on the prohibition of employment of irregular migrants is not considered here either, because there are no jurisdictional rules attached to the criminal offences set out in that Directive.[92]

    As for proposed measures, the Commission has proposed a Directive which would replace the existing Convention and Protocols on protection of the EU's financial interests, and a Directive which would replace the prior Framework Decision on terrorism. These measures are being negotiated by the EP and the Council.[93]

---

[81] [2004] OJ L 335/8.

[82] Convention ([1997] OJ C 195/1); Framework Decision on private corruption ([2003] OJ L 192/54).

[83] Dir 2014/62 ([2014] OJ L 151/1), replacing a prior Framework Decision: [2000] OJ L 140/1.

[84] [2001] OJ L 149/1.

[85] Dir 2013/40 ([2013] OJ L 218/8), replacing a prior Framework Decision: [2005] OJ L 69/67.

[86] [2008] OJ L 300/42.

[87] Framework Decision ([2008] OJ L 328/55), which replaced a prior Joint Action ([1996] OJ L 185/5) as from 28 Nov 2008 (Art 10(1), Framework Decision).

[88] [2002] OJ L 328/1.

[89] Convention ([1995] OJ C 316/48); First Protocol ([1996] OJ C 313/1); and Second Protocol ([1997] OJ C 221/12).

[90] Dir 2014/57 ([2014] OJ L 173/179).

[91] [2003] OJ L 29/55 and [2005] OJ L 255/164 (Framework Decisions); Cases C-176/03 *Commission v Council* [2005] ECR I-7879 and C-440/05 *Commission v Council* [2007] ECR I-9097 (Court judgments); Dirs 2008/99 ([2008] OJ L 328/28) and 2009/123 ([2009] OJ L 280/52). The Dirs do, however, have a specific territorial scope (ie the territorial scope of the measures listed in the Annex to Dir 2008/99, and Art 3 of Dir 2005/35 ([2005] OJ L 255/11), which Dir 2009/123 amended).

[92] Dir 2009/52 ([2009] OJ L 168/24). However, the Dir has a defined territorial scope, as it applies to the employment of an irregular migrant who is 'present on the territory of a Member State, who does not fulfil, or no longer fulfils, the conditions for stay or residence in that Member State' (Art 2(b), Dir 2009/52).

[93] Respectively COM (2012) 363, 11 July 2012 and COM (2015) 625, 2 Dec 2015.

The basic rule for jurisdiction in these measures is that Member States *must* take territorial jurisdiction when a crime was committed partly or wholly in their territory, and *may* take jurisdiction where an act was committed by one of their nationals or for the benefit of a legal person established there (active personality principle).[94] Also, most EU measures set out an 'extradite or prosecute' rule, which requires a Member State which does not extradite its own nationals to prosecute them instead for the offences established by the EU measures.[95]

However, there are several variations on this approach. The 'extradite or prosecute' rule is not set out uniformly,[96] and is in effect being phased out.[97] Several measures spell out in more detail what the territorial principle entails. The PIF Convention specifies that it may apply where a person on the territory assists or induces the commission of a fraud on another Member State's territory, while the Framework Decision on terrorism extends the concept to vessels flying a Member State's flag and aircraft registered there, and the Framework Decision on organized crime specifies that territorial jurisdiction applies whenever the acts take place on national territory, 'wherever the criminal organisation is based or pursues its criminal activities'. The Directive on attacks on information systems (like the prior Framework Decision) requires assertion of such jurisdiction whenever a person is physically present (wherever the relevant information system is located) or against an information system on its territory (wherever the offender is physically located). Similarly, the Directive on sexual exploitation and child pornography requires Member States to assert jurisdiction whenever an offence is committed by means of information and communications technology accessed from its territory, whether or not that technology is based on their territory.[98]

---

[94] For the jurisdiction rules, see: Art 9, Framework Decision on terrorism, n 78 above; Art 10, Directive on trafficking in persons, n 79 above; Art 17, Directive on sexual exploitation and child pornography, n 80 above; Art 8, Framework Decision on drug trafficking, n 81 above; Art 7, Framework Decision on private corruption, n 82 above; Art 7, corruption Convention, n 82 above; Art 8, Directive on counterfeiting currency, n 83 above; Art 9, Framework Decision on payment card fraud, n 84 above; Art 12, Directive on attacks on information systems, n 85 above; Art 7, Framework Decision on organized crime, n 86 above; Art 9, Framework Decision on racism and xenophobia, n 87 above; Art 4, Framework Decision on facilitation of illegal entry and residence, n 88 above; Art 4, PIF Convention, n 89 above; Art 10, Directive on insider dealing, n 90 above; and Art 11, proposed Dir on EU financial interests, n 93 above. On the jurisdiction rules in pre-Amsterdam measures, see the first edition of this book, pp 162–64.

[95] Art 9(3), Framework Decision on terrorism; Art 8(3), Framework Decision on drug trafficking; Art 7(3), Framework Decision on private corruption; Art 8, corruption Convention; Art 10, Framework Decision on payment card fraud; Art 7(3), Framework Decision on organized crime; Art 5, Framework Decision on facilitation of illegal entry and residence; and Art 5, PIF Convention. There is no such rule in the Framework Decision on racism and xenophobia, or in any of the criminal law Directives adopted or proposed after the Treaty of Lisbon. On the nationality exception to extradition, see further II:3.5 above.

[96] The Framework Decision on terrorism requires Member States to establish jurisdiction regardless of the nationality of the fugitive or the location of the offence; but it does not explicitly require Member States to *prosecute*. Also, the Framework Decisions on corruption, drug trafficking, and organized crime require prosecution (in lieu of extradition) regardless of where the offence was committed; the other measures only require it if the offence was committed in a Member State.

[97] The rule appeared in the prior Framework Decisions on sexual offences (Art 8(3)), trafficking in persons (Art 6(3)), and attacks on information systems (Art 10(3)), but was removed when those measures were replaced by Directives. It never appeared in the prior Framework Decision on counterfeiting currency. The rule in the PIF Convention will be replaced if the proposed Directive on this issue is adopted.

[98] The previous Framework Decision referred to access by means of a 'computer system' instead, in the same circumstances. The proposed PIF Directive would assert jurisdiction if information and communications technology was accessed from the territory.

The corruption Convention enables (but does not require) Member States to take a form of 'passive personality' jurisdiction in certain circumstances. More importantly, several measures place additional obligations on Member States, requiring them to take extraterritorial jurisdiction. The Framework Decision on terrorism requires Member States to take jurisdiction based on a broad concept of the active personality principle (including acts committed by 'residents' and legal persons as well as citizens) and jurisdiction based on a broad concept of the protective principle, where acts are committed 'against the institutions or people' of that Member State or an EU institution or body based there. This may be intended to extend as far as the passive personality principle, depending on whether an attack on 'the people' also includes every attack on individual nationals of a Member State. Even wider jurisdiction is not precluded.[99]

This broader approach to extraterritorial jurisdiction is an established trend after the entry into force of the Treaty of Lisbon: all of the Directives adopted or proposed since that Treaty require Member States to impose their jurisdiction on their nationals. The Directives on trafficking in persons and sexual offences against children also require Member States to waive any requirement 'that the acts are a criminal offence at the place where they were performed' or 'that the prosecution can only be initiated following a report made by the victim in the place where the offence was committed, or a denunciation from the State of the place where the offence was committed'. Furthermore, the proposed PIF Directive would require Member States to waive the latter rule, while the Directive on currency counterfeiting also requires Member States to waive the first of those rules as regards certain offences. That Directive additionally requires the Eurozone Member States to take extraterritorial jurisdiction over any counterfeiting of the euro, as long as the offender is in the territory of that Member State and not extradited, or there are counterfeit notes or coins on that Member State's territory.[100]

6.6 Conflicts of Jurisdiction

In light of the encouragement, and in some cases the requirement, for Member States to assert extraterritorial jurisdiction, as well as the possibility that elements of a crime will fall within the territorial jurisdiction of more than one Member State,[101] there are obviously an increasing number of circumstances where multiple Member States will have criminal jurisdiction as regards a particular act. This is problematic because it is objectionable in principle for any person to be prosecuted more than once for the same acts, even by different States, and to that end the EU has banned such multiple prosecutions as a rule—although the ban only applies *after* one of those prosecutions has resulted in a final judgment.[102] But since only one prosecution can normally lead to a

---

[99] For a comparison of the jurisdiction rules in the Framework Decision (before its amendment in 2008) and the UN Conventions on terrorism, see S Peers, 'EU Responses to Terrorism' (2003) 52 ICLQ 227 at 233–34.

[100] The previous Framework Decision on counterfeiting currency took a broader approach, requiring the Eurozone Member States to take jurisdiction regardless of the nationality of the offender and place of commission of the offence in cases of counterfeiting euros.

[101] See II:6.5 above.   [102] See II:6.8 below.

final judgment, it would be better also to avoid multiple *pending* prosecutions against the same person for the same act in different Member States (known as *lis pendens*) as well, in order to prevent wasting the time and resources of the police, prosecution, and judicial authorities and an unjustified burden on the accused. While the obvious way to do this would be to agree binding rules allocating criminal jurisdiction as between Member States, there are, as we have already seen, no such rules agreed at EU or any other level.

In particular, the Council of Europe Member States did not want to agree on a draft Convention to this end, drawn up by the Council of Europe's Parliamentary Assembly in 1965.[103] However, to take some steps towards avoiding multiple prosecutions, Council of Europe members drew up in 1972 a Convention on the transfer of proceedings in criminal matters, which included rules not only on the transfer of proceedings but also on the conflict of pending proceedings and on cross-border double jeopardy.[104]

On the conflict issue, the Council of Europe Convention provides that any State which becomes aware of any proceedings pending in another State party 'against the same person in respect of the same offence' must consider whether it can waive, suspend, or transfer its proceedings.[105] In these circumstances, the State which has discovered the existence of the parallel proceedings must inform that State where proceedings were already underway if it does not intend to waive or suspend proceedings.[106] In that case, 'the States concerned shall endeavour as far as possible to determine' which single State shall 'continue to conduct proceedings', after evaluating each of the circumstances in which the Convention provides for a possible request to transfer proceedings.[107] During this process a judgment on the merits must be suspended for up to thirty days. However, the process does not apply if the trial has already been opened in either State.[108] If agreement is reached, then the rules on the transfer of proceedings in the Convention are applicable:[109] this means that the State which has waived or suspended its proceedings may not continue with a prosecution, unless the State where the prosecution was centralized discontinues or does not institute proceedings.[110]

Within the EU, a Convention on the transfer of proceedings drawn up within the EPC context in 1990 did not generally address the issue of conflicts of jurisdiction.[111] Subsequently, some EU measures contain rules on priority jurisdiction, to be applied in the event that more than one Member State has jurisdiction over an offence. The Framework Decisions on terrorism and organized crime require Member States to take (respectively) 'sequential account' and 'special account' of territorial jurisdiction, followed by active personality, passive personality, and the State where the person was found.[112] For its part, the Framework Decision on attacks on information systems stated

---

[103] Rec 420 of the Parliamentary Assembly, 8 Nov 1965.
[104] ETS 73. About half of the Member States have ratified this Convention. For ratification details, see Appendix I. On the other rules in this Convention, see I:6.7 and II:6.8.
[105] Art 30(1) of the Convention. Political and military offences are excluded.
[106] Art 30(2) of the Convention.
[107] Art 31(1) of the Convention, referring to Art 8 of the Convention.
[108] Art 31(2) of the Convention.   [109] Arts 33 and 34 of the Convention.
[110] Art 21 of the Convention.
[111] As an exception, the Convention addressed the conflicts issues when proceedings were transferred.
[112] Respectively [2002] OJ L 164/3, Art 9(2), and [2008] OJ L 300/42, Art 7(2).

that Member States *may* take sequential account of territorial jurisdiction, followed by active personality, then the state where the person was found.[113] In each of these measures, the aim is to centralize proceedings in a particular Member State, and Member States should use any mechanism within the EU to attempt to coordinate jurisdiction; the Framework Decision on organized crime refers explicitly to the possibility of using Eurojust for this purpose.[114] In comparison, the Framework Decision on counterfeiting the euro and the fraud and corruption Conventions simply encourage Member States to cooperate with a view to centralizing the prosecution in a single Member State, but without setting rules for priority jurisdiction.[115] Since the Treaty of Lisbon, the trend is to eschew such references and remove those which appear in prior legislation,[116] presumably because of the adoption of a Framework Decision specifically on conflicts of jurisdiction in 2009 (discussed below).

More general provisions on the *lis pendens* issue were included in a Greek proposal for a Framework Decision that set out a list of criteria that would apply where prosecutions for the same acts were pending in multiple Member States.[117] Since Member States could not agree on this proposal (which also would have amended the Schengen double jeopardy rules), discussions were suspended pending a communication from the Commission on the issue.[118] The Commission's subsequent Green Paper, which also addressed the connected issue of the cross-border double jeopardy rules,[119] suggested that there should be rules on informing other Member States about (potentially) conflicting pending proceedings, a consultation procedure between the Member States concerned, and possibly a dispute settlement process. There would be a requirement to centralize prosecutions in a single jurisdiction, with criteria to guide the selection of that jurisdiction on a case-by-case basis. Developments in this area would be linked to a review of the double jeopardy rules, which could be reformed (for instance, to withdraw some exceptions to those rules) in light of the creation of an effective system to agree on centralizing the prosecution at an early stage.

Member States were not enthusiastic about these suggestions, so the Commission did not make any legislative proposal. However, ultimately the Council adopted a Framework Decision on conflicts of jurisdiction in 2009, which addresses only the information and consultation aspects of this issue.[120] Member States had to apply the Framework Decision by 15 June 2012.[121] The specific provisions on prioritizing jurisdiction that are set out in a number of earlier Framework Decisions harmonizing substantive criminal law (see above) were not repealed by this Framework Decision,

---

[113] Art 10(4) of the Framework Decision ([2005] OJ L 69/67).

[114] On the role of Eurojust, see II:6.9 below.

[115] Art 7(3) of Framework Decision ([2000] OJ L 140/1); Art 6(2) of PIF Convention ([1995] OJ C 316/48); and Art 9(2) of corruption Convention ([1997] OJ C 195/1).

[116] The special rules in the Framework Decisions on attacks on information systems and on counterfeiting the euro were not retained when those measures were repealed (respectively by Dir 2013/40 ([2013] OJ L 218/8) and Dir 2014/62 ([2014] OJ L 151/1)). The proposed Directive on fraud against EU interests (COM (2012) 363, 11 July 2012) would equally remove the special rule in the prior Convention on this issue.

[117] [2003] OJ C 100/24, Art 3.   [118] See statement in JHA Council press release, 19 July 2004.

[119] COM (2005) 696, 23 Dec 2005; see also the staff working paper (SEC (2005) 1767, 23 Dec 2005).

[120] [2009] OJ L 328/42.

[121] Art 16. All references in this section are to this Framework Decision except where otherwise indicated.

but neither is there any provision governing the relationship between this measure and those earlier acts. The CJEU has ruled on the relationship between the Framework Decision and the Schengen double jeopardy rules.[122]

The 2009 Framework Decision concerns only cases where parallel proceedings might result in the final disposal of the proceedings in multiple Member States, in a violation of the cross-border double jeopardy rules, also known as the *ne bis in idem* principle, as defined in the Schengen Convention rules as interpreted by the Court of Justice.[123] It should be pointed out, however, that the double jeopardy principle is violated not only by the final disposal of a case in multiple Member States, but also as soon as a second *prosecution* is begun (or continued) following the first final judgment issued in a Member State.[124] Moreover the *ne bis in idem* principle applies to Schengen associates, whereas the Framework Decision only applies to EU Member States.[125] Since the double jeopardy rules only apply where the same acts were (allegedly) committed by the same person,[126] a declaration adopted by the Council states that it will consider further measures as regards cases where there are proceedings in multiple Member States as regards different persons being tried in relation to the same or related facts, or in respect of the same criminal organization.[127]

The process established by the Framework Decision also aims to 'reach consensus on any effective solution aimed at avoiding the adverse consequences arising from such parallel proceedings'.[128] The Framework Decision does not apply to EU competition proceedings.[129]

The first obligation under the Framework Decision is for a Member State's authorities which have 'reasonable grounds to believe that parallel proceedings are being conducted in another Member State' to contact the authorities of the other Member State in order to 'confirm the existence' of those proceedings.[130] This authority must supply the contacted authority with basic information about the relevant criminal proceedings underway in that state.[131] The contacted authority must then reply to the contacting authority within any deadline indicated by the latter, or otherwise 'without undue delay'. If the person concerned is in custody, the contacted authority must reply urgently.[132] This authority must indicate whether parallel proceedings are underway and if so, whether a 'final decision' has been delivered in the proceedings.[133]

If parallel proceedings are underway, the authorities concerned must then enter into a consultation process. This consultation has to 'aim to reach consensus on any effective

---

[122] Case C-129/14 PPU *Spasic*, ECLI:EU:C:2014:586. See I:6.8.
[123] Art 1(2)(a). See also the reference to the Schengen double jeopardy rules and case law (recital 3 in the preamble).
[124] See II:6.8 below. [125] See II:6.2.5 above.
[126] See the definition of 'parallel proceedings' in Art 3(a).
[127] Council doc 10225/09, 20 May 2009. See also Art 32 of the Council of Europe Convention on the transfers of proceedings.
[128] Art 1(2)(b). [129] Art 2(2). See II:6.4 above.
[130] Art 5(1). The obligation does not apply when the former authorities are already aware of the existence of such proceedings by other means (Art 5(3)). On the definition of the authorities concerned, see Art 2(d). On the concept of 'reasonable grounds', see recital 5 of the preamble to the Framework Decision.
[131] Art 8(1). [132] Art 6(1).
[133] Art 9(1). Presumably this refers to the definitions which apply pursuant to the Schengen double jeopardy rules (see II:6.8 below).

solution aimed at avoiding the adverse consequences arising from such parallel proceedings'. The process 'may, where appropriate, lead to the concentration of the criminal proceedings in one Member State'.[134] The preamble to the Framework Decision
refers vaguely to other possible solutions, and also indicates that the proceedings could
be concentrated by means of a transfer of proceedings.[135] An indication of the criteria
which may be taken into account during this consultation is set out in the preamble to
the Framework Decision, which refers to guidelines on allocating jurisdiction adopted
by Eurojust in 2003,[136] 'and take into account for example the place where the major
part of the criminality occurred, the place where the majority of the loss was sustained,
the location of the suspected or accused person and possibilities for securing its surrender or extradition to other jurisdictions, the nationality or residence of the suspected
or accused person, significant interests of the suspected or accused person, significant
interests of victims and witnesses, the admissibility of evidence or any delays that may
occur'.[137]

Despite the consultation process established by the Framework Decision, it is clear
that this process does not require authorities to waive or accept jurisdiction unless they
choose to.[138] Moreover, even if the process leads to agreement on the concentration
of proceedings, the Framework Decision does not specify the obvious conclusion that
the other Member State(s) must waive or suspend their proceedings in favour of the
Member State in which proceedings are concentrated.[139] But intriguingly, the preamble
to the Framework Decision does suggest that in Member States that apply the 'legality'
principle (ie mandatory prosecution in principle, once information is available about
an alleged offence), that principle 'should be understood and applied in a way that it is
deemed to be fulfilled when *any* Member State ensures the criminal prosecution of a
particular criminal offence'.[140]

If a consensus cannot be reached, then the issue 'shall where appropriate' be referred
to Eurojust, which, as noted already, has a possible role in attempting to settle conflicts of jurisdiction between Member States.[141] If consensus is reached on concentrating proceedings, then the authorities in the Member State where proceedings are
concentrated must inform the other Member State(s) of the outcome of the process.[142]
However, there is no provision to regulate what happens if the Member State where
proceedings are concentrated declines to continue prosecution (where this decision
falls short of a 'final judgment' for the purpose of the double jeopardy rules) or where

---

[134] Art 10(1).   [135] Recital 4 of the preamble. See II:6.7 below.
[136] See Annex I to the Eurojust 2003 annual report, and more generally II:6.9 below.
[137] Recital 9 of the preamble. These suggestions are similar, but not identical, to the Eurojust guidelines,
n 136 above.
[138] Recital 11 of the preamble.
[139] See the vague recital 13 in the preamble. However, recital 11 in the preamble implies *a contrario* that a
consensus on concentrating proceedings in one Member State will result in the discontinuation of proceedings in the other Member State(s).
[140] Recital 12 of the preamble; emphasis added.
[141] Art 12(2); see II:6.9 below. The Framework Decision does not amend the Eurojust Decision on this
point (see Art 12(1)).
[142] Art 13.

the Member State(s) which have waived or suspended prosecutions decide that they wish to rescind their agreement to concentrate proceedings.

The Framework Decision permits Member States to maintain in force or conclude bilateral or multilateral agreements in order to extend the Framework Decision or to simplify or facilitate the processes which it sets out.[143] Unlike the 'standard' final provisions of many EU measures regulating mutual recognition, this measure does not expressly replace the corresponding provisions of the relevant Council of Europe Convention (in this case, the Convention on transfer of proceedings). The latter Convention should possibly be regarded as falling within the scope of Member States' powers to maintain or conclude treaties dealing with the same subject-matter; and in any event the preamble to the Framework Decision specifies that it is 'without prejudice' to this Convention or any other arrangements between Member States.[144]

Comparing the Framework Decision with the Council of Europe Convention, the latter (unlike the former) does not establish a formal procedure for information exchange between the States concerned once there are grounds to suspect the existence of parallel proceedings. But the Convention does provide for express criteria for considering whether to centralize proceedings, and it clearly provides for the consequences of centralizing prosecution, including regulation of the important issue of when the power to prosecute would revert to the State(s) which have waived its (their) proceedings. The risk is that by creating a system for exchange of information without creating an obligation to centralize jurisdiction, the Framework Decision could lead to more *lis pendens* cases, not fewer, for instance because in some cases the informed Member State's authorities will (or must) begin a prosecution that they would not otherwise have begun (because those authorities would otherwise not have known about those facts). While the preamble to the Framework Decision states that it should not create a conflict where none existed anyway,[145] this depends on how the legality principle (ie the obligation to prosecute which exists in some national laws) is applied in practice, given that the main text of the Framework Decision does not expressly require Member States to waive that principle merely because another Member State is prosecuting an offence. Moreover, the consultation procedure could be (ab)used to 'forum-shop' the location to prosecute which is most convenient to the prosecution, or to manipulate the exceptions to the double jeopardy rules so that a second prosecution could take place even after a final judgment in one Member State.[146] The position of the individual to complain about the location of the prosecution is not enhanced by the Framework Decision.[147]

In 2014, the Commission reported about the application of the Framework Decision in practice.[148] The report notes first of all that only about half of the Member States (fifteen) had implemented it by that point, nearly two years after the deadline. Only two more Member States have implemented it since.[149] Those not implementing it included the UK, which subsequently opted out of the measure in December that year.[150]

---

[143] Art 15.   [144] Recital 15 of the preamble.   [145] Recital 12 in the preamble.
[146] See Art 55 of the Schengen Convention ([2000] OJ L 239), discussed further in II:6.8 below.
[147] Recital 17 in the preamble.   [148] COM (2014) 313, 2 June 2014.
[149] Council doc 5881/4/15, 22 July 2015.   [150] See II:6.4.5 above.

Overall, the Commission stated that it was 'too early to draw general conclusions' about the quality of implementation of the Framework Decision, because few Member States have practical experience in its application. But it does note that some Member States have not applied the key rules on the information to be transferred between authorities. Most Member States permit parallel investigations to take place, even after the consultation process, although they are a waste of time and money. Only Croatia has an express rule (corresponding to the *M* judgment, discussed below)[151] that a final judgment in one Member State must terminate a pending prosecution in another. While the Commission refers to this measure as a 'first step', it does not indicate what further steps should be taken, and indeed it has not taken any since.

How should the Framework Decision be assessed? Ultimately this measure is disappointing, because it does not take sufficient steps to avoid multiple prosecutions, by creating an obligation to centralize prosecutions in principle, subject to objective criteria for the choice of jurisdiction which do not permit either the prosecution or the defence to forum-shop. Those criteria should in particular aim to reduce significantly the application of extraterritorial jurisdiction by Member States. Such jurisdiction is objectionable in principle, unless the suspects would otherwise benefit from impunity from their actions, because of the principle of a State's sovereignty over its territory and the reasonable expectation of a State's citizens and residents that acts they commit on the territory of that State will be subject to the criminal law of that State—over which that State's citizens exercise democratic control. Moreover, where the suspects lack knowledge of the substantive criminal law of, and/or the existence of the extraterritorial jurisdiction asserted by, the State asserting it, this is arguably a breach of Article 7 ECHR.[152] The traditional rationale for asserting extraterritorial jurisdiction was the refusal of many States to extradite their own nationals, but the abolition of this rule in the context of the European Arrest Warrant (EAW) renders this traditional rationale irrelevant.[153]

The lack of harmonization of national jurisdictional rules means that Member States may refuse to apply EU mutual recognition measures on jurisdictional grounds.[154] Some degree of harmonization of these rules could mean that those grounds for refusal could be reconsidered.[155] But in the absence of harmonization, those grounds for refusal should certainly be fully retained and applied, otherwise the effect of the abolition of dual criminality rules, coupled with the removal of the ban on extradition of a State's nationals, risks the possible application of extraterritorial criminal jurisdiction even to acts which were not criminal on the territory where they were committed.

The lack of enthusiasm for this measure is unfortunate, for as the Commission points out in its report, lack of implementation by Member States 'increases significantly the risk of double jeopardy'. But as with other EU criminal law measures,[156] the Commission's indifference to its role of ensuring the effective enforcement of EU law is striking. Many months after it gained the power to bring infringement proceedings

---

[151] II:6.8.   [152] See II:6.3.1 above.   [153] See II:3.5.2 above.
[154] See II:3.5 to II:3.7 above.   [155] See the Commission's Green Paper, n 119 above.
[156] See generally chs 3 and 5 of this volume.

against Member States, it had not brought any Member States to the CJEU to ensure that they transposed the legislation, even three years after the deadline to do so.

6.7 Transfer of Proceedings

One method of addressing jurisdictional issues, in particular conflicts of jurisdiction and the prevention of cross-border double jeopardy, is to establish a formal system for the transfer of criminal proceedings between States. As noted already, a Council of Europe Convention from 1972 sets out such a system, but only about half of EU Member States have ratified it.[157] Even fewer Member States have ratified an earlier Council of Europe Convention on road traffic offences, which provides for both transfer of proceedings and recognition of judgments.[158] Also as noted already, EU Member States agreed an EPC Convention on this issue among themselves, but this Convention did not attract sufficient ratifications to enter into force.[159] However, there is a brief reference to this issue in the Council of Europe Convention on mutual assistance in criminal matters, which all Member States have ratified.[160]

For some time, this issue was not on the EU's agenda, but in July 2009 a group of Member States tabled an initiative for a Framework Decision on this issue,[161] based broadly on the Council of Europe Convention of 1972. However, this proposal was not adopted or agreed before the Treaty of Lisbon entered into force, and has not been tabled since.

6.8 Double Jeopardy

The lack of harmonization of criminal jurisdiction rules and the inadequate or partial rules on the conflict of jurisdiction and the transfer of proceedings create a risk that a person will be tried more than once for the same act or omissions in more than one Member State.[162] As we have seen, this would violate international human rights law if it took place within one Member State,[163] but there is no general ban on cross-border double jeopardy in international human rights instruments. However, the general principles of EU law and the EU Charter of Fundamental Rights ban cross-border double jeopardy.

There are detailed rules on this issue in specific international criminal law instruments, in particular the Council of Europe Conventions on the transfer of criminal

---

[157] On the ratification details, see ibid.

[158] ETS 52. On the ratification details, see Appendix I. On the enforcement of foreign judgments concerning road traffic offences, see II:3.7.1.1 above.

[159] ETS 73. See the ratification information in Appendix I.

[160] Art 21 of that Convention (ETS 30), which refers to the process for transmitting information from one Party to the courts of the other Party with a view to taking proceedings in the latter. The UK, Ireland, and Malta have reservations on this provision.

[161] [2009] OJ C 219/7.

[162] See E Sharpston and J Maria Fernandez-Martin, 'Some Reflections on Schengen Free Movement Rights and the Principle of *Ne Bis in Idem*' (2007–08) 10 CYELS 413, and S Peers, 'Double Jeopardy and EU Law: Time for a Change?' (2006) 8 EJLR 199.

[163] II:6.3.1 above.

proceedings and on the international validity of criminal judgments,[164] although as noted already, not many Member States have ratified these instruments. Nevertheless, such a ban can also be found in EU measures—a reflection of the high level of integration within the EU in the area of criminal law cooperation, and a welcome and distinctive contribution by the EU to the development of international human rights law.

6.8.1 Legal framework

Between the EU Member States, the cross-border double jeopardy principle was first set out in a pre-Maastricht 1987 EPC Convention.[165] Like the prior Council of Europe Conventions, this Convention attracted only limited support.[166] Indeed, the EPC Convention never entered into force as such, but it is applied provisionally by those Member States which have ratified it; this is relevant because those Member States include Ireland, which does not yet apply the Schengen Convention double jeopardy rules.[167] The provisions of the EPC Convention were subsequently inserted without amendment into Articles 54–8 of the Schengen Convention, and now apply to all Member States except Ireland, plus the Schengen associates.[168]

> Article 54 of the Schengen Convention sets out the basic rule:
> A person whose trial has been finally disposed of in one Contracting Party may not be prosecuted in another Contracting Party for the same acts provided that, if a penalty has been imposed, it has been enforced, is actually in the process of being enforced or can no longer be enforced under the laws of the sentencing Contracting Party.

Article 55 then provides for possible exceptions to the rule.

1. A Contracting Party may, when ratifying, accepting or approving this Convention, declare that it is not bound by Article 54 in one or more of the following cases:
   (a) where the acts to which the foreign judgment relates took place in whole or in part in its own territory; in the latter case, however, this exception shall not apply if the acts took place in part in the territory of the Contracting Party where the judgment was delivered;
   (b) where the acts to which the foreign judgment relates constitute an offence against national security or other equally essential interests of that Contracting Party;
   (c) where the acts to which the foreign judgment relates were committed by officials of that Contracting Party in violation of the duties of their office.
2. A Contracting Party which has made a declaration regarding the exception referred to in paragraph 1(b) shall specify the categories of offences to which this exception may apply.
3. A Contracting Party may at any time withdraw a declaration relating to one or more of the exceptions referred to in paragraph 1.

---

[164] Respectively ETS 73 (1972), Arts 35–7, and ETS 70 (1970) Arts 53–5. There are more limited provisions in Art 9 of the Council of Europe Convention on extradition (ETS 24), as revised by Art 2 of the First Protocol to that Convention (ETS 86). For ratification details of these measures, see Appendix I.

[165] The text of this Convention was based roughly on the prior Council of Europe Conventions.

[166] For ratification details, see Appendix I.   [167] II:6.2.5 above.

[168] [2000] OJ L 239. All further references in this section are to the Convention, unless otherwise indicated.

4. The exceptions which were the subject of a declaration under paragraph 1 shall not apply where the Contracting Party concerned has, in connection with the same acts, requested the other Contracting Party to bring the prosecution or has granted extradition of the person concerned.

In practice, according to the Commission, seven Member States have invoked Article 55(1)(a), four have invoked Article 55(1)(b), and none have invoked Article 55(1)(c).[169] The relevant declarations have not, however, been published. It is not clear how the timing of declarations applies as regards Member States which applied the Convention after its integration into the EU legal order.[170]

Next, the Schengen Convention provides that in the event of a second prosecution, 'any period of deprivation of liberty served in the [first] Contracting Party arising from those acts shall be deducted from any penalty imposed'. Also, the second Member State must take account of any prior non-custodial sentence, to the extent provided for by national law (the 'accounting' principle, also known as the 'set-off' rule).[171] Member States must cooperate to exchange information on the potential application of these rules, once the authorities of the second Member State have reason to believe that a charge relates to the same acts which were the subject of a final decision in another Member State.[172] Finally, Member States are authorized to apply a more generous application of double jeopardy (also known as *ne bis in idem*) rules with regard to judgments taken abroad.[173]

As compared to the Council of Europe Conventions with double jeopardy rules:[174] the definition of final judgment is less precise in the Schengen rules;[175] there is only an express restriction on further prosecution in the Schengen rules, not a restriction on further sentencing or enforcement of a sentence; the derogations are narrower in the Schengen rules; the set-off rule is more generous in the Schengen rules; and the Schengen rules provide for contacts between the national authorities concerned. The Schengen rules have obviously taken the Council of Europe rules as a model, but have on the whole strengthened the double jeopardy rule in light of the greater degree of integration between Schengen states. It is striking, though, that the Court of Justice case law on the Schengen rules makes no comparison with the Council of Europe rules.

Specific *ne bis in idem* provisions apply in the EU's fraud and corruption Conventions.[176] The basic rule and the exceptions to it are identical to the Schengen

---

[169] SEC (2005) 1767, 23 Dec 2005, p 47. The Member States invoking Art 55(1)(a) are Austria, Germany, Denmark, Greece, Finland, Sweden, and the United Kingdom, while Austria, Denmark, Greece, and Finland have invoked Art 55(1)(b).

[170] The Commission's information (ibid) clearly assumes that it is possible for Member States which only applied the relevant rules after 1999 (the Nordic States and the UK) to invoke the derogations, but it is not clear whether Member States which joined the EU in 2004 or 2007 can do so.

[171] Art 56.

[172] Art 57. Compare to the exchange of information on multiple pending prosecutions (II:6.6 above).

[173] Art 58.   [174] N 164 above.

[175] However, as will be seen below, the case law on the definition of final judgment in the Schengen rules is consistent with the more precise definitions in the Council of Europe Conventions, as regards acquittals, amnesties (and so probably pardons), lapse of time, and suspended sentences.

[176] Art 7 of the fraud Convention and Art 10 of the corruption Convention (respectively [1995] OJ C 316/48 and [1997] OJ C 195/1). The former Art is extended to the First Protocol to the fraud Convention by Art 7(2) of that Protocol, and to the Second Protocol to the fraud Convention by Art 12(2) of that Protocol

Convention rules, but neither of the more specific Conventions contains a provision on cooperation; there is no requirement to specify which provisions of national law are governed by the derogation for national security; there is no provision on withdrawing derogations; relevant agreements between Member States are not affected by the provisions; and (in the fraud Convention only) there is no reference to the 'accounting' principle. It is not clear whether the fraud and corruption Conventions should be regarded as *lex specialis*, or whether the Schengen rules should be regarded as taking precedence. In any case, it should be recalled that the three instruments have different temporal and territorial scope.[177] On this point, it should be noted that the explanatory memorandum for the fraud Convention asserts that Member States which are already parties to the Schengen Convention have to renew the relevant declarations for this Convention, and those Member States cannot make any declarations besides those already applicable to the Schengen Convention.[178] The legal framework would be simplified if the proposed Directive on the EU's financial interests is adopted, since it would repeal the Convention and Protocols on this issue without retaining a specific double jeopardy rule.[179]

Of the Member States which have ratified the corruption Convention, nine have made declarations concerning derogations from the *ne bis in idem* rule.[180] Equally, nine Member States have derogated from the *ne bis in idem* rule applying to the Convention on the EU's financial interests and its Protocols.[181] As regards the corruption Convention, the explanatory memorandum to the Convention points out that the derogation for public officials (which seven Member States have invoked) is particularly significant, given the subject-matter of the Convention.[182]

As noted above, in 2003, Greece proposed a Framework Decision which would, inter alia, have clarified and altered the Schengen provisions, but discussions were halted in July 2004 pending a Commission communication.[183] The subsequent Green Paper suggested reconsidering the Schengen double jeopardy rules, in particular as regards the clarification of the key aspects of *ne bis in idem*, the conditions for application of the principle, and the derogations from the rule, if an agreement can be reached on a procedure for allocating criminal jurisdiction.[184] The Commission did not follow up this Green Paper with a proposal.[185] Finally, it should be noted that EU mutual recognition

---

([1997] OJ C 221/12). A few Member States have not yet ratified one or both of these Conventions and the relevant Protocols. For information on ratification, see Appendix I.

[177] On the territorial scope, see II:5.2.5 and II:6.2.5 above; on the temporal scope, see I:2.2.2.2 and I:2.2.5 (as regards the Schengen rules), compared to the ratification dates of the relevant Conventions and Protocols.

[178] [1997] OJ C 191/1.   [179] COM (2012) 363, 11 July 2012.

[180] Austria, Denmark, Spain, Italy, and Finland have derogated on all three grounds; Austria and Denmark have moreover listed the national legislation covered by the security exception. Germany has invoked only the territoriality exception; Greece and Hungary have invoked only the security and public official exception; and Sweden has invoked only the territoriality and security exception.

[181] The position is the same as regards the corruption Convention (see n 180 above), except that Spain and Hungary have not derogated, while Slovenia and Slovakia have invoked the security derogation.

[182] [1998] OJ C 391/1.   [183] See II:6.6 above.   [184] COM (2005) 696, 23 Dec 2005.

[185] See, however, the Framework Decision on conflicts of jurisdiction (II:6.6 above), which addresses other aspects of this issue.

instruments contain provisions on *ne bis in idem* as a ground for refusal of recognition of foreign decisions, although these provisions differ greatly.[186]

6.8.2 Interpreting the rules

To date, the CJEU has delivered eleven judgments answering questions sent from national courts on the interpretation of the Schengen double jeopardy rules.[187] One more case is pending.[188] The Court has answered a number of key questions concerning application of the double jeopardy principle, but national courts will probably need to address further questions to the Court in future.

Before examining the substantive issues, it is useful to examine the overall approach adopted by the Court of Justice. First of all, the Court has stressed that the application of double jeopardy principle is not made subject to any harmonization of substantive or procedural criminal law.[189] Moreover, underlying the double jeopardy rule, 'there is a necessary implication that the Member States have mutual trust in their criminal justice systems and that each of them recognises the criminal law in force in the other Member States even when the outcome would be different if its own national law were applied'.[190] Also, 'the integration of the Schengen *acquis* (which includes Article 54 of the [Schengen Convention]) into the framework of the European Union is aimed at enhancing European integration and, in particular, at enabling the Union to become more rapidly the area of freedom, security and justice which it is its objective to maintain and develop'.[191] The objective of Article 54 'is to ensure that no one is prosecuted on the same facts in several Member States on account of his having exercised his right to freedom of movement'.[192] To that end, 'freedom of movement is effectively guaranteed only if the perpetrator of an act knows that, once he has been found guilty and served his sentence, or, where applicable, been acquitted by a final judgment in a Member State, he may travel within the Schengen territory without fear of prosecution in another Member State on the basis that the legal system of that Member State treats the act concerned as a separate offence'.[193] In particular, the double jeopardy rule 'ensures that persons who, when prosecuted, have their cases finally disposed of are left undisturbed'.[194] If the application of the rules was subject to differences between national criminal law, this 'might create as many barriers to freedom of movement within the Schengen territory as there are penal systems in the Contracting States'.[195]

---

[186] See II:3.5 to II:3.7 above.
[187] Cases: C-187/01 and C-385/01 *Gozutok and Brugge* [2003] ECR I-1345; C-469/03 *Miraglia* [2005] ECR I-2009; C-436/04 *Van Esbroek* [2006] ECR I-2333; C-467/04 *Gasparini* [2006] ECR I-9199; C-150/05 *Van Straaten* [2006] ECR I-9327; C-288/05 *Kretzinger* [2007] ECR I-6441; C-367/05 *Kraaijenbrink* [2007] ECR I-6619; C-297/07 *Bourquain* [2008] ECR I-9425; C-491/07 *Turansky* [2008] ECR I-11039; Case C-129/14 PPU *Spasic*, ECLI:EU:C:2014:586; and Case C-398/12 *M*, ECLI:EU:C:2014:1057. In fact, the *Kretzinger* and *Gasparini* cases arguably fell within the scope of the double jeopardy rules in the PIF Convention, but this issue was not raised before the Court of Justice. See the staff working paper for the Commission's report on application of the PIF Convention (SEC (2008) 188, 14 Feb 2008).
[188] Case C-486/14 *Kossowski*.   [189] *Gozutok and Brugge*, para 32 and *van Esbroek*, para 29.
[190] *Gozutok and Brugge*, para 33 and *van Esbroek*, para 30.   [191] *Gozutok and Brugge*, para 37.
[192] *Gozutok and Brugge*, para 38; *Miraglia*, para 32; and *van Esbroek*, para 33.
[193] Case law beginning with *Van Esbroek*, para 34.   [194] *Gasparini*, para 27.
[195] Case law beginning with *Van Esbroek*, para 35.

On the other hand, the Court has also referred to the previous Article 2 EU, according to which 'the European Union set itself the objective of maintaining and developing the Union as an area of freedom, security and justice in which the free movement of persons is assured',[196] but this takes place 'in conjunction with appropriate measures with respect to...prevention and combating of crime'.[197] The Court has reiterated this approach following the entry into force of the Treaty of Lisbon.[198]

Finally, the Court has ruled that the intention of the Contracting Parties to the 1990 Schengen Convention, as revealed by national parliamentary documents in the context of ratifying that Convention or the 1987 EPC Convention on double jeopardy, are not relevant following the integration of the Schengen Convention into the EU legal order.[199] This implies that the integration of the Schengen rules into the EU legal order has an impact as such on their interpretation. Indeed, the Court has ruled that at least some provisions of the Schengen double jeopardy rules must receive an autonomous and uniform interpretation.[200]

As for the substantive issues raised by the double jeopardy rules, the first point to consider is the scope of the rule, which has four elements: the temporal scope, the territorial scope, the personal scope, and the material scope. On the temporal scope, the Court of Justice has ruled repeatedly, beginning with the *Van Esbroek* judgment, that in the absence of any provisions on the issue of temporal scope in the Schengen Convention double jeopardy rules, the rules prohibit a second prosecution in a State applying those rules even where the first prosecution had taken place in another State *before* that State applied those rules.[201]

Next, as regards the territorial scope, the Court of Justice expressly ruled in the *Bourquain* case, where the initial conviction was issued by a French court in Algeria during colonial times, that 'the application of Article 54 cannot, in special circumstances such as those of that conviction, depend on the place where the sentence was pronounced, since the decisive factor is whether the sentence was pronounced by a competent judicial authority of a State which became a Contracting Party to the' Schengen Convention.[202] Moreover, the Court stated that '[s]ince Article 54 ...does not...provide that the person concerned must necessarily have been tried in the territory of the Contracting Parties, that provision, the purpose of which is to protect a person whose

---

[196] Case law beginning with *Gozutok and Brugge*, para 36.

[197] Case law beginning with *Miraglia*, para 34.

[198] *Spasic*, para 61, which refers to Art 3(2), revised TEU. At para 62 of the same judgment, the Court also refers to the JHA criminal law objectives set out in Art 67(3) TFEU.

[199] *Gozutok and Brugge*, para 46. See also the Opinion in that case, dismissing the relevance of the Council working programme on mutual recognition ([2001] OJ C 12/10) for the interpretation of the rules (paras 127–31).

[200] *Spasic*, para 79, referring to the 'execution condition' (discussed below), although the Court has consistently interpreted all aspects of Art 54 of the Convention in an autonomous manner. The Court also ruled that the concept of 'same acts' in the double jeopardy exception in the Framework Decision establishing the European Arrest Warrant should be interpreted uniformly and autonomously, and consistently with the same wording in the Schengen double jeopardy rules (Case C-261/09 *Mantello* [2010] ECR I-11477, paras 38 and 40).

[201] *Van Esbroek*, paras 18–24. See subsequently *Kraaijenbrink* (para 22), *Bourquain* (para 28), and *Turansky* (para 27).

[202] *Bourquain*, para 29.

trial has been finally disposed of against further prosecution in respect of the same acts, cannot be interpreted as meaning that Articles 54 to 58 of the [Schengen Convention] are never applicable to persons who have been tried by a Contracting Party exercising its jurisdiction beyond the territory to which that Convention applies.'[203] With great respect, the Court's analysis is not consistent with at least the English text of the Convention, which refers quite clearly to the disposal of a trial 'in' a Contracting Party, not 'by' or 'in the *courts* of' a Contracting Party.[204]

The Court of Justice has not ruled on whether the *location of the acts* which were the subject of the final judgment is relevant. However, it stands to reason that in the absence of any express rule on this issue in Article 54 of the Convention, or any express derogation in Article 55,[205] the rule applies regardless of where the acts were committed, even if they were committed outside the European Union. This point is ever more relevant to the extent that EU measures on substantive criminal law are requiring or encouraging Member States to assert more extraterritorial jurisdiction.[206]

On the personal scope of the rules, the Court of Justice ruled in *Gasparini* that only the person who had previously been subject to a final judgment within the scope of Article 54 of the Convention could benefit from the rules; his or her co-accused could not benefit from that person's immunity from further prosecution in another Member State pursuant to the double jeopardy rules, unless of course they had previously been subject to such a final judgment themselves.[207]

It follows implicitly from the *Gozutok* and *Spasic* judgments that the nationality of the person concerned is not relevant, given that in those cases third-country nationals invoked the double jeopardy rule without any objection from the CJEU. This makes sense within the context of the States fully applying the free movement rules of Schengen, given the freedom to travel for resident third-country nationals,[208] but this raises further questions in turn: should the interpretation of the rules be different as regards Member States that do not (yet) apply the full Schengen rules, or (in the case of the UK) are not likely to apply them for the foreseeable future? And should the interpretation of the rules be different as regards persons living outside the EU? In either case, EU citizens and their family members should benefit from the rules, since they have the right to move to and from the Schengen area and non-Schengen states or third countries (or between non-Schengen States, or to and from non-Schengen States and third countries) on the basis of EU free movement law.[209] As for third-country

---

[203] *Bourquain*, para 30.

[204] It is possible that the other language versions suggest a different interpretation than the English language version, but in that case the Court should have explained why some language versions were preferable to others (see, for instance, Joined Cases C-261/08 and C-348/08 *Zurita Garcia* and *Choque Cabrera* [2009] ECR I-10143). As the Court rightly observed (para 29 of the *Bourquain* judgment), due to Art 138 of the Schengen Convention, Art 54 could not apply on the basis of the colonial link between France and Algeria at the time of the judgment, because the Convention only applies to the European territory of France.

[205] There is a possible derogation from the rule in Art 54 if the acts took place partly or wholly on the territory of the second Member State, as long as they did not take place partly in the territory of the first Member State (Art 55(1)(a)), but this exception suggests by *a contrario* reasoning that Art 54 is otherwise applicable regardless of where the acts were committed.

[206] See II:6.5 above.   [207] Paras 34–7 of the judgment.   [208] See I:4.9.

[209] See I:6.4.1.

nationals, they should benefit also despite their more limited free movement rights, because the Schengen rules implement human rights principles that should be applicable to all persons.

Another key issue of personal scope has not yet been addressed by the Court: the application of the rules to legal persons. On this point, the Second Protocol to the PIF Convention expressly states that the cross-border double jeopardy principle extends to legal persons,[210] but the other double jeopardy rules, notably the Schengen Convention, are silent on the issue. It is submitted that in light of the corporate criminal liability encouraged by many EC and EU criminal law measures,[211] along with the mutual recognition of criminal law fines applied to legal persons,[212] and given the objective of the Schengen rules to encourage free movement rights, which of course are enjoyed by legal persons as well as natural persons as a matter of EU law, the double jeopardy rules must apply to legal persons as well.[213] This would also be consistent with the application of human rights rules to legal persons.[214] However, this raises certain questions, as regards (for instance) whether a subsidiary of a company which has been subject to final decision in the first Member State should be regarded as the same 'person' as its parent company in a second Member State. Also, the question might even be raised as to whether a final decision against natural persons (ie the managers of a company) in one Member State should preclude the prosecution of the relevant legal person in another Member State, or *vice versa*.[215]

This brings us to the material scope of the rules. As regards legal persons (and often natural persons as well), there is an obvious distinction between administrative and criminal liability,[216] which has been a difficult issue to agree upon in the context of mutual recognition.[217] However, the Court of Justice has ruled that even though there is an EU rule against double jeopardy in administrative law proceedings, there is no rule against double jeopardy in administrative and criminal proceedings.[218] Similarly, in the *Gozutok and Brugge* judgments, the Court ruled that despite the ban on the further prosecution of a person in a second Member State for the same acts, the interests of victims and other persons injured by that person's acts could still be protected by civil proceedings;[219] and in the *Turansky* judgment, the Court ruled that the double jeopardy rule did not prevent multiple *investigations*, as distinct from multiple prosecutions.[220] According to the case law, the distinction, for the purpose of the Schengen rules, as between criminal proceedings on the one hand and investigations, civil proceedings, and administrative proceedings on the other, is based on the ECHR definition of criminal proceedings, as derived from the jurisprudence of the European Court of

---

[210] Art 12(2) of the Second Protocol, n 176 above.   [211] See II:5.5.2.1 above.
[212] See II:3.7.1.1 above.
[213] Although the Court excluded legal persons from the protection of the Framework Decision on crime victims on the basis of a literal interpretation of the personal and material scope of that Framework Decision (Case C-467/05 *Dell'Orto* [2006] ECR I-5557), those considerations do not apply to Art 54 of the Schengen Convention.
[214] See S Trechsel and S Summers, *Human Rights in Criminal Proceedings* (OUP, 2005), 171–2.
[215] On the liability of the management of legal persons, see II:5.5.2.1 above.
[216] As regards legal persons, see ibid.   [217] See II:3.2.2.3 above.
[218] See II:6.3.2 and II:6.4 above.   [219] Para 47 of the judgment.
[220] Para 44 of the judgment.

Human Rights.[221] It is also notable that Article 57 of the Schengen Convention triggers a requirement in principle to consult with another Member State's authorities when a person is *charged*; this arguably corresponds to the concept of a 'criminal charge' for the purposes of Article 6 ECHR. In any event, it is also clear that multiple extradition or surrender proceedings are not covered by Article 54 of the Convention, since multiple requests to obtain the hand-over of a fugitive in relation to the same acts do not amount to multiple prosecutions for those acts.[222]

A final question concerning the material scope of the Schengen rules is their application to private prosecutions. The Court of Justice has not ruled on this issue yet, but it is submitted that in the absence of anything to the contrary, it must follow that private prosecutions are within the scope of the rules, in particular by analogy with the Court's ruling on the scope of the Framework Decision on victims' rights.[223] This would mean not only that a final judgment in a private prosecution in one Member State would in principle preclude further private prosecutions for the same act in another Member State, but also that *mutatis mutandis*, a final judgment in a public prosecution would preclude further private prosecutions, and a final judgment in a private prosecution would preclude further public prosecutions. Arguably, this would only apply to the extent that the law in the first Member State prevented public prosecutions from being brought in that Member State after a private prosecution, and *vice versa*.[224]

Moving on to the core rules in Article 54 of the Convention, the Article contains four elements. First of all, what is meant by the phrase, 'a person whose trial has been finally disposed of'? The Court of Justice first has ruled that the double jeopardy rule applies not merely following a judgment of a court, but also where a prosecutor decides to discontinue proceedings because a person has admitted his or her guilt and made a payment to expiate it.[225] Next, the Court ruled in *Miraglia* that where a first Member State's authorities decide to terminate criminal proceedings merely because a second Member State has also opened them, the double jeopardy rule does not have the effect of requiring the second Member State to terminate proceedings in turn. This could be interpreted as a general rule that a trial cannot be considered 'disposed of' until there is a ruling on the merits of the case, but the Court did not unambiguously state such a general rule at that time.

Further clarification was offered in the judgments in *Van Straaten* and *Gasparini*. In *Van Straaten*, the Court ruled that acquittals due to lack of evidence were within the scope of the rule,[226] although it expressly declined to rule on whether acquittals *not* based on the merits of the case were covered.[227] In *Gasparini*, the Court ruled that a decision to acquit due to a time-bar on further proceedings amounted to a final

---

[221] See II:6.3.2 and II:6.4 above.

[222] See the Opinion in Case C-296/08 PPU *Santesteban Goicoechea* [2008] ECR I-6307.

[223] The Court ruled in para 41 of C-404/07 *Katz* [2008] ECR I-7607: '[t]here is no provision in the Framework Decision which aims to exclude from its scope the situation where, in criminal proceedings, the victim assumes, as in the present instance, the role of the prosecutor in place of the public authorities.'

[224] See the further discussion of the *Turansky* judgment below.

[225] See *Gozutok and Brugge*, particularly paras 25–31 of the judgment.

[226] Paras 54–61 of the judgment. See also para 34 of the prior *Van Esbroek* judgment.

[227] Para 60 of the judgment.

judgment for the purposes of the rules;[228] otherwise the free movement objective of the double jeopardy rule would be undermined.[229] In *Kretzinger*, the Court confirmed that a suspended sentence was covered by the rules,[230] while in *Bourquain*, it ruled that judgments following trials held *in absentia* were covered,[231] even though such judgments were subject to a requirement of an automatic retrial if the person concerned were arrested.[232] On the other hand, in the *Turansky* judgment, the Court ruled that a decision by a police authority which suspended proceedings but which did not definitely bar further prosecution under the law of the first Member State did not qualify as a final decision.[233]

Most recently, in *M*, the CJEU brought the two lines of case law together,[234] clarifying that a 'trial' was not 'disposed of' unless: (a) there was a ruling on the merits (cf *Miraglia*), meaning 'a definitive decision on the inadequacy of [the] evidence', which 'excludes any possibility that the case might be reopened on the basis of the same body of evidence'; and (b) further prosecution was definitively barred within the meaning of the *Turansky* judgment. A Belgian 'non-lieu' decision met both criteria. It is not clear how the ruling in *Gasparini*, where there was no consideration of the merits, is consistent with this analysis.

In the absence of an explanation as to why the concept of 'final judgment' covers time-barring, there is still some uncertainty about the exact scope of this element of the rule, in particular as regards acquittals or other forms of termination of proceedings that have not considered the merits of the case, perhaps due to amnesties or pardons during the proceedings,[235] or the termination of proceedings due to lack of jurisdiction or immunity. These circumstances must of course be distinguished from cases where a prosecution *never began at all* due to time-barring, amnesty, a pardon, lack of jurisdiction, or for any other reason, in which case it is beyond doubt that there is no final judgment for the purposes of the Schengen rules.

There is much to be said for the argument that judgments should only be considered final if they have considered the merits of a case,[236] and indeed the *M* judgment reaffirms this interpretation of Article 54. This approach ensures (relative) legal certainty, and also strikes a reasonable balance between the objectives of ensuring free movement and fighting crime. Assuming that *Gasparini* is still good law, it is therefore necessary to explain how that judgment is consistent with the other case law. The best approach to

---

[228] Paras 22–33 of the judgment. [229] Para 28 of the judgment.

[230] Para 42 of the judgment.

[231] Paras 34–7 of the judgment. See earlier the Opinion in *Kretzinger*, paras 93–100, the Framework Decision on *in absentia* trials ([2009] OJ L 81/24) and the judgment in Case C-306/09 *I.B.* [2010] ECR I-10341.

[232] Paras 38–42 of the judgment, referring, inter alia, to the free movement objective of the rules (paras 41–2).

[233] Paras 30–45 of the judgment. The pending *Kossowski* case concerns a similar issue. The *Mantello* judgment (n 200 above) applied the *Turansky* case law to the double jeopardy exception in the European Arrest Warrant Framework Decision.

[234] Paras 27–33 of the judgment.

[235] This is a distinct issue from an amnesty or a pardon *after* a final judgment, on which see the discussion of the enforcement condition below.

[236] See the convincing arguments in favour of this approach in the *Gasparini* Opinion, and also in the secondary literature: Sharpston and Fernandez-Martin, n 162 above.

this issue is to categorize *Gasparini* as a case where the national court in question terminated proceedings having had an *opportunity* to decide a case on the merits, whereas in a case like *Miraglia* it did not have that chance. While it might be objected that a better approach would be to give the national courts an *effective* opportunity to decide the case on the merits, such an approach should be rejected, as it would be difficult to apply given its inherently subjective nature, and would not take account of the many ways in which EU law facilitates effective prosecutions in cross-border cases (notably by means of the transfer of evidence or fugitives) and the possibility of national courts to deliver *in absentia* judgments if necessary. An alternative approach would be to clarify that statute-barring is an element of the offence, meaning that the substantive merits of the charge *have* been considered if a case is dismissed on such grounds.

Any test that depends to any extent on whether the merits of the case have been assessed will have to define that concept in turn. This issue has already been the subject of disagreement between Advocates-General of the Court of Justice. One has argued that an acquittal on the merits covers cases where either: the issues are 'intrinsic' to the defendant, who cannot be held accountable for his or her acts due to the lack of criminal responsibility (due to age or mental disorder); or the issues are extrinsic to the defendant, such as a valid defence or excuse, the lack of a personal element of the offence, the offence is statute-barred, or the truth of the charges has not been proven.[237] The latter category comprises cases where the acts were not an offence, the defendant did not commit them, or the defendant was not proved to commit them.[238] Obviously, the *Van Straaten* judgment addresses this latter category, ruling that acquittal due to lack of evidence constitutes a ruling on the merits of the case,[239] while the *Gasparini* judgment addresses statute-barring, although the Court's judgment in the latter case does not state whether the termination of proceedings due to a time bar should be considered as an acquittal based on the merits or not. However, a different Advocate-General has disagreed that the termination of proceedings on all of these grounds will amount to acquittals on the merits of the case.[240]

It is submitted that a judgment on the merits of a case must involve a consideration of the substantive elements of the offence, including also any applicable defences or excuses and any ruling that the facts did not constitute an offence. In principle, the personal accountability or situation of the accused should also be regarded as an element of the offence for this purpose. Arguably, termination of proceedings due to lack of jurisdiction, or *lis pendens* in another Member State (cf the *Miraglia* judgment), or the transfer of proceedings to another Member State is not a ruling on the merits of the case; nor was there an opportunity to try the merits of the issues in those cases, considering the proceedings underway in other Member States.[241]

---

[237] Opinion in *Van Straaten*, para 65. This assumes, as suggested above, that statute-barring can be regarded as an element of the offence.

[238] Ibid, para 66.   [239] Para 60 of the judgment.

[240] Opinion in *Gasparini*, note 80. The Opinion particularly rejects the view that decisions on time-bars reflect the merits of the case, and also objects (at para 112) to the view that decisions to terminate proceedings due to the age of criminal responsibility should be subject to mutual recognition.

[241] A jurisdiction rule could be regarded as an element of the offence though, since it concerns where the act took place and/or the person who committed it.

The *M* judgment also addressed the definition of final judgments in the context of appeal or review procedures. It is clear from the Court's ruling that a judgment is not final until a final appeal judgment has been issued.[242] Therefore it is not final as long as an ordinary appeal has been lodged against it, or for as long as the possibility to bring such an appeal still exists (by the defence and/or the prosecution). This judgment also clarified whether a judgment can be regarded as final as long as some possibility of exceptional review exists. Following the Strasbourg case law, the CJEU ruled that a judgment must be regarded as final in such circumstances.[243] This applies equally where national law, in accordance with the exception to the double jeopardy rule set out in the Seventh Protocol to the ECHR, permits a final judgment to be reopened due to new evidence.[244] The CJEU ruled that only the first State could reopen proceedings in such circumstances.[245]

The second element of Article 54 is the definition of the 'same acts'. The Court first addressed this issue in its *van Esbroek* judgment, ruling that the term did not require identical classification of the relevant acts in national criminal law, but rather 'the only relevant criterion is the...identity of the material acts, understood in the sense of the existence of a set of concrete circumstances which are inextricably linked together'. The movement of drugs from one Member State to another (constituting the export of drugs from one Member State and import of drugs into another) 'may, in principle, constitute a set of facts which, by their very nature, are inextricably linked', but 'the definitive assessment' of the issue belongs to 'the competent national courts' to determine whether the acts 'constitute a set of facts which are inextricably linked together in time, in space and by their subject-matter'.[246] The Court did not attach any relevance to the provisions of Article 71 of the Convention, which refers specifically to measures to be taken to combat drug trafficking.[247] Moreover, the Court specifically distinguished the Schengen rules (preventing prosecution for the same '*act*') from the international human rights rules (preventing prosecution for the same '*offence*').[248] Of course, it should be reiterated that the ECHR case law has subsequently aligned itself with the case law of the Court of Justice,[249] and that (as discussed below) the CJEU was subsequently content to align itself with the Strasbourg case law.

These principles have been clarified further in four later judgments. In *Van Stratten*, the Court ruled that the quantities of drugs at issue or the persons who were party

---

[242] Para 33 of the judgment.

[243] Paras 37–9, *M* judgment. For instance, in the UK, the *Criminal Appeal Act 1995* established the Criminal Cases Review Commission to this end (except for Scotland, where there is separate legislation on the same issue). See also Recommendation No. R (2000) 2 of the Committee of Ministers of the Council of Europe to Member States, on the re-examination or reopening of certain cases at domestic level following judgments of the European Court of Human Rights.

[244] See II:6.3.1 above.

[245] Para 39, *M* judgment. It will still remain possible for any relevant new evidence to be transmitted to the *first* Member State, pursuant to the EU and Council of Europe rules on transmission of evidence (see II:3.6 above), in order for that Member State to consider whether the grounds for re-opening a prior judgment exist.

[246] *Van Esbroek*, paras 36–8.

[247] But see the Court's subsequent ruling on the link between Arts 58 and 71 of the Convention in the *Kraajenbrink* judgment (discussed below). On the substance of Art 71, see II:7.7.4 below.

[248] Para 28 of the judgment.   [249] II:6.3.1 above.

to the alleged offences did not have to be identical in the different Member States concerned.[250] In *Gasparini*, the Court ruled that the marketing of goods in a second Member State after the importation of the same goods into a first Member State could in principle constitute the same acts.[251] Next, in *Kretzinger* the Court confirmed that there is no need to have an identity of legal interests for the rule to apply,[252] and that the successive crossing of various Schengen borders with the same contraband goods could therefore be considered in principle to constitute the 'same acts'.[253] Finally, in *Kraajenbrink* the Court ruled that the same criminal intention behind separate actions was not sufficient in itself to constitute the 'same act' for the purpose of the double jeopardy rule; the rule required an objective link between acts, not merely a subjective link.[254]

Next, the third element of Article 54 of the Convention is the 'enforcement condition', ie the requirement that 'if a penalty has been imposed, it has been enforced, is actually in the process of being enforced or can no longer be enforced under the laws of the sentencing' Member State. The 'enforcement condition' was interpreted by the Court of Justice in the *Kretzinger*, *Bourquain*, and *Spasic* judgments. In *Kretzinger*, the Court ruled that in the case of suspended sentences, the 'penalty must be regarded as "actually in the process of being enforced" as soon as the sentence has become enforceable and during the probation period. Subsequently, once the probation period has come to an end, the penalty must be regarded as "having been enforced" within the meaning of that provision'.[255] The judgment did not comment on what would happen if the conditions of probation were breached during the probation period. Logically, this judgment is applicable *mutatis mutandis* to any form of parole or other early release.

The Court also ruled in the *Kretzinger* case that spending a period in detention before the first judgment (whether in police custody or detention on remand) did not satisfy the enforcement condition, even if that period would count against any subsequent custodial sentence imposed.[256] Furthermore, the Court ruled that it was irrelevant as regards the enforcement condition that a judgment *could* be enforced by the sentencing State by means of issuing an EAW;[257] this ruling is presumably applicable by extension to other methods of enforcing judgments pursuant to the EU rules.[258] Next, in the *Bourquain* judgment, the Court ruled that the enforcement condition was still satisfied if it had been impossible in practice for a judgment *ever* to be enforced, due to the disappearance of the convicted person during the entire period when the judgment was in principle enforceable, because Article 54 of the Convention did not require that the judgment must have been enforceable in practice.[259]

---

[250] Paras 40–53 of the judgment.   [251] Paras 55–7 of the judgment.
[252] It should be noted that there is a requirement for the same legal interests to be at stake when the double jeopardy rule applies in the context of EU competition law: see the discussion in the Opinion in *Gasparini* (paras 155–9) and the case law referred to in II:6.4 above.
[253] Paras 28–37 of the judgment.   [254] Paras 23–36 of the judgment.
[255] Para 45–52 of the judgment.   [256] Paras 56–64 of the judgment.
[257] Paras 56–64 of the judgment.
[258] Cf the Framework Decisions on enforcement of financial penalties and custodial penalties: see II:3.7.1 above.
[259] Paras 45–51 of the judgment.

Finally, in the *Spasic* judgment the Court of Justice ruled that the enforcement condition was valid, since it was a legitimate restriction on the rights in Article 50 of the Charter (see the discussion below). It also further interpreted the substance of the rule, holding that where the first judgment in a Member State imposed a small fine as well as a lengthy custodial sentence, the sentenced person could not avoid the second Member State bringing proceedings simply by paying the small fine, and claiming that the enforcement condition was satisfied.

The fourth and last element of Article 54 is that a person 'may not be prosecuted' (the 'non-prosecution obligation') if there has been a final judgment for the same facts (subject to the enforcement condition). Again, this element of the rules was clarified in the *M* judgment, where the Court stated that once final judgment had been given in one Member State, the parallel pending proceedings in a second Member State had to end. Logically, this ruling should apply by analogy to cases where the enforcement condition was not satisfied when the second proceedings start, but becomes satisfied while they are underway.[260]

There is also a separate, but related, question of the scope of the non-prosecution obligation. Does it also amount to an obligation not to sentence a person or enforce a sentence? It is notable that the Schengen Convention, unlike the relevant Council of Europe rules,[261] does not contain an express rule on this point. Also, it is notable that the ECHR double jeopardy rule and the EU Charter of Fundamental Rights both refer to an obligation not to try *or punish* a person again, and this point has been emphasized in the ECHR case law.[262] This point will obviously be moot in cases where the non-prosecution obligation applies before a prosecution starts, or if the non-prosecution obligation applies during the prosecution process, since sentencing and enforcement would be impossible if the prosecution cannot begin, or has to be abandoned. But on the other hand, it would be relevant if a first judgment becomes final or the enforcement condition relating to a first judgment becomes satisfied after the prosecution phase of the second proceedings is completed.[263] It is also possible that the existence of a final first judgment only comes to light, or is confirmed, after the second judgment is delivered,[264] or even that a legal person assumes the criminal liability of another legal person by means of a merger.

On this point, it is submitted that it is only appropriate to draw comparisons between the Council of Europe Conventions and the Schengen rules where that would facilitate

---

[260] This is consistent with the *Muslija* judgment of the ECtHR (II:6.3 above), as noted by the Advocate-General in *Spasic*, para 60.

[261] See n 164 above.   [262] See II:3.3 above.

[263] In the case of a first judgment becoming final, this assumes that the second judgment is not yet final either—otherwise the second judgment (even it was delivered later in time) would have to be considered as the first judgment.

[264] This could be relevant in particular where the first trial was held *in absentia* and the convicted person was not aware of it. It can be assumed that normally an accused person would reveal the existence of a prior final judgment concerning the same facts so as to benefit from the protection of Arts 54 and 56 of the Convention, but it is possible that an accused person in some cases would fail to reveal the prior judgment for tactical reasons (for instance, to avoid disclosing the existence of unfavourable evidence which had been used in the first trial if the second set or prosecutors were unaware of that evidence) or due to mental incapacity.

the objectives of the Schengen rules (cf the different wording of the 'set-off' rules, discussed below), not undermine those objectives. Similarly, the differences in wording between the Schengen double jeopardy rules and the relevant human rights rules are only relevant where the Schengen rules set a higher standard (cf the different definition of the 'same acts', discussed above), not a lower standard. So, disregarding the comparisons with these other measures, it would clearly be more compatible with the underlying objectives of the double jeopardy rules to rule out not only multiple prosecutions but also multiple sentencing or enforcement of sentences, and indeed also to rule out sentencing or the enforcement of a sentence following a second judgment even if a first judgment resulted in an acquittal. Both of these points are also relevant as regards the relationship between the double jeopardy rule and other EU measures, an issue discussed further below.

Moving on to the derogations from the double jeopardy rule set out in Article 55 of the Convention, the Court of Justice has not ruled in any detail on the interpretation of these provisions. However, the Court stated in the *Gozutok and Brugge* judgment that the derogations listed in Article 55 were exhaustive, and moreover that Article 55 referred to the same acts as Article 54.[265] Also, in the *Turansky* judgment, the Court did comment in passing that the important limit on the derogations set out in Article 55(4), which rules out the application of any of the derogations when the second Member State requested the first Member State to start a prosecution or granted extradition in respect of the same facts, was applicable.[266] The Court has been asked in a pending case whether the Article 55 exceptions remain in force after the integration of the Schengen *acquis* into the EU legal order, and if so whether they are invalid for breach of the EU Charter.[267] On the latter point, it should be noted that the *Spasic* judgment did not assess whether *these* provisions were valid in light of the Charter, and the rationale in that judgment for upholding the validity of the enforcement condition (the need to avoid impunity for criminal offences) is not relevant to Article 55, which instead provides for a fully-fledged second prosecution.[268] Arguably this affects the essence of the right in Article 50 of the Charter, in a way that (according to the CJEU's own analysis) the enforcement condition does not.

The limitation in Article 55(4) must surely now be understood as covering cases where an EAW has been issued and executed by the relevant Member States, in particular in light of the particular *ne bis in idem* exception set out in the Framework Decision establishing the EAW.[269] Presumably it also applies to a transfer of proceedings, whether pursuant to the Council of Europe Convention or other arrangements,[270] for example any EU measures which might be adopted on this issue.[271] Logically, it

---

[265] Para 44 of the judgment.   [266] Para 29 of the judgment.   [267] *Kossowski*, pending.
[268] The Advocate-General in *Spasic*, para 77, raised the possibility that the Art 55 derogations may conflict with the Charter right.
[269] See further II:3.5 above.
[270] It should be noted that the Court ruled in the *Turansky* judgment (paras 19 and 28) that Austria had requested Slovakia in the case to bring proceedings pursuant to Art 21 of the Council of Europe mutual assistance Convention (see II:6.7 above), and that it was therefore necessary to examine the Schengen rules because that Council of Europe Convention (unlike the transfer of proceedings Convention) does not regulate the effect of the requested State's taking over proceedings upon the proceedings underway in the requesting State.
[271] On these rules, see II:6.7 above.

should also apply where there has been an agreement between the States concerned on bringing a prosecution pursuant to the Framework Decision on conflicts of jurisdiction or the rules on priority jurisdiction in the EU's substantive criminal law legislation.[272]

The Convention does not make clear whether the derogations must be interpreted autonomously, or in accordance with national law, although it should be recalled that the EU's substantive criminal law measures in some cases specify more precisely when Member States must assert their territorial jurisdiction,[273] and EU measures concerning corruption to some extent define the substance of the 'public official' exception.[274]

Next, the Court of Justice has not yet interpreted Article 56 of the Convention, which sets out a 'set-off' rule as regards periods of detention in the event of a second prosecution. Presumably, as with Article 55, the concept of 'same acts' and final judgments must have the same definition as the concepts in Article 54. An important question regarding Article 56 is the definition of the prior periods of detention which must be deducted from the second sentence. The Convention refers to prior detention 'arising from those acts', wording which differs from the double jeopardy rule in the relevant Council of Europe Conventions ('arising from the *sentence enforced*'). Given the difference in wording, the objectives of the double jeopardy rule, and the EU law principle of proportionality, it therefore seems clear that not only detention arising from a sentence, but also periods spent in police custody and remand connected to the same acts, must also be deducted from the sentence imposed.[275]

One issue raised in the Opinions of Advocates-General has been the scope of Article 56, in two respects. First of all, does Article 56 only apply where a second sentence is imposed pursuant to the application of the derogations in Article 55, or does it also apply where a second sentence is imposed because the enforcement condition set out in Article 54 is not satisfied? The Opinion in *Van Straaten* assumes the former interpretation,[276] while the Opinion in *Kraaijenbrink* argues the latter.[277] It is submitted that the second interpretation is correct, since it best reflects the objectives of the double jeopardy rule and the principle of proportionality, and moreover reflects the literal wording of Article 56, which does not suggest that the set-off rule is limited in scope to cases where the derogation applies.

The second issue is the material scope of Article 56, in particular its application to other forms of penalty besides custodial penalties. While Article 56, by itself, clearly leaves it to the national law of Member States to decide whether non-custodial penalties

---

[272] See II:6.6 above.

[273] Note that this clarification not only impacts upon the application of the territoriality derogation pursuant to Art 55(1)(a), but also upon the *disapplication* of that derogation, since the derogation cannot apply where the final judgment followed the application of territorial jurisdiction by the first Member State.

[274] Art 55(1)(c); see II:5.5.1.2 above.

[275] See by analogy the judgment in *Lanigan* (Case C-237/15 PPU, ECLI:EU:C:2015:474), and generally paras 62–9 of the *Kretzinger* Opinion. Although the judgment in *Kretzinger* rejected the argument that periods spent in pre-trial detention satisfied the enforcement condition set out in Art 54 (see above), this can clearly be distinguished from the question of whether those periods must be deducted from a second sentence pursuant to Art 56, given the different wording and context of the two provisions. It is surely also relevant in this context that, as the Court noted in *Kretzinger*, at least some national laws require periods of pre-trial detention to be deducted from any final sentence (see also para 64 of the *Kretzinger* Opinion).

[276] Note 29 of the Opinion.

[277] Paras 55–66 of the Opinion. See also paras 71–2 of the *Kretzinger* Opinion.

are deducted following a second prosecution, an Opinion of an Advocate-General has argued that the 'set-off' rue is a general principle of EU law, so there is an obligation to take account of non-custodial penalties also despite the express wording of Article 56.[278] Furthermore, Article 49(3) of the EU Charter of Fundamental Rights arguably also sets out this rule, as it provides that '[t]he severity of penalties must not be disproportionate to the criminal offence.'[279] The convincing argument that the set-off rule is a general principle and/or encapsulated within the EU Charter furthermore bolsters the arguments set out above in relation to the deduction of pre-trial detention from all forms of second sentences, and the application of the set-off rule in any case when a second sentence is imposed for the same acts.

The consultation procedure set out in Article 57 of the Schengen Convention has also not been interpreted as such by the Court of Justice, although the Court noted that the procedure was applied in the *Bourquain* case,[280] and was not applied in the *Turansky* case, where the use of the consultation procedure could clearly have clarified the situation.[281] It might be argued that a State's failure to make a request under Article 57, or a requested State's failure to respond promptly (or at all, or accurately) could give rise to or aggravate the damages liability of the State(s) concerned (see below).

As for Article 58 of the Schengen Convention, the Court ruled in the *Kraajenbrink* judgment that there were limits to Member States' power to apply more favourable rules; they could not refrain from prosecuting separate drugs offences pursuant to Article 71 of the Schengen Convention merely because the separate acts were motivated by the same criminal intention.[282] It should be noted that there is no provision of the Schengen Convention which expressly regulates the relationship of the double jeopardy rules with Member States' other international commitments.[283]

Next, the question might arise of the legal effect of the double jeopardy rules. This is a specific application of a general question (the legal effect of third pillar rules in general), and the answer (until the conversion of the double jeopardy rules into an EU measure after the entry into force of the Treaty of Lisbon) depends on the legal effect of third pillar rules in general.[284] At the very least, it is arguable that the rules have indirect effect so that any relevant national law should be interpreted as far as possible by national courts in order to ensure that it is consistent with the Schengen rules as interpreted by the Court of Justice. Moreover, to the extent that the established EC law rules on remedies apply to the third pillar, in particular there should be damages liability for any wrongful prosecution, conviction, or detention in breach of the Schengen rules, if those breaches are sufficiently serious as defined by the relevant EC rules. In the case of wrongful detention, the damages liability also stems from ECHR rules.[285]

---

[278] Ibid; see also para 64 of the *Kretzinger* Opinion.
[279] See note 38 of the Opinion in *Kraaijenbrink*.
[280] Paras 23–4 of the judgment. See also *Mantello*, when the analogous provision in the Framework Decision on the EAW was applied, in the context of the double jeopardy exception to executing an EAW.
[281] Paras 37–8 of the judgment.   [282] Para 35 of the judgment.
[283] See further II:6.11 below.   [284] See II:2.2.2.
[285] See Art 5(5) ECHR. There is also a right to compensation for a wrongful conviction, following a miscarriage of justice as defined in Art 3 of Protocol 7 to the ECHR.

Furthermore, by their nature, the double jeopardy rules, in order to be effective, need to be enforced by the remedies of forestalling or terminating prosecutions, quashing convictions, and releasing from detention or otherwise ending the enforcement of criminal penalties, if possible retroactively (ie by reimbursing a fine which was already paid, with interest). Given that third pillar measures have supremacy over the national law of the Member States, the substantive provisions of the Schengen rules and any associated remedies can be enforced, if necessary, by asking a national court to set aside conflicting national law.[286]

The final two points are closely connected: the relationship between the double jeopardy rule and EU mutual recognition measures on the one hand, and the EU's fundamental rights rules on the other. On the first point, as noted above, the EU's mutual recognition measures usually include provisions concerning refusal of enforcement on grounds of double jeopardy.[287] However, this ground of refusal is not always mandatory, and it is not clear whether the double jeopardy principle in the mutual recognition measures is identical to the principle as set out in the Schengen rules. The Court of Justice has addressed this issue in the *Mantello* ruling,[288] stating that key concepts in the Schengen rules ('final judgment' and 'same acts') apply by analogy to the interpretation of the double jeopardy exception in the Framework Decision establishing the European Arrest Warrant. Presumably the enforcement condition (which also appears in the EAW legislation) must also be interpreted the same way. However, the EAW legislation does not contain an exception equivalent to Article 55 of the Convention, although it does contain similar provisions to Articles 56 and 57.[289]

In contrast to the EAW rules, in most other mutual recognition measures the wording of the double jeopardy exception diverges from the Schengen rules, and is not mandatory. At the very least, since there is no derogation for such mutual recognition measures set out in the Schengen rules (Article 55 being an exhaustive list of derogations, as noted above), the Schengen rules take precedence in the event of a conflict, and are clearly mandatory. So it would not be possible to execute a mutual recognition decision if that amounts to a second proceeding prohibited by the Schengen rules, or arguably if it indirectly facilitates such a second proceeding (taking account of the principle of effectiveness).

The CJEU has also ruled that the existence of mutual recognition measures (the EAW, the legislation on transfer of prisoners and recognition of financial penalties, and the conflict of jurisdiction rules discussed in this chapter) do not mean that the 'enforcement condition' in the Schengen rules is satisfied, since there is no guarantee that such measures will be applied so as to ensure the enforcement of a ruling.[290] Moreover, the Court has briefly addressed other types of links between the double jeopardy rules and

---

[286]　See generally II:2.2.2 above.　　　[287]　For details, see II:3.2.2.3 above.　　　[288]　N 200 above.
[289]　The *Mantello* judgment discusses the equivalent provision to Art 57; on the Art 56 equivalent, see *Lanigan*, n 275 above.
[290]　See initially *Kretzinger*, and subsequently the more elaborate reasoning of the Court on the same point in the *Spasic* judgment.

mutual recognition measures,[291] and links with other EU measures concerning criminal jurisdiction can be discerned.[292]

On the second point (human rights), for many years the Court seemed reluctant to discuss the Schengen double jeopardy rules in that context. However, in its 2014 judgments in *Spasic* and *M*, the CJEU fully aligned the Schengen provisions with Article 50 of the EU Charter of Rights, as well as the relevant ECHR case law, which had already become aligned with the Court of Justice case law.[293] In *Spasic*, the Court ruled that the enforcement condition in Article 54 of the Convention was a limitation upon the right in Article 50 of the Charter, which had to be justified in light of Article 52(1) of the Charter, which addresses limitations on Charter rights.[294] According to the Court's view, the limitation on the right was permissible, given that it was prescribed by law, had a public interest aim (avoiding impunity), observed the essence of the right (leaving the basic double jeopardy rule intact), and was proportionate to its objective, given that the other EU measures in this field, as discussed just above, could not guarantee that impunity for criminal acts would be avoided. The Court has now been asked whether the exceptions set out in Article 55 of the Convention are valid in light of the Charter;[295] and it follows that if the EU legislature wanted to amend the Convention to create any further exceptions to the Schengen rules, those new exceptions could potentially be challenged for breaching the Charter too.

6.9 Eurojust

The interim step between a purely national system of prosecution of crimes and prosecution of crimes by an EU prosecutor is Eurojust, a body intended to coordinate and support national investigations, to facilitate judicial cooperation and mutual recognition, and to assist resolving conflicts of jurisdiction. Following the mandate of the Tampere European Council, the Council adopted a Decision establishing a provisional Eurojust late in 2000.[296] Shortly after the Tampere deadline of end-2001, the Council

---

[291] The *Miraglia* judgment implicitly addressed the relationship with mutual assistance rules, and the *Turansky* case explicitly referred to Art 21 of the Council of Europe mutual assistance Convention. The *Gasparini* judgment interpreted the double jeopardy rules in the context of the Framework Decision on the EAW.

[292] As noted above, the *Turansky* case raises implicit questions about the application of Art 55(4) when proceedings are transferred. Also, the *Miraglia* case could be relevant to the consequences of applying the Framework Decision on conflicts of jurisdiction and/or, by analogy, any future EU rules on the transfer of proceedings.

[293] II:6.3 above.

[294] Art 52(1) requires that '[a]ny limitation' of Charter rights 'must be provided for by law', 'respect the essence of those rights and freedoms', and be '[s]ubject to the principle of proportionality'; moreover 'limitations [on rights] may be made only if they are necessary and genuinely meet objectives of general interest recognised by the Union or the need to protect the rights and freedoms of others'.

[295] *Kossowski*, n 188 above. There are good grounds to find a breach of the Charter. First of all, any national decision to invoke these exceptions must also meet the 'prescribed by law' requirement in Art 52(1) of the Charter, and the failure to publish the national decisions to invoke these exceptions at EU level arguably breaches this rule. Also, as noted above, these national exceptions do not aim to end impunity, but to bring a second prosecution, and so arguably they have no public interest justification and violate the essence of the Charter right as well.

[296] [2000] OJ L 324/2.

adopted a Decision in February 2002, which established Eurojust definitively.[297] This Decision was subsequently amended as regard the financial rules governing Europol,[298] and then again more substantially in 2008, inter alia, in order to strengthen Member States' support for Eurojust (in particular as regards the powers of national members), to give Eurojust a greater role settling conflicts of jurisdiction, to increase the flow of information to Eurojust, and to overhaul the external relations rules.[299] In 2013, the Commission proposed to replace the Decision with a Regulation following the entry into force of the Treaty of Lisbon.[300] This proposal is still under discussion, although the Council has agreed its position on most of the text.[301]

The JHA Council has approved Eurojust's rules of procedure,[302] and its joint supervisory body adopted its own rules of procedure.[303] According to the Court of Justice, a Member State cannot challenge Eurojust's staffing decisions before the Court pursuant to Article 230 EC (as it then was), but disappointed applicants can challenge Eurojust's decisions.[304]

Eurojust is a 'body' of the EU with legal personality,[305] with its seat in The Hague.[306] It is made up of one member seconded by each Member State, who may be a prosecutor, judge, or police officer depending on the national legal system, whose place of work must be at Eurojust. Each member must be assisted by one deputy and one assistant, and may be assisted by more people. The deputy must be able to replace the national member.[307] The Decision specifies that national members must have: a term of office of at least four years; access to the national registers on criminal records, arrested persons, investigations, and DNA; and powers to follow up mutual recognition requests, to issue such requests (in conjunction with a national authority), to execute mutual recognition requests and authorize controlled deliveries in urgent cases, and to participate in joint investigative teams.[308]

The activities of Eurojust are threefold: to coordinate national investigations and prosecutions; to improve cooperation between national authorities, in particular by facilitating judicial cooperation and mutual recognition; and to support in other ways the effectiveness of national investigations and prosecutions.[309] Eurojust may also become involved in assisting investigations and prosecutions involving only one Member State and a non-Member State once Eurojust has concluded an agreement

---

[297] [2002] OJ L 63/1. See the Eurojust website: <http://www.eurojust.europa.eu/pages/home.aspx>.

[298] [2003] OJ L 245/44.

[299] [2009] OJ L 138/14, which took effect on 4 June 2009 (Art 3). See the earlier Commission communication (COM (2007) 844, 23 Oct 2007). Member States had until 4 June 2011, if necessary, to amend their national law to comply with these amendments (Art 2). The Decision has not been codified. All further references in this section are to the Eurojust Decision as amended, unless otherwise indicated.

[300] COM (2013) 535, 17 July 2013.

[301] Council doc 6643/15, 27 Feb 2015. The Council has agreed on all of the text except for the provisions concerning links with the EPPO, in light of the ongoing discussion on the proposed EPPO negotiation (see II:6.10 below).

[302] [2002] OJ C 286/1 and [2005] OJ C 68/1.　　　[303] [2004] OJ C 86/1.

[304] Case C-160/03 *Spain v Eurojust* [2005] ECR I-2077.　　　[305] Art 1.

[306] [2004] OJ L 29/15.　　　[307] Art 2, as amended.

[308] Arts 9–9f, as amended. On controlled deliveries and joint investigation teams, see II:7.7 and II:7.9 below.

[309] Art 3(1), as amended.

with the relevant non-Member State (see below) or where there is an 'essential interest' in specific cases.[310] It may also become involved in investigations involving only one Member State and the EU.[311]

Eurojust's competence encompasses the crimes which Europol is competent to address, plus other offences committed in conjunction with any of the crimes over which it is competent.[312] Eurojust may also assist in other investigations at the request of a Member State's authorities.[313] It has established an 'on-call coordination centre' to deal with urgent requests.[314] When it acts through its individual members, it can, inter alia, request Member States' authorities to begin investigations or prosecutions, accept that one of them is in a better position to undertake a prosecution, coordinate between authorities, set up a joint investigation team, or to take special investigative measures.[315] When acting as a college, it can do many of the same things, plus it also has a distinct role suggesting resolutions of conflicts of jurisdiction or recommending the settlement of disputes regarding the application of mutual recognition measures.[316] On the issue of conflicts of jurisdiction, several EU substantive criminal law measures also specify a role for Eurojust in advising which Member State should exercise jurisdiction over cross-border offences, and the Framework Decision on conflicts of jurisdiction requires Member States to send a dispute over jurisdiction to Eurojust, 'where appropriate', if it cannot be agreed by means of consultation.[317] Member States have to motivate 'without undue delay' any refusals to comply with a request from a national member or the College, as well as any decision not to comply with an opinion by the College in the context of dispute settlement.[318]

In order to support Eurojust's activities, Member States must appoint national correspondents and establish a national coordination system for Eurojust.[319] Also, Member States must exchange extensive information with Eurojust,[320] and there are detailed rules on data protection.[321]

The provisions on the status and operation of Eurojust apply EU rules to Eurojust's staff and budget and provide for annual reports to the EP and the Council.[322] As for external relations, the Eurojust Decision has specific provisions on relations with the European Judicial Network, other EU bodies (Europol, OLAF, Frontex, and the Council as regards foreign policy), and third states and bodies, including provisions on sending and receiving liaison officers and executing requests for judicial cooperation from third States.[323]

In practice, Eurojust suffered from its limited competence as a provisional unit until 2002, a delay until it could take up permanent offices in The Hague in 2003, a shortage

---

[310] Art 3(2).   [311] Art 3(3).

[312] Art 4(1), as amended. On the competence of Europol, see II:7.8 below.   [313] Art 4(2).

[314] Art 5a, as inserted.   [315] Art 6(1)(a), as amended.   [316] Art 7, as amended.

[317] See II:6.6 above, and also the Eurojust guidelines on jurisdiction in the Annex to the 2003 annual report.

[318] Art 8, as amended. Member States may decline to give reasons for refusing to accede to requests on grounds of national security or protecting individual safety.

[319] Art 12, as amended.   [320] Art 13, as amended.   [321] Arts 14–24, as amended.

[322] Arts 28–39, as amended.

[323] Arts 25a–27b, as amended; on the judicial network and the liaison magistrates, see II:3.8 above.

of support staff until 2003, and Member States' tardiness in appointing data protection officers and amending national law to conform to the initial Eurojust decision.[324] Nevertheless, Eurojust has been used increasingly in practice, with the number of cases referred to Eurojust by national authorities rising ten-fold, from 180 in 2001 to 1,804 in 2014. Eurojust has in particular made a number of recommendations to Member States' authorities pursuant to the Decision, including on the issue of conflicts of jurisdiction.

As for Eurojust's external relations, an agreement with Europol came into force in 2004 and was revised in 2009,[325] and a memorandum with OLAF was agreed in 2003, although the relationship with OLAF was considered unsatisfactory until a formal agreement was negotiated in 2008. Europol has also agreed Memoranda of Understanding with the European Judicial Training Network, the European Police College, Frontex (the EU borders agency), the EU Fundamental Rights Agency, and the EU Drugs Monitoring Agency. Treaties with Norway, Iceland, Liechtenstein, Switzerland, the Former Yugoslav Republic of Macedonia, Moldova, the USA, and several international bodies are in force.[326]

Eurojust also has a role in other Council measures, in particular as regards the EAW, where it can be asked to address the issue of competing warrants and must be informed of delays in the execution of warrants.[327] In practice, Eurojust has adopted guidelines on competing warrants, and receives reports of dozens of delayed executions of EAWs every year. Furthermore, Council Decisions on the exchange of information on terrorism provide for a role for Eurojust,[328] and another Council Decision gives Eurojust access to the Schengen Information System; this took effect in December 2007.[329] Eurojust also has access to the Customs Information System (CIS).[330]

The proposed Regulation on Eurojust would first of all strengthen the powers of national members, by providing for a common list of operational powers which they should all have. It would also: restructure the Eurojust College system; create a new Executive Board, which would prepare College decisions and take over some administrative tasks; spell out more detail on the role of the Administrative Director; update the rules on data protection, budgets, and staff in line with parallel legal developments; apply the usual EU external relations rules to Eurojust; and increase the role of the European Parliament and national parliaments in the evaluation of Eurojust's activities, as provided for in Article 85 TFEU. In the meantime, the Council made detailed recommendations to Member States as regards the best approach to implement their current legal obligations, in an evaluation concluded in 2014.[331]

---

[324] See the annual reports for 2001–09, available on the Eurojust website, as well as the report in COM (2004) 457, 6 July 2004.

[325] See II:7.8 below.

[326] For the texts, see: <http://www.eurojust.europa.eu/about/Partners/Pages/eu-institutions-agencies-and-bodies.aspx>.

[327] Arts 16 and 17 of the EAW Framework Decision ([2002] OJ L 190/1).

[328] [2003] OJ L 16/68, replaced by later Decision ([2005] OJ L 252/23).

[329] [2005] OJ L 68/44. On the SIS, see II:7.6.1.1 below.

[330] Art 12 of the CIS Decision ([2009] OJ C 323/20), which applied from 27 May 2011 (Art 36(2) of the Decision). On the CIS, see II:7.6.1.2 below.

[331] Council doc 14536/2/14, 2 Dec 2014.

6.10 European Public Prosecutor

The Commission initially suggested during negotiation of the Treaty of Nice in 2000 that provisions on a European Public Prosecutor should be inserted into the EC Treaty (as it then was), but the suggestion was not taken up.[332] Subsequently in 2001, it attempted to lay the groundwork for further consideration of the idea by releasing a Green Paper,[333] arguing that the existing and contemplated arrangements for judicial cooperation and investigation related to the EU's financial interests were (and would be) ineffective. The Commission argued in particular that the legal framework was inadequate as regards lack of ratification of the PIF Convention and its Protocols, traditional judicial cooperation was 'cumbersome and inappropriate' (without citing details), judges often did not follow up investigations by OLAF (the Commission's anti-fraud unit), and evidence was often inadmissible or (in the case of tax and banking information) inaccessible. Furthermore, the Public Prosecutor would increase the effectiveness of internal investigations within the EU institutions, and would enhance protection of fundamental rights, by speeding up proceedings and reducing the need for pre-trial detention.

As to the details, the Commission proposed that the Public Prosecutor would centralize the investigation and prosecution of the crimes within his or her remit, but that trials would subsequently take place within the criminal courts of a Member State. The existing substantive criminal law in this area could perhaps be supplemented, and rules on penalties for such crimes could be adopted. So could rules on limitation periods. There would have to be agreement on whether prosecution would be mandatory or discretionary, and on the division of competence between the Public Prosecutor and national prosecuting authorities. The Public Prosecutor would enjoy extensive investigatory powers and would choose in which Member State's courts a trial would take place, subject to established criteria for making this choice. Evidence gathered lawfully in one Member State would have to be admitted before the courts of any other Member State, and there would have to be detailed rules on judicial review of the Public Prosecutor.

According to the Commission's communication on the follow-up to the Green Paper,[334] the majority of those responding to the Green Paper were supportive of the idea of a European Public Prosecutor, although most had reservations about the details. In particular, many called for an enlarged competence for the Prosecutor, a greater degree of approximation of relevant substantive criminal law, more limited investigatory powers for the Prosecutor, and further harmonization of the law of evidence and defence rights.

Article 86 TFEU, as inserted by the Treaty of Lisbon, gives the Council the power (not the obligation) to establish the EPPO, with the option to extend his or her competence to areas other than the EU's financial interests, and accepts the model of the Prosecutor

---

[332] See Annex I to the subsequent Commission Green Paper on the Public Prosecutor (COM (2001) 715, 11 Dec 2001).
[333] Ibid.   [334] COM (2003) 128, 19 Mar 2003.

bringing prosecutions in national courts.[335] The Commission proposed a Regulation creating the EPPO in 2013,[336] and discussions on this proposal are continuing.[337]

The proposed Regulation establishes the EPPO as a new office of the EU with powers of investigation and prosecution. It aims to ensure the independence of the Office, alongside its accountability to other EU institutions. Only the CJEU can dismiss the EPPO. There would also be European Delegated Prosecutors, who would be appointed and dismissed by the European Public Prosecutor, but also linked to national prosecution systems.

The EPPO would have to comply with the EU Charter of Rights, along with the principles of proportionality and legality. Member States will be obliged to assist EPPO investigations. At least at first, the EPPO will only have competence as regards fraud against the EU's financial interests, to be defined in a proposed Directive currently under discussion.[338] Some offences would always fall within EPPO competence, while some would only be within EPPO jurisdiction if there are connecting links.

There are detailed rules of procedure on investigations, prosecutions, and trial proceedings, specifying how national courts would control the EPPO, the specific powers of the EPPO (which will be further specified in national law), and the use of evidence in national courts. Suspects will be protected by detailed safeguards, based on the EU Charter, EU legislation on suspects' rights and other rights not yet addressed by EU legislation.[339] As for judicial review, the EPPO's close relationship with national legal systems justify subjecting it to judicial review in national courts, not the EU courts, although it would remain possible for national courts to ask the CJEU for a preliminary ruling on the interpretation of the EPPO Regulation. There would also be detailed provisions on data protection, budgeting, staff, and relations with other EU bodies or third States.

The EPPO seems likely to be established in the near future, but it is unfortunate that the need for the Office was not questioned, given the argument that there were other means that might have achieved the same objective of ensuring more effective prosecutions in defence of the EU's financial interests. Examining in turn the specific arguments made by the Commission for the EPPO (summarized above), the PIF Convention and both of its Protocols have now been ratified; judicial cooperation has been speeded up by adopted EU measures (the mutual assistance Convention and its Protocol, the Framework Decisions on the arrest warrant, freezing orders, evidence warrant, financial penalties, custodial penalties, probation, and pre-trial supervision) and will be further speeded up by the European Investigation Order as from 2017;[340] the legislation on OLAF has been updated,[341] and further measures strengthening the relationship between OLAF and national prosecutors and/or Eurojust could be adopted; and the Protocol to the Mutual Assistance and the Framework Decisions on freezing orders have made tax or banking information more accessible. Finally, as regards individual

---

[335] See further II:6.2.3 and II:6.2.4 above.   [336] COM (2013) 534, 17 July 2013.

[337] In June and Dec 2015, the Council agreed its position on parts of the proposed Reg: Council docs 10264/15, 24 June 2015 and 14718/15, 30 Nov 2015.

[338] See II:5.5 above.   [339] On the EU legislation, see II:4.6 above.

[340] See generally 3 of this volume.   [341] See II:7.4.6 below.

rights, as noted already, the speed of proceedings has been increased already by the application of the EAW and the Framework Decision on pre-trial supervision should (if applied correctly and fully) reduce detention in cross-border cases. It should be reiterated that in all mutual recognition measures adopted or agreed to date, the dual criminality principle has been dropped as regards crimes against the EU's financial interests, except for a few cases where Member States could insist on retaining the principle.

Moving on to the detailed aspects of Public Prosecutor's role as proposed by the Commission, it is possible to harmonize the substantive criminal law as regards the EU's financial interests further, including the adoption of harmonized rules on penalties and limitation periods, without creating a Public Prosecutor. Indeed, the proposed Directive on this issue already addresses these points.[342] Furthermore, a case could be made that the EU should regulate national prosecutions in this area, for example as to whether prosecutions should be mandatory, the extent of investigatory powers, and the decision on where to prosecute (going further to allocate jurisdiction than the 2009 Framework Decision on conflicts of jurisdiction).[343]

The second basic problem is that the model of centralized prosecution and decentralized trials proposed by the Commission—and now enshrined in Article 86 TFEU, following the entry into force of the Treaty of Lisbon—is half-baked. This model was notably *not* followed by the Rome Statute creating the International Criminal Court, and its defects are obvious: the rules relating to investigations and prosecutions on the one hand and trials on the other cannot be separated any more than eggs can be extracted from omelettes. In particular, this model risks lowering the protection of the rights of criminal defendants, since that protection is provided at different stages in the criminal procedure in different Member States. Time will tell if the EPPO, once operational, actually significantly enhances the effectiveness of prosecutions in this area of law.

6.11 External Relations

The Framework Decision on conflicts of jurisdiction contains a general provision permitting Member States to sign agreements which facilitate the objectives of that Framework Decision.[344] Unlike the EU's mutual recognition measures,[345] that Framework Decision does *not* require Member States to disapply the corresponding provisions of the relevant Council of Europe Convention (on the transfer of proceedings) or any other treaties,[346] which is significant because the provisions in the transfer of proceedings Convention are, on the whole, better than those of the Framework Decision.[347] On the other hand, as noted above, the Schengen Convention does not expressly clarify the relationship of the double jeopardy provisions with any other international measures.[348] There are very specific rules governing the external relations of Eurojust, and further specific rules are proposed for the EPPO.[349]

---

[342] See II:5.5 and II:5.6 above.   [343] See II:6.6 above.   [344] [2009] OJ L 328/42, Art 15.
[345] See II:3.9 above.   [346] See explicitly para 15 in the preamble to the Framework Decision.
[347] See II:6.6 above.
[348] II:6.7 above. Compare Art 58 of the Convention with Arts 48, 59, and 67 ([2000] OJ L 239).
[349] II:6.9 and II:6.10 above.

It should be kept in mind that although the Court of Justice has taken an assertive approach as regards the EU's exclusive competence over issues of civil jurisdiction,[350] the case in question concerned a fully harmonized set of jurisdiction rules, including effective *lis pendens* provisions, leaving the rules on conflicting judgments (the equivalent of the criminal law double jeopardy rules) somewhat secondary.[351] As we have seen, the position as regards criminal law is rather different. There is also a declaration to the Treaty of Lisbon on the EU's external competence over civil law, but arguably it does nothing more than confirm that EU competence can only become exclusive when the relevant internal law is fully harmonized.[352] So as the law now stands, it is probably the case that the EU has exclusive competence over any international treaty provisions that could impact upon the EU's double jeopardy rules, but shares competence with the Member States as regards any other rules relating to criminal jurisdiction.[353]

6.12 Conclusions

EU action in this field is a mixture of welcome developments and disappointing shortcomings. The rules on double jeopardy, as interpreted by the Court of Justice, are generally very welcome, although a number of issues relating to these rules could still be clarified, in particular the relationship with the specific double jeopardy rules in EU mutual recognition measures that include only an optional double jeopardy exception. In other areas, the EU's substantive criminal law measures increasingly do too much to encourage or require extraterritorial jurisdiction, in the absence of any particular need (in light of the possibility of extraditing States' nationals, and other developments in the area of mutual recognition), and without any effective system (in light of the weakness of the Framework Decision on conflicts of jurisdiction) to ensure that individuals are not subjected to multiple prosecutions—which in any event waste the scarce time and money of prosecutors, police, and judges.

The EU should be bolder in ensuring not only that the useful rules on conflicts of jurisdiction and transfers of proceedings in the Council of Europe Convention on transfers of proceedings apply to all Member States, but also further developing those rules. There should be a prima facie obligation to centralize a prosecution in the Member State where the alleged criminal activity took place, subject to reasonable exceptions in the interests of justice, while clearly ruling out forum-shopping by the prosecution or the defence. A rule establishing that there can only be a single prosecution, determined by objective and fair criteria, would contribute significantly to the development of an EU criminal justice model.

---

[350] *Opinion 1/2003* [2006] ECR I-1145. See further II:8.9 below.

[351] Moreover, the double jeopardy rules apply even if the judgments in question are not conflicting.

[352] See II:3.9 above.

[353] See the Council conclusions on cooperation with the Council of Europe as regards criminal law ([2009] OJ C 50/8).

7

Policing and Security

7.1 Introduction

The effective prevention and investigation of crime, particularly violent crime, is understandably a basic desire of the public in every society. But in this area there is the most acute tension between civil liberties and security objectives. Obviously, the greater the level of supervision and control of the public, the easier it is to prevent crime and to investigate it more effectively. Yet, even leaving aside their cost and practicality, such measures erode the extent of freedom in our society. There is therefore a continuing debate over the right balance to be struck between the two objectives, and this debate has been affected by the ever-greater sophistication of security technology (in particular, the development of information systems) and the perceived increase in the intensity of the threat posed by international terrorism since the terrorist attacks of 11 September 2001 and later attacks within Europe.

Within national legal and political systems, security-minded national executives and law enforcement authorities must justify further restrictions on civil liberties in the interests of greater security before national parliaments and courts. There are also systems of accountability for law enforcement operations. But until the entry into force of the Treaty of Lisbon, EU policing law was not subject to any effective parliamentary or judicial control or supervision of the executive, or to a developed framework for the accountability of operations, and therefore offered an escape from these national constraints. Even the enhanced parliamentary and judicial control that has applied to measures adopted after the entry into force of the Treaty of Lisbon does not necessarily mean that operational measures in this area are subject to effective scrutiny.

This chapter focuses on law enforcement within the European Union, beginning as always with an examination of the institutional framework as it has developed over time, an overview of measures adopted, and an examination of the relevant issues of legal competence, territorial scope, human rights, and overlaps with non-JHA EU law. It then analyses in turn EU measures concerning crime prevention, the collection and exchange of data relating to policing, other forms of cooperation between national law enforcement authorities, the operation of Europol (the EU's law enforcement agency), and cross-border police operations. Finally, it examines the issues of administrative cooperation and EU funding and EU external relations in the field of policing law.

The closely related issue of criminal procedure, including EU measures on the rights of criminal suspects (which impact upon the police) is examined in Chapter 4 of this volume, and the underlying issue of substantive criminal law is addressed in Chapter 5 of this volume. This book observes the English distinction between the *investigation* of crime by the police or similar authorities (addressed in this chapter) and the prosecution and trial process before the courts (addressed in Chapters 3 and 6), although of course in many continental countries investigations form part of the judicial process.[1]

This chapter examines together EU measures concerning the prevention and investigation of specific crimes, such as drug trafficking and terrorism, although it should be recalled that the EU has also harmonized the substantive law (Chapter 5) and simplified mutual recognition of criminal measures (Chapter 3) as regards specified crimes.

Finally, one particular feature of EU law in this area is the continued substantial use of soft law, which is referred to throughout as appropriate. Of course, policing and security measures cannot be fully examined without an understanding of practice, although the paucity of information made available has limited the possibility to analyse the operational aspects of the EU measures discussed in this chapter.

7.2 Institutional Framework and Overview

7.2.1 Cooperation prior to the Treaty of Amsterdam

Before the Maastricht Treaty entered into force, EU leaders had already agreed on the principle of establishing an EU police agency, Europol, and EU ministers had already adopted a Ministerial Agreement on the creation of that body.[2] With the entry into force of the Treaty on European Union (TEU), this intergovernmental cooperation was formalized. Article K.1(8) and (9) TEU included, as matters of common interest, 'customs cooperation' and 'police cooperation for the purposes of preventing and combatting terrorism, unlawful drug trafficking and other serious forms of international crime', possibly including aspects of customs cooperation, 'in connection with a Union-wide system for exchanging information within' Europol. However, Article K.2(2) asserted that Title VI EU would not 'affect the exercise of the responsibilities incumbent upon Member States with regard to the maintenance of law and order and the safeguarding of internal security'. There was no possibility for the Commission to propose measures.

During the Maastricht period (November 1993 to May 1999), there were a number of important developments as regards policing and customs cooperation. The negotiations on the Europol Convention and on a Convention establishing a Customs Information System (CIS) Convention were concluded in July 1995.[3] In 1998, negotiations were concluded on the Naples II Convention, which governs cross-border operations and exchanges of information by customs officers.[4] Other measures included Joint Actions establishing directories of expertise on counter-terrorism and organized crime, and concerning the exchange of liaison officers, customs and business cooperation in drug trafficking, the exchange of information on chemical profiling of drugs, security cooperation, and targeting criteria for police.[5] Three other Joint Actions established funding

---

[1] The specific issue of search and seizure is addressed in II:3.6 above, due to its link with mutual judicial assistance.

[2] See II:7.8 below.

[3] See ibid and II.7.6.1.2 below. See also II.7.4.1 below, on the Reg paralleling the CIS Convention.

[4] See II.7.6.3, II.7.7.1, and II.7.9 below.   [5] See particularly II.7.6.3 and II.7.7.4 below.

programmes related to law enforcement.[6] The Council also adopted a large number of soft law measures in the area of policing.[7]

Meanwhile, the Schengen states engaged in more intensive cooperation regarding policing matters. In particular, the Schengen Convention contains detailed rules specific to police cooperation, on: the exchange of information among police authorities;[8] hot pursuit or surveillance by the police of one Member State across the borders into another Member State;[9] the improvement of cross-border police communications;[10] the registration of visiting foreigners (including EU citizens) for the benefit of the police;[11] and the posting of liaison officers.[12] The Convention also includes parallel measures regarding drugs and firearms,[13] along with the creation of the Schengen Information System (SIS), which contains data relevant to the police (along with authorities responsible for immigration and criminal law).[14] Schengen cooperation also entailed the adoption of Decisions of the Schengen Executive Committee on a number of measures.[15]

7.2.2 Treaty of Amsterdam

7.2.2.1 Institutional framework

The Treaty of Amsterdam extensively revised the third pillar rules relating to police cooperation. In the revised version, according to the previous Article 29 TEU, the objectives of the third pillar were to be achieved partly through 'closer cooperation between police forces, customs authorities and other competent authorities in the Member States, both directly and through the European Police Office (Europol), in accordance with' the previous Articles 30 and 32 TEU.[16] The previous Article 30 TEU provided that:

1. Common action in the field of police cooperation shall include:
   (a) operational cooperation between the competent authorities, including the police, customs and other specialised law enforcement services of the Member States in relation to the prevention, detection and investigation of criminal offences;
   (b) the collection, storage, processing, analysis and exchange of relevant information, including information held by law enforcement services on reports on suspicious financial transactions, in particular through Europol, subject to appropriate provisions on the protection of personal data;
   (c) cooperation and joint initiatives in training, the exchange of liaison officers, secondments, the use of equipment, and forensic research;
   (d) the common evaluation of particular investigative techniques in relation to the detection of serious forms of organised crime.
2. The Council shall promote cooperation through Europol and shall in particular, within a period of five years after the date of entry into force of the Treaty of Amsterdam:
   (a) enable Europol to facilitate and support the preparation, and to encourage the coordination and carrying out, of specific investigative actions by

---

[6] See II.7.10 below.   [7] See particularly II.7.7.4 below.
[8] See II.7.6 below. The Convention is in [2000] OJ L 239/1.   [9] See II.7.9 below.
[10] See II.7.7.4 below.   [11] See ibid.   [12] See II.7.6.3 below.   [13] See ibid.
[14] See II.7.6.1.1 below.   [15] See ibid, II.7.4.7, II.7.6.3, and II.7.7.4 below.
[16] For the objectives, see II:5.2.2 above.

the competent authorities of the Member States, including operational actions of joint teams comprising representatives of Europol in a support capacity;

(b) adopt measures allowing Europol to ask the competent authorities of the Member States to conduct and coordinate their investigations in specific cases and to develop specific expertise which may be put at the disposal of Member States to assist them in investigating cases of organised crime;

(c) promote liaison arrangements between prosecuting/investigating officials specialising in the fight against organised crime in close cooperation with Europol;

(d) establish a research, documentation and statistical network on cross-border crime.

The previous Article 32 TEU provided that:

> The Council shall lay down the conditions and limitations under which the competent authorities referred to in Articles 30 and 31 may operate in the territory of another Member State in liaison and in agreement with the authorities of that State.

The previous Article 33 TEU copied the guarantee of national competence over law and order and security found in the original Article K.2(2) TEU. The policing provisions of the TEU were not amended at all by the subsequent Treaty of Nice.

Customs cooperation continued to fall within the scope of the third pillar, as customs was expressly referred to in the previous Articles 29 and 30(1)(a) TEU. The Treaty of Amsterdam did, however, create a new legal base for customs cooperation falling within the scope of the first pillar.[17]

Many of the measures foreseen in the previous Article 30(1) TEU had already been agreed in some form, noted above. Similarly, liaison officers (Article 30(2)(c)) were already connected to Europol and its precursor organization.[18] But Articles 30(2)(a) and (b) were new.

As for the relevant Schengen *acquis*, the Council easily agreed on the allocation of most of the policing provisions of the Schengen Convention and the related Executive Committee Decisions to the previous Articles 30 and 32 EU,[19] although certain drugs and firearms provisions were allocated to the first pillar (or not allocated at all). However, it could not originally agree on how to allocate the *acquis* relating to the SIS, so it allocated it by default to the third pillar.[20]

7.2.2.2 Implementing the Treaty of Amsterdam

As with other fields of Justice and Home Affairs (JHA) cooperation, the objectives of the EU in this area were set out in the 1999 Tampere European Council conclusions, which referred in particular to: the development of a crime prevention network; the establishment of joint investigation teams, including the participation of Europol representatives; the creation of a 'European Police Chiefs operational Task Force' which

---

[17] The previous Art 135 EC; see II.7.4.1 below.   [18] II.7.6.3 below.   [19] [1999] OJ L 176/17.
[20] On the issue of allocation of the SIS, see further I:2.2.2.2 and I:2.4.

would exchange 'experience, best practices and information on current trends in cross-border crime and contribute to the planning of operative actions'; the strengthening of Europol by 'receiving operational data from Member States and authorising it to ask Member States to initiate, conduct or coordinate investigations or to create joint investigative teams in certain areas of crime'; the creation of a 'European Police College for the training of senior law enforcement officials', starting as a 'network of existing national training institutes'; the adoption of a 2000–04 Drugs Strategy; the improvement of the exchange of information between financial intelligence units (FIUs) as regards money laundering; and the extension of Europol's competence to money laundering in general.

In order to implement this agenda, as regards crime prevention, the Council adopted an initial Decision establishing a crime prevention network, and later amended that decision in 2009.[21] Joint investigative teams were to be established in accordance with a Framework Decision.[22] A Police Chiefs task force was established.[23] Europol's competence was expanded, and three Protocols to the Europol Convention provided for a number of changes to its operations; subsequently the Europol Convention and its Protocols were replaced by a third pillar Decision, which made further changes to the legal framework governing Europol.[24] The Police College was promptly established in 2000, and its status was subsequently transformed in 2004 and 2005.[25] An anti-drugs strategy was adopted, and implemented, inter alia, by several law enforcement measures.[26] Finally, a Decision establishing financial intelligence units was quickly adopted.[27]

After the adoption of the Tampere programme, the European Council returned to policing and security issues several times, in particular following the terrorist offences of September 2001 in the United States, March 2004 in Madrid, and July 2005 in London, by holding emergency summits and/or adopting declarations with detailed agendas for further anti-terrorist measures—most of which have an impact well beyond terrorist crimes.[28] In another priority area, the Council adopted an organized crime action plan.[29] The 2004 Hague Programme set out objectives for this field, concerning in particular implementation of the anti-terrorist plan and measures on data retention, passenger name records, and the enhanced mutual access to national police databases.[30] Moreover, a number of measures in this area were taken from the text of a Convention initially agreed among a group of Member States (the Prum Convention).[31]

More specifically, in the area of customs, a Protocol to the CIS Convention concerning customs files was signed in May 2003, and ultimately the CIS Convention and its Protocols were, like the Europol Convention, replaced by a third pillar Council Decision.[32] A detailed strategy for EU customs cooperation was also agreed in 2003, and updated in 2009.[33] There were also many amendments to the Schengen rules on policing, as regards: the extension of the rules on cross-border surveillance;[34] amendment

---

[21] II.7.5 below. [22] II.7.9.4 below. [23] II.7.7.3 below. [24] II.7.8 below.
[25] II.7.7.2 below. [26] See particularly II.7.7.4 below. [27] See ibid.
[28] See the Statewatch analysis, online at: <http://www.statewatch.org/news/2004/mar/swscoreboard.pdf>.
[29] [2000] OJ C 124/1. [30] [2005] OJ C 53/1.
[31] For the text of the Prum Convention, see Council doc 10900/05, 7 July 2005.
[32] II.7.6.1.2 below. [33] [2003] OJ C 247 and [2009] OJ C 260/1. [34] II.7.9.2.below.

of the rules on the exchange of information among police;[35] changes to the rules establishing the SIS; the adoption of legislation to establish a second-generation Schengen Information System ('SIS II');[36] and amendments to the Schengen and EU rules on liaison officers.[37]

Investigations were facilitated by Decisions concerning, inter alia, Internet child pornography, currency counterfeiting, and vehicle crime, as well as soft law concerning other types of crime, while control of persons was the subject of a Decision on football match security and soft law on summit meetings. The Council was keen to establish networks dealing with particular forms of crime, for example for the protection of VIPs, as regards corruption, and for the investigation and prosecution of war crimes.[38] Furthermore, the Council adopted fresh funding measures related to law enforcement, when the pre-Amsterdam measures expired.[39]

A particular focus of EU activity was the exchange of information regarding investigations, not just by developing the rules governing Europol, the SIS, and the Schengen rules on police information exchange (as mentioned above), but by further controversial measures, in particular concerning the adoption of rules on telecoms data retention (requiring the private sector to keep information on telephone and Internet use in case law enforcement services request it), the exchange of information on passengers, the enhancement of national police services' access to each others' databases, and the access by law enforcement services to the VIS.[40] The Council also adopted a Framework Decision which harmonized aspects of national law regarding data protection in the criminal law and policing sector.[41]

Particular attention was paid to the evaluation of Member States' compliance with EU measures in this field. Evaluation of compliance was carried out in accordance with a 1997 Joint Action, a Schengen Executive Committee decision, and a 2002 Decision regarding evaluation of compliance with anti-terrorism measures.[42]

Finally, it should be noted that there were no references to the Court of Justice from national courts on any EU police cooperation measures before the entry into force of the Treaty of Lisbon. However, annulment actions were brought against EC measures which arguably should have been adopted as third pillar acts,[43] and against a third pillar measure which arguably should have permitted greater participation for the UK.[44]

7.2.3 Treaty of Lisbon

Following the entry into force of the Treaty of Lisbon on 1 December 2009, police cooperation within the EU is primarily governed by Articles 87–9 of the Treaty on the

---

[35] II.7.6.3 below.   [36] II.7.6.1.1 below.   [37] II.7.6.3 below.
[38] On all these measures, see II.7.7.4 below.   [39] II.7.10 below.   [40] II.7.6 below.
[41] [2008] OJ L 350/60; see II.7.6.1 below. On the legal effect of Framework Decisions, see Case C-105/03 *Pupino* [2005] ECR I-5285 and further II:2.2.2 above.
[42] See respectively [1997] OJ L 344/7; [2000] OJ L 239/138; and [2002] OJ L 349/1. See also the Joint Action evaluating candidate Member States (II.7.11 below).
[43] Joined Cases C-317/04 and C-318/04 *EP v Council and Commission* [2006] ECR I-4721 and Case C-301/06 *Ireland v Council and EP* [2009] ECR I-593. See II.7.4.3.2 below.
[44] Case C-482/08 *UK v Council* [2010] ECR I-10413, concerning the validity of the Decision on police access to the VIS ([2008] OJ L 218/129). See II.7.2.5 below.

Functioning of the European Union (TFEU) (Chapter 5 of Title V of Part Three of that Treaty), along with Article 84 TFEU, which concerns crime prevention.

Article 84 TFEU provides as follows:

The European Parliament and the Council, acting in accordance with the ordinary legislative procedure, may establish measures to promote and support the action of Member States in the field of crime prevention, excluding any harmonisation of the laws and regulations of the Member States.

Articles 87 TFEU sets out the general provisions on police cooperation, replacing the prior Article 30(1) TEU:

1. The Union shall establish police cooperation involving all the Member States' competent authorities, including police, customs and other specialised law enforcement services in relation to the prevention, detection and investigation of criminal offences.
2. For the purposes of paragraph 1, the European Parliament and the Council, acting in accordance with the ordinary legislative procedure, may establish measures concerning:
    (a) the collection, storage, processing, analysis and exchange of relevant information;
    (b) support for the training of staff, and cooperation on the exchange of staff, on equipment and on research into crime-detection;
    (c) common investigative techniques in relation to the detection of serious forms of organised crime.
3. The Council, acting in accordance with a special legislative procedure, may establish measures concerning operational cooperation between the authorities referred to in this Article. The Council shall act unanimously after consulting the European Parliament.

    In case of the absence of unanimity in the Council, a group of at least nine Member States may request that the draft measures be referred to the European Council. In that case, the procedure in the Council shall be suspended. After discussion, and in case of a consensus, the European Council shall, within four months of this suspension, refer the draft back to the Council for adoption.

    Within the same timeframe, in case of disagreement, and if at least nine Member States wish to establish enhanced cooperation on the basis of the draft measures concerned, they shall notify the European Parliament, the Council and the Commission accordingly. In such a case, the authorisation to proceed with enhanced cooperation referred to in Article 20(2) of the Treaty on European Union and Article 329(1) of this Treaty shall be deemed to be granted and the provisions on enhanced cooperation shall apply.

    The specific procedure provided for in the second and third subparagraphs shall not apply to acts which constitute a development of the Schengen *acquis*.

Article 88 TFEU concerns Europol, and replaced the previous Article 30(2) TEU:

1. Europol's mission shall be to support and strengthen action by the Member States' police authorities and other law enforcement services and their mutual cooperation in preventing and combating serious crime affecting two or more Member

States, terrorism and forms of crime which affect a common interest covered by a Union policy.

2. The European Parliament and the Council, by means of regulations adopted in accordance with the ordinary legislative procedure, shall determine Europol's structure, operation, field of action and tasks. These tasks may include:

(a) the collection, storage, processing, analysis and exchange of information, in particular that forwarded by the authorities of the Member States or third countries or bodies;

(b) the coordination, organisation and implementation of investigative and operational action carried out jointly with the Member States' competent authorities or in the context of joint investigative teams, where appropriate in liaison with Eurojust.

These regulations shall also lay down the procedures for scrutiny of Europol's activities by the European Parliament, together with national Parliaments.

3. Any operational action by Europol must be carried out in liaison and in agreement with the authorities of the Member State or States whose territory is concerned. The application of coercive measures shall be the exclusive responsibility of the competent national authorities.

Finally, Article 89 TFEU, in place of the prior Article 32 TEU, now governs cross-border operation measures:

The Council, acting in accordance with a special legislative procedure, shall lay down the conditions and limitations under which the competent authorities of the Member States referred to in Articles 82 and 87 may operate in the territory of another Member State in liaison and in agreement with the authorities of that State. The Council shall act unanimously after consulting the European Parliament.

Taking these provisions in turn, Article 84 TFEU essentially provides for the affirmation of the prior status quo,[45] providing, as before, for EU support for national measures concerning crime prevention without any harmonization of national law. But the decision-making procedure changed to qualified majority voting (QMV) in the Council and co-decision with the European Parliament (EP) (known as the 'ordinary legislative procedure' since the Treaty of Lisbon entered into force).[46] Another change is the use of 'Community' instruments in place of third pillar acts previously. So it is possible to adopt Directives on the subject of crime prevention, whereas Framework Decisions were never used in this area.

As for the general rules on police cooperation (Article 87 TFEU), compared to the prior rules, the decision-making procedure changed as regards non-operational police cooperation (Article 87(2) TFEU) from the previous unanimity in Council and consultation of the EP to QMV and co-decision (the 'ordinary legislative procedure', since the Treaty of Lisbon). However, the previous decision-making rules were retained as regards operational cooperation (Article 87(3) TFEU); these are described as a type of 'special legislative procedure',[47] but in some cases there is a possible fast-track to

---

[45] On which, see II.7.5 below.   [46] On this procedure, see Art 294 TFEU.
[47] See Art 289(2) TFEU.

enhanced cooperation in the event of a national veto.[48] The EU's competence was amended slightly.[49]

Comparing Article 87(2) TFEU to the prior Article 30(1)(b) to (d) TEU, Article 87(2)(a) is nearly identical to the prior Article 30(1)(b), except that a specific example of the content of these powers was dropped (suspicious financial transactions), along with references to Europol and to data protection rules. The first change is immaterial, since reports on suspicious financial transactions fall within the scope of this provision anyway. Secondly, the change concerning Europol simply takes account of Article 88(2)(a) TFEU. The third change takes account of the inclusion of a general legal base for data protection in the TFEU (Article 16), which clearly confers power on the EU to adopt data protection rules covering both the previous first pillar and the previous third pillar,[50] subject to a declaration attached to the Final Act of the Treaty indicating that specific provisions will be adopted to address national security concerns.[51]

Next, Article 87(2)(b) is very similar to the previous Article 30(1)(c) TEU, with minor changes to the wording regarding training, staff exchange, and research, and a more significant change as regards dropping any reference to liaison officers.[52] Article 87(2)(c), compared to the previous Article 30(1)(d) TEU, confers power to adopt common investigative techniques, rather than just a common *evaluation* of such techniques, suggesting a possible greater degree of harmonization in this area. Finally, the power over police operations set out in Article 87(3) is prima facie identical to the competence set out in the previous Article 30(1)(a) TEU.

Moving on to Europol (Article 88 TFEU), the decision-making procedure was changed fully to QMV in Council and co-decision with the EP (the ordinary legislative procedure) with no exceptions provided for. However, only Regulations, not any other form of EU act, have to be used as regards Europol. Compared to the previous Article 30(2) TEU, there is an express exclusion from exercising 'coercive measures' and a requirement to act in liaison and agreement with each Member State as regards 'operational action'. More specifically, 'investigative and operational action' has to be carried out either 'jointly' with Member States or 'in the context of joint investigative teams'. The reference to specific rules concerning EP and national parliamentary scrutiny of Europol is new.

Overall, Europol is no longer assigned a role *supporting*, *facilitating*, and *requesting* action by national police forces, but rather (implicitly) a role in *partnership* with national forces. But the partnership is not fully equal since Europol cannot have the capacity to apply coercive measures. Moreover, the Treaty does not refer to any *independent* role for Europol to act fully by itself, although since the listed powers are non-exhaustive ('may include') it would be possible to adopt rules to that effect—as long

---

[48] This process could also be invoked as regards Art 86 TFEU, concerning the possible creation of a European Public Prosecutor (see II:6.2.3 above). On this procedure, referred to as a 'pseudo-veto' in this book, see II:2.2.3.4.2 above.

[49] See II.7.2.4 below.   [50] On the competence issues which arise, see II.7.2.4 below.

[51] Declaration 20 to the Final Act of the Treaty of Lisbon.

[52] On the competence issues which arise regarding liaison officers, see II.7.2.4 below.

as Europol would not thereby carry out operational action independently, or exercise coercive powers, in light of the limits on its powers set out in Article 88(3).

Finally, Article 89 TFEU (as regards cross-border operations) essentially copied the prior Article 32 TEU with no substantive amendments, either to decision-making rules (again described as a 'special legislative procedure') or competence.

As regards all aspects of police cooperation, the extended jurisdiction of the Court of Justice applies, subject to the transitional period applying to pre-existing third pillar measures (which expired in December 2014) and to the special derogation applying to law enforcement measures, which could be particularly relevant to police cooperation.[53]

All of the police cooperation rules are also affected by the general provisions in Title V of the TFEU,[54] particularly the provisions relating to: the evaluation of national implementing measures;[55] the establishment of the standing committee on security;[56] national competence for law and order measures (which is identical to the prior Article 33 TEU);[57] security cooperation between Member States;[58] administrative cooperation between Member States;[59] and the adoption of anti-terrorist sanctions measures.[60] It also remains possible for a group of Member States to make proposals for measures in this field.[61]

The remaining provisions permitting unanimous voting in this area (as regards cross-border police action and operational police cooperation) are subject to the possibility of simplified treaty amendment to introduce QMV in Council and co-decision by the EP.[62] Furthermore, a group of Member States can request to apply enhanced cooperation in this area, with the possibility that they can change the relevant decision-making procedures between themselves.[63] The revised and extended rules on JHA opt-outs also apply to policing issues.[64]

As regards the rest of the Treaty of Lisbon, the revised rules on human rights (accession of the EU to the ECHR and the enhanced status of the Charter) could impact upon the area of police cooperation. The previous Article 135 EC on customs cooperation was amended to drop the prior limitation concerning the application of criminal law or criminal justice.[65] Finally, the specific power to adopt measures on civil protection and the 'solidarity' clause introduced by the Treaty of Lisbon will also impact upon the issues discussed in this Chapter.[66]

In practice, the most significant developments in this field since the Treaty of Lisbon entered into force have been a Regulation re-establishing Europol and a Directive on passenger name records (PNR) data (both agreed in late 2015), along with the treaties with third states on PNR.[67] There has also been new legislation on the European Police College, and SIS II began operations in 2013.[68] The Council also adopted a decision establishing a committee on operational security (known as 'COSI', based on the

---

[53] Art 275 TFEU. See further II:2.2.3.3 (transitional rules) and II:2.2.3.2 above (derogation).
[54] See I:2.2.3.2 and II:2.2.3.2.   [55] Art 70 TFEU.   [56] Art 71 TFEU.
[57] Art 72 TFEU.   [58] Art 73 TFEU. See also Art 4(2), revised TEU.   [59] Art 74 TFEU.
[60] Art 75 TFEU. On the substantive measures concerned, see II.7.4.5 below.   [61] Art 76 TFEU.
[62] See Art 48(7), revised TEU.
[63] For a discussion of the enhanced cooperation rules, see I:2.2.5.5.   [64] II.7.2.5 below.
[65] Art 33 TFEU. See further II.7.4.1 below.
[66] Arts 196 and 222 TFEU. See further II.7.4.7 below.
[67] See respectively II.7.8, II.7.6, and II.7.11 below.   [68] See respectively II.7.7 and II.7.6 below.

French acronym).[69] There have been no references to the Court of Justice on policing measures, but the Court has been active in closely related areas of the rest of EU law (on the issue of data retention, for instance).[70]

7.2.4 Competence issues

Before the entry into force of the Treaty of Lisbon, the most difficult competence issues regarding EU policing and security were the extent of the cross-over with EC legislation (as it then was), in particular as regards the use of private-sector data by law enforcement agencies. These issues are examined further below.[71]

As for the competence issues arising after the entry into force of the Treaty of Lisbon, first of all a number of the general provisions of Title V of the TFEU raise questions, given that they are subject to different decision-making procedures than all of the specific policing provisions of the Treaty. The scope of the legal bases for measures concerning evaluations (Article 70 TFEU), the creation of the standing committee on internal security (Article 71 TFEU), and anti-terrorist sanctions (Article 75 TFEU) has been examined already in this book.[72] So has the specific rule in Article 72 TFEU (previous Article 33 EU), which refers to Member States' responsibilities as regards law, order, and security; this provision simply confirms that the implementation of EU policing measures is left to the Member States' authorities, particularly as regards coercive measures.[73] It should also be noted that the Treaty provides for a specific restriction of competence as regards intelligence cooperation.[74] Finally, as regards the power to adopt measures on administrative cooperation (Article 74), this is distinct from the powers to adopt measures concerning law enforcement *practitioners*, and so has limited scope as compared to the policing powers set out in Articles 84 and 87–9 TFEU.

Next, as noted already,[75] Article 16 TFEU, the legal base for measures concerning data protection, applies not only to the former first pillar but also to the former third pillar, and provides for the use of the ordinary legislative procedure (and therefore, the power of consent for the EP as regards the conclusion of treaties). The measures to be adopted on this issue will often cross over with the substantive rules on the exchange of information as such between law enforcement authorities, but there is no problem having a joint legal base of Articles 16 and 87(2) TFEU, because the decision-making procedure is the same and the possible conflict of rules regarding territorial scope has been resolved by specific provisions in the opt-out Protocols relating to the UK, Ireland, and Denmark.[76]

The other competence issues relevant to EU policing law fall into three main categories: the distinction between policing law and the non-JHA provisions of the Treaties; the distinction between policing law and criminal law; and the distinction between the different powers relating to policing law. The first category of issues is discussed below,[77] while the second and third are discussed in turn in this section.

---

[69] See [2010] OJ L 52/50 (discussed further in II:2.2.3.2 above).   [70] See II.7.6.5 below.
[71] II.7.4.3.2.   [72] I:2.2.3.2 and II:2.2.3.2.
[73] See the interpretation of Art 72 TFEU in II:2.2.3.2 above.
[74] See Art 73 TFEU and Art 4(2), revised TEU, discussed in ibid.   [75] II.7.2.3 above.
[76] II.7.2.5 below.   [77] II.7.4.

The distinction between the policing and criminal law provisions is significant to the extent that several policing provisions (Articles 87(3) and 89 TFEU) are subject to a special legislative procedure, whereas most criminal law provisions are subject to the ordinary legislative procedure. However, Article 86 TFEU is subject to a special legislative procedure; and certain criminal law provisions (Articles 82(2) and 83 TFEU)—but no policing law provisions—are subject to an emergency brake procedure.[78] As discussed in other chapters, any criminal procedure or substantive criminal law measures which also address investigations by police need a dual legal base from the policing provisions of the Treaty.[79] Any involvement by Eurojust or the European Public Prosecutor in investigations requires the *lex specialis* of Articles 85 or 86 TFEU, and any rule concerning jurisdiction over investigations (as distinct from prosecutions) falls within the scope of the policing provisions.[80]

As for the distinctions between the different legal bases relating to EU policing law, there are four different issues. First, and most obviously, it is necessary to distinguish between the non-operational police cooperation within the scope of Article 87(2) TFEU, and the operational police cooperation within the scope of Article 87(3) TFEU, because the former provisions are subject to the ordinary legislative procedure, while the latter provisions are subject to a special legislative procedure, in particular involving unanimity.[81] Secondly, it is necessary to distinguish within Article 87(3) the issues that can be the subject of fast-track enhanced cooperation in the event of a veto (because they do not build upon the Schengen *acquis*) and those which cannot (because they build upon that *acquis*). Thirdly, it is necessary to distinguish the legal base concerning Europol from the legal bases concerning operational powers (ie Articles 87(3) and 89), again because of the different decision-making process; this includes the definition of the limits on Europol's powers. Fourthly, it is necessary to distinguish Articles 87(3) and 89, again because of the fast-track route to enhanced cooperation that applies to the former (in part), but not the latter.[82]

First of all, there is extensive prior practice of the Council adopting policing measures on various legal bases before the Treaty of Lisbon, but it should be kept in mind that the mere practice of the institutions does not establish a legally binding precedent.[83] Moreover, many of the Council's decisions regarding legal bases could be questioned: for instance, the Decision establishing SIS II, which was in part adopted on the legal base of the previous Article 30(1)(a) TEU, addressed operational police cooperation marginally, to the extent that it set out rules for action following policing alerts;[84] but essentially it concerned only the collection of information, and should have had only Article 30(1)(b) TEU (now Article 87(2)(a) TFEU) as a legal base. Also, the specific legal base for measures concerning liaison officers (previous Article 30(1)(c)

---

[78] On this procedure, see II:2.2.3.4.1 above. Note that the combination of a legal base subject to the emergency brake with a legal base which is not is not per se a problem: see II:3.2.4 above.

[79] See II:3.2.4 and II:6.2.4 above.   [80] See II:7.2.4 above.

[81] It is assumed that this analysis applies *mutatis mutandis* to distinguish Arts 87(2) and 89 TFEU.

[82] As with the emergency brake, however, a dual legal base should not be impossible per se (see the discussion in II:3.2.4 by analogy).

[83] *Opinion 1/94* [1994] ECR I-5273.   [84] Arts 33, 37, and 39 of the Decision ([2007] OJ L 205/63).

TEU) was repealed by the Treaty of Lisbon, so any further measures on this issue will need a legal base which reflects the specific tasks of the liaison officers.[85]

The starting point for deciding on the correct legal base, according to the case law of the Court of Justice,[86] is to look at the aim and content of each measure. It must be kept in mind, in particular, that the legal base for operational cooperation concerns cooperation *between* the services of *different* Member States, ie there must be a specific cross-border element. Of course, the distinction between operational and non-operational policing measures is difficult to define precisely, as there is an obvious link between the exchange of data in particular on the one hand and police cooperation on the other—since the operational activity of law enforcement bodies will often be based on information received, and will also often result in the collection of information which can then be exchanged. However, the concept of operational cooperation must be distinct from the exchange and analysis of information, since Article 87 TFEU requires a distinction to be made between these issues. In the absence of any positive definition of 'operational measures' in the Treaty, the concept should be defined *a contrario* as compared to the specific powers set out in Article 87(2), and should, in particular, include coercive measures (on which, see the discussion of Article 88 below). By analogy with case law on competence in other areas of EU law, it is arguable that Article 87(3) is an exception which has to be interpreted narrowly.[87]

Secondly, there is case law of the Court of Justice defining the concept of a measure building upon the Schengen *acquis*.[88] According to this jurisprudence, the concept must be defined by analogy with the legal base case law, although sometimes the two tests lead to different results: the Court of Justice of the European Union (CJEU) ruled that the Decision giving law enforcement officers access to the Visa Information System (VIS) had a policing legal base, but built upon the *visa* aspects of the Schengen *acquis*. It can be deduced that the concept of 'building upon' the *acquis* has a wider scope as regards external borders and visas issues than policing matters, given that the former issues are more directly connected to the core Schengen principle of abolishing internal border controls. Certainly, it is implicitly possible that a measure builds upon the Schengen *acquis* even if it does not amend an existing measure which forms part of that *acquis*.

Moving on to the third issue, what is the distinction between Europol's powers pursuant to Article 88 on the one hand, and the provisions of Article 87(3) and 89 on the other? The obvious dividing line is that the latter provisions refer to *Member States'* authorities as distinct from Europol, and so a measure solely dealing with Europol (including the relationship of national law enforcement bodies *with Europol*) falls within the scope of Article 88, while measures which only govern operational actions by national authorities fall within the scope of the other provisions. Any measure

---

[85] Since the pre-Lisbon measures on this issue concern the exchange of information by liaison officers (see II.7.6.3 below), the correct legal base for further measures would be Art 87(2)(a), unless the officers are given other tasks.

[86] See the summary of the case law in I:3.2.3.

[87] See Case C-268/06 *Impact* [2008] ECR I-2483.

[88] See Cases C-77/05 *UK v Council* [2007] ECR I-11459, C-137/05 *UK v Council* [2007] ECR I-11593, and C-482/08 *UK v Council* [2010] ECR I-10413.

governing both issues will need joint legal bases (if this is legally feasible). The prospect of legislation on Europol circumventing the unanimity requirement of Articles 87(3) and 89 (ie by adopting legislation permitting Europol to have powers that national bodies cannot) is ruled out by the limits on Europol's power set out in Article 88(3) TFEU (ie the ban on exercising 'coercive powers' and operational action without Member States' approval); and those limits cannot in turn be circumvented by the use of Articles 87(3) or 89, because, as noted already, the latter provisions only confer power to regulate Member States' authorities.

This brings us to the interpretation of the 'coercive powers' exception set out in Article 88(3). At the very least, 'coercive measures' must refer to authorized violence (ie the use of physical force) against individuals or other forms of constraint, including detention. It has been argued convincingly that the concept also extends to arrest, search and seizure, the power to examine books and records, and the interception of telecommunications.[89]

Fourth, as for the distinction between Articles 87(3) and 89, the former Article is the legal base for measures concerning 'operational cooperation between' the national law enforcement officers of different Member States, while the latter Article concerns the 'conditions and limitations' which apply when law enforcement officers from one Member State wish to 'operate' in another Member State. There is little to distinguish the two provisions, considering that measures adopted on the basis of Article 87(3) will often involve some movement of law enforcement officers between Member States (since this is obviously a form of 'operational' activity), while the latter provision requires close links between the law enforcement officers who move and the host Member State's authorities ('in liaison and in agreement'). The best view is that Article 89 alone applies where the 'guest' law enforcement officials play an essentially *independent* role in the host State's territory (leaving aside the liaison with and agreement of the host State's authorities), while Article 87(3) alone applies where the guest officers and the home State's officers work together *jointly*, or where law enforcement authorities coordinate their operational actions in different Member States. Arguably, where EU measures regulate the issue of the operational powers of guest officers in a host State in the context of a joint operation, then a *dual* legal base of both Articles 87(3) and 89 will be required.

7.2.5 Territorial scope

The policing rules in the Schengen *acquis* applied to the UK from 1 January 2005, except for the SIS provisions, which applied from April 2015. These rules will also apply to Ireland, as soon as the latter's opt-ins to the Schengen *acquis* fully enter into force.[90] Due to their geographical position and political reservations, both States have opted out of the Schengen rules on hot pursuit by police officers, and Ireland has also opted out of the rules on cross-border surveillance. One particular dispute in this area was

---

[89] N Grief, 'EU Law and Security' (2007) 32 ELRev 752 at 759 and 761.
[90] See further II:2.2.5.1 above. On the content of the Schengen *acquis* as regards policing, see II.7.2.1 above.

the question of whether the UK and Ireland can fully participate in the third pillar Decision which gave law enforcement bodies access to the VIS; the UK lost its legal challenge on this point.[91]

After the entry into force of the Treaty of Lisbon, the UK and Ireland have the capacity to opt out of new measures in this area, subject to special rules if they opt out of measures amending acts which already apply to those States. In practice they have opted in to the proposals on passenger name records and Eurodac, but the UK has opted out of the proposals on the European Police College and Europol.

When the UK applied its block opt-out from pre-Lisbon policing and criminal law measures as of 1 December 2014, it decided to opt back in to the most policing issues, namely: the pre-Lisbon legislation on: Europol; the Customs Information System; the Naples II Convention on cooperation between customs administrations; the Decisions on combating child pornography, setting up a Secretariat for data protection authorities, Financial Intelligence Units, Asset Recovery Offices, and security in relation to football matches; and the Framework Decisions on joint investigation teams, and ad hoc exchange of police information.[92] However, it opted out of a long list of relatively minor measures:[93] Joint Actions on counter-terrorism, drug trafficking, chemical profiling of drugs, an organized crime directory, cooperation on law and order and security, and the targeting of police information; Decisions on the exchange of information on counterfeit travel documents, exchanging information with Interpol, the exchange of information on terrorist offences, liaison officers, the Prum Decisions on police cooperation, and the European Crime Prevention Network (EUCPN); and a few Schengen measures (Decisions of the Schengen Executive Committee, and rules on the integration of the SIS to the second-generation system).

The block opt-out did not, however, apply to acts adopted after the entry into force of the Treaty of Lisbon, which the UK had opted in to, or to pre-Lisbon acts amended since that Treaty of Lisbon, which the UK had opted in to.[94] The UK can still opt back into to further pre-Lisbon measures in future, and in fact the Council adopted a measure on the consequences of the UK's block opt-out, requiring the UK to consider whether it wished to opt back in to the 'Prum' decisions on information exchange by autumn 2015.[95] Until the UK does so, its law enforcement officials cannot access the Eurodac database.[96]

The pre-Lisbon Schengen and EU policing rules fully apply to Denmark,[97] but Denmark is not subject to any measures in this area adopted after the Treaty of Lisbon, except those building upon the Schengen *acquis*. In December 2015, Denmark held a

---

[91] [2008] OJ L 218/129; see Case C-482/08 *UK v Council* [2010] ECR I-10413. On the substance of this Decision, see II.7.6.1.3 below; on the VIS generally, see I:4.8.

[92] See the Council and Commission decisions authorizing the UK to opt back in to these measures ([2014] OJ L 345/1 and 6).

[93] See the list of the measures which the UK opted out of: [2014] OJ C 430/17.

[94] In the field of policing, this is relevant to the EU Mutual Assistance Convention and its Protocol: see the list of such measures in [2014] OJ C 430/23.

[95] [2014] OJ L 343/11. If the UK does not opt back in to the Prum Decision it must repay funds it received to help it prepare to join the system: [2014] OJ L 343/17. In autumn 2015, the UK government announced its intention to opt back in.

[96] Art 3 of the transitional decision (ibid).   [97] See further II:2.2.5.2 above.

referendum on whether to move towards a partial opt-in to JHA measures. A group of political parties had agreed to seek an opt-in to the legislation on Europol and passenger name records, but not JHA funding. The parties had not yet decided whether to seek an opt-in to post-Lisbon measures on the European Police College. However, the public voted against the idea of the partial opt-in.

For all three countries, there are specific provisions on data protection, which provide that those Member States are not bound by measures adopted on the basis of Article 16 TFEU, to the extent that they are not bound by the underlying policing measure in question.[98]

As for the new Member States, the EU's policing rules all applied immediately, except for the rules on cross-border surveillance and hot pursuit and on the SIS, which only applied once the Schengen *acquis* was fully extended to the new Member States (entailing abolition of border controls between old and new Schengen States).[99] It follows that those rules do not yet apply to Cyprus, Romania, Bulgaria, and Croatia, since the Schengen *acquis* does not yet fully extend to those States.

Norway and Iceland have applied all the Schengen policing rules (and subsequent measures building upon them) since 2001, when their Schengen accession treaty entered into force.[100] Switzerland has done the same since its Schengen accession treaty came into force in 2008, and Liechtenstein followed in 2011.[101]

Norway and Iceland (but not Switzerland and Liechtenstein) have also agreed a separate treaty with the EU as regards their participation in most of the provisions of the 'Prum Decision',[102] which puts into force within EU law many of the provisions of the Prum Convention, which had earlier been agreed between a group of Member States in 2005.[103] This treaty also applies to the relevant provisions of a Decision which implements the Prum Decision, but does not apply to a separate Decision on special intervention units, which was also carved out of the Prum Convention.[104]

7.3 Human Rights

7.3.1 International human rights law

Police operations and investigations raise questions in particular about the right to life, freedom from torture, rights regarding detention, and the gathering of evidence. The latter two points are best addressed as aspects of criminal procedure,[105] and the other

---

[98] See II:2.2.5.1 and II:2.2.5.2 above.   [99] See further II:2.2.5.3 above.

[100] [1999] OJ L 176/35. See further I:2.2.5.4.

[101] [2008] OJ L 53/52 (treaty with Switzerland) and [2011] OJ L 160 (Protocol with Liechtenstein). See further I:2.2.5.4. Also see the EU-Swiss treaty on judicial cooperation against fraud ([2009] OJ L 46/6, in force as regards most Member States, the EC, and Switzerland on 8 Apr 2009 (see [2009] OJ L 177/7)), contains some policing provisions. So does the proposed treaty on the same topic with Liechtenstein (COM (2009) 644, 23 Nov 2009).

[102] [2008] OJ L 210/1. Norway and Iceland will participate in all of the provisions of the Decisions except the institutional clauses (see Art 1 of the treaty). On the substance of the Prum Decision, see II.7.6.2, II.7.6.3, and II.7.9.4 below.

[103] [2009] OJ L 353/1. The treaty has been signed, but is not yet in force.

[104] See respectively [2008] OJ L 210/12 and 73. On the latter Decision, see II.7.9.5 below.

[105] See chs 3 and 4 of this volume.

points have limited relevance to EU law given the limitations upon both EU policing bodies and national police forces operating across borders pursuant to EU law. The focus in this chapter is therefore on the issues most affected by EU policing measures, particularly data protection and privacy rights in the context of police surveillance, monitoring, and exchange and storing of information, the impact of EU policing measures on freedom of expression and assembly, and the impact of EU anti-terrorist sanctions.[106]

The starting point on the issue of privacy and data protection is Article 8(1) of the European Convention on Human Rights (ECHR), which recognizes the 'right to respect for...private and family life...home...and correspondence'. However, Article 8(2) ECHR provides that public authorities may interfere with the exercise of this right if the interference 'is in accordance with the law and is necessary in a democratic society in the interests of national security, public safety', and, inter alia, 'the prevention of disorder or crime'.

There is an obvious tension between the right to privacy and the interests of law enforcement and state security, in particular because of the nearly 'zero-sum' relationship between the two objectives: any increase in State surveillance and control could in principle potentially lead to an increase in the effectiveness of crime prevention and police investigations. Of course, this assumes that the competence and integrity of law enforcement and security service officials and the accuracy and efficiency of the technology they are using is beyond doubt; but unfortunately such assumptions are sometimes misplaced. Furthermore, it may be a more efficient use of resources for law enforcement and security services to concentrate their surveillance efforts upon a small number of criminal suspects and their associates, rather than the entire society. Finally, it is often argued that only people with something to hide should be concerned about maintaining their privacy from law enforcement or security service officials, but quite apart from the risks posed by technical and human failings, there is surely something intrinsically so valuable about our privacy that a degree of it must be protected, even if this comes at the cost of a greater risk to public safety. Quite simply, there has to be a balance between privacy on the one hand and combating crime and security risks on the other; but the precise place to draw the line is more and more contested as technology allows for ever wider interference with privacy, in particular the mass surveillance of most of the population, and the perceived risk from serious crime and terrorism increases.

Some indication of where to draw the line can be gleaned from the jurisprudence of the Strasbourg organs, which have addressed the application of Article 8 to policing activities on a number of occasions. A leading judgment of the European Court of Human Rights is *Klass*,[107] which ruled that telephone tapping (interception) was an interference with Article 8 rights, but that the German measures attacked in that case did not breach Article 8 because the interference had a legitimate aim and the safeguards on interception were sufficient. As in many subsequent cases in this field, the judgment turned on whether the national measures were 'in accordance with the law',

---

[106] The last of these issues is discussed in II.7.4.5 below.   [107] *Klass v Germany* (A-28).

meaning that there must be a basis for interferences with Article 8 rights in domestic law, such domestic laws have to be accessible, and the circumstances of their application to individuals has to foreseeable. The following principles were established:

> ...The Court has...to accept that the existence of some legislation granting powers of secret surveillance over the mail, post and telecommunications is, under exceptional conditions, necessary in a democratic society in the interests of national security and/or for the prevention of disorder or crime....Nevertheless, the Court stresses that this does not mean that the Contracting States enjoy an unlimited discretion to subject persons within their jurisdiction to secret surveillance. The Court, being aware of the danger such a law poses of undermining or even destroying democracy on the ground of defending it, affirms that the Contracting States may not, in the name of the struggle against espionage and terrorism, adopt whatever measures they deem appropriate. The Court must be satisfied that, whatever system of surveillance is adopted, there exist adequate and effective guarantees against abuse. This assessment has only a relative character: it depends on all the circumstances of the case, such as the nature, scope and duration of the possible measures, the grounds required for ordering such measures, the authorities competent to permit, carry out and supervise such measures, and the kind of remedy provided by the national law.[108]

It is clear that while some interference with the right to privacy must be permitted in the interests of security and combating crime, the discretion granted to States cannot be absolute, or the very principle of a free society underlying the Convention would be threatened. Later case law elaborated on these principles, condemning Member States for interfering with privacy without a clear legal basis.[109]

A series of intertwined cases have addressed the particular privacy issues arising from data protection. In *Leander*,[110] the Human Rights Court found, by analogy with *Klass*, that it was a legitimate interference with the right to privacy for States to establish a security file on citizens and to vet applicants for public service, provided that sufficient safeguards were put in place. Subsequently, the Court referred to the Council of Europe's data protection Convention (see below) when ruling on the application of Article 8 to data files kept by security services.[111] Further cases condemned actions by law enforcement authorities in obtaining and/or storing or further transferring data such as recorded video footage, or taped conversations even as regards footage taken from security cameras in a public street or in police stations or prison cells.[112] Member States have also violated Article 8 ECHR when they kept personal data for longer than necessary.[113] Furthermore, the Human Rights Court has confirmed that storing cell

---

[108] Paras 48–50 of the judgment (ibid).

[109] See *Malone v UK* (A-82); *Kruslin v France* (A-176-A); *Huvig v France* (A-176-B); *Halford v UK* (Reports 1997-III); *Kopp v Switzerland* (Reports 1998-II); *Valenzeula Contreras v Spain* (Reports 1998-III); *Lambert v France* (Reports 1998-V); *Khan v UK* (Reports 2000-V); *Doerga v Netherlands*, 27 Apr 2004, *Vetter v France*, 31 May 2005; and *Wisse v France*, 20 Dec 2005.

[110] *Leander v Sweden* (A-116).

[111] For instance, *Amann v Switzerland* (Reports 2000-II), *Rotaru v Romania* (Reports 2000-V); Art 13 ECHR was also violated in both cases due to the lack of a remedy in relation to the data.

[112] See *P.G. and J.H. v UK* (Reports 2001-IX), *Peck v UK* (Reports 2003-I), and *Perry v UK* (Reports 2003-IX).

[113] *Segerstedt-Wiberg v Sweden*, 6 June 2006.

samples, DNA information, and fingerprints falls within the scope of Article 8, and that the indefinite retention of such information from all persons who are charged, but not convicted, of any offence violates Article 8.[114] But on the other hand, establishing a database on offenders does not violate Article 8 if access to information is limited and subject to a duty of confidentiality,[115] and States have an obligation to waive the anonymity of Internet users if necessary in order to ensure that serious criminal offences which amount to a violation of privacy are prosecuted.[116]

Further detailed rules on data protection are set out in the 1981 Council of Europe data protection Convention, which has been ratified by all EU Member States.[117] The Convention applies to personal data processed by automatic means,[118] and its key provision requires States to apply key 'data quality' principles: data must be 'obtained and processed fairly and lawfully'; 'stored for specified and legitimate purposes and not used in a way incompatible with those purposes'; 'adequate, relevant and not excessive in relation to the purposes for which they are stored'; 'accurate and, where necessary, kept up to date'; and 'preserved in a form which permits identification of the data subjects for no longer than is required for the purpose for which those data are stored.'[119] Certain data (known in practice as 'sensitive data') cannot be processed unless there are 'appropriate safeguards' (data revealing racial origin, political opinion, or religious beliefs, concerning health and sexual life, or relating to criminal convictions).[120] Individuals have the right: to establish the existence of a file on them, its purpose, and details about the controller of the file; to obtain confirmation of whether their personal data is being stored, as well as obtaining access to the data; to obtain rectification or erasure of the data if it has been kept in violation of national law; and to have a remedy in relation to any of these rights.[121] However, derogations from these rights and the rules on data quality and sensitive data are permitted if they are 'provided for by the law' of the relevant State and constitute 'a necessary measure in a democratic society in the interests of', inter alia, 'protecting State security, public safety,...or the suppression of criminal offences.'[122]

A Protocol of 2001, in force in 2004 and ratified by a majority of EU Member States,[123] supplements the Convention with two provisions, requiring States to establish a supervisory authority to facilitate the application of the Convention and prohibiting transmission of data to States or organizations which have not ratified the Convention unless they provide an 'adequate level of protection' for the data, or inter alia, 'legitimate prevailing interests, especially important public interests' justify the transfer. A further agreement, not yet in force, permits the EC (now the EU) as such to become party to the Convention.

As for the freedoms of expression and assembly, those rights are protected by Articles 10 and 11 ECHR, but again those rights may be limited on grounds similar to those

---

[114] *S and Marper v UK*, 5 Dec 2008.   [115] *Bouchacourt and others v France*, 17 Dec 2009.
[116] *KU v Finland*, 2 Dec 2008.   [117] ETS 108.
[118] For the definitions of these concepts, see Art 2 of the Convention.
[119] Art 5 of the Convention.   [120] Art 6 of the Convention.
[121] Art 8 of the Convention.   [122] Art 9 of the Convention.
[123] ETS 181; for ratification details, see Appendix I.

permitting interference with Article 8 rights, provided that the interference is 'prescribed by law' and is 'necessary in a democratic society'. Although there is limited case law of the Strasbourg Court concerning demonstrations as such, it is clear that national authorities should not in principle restrict the movement of persons, even across *de jure* or *de facto* borders, who wish to participate in meetings or demonstrations.[124]

7.3.2 Application to EU law

The protection of privacy is recognized as a general principle of EU law,[125] as are data protection rights;[126] both rights are also recognized by the EU Charter of Fundamental Rights.[127] There is also detailed EU legislation on the specifics of data protection: within the scope of Community law (as it was before the Treaty of Lisbon), there is a Directive (applicable to Member States) and a Regulation (applicable to the EU institutions and bodies),[128] while within the scope of the third pillar (as it was before the Treaty of Lisbon) there is both a general Framework Decision and separate rules in specific third pillar acts. The third pillar measures are discussed further below.[129] As noted above, following the entry into force of the Treaty of Lisbon, there is a single legal base for measures governing data protection issues (Article 16 TFEU). The Commission proposed legislation to replace the Directive with a Regulation and the Framework Decision with a Directive in 2012; these proposals will likely be adopted in the near future.[130]

The EC data protection measures are similar and essentially set out the principles of the Council of Europe Convention (and also the Protocol to that Convention, even though it was opened for signature later) in greater detail. In particular, the EC measures guarantee the free flow of data between Member States, but establish an elaborate regime regarding the transfer of data outside the EU. In particular, a detailed procedure is established to determine whether a third State has an 'adequate level of protection'; there may be a Commission decision or negotiation of a treaty to be concluded by the Council to this end.[131] The EU measures, unlike the Council of Europe Convention, set out detailed rules on when personal data may be processed; this includes cases where the controller is subject to a legal obligation, or where necessary to carry out a task in the public interest or the exercise of official authority.[132] There are also more detailed provisions on individual remedies and the powers of supervisory authorities;[133] the Regulation creates a European Data Protection Supervisor to exercise those powers as regards EC bodies.[134] However, the EC measures do not apply to the processing of data

---

[124] *Chorherr v Austria* (A-226-B); *Piermont v France* (A-314); and *Djavit An v Turkey* (Reports 2003-III). See also I:3.3.1.

[125] See the case law referred to in I:6.3.1.   [126] Case C-369/98 *Fisher* [2000] ECR I-6751.

[127] Arts 7 and 8 ([2007] OJ C 303).

[128] Respectively Dir 95/46 ([1995] OJ L 281/31) and Reg 45/2001 ([2001] OJ L 8/1). On the implementation of the Dir, see the Commission's report (COM (2003) 265, 15 May 2003).

[129] See II.7.6.4 below.   [130] COM (2012) 10 and 11, 25 Jan 2012.

[131] Arts 25 and 26 of the Directive. The CJEU has clarified that an 'adequate' level of data protection means a very similar level of protection to the EU, and that data cannot be transferred to a third State if it will be subject there to mass surveillance without sufficient safeguards: see Case C-362/14 *Schrems*, ECLI:EU:C:2015:650. On the consequences of this judgment, see COM (2015) 566, 6 Nov 2015.

[132] Art 7 of the Directive.   [133] Arts 22 and 28 of the Directive.

[134] Arts 41–8, Reg 45/2001, n 128 above.

'by a natural person within the course of a purely personal or household activity', or to 'an activity which falls outside the scope of Community law, such as those provided for by Titles V and VI of the Treaty on European Union [the second and third pillars] and in any case to processing operations concerning public security, defence, State security (including the economic well-being of the State when the processing operation relates to State security matters) and the activities of the State in areas of criminal law'.[135] Even though the Treaty of Lisbon has repealed the former Title VI of the TEU, the data protection rules adopted within the framework of the former third pillar remain valid until the planned amendments replace them, due to the continuing exclusion of matters relating to criminal law and public security from the Directive.

The Court of Justice has ruled several times on the application of the Directive, defining its scope broadly to include: data processing within a single Member State; interpreting the 'household' exception from its scope narrowly; aligning the interpretation of the data protection rights and possible exceptions with the jurisprudence of the Human Rights Court on Article 8 ECHR; ruling that the regime on external transfers of data does not apply to material posted on websites; limiting the information on EU citizens who have moved to another Member State which it is necessary to store in the public interest; addressing the balance between data protection rights and the freedom of expression; specifying the extent of the obligation to keep information on data processing; and clarifying the extent of the required independence of supervisory authorities.[136] The Court also ruled that the Directive does not apply to the transfer of data from EU airlines to American law enforcement authorities, given the public security context of the issue.[137]

More recently, in its best known judgment on the Directive, the Court has subjected Google's search engine listings to a filtering process in the interests of data protection, often called the 'right to be forgotten' in practice.[138] Furthermore, the CJEU has ruled that home security cameras fall within the scope of the Directive, if they record activity outdoors.[139] However, the Court was not so rigorous about the application of the Directive to national passport databases.[140]

As for the Regulation on data protection as regards the EU institutions, the Court of Justice has ruled that it takes priority over the EU's legislation on access to documents, meaning that anyone who wishes to know the names of persons who have lobbied the Commission on particular issues must show a legitimate interest in obtaining access to that data, unless the lobbyists have consented to the release of their names.[141] There

---

[135] Art 3(2) of the Directive.
[136] For instance, see Cases: C-465/00, C-138/01, and C-139/01, *Osterreichischer Rundfunk* [2003] ECR I-4989; Case C-101/01 *Lindqvist* [2003] ECR I-12971; C-524/06 *Huber* [2008] ECR I-9705; C-73/07 *Satamedia* [2008] ECR I-9831; C-553/07 *Rijkeboer* [2009] ECR I-3889; and C-518/07 *Commission v Germany* [2010] ECR I-1885.
[137] Joined Cases C-317/04 and C-318/04 *EP v Council and Commission* [2006] ECR I-4721. See the discussion of the legal base issue in II.7.4.3.2 below, the human rights issues in II.7.6.3 below, and the external relations context in II.7.11 below.
[138] Case C-131/12 *Google Spain*, ECLI:EU:C:2014:317.
[139] Case C-212/13 *Rynes*, ECLI:EU:C:2014:2428.
[140] Cases C-446/12 to C-449/12 *Willems and others*, ECLI:EU:C:2015:238.
[141] Case C-28/08 P *Bavarian Lager II* [2010] ECR I-6055. For a similarly strict approach as regards the release of information on the beneficiaries of EU agricultural spending, see Joined Cases C-92/09 and C-93/09 *Volker and Schecke* [2010] ECR I-11063.

is also a separate Directive providing for additional specific rules relating to data protection in the field of electronic communications (known generally as the 'e-privacy Directive).[142] The Court of Justice has ruled that the e-privacy Directive does not preclude Member States from requiring Internet service providers to make available to copyright holders information on illegal downloads of their music, subject to the principle of proportionality.[143] Finally, there was also a separate Directive establishing a requirement for telecommunications service providers to retain data on their customers, for use by the law enforcement authorities.[144] This 'data retention' Directive was struck down by the CJEU in 2014 for violation of the rights to privacy and data protection, in a key judgment that attempts to reconcile privacy and security concerns.[145]

The Court of Justice has addressed the interface between the freedom of expression and assembly and police action to enforce EU law rules on free movement of goods, in a case in which national police permitted demonstrators to block the movement of goods between Member States for a period.[146] In the Court's view, Member States in principle must use police action to enforce EU free movement rights, which are a public interest which can in principle justify limitations on the rights set out in Articles 10 and 11 ECHR. On the other hand, the protection of human rights is a legitimate ground justifying a restriction by Member States upon free movement rights. To reconcile the conflicting rules, the Court stated that 'the interests involved must be weighed having regard to all the circumstances of the case in order to determine whether a fair balance was struck between those interests'.[147] In all the circumstances of this case, a correct balance was struck.

7.4 Impact of Other EU Law

JHA customs cooperation is obviously closely linked with non-JHA EU law, given the EU's powers to regulate customs issues both as regards trade between Member States and the external trade between the EU and the rest of the world. Moreover, there are a number of links between police cooperation and non-JHA EU law, particularly as regards free movement law and private sector links with law enforcement activities. There are also important non-JHA EU measures on, inter alia, transport security, infrastructure protection, anti-terrorist sanctions, anti-fraud measures, and civil protection.[148] It is still necessary to draw distinctions between these areas of law and policing measures even after the entry into force of the Treaty of Lisbon, at least due to the differences in territorial scope of the measures concerned.

---

[142] Dir 2002/58, [2002] OJ L 201/37, amended in 2009 (Dir 2009/136, [2009] OJ L 337/11).

[143] See Cases: C-275/06 *Promusicae* [2008] ECR I-271; C-70/10 *Scarlet Extended* [2011] ECR I-11959; and C-461/10 *Bonnier Audio*, ECLI:EU:C:2012:219.

[144] Dir 2006/24 ([2006] OJ L 105/1), discussed further in II.7.4.3.2 and II.7.6.3 below. The Court of Justice had upheld the internal market legal basis of this Dir: C-301/06 *Ireland v Council and EP* [2009] ECR I-593.

[145] See II.7.6.5 below.

[146] C-112/00 *Schmidberger* [2003] ECR I-5659. See further II.7.4.2 below.

[147] Para 81 of the judgment.

[148] Note also the application of Art 16 TFEU to data protection issues in both the former first pillar and the former third pillar (see II.7.2.4 above).

7.4.1 Customs cooperation

As regards customs cooperation, the EU has both a third pillar Convention (replaced by a Decision in 2009) establishing a Customs Information System as regards criminal offences, and a first pillar Regulation (adopted pursuant to Community law, as it then was) establishing that system as regards administrative offences.[149] The Regulation was amended in 2008, inter alia, in order to match the 2003 Protocol to the third pillar Convention.[150] A further amendment to the Regulation was adopted in 2015.[151]

When adopted in 1997, this Regulation had to have the legal base of Article 308 EC (the 'residual powers' clause),[152] but the Treaty of Amsterdam subsequently inserted a new Article 135 into the EC Treaty, allowing the adoption of measures using the co-decision procedure (as it then was) 'in order to strengthen customs cooperation between the Member States and between the latter and the Commission'. Until the entry into force of the Treaty of Lisbon, this Article expressly provided that '[t]hese measures shall not concern the application of national criminal law or national administration of justice' and that measures could only be taken '[w]ithin the scope of application of' the EC Treaty. The Treaty of Lisbon has since removed these restrictions.[153]

In practice, Article 135 EC was used to adopt several measures with an impact on security. Following the events of 11 September 2001, the US tightened its control of foreign goods shipped to the US on security grounds, and ultimately the EC (as it then was) agreed a treaty with the US on container security.[154] More broadly, the Commission issued a communication on the role of customs in ensuring security at the external borders,[155] and security-related amendments to the EU customs code were adopted in 2005.[156] EU customs powers are also relevant to combating breaches of intellectual property law.[157]

Furthermore, a Regulation requiring Member States to control the movement of large volumes of cash at external borders was also adopted in 2005.[158] This Regulation is complementary to EU legislation on money laundering, and requires persons to make a declaration if they are carrying more than €10,000 across the external border of a Member State.[159] The EU also adopted a new customs code in 2008,[160] and replaced it in 2013.[161]

---

[149] Reg 515/97 ([1997] OJ L 82/1). On the Convention (now Decision), and on the application of both measures, see II.7.6.1.2 below.

[150] Reg 766/2008 ([2008] OJ L 218/48).

[151] Reg 2015/1525 ([2015] OJ L 253/1). The legislation has not been codified.

[152] The Commission's argument for use of the EU's 'internal market' powers to adopt the Reg instead was rejected by the Court of Justice: Case C-209/97 *Commission v Council* [1999] ECR I-8067. The Treaty of Lisbon replaced Art 308 EC (following amendment) with Art 352 TFEU.

[153] See Art 33 TFEU.   [154] [2004] OJ L 304/32.

[155] COM (2003) 452, 24 July 2003. See the parallel issues concerning external border controls on persons (I:3.6).

[156] Reg 648/2005 ([2005] OJ L 117/13).

[157] See further II:5.4.1 and II:5.5.1.1 above, and also the Commission communication and Council resolution on this issue (COM (2005) 479, 11 Oct 2005 and [2006] OJ C 67/1).

[158] Reg 1889/2005 ([2005] OJ L 309/9), applicable from 15 June 2007 (Art 11). On the application of the Reg, see the Commission report (COM (2010) 455, 12 Aug 2010). Penalties for breach of these rules must be proportionate: Case C-255/14 *Chmielewski*, ECLI:EU:C:2015:47.

[159] On EU money laundering legislation, see II:5.5.1 above.

[160] Reg 450/2008 ([2008] OJ L 145/1).   [161] Reg 952/2013 ([2013] OJ L 269/1).

The cash checks Regulation and the revised customs code raised issues about the scope of EC powers (as they then were) as regards criminal law, and in particular the interpretation of the limitation on the scope of the former Article 135 EC—although it should be noted that both measures entailed the use of other legal bases as well. Since both measures were stripped of detailed proposed criminal provisions,[162] they fell within the scope of EC powers at the time.[163]

7.4.2 Police cooperation

As for police cooperation, it is clear that Member States can deny access to employment as a police officer to nationals of other Member States,[164] but policing employment falls within the scope of EU discrimination law. The result is that Member States' decisions to ban women from policing jobs are justiciable, and while certain police duties can be barred to women, it might be disproportionate to ban women from serving as reserve police officers and separate recruitment systems for male and female police officers might also breach EU law.[165] Furthermore, Member States are precluded from arguing that policing difficulties justify state action which restricts free movement rights. If they wish to argue that free movement rights must be suspended, or that their illegal state aid cannot be reclaimed, because of public unrest, they must show that such unrest will occur and that they are unable to meet the anticipated unrest from the police resources available to them.[166]

Moreover, the Court of Justice has ruled that Member States' discretion over police operations may be curtailed in cases of omissions, if Member States refrain from taking the necessary steps to ensure free movement of goods in spite of action by private parties.[167] According to the Court, Member States 'retain exclusive competence as regards the maintenance of public order and the safeguarding of internal security',[168] and thus have a 'margin of discretion' when deciding how best to combat threats to free movement, a 'fundamental principle' of the Treaty. But although the EU institutions cannot prescribe what policing operations the Member States must undertake to ensure free movement, the Court of Justice has asserted power to review whether a

---

[162] Compare the final cash checks Reg with the original proposal (COM (2002) 328, 25 June 2002) and the final customs code (2008 version) with Art 22 of the original proposal (COM (2005) 608, 30 Nov 2005).

[163] On this issue, see further II:5.4.1.1 above, which also discusses further the similar limitations on EC power set out in the former Art 280(4) EC (now Art 325 TFEU after the Treaty of Lisbon). On the legal base of the cash checks legislation, see the 1st Report of the House of Commons Select Committee on European Scrutiny (2004–05), with further references.

[164] See Case 149/79 *Commission v Belgium* [1979] ECR 1845 (night watchmen working for the State excluded from free movement rights); Commission communication on Art 39(4) EC ([1988] OJ C 72/2).

[165] Cases 222/84 *Johnston* [1986] ECR 1651 and 318/86 *Commission v France* [1988] ECR 3659.

[166] Case 231/83 *Cullet* [1985] ECR 305; Case C-280/95 *Commission v Italy* (tax breaks for truckers) [1998] ECR I-259. See also *R. v Coventry City Council, ex parte Phoenix Aviation and Others* [1995] All ER 37 (QB) and subsequently Case C-175/97 *Commission v France* [1998] ECR I-963.

[167] Case C-265/95 *Commission v France* (revolting farmers) [1997] ECR I-6959.

[168] The Court's wording is almost identical to the initial Art K.2(2) EU and the previous Art 100c(5) EC, which were in force at the time of the judgment, although it made no reference to those provisions. As noted above (II.7.2.2.1 and II.7.2.3), these provisions are identical to the subsequent Art 33 EU, and now Art 72 TFEU.

Member State has 'adopted appropriate measures' to that end. In *Commission v France*, ongoing attacks by farmers' groups on foreign produce had been met by relative inaction by the French police, and while the Court accepted in principle that police forces might appropriately refrain from interfering in a dispute for fear of sparking broader unrest, this could only apply to a specific incident and the Member State (as in *Cullet* and *Commission v Italy*) bears the burden of proof in showing that it would not be able to respond effectively. Therefore, France had breached Article 28 EC taken with Article 10 EC (the 'solidarity' clause).[169]

This principle raises two important questions. First, what limits exists upon Member States' obligation to spend their police resources in order to ensure the free movement of goods? The UK courts wrestled with this question when one county police force decided that it would only offer policing on certain days to protect the legal export of veal crates from a nearby port, because of the huge cost of preventing the exports from being blocked by animal rights protesters. The exporters sued to quash this decision and claim damages. Ultimately, the House of Lords, hearing the appeal after the Court of Justice's *Commission v France* ruling, dismissed the case.[170] Lord Slynn declined to rule on whether the police force had violated Articles 29 and 10 EC (now Article 35 TFEU and Article 4(3), revised TEU), because even if it had, it could defend its relative inaction under the 'public policy' defence of Article 30 EC (now Article 36 TFEU), because it had done as much as it reasonably and proportionately could in light of other legitimate claims upon it. Lord Cooke ruled that the police force had breached Article 29 EC taken alone, but could defend its inaction under Article 30, even after embarking upon a slightly more stringent review than Lord Slynn had undertaken. However, Lord Hoffman ruled that the force's inaction was not a measure which could be challenged under Articles 29 and 10 EC, because under the circumstances, the exporters' rights were not directly effective. With great respect, this does not dispose of the issue (even if it is correct), because damages can still be claimed under EU law even if a Member State breaches an EU law right which is not directly effective.[171] Lord Hoffman further took the view that when relying on the exception in Article 30, Member States could not invoke local police force discretion but only national-level discretion—a *caveat* that would make it difficult for locally-based police forces (like most English forces) to rely on Article 30. The multiplicity of reasoning in this case did not clarify matters much for lower British courts that might be faced with similar disputes in future.[172]

In comparison with the *Commission v France* ruling, the later judgment in *Schmidberger* sets out circumstances in which police inaction is justified, in particular due to the human rights context of that case.[173] In this case: the demonstration had been authorized by the authorities; the restriction on free movement was limited in

---

[169] These provisions are now Art 34 TFEU and Art 4(3), revised TEU, respectively.

[170] *R. v Chief Constable for Sussex, ex parte International Traders' Ferry* [1995] 3 CMLR 485 (QB); [1997] 2 CMLR 164 (CA); [1998] 3 WLR 1260 (HL).

[171] Joined Cases C-6/90 and 9/90 *Francovich and Bonifaci* [1991] ECR I-5357.

[172] Lord Nolan agreed with Lord Slynn, while Lord Hope problematically agreed with *both* Lord Slynn and Lord Hoffman.

[173] Case C-112/00 [2003] ECR I-5659, paras 82–93 of the judgment.

time and space; the demonstration was not aiming to restrict trade in foreign goods per se (or indeed to destroy foreign goods); the authorities took steps to limit the disruption to free movement; there was no creation of a 'general climate of insecurity'; and the alternatives to permitting the demonstration might have resulted in more serious disruption to free movement and would have impinged more upon the freedoms of expression and assembly.

In the meantime, there was legislative action by the EU, in the form of a Council Regulation and a Resolution of the Council and the Member States adopted in 1998.[174] The former requires Member States to inform other Member States and the Commission of obstacles to trade, which may include a Member State's inaction in response to acts of private parties, to take 'all necessary and proportionate steps' to assure free movement, and to reply very quickly to possible urgent requests from the Commission to take action. Fundamental rights, such as the right or freedom to strike, are expressly protected. The accompanying Resolution makes clear that the Commission requests under the Regulation will be part of the infringement procedure under Article 226 EC (now Article 258 TFEU), thus speeding up that procedure considerably. Member States also undertook to inform injured parties of effective remedies for their damages; furthermore, the Resolution allows for possible emergency Council meetings and raises the possibility of amending the Court of Justice's Rules of Procedure to expedite the hearing of relevant infringement actions which reach the Court. However, the Commission is not required to apply the procedure in the Regulation before using Article 258 TFEU.[175] A Commission report on the application of the Regulation expressed some disappointment at the lack of clarity in the Regulation and the lack of full implementation by Member States, but the further actions suggested by the Commission (clarification and/or amendment of the Regulation) have not materialized.[176]

EU free movement law thus has an important impact upon the interests which national policing must protect and upon the operational decisions of police forces. It requires the interests of free trade to be protected in principle and in practice. Although national police forces have historically represented the inner core of state sovereignty, they can no longer be deployed purely in pursuit of national goals, with purely national decisions about operations and without any accountability to 'foreign' citizens, governments, or courts. As we shall see, EU policing law measures have affected national policing law even more substantially.

7.4.3 The private sector and security

7.4.3.1 Private security industry

Despite its links with law enforcement authorities, the sizable and significant private security industry essentially falls outside the scope of JHA law, due to its nature as an economic activity. The Court of Justice has delivered a series of judgments against

---

[174] Reg 2679/98 ([1998] OJ L 337/8); [1998] OJ L 337/10 (Resolution).
[175] Case C-320/03 *Commission v Austria* [2005] ECR I-9871.
[176] COM (2001) 160, 22 Mar 2001.

various national restrictions which infringe, in the field of private security, the free movement of workers, freedom of establishment, and the freedom to provide services set out in the previous Articles 39, 43 and 49 EC (now Articles 45, 49, and 56 TFEU).[177] In these cases, the Court has consistently ruled that private security activities do not fall within the exceptions for 'public employment' or 'official authority' in the relevant Treaty Articles, because private security staff are not state employees and merely contributing to public security does not constitute an exercise of official authority. Nor do the Treaty exceptions for 'public policy, public security or public health' apply, because those exceptions do not remove entire sectors of economic activity from the scope of the free movement rules.

More precisely, Member States cannot justify directly discriminatory rules which require managers or staff, including self-employed persons, to have the nationality of the host State, or which ban foreign companies altogether from providing security services.[178] Residence requirements for managers or staff are not justified, since checks on non-residents could be carried out and guarantee requirements could be imposed on non-residents.[179] Similarly, host Member States cannot require security companies to have a place of business in the host State (or parts of it),[180] or demand prior authorization or a licence for the company, managers, or staff from the host State government,[181] to insist on a bank guarantee or to control the prices of private security services.[182] Nor can a host State: require staff to carry a special national identity card;[183] ban natural persons from providing security services or require persons providing security services to have a minimum share capital;[184] regulate the numbers of staff providing a private security service (except as regards the transport of explosives);[185] insist that security staff make an oath of allegiance to the host State;[186] or make security staff hold a professional certificate issued by the host State, although the Commission has generally failed to establish that Member States have infringed EU rules on mutual recognition of qualifications in this sector.[187]

Also, the private security sector is subject to EU rules on posted workers, which must be applied more flexibly in this sector as compared to construction.[188] However, private security has been excluded from general EU legislation on the provision of services.[189]

---

[177] Cases: C-114/97 *Commission v Spain (I)* [1998] ECR I-6717; C-355/98 *Commission v Belgium* [2000] ECR I-1221; C-283/99 *Commission v Italy (I)* [2001] ECR I-4363; C-171/02 *Commission v Portugal* [2004] ECR I-5645; C-189/03 *Commission v Netherlands* [2004] ECR I-9289; C-514/03 *Commission v Spain (II)* [2006] ECR I-963; and C-465/05 *Commission v Italy (II)* [2007] ECR I-11091.

[178] *Commission v Spain (I)* and *Commission v Italy (I)*, n 177 above.

[179] *Commission v Spain (I)* and *Commission v Belgium*, n 177 above.

[180] *Commission v Belgium, Commission v Portugal*, and *Commission v Italy (II)*, n 177 above.

[181] *Commission v Belgium, Commission v Portugal, Commission v Netherlands, Commission v Spain (II)*, and *Commission v Italy (II)*, n 177 above.

[182] *Commission v Italy (II)*, n 177 above.

[183] *Commission v Belgium* and *Commission v Netherlands*, n 177 above.

[184] *Commission v Portugal* and *Commission v Spain (II)*, n 177 above.

[185] *Commission v Spain (II)* and *Commission v Italy (II)*, n 177 above.

[186] *Commission v Italy (II)*, n 177 above.

[187] *Commission v Portugal* and *Commission v Spain (II)*, n 177 above. However, in the latter case, Spain infringed EU law as regards recognition of the qualifications of private detectives.

[188] Case C-165/98 *Mazzoleni* [2001] ECR I-2189.

[189] See Dir 2006/123 ([2006] OJ L 376/36), Art 2(2)(k).

Finally, the private security sector is subject to a Council Recommendation adopted in 2002,[190] which encourages Member States to exchange experience and best practices regarding the handling of information supplied by the private security sector. The Recommendation was adopted in place of a proposed Decision,[191] which was rightly criticized for infringing EC competence (as it then was), since it concerned the regulation and activities of the private security sector; it is clearly implicit in the Court's case law that only first pillar measures could then address such issues.

An appropriate degree of regulation of private security activities is in the public interest in order to guarantee appropriate ethical standards, and in particular to ensure that no convicted criminals or persons disqualified in disgrace from the police or military take up private security activities. In the absence of at least an EU framework for exchanging information on national legislation or the qualifications of individuals, there is a risk that justified national regulation of private security could be undercut. There may even be a case for establishing common minimum EU standards for regulation of private security activities. It is unfortunate that the Commission has concentrated on infringement actions without also examining these broader issues.

7.4.3.2 *Private sector security cooperation*

In several areas, controversial EU legislation requires the private security to take extensive—and expensive—measures in pursuit of security objectives.[192] In particular, EU law requires the passenger transport industry to transmit information on passengers to Member States' immigration authorities (and non-EU law enforcement bodies), and the financial services industry to transmit information on its customers to American law enforcement bodies. It previously required the telecommunications industry to retain substantial amounts of data on its customers, because that data may be of later use to law enforcement agencies, but the measure concerned was struck down by the CJEU.[193]

First of all, as for the legal bases applicable to these measures, the Court of Justice ruled that the transfer of passenger name records (PNR) to the USA was outside the scope of the data protection Directive adopted by the EC (as it then was), because the basic purpose of the measures concerned was to regulate the use of that data by the American law enforcement bodies concerned.[194] On the other hand, the Court ruled that the EC Directive (as it then was) on data retention by the telecom industry fell within the EC's internal market powers, because this legislation essentially concerned the regulation of private sector activity, not the use of the data by the law enforcement authorities.[195]

---

[190] [2002] OJ C 153/1.
[191] [2002] OJ C 42/15.
[192] The details and merits of these measures are considered in II.7.6.3 and II.7.6.5 below.
[193] On the external relations context of the latter two measures, see II.7.11 below.
[194] Joined Cases C-317/04 and C-318/04 *EP v Council and Commission* [2006] ECR I-4721.
[195] Case C-301/06 *Ireland v Council and EP* [2009] ECR I-593, concerning Dir 2006/24 ([2006] OJ L 105/54). The relevant Directive was later struck down on human rights grounds instead: see II:7.6.5 below.

It might be argued that these judgments are inconsistent, although in principle the distinction between the regulation of the use of the data concerned and the regulation of its initial collection is defensible. But with respect, the better approach would have been to uphold the Community's powers to regulate both issues, given the impact of both measures on the competition between private sector actors (an argument which was decisive in the data retention judgment, but dismissed in the PNR judgment), and (by analogy) the Court's ruling in another case that if a measure fell partly within the scope of EC law and partly within the scope of the second pillar (as they then were), the Community's powers always took priority.[196] This reasoning is comparable to Court judgments regarding the EU's common commercial policy, where a measure regulating foreign trade has a foreign or defence policy impact.[197]

7.4.4 Transport security and infrastructure protection

Following the terrorist offences of 11 September 2001, the EU institutions were quick to adopt a Regulation on the security of civil aviation, addressing the safety of airports and aircraft, including a requirement for Commission monitoring and the development of national aviation safety plans.[198] In light of experience with the application of the Regulation, a revised Regulation was adopted in 2008.[199] A series of Commission implementing measures address in more detail issues such as screening of staff, searching of passengers, the performance standards of X-ray machines, and items prohibited on board aircraft.[200] Initially most of these measures were not public, including the rules setting out which items passengers were prohibited from carrying on board aircraft. Following prosecution of a man who carried on board a tennis racket in breach of these unpublished rules, the Court of Justice ruled that those rules were unenforceable,[201] and they were mostly duly published.[202] Subsequently, the EU institutions adopted a Regulation on maritime security and a Directive on port security;[203] there is also extensive legislation governing the transport of dangerous goods.[204]

---

[196] Case C-91/05 *Commission v Council* [2008] ECR I-3651.

[197] See Cases C-70/94 *Werner* [1995] ECR I-3189, C-83/94 *Liefer* [1995] ECR I-3231, and C-124/95 *Centro-com* [1997] ECR I-81.

[198] Reg 2320/2002 ([2002] OJ L 355/1).

[199] Reg 300/2008 ([2008] OJ L 97/72). The Commission has proposed to replace this Reg with an amended version: COM (2015) 613, 7 Dec 2015.

[200] See most recently Commission Reg 2015/187 ([2015] OJ L 31/18). For an overview of these measures and of the application of the Reg in practice, see the Commission's annual reports (most recently, COM (2015) 360, 23 July 2015). See also the Commission communication on body scanners (COM (2010) 311, 15 June 2010).

[201] Case C-345/06 *Heinrich* [2009] ECR I-1659.

[202] Commission Reg 820/2008 ([2008] OJ L 221/8).

[203] Respectively Reg 725/2004 ([2004] OJ L 129/6) and Dir 2005/65 ([2005] OJ L 310/28); Member States had to implement the Directive by 15 June 2007 (Art 18). See also the earlier communication on maritime security (COM (2003) 229, 2 May 2003), the report on financing transport security (COM (2006) 431, 1 Aug 2008), and the report on the application of the Dir (COM (2009) 2, 20 Jan 2009). On the external competence resulting from the Reg, see Case C-45/07 *Commission v Greece* [2009] ECR I-701.

[204] Dir 2008/68 ([2008] OJ L 260/13); and see further: <http://ec.europa.eu/transport/road_safety/topics/dangerous_goods/index_en.htm>.

Furthermore, due to the risk that terrorist attacks would affect energy, food, or water supplies, the Council adopted a Directive establishing a European critical infrastructure protection programme in 2008.[205] Since the entry into force of that Treaty, any further measures in this field could be adopted on the basis of the ordinary legislative procedure, as a civil protection measure.[206]

7.4.5 Anti-terrorist sanctions

The EU's well-known and controversial anti-terrorist sanctions measures address three categories of persons and groups. [207] First of all, there are measures establishing sanctions against persons or groups deemed by the UN Security Council to be connected with against Al-Qaeda and the Taliban. For this first category, before the entry into force of the Treaty of Lisbon, the EU adopted a foreign policy measure which is implemented by an EC (now EU) measure establishing a list of the persons concerned.[208] The measures (as amended) list the persons and groups considered to be terrorists; to this end, the EU has simply listed those persons and groups which a committee of the Security Council considers to be terrorists, apparently on the basis of allegations from Western intelligence agencies. It appears that the names of any non-EU citizens on the UN list are also added to the SIS, in order to list them as persons to be denied entry into the EU.[209]

It was assumed in practice that, before the entry into force of the Treaty of Lisbon this EC legislation had to be adopted on the basis of the prior Article 308 EC, which gave the EC (as it when was) the residual power to adopt measures which impacted upon the common market. The more specific power for the EC to adopt measures relating to economic and financial sanctions against third States (Article 301 EC) was rejected as unsuitable, since the persons and groups concerned did not control States. This approach was approved by the Court of Justice.[210] After the entry into force of the Treaty of Lisbon, there were two possible competing legal bases for the legislation concerned: Article 215 TFEU, which provides for the adoption of economic and financial sanctions against third States *or* non-State entities, and Article 75 TFEU, which provides for the adoption of financial sanctions against terrorists. The latter legal base, which is within the JHA provisions of the TFEU, gives more power to the EP. According to the CJEU, Article 215 TFEU is the correct legal base for such measures.[211]

---

[205] Dir 2008/114 ([2008] OJ L 345/75). Member States had to implement this Directive by 12 Jan 2011 (Art 12). Also on this subject, see the earlier Commission communication (COM (2004) 702, 20 Oct 2004) and Green Paper (COM (2005) 576, 17 Nov 2005), and the Commission communications on critical infrastructure protection (COM (2006) 786, 12 Dec 2006) and protection of critical infrastructure from cyber-attacks (COM (2009) 149, 30 Mar 2009).

[206] See the discussion of Art 196 TFEU and of other civil protection measures, in II.7.4.7 below.

[207] From a huge literature, see C Eckes, *EU Counter-Terrorist Policies and Fundamental Rights: The Case of Individual Sanctions* (OUP, 2009) and the contributions in (2009) 29 YEL with further references.

[208] Reg 881/2002 ([2002] OJ L 139/9), replacing Reg 337/2000 ([2000] OJ L 43/1).

[209] Council doc 9358/02, 28 May 2002. The legislation establishing SIS II provides expressly for this practice (see I:3.7).

[210] Joined Cases C-402/05 P and C-415/05 P *Kadi and Al Barakaat* [2008] ECR I-6351.

[211] Case C-130/10 *EP v Council*, ECLI:EU:C:2012:472. See the more detailed discussion of the legal base issue in II:2.2.3.2 above.

The other categories of sanctions concern those persons or groups which the EU has *autonomously* decided are terrorists, and who are either based outside the EU (the second category, ie 'international terrorists') or inside the EU (the third category, ie 'domestic terrorists'). This policy began following the terrorist attacks of 11 September 2001, and comprises a package of four acts which were originally adopted in December 2001,[212] and have subsequently been amended.[213] The package includes two Common Positions adopted jointly on the basis of the prior Articles 15 and 34 EU (therefore addressing both foreign police and police/criminal law issues), an EC (now EU) Regulation implementing the second Common Position, and an EC (now EU) Decision further implementing that Regulation.

As to the substance, the first Common Position essentially transposes UN Security Council Resolution 1373/2001 on the suppression of terrorism, although the Common Position makes several provisions of the Resolution mandatory,[214] and alters the obligation for States to refrain from active or passive support for terrorism into an obligation for *individuals* to refrain from such support.[215] Since the Resolution does not define 'terrorism', it is equally unclear how the Common Position defines the term.

The second Common Position does define terrorism, by copying the definition that had been agreed by the Council in the context of the (then) proposed Framework Decision on terrorism, since adopted in June 2002.[216] However, the Common Position does not include the human rights provisions set out in the preamble and main text of the Framework Decision or in the statements attached to it. Nor it is limited (as is the Framework Decision) to acts committed on the territory of the EU or against EU citizens, institutions, or Member States. This distinction is crucial since there is no legal or ethical case for using political violence in a democracy, but the position may arguably be different in a non-democratic State.[217]

The impact of this second Common Position is that (by means of the Regulation and Decision), sanctions consisting of a freezing of all assets and a ban on the transfer of any sort of funds (including wages and social benefits) must be applied to all *international* terrorists, while *domestic* terrorist persons and groups are not covered by such sanctions. Both the international and domestic terrorists are subject to intensified police and judicial cooperation, an issue considered later in this chapter.[218]

The obvious problem with these measures is that persons and groups are listed as terrorists without any criminal trial or any alternative form of hearing at which they could dispute the categorization. As the result of the listing, for the first and second categories of persons and groups, is the freezing of all assets and income in the EU, except for a derogation to meet basic needs, the impact is substantial and indefinite. The sanctions were inevitably challenged in the EU courts directly by some of the persons and

---

[212] Common Positions 2001/930 and 931 ([2001] OJ L 344/90 and 93); Reg 2580/2001 ([2001] OJ L 344/70) and Decision 2001/927 ([2001] OJ L 344/83).

[213] The latest text of the second Common Position (now a Decision, after the entry into force of the Treaty of Lisbon) is in [2015] OJ L 82/107.

[214] Compare Arts 13–17 of the Common Position to para 3 of the Resolution.

[215] Compare Art 4 of the Common Position to para 2(a) of the Resolution.

[216] On this definition, see II:5.5.1.2 above.   [217] See ibid.

[218] See II.7.6.3 and II.7.7.4 below.

groups subjected to them, and through the national courts by other persons and groups indirectly affected by them. Moreover, the EU sanctions regime was questioned in the context of the broader public debate about the proportionality and legality of the international community's response to the 11 September terrorist attacks.

First of all, as for the first category of alleged terrorists (persons or groups with supposed links to Al-Qaeda or the Taliban, in the view of the Security Council), the Court of First Instance (as it then was) would not, in effect, rule on the legality of the listing of such persons or groups, on the grounds that the EC/EU was bound by the decisions of the Security Council, which took priority over all other legal obligations as a matter of international law. In the view of the Court, it would be possible for *jus cogens* principles to take priority over Security Council decisions, but the actions of the Security Council did not constitute a breach of those principles.[219]

However, on appeal to the Court of Justice, these rulings were overturned.[220] In the view of the Court, the EU could not avoid a full review of the legality of its decisions, even where its actions were based on resolutions of the Security Council, due to the fundamental rule that EU measures had to be accountable from a human rights perspective. As to the merits of the case, the procedure for listing the persons and groups concerned had 'patently' not respected the rights of the defence and did not provide for effective judicial review, since the persons and groups concerned had a right to know the reasons for the listing either at the time they were listed or as soon as possible thereafter. There was, however, no right to be told the reasons for the listing in advance, since the listing needed to have a 'surprise effect' in order to achieve the purpose of the rules. While considerations of safety and international relations meant that some information could legitimately be withheld from the persons concerned, this did 'not mean, with regard to the principle of effective judicial protection, that [sanctions] measures... escape all review by the Community judicature once it has been claimed that the act laying them down concerns national security and terrorism.' The failure to communicate any evidence to the persons or groups concerned meant that their rights to be heard, and to effective judicial protection, had been breached. For similar reasons, their right to property had also been breached on procedural grounds, although substantively the restriction on their right to property was justified in the public interest.

Given that this judgment was decided on essentially procedural grounds, the Council and Commission took the view that the persons and groups concerned could simply be re-listed as terrorists, following the communication to them of the reasons for the listings. This re-listing was in turn successfully challenged.[221] Moreover, the basic framework for adopting sanctions measures against persons or groups allegedly linked to Al-Qaeda has been amended to take account of the *Kadi* judgment, in order to provide

---

[219] Cases T-306/01 *Yusuf* [2005] ECR II-3633 and T-315/01 *Kadi* [2005] ECR II-3649, followed in Cases T-49/04 *Hassan* [2006] ECR II-52* and T-253/02 *Ayadi* [2006] ECR II-2139.

[220] *Kadi and Al Barakaat* (n 210 above), followed in Joined Cases C-399/06 P and C-403/06 P *Hassan and Ayadi* [2009] ECR I-11393, Case T-318/01 *Othman* [2009] ECR II-1627, and Joined Cases T-135-138/06 *Al-Faqih and others* [2010] ECR I-208*.

[221] Cases T-85/09 *Kadi II* [2010] ECR II-5177 (General Court) and C-584/10 P, C-593/10 P and C-595/10 P, ECLI:EU:C:2013:518 (Court of Justice). The Commission was subsequently condemned for failure to act to de-list names from the list: Case T-306/10 *Yusef*, ECLI:EU:T:2014:14.

for a statement of reasons for persons or groups added to the list in the future, as well as those already on the list who request one. In the latter case the Commission will review the sanctions decision if the persons or groups concerned make observations, and forward such observations to the UN Sanctions Committee; it does not have the power to remove the person or group from the list (or to refuse to accept a new listing made by the Security Council).[222]

Furthermore, there have been references from national courts concerning the extent of the financial sanctions as regards third parties. The Court of Justice has confirmed that the sanctions extend to a ban on completing the process of selling a property to the persons or groups concerned,[223] and to raising money for a listed organization, although a prosecution to this end is tainted by the illegality of the listings decision.[224] On the other hand, the EU rules do not require Member States to refuse to pay social benefits to the family members of the persons concerned.[225]

As for the second category of alleged terrorists (ie the 'international terrorists' designated by the EU), right from the outset the Court of First Instance (as it then was) accepted to rule on the merits of challenges to the EU listings, given that the names of the persons and groups concerned had been decided on by the EU institutions, not designated by the UN Security Council. The leading case is *OMPI I*, in which the Court decided from the outset that the right to a hearing, to reasons, and to effective judicial protection apply to the second category of sanctions measures.[226] The basic rules in the relevant legislation require the listing to take place on the basis of 'precise information or material in the relevant file which indicates that a decision has been taken by a competent authority' as regards the persons or groups concerned, 'irrespective of whether it concerns the instigation of investigations or prosecution for a terrorist act, an attempt to perpetrate, participate in or facilitate such an act based on serious and credible evidence or clues, or condemnation for such deeds'; a 'competent authority' is a judicial authority or its equivalent, and the list has to be reviewed every six months.[227] There is therefore a two-step procedure, with a right to a fair hearing at both the national and EU level. At EU level, the person concerned has the right to a hearing as regards whether there is information in the file indicating that a relevant decision has been taken by a national competent authority (in the case of an initial listing), or the reasons for maintaining the listing (following a review). This does not entail a review of the merits of the national decision, which is in principle a matter for national law and procedure. As with the first category of sanctions, the initial decision to freeze funds can be taken in advance of a hearing; but the decisions to maintain the persons or groups on the sanctions list cannot. The statement of reasons must set out precisely how the

---

[222] Reg 1286/2009 ([2009] OJ L 346/42), particularly new Arts 7a and 7c. This raises the question as to whether the Commission's review of the listing can at least be challenged in the EU courts; the basic right of judicial review surely suggests that it can. This Reg was unsuccessfully challenged by the EP on legal base grounds, n 211 above.

[223] Case C-117/06 *Möllendorf and Möllendorf-Niehuus* [2007] ECR I-8361.

[224] Case C-550/09 *E and F* [2010] ECR I-6213, by analogy (the case concerned a group covered by the second category of sanctions measures).

[225] Case C-340/08 *M and Others* [2010] ECR I-3913.   [226] Case T-228/02 [2006] ECR II-4665.

[227] Art 1(4) to (6) of Common Position 2001/931, n 212 above.

criteria for imposing the sanctions are satisfied. Applying these rules to the case, there had been no communication of evidence or reasons at all—it was not even clear which national decision was the basis of the Council's listing decision—and so judicial review was impossible; the decision was therefore invalid on procedural grounds.

This case was followed by a number of other annulments of decisions to list various groups and persons as terrorists, because of the same procedural flaws.[228] However, from 2007, the Council improved its procedural standards in light of the Court's case law, and gave a statement of reasons to each group or person on its list. A series of new challenges have followed, in which the Court of First Instance (as it then was) has ruled that there are good reasons for a listing if a person or group has been convicted of terrorist offences,[229] but that conversely the Council had to take account of subsequent developments, in particular the termination of the national decision which gave rise to the original listing.[230] The Court also clarified that national court judgments relating to immigration law issues did not constitute a decision which could justify a listing at EU level.[231] Certainly a national decision cannot be a valid reason for an EU listing if the Member State concerned refused to supply any of the reasons for that decision.[232] On the other hand, a decision by a prosecutor to investigate someone for terrorist offences was sufficient.[233] Listing decisions have also been struck down for inadequate reasoning,[234] and for not sufficiently checking whether a listing originating from a third State met sufficient human rights standards.[235]

As for references from national courts, as noted above, the Court of Justice has confirmed that raising money for a listed organization falls within the scope of the sanctions, although a prosecution to this end is tainted by the illegality of the listings decisions taken before the Council's procedures were improved in 2007.[236] The references relating to the first category of sanctions (as regards property sanctions and family members) are also relevant by analogy.[237] The Court also took a lenient view toward the restriction of broadcasts by alleged terrorist organizations.[238]

---

[228] Cases: T-47/03 *Sison v Council* [2007] ECR II-2047; Case T-327/03 *Al-Aqsa v Council* [2007] ECR II-79*; T-229/02 *PKK v Council* [2008] ECR II-45*; and T-253/04 *Kongra-Gel and Others v Council* [2008] ECR II-46*. The *PKK* case had initially been dismissed as inadmissible by the CFI (Case T-229/02 *PKK and KNK v Council* [2005] ECR II-539), on the grounds of the lack of legal form of the group concerned, but the Court of Justice overturned that decision on appeal, on the highly convincing grounds that if the group concerned has sufficient legal existence to be subject to sanctions, it must have sufficient legal existence to challenge them (Case C-229/05 P *PKK and KNK* [2007] ECR I-439).

[229] Joined Cases T-37/07 and T-323/07 *El-Morabit*, judgment of 3 Sep 2009, unreported.

[230] Case T-256/07 *PMOI II* [2008] ECR II-3019. See, however, Joined Cases C-539/10 P and C-550/10 P *Al Aqsa*, ECLI:EU:C:2012:711, in which the CJEU (overturning Case T-348/07 *Al-Aqsa* [2010] ECR II-4575) ruled that a repeal of a national decision did not necessarily mean that a group had to be removed from the EU list.

[231] Case T-341/07 *Sison II* [2009] ECR II-3625. The Council did not act sufficiently unlawfully for the applicant in this case to claim damages successfully, however: [2011] ECR II-7915.

[232] Case T-284/08 *PMOI III* [2008] ECR II-3487, which was unsuccessfully appealed by France (Case C-27/09 P, [2011] ECR I-13427).

[233] Case T-49/07 *Fahas* [2010] ECR II-5557.

[234] Case T-400/10 *Hamas*, ECLI:EU:T:2014:1095, on appeal to the Court of Justice (C-79/15 P).

[235] Case T-208/11 and C-508/11 *LTTE*, ECLI:EU:T:2014:885, on appeal to the Court of Justice (C-599/14 P).

[236] *E and F*, n 224 above.   [237] *Möllendorf and M*, nn 223 and 225 above.

[238] Joined Cases C-244/10 and C-245/10 *Mesopotamia Broadcasting* [2011] ECR I-8777.

Finally, as for the third category of alleged terrorist groups and persons (the 'domestic terrorists' subjected only to police and judicial cooperation by the EU, but not to economic sanctions), the European Court of Human Rights dismissed their arguments because they were not sufficiently affected by EU measures to claim 'victim' status,[239] and the Court of First Instance dismissed their claim for damages as regards the EU measures due to its lack of jurisdiction.[240] On appeal, the Court of Justice confirmed that the EU courts had no jurisdiction to hear damages actions against the EU institutions as regards third pillar Common Positions, but referred to the prospect of bringing such claims before national courts. The Court of Justice also stated that Common Positions could not in themselves have any binding impact on individuals, and the validity of any Common Position which nevertheless appeared to have such an effect could be referred to the Court of Justice by national courts.[241]

The EU Courts' case law on these issues is transformed from the original position of effectively refusing to review the EU's sanctions decisions. As regards listings made by the UN Security Council, the *Kadi* judgments of the Court of Justice are highly welcome, but arguably, in the absence of sufficient procedural rights for individuals at UN level, it must be possible in principle for the EU to withdraw or to refuse to apply a UN decision in some cases, where the evidence available is insufficient. As for the second category of sanctions, the case law of the EU courts broadly sets the right balance, but it might be desirable to review the underlying rules relating to national decisions, in order to ensure that basic procedural standards are being applied before a listing is made,[242] for instance to set reasonable time limits to begin or conclude prosecutions in order to justify continued listings. Finally, as for the third category, the allegation of terrorism is serious enough that it must be judicially reviewable, even in the absence of parallel financial sanctions against the alleged terrorists. Decisions in this category made before the Treaty of Lisbon arguably already met the criteria in the *SEGI* judgment for judicial review of the listings, and certainly any decision made or confirmed after that Treaty entered into force is indisputably reviewable.

7.4.6 OLAF

Following extensive criticism of the Commission's anti-fraud unit, UCLAF, created in 1987, the EU institutions decided to create a replacement body, OLAF, pursuant to legislation adopted in 1999.[243] Following an assessment of the functioning of OLAF,[244]

---

[239] Decision in *Segi and others v 15 Member States* (Reports 2002-V).

[240] Order of the Court of First Instance in Case T-338/02 *SEGI and others* [2004] ECR II-1647. See by analogy also the order in Case T-299/04 *Selmani* [2005] ECR II-20*.

[241] Cases C-354/04 P *Gestoras pro Amnistia* [2007] ECR I-1579 and C-355/04 P *SEGI* [2007] ECR I-1657. See the discussion of the legal effect and jurisdiction issues in II:2.2.2 above.

[242] Cf the legislation being adopted in order to underpin mutual recognition in criminal matters: see II:4.6 above.

[243] Reg 1073/1999, Inter-Institutional Agreement, and Commission Decision ([1999] OJ L 136). For the background, see the first edition of this book, pp 204–05.

[244] COM (2003) 154, 2 Apr 2003. See the Council conclusions on the report (press release of Environment Council, 22 Dec 2003). See also the critical Court of Auditors report on OLAF ([2005] OJ C 202/1). OLAF also allegedly withheld information from the Commission as regards to allegations of corruption at Eurostat, the EU's statistics body, and allegedly libelled a journalist.

this legislation was overhauled in 2013,[245] and the Commission has proposed further amendments to increase procedural guarantees.[246]

OLAF, an independent body but situated within the Commission, has both an 'internal affairs' function within the EU, examining allegations of fraud, and an 'external' function examining allegations within the Member States within the context of EU law. However, it does not have police or prosecution powers, and must hand over information to national authorities for prosecution and/or EU bodies to take disciplinary action. It also has a role in drafting relevant EU legislation and in EU operations, for example operating the Customs Information System (CIS) and contributing to combating euro counterfeiting.[247] OLAF's powers extend to all EU bodies; attempts by the EU's Central Bank and Investment Bank to avoid OLAF's remit were illegal.[248] An attempt by MEPs to challenge the principle that OLAF could search their offices was dismissed as inadmissible.[249] OLAF's powers to conduct investigations in Member States are set out in an earlier Regulation.[250]

For their part, the EU courts have begun to exercise effective judicial control over OLAF in the context of staff cases,[251] but their review of OLAF's actions towards journalists has been less searching.[252] The General Court's conclusion that a Commissioner was not really forced to resign after an OLAF investigation is hugely unconvincing,[253] and the judicial review of access to OLAF documents has not been rigorous.[254]

OLAF (and its predecessor) have faced difficulties accomplishing their objectives in practice due to complaints about their ineffectiveness, as well as concerns about the procedural rights of those under investigation, including the (in)adequacy of judicial control by the EU courts. In part, these difficulties are connected to the underlying dispute between Member States as to the division of power in this area, and in particular whether the EU should develop a public prosecutor and/or develop the role of Europol and Eurojust instead.[255]

---

[245] Reg 883/2013 ([2013] OJ L 248/1).   [246] COM (2014) 340, 11 June 2014.

[247] On the CIS, see II.7.6.1.2 below. For an overview of OLAF, see House of Lords, Committee on European Union, *Strengthening OLAF, the European Anti-Fraud Office*, 24th Report, 2003–04.

[248] Cases C-15/00 *Commission v ECB* [2003] ECR I-7147 and C-15/00 *Commission v EIB* [2003] ECR I-7281.

[249] Case T-17/00 *Rothley* [2002] ECR I-579 (see interim measures ruling, [2000] ECR II-2085), upheld on appeal (Case C-167/02 P *Rothley* [2004] ECR I-3149).

[250] Reg 2185/96 ([1996] OJ L 292/2).

[251] See Cases: T-215/02 *Gómez-Reino* [2003] ECR II-1685; C-471/02 P (R) *Gómez-Reino* [2003] ECR I-3207; T-96/03 *Camos Grau* [2004] ECR II-707; and particularly T-309/03 *Camos Grau* [2006] ECR II-1173 and T-48/05 *Franchet and Byk* [2008] ECR II-1585. However, see the appeal judgment in T-261/09 P *Violetti*, ECLI:EU:T:2010:215 (overturning the Civil Service Tribunal judgment in F-5/05 and 7/05 *Violetti*, ECLI:EU:F:2009:39) and the judgments in Case C-220/13 P *Nikolaou*, ECLI:EU:T:2014:2057 and Case F-73/13 *AX*, ECLI:EU:F:2015:9.

[252] Case T-193/04 *Tillack* [2006] ECR I-3995.

[253] Case T-562/12 *Dalli*, ECLI:EU:T:2015:270. The judgment has been appealed to the CJEU (Case C-394/15, pending).

[254] Case T-447/11 *Catinis*, ECLI:EU:T:2014:267.

[255] On the idea of the prosecutor, see II:6.10 above. On the issues arising from OLAF, see W Hetzer, 'Fight Against Fraud and Protection of Fundamental Rights in the European Union' (2006) 14 IJCCLCJ 1: 20.

7.4.7 Other measures

A broad array of non-JHA EU law issues overlap with law enforcement issues in general, and anti-terrorism policy in particular. Coordinated reactions to the effects of terrorist attacks fall within the scope of EU civil protection rules, most particularly the general EU civil protection coordination mechanism and the EU civil protection funding programme.[256] Moreover, the Commission has specifically taken account of anti-terrorism issues within the scope of civil protection policy, drawing up an action plan on nuclear, radiological, biological, and chemical threats,[257] and addressing in detail the issue of preparedness and consequence management in the fight against terrorism, calling especially for a centralized Commission alert system and a third pillar law enforcement network to be managed by Europol.[258] The latter communication was endorsed by the Council, and resulted in the creation of a Commission alert system at the end of 2005.[259] Furthermore, the Council established a specific civil protection funding programme concerning terrorism-related issues,[260] although subsequently the issue falls within the scope of the EU's Internal Security Fund.[261]

Before the entry into force of the Treaty of Lisbon, the EU's civil protection measures were adopted on the basis of the former Article 308 EC, which provided for a residual power for the EC to adopt measures to achieve its objectives, in the absence of any more specific legal basis, by means of a unanimous vote in Council and consultation of the EP. The Treaty of Lisbon introduced a specific legal base for civil protection measures, entailing the use of the ordinary legislative procedure, as well as a 'solidarity clause',[262] which provides for joint action 'in a spirit of solidarity if a Member State is the object of a terrorist attack or the victim of a natural or man-made disaster'. The Council can adopt measures to this end following a joint proposal of the Commission and High Representative, by qualified majority voting in most cases, but must vote unanimously where defence matters are concerned. The EP is only informed of the adopted measures. Due to the different decision-making procedures, there is a possible conflict between the civil protection legal base and the solidarity clause. In practice, the Council adopted a Decision implementing the solidarity clause in 2014.[263]

Measures against the financing of terrorism involve, as well as the sanctions and customs legislation discussed above, the application of EU legislation concerning money laundering and (indirectly) the regulation of wire transfers and of payments more

---

[256] For the mechanism, see [2001] OJ L 297/7, recast in 2007 ([2007] OJ L 314/7); for the funding programme, see originally [1999] OJ L 327/53, extended to end-2006 ([2005] OJ L 6/7), and later established for 2007–13 ([2007] OJ L 71/9) and 2014/2020 (Decision 1313/2013, [2013] OJ L 347/924). See generally Council conclusions on civil protection ([2005] OJ C 304/1).

[257] See: COM (2001) 707, 28 Nov 2001 (communication on state of alert against emergencies); COM (2002) 302, 11 June 2002 (report on implementation); COM (2004) 200, 25 Mar 2004 (reinforcing civil protection capacity); Council doc 15480/04, 1 Dec 2004 (revised programme on the consequences of terrorist attacks); and COM (2009) 273, 24 June 2009 (action plan on chemical, biological, radiological, and nuclear security).

[258] See COM (2004) 701, 20 Oct 2004.

[259] See respectively Council conclusions (Council doc 15232/04, 25 Nov 2004) and amendment to Commission Rules of Procedure ([2006] OJ L 19/20).

[260] [2007] OJ L 58/1; see further II.7.10 below.

[261] Reg 513/2014 ([2014] OJ L 150/93). The 2007 Decision was repealed by Decision 2015/457 ([2015] OJ L 76/1).

[262] Art 222 TFEU.   [263] [2014] OJ L 192/53.

generally.[264] The EU has also developed policy in this area,[265] in particular as regards regulation of the non-profit sector.[266] Of course, it should be recalled that financial regulation measures are relevant to other forms of organized crime as well.[267]

The EU has also developed a policy on the radicalization of potential terrorists, which focuses upon disrupting recruitment by terrorist networks, ensuring that moderate voices are more successful than extremists, and promoting equality and integration within the EU and supporting good governance and conflict resolution outside it.[268] However, the concrete implementation of the strategy is left entirely to Member States.

A final area of EU law of particular relevance to terrorism is the regulation of explosives. This issue was first regulated by EU internal market legislation dating from 1993.[269] Subsequently, the Commission adopted an action plan to enhance the security of explosives,[270] culminating in further EU legislation controlling explosives precursors, adopted in 2013.[271]

The related issue of firearms regulation is addressed by: a Directive dating from 1991, as amended in 2008; provisions of the Schengen Convention;[272] and a Regulation establishing an import/export regime for firearms, dating from 2012.[273] Due to the overlap between these measures, only some of the provisions of the Schengen *acquis* were allocated to the EC/EU legal order.[274] Furthermore, the EU has concluded the Protocol to the UN Convention on Organized Crime concerning firearms,[275] and authorized Member States to ratify the arms trade treaty.[276]

---

[264] On EU money laundering legislation, see II:5.5 above; see also Reg 1781/2006 on wire transfers ([2006] OJ L 345/1), replaced by Reg 2015/847 ([2015] OJ L 141/1) from 26 June 2017 (Art 27), and Dir 2007/64 on payment services ([2007] OJ L 319/1).

[265] See generally, as regards terrorism finance, COM (2004) 700, 20 Oct 2004); the subsequent EU strategy (Council doc 16089/04, 14 Dec 2004), and regular Council reports on the implementation of the strategy (see most recently Council doc 14744/05, 21 Nov 2005).

[266] See Conclusions of the JHA Council (Council press release, 1–2 Dec 2005) and Commission communication and Recommendation (COM (2005) 620, 29 Nov 2005).

[267] See Commission communication concerning organized crime in the financial sector (COM (2004) 262, 14 Apr 2004).

[268] Council doc 14781/1/05, 24 Nov 2005; see earlier Commission communication (COM (2005) 313, 21 Sep 2005) and the more recent communication on strengthening the EU response (COM (2013) 941, 15 Jan 2014).

[269] Dir 93/15 ([1993] OJ L 121/20), implemented by Commission Decisions setting out a standard form for intra-EU transfers ([2004] OJ L 120/43, amended in [2010] OJ L 155/54) and establishing rules on the traceability of explosives ([2008] OJ L 94/8). On implementation of the Dir, see Case C-327/98 *Commission v France* [2000] ECR I-1851 and Council conclusions (press release of JHA Council, 2 Oct 2003).

[270] COM (2007) 651, 6 Nov 2007; see earlier COM (2005) 329, 18 July 2005.

[271] Reg 98/2013 ([2013] OJ L 39/1). The Reg applied from 2 Sep 2014 (Art 19).

[272] Dir 91/477 ([1991] OJ L 256/51), amended by Dir 2008/51 ([2008] OJ L 179/5) and Arts 77–91 of the Convention ([2000] OJ L 239). There is also a Schengen Executive Committee Decision on illegal trade in firearms: [2000] OJ L 239/469. Member States had to implement Dir 2008/51 by 28 July 2010 (Art 2(1), Dir 2008/51). The Commission has reported on the issue of whether to simplify the categorization of firearms (COM (2012) 415, 26 July 2012), evaluated the Directive more generally (COM (2015) 721, 18 Nov 2015), and adopted an implementing Decision on deactivation of firearms ([2015] OJ L 333/62).

[273] Reg 258/2012 ([2012] OJ L 94/1), applicable from 30 Sep 2013 (Art 22).

[274] Arts 82 and 91 of the Convention (concerning derogations from the rules and exchanges of information respectively). These provisions, and the Executive Committee Decision, were allocated to Art 95 EC, now Art 114 TFEU (see Decision allocating the *acquis*, [1999] OJ L 176/17).

[275] [2014] OJ L 89/7. Member States have also signed or ratified this Protocol. For ratification details, see Appendix I.

[276] [2014] OJ L 89/44.

There is an obvious need for consolidation of the disparate measures regulating fire-arms within the EU. In 2013, the Commission issued a communication suggesting a number of possible reforms to EU legislation on firearms, including the adoption of criminal law,[277] and subsequently proposed a number of amendments to the law in 2015.[278]

There are links between the EU's policing measures and the EU's powers over immigration, particularly as regards the Schengen Information System, which is addressed both by EU policing legislation and EU immigration legislation, as well as non-JHA EU legislation concerning access to the SIS by vehicle registration authorities.[279] EU immigration legislation has also established a Visa Information System (VIS), which law enforcement authorities now have access to.[280] There are also EU immigration law measures concerning trafficking and smuggling in persons,[281] and links between the EU's border control agency and EU policing law.[282] Finally, EU immigration law measures relating to passenger data are connected with third pillar measures.[283]

Offences against children are addressed by a Recommendation on the protection of minors and human dignity in the audio-visual field,[284] and by a Decision establishing a 'safer Internet action plan' funding programme.[285] There is also an EU funding programme addressing the health aspects of violence against women and children.[286] The development of EU policy on crime statistics also has a non-JHA legal base, after the entry into force of the Treaty of Lisbon.[287] However, the Commission's proposal for legislation on this issue was rejected and withdrawn.[288]

Another area of non-JHA EU law with security implications is the field of research, where the Commission first of all managed a preparatory action on security research funding from 2004,[289] and security research subsequently formed part of the EU's overall research programmes.[290]

---

[277] COM (2013) 716, 21 Oct 2013.

[278] COM (2015) 750, 18 Nov 2015. See also the communication on security as regards firearms and explosives (COM (2015) 624, 3 Dec 2015).

[279] For details, see II.7.6.1.1 below. On the legal base issues relevant to the SIS, see I:2.4.2.

[280] See II.7.6.1.3 below.   [281] See I:7.5.3, I:7.5.4, and I:7.6.2.   [282] See I:3.10.1.

[283] See II.7.4.3.2 above.

[284] [1998] OJ L 270/48, amended in 2006 ([2006] OJ L 378/72). See the report by the Commission on implementation of the Recommendation (COM (2011) 556, 13 Sep 2011).

[285] The 1999–2004 programme was set out in Decision 276/1999 ([1999] OJ L 33/1, extended and amended in [2003] OJ L 162/1); the 2004–08 programme was set out in Decision 854/2005 ([2005] OJ L 149/1); and the 2009–13 programme was set out in Decision 1351/2008 ([2008] OJ L 348/118). On the policing law aspects of this issue, see II.7.7.4 below; see also the criminal law legislation (II:5.5.2.1 above).

[286] Daphne I programme ([2000] OJ L 34/1); Daphne II programme ([2004] OJ L 143/1); and Daphne III programme ([2007] OJ L 173/19). The Daphne programme now forms part of the citizenship, equality, and human rights programme for 2014–20 (Reg 1381/2013, [2013] OJ L 354/62).

[287] See COM (2006) 437, 7 Aug 2006 and Art 338 TFEU (the legal base for statistics measures), which applies to policing and criminal law issues after the entry into force of the Treaty of Lisbon.

[288] COM (2011) 335, 8 June 2011 (proposal); [2014] OJ C 153/3 (withdrawal).

[289] See Commission communication (COM (2004) 72, 3 Mar 2004); Commission Decision on implementation ([2004] OJ L 67/18); and a further communication in response to a report on Security Research by a 'Group of Personalities' (COM (2004) 590, 7 Sep 2004).

[290] See Art 2(1)(i)(j) of Decision 1982/2006 ([2006] OJ L 412/1), establishing the 7th Research Framework Programme. Security research is now integrated into the replacement 'Horizon 2020' programme (Reg 1291/2013, [2013] OJ L 347/104). For critiques, see B Hayes, *NeoConOpticon: The EU's Security-Industrial Complex* (Transnational Institute and Statewatch, 2009), online at: <http://www.statewatch.org/analyses/

EU external policies concerning development and association also provide a frame-work for encouraging alignment with the EU's policing and security objectives, although the use of development funds explicitly for anti-terrorist measures was suc-cessfully challenged in the absence of a specific legal base.[291]

Finally, various non-JHA EU law measures have an impact on the fight against counterfeiting the euro, and on anti-drug policy, in conjunction with EU policing measures.[292]

7.5 Crime Prevention

Before the Treaty of Amsterdam entered into force, the Council adopted a broad-ranging Resolution on crime prevention.[293] Subsequently, in 2001 the Council adopted a Decision establishing a crime prevention network,[294] and a specific Decision on fund-ing measures for crime prevention, later incorporated into broader law enforcement funding programmes.[295] The Network originally consisted of contact points desig-nated by Member States, supported by a Secretariat provided by the Commission, and its objectives included: facilitating cooperation and the exchange of information and experience; the collection, analysis, and evaluation of information on crime preven-tion activities; helping to identify and develop the main areas for research, training, and evaluation as regards crime prevention; and organizing conferences, seminars, and similar meetings on crime prevention and disseminating the results. It had to submit annual reports on its activities, and the Council had to evaluate the application of the Decision in 2004.

The initial annual reports of the Network established a focus on juvenile, urban, and drug-related crime, as well as issues of crime statistics, crime proofing, fear of crime, and crime-prevention partnerships. The Network was hindered in practice by funding issues, since only its secretariat was funded from the EU budget, although it was able to achieve some its objectives as regards holding conferences and producing reports.[296]

In 2004, the Commission released a communication on crime prevention,[297] which suggested that: a solution must be found for the Network's funding and support

---

neoconopticon-report.pdf> and B Hayes, *Arming Big Brother: The EU's Security Research Programme* (Transnational Institute and Statewatch, 2006), online at: <http://www.statewatch.org/analyses/bigbrother. pdf>. See also the Commission communication on a public/private dialogue in the field of European secur-ity research and innovation (COM (2007) 511, 11 Sep 2007) and the subsequent communication on the issue (COM (2012) 417, 26 July 2012).

[291] Case C-403/05 *EP v Commission* [2007] ECR I-9045; see now the EU development policy legislation that explicitly addresses such issues: Reg 1717/2006, [2006] OJ L 317/1, and now Art 5(3)(c)(iv) of Reg 233/2014 ([2014] OJ L 77/44).

[292] For details of both topics, see II.7.7.4 below.

[293] [1998] OJ C 408/1. For more on crime prevention prior to the Treaty of Amsterdam, see the first edi-tion of this book, at pp 192–93.

[294] [2001] OJ L 153/1. See website: <http://www.eucpn.org/>. See also the Commission communication (COM (2000) 786, 29 Nov 2000).

[295] II.7.10 below.

[296] Council docs: 7632/03, 26 Mar 2003 (2002 report); 13421/04, 13 Oct 2004 (2003 report); and 11140/05, 15 July 2005 (2004 report).

[297] COM (2004) 165, 12 Mar 2004; [2004] OJ C 92/2.

problems; the Network should focus further on particular types of crime; the Network should draw up a list of good practices; there should be a system of monitoring and evaluation of national crime prevention policies; and the EU should harmonize rules on crime statistics. The 2004 evaluation of the Network also addressed funding issues and called for further prioritization on specific forms of crime, and this approach was also supported by the Hague Programme and by Council conclusions on the evaluation of the Network.[298]

The later annual reports on the operation of the Network detailed the amendment of its structure to include an operational board, the development of an independent website, and the greater focus of its work.[299] Eventually, the original Council Decision was replaced by a revised Decision just before the Treaty of Lisbon entered into force in 2009,[300] which, inter alia, established an Executive Committee charged with developing a long term strategy for the Network, gave more clearly defined roles and objectives to national representatives, and allowed the Network's Board more flexibility as regards the organization of its Secretariat.

The Commission produced an evaluation of the Network in 2012.[301] According to this report, the previous shortcomings of the Network had been addressed, and it had published more focused analyses, such as thematic papers and crime prevention monitors. However, the Network did not always link to crime prevention priorities, its reports were not always tailored to target groups, and its profile was still low. The Commission recommended a modest upgrade to the budget of the Network for now, rather than transforming it into an Observatory for crime prevention as suggested by the Stockholm Programme.[302]

7.6 Exchange of Information

The main focus of EU measures concerning policing has been the facilitation of the 'free movement of investigations' by facilitating the gathering, transfer, and/or analysis of information—although of course there is a close connection and overlap between gathering and analysing information and operational activities.[303] In fact, EU measures concerning operational activities frequently contain specific ancillary provisions on exchange of information.[304]

This section examines in turn: the development of EU-wide databases; access to national databases; the ad hoc exchange of information between national authorities; and the rules on personal data protection as regards policing and criminal law. The

---

[298] Council doc 13419/04, 13 Oct 2004. See point III.2.6 of the Hague Programme ([2005] OJ C 53/1) and Council doc 14649/04, 17 Nov 2004. See subsequent progress report (Council doc 13945/1/05, 29 Nov 2005).

[299] Council docs: 11131/06, 4 July 2006 (2005 report); 6683/07, 5 Mar 2007 (2006 report); 8815/08, 28 Apr 2008 (2007 report); 9397/09, 4 May 2009 (2008 report); and 7025/10, 3 Mar 2010 (2009 report).

[300] [2009] OJ L 321/44.   [301] COM (2012) 717, 30 Nov 2012.

[302] [2010] OJ C 115, point 4.3.2.   [303] On the operational measures, see II.7.7 below.

[304] See, for example, Art 4 of the Decision on protection of the euro against counterfeiting ([2001] OJ L 329/1) and Art 2 of the 2003 Decision on war crimes, etc. ([2003] OJ L 118/12). On the distinction between the legal bases for data exchange on the one hand, and operational cooperation on the other, see II.7.2.4 above.

specific rules relating to Europol, which is also primarily concerned with information exchange and analysis, are discussed further below.[305]

In general terms, following an overview of EU information exchange systems in 2010,[306] the Commission concluded in 2012 that there was no further need for information exchange systems at EU level.[307] However, the 2015 security strategy revives an old idea for a police records information system.[308]

7.6.1 EU databases

The EU has established two major information systems relating, inter alia, to policing and customs: the Schengen Information System (SIS), for the use of national immigration, border control, police, and customs authorities; and the Customs Information System (CIS), for the use of the customs authorities. Also, law enforcement authorities have access to the EU's database of information on visa applicants, the Visa Information System (VIS), and to Eurodac, the database containing asylum-seekers' fingerprints.[309] Furthermore, the Commission has suggested the interoperability and further development of EU databases.[310] Most of these databases (SIS, VIS, and Eurodac) are managed by an agency, known as EU-LISA.[311]

7.6.1.1 Schengen Information System

The SIS went into operation with the entry into effect of the Schengen Convention in March 1995.[312] In addition to the relevant provisions of the Convention, the SIS was also the subject of a number of implementing measures adopted by the Schengen Executive Committee.[313] The power of the Executive Committee and its working groups was transferred by the Treaty of Amsterdam to the Council and its working groups.[314] Furthermore, the Council has adopted a catalogue of best practices and recommendations regarding the SIS.[315]

The SIS was established firstly for the use of national police, customs, and border control authorities when making checks on persons at external borders or within

---

[305] II.7.8.   [306] COM (2010) 385, 20 July 2010.   [307] COM (2012) 735, 7 Dec 2012.

[308] COM (2015) 185, 28 Apr 2015. Law enforcement bodies might also be granted access to the data included in the planned EU entry-exit system (I:3.6).

[309] See II.7.6.1.3 and II.7.6.1.4 below.   [310] COM (2005) 597, 24 Nov 2005.

[311] The Agency was established by Reg 1077/2011 ([2011] OJ L 286/1).

[312] Arts 92–119 of Schengen Convention ([2000] OJ L 239). On the overall framework of Schengen integration, see I:2.2.2.2.

[313] These Decisions concerned: a financial regulation; a contract for a preliminary study on SIS II; contributions from Norway and Iceland; the development of the SIS; the number of national connections; a help-desk budget; installation expenses; the adoption of the 'Sirene manual' (explained below); and a catch-all decision authorizing the SIS technical *acquis* ([2000] OJ L 239, respectively 439 and 444, 440, 441, 442, 452, 453, 454, 457, and 144). There were also declarations on the definition of 'alien' and the structure of the SIS ([2000] OJ L 239/458 and 459). The Sirene manual was published later: [2003] OJ C 38/1. See also the Decisions on declassification of parts of the manual: [2003] OJ L 8/34; [2007] OJ L 179/52; and [2008] OJ L 149/78.

[314] In addition to the measures discussed below, the Council adopted several measures concerning SIS contracts and Decisions on the Joint Supervisory Body secretariat (see I:2.2.2 and [2000] OJ L 271/1).

[315] See Council doc 16613/3/08, 8 May 2009.

Schengen states; and secondly, for the use of immigration officers when administering third-country nationals, in particular when deciding whether to issue visas or residence permits.[316] To that end, Member States could enter certain types of information about or relating to persons (certain personal details and an indication of whether they were armed or dangerous) as well as specified information on vehicles and objects.[317] There were six broadly defined reasons for which information could be included on the SIS (types of SIS 'alerts'):

a) when a person was 'wanted for arrest for extradition purposes' (subsequently including the European Arrest Warrant);[318]

b) when a person had been listed to be refused entry to all the Schengen States;[319]

c) when a person had disappeared or needed to be placed in a secure location to protect his or her safety;[320]

d) when a judicial authority in one Member State wanted to know the whereabouts of a person (such as a witness or a person being prosecuted) in another Member State during the course of a prosecution;[321]

e) when one Member State wanted others to subject a vehicle or person to discreet surveillance or checks, because of 'clear evidence' that the person 'intends to commit, or is committing numerous and extremely serious offences' or 'where an overall evaluation of the person', particularly his or her prior offences, 'gives reasons to suppose' that he or she 'will also commit extremely serious offences in future', or because the security services believe that the person is a 'serious threat';[322] and

f) where objects were sought 'for the purposes of seizure of for evidence in criminal proceedings'.[323]

SIS data could be accessed by relevant national policing, border control, immigration, or customs authorities, but officials could only search the data necessary for the performance of their tasks.[324] The original SIS rules were amended in 2004 and 2005 in order to make certain changes which the Member States desired that could be implemented within the previous technical framework.[325] Inter alia, these amendments: inserted express references for the first time to the 'Sirene' system (a supplementary system for

---

[316] Art 92(1), Schengen Convention, n 312 above. On the operation of SIS in practice, see, for instance, Cases: C-503/03 *Commission v Spain* [2006] ECR I-1097; C-150/05 *Van Straaten* [2006] ECR I-9327; and C-123/08 *Wolzenburg* [2009] ECR I-9621.

[317] Arts 94(3), 99(4), and 100(3).   [318] Art 95; see II:3.5 above.

[319] Art 96; see I:3.7, I:4.7, and I:4.9.

[320] Art 97; see the Schengen Executive Committee declaration on the abduction of minors ([2000] OJ L 239/436). The Commission has proposed to repeal the latter measure, on the grounds that it is obsolete: COM (2014) 714, 28 Nov 2014.

[321] Art 98; see II:3.6.1 above.   [322] Art 99.   [323] Art 100; see II:3.6.1 above.

[324] Art 101.

[325] Reg 871/2004 ([2004] OJ L 162/29) and third pillar Decision ([2005] OJ L 68/44). These measures amended Arts 92, 94, 99–101, 103, and 113 of the Schengen Convention, and inserted Arts 101A, 101B, 112A, and 113A into the Convention. Different provisions of these measures applied from different dates: see Art 2(2) of the Reg, Art 2(3) of the Decision, and Decisions in [2005] OJ L 158/26, [2005] L 271/54, [2005] L 273/25 and 26, [2006] OJ L 81/45 and 46, and [2006] OJ L 256/15 and 18.

the exchange of information between Member States following a 'hit' in the SIS); gave access to SIS data for judicial authorities, Europol, and Eurojust; permitted national security services to place the names of persons into the SIS without prior consultation of other Member States; and expanded the list of objects that could be placed under surveillance or listed as wanted in the SIS. A further Regulation was adopted in 2005, giving access to SIS data by vehicle registration authorities.[326] Finally, a Regulation and a parallel third pillar Decision adopted in 2004 conferred power upon the Commission to amend the 'Sirene manual', which regulates the use of the Sirene system.[327]

In order, inter alia, to add additional categories of data to the SIS (notably finger-prints and photographs), the EU decided to develop a second-generation SIS ('SIS II') to take the place of the original SIS. Parallel EC and third pillar measures adopted in 2001 (under the legal framework which applied before the entry into force of the Treaty of Lisbon) conferred power upon the Commission until the end of 2006 to man-age the development of SIS II, which was funded from the EU budget.[328] Since SIS II was not operational by the end of 2006, these measures were amended at that time to extend their application to the end of 2008 and to designate Strasbourg, France as the main location of SIS II and an Austrian location as the main location of the back-up system.[329] When it became obvious that SIS II would not be operational by the end of 2008, the EU adopted fresh parallel measures which regulated in detail the pro-cess of migration from SIS to SIS II.[330] These measures were amended in 2010, inter alia, extending their validity to the end of 2013.[331] Pursuant to these measures, the Commission released a number of reports on its management of the SIS II project.[332] In the event, SIS II began operations in April 2013.[333]

As for the legislative framework, in order to establish SIS II, the Council adopted three measures (a Regulation concerning immigration aspects, a Decision concerning

---

[326] Reg 1160/2005 ([2005] OJ L 191/18), applicable from 11 Jan 2006.

[327] Reg 378/2004 ([2005] OJ L 64/5); Decision ([2005] OJ L 64/45). The Commission used these powers to adopt new versions of the Sirene manual in 2006: [2006] OJ L 317.

[328] Reg 2424/2001 and Decision 2001/886/JHA ([2001] OJ L 328/1 and 4).

[329] Reg 1988/2006 and Decision 2006/1007/JHA ([2006] OJ L 411/1 and 78). Measures implementing these acts were subsequently adopted: Commission Decisions on the network requirements for SIS II devel-opment ([2007] OJ L 79/20 and 29); Council Reg 189/2008 and Decision 2008/173 ([2008] OJ L 57/1 and 14) on tests of SIS II. The Commission has proposed to repeal the 2008 measures, on the grounds that they are obsolete since SIS II began operations: COM (2014) 713 and 715, 28 Nov 2014.

[330] Reg 1104/2008 and Decision 2008/839 ([2008] OJ L 299/1 and 43). These measures, inter alia, inserted an Art 92A into the Schengen Convention and amended Art 119 of that Convention. The Commission adopted Decisions implementing these measures, in order to change the date of migration to SIS II from Sep 2009 to June 2010: [2009] OJ L 257/26 and 41. These measures were replaced by Regs 1272/2012 and 1273/2012 ([2012] OJ L 359/21 and 32), which expired after SIS II data was migrated (Arts 20 and 21 of each Reg).

[331] [2010] OJ L 155/19 and 23.

[332] The reports available online are: SEC (2008) 35, 17 Jan 2008 (Jan–June 2007); COM (2008) 239 and SEC (2008) 552, 7 May 2008 (July–Dec 2007); COM (2008) 710, 10 Nov 2008 (Jan–June 2008); COM (2009) 133, 24 Mar 2009 (July–Dec 2008); COM (2009) 555, 22 Oct 2009 (Jan–June 2009); COM (2010) 221, 6 May 2010 (July – Dec 2009); COM (2010) 633, 5 Nov 2010 (Jan–June 2010); COM (2011) 391, 6 July 2011 (July–Dec 2010); COM (2011) 907, 20 Dec 2011 (Jan–June 2011); COM (2012) 334, 22 June 2012 (July–Dec 2011); COM (2012) 587, 11 Nov 2012 (Jan–June 2012); COM (2013) 305, 27 May 2013 (July–Dec 2012); and COM (2013) 777, 3 Dec 2013 (Jan–May 2013).

[333] Council decisions ([2013] OJ L 87/8 and 10).

criminal law and policing aspects, and a Regulation on access by vehicle registration authorities) in 2006 and 2007.[334] When SIS II began operations, these rules fully replaced the previous Schengen Convention rules (as already amended) and Executive Committee Decisions.[335] Compared to the previous SIS rules, the types of alert are the same, although the grounds for issuing immigration alerts have been altered, the extradition alerts include more data relating to the European Arrest Warrant, and there are minor changes to other policing and criminal law alerts.[336] Categories of data were expanded to include photographs and fingerprints, and links between alerts were established.

The operation of SIS II is funded from the EU budget, and operational management of the SIS has, as noted above, been handed over to an EU agency. There have also been changes to the rules governing data protection.[337] The Commission has used the power to implement these measures in order to adopt a new version of the Sirene manual,[338] as well as rules on security of SIS II.[339]

7.6.1.2 Customs Information System

The CIS Convention was opened for signature in 1995,[340] but only entered into force on Christmas Day 2005, following ratification by all of the first fifteen Member States.[341] Previously the Convention had applied provisionally in those Member States which had ratified an Agreement on provisional application, which had entered into force on 1 November 2000, following its ratification by a majority of the first fifteen Member States.[342] The CIS began operations on 24 March 2003, once the technical requirements for operation of the system were satisfied. As noted above, the CIS Convention was closely intertwined with a Regulation setting up a nearly identical system of information exchange (also called the CIS) to detect breaches of legislation outside the JHA context (ie in relation to international trade regulations).[343]

There were also three Protocols to the CIS Convention. First of all, a Protocol on the jurisdiction of the Court of Justice to interpret the Convention on references from national courts was agreed in 1996, and entered into force at the same time as the Convention.[344] Secondly, a Protocol signed in 1999 aligned the definition of 'money laundering' in the CIS Convention with that in the Naples II Convention on customs operations,[345] and allowed the third pillar CIS system to keep data on licence plates, in line with the parallel CIS Regulation;[346] this Protocol entered into force on 14 April

---

[334] See respectively Reg 1987/2006 ([2006] OJ L 381/4), Decision 2007/533 ([2007] OJ L 205/63, and Reg 1986/2006 ([2006] OJ L 381/1).
[335] Arts 68 and 69 of the Decision (ibid).   [336] Arts 26–39 of the Decision (ibid).
[337] Arts 56–63 of the Decision (ibid).
[338] Successive versions in: [2008] OJ L 123; [2011] OJ L 137/1; [2013] OJ L 71/1; and [2015] OJ L 44/75. The list of authorities with access to SIS II data is published in [2005] OJ C 208/1.
[339] [2010] OJ L 112/31.   [340] [1995] OJ C 316/33.
[341] All of the newer Member States also ratified the Convention (except Croatia, which joined the EU after its replacement).
[342] [1995] OJ C 316/58.   [343] II.7.4.1.   [344] [1997] OJ C 151/15.
[345] [1998] OJ C 24/1. On this Convention, see II.7.7.4 and II.7.9 below.
[346] [1999] OJ C 91/1.

2008.[347] Finally, a Protocol signed in 2003 established a Customs Files Information System as part of the CIS; this Protocol entered into force on 15 October 2007.[348]

In November 2009, the Council adopted a third pillar Decision which replaced the CIS Convention and its substantive Protocols as from 27 May 2011.[349] According to this Decision, the CIS is implemented and applied by a committee made up of Member States' representatives, which oversees the functioning of the CIS, reporting annually to the Council, with the Commission taking part.[350] The CIS is confined to assisting in 'preventing, investigating and prosecuting serious contraventions of national [customs] laws', namely the movement of goods which Member States can ban or restrict in accordance with EU law, cash checks, the property or proceeds of international drug trafficking, and EU rules on indirect tax, agriculture, and trade.[351] The CIS cannot store the very sensitive data referred to in the Framework Decision on data protection.[352] The reasons for storage of data in the CIS are limited to the purposes of 'sighting and reporting, discreet surveillance, specific checks and strategic or operational analysis'.[353] Direct access to the CIS system is limited to national customs authorities and other national law enforcement authorities, along with Europol and Eurojust.[354] Member States may use CIS information 'for administrative or other purposes', or pass it on to non-Member States and international or regional organizations, if the Member State supplying the information agrees.[355]

The 2004 annual report on the operation of the CIS indicated that it initially suffered from a 'very low level of use', due to training shortfalls, technical problems, and delayed ratification of the CIS Convention.[356] A team of experts produced an assessment with an action plan of recommendations to improve the situation,[357] but the 2005 report still reported a 'very low level of use'.[358] The 2006 report indicated that there was a 'significant increase in the use of CIS' since the start, but that 95% of the data in the CIS was inputted by only five Member States.[359] According to the 2007 report, there was a further increase in the use of the CIS, but a drop in the number of active cases; most data was still inputted by only a small number of Member States.[360] The 2008 report indicated that there were fewer active third pillar CIS files, but increasing consultation of those files; only a few files were at first included in the new customs files database.[361]

---

[347] All Member States have ratified this Protocol.　　　[348] [2003] OJ C 139/1.

[349] [2009] OJ L 323/20. On the background to the Decision, see Council doc 14600/1/08, 3 Nov 2008.

[350] Art 27, CIS Decision (ibid).　　　[351] Arts 1(2) and 2(1), CIS Decision.

[352] Art 4(5), CIS Decision, referring to Art 6 of the Framework Decision, on which see II.7.6.4 below.

[353] Art 5(1), CIS Decision. For the definitions of 'strategic analysis' and 'operational analysis', see Art 2(4) and (5) of the Decision.

[354] Arts 7(1), 11, and 12, CIS Decision.

[355] Art 8, CIS Decision. The Council can also decide to give access to national or international organizations: Art 7(3) of the Decision.

[356] Council doc 7361/1/04, 26 Apr 2004. In particular, only forty-five first pillar and twenty-seven third pillar cases had been inputted.

[357] See Council doc 9085/1/04, 2 June 2004.

[358] See Council doc 12701/1/05, 13 Oct 2005. By Sep 2005, 164 third pillar cases had been inputted.

[359] Council doc 14694/2/06, 12 Jan 2007. By Oct 2006, over 600 third pillar cases had been inputted.

[360] Council doc 16245/07, 7 Dec 2007. By Nov 2007, over 1,000 third pillar cases had been inputted. Eight Member States had inputted 93% of the data.

[361] Council doc 15651/08, 13 Nov 2008, referring to 287 active third pillar cases (the total number of cases was no longer listed). There were thirteen third pillar files in the customs files database, which was operational from 15 Sep 2008 following the entry into force of the 2003 Protocol to the Convention (n 330

The final annual report on use of the system showed a further modest increase in its use.[362]

7.6.1.3 Access to the Visa Information System

In 2008, the Council adopted a Regulation establishing the Visa Information System, on the basis of the EU's powers over visas.[363] Simultaneously, it adopted a third pillar Decision giving law enforcement authorities and Europol access to the data to be held in the VIS, when it begins operations.[364] The UK unsuccessfully challenged the validity of this measure, on the grounds that it was not allowed to participate fully due to its non-participation in the VIS itself.[365] The Decision requires Member States to designate the law enforcement authorities which will have access to the VIS, for the purpose of preventing, detecting, or investigating terrorism or the other thirty-two 'serious crimes' referred to in the list set out in the Framework Decision establishing the European Arrest Warrant (EAW).[366] There is a special process for law enforcement authorities to request access to the data, subject to the conditions that the access is 'necessary for the purpose of the prevention, detection or investigation' of the relevant offences; that access is 'necessary in a specific case', and there are 'reasonable grounds to consider' that access to the data will 'substantially contribute to the prevention, detection or investigation of any of the criminal offences' in question.[367] Law enforcement authorities only have access to certain data,[368] and Europol has access to the data for very specific purposes.[369] Their access was put into effect from 1 September 2013,[370] although in 2015 the relevant decision was annulled on procedural grounds, and had to be replaced.[371]

As for the merits of police access to the VIS, it might be doubted that the VIS data will be of much use to police except possibly identifying fingerprints left at a crime scene or providing further information about a suspect for the purpose of tracing him or her. The VIS Regulation and the parallel third pillar Decision leave lots of discretion to give extensive access to the police services, but at least a prior check will apply in principle before access is granted. But it might be doubted whether this procedure will be independent or critical of police requests. At least it is certainly welcome that access for the police is limited to specific cases, with no general power to search the entire database to produce 'risk assessments'.

above) and the 2008 amendments to the CIS Regulation (II.7.4.1 above). This report contains a number of criticisms of the operation of the system.

[362] Council doc 7036/3/11, 23 May 2011.
[363] Reg 767/2008 ([2008] OJ L 218/60). The VIS began operations in 2011. For details, see I:4.8.
[364] [2008] OJ L 218/129. See also Art 3 of Reg 767/2008, n 363 above.
[365] Case C-482/08 *UK v Council* [2010] ECR I-10413. The special rule concerned is set out in Art 6 of the Decision.
[366] Arts 3(1) and 2(1)(d) and (e) of the Decision. For the EAW Framework Decision ([2002] OJ L 190/1), see II:3.5 above.
[367] Arts 4 and 5(1) of the Decision.   [368] Art 5(2) of the Decision.
[369] Art 7 of the Decision.
[370] Council Decision ([2013] OJ L 198/35). For the list of agencies with access, see [2013] OJ C 236.
[371] Case C-540/13 *EP v Council*, ECLI:EU:C:2015:224 (judgment) and [2015] OJ L 284/146 (replacement decision). See discussion in II:2.2.3.3 above.

7.6.1.4 Access to Eurodac

Eurodac, the EU system for the comparison of asylum seekers' fingerprints for the purpose of applying the EU rules on asylum applications, was established by legislation adopted in 2000 and became operational in 2003.[372] The legislation establishing Eurodac was revised in 2013, giving law enforcement authorities and Europol access to the Eurodac database as from July 2015.[373]

The 2013 Regulation requires Member States to designate the law enforcement authorities which will have access to Eurodac for 'law enforcement purposes', which is defined as 'the prevention, detection, or investigation of terrorism or other serious criminal offences', as further defined respectively in the Framework Decision on terrorism and the Framework Decision establishing the European Arrest Warrant.[374] Member States must list the authorities with access, and their requests must be subject to independent verification.[375] There is a detailed special procedure for law enforcement authorities or Europol to request access to Eurodac data, subject to the conditions that the access is 'necessary for the purpose of the prevention, detection or investigation' of the relevant offences; that access is 'necessary in a specific case', and there are 'reasonable grounds to consider' that access to the data will 'substantially contribute to the prevention, detection or investigation of any of the criminal offences' in question.[376] There are specific data protection rules for law enforcement authorities.[377]

7.6.2 Access to national databases

In 2008, the Council adopted a Decision (known informally as the 'Prum Decision'),[378] which incorporates a large number of provisions from the Prum Convention, a separate treaty agreed originally in 2005 between a small group of Member States.[379] This Decision includes, inter alia, rules on access by one Member States' authorities to another Member States' databases as regards fingerprint data, DNA data, and vehicle registration information.[380] This Decision also includes a number of other provisions discussed elsewhere in this Chapter,[381] and there is also another Decision, adopted at the same time and similarly carved out of the Prum Convention, concerning cross-border movement of special intervention units in crisis situations.[382] A parallel Decision sets out rules which implement the details of the Prum Decision.[383] It should be noted that

---

[372] See Reg 2725/2000 ([2000] L 316/1); see I:5.8.

[373] Reg 603/2013 ([2013] OJ L 180/1), applicable since 20 July 2015 (Art 46).

[374] Arts 1(2) and 2(1)(i) to (k) of the Reg.

[375] Arts 5 and 6 of the Reg. On Europol access, see Art 7.   [376] Arts 19–22 of the Reg.

[377] Art 33 of the Reg; see also Art 35(2), which bans transfers to countries where there is a risk of torture, inhuman or degrading treatment, or any other violation of the data subject's fundamental rights. There is a general ban on transfers to third States in Art 35(1), with an exception for the Schengen associates, which also apply the Dublin rules (Art 35(3)). The latter States are negotiating treaties with the EU for law enforcement access to Eurodac data.

[378] [2008] OJ L 210/1.   [379] On the background to the Prum Convention, see II.7.2.3 above.

[380] Arts 2–12 of the Decision. These provisions had to be applied by Member States by 26 Aug 2011: see Arts 36(1) and 37.

[381] See II.7.6.3 and II.7.9 below.   [382] [2010] OJ L 218/73. See II.7.9.5 below.

[383] [2008] OJ L 210/12.

these provisions of the Prum Decision and the relevant provisions of the implementing Decision will be extended to Norway and Iceland by means of a separate treaty, which does not apply to the separate Decision on special intervention units.[384]

First of all, as regards DNA data,[385] the Prum Decision requires Member States to establish files of such data in order to assist with criminal investigations. Reference data from these files (which cannot as such be used to identify individuals) must be available for searching automatically by other Member States' authorities. In the event of a match, further data shall be supplied to the requesting Member State. If there is no DNA profile available for a particular individual, the requested State shall obtain DNA samples from that person if requested by another Member State, if the national law of both States permits it.

As regards fingerprint data, similarly Member States must make anonymized reference data from their national files available for automatic searches to other Member States, and supply further data in the event of a match.[386] Finally, as regards vehicle registration data, Member States must open up their national registers to searches by other Member States' authorities, as regards searches for information on owners or vehicles.[387]

According to the Commission report on implementation of the Prum Decision,[388] a number of Member States had failed to implement the information exchange provisions of that Decision on time.[389] But many Member States were using the system routinely, leading to approximately 2,600 fingerprint matches, 20,700 DNA matches, and 260,300 vehicle registration matches in 2011. The lack of rules on follow-up actions to a hit (as compared to the Sirene system, established for the SIS) was a problem in practice.

7.6.3 Ad hoc exchange of information

Many EU measures have been adopted dealing with the exchange of information on a case-by-case basis and/or in specific areas. First of all, general rules on the exchange of information on a case-by-case basis between national law enforcement authorities are set out in a Framework Decision adopted in 2006, which replaced prior rules in the Schengen Convention.[390] This Framework Decision, inter alia, specifies that Member States shall not apply different rules for providing information and intelligence to other Member States than the rules which apply to such provision within the same Member State, including rules on judicial authorization of information transfer.[391] If judicial authorization is required for the requested authority to access the information

---

[384] [2009] OJ L 353/1. The treaty has been signed, but is not yet in force. See further II.7.2.5 above.
[385] Arts 2–7, Prum Decision.   [386] Arts 8–11, Prum Decision.
[387] Art 12, Prum Decision.   [388] COM (2012) 732, 7 Dec 2012.
[389] For the latest state of play on implementation, see Council doc 5015/5/15, 28 July 2015.
[390] [2006] OJ L 386/89, known in practice as the 'Swedish Framework Decision'. It had to be implemented by 19 Dec 2008 (Art 11(2)) and replaced Art 39(1) to (3) and 46 of the Schengen Convention ([2000] OJ L 239), as well as two Schengen Executive Committee Decisions (Art 12). See the guidelines on the implementation of the Framework Decision (Council doc 9512/1/10, 17 Dec 2010).
[391] Art 3(3).

or intelligence, it must ask for that authorization in the event of a request for that intelligence or information from another Member State's authority.[392]

The Framework Decision sets a time limit of eight hours for responding to 'urgent' requests for information and intelligence as regard offences to which dual criminality no longer applies pursuant to the Framework Decision establishing the European Arrest Warrant.[393] In non-urgent cases relating to the same offences, Member States should respond within one week, if the information is in a database which the requested law enforcement authority can directly access.[394] In all other cases, the requested authority must respond to requests for information within fourteen days.[395] Furthermore, there is a requirement to exchange information spontaneously, ie without a request from other Member States' authorities.[396] Member States can refuse to reply to a request 'only' if there are reasons to assume that supply of the information would 'harm essential national security interests of the requested Member State', or 'jeopardise the success of a current investigation or a criminal intelligence operation or the safety of individuals', or would 'clearly be disproportionate or irrelevant with regard to the purposes for which it has been requested.'[397] A request *may* also be refused if the offence in question is punishable by imprisonment of one year or less in the requested Member State, and *shall* be refused if any required judicial authorization has not been obtained.[398]

The Commission reported on the application of the Framework Decision in practice in 2011.[399] By the end of 2010, about two-thirds of the Member States had applied the measure, but most (except for Germany and France) had used the rules only a handful of times each year. A later evaluation by the Council in autumn 2012 indicated that five Member States still did not apply the rules, and in some Member States the process of information exchange was slowed down because it needed judicial approval.[400]

Furthermore, the cross-border exchange of information is greatly facilitated by the exchange of liaison officers between Member States.[401] Another general measure is an EU Decision of 2005 which facilitates the exchange of information between Member States on criminal records, followed up by further measures adopted in 2009.[402]

As regards customs, the Naples II Convention also sets out rules on the exchange of information upon request, as well as spontaneous assistance.[403] Also, an early Joint Action vaguely encourages the exchange of information and intelligence between and the development of risk analysis techniques by customs authorities.[404]

---

[392] Art 3(4).

[393] Art 4(1), referring to Art 2(2) of the EAW Framework Decision: [2002] OJ L 190/1. For exceptions to this rule, see Art 4(2).

[394] Art 4(3).   [395] Art 4(4).   [396] Art 7.   [397] Art 10(1).

[398] Art 10(2) and (3), referring to Art 3(4).

[399] SEC (2011) 593, 13 May 2011, available as Council doc 10316/11, 18 May 2011.

[400] Council doc 14755/1/12, 15 Nov 2012. See the earlier assessment of compliance (Council doc 15278/11, 14 Oct 2011) and Council conclusions (Council doc 15277/11, 14 Oct 2011).

[401] Arts 47(2)(b) and 125, Schengen Convention, n 390 above; Schengen Executive Committee Decision on liaison officers ([2000] OJ L 239/411); Art 6(3)(b) and (d), Naples II Convention ([1998] OJ C 24/1); and Decision on liaison officers ([2003] OJ L 67/27), as amended ([2006] OJ L 219/31). See also the Resolution on posting of drugs liaison officers to Albania (II.7.11 below). On the past and present legal base for measures concerning liaison officers, see II.7.2.4 above.

[402] [2005] OJ L 322/33 and [2009] OJ L 93/23 and 33. See further II:3.6.1.4 above.

[403] Arts 8–10 and 13–18 ([1998] OJ C 24/1).

[404] [1997] OJ L 159/1. The Commission has proposed to repeal this measure, on the grounds that it is obsolete in light of the CIS and the Naples II Convention: COM (2014) 715, 28 Nov 2014.

Measures concerning terrorism comprise Decisions implementing the EU's Common Position on terrorism as regards police and judicial cooperation,[405] which require the transmission of information concerning terrorist groups or individuals on the EU list to Europol and Eurojust, and a number of soft law measures;[406] one of the latter is questionable on human rights grounds due to the link between terrorists and non-violent protesters which it initially alleged.[407] The Prum Decision also provides for the exchange of information, even without request, 'as is necessary because particular circumstances give reason to believe that the data subjects will commit criminal offences as' provided for in the EU legislation defining terrorism.[408]

The Council has also adopted a number of measures on football security in particular and cooperation on public order more generally.[409] One of these relates particularly to security at summits, and concerns the exchange of information on persons where there are 'substantial grounds for believing that they intend to enter the Member State with the aim of disrupting public order and security at the event or committing offences relating to the event.[410] The Prum Decision also provides for the exchange of non-personal or personal data relating to such meetings, in the latter case 'if any final convictions or other circumstances give reason to believe that the data subjects will commit criminal offences at the events or pose a threat to public order and security'.[411]

In the sphere of drugs, the Council has adopted a Joint Action on the exchange of chemical profiling information, in order to assist 'strategic' analysis of the sources and routes of drug traffickers and the trends in drug production.[412] A later Decision regulates the transmission of samples of controlled substances between Member States.[413] The related field of money laundering is addressed by a Decision requiring Member States to establish financial intelligence units.[414]

As regards immigration offences, the Council has adopted a Decision concerning the exchange of information on counterfeit travel documents,[415] and a Common Position requiring the transfer of data on lost, stolen, or misappropriated passports to Interpol.[416] The Commission has reported that most Member States are implementing

---

[405] [2003] OJ L 16/68, replaced by later Decision ([2005] OJ L 252/23).

[406] Recommendation on cooperation on terrorist financing ([1999] OJ C 373/1); Recommendation on assessing the risk of terrorism against visiting persons ([2001] OJ C 356/1); and Recommendation on exchange of information on terrorists (unpublished; on file with the author).

[407] The Recommendation on exchange of information on terrorists, n 406 above; for criticism, see S Peers, 'EU Responses to Terrorism' (2003) 52 ICLQ 227 at 241–43.

[408] [2008] OJ L 210/1, Art 16. For the legislation referred to, see II:5.5.2.1 above.

[409] Resolution on football hooliganism ([1996] OJ C 131/1); Recommendation on football hooliganism ([1996] OJ C 193/1); Joint Action on cooperation on law, order, and security ([1997] OJ L 147/1); Decision concerning security in connection with football matches with an international dimension ([2002] OJ L 121/1); Council conclusions on implementation of the Decision (press release of JHA Council, 29 Apr 2004); and a Resolution on security at summits ([2004] OJ C 116/18). The Commission has proposed to repeal the 1997 Joint Action, on the grounds that it is obsolete in light of the Prum Decision and the later Decision on football matches: COM (2014) 715, 28 Nov 2014.

[410] Point 1 of the 2004 Resolution (ibid).   [411] Arts 14–15 of the Decision, n 208 above.

[412] [1996] OJ L 322/5. The Commission has proposed to repeal this measure, on the grounds that Europol has taken over this activity: COM (2014) 715, 28 Nov 2014.

[413] [2001] OJ L 150/1.

[414] [2000] OJ L 271/4. See the Commission review of implementation (COM (2007) 827, 20 Dec 2007), and also the CJEU ruling in Case C-212/11 *Jyske Bank*, ECLI:E:C:2013:270, concluding that the Decision did not preclude national law restricting the free movement of capital in order to combat money laundering.

[415] [2000] L 81/1.   [416] [2005] OJ L 27/61.

this Common Position, resulting in a significant increase in the data transmitted and accessed by Member States.[417]

But the most controversial measures in this area both concern the exchange of data from the private sector to law enforcement authorities. First of all, the EU has treaties with the USA, Canada, and Australia requiring the exchange of passenger data with those States' authorities,[418] although the most recent such treaty is being assessed by the CJEU for compliance with fundamental rights.[419] There is also a Directive regulating the transfer of passenger data to immigration authorities of EU Member States, which leaves open to Member States the possibility of further requiring transfer of this data for law enforcement purposes.[420] In 2007, the Commission proposed a Framework Decision on the transfer of such data to law enforcement authorities, but this measure was not agreed before the entry into force of the Treaty of Lisbon.[421] In its place, the Commission tabled a proposed Directive on this issue in 2011, which was agreed by the Council and EP in 2015.[422]

The second particularly controversial issue is the requirement that telecommunications companies collect data and then share it with law enforcement authorities. On this point, the Council has adopted a number of non-binding measures, in particular a Resolution on the interception of telecommunications.[423] The mutual assistance Convention also contains provisions on interception,[424] which concern requests from one Member State to another to intercept telecommunications and the facility, subject to certain conditions, to intercept the telecommunications of a person who is on the territory of another Member State. From May 2017, these rules will be replaced by provisions in the Directive on the European Investigation Order.[425]

But the most hotly disputed issue was the adoption of a Directive in 2006 requiring Member States to compel telecommunications companies to retain traffic and location data not just as regards suspected criminal suspects or their associates, but the entire population (the 'data retention Directive').[426] The background to the Directive dates to 2002, when the EP and Council adopted a Directive on the specific issue of telecommunications privacy, which states that Member States *may* adopt measures derogating from the Directive's rules on privacy of communications, traffic data, and location data:[427]

---

[417] COM (2006) 167, 21 Apr 2006.

[418] See II:7.11 below. On the legal base issues, see I:7.4.3.2.

[419] COM (2013) 528, 18 July 2013 (text of treaty); *Opinion 1/2015*, pending (CJEU case).

[420] Dir 2004/82 ([2004] OJ L 261/24). For details, see I:7.5.2.

[421] COM (2007) 654, 6 Nov 2007.

[422] COM (2011) 32, 2 Feb 2011 (proposal); Council doc 14670/15, 2 Dec 2015 (agreed text).

[423] [1996] OJ C 329/1, discussed further in the first edition of this book, pp 199–200. See also the Council conclusions on information technology and the investigation and prosecution of organized crime (press release, 19 Dec 2002 JHA Council) and on mobile phone cards (press release, 8 May 2003 JHA Council).

[424] Arts 17–22 of the Convention ([2000] OJ C 197/1).

[425] Arts 30 and 31, Dir 2014/41 ([2014] OJ L 130/1).

[426] Dir 2006/24 ([2006] OJ L 105/54), which Member States had to implement by 15 Sep 2007 (Art 15(1)). The legal base of this measure in the first pillar (rather than the third) was disputed unsuccessfully: see II.7.4.3.2 above. On the detailed background to the Directive, see <http://www.statewatch.org/soseurope.htm>, 'surveillance of telecommunications' section. On the issues, see P Breyer, 'Telecommunications Data Retention and Human Rights: The Compatibility of Blanket Traffic Data Retention with the ECHR' (2005) 11 ELJ 373.

[427] Art 15(1), Dir 2002/58 ([2002] OJ L 201/37). This Directive was also amended by Dir 2009/136 ([2009] OJ L 337/11).

...when such restriction constitutes a necessary, appropriate and proportionate measure within a democratic society to safeguard national security (i.e. State security), defence, public security, and the prevention, investigation, detection and prosecution of criminal offences.... To this end, Member States may, inter alia, adopt legislative measures providing for the retention of data for a limited period justified on the grounds laid down in this paragraph. All the measures referred to in this paragraph shall be in accordance with the general principles of Community law, including those referred to in Article 6(1) and (2) of the Treaty on European Union.

The data retention Directive took this further by *requiring* Member States to compel telecommunications providers to retain traffic and location data on customers (although not the content of communications). Member States were allowed to postpone application of that Directive to Internet connections (including e-mails) for eighteen months; no fewer than sixteen Member States did so.[428]

The retention obligation also applied to unsuccessful calls (calls where the phone rang, but no-one answered, or where the phone was engaged), although not to unconnected calls (calls which were never connected to a line at the other end). The purpose of retaining the data was to assist 'the investigation, prosecution and detection of serious crime, as defined by each Member State in its national law';[429] the 2002 Directive still applied to the retention of other types of data (in particular as regards the content of communications, or unconnected calls), or data retained for other purposes (for security services, and arguably for crime prevention and to assist investigation of *less* serious crime).[430] As for access to the data, the conditions of access were defined by reference to national law, although this was subject to the necessity and proportionality principles and observance of, inter alia, the ECHR.[431] The data had to be kept for at least six months and no more than two years; but the legal base of the Directive permitted Member States to retain pre-existing national law which required retention for more than two years on public security grounds, and the Directive furthermore permitted Member States to introduce new laws which had the same effect. In both cases, there was a procedure for Commission approval of the national law, but the Commission could apparently take into account only internal market issues, not human rights principles.[432]

The CJEU ruled against several Member States for failure to apply the Directive.[433] In fact, the CJEU then fined Sweden for non-compliance with the first judgment.[434] According to a Commission report on the evaluation of the Directive in 2011, the Directive was useful for law enforcement but gave rise to concerns about privacy,

---

[428] Art 15(3) of the Directive (permitting a delay until 15 Mar 2009) and attached declarations.

[429] Art 1(1) of the Directive.

[430] See Art 11 of the Directive, inserting an Art 15(1a) into Dir 2002/58. The 2002 Directive still applied to retention of data for civil proceedings: see judgment in C-461/10 *Bonnier Audio*, ECLI:EU:C:2012:219.

[431] Art 4 of the Directive.   [432] See Art 95(4)–(10) EC and Art 12 of the Directive.

[433] Cases: C-185/09 *Commission v Sweden* [2010] ECR I-14*; C-189/09 *Commission v Austria* [2010] ECR I-99*; C-202/09 *Commission v Ireland* [2009] ECR I-203*; and C-211/09 *Commission v Greece* [2009] ECR I-204*.

[434] Case C-270/11 *Commission v Sweden*, ECLI:EU:C:2013:339.

and indeed had been struck down in several national constitutional courts.[435] The Commission intended to table amendments to the Directive, but in the event in its 2014 ruling in *Digital Rights and Seitlinger*, discussed further below, the CJEU ruled that the Directive was invalid for breach of fundamental rights.[436] At time of writing, the Commission was not intending to propose a replacement to the Directive, but Member States' optional decisions to retain data pursuant to the 2002 Directive were being challenged in national courts in light of the Court's ruling in *Digital Rights and Seitlinger*. The CJEU has been asked to clarify this point.[437]

Finally, the EU and the USA decided in 2007 to regulate the informal arrangements by which US anti-terrorist investigators had access to all data concerning financial transfers within the EU.[438] These arrangements subsequently took the form of a treaty, originally rejected by the EP but then approved after renegotiation.[439]

7.6.4 Data protection

The key question from a civil liberties perspective regarding all of the EU measures relating to exchange of information is the rules on data protection. These rules can be found either in a general measure adopted in 2008 (which may be replaced in the near future), or in specific policing measures—or sometimes in both. This section examines the general and the specific data protection rules in turn.

7.6.4.1 General rules on data protection

In 2008, after difficult negotiations, the Council adopted a Framework Decision regulating data protection within the context of policing and criminal law.[440] The purpose of the Framework Decision is:[441]

> ...to ensure a high level of protection of the fundamental rights and freedoms of natural persons, and in particular their right to privacy, with respect to the processing of personal data in the framework of police and judicial cooperation in criminal matters, provided for by Title VI of the Treaty on European Union, while guaranteeing a high level of public safety.

The Framework Decision applies to the transmission of personal data 'for the purpose of the prevention, investigation, detection or prosecution of criminal offences or the execution of criminal penalties,' if those data 'are or have been transmitted or made available' either 'between Member States,' or 'by Member States to authorities or to information systems established on the basis of Title VI of the [former TEU]', or 'to the competent authorities of the Member States by authorities or information systems established on the basis of the [TEU or the former EC Treaty].'[442] However, unlike the

---

[435] COM (2011) 225, 18 April 2011.   [436] II.7.6.4.   [437] Case C-203/15, *Tele2Sverige*.
[438] [2007] OJ C 166/18 and 27.   [439] See II:7.11 below.
[440] [2008] OJ L 350/60. Member States had to implement this measure by 27 Nov 2010: Art 29(1). All references in this sub-section are to this Framework Decision, unless otherwise indicated.
[441] Art 1(1).   [442] Art 1(2).

EC data protection Directive,[443] the Framework Decision does not apply to the processing of data within a Member State, and it permits Member States to apply higher standards regarding the processing of data at national level.[444] It is also 'without prejudice to essential national security interests and specific intelligence activities in the field of national security'.[445] Like the data protection Directive, the Framework Decision applies to the processing of personal data 'wholly or partly by automatic means, and to the processing otherwise than by automatic means, of personal data which form part of a filing system or are intended to form part of a filing system'.[446]

The main substantive provisions of the Framework Decision on data protection provide for the application of the basic data protection principles of lawfulness, proportionality, and purpose limitation, although in a vaguer form than in the data protection Directive.[447] There are also obligations as regards rectification, erasure, and blocking, which differ in some respects from those in the data protection Directive.[448] The obligations to establish time limits for erasure and review and the qualified ban on the processing of 'sensitive' data are broadly similar to the rules in the Directive,[449] as is the ban on taking automated individual decisions, except where this is authorized by a law which lays down necessary safeguards.[450] Member States are required to verify data quality,[451] and there are general rules relating to time limits for keeping data.[452]

The Framework Decision contains specific rules on logging and documentation and exceptions from the purpose limitation rule, as regards data received from other Member States.[453] Member States may set rules on the receipt of data by other Member States or EU agencies, provided that they do not apply restrictions above those applicable in similar domestic cases.[454] There are specific rules on the transfer of data to third states or international bodies, which differ significantly from the rules in the Directive (Article 13);[455] the Framework Decision also confers protection for pre-existing treaties of the EU or its Member States with third states.[456] Furthermore, there are special rules on the transmission of data to private parties in Member States, and a requirement for the recipient of the data to inform the sending authority about the use made of the data, on its request.[457]

As for the rights of data subjects, the right to information for the data subject differs significantly from the rules in the Directive;[458] the right of access to data is weaker than the Directive;[459] there are similar rights to rectification, erasure, or blocking, and

---

[443] Dir 95/46 ([1995] OJ L 281/31); see II.7.3.2 above.
[444] See respectively recital 7 in the preamble, and Art 1(5).
[445] Art 1(4). See the discussion of Art 72 TFEU, in II:2.2.3.2 above. [446] Art 1(3).
[447] Art 3. [448] Compare Art 4 of the Framework Decision to Art 12 of the Dir.
[449] Compare Arts 5 and 6 of the Framework Decision to Arts 6(1)(e) and 8 of the Dir.
[450] Compare Art 7 of the Framework Decision to Art 15 of the Dir.
[451] Art 8; compare to Art 6(1)(d) of the Dir. [452] Art 9; compare to Art 6(1)(e) of the Dir.
[453] Arts 10 and 11. [454] Art 12.
[455] Compare Art 13 of the Framework Decision to Arts 25 and 26 of the Dir. Also, the Framework Decision only applies to external movements of personal data where that data was *first transferred between Member States*; the Dir contains no such limitation.
[456] Art 26; there is no equivalent in the Dir. [457] Arts 14 and 15.
[458] Compare Art 16 of the Framework Decision to Arts 10 and 11 of the Dir.
[459] Compare Art 17 of the Framework Decision to Art 12(a) of the Dir.

to compensation;[460] and the right to a judicial remedy is essentially identical.[461] There are also broad similarities with the Directive as regards the rules on confidentiality, data security, the creation of and relations with national supervisory authorities, and penalties for breach of the Framework Decision.[462]

According to a Commission report on the application of the Framework Decision,[463] most Member States are compliant with it but some had difficulties distinguishing between national data and data transmitted to other Member States. Others had questions about the rules on transfers to third countries.

Overall, as compared to the data protection Directive, the Framework Decision on data protection is generally similar, with a number of differences of detail, which mostly (but not entirely) set lower standards than the Directive. The most significant differences are the territorial scope of the measures, ie the limitation of the Framework Decision to data exchanged between Member States, and the quite different standards as regards data transferred to third States. Furthermore, of course, the Framework Decision is not directly effective.

However, the Framework Decision will likely be replaced by a Directive in the near future,[464] leading to an improvement in the standards applicable in this field.

7.6.4.2 *Specific rules on data protection*

The Framework Decision expressly specifies that where third pillar acts adopted beforehand which concern personal data exchange between Member States or Member States' law enforcement authorities' access to data held in information systems established pursuant to EC legislation (as it was then) set out 'specific conditions' regarding the use of such data by the receiving Member State, those rules have priority over the rules in the Framework Decision.[465] Two clauses in the preamble to the Framework Decision address this issue further, setting out two categories of prior measures. First of all, the preamble refers to those acts which establish a 'complete and coherent set of rules covering all relevant aspects of data protection (principles of data quality, rules on data security, regulation of the rights and safeguards of data subjects, organisation of supervision and liability)', in more detail than the Framework Decision, 'in particular' the rules on Europol, Eurojust, the SIS, the CIS, and access to other Member States' databases in the Prum Decision.[466] Presumably the specific rules in these measures apply entirely instead of the rules in the Framework Decision.

Secondly, the preamble refers to prior third pillar acts which have data protection rules which are 'more limited in scope', including rules governing the purpose for which a receiving Member State can use data, but otherwise referring to the Council of Europe data protection Convention or to national law. In this case, those specific rules in these

---

[460] Compare Arts 18 and 19 of the Framework Decision to Arts 12(b) and 23 of the Dir.
[461] Compare Art 20 of the Framework Decision to Art 22 of the Dir.
[462] Compare Arts 21–4 of the Framework Decision to Arts 16, 22, 18, 24, and 28 of the Dir.
[463] COM (2012) 12, 25 Jan 2012.
[464] COM (2012) 10, 25 Jan 2012 (proposal). Negotiations on this proposal may be finished by the end of 2015.
[465] Art 28.   [466] Para 39 of the preamble.

measures (no such measures are named) apply instead of the Framework Decision if they are 'more restrictive' than the Framework Decision, but otherwise the Framework Decision applies.[467] Arguably this applies in particular to: the 'Swedish' Framework Decision on the exchange of police information and intelligence;[468] the data protection rules in the Schengen Convention generally;[469] the Decision on police access to the VIS;[470] the other aspects of data exchange under the Prum Decision;[471] the exchange of information among customs authorities pursuant to the Naples II Convention,[472] and exchanges between judicial authorities under the mutual assistance Convention.[473]

What about the measures adopted after the entry into force of the Framework Decision? First of all, the Decision establishing the CIS,[474] which replaced the CIS Convention and its Protocols as from 27 May 2011,[475] contains a number of specific references to the data protection Framework Decision, which applies to the CIS unless otherwise provided for in the Decision.[476] Secondly, the Decision establishing Europol, and the amendment to the Decision establishing Eurojust, each specify that the Framework Decision applies to the processing by Member States of the data transmitted between the Member States and Eurojust or Europol, but that the data protection rules applying to Eurojust and Europol as such are not affected by the Framework Decision, because of the 'particular nature, functions and competences of' those bodies.[477] Several measures simply state that the Framework Decision applies to any personal data exchanged pursuant to that measure.[478] Next, the Decision on criminal records states that the Framework Decision 'should' apply in the context of computerized exchange of data between Member States, while allowing Member States to set higher levels of protection,[479] but the *Framework Decision* on criminal records exchange, which the Decision on this issue implements, states that the specific data protection rules in this Framework Decision complement the general data protection rules in force, with no reference to the Framework Decision on data protection.[480]

As for proposed measures, the proposed Directive on passenger name records applies the Framework Decision as regards some issues, but has stricter standards on transfers to third States.[481]

---

[467] Para 40 of the preamble.   [468] [2006] OJ L 386/89; see Art 8.
[469] [2000] OJ L 239, Arts 126–30.   [470] [2008] OJ L 218/129, Arts 8–16.
[471] [2008] OJ L 210/1, Arts 13–16; and see the data protection rules in Arts 24–32.
[472] Art 25 of the Convention ([1998] OJ C 24).
[473] Art 23 of the Convention ([2000] OJ C 197/1).   [474] [2009] OJ L 323/20.   [475] Art 34.
[476] Art 20.
[477] [2009] OJ L 138/14, recital 13 in the preamble (Eurojust) and [2009] OJ L 121/37, recital 12 in the preamble (Europol).
[478] Before the Treaty of Lisbon, see the Framework Decisions on conflicts of jurisdiction ([2009] OJ L 328/42), recital 18 in the preamble and on the recognition of pre-trial supervision orders ([2009] OJ L 294/20), recital 19 in the preamble. After the Treaty of Lisbon, see: Dir 2011/99 on protection orders ([2009] OJ L 338/2), recital 36 in the preamble; Dir 2014/41 on the European Investigation Order ([2014] OJ L 130/1), Art 20; and Reg 603/2013 on Eurodac ([2013] OJ L 180/1), Arts 33–5.
[479] [2009] OJ L 93/33, recital 18 in the preamble.
[480] [2009] OJ L 93/23, recital 13 in the preamble.
[481] COM (2012) 32, 2 Feb 2012, Arts 8, 11, and 12.

Finally, although the data protection Framework Decision states that treaties agreed after its adoption should be subject to its rules, none of the treaties adopted subsequently refer to the Framework Decision.[482]

7.6.5 Assessment

Are the EU rules on information exchange and data protection adequate? First of all, as for the three most controversial measures, each provides for mass exchange of information on a large proportion of the population, not just criminal suspects, and thus is particularly difficult to justify in light of the jurisprudence of the European Court of Human Rights and the CJEU.[483] The treaty on transfers of financial information to the USA at first sight limits itself to requests in specific cases only, but as the European Data Protection Supervisor has pointed out, in practice the information concerned will still be transferred in bulk, and Europol is an unsuitable body to carry out a supervisory function.[484]

As for passenger name data exchange, the EP had rightly argued before the Court of Justice that the treaty with the US does not guarantee an 'adequate level of protection' for personal data, as required by EU data protection law, in particular because the measures are not sufficiently prescribed by law, the amount of data to be transferred and the period of storage are disproportionate, judicial review is not adequate, and there are insufficient controls on the further exchange of data with other authorities.[485] However, the Court of Justice did not rule on this part of the complaint. It remains to be seen what the Court will rule on the later complaint relating to the treaty with Canada.[486]

Finally, as for the data retention Directive, as noted already, the CJEU struck it down in the landmark judgment in *Digital Rights and Seitlinger*.[487] According to the CJEU, first of all the Directive interfered with the protection of the rights to privacy and data protection, so the question was whether this interference could be justified.[488] The Court carried out this assessment pursuant to Article 52 of the EU Charter of Fundamental Rights, which states that any limitation upon Charter rights must be laid down by law, respect the essence of the right, and subject to the principle of proportionality, limit rights and freedoms only if it is necessary and genuinely meets public interest objectives and the rights and freedoms of others.

In the Court's view, there was a public interest justification (public safety) for the restriction of the Charter rights at issue. Also, the 'essence' of the rights was not affected, because (as regards the right to privacy) the content of communications was not recorded, and (as regards the right to data protection) certain data processing and data security rules had to be respected. Therefore the key issue was the proportionality

---

[482] On those treaties, see II:7.11 below.   [483] See II.7.3.1 above.
[484] See: <http://www.edps.europa.eu/EDPSWEB/webdav/site/mySite/shared/Documents/Consultation/Opinions/2010/10-06-22_Opinion_TFTP_EN.pdf>.
[485] See Joined Cases C-317/04 and C-318/04 *EP v Council and Commission* [2006] ECR I-4721.
[486] *Opinion 1/2015*, pending.
[487] Joined Cases C-291/12 and C-594/12, ECLI:EU:C:2014:238.
[488] On the human rights framework, see II:7.3.2 above.

of the interference with Charter rights. On this point, the Court indicated that judicial review of the EU legislature's discretion should be 'strict' in this case, applying factors such as the area of law concerned, the nature of the right, the nature and seriousness of the infringement and the objective pursued. Here, it followed from the nature of the right and the nature and seriousness of the infringement that the EU legislature's discretion was reduced; the CJEU took no account expressly of the objective being pursued.

The first aspect of proportionality (the appropriateness of the interference with the right for obtaining the objective) was fulfilled, because the data concerned might be useful to investigations. However, the CJEU found that the Directive was problematic as regards the second facet: the necessity of the measure in question. Crucially the Court ruled that the important objective of investigating serious crime and terrorism did 'not, in itself' justify data retention. Its analysis proceeded by setting out the general importance of safeguards as regards the protection of privacy and data protection rights (building upon the case law of the European Court of Human Rights). These safeguards are even more necessary when data is processed automatically, with a risk of unlawful access. Applying this test, the Court gave three reasons why the rules on data retention in the Directive were not strictly necessary. First of all, the Directive had an extremely broad scope, given that it applied to all means of electronic communication, which have 'widespread and growing importance' in everyday life, without being sufficiently targeted. Indeed, it 'entails an interference with the fundamental rights of practically the entire European population'. In other words (the Court does not use the term), it amounts to mass surveillance.

Secondly, besides the 'general absence of limits' in the Directive, it failed to limit access to the data concerned by law enforcement authorities, and the subsequent use of that data, sufficiently precisely. In particular: it referred generally to 'serious crime' as defined in national law; it did not restrict the purpose of subsequent access to that data; it did not limit the number of persons who could access the data; and it did not control access to the data by means of a court or other independent administrative authority. Thirdly, the Directive did not set out sufficient safeguards, as regards: the data retention period, for instance as regards the categories of data to be retained for the whole period; the protection of the data from unlawful access and use (here the CJEU criticizes the possible limits on protection measures due to reasons of cost); the absence of an obligation to destroy the data; and the omission of a requirement to retain the data within the EU only.

The Court's ruling is open to alternative interpretations: does it rule out all mass surveillance, or just mass surveillance without specific safeguards? If the former, how to define mass surveillance? Does it apply equally to purely optional surveillance imposed by Member States pursuant to the 2002 Directive on telecommunications privacy? The CJEU has been asked to answer these questions, and its answers are eagerly awaited.[489] But in any event, the judgment sends the signal that there are significant limits on the degree of interference with the privacy rights of the general population that can be accepted, even when there are grave concerns about terrorist threats.

---

[489] *Opinion 1/2015* and *Tele2Sverige*, nn 486 and 437 above.

Moving on to the EU's data protection rules, the Framework Decision is problematic due to its limited scope of application and relatively low standards overall, as compared to the EU's data protection Directive. The EU's more specific data protection rules create a fragmented system and neither these measures nor the Framework Decision explain their relationship to each other sufficiently clearly. As for the substance, the grounds to refuse access to information about their data to data subjects are so broad that any effective scrutiny of the processes depends upon the supervisory authorities, but it is doubtful that they have the money or resources to perform this function effectively.

7.7 Other forms of Police Cooperation

As explained at the outset of this chapter,[490] while the Treaty of Amsterdam made a distinction between policing operations and issues such as training, research, and investigative techniques, this distinction did not have any relevance until the entry into force of the Treaty of Lisbon, which set out different decision-making procedures in Article 87 TFEU for operational police cooperation on the one hand and non-operational police cooperation on the other. While it is therefore necessary to distinguish between these two types of cooperation as regards measures adopted after the entry into force of the Treaty of Lisbon,[491] no clear distinction between them was made beforehand. So the discussion in this section of the measures which were adopted previously does not seek to draw that distinction retroactively. Rather it first examines certain specific measures which have been adopted, as regards controlled deliveries, the European Police College, and the Police Chiefs' Task Force, and then examines other forms of cooperation generally, bringing together the various instruments affecting different forms of crime.

7.7.1 Controlled deliveries

In order to increase the effectiveness of investigations into the criminal organizations behind the import or export of drugs or other illegal products, EU measures facilitate 'controlled deliveries', under which national law enforcement officers do not intercept shipments at the border, but rather allow the products to cross the territory under surveillance, in the hope of finding out more information about the criminal networks involved.

Controlled deliveries were first mentioned in the Schengen Convention, when Member States undertook to permit them as regards drug trafficking, subject to prior authorization and the guarantee that Member States would retain responsibility and control over and the right to intervene as regards deliveries carried out on their territory.[492] A similar provision, applicable 'in the framework of criminal investigations into extraditable offences', appears in the EU's mutual judicial assistance Convention.[493]

---

[490] II.7.2.3.
[491] For analysis of this issue, see II.7.2.4 above. The measures adopted concerning the cross-border movement of police officers are considered separately in II.7.9 below.
[492] Art 73 of the Convention ([2000] OJ L 239).
[493] Art 12 of the Convention ([2000] OJ C 197).

From May 2017, this provision of the Convention will be replaced by the Directive establishing a European Investigation Order, which requires a request for a controlled delivery to be accepted unless the grounds for refusal apply.[494] As for customs, the Naples II Convention requires Member States to permit controlled deliveries for customs supervision of other types of goods, again as regards all extraditable offences.[495]

7.7.2 European Police College

As called for by the Tampere European Council, the European Police College was established by a Decision in December 2000.[496] The College was established as a network of national training institutes, and its governing board is made up of the directors of the national institutes for training senior police officers. Its main task is to provide training for senior police officers, along with training of trainers and development of training programmes; it is also obliged to develop links with third countries.

A report on the first three years of operation of the College indicated that there were practical difficulties with the framework established by the initial Decision, in particular the lack of legal personality for the College, an under-funded permanent Secretariat, and the lack of a permanent seat.[497] Due to an ongoing dispute about the seat of various EU bodies, the College had been located provisionally in Denmark in facilities offered by the Danish government. The secretariat comprised only three staff, and the College finances were precarious in the absence of regular funding from the EU budget.

Subsequent to this report, and to a European Council summit agreement in December 2003 on the location of various EU institutions,[498] the Council adopted further decisions respectively conferring legal personality upon the College and officially setting the seat of the College in Bramshill in the United Kingdom.[499] Subsequently, the Decision establishing the College was overhauled, with effect from the start of 2006, to integrate it into the EU institutional framework, in particular funding the College from the EU budget, and applying EU rules on privileges and immunities, budgeting, and staff.[500] The 2005 Decision also elaborates on the functions of the College's Governing Board and Director.

Following the entry into force of the Treaty of Lisbon, the rules establishing the College were amended again. First of all, a Regulation provided for moving the College to Hungary, since the UK no longer wished to host it.[501] Secondly, a further Regulation adopted in 2015 overhauled the legal framework of the College again.[502] The revised rules involve the Police College in the Commission's planned law enforcement training system,[503] clarify and update its objectives, and improve its governance.

---

[494] Art 28, Dir 2014/41 ([2014] OJ L 130/1); see II:3.6.1.3 above.

[495] Art 22, Naples II Convention ([1998] OJ C 24).

[496] [2000] OJ L 336/1. See the College website: <http://www.cepol.net>.

[497] Council doc 15722/03, 9 Dec 2003.   [498] [2004] OJ C 20/18.

[499] [2004] OJ L 251/19 and 20. See also the JHA Council conclusions on the College report (press release of JHA Council, 19 Feb 2004).

[500] [2005] OJ L 256/63.   [501] Reg 543/2014 ([2014] OJ L 163/5).

[502] Reg 2015/2219 ([2015] OJ L 319/1).   [503] See COM (2013) 172, 27 Mar 2013.

7.7.3 Police Chiefs' Task Force

Following the decision, as set out in the Tampere conclusions, to create a task force of EU police chiefs, the task force was established in the spring of 2000 and has met regularly since then. However, the task force has never been placed on a formal footing by any formal EU measure—even by an EU soft law measure—or by its establishment as a Council working group. After much discussion, it decided to focus inter alia upon planning joint operations and making policy recommendations to the Council.[504] In the Commission's view, '[t]here is general agreement, however, that so far, these efforts have not led to an operational added value at EU level'.[505] Subsequently, it was decided that the Task Force would meet within the framework of Europol as regards its operational tasks, and within Council structures as regards its strategic tasks.[506] The Task Force has been criticized for its unclear legal status and the lack of transparency of its proceedings (since the Council claims that the EU access to documents rules do not apply to it), in light of its apparently significant role in operations and policy development.[507]

7.7.4 Other measures

There are a number of general EU measures in this area. First of all, the Schengen Convention contains provisions on enhancing communications between border police forces and requiring Member States to ensure that hotel staff register foreigners staying in commercial accommodation.[508] The Schengen Executive Committee also adopted Decisions, now integrated into EU law, concerning crime prevention and detection in the context of cross-border police cooperation, a Handbook on cross-border police cooperation, police telecommunications, and principles governing the payment of informers.[509] The Council, in the Maastricht period, adopted a parallel Resolution regarding use of informers.[510] Subsequently, the Council adopted a catalogue of best practices and recommendations regarding Schengen police cooperation.[511] The Council has adopted conclusions concerning police professional standards applicable to international police operations, with a view towards developing such standards, but has not addressed this issue further.[512] Finally, the Council has adopted a Framework Decision governing forensic standards.[513]

As for specific issues, first of all, the Schengen Convention contains a number of provisions on drugs.[514] Member States 'undertake' to adopt 'all necessary measures to

---

[504] For a summary of developments, see the Statewatch analysis by T Bunyan, *The EU's Police Chief Task Force (PCTF) and Police Chiefs Committee*, online at: <http://www.statewatch.org/news/2006/mar/pctf.pdf>, and the Commission's communication on police cooperation (COM (2004) 376, 19 May 2004), 19–21.
[505] Ibid, 21.   [506] See press release, JHA Council of 19 Nov 2004.
[507] See Bunyan, n 504 above.   [508] Arts 44 and 45 of the Convention ([2000] OJ L 239).
[509] Respectively [2000] OJ L 239/407, 408, 409, and 417. The first of these measures was repealed by the 2006 Framework Decision on police cooperation ([2006] OJ L 386/89, Art 12(2)), on which see II.7.6.3 above. The Commission has proposed to repeal the second measure, on the grounds that it is obsolete: COM (2014) 714, 28 Nov 2014.
[510] [1997] OJ C 10/1.   [511] Council doc 10842/09, 16 June 2009.
[512] Council doc 14633/04, 15 Nov 2004, adopted by the Dec 2004 JHA Council.
[513] [2009] OJ L 322/14, applicable from 20 Nov 2013 (DNA data) and 30 Nov 2015 (fingerprints) (Art 7).
[514] Arts 70–6 of the Convention and an Executive Committee Decision ([2000] OJ L 239/463). Arts 70 and 74 were not integrated into the EU legal order (see Council Decision, [1999] OJ L 176/1). Arts 71–3 were allocated to the third pillar, Art 75 and the Executive Committee Decision were allocated to Art 95 EC,

prevent and punish the illicit trafficking' in drugs, and 'to prevent and punish by administrative and penal measures the illegal export... as well as the sale, supply and handing over' of drugs. To 'combat the illegal import' of drugs, checks on external borders must be increased.[515] Member States must also provide for seizure and confiscation of the proceeds of drug trafficking, and undertake to permit 'controlled deliveries' regarding drug trafficking.[516] Individuals who move between Member States can carry drugs necessary for their treatment, as long as they carry a certificate.[517] Finally, Member States shall, 'where necessary', adopt measures to control drugs which are subject to greater restriction in other Member States.[518]

EU measures against narcotic drugs have been developed in the framework of successive multi-annual Action Plans.[519] Over the years, EU action has included further measures concerning substantive criminal law, particularly harmonizing the law concerning drug precursors, drug trafficking, and synthetic drugs.[520] Specific anti-drugs measures concerning the harmonizing of policing have comprised Resolutions or Recommendations on: coordination between police and customs regarding combating drugs;[521] drugs statistics;[522] drugs indicators;[523] generic classification of new synthetic drugs;[524] drug abuse in prisons;[525] investigation methods (in particular suggesting simultaneous investigation into criminal assets);[526] cooperation between national authorities;[527] training of drugs law enforcement officers;[528] and guidelines for taking samples of seized drugs.[529] A Joint Action addresses customs/business cooperation against drug trafficking.[530]

Non-policing measures have included Resolutions and Recommendations on the recreational use of drugs,[531] prevention and reduction of health-related harm associated with drug dependence,[532] the incorporation of drug prevention in the school curriculum,[533] inclusion of substance abuse in the university curriculum,[534] drug dependencies and national health care,[535] the role of families,[536] and road accidents.[537] The EU also has established an agency monitoring the use of narcotic drugs,[538] and its health funding programmes address drug-related issues.[539]

---

and Art 76 was allocated jointly to the third pillar and to Arts 95 and 152 EC (see Council Decision, [1999] OJ L 176/17). Arts 95 and 152 are now Arts 114 and 168 TFEU.

[515] Art 71.   [516] Arts 72 and 73; on 'controlled deliveries', see further II.7.7.1 above.

[517] Art 75 and Executive Committee Decision, n 509 above. Furthermore, restrictions on cross-border purchases of prescription drugs will, to an extent, violate EU free movement rules: see Cases C-62/90 *Commission v Germany* [1992] ECR I-2575 and C-322/01 *Doc Morris* [2003] ECR I-14887.

[518] Art 76.   [519] The most recent Plan is set out in [2012] OJ C 402/1.

[520] See II:5.5.1.2 above.   [521] [1996] OJ C 375/1, replaced by [2006] OJ L 124/1.

[522] Council doc 12411/01, 10 Oct 2001.   [523] Council doc 13932/01, 15 Nov 2001.

[524] See JHA council press release, 28 Nov 2002.

[525] See JHA council press release, 27–8 Feb 2003.   [526] [2002] OJ C 114/1.

[527] [2002] OJ C 114/3.   [528] [2004] OJ C 38/1.   [529] [2004] OJ C 86/10.

[530] [1996] OJ L 322/3.   [531] Council doc 5095/3/02, 15 Apr 2002.

[532] [2003] OJ L 165/31. See earlier Conclusions on the health aspects of drugs ([1997] OJ C 241/7).

[533] See JHA Council press release, 13 June 2002.

[534] See Agriculture Council press release, June 2003.   [535] See ibid.

[536] [2004] OJ C 97/4.   [537] [2004] OJ C 97/1.

[538] Reg 302/93 ([1993] OJ L 36/1), recast by Reg 1920/2006 ([2006] OJ L 376/1).

[539] Initially there was a specific measure on drug-related matters (Decision 102/97, [1997] OJ L 19/25, extended by Decision 521/2001, [2001] OJ L 79/1). Drug-related health measures then formed part of the EU's general health funding programme (Decision 1786/2002, [2002] OJ L 271/1), and now again form a

EU measures combating terrorism usually address the exchange of information,[540] but the EU has also adopted a Joint Action establishing an inventory of expertise on this issue,[541] as well as a 2002 Recommendation on the drawing up of terrorist profiles.[542]

Another issue to which the EU has devoted considerable effort is the fight against organized crime. In this field,[543] measures comprise a Joint Action establishing an inventory of competences concerning organized crime,[544] a Resolution on policing international crime routes,[545] a Resolution establishing a model protocol on public/private partnerships against organized crime,[546] and Council conclusions on an administrative approach to tackling organized crime.[547]

Measures concerning trafficking in persons comprise a number of soft law measures, in particular a Recommendation of November 2003 concerning the law enforcement response to trafficking.[548] As regards missing children, a Council Resolution addresses the role of civil society in assisting police investigations.[549] Also, a Decision concerning child pornography sets out a number of measures in order to combat this crime.[550]

As for public order, the Council has adopted a Resolution on a Handbook containing detailed suggestions regarding public order at football matches.[551] Following conflicts between police and protestors at EU summits ('European Council' meetings), the Council adopted detailed conclusions in July 2001, a manual concerning security at summits in November 2002,[552] and a Resolution on security at summits in April 2004.[553]

High-technology crime has been addressed by a Council Recommendation on Member States' creation of 24-hour specialized contact points,[554] and a number of aspects of vehicle crime have been addressed by a Council Decision of 2004.[555] The EU has created formal networks of national officials to encourage operational cooperation as regards: the protection of public figures;[556] the exchange of information and

---

separate programme (still with the legal base of health policy): Decision 1750/2007, [2007] OJ L 257/23. Drugs issues now form part of the current health funding programme (Reg 282/2014 [2014] L 86/1).

[540] See II.7.6.3 above, and also II.7.4.5 above (sanctions) and II.7.9.4 below (joint investigations).

[541] [1996] OJ L 273/1. The Commission has proposed to repeal this measure, on the grounds that Europol has taken over this activity: COM (2014) 715, 28 Nov 2014.

[542] See text at: <https://www.consilium.europa.eu/ueDocs/cms_Data/docs/polju/en/EJN280.pdf>.

[543] See also the Commission communication on a strategy against organized crime (COM (2005) 232, 2 June 2005).

[544] [1996] OJ L 342/2. The Commission has proposed to repeal this measure, on the grounds that Europol has taken over this activity: COM (2014) 715, 28 Nov 2014.

[545] [1999] OJ C 162/1.   [546] [2004] OJ C 116/20.

[547] Council doc 14125/2/04, 24 Nov 2004, adopted by the Dec 2004 JHA Council.

[548] Council doc 15028/03, 19 Nov 2003. See also Council conclusions on trafficking in persons ([2003] OJ C 137/1), a Council resolution on the law enforcement response ([2003] OJ C 260/4), a Commission decision establishing an expert group of advisors ([2003] OJ L 79/25), and an Action Plan against human trafficking ([2005] OJ C 311/1). See further I:7.5.4 above.

[549] [2001] OJ C 283/1.

[550] [2000] OJ L 138. See also the measures referred to in II.7.4.7 above.

[551] [1999] OJ C 196/1, replaced by subsequent Resolutions ([2002] OJ C 22/1, [2006] OJ C 322/1, and [2010] OJ C 165/1).

[552] Council doc 12637/3/02, 12 Nov 2002.   [553] See also II.7.6.3 above.

[554] [2001] OJ C 187/5.   [555] [2004] OJ L 389/28.

[556] Council Decision ([2002] OJ L 333/1), amended in 2009 ([2009] OJ L 283/62); see implementation in [2003] OJ C 260/6.

contact points concerning genocide, crimes against humanity, and war crimes;[557] asset recovery;[558] and anti-corruption.[559]

Finally, the EU and EC have adopted a number of related instruments concerning the protection of the euro from counterfeiting.[560] Framework Decisions (and later a Directive) have harmonized the substantive law and extended mutual recognition to sentences in this field.[561] Other early measures comprised a Regulation which laid down detailed obligations regarding counterfeit notes and coins,[562] a parallel third pillar Decision concerning criminal investigations,[563] and an EU funding programme, 'Pericles'.[564] Subsequently the Council adopted a further Recommendation on the issue,[565] and the Commission established a scientific centre to assist cooperation against euro counterfeiting.[566] The European Central Bank has also adopted measures.[567]

7.8 Europol

Europol had an embryonic existence for over five years in the form of the Europol Drugs Unit (EDU). The EDU was created before the TEU entered into force, by a Ministerial agreement in June 2003, and initially focused solely on combating drug trafficking and associated criminal organizations and money laundering.[568] Its legal status was subsequently based on a 1995 Council Joint Action, which also expanded its role to cover trafficking in nuclear and radioactive substances, 'crimes involving clandestine immigration networks', and 'illicit vehicle trafficking'.[569] Its role was expanded again by a 1996 Joint Action, which gave it the mandate to cover 'traffic in human beings'.[570] The EDU's role was to exchange information (including personal information) about investigations and to prepare 'general situation reports and analyses of criminal activities', but it lacked a central database and so information could only be exchanged between Member States' liaison officers on the basis of each officer's national data protection law.[571]

The EDU was finally replaced by Europol as from 1 July 1999, when Europol began operations because the Europol Convention, signed in 1995,[572] had entered into force

---

[557] Council Decisions ([2002] L 167/1 and [2003] OJ L 118/12).

[558] [2007] OJ L 332/103. For analysis of the role of asset recovery offices, see the Commission communication on crime proceeds (COM (2008) 766, 20 Nov 2008).

[559] [2008] OJ L 301/38.

[560] For further information, see: <http://ec.europa.eu/economy_finance/euro/anti-counterfeiting/index_en.htm>.

[561] See II:5.5.1.2 and II:3.7.2 above.   [562] Reg 1338/2001 ([2001] OJ L 181/6).

[563] [2001] OJ L 329/1.

[564] [2001] OJ L 339/50; the programme was extended ([2006] OJ L 26/40 and [2006] OJ L 330/28). For the 2014–20 programme, see Reg 331/2014, [2014] OJ L 103/1.

[565] Council doc 6927/5/03, 22 Sep 2003, adopted by the JHA Council, 2–3 Oct 2003.

[566] See Council Decision conferring power on Commission ([2003] OJ L 325/44) and Commission Decision establishing the Centre ([2005] OJ L 19/73).

[567] See ECB Recommendation on euro counterfeiting ([1999] OJ C 11/13), Decision on access to counterfeit monitoring system ([2001] OJ C 337/49), and treaties with Interpol ([2004] OJ C 134/6) and Europol (II.7.11 below).

[568] T Bunyan, ed., *Key Texts on Justice and Home Affairs in the European Union* (1997), 47.

[569] [1995] OJ L 62/1.   [570] [1996] OJ L 342/4.

[571] On the EDU in practice, see p 211 of the first edition of this book.   [572] [1995] OJ C 316/1.

on 1 October 1998, and the last of various required supplementary measures had entered into force.[573] This institutional framework was supplemented by five Protocols to the Convention:

a) a Protocol signed in 1996, which conferred jurisdiction upon national courts to refer questions on the Europol Convention to the Court of Justice;[574]

b) a Protocol signed in 1997, which provided for privileges and immunities for Europol staff;[575]

c) a Protocol signed in 2000, which extended Europol's competence to cover all forms of money laundering;[576]

d) a Protocol signed in 2002, which expressly permitted Europol to participate in joint investigative teams and to ask the competent authorities of Member States to begin investigations;[577] and

e) a Protocol signed in 2003, which made a number of amendments to the Convention,[578] inter alia as regards extensions of Europol's competence, further communication of data to third states and bodies, an enhanced role for the EP, and rules on a right of access to Europol documents.

There were also a large number of secondary measures adopted by the Council or Europol's Management Board.[579]

However, as from 1 January 2010, the basic legal acts governing Europol (the Convention and Protocols) were replaced by a third pillar Council Decision (the 'Europol Decision') adopted in 2009.[580] From that point on, EU rules on staff and budgets (including finance from the EU budget) have applied to Europol.[581] A parallel Regulation specifies that Europol staff do not have immunity when they participate in joint investigation teams.[582] The Europol Decision is supplemented by a number of implementing measures,[583] and the Council has also adopted a Decision establishing a joint secretariat for the data protection authority for Europol, the SIS, and the CIS.[584] In 2015, the EU institutions agreed on a Regulation that will refound Europol following the entry into force of the Treaty of Lisbon.[585]

---

[573] [1999] OJ C 185/1.

[574] [1996] OJ C 299/1, in force 29 Dec 1998. Some Member States opted out of the Court's jurisdiction. No cases have yet been referred to the Court.

[575] [1997] OJ C 221/1, in force 1 July 1999.   [576] [2000] OJ C 358/1, in force 29 Mar 2007.

[577] [2002] OJ C 312/1, in force 3 Apr 2007. See also two earlier Council Recommendations on these issues: [2000] OJ C 289/8 and C 357/7.

[578] [2003] OJ C 358/1, in force 18 Apr 2007.

[579] For more details of the legal framework governing Europol before 2010, see the second edition of this book, pp 536–8.

[580] [2009] OJ L 121/27. All further references in this section are to this Decision, unless otherwise noted.

[581] Arts 39 and 42–4.   [582] Reg 371/2009, [2009] OJ L 121/1.

[583] Rules of procedure of the Joint Supervisory Board [2010] OJ C 45/2; Management Board decision on appointment of the Director and Deputy Directors ([2009] OJ L 348/3); Management Board decision on conditions for data processing ([2009] OJ L 348/1); Council decision on confidentiality rules ([2009] OJ L 332/17); Management Board decision on the rules for analysis work files ([2009] OJ L 325/14); Council decision on the States which Europol can sign treaties with ([2009] OJ L 325/12); and Council decision on Europol's relations with external partners ([2009] OJ L 325/6).

[584] [2000] OJ L 271/1.   [585] Council doc 14713/15, 1 Dec 2015.

Europol is an international organization with legal personality,[586] headquartered in the Hague.[587] Its chief organ is a Management Board, made up of one representative from each Member State with one from the Commission and taking most decisions by a two-thirds vote,[588] although day-to-day management is in the hands of a Director and Deputy Directors.[589] The Board must report annually to the Council on both the previous year's activities and plans for the previous year, and the Council forwards these reports to the European Parliament.[590]

Europol's main tasks are to: 'collect, store, process, analyse and exchange information and intelligence'; inform national authorities of information about criminal activities; aid national investigations; ask national authorities to begin or coordinate investigations; to provide intelligence and support as regards major events; and to draw up threat assessments and strategic analyses.[591] These tasks include analysis of Internet information, and it has the additional tasks of developing knowledge of investigative procedures, advising on investigations, and providing strategic intelligence.[592] It may also assist with 'support, advice and research' as regards training national staff, technical support, crime prevention methods, and technical and forensic police methods and investigative procedures,[593] and acts as the central office for coordinating action against euro counterfeiting.[594] Europol's external relations are considered later in this Chapter.[595]

Europol has competence over 'organised crime, terrorism and other forms of serious crime' listed in the Annex to the Europol Decision, as long as those crimes '[affect] two or more Member States in such a way as to require a common approach by the Member States owing to the scale, significance and consequences of the offences'.[596] It has competence also over specified 'related criminal offences'.[597] Europol has also been given further tasks in various legislative measures adopted by the Council,[598] as well as the role of supervisory body as regards transfers of financial data to the United States.[599] It has also been given access to the data in the SIS, SIS II, VIS, CIS, and Eurodac.[600]

In concrete terms, Europol can participate in joint investigation teams, request national authorities to begin investigations, establish information systems (in particular the Europol Information System), and open analysis work files.[601] Member States must establish national units for relations with Europol, which shall send liaison officers to it.[602]

---

[586] Art 2(1).　　[587] Protocol 6 to the consolidated Treaties.　　[588] Art 37.　　[589] Art 38.
[590] Art 37(10).　　[591] Art 5(1).　　[592] Art 5(2) and (3).　　[593] Art 5(4).
[594] Art 5(5), referring to the earlier Decision on this issue ([2005] OJ L 185/35).　　[595] II.7.11.
[596] Art 4(1). The Annex lists a further twenty-four crimes, with definitions of four of them.
[597] Art 4(3).
[598] See particularly: the Council Resolution concerning international crime routes ([1999] OJ C 162/1); Art 2 of the Decision concerning child pornography ([2000] OJ L 138); Arts 3 and 4(1) of the Decision on counterfeiting the euro ([2001] OJ L 329/1); Art 8 of the Decision on liaison officers ([2003] OJ L 67/27), as amended ([2006] OJ L 219/31); Art 7 of the Decision on vehicle crime ([2004] OJ L 389/28); the Recommendation on use of joint investigation teams ([2003] OJ C 121/1, subsequently amended in [2010] OJ C 70/1); the Decisions on exchange of information on terrorism ([2003] OJ L 16/68 and [2005] OJ L 253/22); and the Decision on procedure for banning designer drugs ([2005] OJ L 127/32).
[599] Art 4 of the 'Swift' treaty ([2010] OJ L 195/1).　　[600] See Art 21 and further II.7.6.1 above.
[601] Arts 6–7 and 10–16.　　[602] Arts 8–9.

Under its current legal framework, is Europol sufficiently accountable? It must be admitted that Europol does not have powers as extensive as those of national police authorities; in particular, it lacks the power to arrest, question, and detain suspects. Nevertheless, there is still insufficient national or European parliamentary accountability as regards the powers Europol does exercise, and the position regarding judicial control is not clear. While Europol's annual reports are somewhat informative, they inevitably reflect the position of the agency; there is an obvious need for a continuing independent and objective scrutiny and evaluation of Europol in practice.[603]

7.9 Cross-Border Operations

There are no specific principles to determine which State has jurisdiction over an investigation when there are several possible 'home' States. Investigating authorities presume jurisdiction to investigate a crime based on the jurisdiction rules which apply in their home State,[604] and the Court of Justice has confirmed that multiple investigations do not breach the rule on cross-border double jeopardy.[605]

While the basic rules concerning operations by police officers are set out in the Schengen Convention, the basic rules concerning customs operations are set out in the Naples II Convention,[606] which entered into force in all Member States in 2009. The latter Convention sets out basic rules regarding all types of operations, as well as special rules for each type.[607] As well as the measures discussed below, the Convention allows one Member State's customs investigators to request another's to carry out surveillance or enquiries on their own territory.[608] Certain relevant provisions also appear in the EU's mutual judicial assistance Convention,[609] which is in force in a large majority of Member States.[610] The Convention contains general rules on the civil and criminal liability of national officials involved in operations.[611]

7.9.1 Hot pursuit

The Schengen Convention and Naples II Convention provide for hot pursuit by police and customs officers respectively.[612] Schengen rules permit the police officers from specified forces from the 'home State' of an investigation to chase persons across a land border without authorization of the 'host State' if there is not enough time to inform

---

[603] For more detailed criticism and analysis, see S Peers, 'Governance and the Third Pillar: The Accountability of Europol' in D Curtin and R Wessel, eds., *Good Governance and the European Union* (Intersentia, 2005), 253.

[604] See II:6.5 above.

[605] Case C-491/07 *Turansky* [2008] ECR I-11039. Nevertheless, overlapping investigations, unless coordinated effectively, may lead to wasted resources (due to the EU ban on prosecuting a person after a prior final judgment relating to the same acts in another Member State: see II:6.8 above) or an uncooperative 'turf battle'.

[606] Ibid; explanatory report at [1998] OJ C 189/1.

[607] The basic rules, including rules on liability of officers, are in Art 19; the specific rules are in Arts 20–4.

[608] Arts 11 and 12 ([1998] OJ C 24).   [609] [2000] OJ C 197/1.

[610] See ratification details in Appendix I.   [611] Arts 15 and 16 of the Convention.

[612] Arts 41 and 20 of each Convention respectively.

the host State authorities or for the latter to reach the scene.[613] In view of the sensitivity of this power, the pursuit is essentially governed by the host State's law. The pursuing officers must inform host State authorities of their pursuit as soon as possible and the latter can order a stop to the pursuit. A number of additional conditions are attached:

a) police can only chase persons who have escaped a custodial sentence or provisional custody, or who were apprehended committing or participating in certain crimes;[614]

b) a host State may limit home State police to acting within a specified area or for a specified time;

c) a host State may prohibit home State officers from apprehending a suspect; if it does not, then the pursuing officers may 'detain' the person being pursued until the host State officers can make an arrest or establish the person's identity;

d) home State officers are subject to host State laws and to the instructions of host State authorities;

e) home State officers must be identifiable from their vehicle, uniform, or armband, and cannot enter private homes or places not accessible to the public;

f) home State officers may carry service weapons, but can only use them in 'legitimate self-defence';

g) a person who is 'apprehended' by home State officers (see the rule in (c), above) may be handcuffed during the transfer and subjected only to a security search by those officers; items he or she is carrying may be seized by those officers;[615]

h) the home State officers must always account for each operation before the host State's authorities and must assist in any subsequent enquiries if requested by the host State.

It is implicit that if the pursuing police catch the person they are chasing, they cannot simply take him or her back across the border, but must hand the person they have caught over to the host State authorities and arrange to issue an extradition request (or presumably now issue a European arrest warrant, in most cases).[616] The pursued person may be questioned by the host State authorities after arrest, whatever his or her nationality; this is subject to the host State's national law. But if the apprehended person is not a national of the host State, he or she must be released by those authorities within six hours (discounting midnight to 9.00 a.m.) unless an extradition request has been

---

[613] Art 44 of the Convention provides that the technical means to ensure quick communication, particularly in hot pursuit cases, should be established.

[614] The specified crimes are (at each host State's discretion) either all extraditable offences or the following serious crimes: murder; manslaughter; rape; arson; forgery; aggravated burglary and robbery and receiving stolen goods; extortion; kidnapping and hostage taking; trafficking in human beings; drug trafficking; breach of the laws on arms and explosives; wilful damage through use of explosives; illicit transportation of toxic and hazardous waste; and hit-and-run driving. Note that 'escaping arrest' is not included.

[615] It might be questioned whether the search and seizure powers cover only the person, and items on the person, of the person who was caught, or whether they would also cover a search of the *vehicle* and objects within it.

[616] On the scope of application of the European Arrest Warrant, see II:9.5 above.

made. It is not specified who the extradition request may be made by. This appears to mean that the host State authorities cannot lay charges against the person even if he or she is wanted in that State, or has been convicted of an offence and escaped a custodial sentence, unless they send an extradition request to the *home* State.

Home State officers are treated as host State officers if they commit, or are victims of, offences,[617] and are liable for any damages under the host State's law.[618] The host State must repair any damage under its own law and can claim reimbursement of such costs from the home State, but is discouraged from doing so. Member States may make bilateral arrangements providing for more extensive hot pursuit.

There is no limitation regarding the particular methods used to flee across a land border, so in theory the rules could cover persons fleeing by foot or on a bicycle, although in practice the rules are obviously largely relevant to persons fleeing by car (or perhaps motorcycle); they are also applicable in principle to railways.

The Schengen provisions have been amended by a Council Decision adopted in 2000, which allows Member States to change the name of the police forces which have the power to conduct cross-border operations.[619]

The Naples II Convention obviously took the Schengen rules as a model. Hot pursuit, along with other 'special forms of cooperation', can be allowed for the 'prevention, investigation and prosecution' of illicit trafficking in drugs (including precursors), weapons, arms, explosives, cultural goods, dangerous and toxic waste, nuclear material and items for use in manufacturing atomic, biological, or chemical weapons, as well as trade in goods prohibited by national or EU law or illegal trade in goods to evade tax or to obtain authorized payments which would have 'considerable' cost to the national or EU budget.[620] The differences from the Schengen rules are that hot pursuit can be granted for any extraditable offence falling among the offences listed above, but not for persons escaping a custodial sentence or provisional custody; pursuit is allowed by sea as well as land; pursuit on the high seas is governed by relevant international law; a host State can ban home State officers from carrying service weapons generally, or in a specific case; and Member States can opt out of all or part of the hot pursuit rules altogether.[621]

7.9.2 Surveillance

Again, the chief provisions derive from the Schengen Convention.[622] Unlike hot pursuit, advance approval of the host State is necessary before observation can be carried out as a general rule, but cross-border observation is allowed without prior approval on similar grounds to those justifying hot pursuit. In particular, according to the initial version of the rules, police officers from a specified force in the home State of the investigation may enter another Member State with prior approval to 'continue their observation' of a person who is 'presumed to have participated in' an extraditable criminal

---

[617] Art 42 of the Convention.   [618] Art 43 of the Convention.   [619] [2000] OJ L 248/1.
[620] Art 19(2).
[621] The UK, Greece, Ireland, Slovenia, Latvia, and Poland have declared that they are not bound by Art 20; Lithuania has declared that it is not bound in the absence of any reciprocity from neighbouring States.
[622] Art 40, Schengen Convention.

offence, or without prior approval 'where prior authorisation cannot be requested... for particularly urgent reasons' to observe a person 'presumed to have committed' one or more of thirteen serious crimes.[623] The conditions for observation are similar to those governing hot pursuit, except that observing officers need not be publicly identifiable (for obvious reasons);[624] a host State may ban carrying of service weapons in particular cases; the home State officers can never challenge or arrest the observed person (so there need be no rules on arrests or detention); there is no possibility to limit the surveillance to a certain period or area, or to following a person across land borders only (a point of particular relevance to the UK);[625] and the observing officers need only give a report of their activities, usually written, to the host State. The offences and damages rules are the same as for hot pursuit.[626]

The Council adopted a Decision making a technical amendment to Article 40 of the Schengen Convention in 2000,[627] followed by a more substantive amendment in 2003.[628] This entailed two changes to the rules. Firstly, police officers can keep under surveillance not only suspects, but also persons 'who can assist in identifying or tracing' a suspect, subject always to prior authorization. Secondly, the list of crimes for which previously unauthorized surveillance of suspects could take place was enlarged to add six further crimes and to amend the definition of two others.[629] The Directive establishing a European Investigation Order did not affect these rules.[630]

The Naples II provisions[631] allow surveillance where 'there are serious grounds for believing [a person is] involved in one of the infringements' referred to in the special cooperation rules.[632] Otherwise the Naples II rules are the same as the original Schengen rules, except that a Member State can opt out of the provisions entirely and host Member States can impose a general ban on home State officers carrying firearms.[633]

7.9.3 Covert operations

'Covert operations' going beyond the scope of surveillance were not mentioned in the Schengen Convention. However, as regards customs officers, the Naples II Convention

---

[623] These are the same crimes as the crimes to which Schengen states can limit hot pursuit under the Schengen hot pursuit rules (see II.7.9.1 above), with the exception of hit and run driving.

[624] However, they must carry proof of their authority and (usually) their approval to observe.

[625] Indeed, unlike hot pursuit, surveillance will likely sometimes be carried out in a distant Member State, not an adjoining one. However, the host State may attach conditions to its authorization of surveillance, which might include conditions concerning the time and place of the surveillance.

[626] Arts 42 and 43, Schengen Convention.   [627] [2000] OJ L 248/1.

[628] [2003] OJ L 260/37. This Decision applied from 11 Oct 2003 (Art 3).

[629] The additional crimes are serious fraud, smuggling of 'aliens', money laundering, illicit trafficking in nuclear and radioactive substances, organized crime, and terrorism (the last two crimes as defined by EU measures: see further II:5.5 above). The amended definitions concern the replacement of 'rape' by serious sexual offences and the broadening of 'forgery of money' to include counterfeiting and forgery of all means of payment.

[630] Dir 2014/41, recital 9 in the preamble ([2014] OJ L 130/1).

[631] Art 21, Naples II Convention. Greece, Slovenia, Latvia, and Ireland have declared that Art 21 is inapplicable to them.

[632] See Art 19 of the Convention. The infringements need *not* necessarily be extraditable offences.

[633] There is also a Danish declaration, limiting surveillance without approval to extraditable offences.

provides for such actions, although Member States may opt out of this provision in its entirety.[634] If a Member State wishes to 'make contact with subjects and other persons associated with them' in another Member State, it may ask another Member State to allow its customs officers or 'officers acting on behalf' of its administration to enter 'under cover of a false identity'. Presumably this means that private detectives authorized by a State might be sent.[635]

There is no rule restricting covert investigations to certain types of offences, and no list of general conditions attaching to the authorization of the investigations. Instead, the host State's rules on such investigations apply, and the host State is given great latitude to restrict or lay conditions upon the scope of the home State agents' undercover work.

As for cross-border covert operations by the police, the EU's Convention on mutual assistance in criminal matters applies.[636] The rules in this Convention are even vaguer than those in the Naples II Convention, leaving the 'duration', 'the detailed conditions' and 'the legal status of the officers concerned' to be agreed between the relevant Member States. In general, the investigations must take place under the host State's rules, with much latitude to that State to set conditions. The rules in the Convention will be replaced, from May 2017, by the provisions in the Directive establishing a European Investigation Order (EIO).[637] The Directive still leaves latitude to the States involved to agree terms, but no longer allows for a reservation on this issue. A requested State will be obliged to accept a request for an EIO for a covert operation unless the general rules for refusals apply, no agreement could be reached on the terms of the covert operation, or such an operation would not be authorized for a similar domestic case.

The accountability problems arising from undercover police operations would be magnified if there is extensive use of cross-border undercover investigations—which the EIO Directive appears to encourage. However, it is likely that there was already some *de facto* cross-border undercover work which the two Conventions (and now the Directive) have simply legitimized.

7.9.4 Joint operations and investigations

The issue of joint operations and joint investigation teams was first explicitly addressed by the EU's Convention on mutual criminal assistance, which provides for two or more Member States to set up a joint investigation team 'for a specific purpose and a limited period', which may be extended.[638] Teams may be set up 'in particular' where one Member State is conducting a 'difficult and demanding' investigation with links to other Member States, or where Member States are conducting overlapping investigations which should be coordinated. The leader of the team shall be a representative of the Member State in which the team operates; the team is also subject to the laws of that State. Those team members 'seconded' by other Member States may normally participate in investigations and may be given tasks by the team leader.

---

[634] Art 23 of the Convention (ibid). Greece, Denmark, Slovenia, Latvia, and Ireland have opted out.
[635] For the implications of EU law on this, see II.7.4.3.1 above.
[636] Art 12 of the Convention ([2000] OJ C 197/1).   [637] Art 29 of the Directive, n 630 above.
[638] Art 13 of the Convention, n 636 above.

While the team does not have power to operate as such in multiple Member States, it may request the assistance of authorities in Member States other than the Member State where the team operates. Information gathered by the team which would not be otherwise available to a Member States' authorities can be used, subject to limited safeguards. Subject to national law and international rules, persons other than national officials can form part of the team, in particular staff members of EU bodies (a reference to Europol, Eurojust, and OLAF).[639]

In order to apply the provisions of the Convention as early as possible, a Framework Decision comprising the text of the relevant Convention Articles was adopted in 2002;[640] it will cease to apply once all Member States have ratified the Convention.[641] The early adoption of these provisions had the particular objective of facilitating investigations into terrorism, but the Framework Decision is in no way limited to such investigations. Member States had to apply the Framework Decision by 1 January 2003,[642] and its use was encouraged by a Council Recommendation which set out a model agreement establishing a team which Member States could use.[643]

According to a Commission report, only fourteen Member States had applied the Framework Decision in their national law by August 2004, and there were some deficiencies in their application of the measure.[644] The Commission did not report whether any teams had been established or whether they were effective, although it appears that only one team was formed by spring 2005.[645] Nor has the Council assessed the application of the Framework Decision, as required.[646] The Framework Decision was not amended or repealed by the Directive establishing the European Investigation Order.[647]

In addition to this measure, the Council adopted in April 2002 a Recommendation establishing multinational police anti-terrorist teams.[648] It is unclear, given the background to this measure, whether it is intended to deal with criminal investigations, non-criminal investigations, or both.[649] There is no clear definition of 'terrorism', and previous scandals involving similar investigations in Member States give rise to doubts that there will be sufficient accountability and control of these teams.[650]

Next, in 2008 the Council adopted the 'Prum Decision', which includes much of the text of the Prum Convention, which was originally agreed between a group of Member

---

[639] On Europol participation, see II.7.8 above.   [640] [2002] OJ L 162/1.

[641] Art 5, Framework Decision.   [642] Art 4(1), Framework Decision.

[643] [2003] OJ C 121/1, subsequently amended ([2010] OJ C 70/1).

[644] COM (2004) 858, 7 Jan 2005.

[645] See the outcome of proceedings of the Police Chiefs' Task Force meeting on 12 May 2005 (Council doc 9494/05, 30 May 2005), 9.

[646] Art 4(2), Framework Decision. However, on the application in practice, see the report of the first meeting of experts (Council doc 15227/05, 2 Dec 2005) and the guidelines agreed (Council doc 8160/2/04, 25 May 2004).

[647] Art 3 of Dir 2014/41 ([2014] OJ L 130/1), which provides that the Directive only applies if the joint team ask for assistance from another country.

[648] Unpublished (on file with the author).

[649] For details, see S Peers, 'EU Responses to Terrorism' (2003) 52 ICLQ 227 at 239–40.

[650] For instance, on the 'Gladio' network, see Statewatch Briefing, July 1991, and the annexed EP Resolution of 22 Nov 1990, which stated that 'security services (or uncontrolled branches thereof) were involved in serious cases of terrorism and crime as evidenced by various judicial enquiries'.

States.[651] This Decision includes rules on joint patrols and other joint operations, as well as on assistance in connection with mass gatherings, disasters, and serious accidents, which can include notification of such situations, coordination of joint responses, as well as dispatching personnel and equipment onto the territory of another Member State.[652] There are related provisions governing the use of arms and ammunition, protection of guest officers, civil and criminal liability, and the applicable employment relationship.[653] The Commission's report on the application of the Prum Decision indicated that these provisions were rarely used.[654]

Finally, for many years, EU customs administrations have been carrying out several joint operations each year, without any formal binding legal framework. A Council Resolution of 1997 established a Handbook, which sets out a standard procedure for deciding upon operations and evaluating them,[655] and a subsequent Guide sets out even more detailed procedures to be followed.[656] Due to the difficulties of planning and carrying out joint operations, the idea of a permanent operational coordination unit has been considered,[657] but the idea has not yet been implemented. Regular reports on the joint customs operations indicate that they are generally considered successful, resulting in the seizure in particular of significant quantities of drugs and smuggled cigarettes.[658]

7.9.5 Special intervention units

In 2008, the Council adopted a Decision governing the movement of 'special intervention units' from one Member State to another.[659] Like the Prum Decision, this measure is also taken from the text of the Prum Convention. According to the Decision, a 'special intervention unit' is 'any law enforcement unit of a Member State which is specialised in the control of a crisis situation',[660] and a 'crisis situation' is defined as 'any situation in which the competent authorities of a Member State have reasonable grounds to believe that there is a criminal offence presenting a serious direct physical threat to persons, property, infrastructure or institutions in that Member State, in particular those situations referred to in' the Framework Decision defining terrorism.[661]

The Decision provides that one Member State can request another for the assistance of a special intervention team to deal with a crisis situation. The requested Member State is entirely free to refuse.[662] According to the agreement between the two Member States, assistance may entail 'providing the requesting Member State with equipment and/or expertise and/or of carrying out actions on the territory of that Member State, using weapons if so required.'[663] If actions are authorized by officers of the requested State on the requesting State's territory, those officers would be operating under the

---

[651] [2008] OJ L 210/1. On the background to the Prum Decision, see II.7.2.3 above. On the substance of the rest of the Decision, see II.7.6.2 and II.7.6.3 above.

[652] Arts 17–18 of the Prum Decision, ibid.   [653] Arts 19–23 of the Prum Decision, ibid.

[654] COM (2012) 732, 7 Dec 2012.   [655] [1997] OJ C 193/5.

[656] Council doc 8249/2/05, 12 Sep 2005.   [657] Council doc 9335/1/04, 16 July 2004.

[658] See, for instance, the report on operations in 2003 (Council doc 10036/1/04, 6 July 2004), and previously the first edition of this book, pp 203–4.

[659] [2008] OJ L 210/73. This Decision applied from 23 Dec 2009 (Art 9).   [660] Art 2(a).

[661] Art 2(b). On the Framework Decision, see II:5.5.2.1 above.   [662] Art 3(1).   [663] Art 3(2).

'responsibility, authority and direction' of the requesting State and in accordance with its law; at the same time, such officers would also have to act within the limits of the powers of their own law.[664] The rules on civil and criminal liability in the 'Prum Decision' apply.[665] There are also provisions on meetings and joint training, costs, and the maintenance in force or conclusion of treaties on the same subject.[666]

7.10 EU Funding

During the Maastricht period, the EU Treaty provided that operational spending on JHA should normally be funded by Member States, with the EU budget to be used if the Council obtained the unanimous approval of the Member States. The position was reversed by the Treaty of Amsterdam, with the EU budget to be used unless the Council decided otherwise, with a unanimous vote.[667]

Under the Maastricht rules, the Council adopted Joint Actions on the 'STOP' programme on combating sexual exploitation,[668] the 'Oisin' programme on support for law enforcement,[669] and the 'Falcone' programme on combating international organized crime.[670] Following the entry into force of the Treaty of Amsterdam, the Oisin and STOP programmes were extended for 2001–02, joined by a programme concerning crime prevention (Hippocrates).[671] All the third pillar programmes were then replaced by a general third pillar funding programme, 'AGIS', running from 2003 to 2007,[672] and subsequently by programmes on law enforcement and terrorism-related civil protection, which ran from 2007–13 and will run from 2014–20.[673]

As for EU databases and agencies, the costs of the third pillar aspects of SIS II development had to be charged to the EU budget, as there was not unanimous support for charging the costs to Member States' budgets.[674] SIS II operations have been funded from the EU budget since SIS II became operational.[675] Although the European Police College and Europol were initially funded by Member States, they have been funded from the EU budget since the start of 2006 and 2010 respectively.[676] The costs of the Customs Information System have largely been charged to the EU budget since 2011.[677]

7.11 External Relations

Before the entry into force of the Treaty of Lisbon, the EU agreed treaties with the USA, Canada, and Australia as regards passenger name data,[678] with Norway and Iceland

---

[664] Art 3(3).   [665] Art 4.   [666] Arts 5–7.   [667] See II:2.7 above.

[668] [1996] OJ L 322/7, applicable initially from 1996 to 2000.

[669] [1997] OJ L 7/5, applicable initially from 1997 to 2000.

[670] [1998] OJ L 99/8, applicable initially from 1998 to 2002.   [671] [2001] OJ L 186/4, 7, and 11.

[672] [2002] OJ L 203/5.

[673] For 2007–13, see [2007] OJ L 58/7 and 1. The latter measure was adopted on the basis of the former Art 308 EC; see now Art 196 and 222 TFEU. For 2014–20, see Reg 513/2014 establishing a policing fund, as part of the Internal Security Fund ([2014] OJ L 150/93).

[674] See JHA Council conclusions, 28/29 May 2001.   [675] See II.7.6.1.1 above.

[676] See respectively II.7.7.2 and II.7.8 above.   [677] [2009] OJ L 323/20, Art 31.

[678] See [2004] OJ L 183/83 and L 235/11 (US agreement) and the subsequent agreements in [2006] OJ L 298/27 and [2007] OJ L 204; [2006] OJ L 82/14 (Canada); and [2008] OJ L 213/47 (Australia). See also the

as regards the extension of the Prum Decision to those States,[679] and with the USA as regards access to financial information for anti-terrorist purposes. After the entry into force of the Treaty of Lisbon, the EP gained the power of consent over these measures, and voted down the original version of the treaty on exchange of financial information, which was then renegotiated (with the EP's approval).[680] The Commission is also negotiating a general treaty with the USA on sharing of information in this area. Furthermore, the EU has fresh treaties with the USA and Australia on passenger name data,[681] and has agreed a further treaty on this issue with Canada,[682] although the CJEU has been asked to review this treaty for compatibility with fundamental rights.[683]

There have been several other external measures in this area,[684] in particular the treaties between Europol and third States or bodies, pursuant to rules adopted to implement the Europol Convention, and later the Europol Decision.[685]

7.12 Conclusions

EU law on policing and security has not gone so far as to create EU-wide police forces, or to give national police forces the jurisdiction to exercise their full powers on the territory of another State. Rather there are a large number of specific measures concerning the facilitation of operational cooperation and allowing for limited cross-border operations, EU bodies with limited (but significant) powers, and a number of measures with substantial impact on data protection, in particular the creation and development of large databases. The underlying problems, which can be linked to the initial lack of adequate parliamentary and (initially) judicial control of EU measures, are the insufficiencies of the rules (where they exist at all) on accountability of operations or the protection of personal data, and in particular the lack of public accountability through the means of regular reporting on or objective evaluation of the application of most EU measures in practice.

Statewatch observatory on this issue, online at: <http://www.statewatch.org/pnrobservatory.htm>, and the Commission communication on a global EU policy on this issue (COM (2003) 826, 16 Dec 2003) and the Council discussion paper on the same issue (Council doc 10838/15, 14 July 2015). On the legal base issues, see I:7.4.3.2.

[679] [2009] OJ L 353/1; see II.7.2.5 above.

[680] [2010] OJ L 8 (first treaty); [2010] OJ L 195/1 (second treaty). The treaty with Norway and Iceland has not yet been concluded.

[681] [2012] OJ L 186/4 (Australia); [2012] OJ L 215/5 (USA).

[682] COM (2013) 528, 18 July 2013.   [683] *Opinion 1/2015*, pending.

[684] See the Action Plan with Russia concerning organized crime ([2000] OJ C 106/5), the JHA Action Plan with Ukraine ([2003] OJ C 77/1), the pre-accession pact on organized crime ([1998] OJ C 220/1), the Joint Action on evaluation of candidates' compliance with the JHA *acquis* ([1998] OJ L 191/8), and the Resolution on the posting of drugs liaison officers to Albania ([2003] OJ C 97/6).

[685] II.7.8 above. For an overview of the framework for Europol external relations, see C Rijken, 'Legal and Technical Aspects of Cooperation Between Europol, Third States and Interpol' in V Kronenberger, ed., *The European Union and the International Legal Order: Discord or Harmony?* (Asser, 2001), 577. For a detailed analysis and critique of the practice, see S Peers, 'Governance and the Third Pillar: The Accountability of Europol' in D Curtin and R Wessel, eds., *Good Governance and the European Union* (Intersentia, 2005), 253. The texts of most of the agreements in force can be found online at: <http://www.europol.europa.eu/index.asp?page=agreements>.

Although in principle the Treaty of Lisbon has remedied these flaws, many of the pre-Lisbon measures have not been reviewed yet. While the CJEU has been willing in recent years to ensure more rigorous respect for civil liberties, the measures it has interpreted are very much the tip of the iceberg. Overall, EU measures have failed to strike the right balance between the objective of ensuring public security and the protection of civil liberties, and some EU measures moreover contribute towards the creation of a 'surveillance society' across Europe.

8

Civil Cooperation

8.1 Introduction

The substantive details of civil cooperation within the European Union are beyond the scope of this book, which focuses on matters within the scope of interior and home affairs ministries. Instead, this chapter briefly describes the place of civil cooperation within the EU legal system. It will be seen that there are some broad similarities with the issues which arise regarding the mutual recognition principle in the area of criminal law (see Chapter 3 of this volume).

8.2 Institutional Framework and Overview

8.2.1 Cooperation prior to the Treaty of Amsterdam

8.2.1.1 Cooperation prior to the Maastricht Treaty

Right from the creation of the European Community (as it initially was), it was envisaged that Member States would wish to cooperate on civil law matters and that such cooperation would have a close relationship with the economic integration which the Community was intended to focus on. Therefore, such cooperation was provided for even in the original Treaty of Rome, in Article 220 EEC. This Article provided that:

> Member States shall, so far as is necessary, enter into negotiations with each other with a view to securing for their nationals:
> - the protection of persons and the enjoyment and protection of rights under the same conditions as those accorded by each State to its own nationals,
> - the abolition of double taxation within the Community,
> - the mutual recognition of companies or firms within the meaning of the second paragraph of Article 58,[1] the retention of legal personality in the event of transfer of their seat from one country to another, and the possibility of mergers between companies or firms governed by the laws of different countries,
> - the simplification of formalities governing the reciprocal recognition and enforcement of judgments of courts or tribunals and of arbitration awards.

In 1968, agreement was reached on Conventions falling within the third and fourth indents. One Convention was agreed on the mutual recognition of companies[2] and a second was agreed on the recognition and enforcement of civil and commercial judgments, along with the rules governing jurisdiction over proceedings. The former

---

[1] Now Art 54 TFEU.   [2] Published in *EC Bulletin* 2/69.

Convention was not ratified by all Member States and has long been abandoned, but the latter, known as the Brussels Convention, was a resounding success, later extended to all of the first fifteen Member States[3] and even to non-Member States (Norway, Iceland, and Switzerland) in the form of a parallel Convention, the Lugano Convention.[4] Much later, the Member States agreed a Convention on the arbitration of double taxation disputes, falling within the scope of the second indent.[5]

Article 220, renumbered Article 293 by the Treaty of Amsterdam, and subsequently repealed by the Treaty of Lisbon, did not provide expressly for interpretation of the measures adopted pursuant to it by the EU's Court of Justice, but it was presumed that the Court's jurisdiction could be extended to such measures. Protocols on the Court's interpretation of the 1968 Conventions were agreed in 1971,[6] although no such Protocol was agreed for the Tax Arbitration Convention. The Protocol on the Court's interpretation of the Brussels Convention resulted in over a hundred rulings by the Court.

The Member States later decided that they also wished to adopt further Conventions which were closely related to the EC legal system, but which did not fall within the scope of Article 220. The solution was to agree 'purely' intergovernmental Conventions on: the creation of a Community patent;[7] the rules governing choice of law in contract (the Rome Convention);[8] the abolition of legalization of documents; and the simplification of proceedings for recovery of maintenance payments under the Brussels Convention.[9] It was decided that the Court of Justice would have jurisdiction over the Patent Convention and the Rome Convention,[10] although the Patent Convention never came into force and the Protocols on the Court's jurisdiction to interpret the Rome Convention in the first fifteen Member States only came into force on 1 August 2004.[11] The latter Protocols have resulted to date in several references to the Court of Justice from national courts.[12]

---

[3] See the consolidated version of the Convention after the accession of Austria, Sweden, and Finland ([1998] OJ C 27/1).

[4] [1988] OJ L 319/9. This Convention also applied to Sweden, Finland, and Austria before they ratified the Brussels Convention after becoming EU Member States, and to Poland before it joined the EU.

[5] [1990] OJ L 225/10. The Convention was subsequently extended to Member States joining the EU later: see [1996] OJ C 26/1; [2005] OJ C 160/1; [2008] OJ L 174/1; and [2014] OJ L 358/19. It was also amended by a Protocol ([1999] OJ C 202/1).

[6] N 3 above (Protocol to Brussels Convention); D Anderson, *References to the European Court* (Sweet and Maxwell, 1995), 377 (company recognition Convention).

[7] Convention on Community Patent ([1976] OJ L 17/18), amended by 1989 Agreement ([1989] OJ L 401/1).

[8] See the consolidated version of Convention after the accession of the first fifteen Member States ([1998] OJ C 27/34). The Member States joining in 2004 (along with the first fifteen Member States) signed an accession treaty to the Rome Convention in April 2005 ([2005] C 169/1), which entered into force on 1 May 2006 (for ratification details, see Appendix I). See the subsequent consolidated version of the Convention ([2005] OJ C 334/1). Romania and Bulgaria became parties to the Convention on 15 Jan 2008, pursuant to a Council Decision ([2007] OJ L 347/1).

[9] Not published in the OJ; see respectively UK government Command Papers 626 (1989) and 1604 (1991) and Appendix I for ratification details.

[10] See Protocols to the latter ([1989] OJ L 48/1).

[11] [2004] OJ C 277/1. In fact, Ireland opted out of the Court's jurisdiction over the Rome Convention. The two Protocols also apply to the newer EU Member States pursuant to the accession treaty to the Rome Convention and the Council Decision extending that Convention to Romania and Bulgaria, n 8 above.

[12] See II:8.5.3 below.

It should be emphasized that in civil law matters, the question of which State's courts have *jurisdiction* over a dispute is distinct from the question of which *law* applies to the dispute, as it is possible for courts to apply foreign civil law. The Brussels Convention addressed the former issue, while the Rome Convention addressed the latter.

8.2.1.2 Cooperation from Maastricht to Amsterdam

Article K.1(6) of the EU Treaty listed 'judicial cooperation in civil matters' as a common interest of the Member States falling within the scope of the third pillar, although Article K.3(2)(c) of the EU Treaty was expressly 'without prejudice' to Article 220 EC (later Article 293 EC, and now repealed). Member States agreed measures under both of these overlapping legal bases during the Maastricht period. First, Article 220 EC was used to draw up a Convention on choice of law and jurisdiction in insolvency proceedings in 1995,[13] although the prospect of ratification of this Convention lapsed when the UK did not sign it within the six-month period allotted for the Member States' signatures. Secondly, in 1997 and in 1998 the third pillar powers were used by the Council to draw up Conventions on the service of documents and on jurisdiction over and enforcement of matrimonial judgments, including decisions on parental responsibility connected to the judgment concerning dissolution of the marriage.[14] The Council also reached agreement in 1999 on amendments to the Brussels Convention.[15]

8.2.2 Treaties of Amsterdam and Nice

8.2.2.1 Institutional framework

The Treaty of Amsterdam transferred the issue of civil cooperation from the third pillar to the first with effect from 1 May 1999. Powers regarding this issue were conferred by Article 65 EC, which provided as follows:

> Measures in the field of judicial cooperation in civil matters having cross-border implications, to be taken in accordance with Article 67 and insofar as necessary for the proper functioning of the internal market, shall include:
> (a) improving and simplifying:
>   – the system for cross-border service of judicial and extra-judicial documents;
>   – cooperation in the taking of evidence;
>   – the recognition and enforcement of decisions in civil and commercial cases, including decisions in extrajudicial cases;
> (b) promoting the compatibility of the rules applicable in the Member States concerning the conflict of laws and of jurisdiction;

---

[13] (1996) 35 ILM 1223.

[14] [1997] OJ C 261/1 and [1998] OJ C 221/1 respectively. The latter became known as the Brussels II Convention.

[15] See Press Release of JHA Council, 27/28 May 1999, and the Commission's earlier proposal for amendments (COM (1997) 609, 26 Nov 1997; [1998] OJ C 33/3 and 30).

(c) eliminating obstacles to the good functioning of civil proceedings, if necessary by promoting the compatibility of the rules on civil procedure applicable in the Member States.

These provisions were not subjected to any form of deadline, although they were covered by: the special institutional rules of Articles 67 and 68 EC, including the restrictions on the jurisdiction of the Court of Justice; the general 'opt-outs' of the UK, Ireland, and Denmark from Title IV EC; and the possibility of adopting measures on related administrative cooperation under Article 66.[16] As a result of the applicability of Article 67 EC, EC civil law measures were initially subject to unanimous voting in the Council, mere consultation of the European Parliament, and (for the initial five years after entry into force of the Treaty of Amsterdam) a shared right of initiative of the Commission and the Member States.

However, the Treaty of Nice brought about an important change in the institutional framework, as from its entry into force on 1 February 2003. It inserted a new Article 67(5) into the EC Treaty, which, inter alia, provided that civil law measures, except for 'aspects relating to family law', would immediately be subject to the co-decision procedure set out in Article 251 EC, giving equal voting powers to the EP and entailing qualified majority voting (QMV) in the Council and a Commission monopoly on proposals for legislation. Family law measures were still subject to the general decision-making rules set out in Article 67 (unanimity in Council and consultation of the EP), and remained subject to unanimity and consultation even after most of Title IV of the EC Treaty became subject to QMV and co-decision in May 2004 and January 2005.[17] However, since 1 May 2004, family law measures could only be adopted following a proposal from the Commission. It should also be recalled that a Protocol attached to the EC Treaty by the Treaty of Nice changed the decision-making rules applicable to Article 66 EC as from 1 May 2004, so that, from that date, measures on administrative cooperation were adopted by a qualified majority vote in the Council with consultation of the EP. Furthermore, in December 2005, the Commission urged that the Council adopt a decision pursuant to Article 67(2) EC, requiring a unanimous vote after consultation of the EP, in order to amend the decision-making rules to apply the co-decision procedure and QMV in Council to the issue of maintenance.[18] However, the Council did not act on this suggestion.

The Final Act of the Treaty of Amsterdam also included a Declaration (no. 20) relating to Article 65 EC. This Declaration stated that measures adopted pursuant to Article 65 'shall not prevent any Member State from applying its constitutional rules relating to freedom of the press and freedom of expression in other media'. In fact, the Declaration appears to be a reaction to the *Shevill* judgment of the Court of Justice, which ruled on the application of the Brussels Convention to cross-border defamation claims.[19]

---

[16] On the institutional rules, see II:2.2.2 above; on the opt-outs, see II:8.2.5 below; on Art 66, see II:8.2.4 below.

[17] On these developments, see II:2.2.2 above.   [18] COM (2005) 648, 15 Dec 2005.

[19] Case C-68/93 [1995] ECR I-415.

8.2.2.2 *Overview of practice*

The EC's first priority after the entry into force of the Treaty of Amsterdam was to transpose the civil cooperation Conventions which had been agreed or adopted during the Maastricht period into EC legislation.[20] To this end, by the end of 2000 the EC had adopted legislation concerning: the service of documents; jurisdiction over divorce matters and recognition of divorce judgments; jurisdiction, choice of law, and recognition of judgments regarding insolvency proceedings (the 'insolvency regulation'); and the general rules concerning jurisdiction over and recognition of civil and commercial judgments (the 'Brussels Regulation', replacing the Brussels Convention).

In the meantime, the Tampere European Council, meeting in autumn 1999, had set key political objectives for the development of EC law on civil judicial cooperation. According to the European Council, the 'cornerstone' of judicial cooperation, for civil law as well as criminal law, was the principle of 'mutual recognition', applying 'both to judgements and to other decisions of judicial authorities.' The development of this principle by EC law would entail the further reduction of 'intermediate measures' which apply to the recognition and enforcement of judgments issued in other EU Member States (known as 'exequatur'). Exequatur was to be abolished entirely in particular cases (small claims and some family law judgments), possibly subject to the adoption of minimum standards in civil procedure.

The detailed application of these principles was subject to a mutual recognition programme, to be drawn up by the end of 2000.[21] This programme first called upon the EC to adopt measures concerning mutual recognition of judgments in areas where it had not already acted: property rights related to dissolution of marriage and the separation of unmarried couples; property rights related to succession; and judgments on parental responsibility where the parents are unmarried or which were taken after the dissolution of the marriage relationship. Where the EC had already acted, it should further develop the degree of mutual recognition, by gradually abolishing the barriers to the recognition of judgments from other Member States (the exequatur process and the grounds for refusing recognition). The programme also addressed the prospect of adopting measures ancillary to mutual recognition, comprising: minimum standards in civil procedure or harmonization of civil procedure (particularly regarding parental responsibility and service of documents); improved enforcement of judgments (particularly concerning information on debtors' assets); and general improvement of civil cooperation (particularly the creation of a Judicial Network, a system for obtaining evidence, adoption of rules on legal aid, provision of public information, and harmonization of conflict of law rules).

In order to implement this work programme, in the lead up to the entry into force of the Treaty of Nice, the EC adopted legislation concerning the cross-border taking of evidence, civil law spending programmes, the creation of a Judicial Network

---

[20] For more detailed references to the legislation adopted, see II:8.5 and II:8.6 below. As regards EU funding measures and external relations issues, see also II:8.8 and II:8.9 below. On the 'common frame of reference' for contract law, see II:8.7 below.

[21] [2001] OJ C 12/1.

concerning civil matters, and legal aid. Work also began on the development of a 'common frame of reference' for European contract law.

Following the extension of QMV and co-decision to civil law matters (except for family law) in 2003, the EC adopted legislation concerning enforcement orders, small claims, payment orders, mediation, and choice of law regarding both contractual and non-contractual obligations, in particular replacing the Rome Convention on conflict of law in contracts. It also amended the legislation concerning the service of documents and the civil law Judicial Network, and adopted a new civil law funding programme. In the sphere of family law, the EC adopted legislation regarding maintenance claims, and amended the rules concerning jurisdiction over family law matters, inter alia, extending the relevant Regulation to include certain issues relating to children. Furthermore, it adopted legislation authorizing Member States to conclude treaties within the sphere of EC exclusive external competence, subject to certain conditions. In the meantime, the Hague Programme, adopted in 2004, reiterated the basic focus on mutual recognition, set a date of 2011 for completion of the civil law mutual recognition work programme, and specified a number of further measures to be adopted to accomplish this.[22]

The fairly intense legislative activity in this area was matched by an increasing involvement of the Court of Justice.[23] It is notable that the restrictions on the Court's jurisdiction did not prevent a generally increasing flow of references from national courts as regards Title IV civil law legislation, although it might have been expected that the Court would have received an even greater number of cases if the restrictions on its jurisdiction had not been in place.[24]

More precisely, the number of cases reaching the Court gradually rose to a peak of ten to fifteen a year between 2007 and 2009.[25] The large majority of these cases concerned the main regulation on jurisdiction over civil and commercial judgments and the recognition of such judgments. The Regulations on family law, insolvency, and service of documents also attracted several references each,[26] while the legislation on the transmission of evidence attracted two references. There were no references on external civil law treaties concluded by the EC,[27] or on the legislation concerning simplified recognition of judgments (enforcement order, payment orders, small claims) or conflicts of law. However, the latter measures were all quite recent at the time. Two references were subjected to the emergency ruling procedure for Justice and Home Affairs (JHA) matters which was established in 2008.[28]

EC civil law legislation did not attract other types of legal proceedings (annulment actions or infringement actions) except for one request for an opinion relating to a

---

[22] [2005] OJ C 53, point 3.4. See also the work programme for implementation of the Hague programme, point 4.3 ([2005] OJ C 198/1). The common frame of reference in contract law was to be adopted by 2009; on this issue, see II:8.7 below.

[23] See Art 68 EC.

[24] Compare with the numbers of cases after the entry into force of the Treaty of Lisbon (II:8.2.3 below).

[25] S Peers, 'Mission Accomplished? EU Justice and Home Affairs Law and the Treaty of Lisbon' (2011) 48 CMLRev 661.

[26] Respectively eight, six, and four references. Also, several cases concerning the Brussels Regulation clarified its relationship with the insolvency Reg: see II:8.5.1 below.

[27] On the question of the Court of Justice's jurisdiction over such treaties, see II:8.9 below.

[28] On that procedure, see II:2.2.2 above.

planned external treaty.[29] The Court did not address the issue of 'mixed jurisdiction' (where a case related to civil law measures as well as measures subject to the Court's non-JHA jurisdiction), despite the large number of cases where civil law legislation and internal market issues overlapped.[30]

8.2.3 Treaty of Lisbon

Following the entry into force of the Treaty of Lisbon on 1 December 2009, the legal basis for civil cooperation measures within the EU is now Article 81 of the Treaty on the Functioning of the European Union (TFEU), which provides as follows:

1. The Union shall develop judicial cooperation in civil matters having cross-border implications, based on the principle of mutual recognition of judgments and of decisions in extrajudicial cases. Such cooperation may include the adoption of measures for the approximation of the laws and regulations of the Member States.

2. For the purposes of paragraph 1, the European Parliament and the Council, acting in accordance with the ordinary legislative procedure, shall adopt measures, particularly when necessary for the proper functioning of the internal market, aimed at ensuring:

    (a) the mutual recognition and enforcement between Member States of judgments and of decisions in extrajudicial cases;
    (b) the cross-border service of judicial and extrajudicial documents;
    (c) the compatibility of the rules applicable in the Member States concerning conflict of laws and of jurisdiction;
    (d) cooperation in the taking of evidence;
    (e) effective access to justice;
    (f) the elimination of obstacles to the proper functioning of civil proceedings, if necessary by promoting the compatibility of the rules on civil procedure applicable in the Member States;
    (g) the development of alternative methods of dispute settlement;
    (h) support for the training of the judiciary and judicial staff.

3. Notwithstanding paragraph 2, measures concerning family law with cross-border implications shall be established by the Council, acting in accordance with a special legislative procedure. The Council shall act unanimously after consulting the European Parliament.

    The Council, on a proposal from the Commission, may adopt a decision determining those aspects of family law with cross-border implications which may be the subject of acts adopted by the ordinary legislative procedure. The Council shall act unanimously after consulting the European Parliament.

---

[29] *Opinion 1/03* [2006] ECR I-1145; see II:8.9 below.

[30] On the mixed jurisdiction issue, see generally I:2.4; on the overlaps between civil law and internal market issues in the case law, see II:8.4 below. This issue is now moot after the entry into force of the Treaty of Lisbon, except where there is a difference in territorial scope between civil law measures and other EU law measures.

The proposal referred to in the second subparagraph shall be notified to the national Parliaments. If a national Parliament makes known its opposition within six months of the date of such notification, the decision shall not be adopted. In the absence of opposition, the Council may adopt the decision.

The list of specific issues appearing within the scope of Article 81 TFEU is the same as the list in the prior Article 65 EC, with the addition of 'a high level of access to justice', 'the development of alternative methods of dispute settlement', and 'support for the training of the judiciary and judicial staff'. However, as we have seen, the EC had previously already used Article 65 EC to address such matters. There have been minor amendments to the wording as regards the items which remain in the list, for example the addition of the word 'mutual' to the item concerning recognition of judgments. Moreover, the issue of mutual recognition has been 'promoted' to the top of the list; this is consistent with the revised wording of Article 81(1) TFEU, which specifies that judicial cooperation on civil matters is 'based on' mutual recognition. This Treaty amendment entrenched the political decision taken back in 1999 in Tampere, as noted above, to prioritize the issue of mutual recognition as regards civil and criminal law cooperation in the EU.

The *chapeau* of Article 81 TFEU is wider than the *chapeau* of Article 65 EC, as the prior requirement that civil law measures must be 'necessary for the proper functioning of the internal market' is now qualified by the word 'particularly'. It seems obvious that a necessary link to the functioning of the internal market is no longer required for civil law measures.[31] On the other hand, the words 'shall include' no longer precede the list of specific measures which could be adopted; the obvious implication is that this list is now exhaustive. This interpretation is confirmed by the decision to add some additional items (reflecting the practice under the Treaty of Amsterdam) to this list. The explicit references in the Treaty to approximation of national law and the principle of mutual recognition are also changes from the prior Article 65 EC.

As for decision-making, the normal rule remains the co-decision procedure (now renamed the 'ordinary legislative procedure') with, as before, an exception for 'family law', which is still subject to unanimous voting in the Council and consultation of the EP (now referred to as a type of 'special legislative procedure'). The latter exception is now worded slightly differently, no longer referring to 'aspects' of family law (except as regards the Council's changes to decision-making rules). That possibility of changing the decision-making rules (Article 81(3) TFEU) differs from the prior Article 67(2) EC (which was repealed by the Treaty of Lisbon) in that the proposal to change the rules must be issued by the Commission, and there is a procedure establishing a form of control by national parliaments. In fact, the enhancement of national parliamentary powers on this point means that a decision to amend the decision-making rules relating to family law is more difficult to adopt after the entry into force of the Treaty of Lisbon than it would have been previously. Also, it is arguable that Article 81(3) TFEU only allows *some* 'aspects' of family law, not all aspects, to be adopted using the co-decision

---

[31] This interpretation is shared by Advocate-General Sharpston: see the Opinion in Case C-353/06 *Grunkin and Paul* [2008] ECR I-7639, note 2.

procedure, whereas the use of the prior Article 67(2) EC was not subject to such limitations. In any event, there has been no suggestion to change the decision-making rules in practice.

There has been fairly extensive legislative activity in this area since the Treaty of Lisbon entered into force. In particular, the EU has adopted Regulations on: choice of law and jurisdiction in inheritance matters;[32] conflict of law in divorce cases (Rome III);[33] protection orders;[34] and account preservation orders.[35] It has also recast the general rules on civil jurisdiction and mutual recognition of judgments, as well as the insolvency Regulation,[36] and amended the legislation on small claims.[37] Proposals to adopt new rules on the issue of matrimonial property (and the property of civil partnerships) are under discussion.[38] So are discussions in the related fields of recognition of civil status documents,[39] as well as rules on a European contract law.[40]

The Treaty of Lisbon rules also fully removed the restrictive provisions on the Court of Justice's jurisdiction over civil matters, just as they were removed almost entirely as regards all JHA matters.[41] Following the entry into force of the Treaty of Lisbon, there have been around twenty to thirty references a year from national courts concerning EU civil law legislation. Overall, the number of references from national courts in this area has increased modestly as a result of the Treaty of Lisbon.

Next, the changes to the Protocols concerning the opt-outs of the UK, Ireland and Denmark changed the legal framework for those countries' opt-outs somewhat,[42] and a declaration concerning EU external relations powers attempts to clarify the limits of EU external competence in this field.[43] Also, as noted above, the previous Article 293 EC was repealed by the Treaty of Lisbon; this resolved any uncertainty about the relationship between Articles 65 and 293 EC.

In addition, the legal basis for civil law measures is subject to the general provisions of Title V of Part Three of the TFEU, in particular the clauses setting out the objectives of Title V and providing for the adoption of measures regarding administrative cooperation. While the latter provision (Article 74 TFEU) is unchanged as compared to the prior Article 66 EC,[44] the former provision (Article 67 TFEU) now refers expressly to 'respect for fundamental rights and the different legal systems and traditions of the Member States', and refers also now to the principle of mutual recognition in civil matters, describing this as a means of fulfilling an EU obligation to 'facilitate access to justice'.[45]

The revised civil law provisions of the Treaty are also subject to the general amendments which the Treaty of Lisbon made to the rest of the Treaties, including the general *passerelle* clause[46] and the changes to the rules on enhanced cooperation. The latter

---

[32] See II:8.5.1 below.   [33] See II:8.6 below.   [34] See II:8.5.1 below.
[35] See II:8.5.1 below.   [36] See II:8.5.1 below.   [37] See II:8.5.6 below.
[38] See II:8.6 below.   [39] See II:8.4 below.   [40] See II:8.7 below.
[41] See II:2.2.3.1 above. There was no five-year transitional period for civil law matters.
[42] See II:2.2.5 above.   [43] See II:8.9 below.
[44] In particular, measures must still be adopted by QMV in Council and consultation of the EP, on the basis of a Commission proposal (as far as civil law is concerned).
[45] For more on the general provisions of Title V, see I:2.2.3.2.   [46] Art 48(7), revised TEU.

changes have proven to be relevant to the adoption of civil law measures by means of enhanced cooperation.[47]

8.2.4 Competence issues

There are four key questions concerning EU civil law competence. First, what is the definition of 'judicial cooperation in civil matters'? Secondly, to what extent is the EU prevented from regulating purely national matters, in light of the restrictions on EU competence to matters having 'cross-border implications'?[48] A parallel question arises as regards the EU's *external* powers in light of this provision; this is considered below.[49] Thirdly, what is the distinction between the legal base of Article 81 TFEU and, where relevant, Article 74 TFEU,[50] and the legal bases relating to the internal market (Articles 114 and 115 TFEU),[51] or indeed the residual powers clause of the Treaty (Article 352 TFEU[52])? Finally, how is the exercise of the EU's civil law powers to be divided between the three different decision-making procedures applicable: the normal rule (QMV and co-decision), the 'family law' exception (unanimity and consultation), and the rule for administrative cooperation (QMV and consultation)? All four of these issues arose prior to the entry into force of the Treaty of Lisbon, but are still relevant following its entry into force, while taking into account the abolition of the requirement that EC civil law measures must always be 'necessary for the proper functioning of the internal market'. A fifth issue, as to whether the EC's civil law powers under the prior Article 65 EC were exhaustive or non-exhaustive, has, as noted above,[53] been answered by the Treaty of Lisbon. However, this issue, along with the 'internal market' requirement, is still of historical relevance in case of any challenge to the validity of EC acts adopted before the entry into force of the Treaty.[54]

The EU's civil law competence after the Treaty of Lisbon remains unchanged from the EC's civil law competence as it existed beforehand, apart from the removal of the internal market requirement and the move to an exhaustive list of powers. Therefore the case law on Article 65 EC remains largely still relevant to the interpretation of Article 81 TFEU.

Starting with the definition of 'judicial cooperation in civil matters', the Court of Justice's case law on the Brussels Convention consistently ruled that public-law actions were outside the scope of the Convention,[55] although the Convention did apply where

---

[47] See the discussion of the Rome III Regulation (II:8.6 below), concerning conflict of law on divorce. On the changes made by the Treaty of Lisbon to the enhanced cooperation rules generally, see I:2.2.5.5.

[48] On the parallel issue relating to EU criminal law competence, see II:3.2.4 above.   [49] II:8.9.

[50] Formerly Arts 65 and 66 EC.   [51] Formerly Arts 94 and 95 EC.

[52] Formerly Art 308 EC.   [53] II:8.2.3.

[54] On the non-exhaustiveness of the powers conferred by the prior Art 65 EC, see p 372 of the second edition of this book.

[55] See Case C-292/05 *Lechoritou* [2007] ECR I-1519, with further references. On the same issue regarding the Brussels I Reg, see the judgments in *Apostolides* (Case C-420/07 [2009] ECR I-3571, paras 40–6) and Case C-645/11 *Sapir*, ECLI:EU:C:2012:228 (distinguishing *Lechoritou*, as regards a system for compensating victims of a totalitarian regime). On state immunity and employment law, see C-154/11 *Mahamdia*, ECLI:EU:C:2012:491. The exception is now in the 2012 replacement for the Brussels Reg (Art 1(1), Reg 1215/2012, [2012] OJ L 351/1).

a public authority was merely substituting itself for a private individual in private law proceedings.[56] However, in a case concerning the Brussels II Regulation, the Court of Justice determined that an action by a public authority to take a child into care was within the scope of the rules in the Regulation relating to parental responsibility.[57] The Court explained its ruling by reference to the wording of the Regulation, rather than the legal base in the EC Treaty. With respect, this begs the question, because the Regulation cannot govern a dispute which is outside the scope of the legal basis used to adopt it. However, the Advocate-General's Opinion in this case did address the question of the legal base, arguing that 'civil matters' had an autonomous meaning in EC law, including 'State measures which affect private law relationships such as the exercise of parental responsibility, even if corresponding measures are classified as measures of public law in some Member States'.[58] This interpretation, if correct, means that in principle the powers conferred by Article 81 TFEU are potentially quite wide, as they can be exercised as long as there is a nexus between state action and private law relationships.

Subsequently, in the particular context of the Regulation on service of documents, which applies from an early point in proceedings, the Court ruled that documents in a case which arguably fell outside the scope of 'civil and commercial' proceedings still had to be served, unless they were manifestly outside the scope of the concept.[59] The issue of scope would be argued at a later point in the proceedings.

As for the restriction of Article 81 TFEU to 'judicial cooperation', the scope of the EU's competence on this point was addressed in the *Roda Golf* judgment.[60] In its judgment in that case, the Court of Justice ruled that the EU legislation on service of documents did not apply only as regards legal proceedings. In the Court's view, taking account of the requirement in Article 65 EC that EC civil law legislation must be necessary for the functioning of the internal market, 'the judicial cooperation referred to by that article … cannot be limited to legal proceedings alone. That cooperation may manifest itself both in the context of and in the absence of legal proceedings if that cooperation has cross-border implications and is necessary for the proper functioning of the internal market'.[61] Of course, with the abolition by the Treaty of Lisbon of the requirement of a link to the proper functioning of the internal market, the EU is even freer to adopt measures which do not have a link to legal proceedings. But in order to take due account of the legal base in the Treaty, it will still be necessary that there is some sort of *judicial* involvement in the relevant proceedings, such as mediation or arbitration.

On the second point, in practice, the application of the 'cross-border implications' clause has been a source of continued controversy,[62] with the Commission usually

---

[56] See, for instance, Case C-433/01 *Blijdenstein* [2004] ECR I-981. The Court has applied this principle to rule that the Brussels Regulation applies where a public authority sues a private company in tort to recover tax revenues lost due to fraud: Case C-49/12 *Sunico*, ECLI:EU:C:2013:545. The Reg also applies to fines to enforce a civil law judgment (Case C-406/09 *RealChemie* [2011] ECR I-9773) and to damages for breach of competition law (Case C-302/13 *flyLAL-Lithuanian Airlines*, ECLI:EU:C:2014:2319).

[57] C-435/06 *C* [2007] ECR I-10141.   [58] Para 52 of the Opinion in *C* (ibid).

[59] Joined Cases C-226/13, C-245/13, C-247/13, and C-578/13 *Fahnenbrock and others*, ECLI:EU:C:2015:383.

[60] Case C-14/08 *Roda Golf and Beach Resort* [2009] ECR I-5439.

[61] Para 56 of the judgment (ibid).

[62] The CJEU has ruled that where the domicile of a defendant is unknown, a cross-border element might be presumed based on his or her nationality: Case C-327/10 *Lindner* [2011] ECR I-11543.

asserting that EU legislation in this area should harmonize rules applicable not only to disputes having elements linked to more than one Member State but also rules applicable to purely national disputes.[63] Most Member States have, however, objected to this interpretation, with the result that the Council (along with the EP) has only proven willing to adopt measures limited specifically to cross-border disputes, and has consistently amended Commission proposals to this effect.[64] The Council legal service has apparently backed this view, arguing that domestic law can only be harmonized where this is purely ancillary to measures concerning cross-border litigation.[65] In fact, the UK only opted in to the relevant measures on the expectation that their scope would be limited essentially to cross-border disputes.[66]

The Commission's argument in the explanatory memoranda to the proposal on payment orders was that Article 65 EC (and presumably, now Article 81 TFEU) does not expressly limit the scope of EC measures to cross-border litigation. In its view, pursuant to Article 65 (now 81), legislation can also be adopted which plays an instrumental role in the working of the internal market; the optional nature of the EC rules should also be taken into account. In the case of mediation, the Commission argued in its explanatory memorandum that it would not be feasible to limit its proposal to cross-border cases only, since this would be arbitrary, produce discriminatory effects, reduce the practical impact of the legislation, increase legal uncertainty, allow the parties to determine the application of the Directive, and lead to the creation of parallel regimes, which would 'run counter to the principles of the internal market'. As for small claims, the Commission argued in its explanatory memorandum that Article 65 (now 81) only requires that a 'matter', rather than a 'measure', has cross-border implications, and that Article 65 should be interpreted in light of sub-paragraph (c) (now Article 81(2)(f)), which permits harmonization of national civil law. In this case, the matter had cross-border implications because 'most economic operators and consumers will sooner or later' become involved in litigation abroad. Again, dual legal regimes would create discrimination.

The Court of Justice has not yet had occasion to rule on this issue, but in a case concerning the 'external' scope of the Brussels Convention, it ruled that like the EC's internal market powers, the Convention could apply:

> ... [T]he uniform rules of jurisdiction contained in the Brussels Convention are not intended to apply only to situations in which there is a real and sufficient link with the

---

[63] See the explanatory memoranda to the proposals on legal aid (COM (2002) 13, 18 Jan 2002); payment orders (COM (2004) 173, 19 Mar 2004); mediation (COM (2004) 718, 22 Oct 2004); and small claims (COM (2005) 82, 15 Mar 2005). The Commission did not suggest that the EU rules on payment orders and small claims would replace national law applicable to domestic proceedings, but rather operate *as an option* alongside domestic rules.

[64] There are precise definitions of 'cross-border' limits set out in several measures: see II:8.5.5 to II:8.5.7 below.

[65] See Council docs 11289/04, 20 July 2004 and 12283/04, 17 Sep 2004, particularly para 14.

[66] See Council docs 8560/02, 6 May 2002 (legal aid); 10965/04, 29 June 2004 (payment orders); 9622/05, 1 June 2005 (mediation); and 10775/05, 30 June 2005 (small claims). All of these opt-in letters except the last one refer to advice of the Council legal service supporting the UK position. It appears that in the case of small claims, this omission is simply because the legal service opinion had not been released by the time of the UK opt-in.

working of the internal market, by definition involving a number of Member States. Suffice it to observe in that regard that the consolidation as such of the rules on conflict of jurisdiction and on the recognition and enforcement of judgments, effected by the Brussels Convention in respect of cases with an international element, is without doubt intended to eliminate obstacles to the functioning of the internal market which may derive from disparities between national legislations on the subject (see, by analogy, as regards harmonisation directives based on Article 95 EC intended to improve the conditions for the establishment and working of the internal market, Joined Cases C-465/00, C-138/01 and C-139/01 *Österreichischer Rundfunk and Others* [2003] ECR I-4989, paragraphs 41 and 42).[67]

In the *Rundfunk* judgment referred to, the Court of Justice found that the application of EC internal market legislation (in this case, the data protection directive) was not limited to cases with a cross-border element. Rather, the EC's powers set out in Article 95 EC (now Article 114 TFEU) allow it to harmonize national laws applicable to purely national situations, provided that the national laws in question need to be harmonized in order to ensure the functioning of the internal market.[68] In his Opinion in the *Owusu* case, the Advocate-General argued that the same reasoning applied to legislation based on Article 65 EC (now Article 81 TFEU),[69] an issue not considered by the Court's judgment. If this is correct, then the EU's civil law powers clearly can serve as a basis for the adoption of harmonization of national civil law.

Which interpretation is correct? First of all, as noted above, the focus on the 'internal market' requirement is now only of historical interest following the entry into force of the Treaty of Lisbon. The remaining requirement, which also applied even before the entry into force of the Treaty of Lisbon, is that EU civil law measures must concern 'matters having cross-border implications'. While it is true that measures based on the EU's internal market powers must have some relationship to cross-border issues, because the internal market is not a purely domestic concept, the different wording of the civil law Article should not be ignored, as it was presumably inserted by the drafters of the Treaty of Amsterdam (and confirmed by the drafters of the Treaty of Lisbon) to limit the scope of the civil law powers as compared to the internal market powers.[70] Contrary to the Commission's view, the 'cross-border' requirement must be viewed as a limitation on the internal market, not the other way around, since the EU in any event would enjoy internal market powers and this interpretation would render the additional 'cross-border' restriction on the EU's powers superfluous.

As for the Commission's further arguments, it is doubtful whether the cross-border criterion is met by measures which harmonize the law applicable to purely national

---

[67] Judgment in Case C-281/02 *Owusu* [2005] ECR I-1383, para 34.

[68] For more on this issue, see the discussion of the third competence issue, below. Since the Treaty of Lisbon has made only minor amendments to Art 95 EC (now Art 114 TFEU), it is presumed that the prior case law on the scope of this Art is still relevant.

[69] Paras 187–213 of the Opinion, n 67 above.

[70] The Court of Justice has made clear that the EC and EU Treaties should be interpreted with regard to the intentions of the drafters of the Treaty of Amsterdam: Cases C-11/00 *Commission v European Central Bank* [2003] ECR I-7147, paras 100, 103, and 130; and C-15/00 *Commission v European Investment Bank* [2003] ECR I-7281, para 131.

disputes, even on an optional basis. Although the Treaty does not require that measures be linked to cross-border litigation, in particular since there is no requirement that legislation adopted on the basis of Article 81 TFEU be limited to legal proceedings (see above), the 'implications' to be regulated explicitly require a cross-border element and must concern '*judicial* cooperation'. So the additional 'cross-border' requirement must mean that measures based on Article 81 must focus on litigation or other forms of judicial proceeding with a cross-border element. The power to regulate 'obstacles to the good functioning of civil proceedings' set out in Article 65(c) EC (now 81(2)(f) TFEU) cannot be divorced from the general limitations on the powers set out in the *chapeaux* of those Articles; it follows that the power conferred by Article 81(2)(f) can only be exercised where such measures would be ancillary to the object of facilitating proceedings with a cross-border element. Furthermore, the *chapeau* of Article 81 makes no distinction as to whether the measures proposed to harmonize domestic proceedings are optional or not; this point goes instead to the issue of proportionality and subsidiarity. Far from being alien to internal market law, distinct regimes for foreign and domestic cases are entrenched within it, in particular as regards free movement of persons.[71] It is rather doubtful that 'most' consumers will become involved in foreign litigation, or even domestic litigation; and in any event, this would not preclude having different rules for foreign and domestic cases. Also, it is not unfeasible to have different rules for foreign and domestic cases, as the adopted legislation in question proves; nor did it prove necessary to develop different definitions of 'foreign' cases for each EU measure, as a standard rule was developed.[72] Persons entering into legal relations across borders already have accepted that different substantive and procedural rules, including foreign courts, may well become involved if they need to enter into litigation; even the Commission's proposals on payment orders and small claims make a *renvoi* to different national laws as regards some issues. Arguments about the practical impact of legislation are irrelevant to the question of the extent of powers conferred upon the EU. A distinction based on the foreign or domestic nature of proceedings would be no more arbitrary and create no more legal uncertainty than other exclusions from the scope of EU civil legislation or the different rules applying to different categories within the scope of that legislation.

Finally, the Court's judgment in *Owusu* concerned the extent of the Member States' powers pursuant to the former Article 293 EC (now repealed), not the extent of the EC's powers pursuant to Article 65 EC (now Article 81 TFEU).

The conclusion is that the Council's and EP's practice reflects a legal requirement, which moreover continues to exist after the entry into force of the Treaty of Lisbon, because the EU lacks the power pursuant to the Treaty provisions on civil cooperation to harmonize national civil procedural law in domestic proceedings except where this

---

[71] See I:6.4.1 and also the Opinion in Case C-265/07 *Caffaro* [2008] ECR I-7085 (para 32), which contrasts the cross-border limits of measures adopted pursuant to the EU's civil law powers with the domestic impact of internal market legislation.

[72] See II:8.5.5 to II:8.5.7 below for details, although note that in one of the four measures concerned (the mediation Directive) it was necessary to elaborate on the question of the date at which the cross-border effect is to be determined.

is purely ancillary to measures solely concerning the regulation of litigation or comparable proceedings with a cross-border element. It should be noted, however, that according to the CJEU, it is not necessary to show a specific effect on the internal market in every individual case for EU civil cooperation legislation to apply; it is sufficient to show only that the procedure in question falls within the scope of that legislation.[73]

This brings us to the third issue: the distinction between the civil law powers on the one hand, and the internal market powers and Article 352 TFEU (former Article 308 EC) on the other. With the abolition of the requirement that EU civil law measures be necessary to ensure the proper functioning of the internal market, there is less likely to be a conflict between the EU's civil law powers and its internal market powers,[74] but the issue is still relevant because Article 81 TFEU clearly does not preclude civil law measures from having a connection with the internal market. As for the relationship between the civil law powers and the former Article 293 EC, the issue is now irrelevant following the repeal of Article 293 by the Treaty of Lisbon, but it remains of historical importance in the event of a validity challenge to pre-Lisbon legislation.[75]

The relationship between the EU's civil law powers and its internal market powers is more complex. Article 114 TFEU (although not Article 115) applies 'save where otherwise provided in the Treaties', and so can be trumped by a *lex specialis*.[76] Also, Article 114(2) sets out express exclusions from the scope of that Article (free movement of persons, fiscal provisions, and the rights and interests of employed persons). It follows that Article 81 applies instead of Article 114 where the two provisions overlap, and that in any event Article 114 cannot be used as a basis for measures concerning civil proceedings which concern matters falling within the scope of Article 114(2). This distinction has implications for the territorial scope of the measures,[77] decision-making (as far as family law measures and administrative cooperation are concerned),[78] and the non-application to EU civil law legislation of the national derogations and safeguards permitted by Article 114(4) to (10) TFEU.

---

[73] Case C-223/14 *Tecom Mican*, ECLI:EU:C:2015:383. This judgment concerned the service of documents Reg (on which, see II:8.5.2 below), but it should logically apply by analogy to all civil cooperation measures.

[74] On the link between the internal market and the civil law legislation under Art 65 EC, see the Opinions in *Apostolides* (n 55 above), para 37, and *Roda Golf* (n 60 above), paras 53–6.

[75] See the analysis in the second edition of this book, p 369.

[76] The scope of Art 114 TFEU (formerly Art 95 EC, and prior to that Art 100a EC) has been much litigated. See, for example, Cases: C-300/89 *Commission v Council* [1991] ECR I-2867; C-70/88 *Parliament v Council* [1991] ECR I-4529; C-155/91 *Commission v Council* [1993] ECR I-939; C-187/93 *Parliament v Council* [1994] ECR I-2857; C-359/92 *Germany v Council* [1994] ECR I-3681; C-350/92 *Spain v Council* [1995] ECR I-1985; C-84/94 *UK v Council* [1996] ECR I-8755; C-233/94 *Germany v Council and EP* [1997] ECR I-2405; C-209/97 *Commission v Council* [1999] ECR I-8067; C-269/97 *Commission v Council* [2000] ECR I-2257; C-376/98 *Germany v Council and EP* [2000] ECR I-8419; C-491/01 *BAT* [2002] ECR I-11453; C-377/98 *Netherlands v Council and EP* [2001] ECR I-7079; C-338/01 *Commission v Council* [2004] ECR I-4829; C-434/02 *Arnold Andre* [2004] ECR I-11825; C-210/03 *Swedish Match* [2004] ECR I-11893; C-154/04 and C-155/04 *Alliance for Natural Health and others* [2005] ECR I-6451; C-66/04 *UK v Council and EP* [2005] ECR I-10553; C-533/03 *Commission v Council* [2006] ECR I-1025; C-436/03 *EP v Council* [2006] ECR I-3733; C-217/04 *UK v Council and EP* [2006] ECR I-3771; C-317/04 and C-318/04 *EP v Council and Commission* [2006] ECR I-4721; C-380/03 *Germany v Council and EP* [2006] ECR I-11573; C-301/06, *Ireland v Council and EP* [2009] ECR I-593; and C-58/08 *Vodafone* [2010] ECR I-4999.

[77] See II:8.2.5 below.

[78] For other measures, Arts 81 and 114 TFEU are subject to the same decision-making procedure, leaving aside the impact on decision-making of the limited territorial scope of Art 81.

Nevertheless, it should not be concluded that all civil law matters fall within the scope of Article 81 TFEU. There are no grounds to argue that Article 81 in any way governs *substantive* civil law, so it remains open for the EU to use the internal market power to adopt measures on that subject, if they fall within the scope of that legal base. Such legislation could include provisions on civil procedure to the extent that those provisions are purely ancillary to the substantive rules.[79] This possibility is provided for explicitly as regards rules on conflict of law.[80] The internal market power can also be used to adopt measures on administrative law or administrative procedure which fall within the scope of that legal base, so it is necessary to distinguish between administrative proceedings and 'judicial cooperation in civil matters'; the scope of the latter phrase was examined above. The more difficult question is whether legislation on civil procedure which falls outside the scope of Article 81 (because it fails the 'cross-border' criterion) can be adopted pursuant to Article 114 (because it nevertheless meets the internal market criterion). It is arguable that such measures cannot be adopted pursuant to Article 114, because Article 81 is a *lex specialis* as regards civil law and allowing the adoption of such measures pursuant to Article 114 would circumvent the intentions of the drafters of the Treaty of Amsterdam (confirmed by the Treaty of Lisbon) to limit the scope of the EU's powers in this area, by analogy with the Court's conclusion that the EU's internal market powers could not be used to circumvent a Treaty ban on harmonization of public health law.[81] However, the contrary view has been assumed in an Opinion of an Advocate-General, which compares the cross-border limitation in the scope of EU civil law measures with the regulation of 'execution procedures carried out within a single Member State', pursuant to a directive adopted on the basis of Article 95 EC (now Article 114 TFEU).[82] It might be argued that the issue of harmonizing civil law pursuant to the EU's internal market powers is a distinct question from harmonizing Member States' law regarding public health, because in the latter case (but not the former) the Treaty contains an express ban on harmonization of national law.[83]

As for Article 352 TFEU, it only applies in the event that another Treaty Article (ie Article 81, 114, or 115) does not give the EU the necessary powers to act. Following the Treaty of Lisbon, there is no longer a requirement for a link between the use of Article 352 and the operation of the common market,[84] and it is expressly confirmed that the Article cannot be used to circumvent limits on the competence of the EU set out in other Treaty provisions.[85] It is conceivable that a civil law measure which does not satisfy either the criterion of a cross-border link set out in Article 81 or the requirements relating to internal market law set out in Article 114 or 115 would be able, nonetheless,

---

[79] On ancillary legal bases, see particularly Case C-211/01 *Commission v Council* [2003] ECR I-8913.

[80] See discussion of the legislation in II:8.4 and II.8.5.3 below. See also the proposal for EC signature on the Hague Convention on the law applicable to certain rights in respect of securities held with an intermediary (COM (2003) 783, 15 Dec 2003; the proposal was later withdrawn), which was based on internal market legal bases, rather than civil law legal bases, in light of the existing internal market legislation on this topic.

[81] See the first tobacco advertising judgment: Case C-376/98 *Germany v EP and Council* (n 76 above), para 79.

[82] Opinion in *Caffaro*, n 71 above.

[83] The tobacco advertising case referred to Art 129(4), subsequently Art 152(3)(c) EC; see now Art 168(5) TFEU.

[84] Art 352(1) TFEU.   [85] Art 352(3) TFEU.

to satisfy the requirements of Article 352.[86] However, the question would again arise as to whether the ban on the use of Article 352 to circumvent restrictions on harmonization would apply where the ban on harmonization is arguably implied (as in the case of Article 81 and harmonization of purely national civil law), rather than express.

The fourth question is the division of competence *within* Title V as regards civil law matters within its scope. There are three different decision-making procedures: the ordinary legislative procedure for Article 81 measures in general; the exception in Article 81(3) TFEU for unanimity in the Council and consultation of the EP as regards 'measures concerning family law'; and QMV in Council and consultation of the EP for administrative cooperation measures (Article 74).[87] What is covered by the family law exception? That exception must surely cover legislation such as Regulation 2201/2003, which solely concerns family law proceedings;[88] conversely, it surely would not apply to the Regulations of 2000 and 2015 which solely concern insolvency proceedings,[89] or to the Rome II and Rome I Regulations on conflict of laws, which exclude family law disputes (including maintenance) from their scope.[90] The Commission has convincingly argued that its proposal relating to jurisdiction and choice of law regarding inheritance did not fall within the scope of the family law exception, because most national legal systems regard inheritance law as a property law issue, inheritance law does not regulate the family relationships between individuals, and the family law exception must be interpreted strictly.[91]

But the majority of civil law measures adopted to date could be described as 'mixed' measures, partly related to family law and partly related to other matters. The Brussels I Regulation applies to maintenance payments as well as many other types of civil and commercial proceeding,[92] until the specific Regulation on maintenance proceedings becomes applicable.[93] Similarly, the Regulation establishing a European Enforcement Order originally applied to maintenance disputes, as it has the same scope as the Brussels I Regulation,[94] until the maintenance Regulation became applicable.[95] Furthermore, prima facie it appears that the EU legislation on the service of documents, requests to obtain evidence, the European Judicial Network, legal aid, payment orders, civil law funding programmes, and mediation also applies partly to family law issues and partly

---

[86] On the previous requirement of a link to the common market for the use of the prior Art 308 EC, see Joined Cases C-402/05 P and C-415/05 P *Kadi and Al Barakaat* [2008] ECR I-6351 and Case C-166/07 *EP v Council* [2009] ECR I-7135.

[87] It is assumed in the following analysis that Arts 74 and 81(3) TFEU have the same meaning as the prior Treaty provisions which they replaced (Arts 66 and 67(5) EC), given that neither Art has been substantively amended by the Treaty of Lisbon.

[88] [2003] OJ L 338/1.   [89] See II:8.5.1.

[90] See Art 1(2)(a) and (b) of the Rome II Reg (Reg 864/2007, [2007] OJ L 199/40) and Art 1(2)(b) and (c) of the Rome I Reg (Reg 593/2008, [2008] OJ L 177/6).

[91] COM (2009) 154, 14 Oct 2009. On the requirement to interpret exceptions from the normal competence rules in the Treaty strictly, see by analogy Case C-268/06 *Impact* [2008] ECR I-2483.

[92] Art 5(2), Reg 44/2001 ([2001] OJ L 12/1).

[93] Reg 4/2009 ([2009] L 7/1), Art 68(1). On the question of when the Reg became applicable, see II:8.6 below.

[94] Reg 805/2004 ([2004] L 143/15), Art 2.

[95] Art 68(2), Reg 4/2009, n 93 above. Note though that the enforcement order regulation continues to apply to Member States that do not apply the standard rules on conflict of law in maintenance disputes: this means the UK (see II:8.2.5 below).

to other issues.[96] For the most part, this is confirmed by Regulation 2201/2003[97] and the maintenance Regulation.[98] So any amendments to these measures could be considered as 'mixed' legislation.

There are two possible interpretations of the family law exception. Either it applies only where the EU adopts legislation essentially solely related to family law proceedings, or it applies to general rules which govern both family law and non-family law proceedings. In the latter case the exception would mean that such measures would have to be adopted on a dual legal base, which would entail adopting separate measures, since the two decision-making procedures would be incompatible.[99] The better interpretation is the former one, since an exception from the general rule should be construed strictly. Moreover, the words 'aspects relating to' support this interpretation, as they suggest that only specific rules for family law proceedings are covered by the exception. In practice, this is the interpretation applied by the EU institutions, as evidenced by the application of the co-decision procedure to the Regulation establishing a European Enforcement Order, which applied (until the maintenance Regulation became applicable) to proceedings concerning maintenance but does not set out special rules in that respect. Similarly, the legislation on payment orders and mediation and the revised rules on service of documents were adopted without any apparent doubt that the general decision-making rule applied. The Commission expressly confirmed this interpretation when it invited the Council to extend co-decision and QMV to maintenance issues.[100]

More difficult questions could arise where legislation does not solely set out general rules applicable to both family and non-family civil proceedings, but contains both general rules applicable to civil law proceedings *and* specific rules relating to family law proceedings. Such legislation would be covered by a dual legal base after February 2003; this would therefore entail adoption of separate measures. But if the institutions adopted only an amendment to the general rules in the legislation or only an amendment to the specific family law rules in it, then the respectively different decision-making procedures would apply. So, for instance, the Council was correct to decide that the amendment to the Brussels I Regulation that altered the specific rules in that Regulation applicable to maintenance payments had to be adopted by unanimity in the

---

[96] See respectively: Reg 1348/2000 ([2000] OJ L 160/37), replaced by Reg 1393/2007 ([2007] OJ L 324/79); Reg 1206/2001 ([2001] OJ L 174/1); Decision 2001/470 ([2001] OJ L 174/25), amended in 2009 ([2009] OJ L 168/35); Dir 2003/8 ([2003] OJ L 26/41); Reg 1896/2006 ([2006] OJ L 399/1); the most recent funding programme (Reg 1382/2013, [2013] OJ L 354/73); and Dir 2008/52 ([2008] OJ L 136/3). However, maintenance and matrimonial property disputes are excluded from the small claims Regulation (Reg 861/2007, [2007] OJ L 199/1, Art 2(2)(b)).

[97] N 88 above. See the references in Reg 2201/2003 to: Reg 1348/2000 (recital 15 of the preamble and Art 18); Reg 44/2001 (recitals 9 and 11 of the preamble); Reg 1206/2001 (recital 20 of the preamble); and Decision 2001/470 (recital 25 of the preamble and Arts 54 and 58(2)). There is no reference to Dir 2003/8, however. See also subsequently the references to Reg 2201/2003 in the preamble to Dir 2008/52 (recitals 20 and 21). The issues addressed by Reg 2201/2003 presumably fall outside the scope of Reg 1896/2006 on payment orders, because the former Reg does not concern pecuniary claims.

[98] N 93 above. See the references in Reg 4/2009 to Decision 2001/470 (recital 39 of the preamble and Arts 70 and 71(3)) and Dir 2003/8 (recital 36 of the preamble and Art 68(3)).

[99] For more detail on this issue, see the analysis in II:3.2.4 above.

[100] COM (2005) 648, 15 Dec 2005.

Council, given that the issue of maintenance payments is inseparable from the substance of family law.

As for Article 74 TFEU, it should be interpreted consistently whether it applies to civil law, immigration and asylum law, or policing and criminal law.[101] This means that it cannot be used to adopt measures relating to the substance of civil proceedings as such, but solely to adopt measures concerning administrative cooperation. Also, EU funding programmes fall within the scope of Article 74 when they are intended primarily to fund cooperation between administrations (even as regards family law specifically), but will fall within the scope of Article 81 if they have other purposes within the 'field' of judicial cooperation, in particular the purposes relating to private practitioners or to judges (who, due to their independence, cannot be considered to form part of the administration).

The practice of the institutions to date is not clear, because the relevant measures adopted to date (all before the Treaty of Lisbon) did not set out whether the EC was acting on the basis of the previous Article 65 EC or of the previous Article 66 EC. But if we apply the criteria set out above, the Decision establishing the European Judicial Network fell within the scope of Article 65 EC (now Article 81 TFEU), not Article 66 EC (now Article 74 TFEU), because it addresses both administrative cooperation and cooperation between practitioners, but has the primary aim of facilitating the latter. This was confirmed when the 2009 amendment to this Decision was adopted using the co-decision procedure.[102] Similarly, the civil law funding measures of 2001, 2002, and 2007 were (or are) not limited in scope to facilitating administrative cooperation, and so fell (or fall) within the scope of Article 65 EC (now Article 81 TFEU). This means that the 2007 and 2013 funding legislation was correctly adopted pursuant to the co-decision procedure.[103]

8.2.5 Territorial scope

The UK and Ireland exercised the possibility to opt in to all proposed civil law measures up until 2005/06. Since that point, those Member States have opted in to the majority of new measures, with some exceptions. In particular, the UK (but not Ireland) opted out of the proposals on maintenance and conflicts of law in contract, and then both the UK and Ireland opted out of the Rome III Regulation on choice of law regarding divorce and the Regulation on choice of law and jurisdiction over inheritance law.[104] The UK has also opted out of the Regulation establishing an Account Preservation Order, and both the UK and Ireland have opted out of the proposals relating to matrimonial property and the property of civil partnerships.

On the other hand, the UK subsequently chose to opt in to the maintenance and conflict of law Regulations *after* their adoption, having successfully *de facto* negotiated

---

[101] On the application of Art 74 to immigration and asylum law, see I:3.2.4; on criminal law, see II:3.2.4 above. See also the discussion of the general provisions of Title V in I:2.2.3.2.
[102] On the substance of the Decision, see II:8.8.2 below.
[103] On the substance of these measures, see II:8.8.1 below.
[104] On the opt-outs for the UK and Ireland generally, see II:2.2.5.1 above.

changes to the proposed texts despite being formally a *non-participant* in the Council discussions. The UK opt-ins were then duly approved by the Commission.[105] However, as regards the maintenance Regulation, the UK and the other Member States agreed to separate the issue of conflict of law in maintenance matters from the main Regulation; this issue is instead addressed in a separate international treaty which the EU has concluded, but in which the UK does not participate.[106] The consequence of the UK's non-participation in these conflict rules is that UK maintenance judgments are subject to an 'exequatur' process before they can be enforced in other Member States (although the Regulation on the European Enforcement Order could still apply to uncontested UK maintenance judgments), whereas judgments will circulate more easily within the Member States which will share common conflict of law rules on this issue. It should be recalled that after the entry into force of the Lisbon Treaty, there are special rules governing the position if the UK and Ireland opt out of measures amending acts which they are already bound by.

As for Denmark, it is fully excluded from civil law legislation as such, until and unless it exercises the option granted to it following the entry into force of the Lisbon Treaty to adopt a case-by-case opt-in system very similar to that which applies to the UK and Ireland.[107] Nevertheless, it should be recalled that during the period when civil law matters were addressed intergovernmentally, Denmark ratified the Brussels and Rome I Conventions and then later signed the Brussels II and service of documents Conventions during the Maastricht era. The Rome I Convention (but not its replacement Regulation) remains in force between Denmark and the other Member States.

In order to retain Danish participation in some of the other measures following their integration into the EU legal order, Denmark and the EU (then the EC) negotiated separate treaties which affiliate Denmark to the Brussels I Regulation and the service of documents Regulation (but not to the Brussels II or Rome I Regulations).[108] The treaties provide that Denmark is not obliged to accept subsequent amendments to or measures implementing the EU legislation, but in the event that it refuses to accept such amendments or implementing measures, the main agreement(s) will be terminated, unless the parties decide otherwise.[109] In accordance with these provisions, Denmark has notified its acceptance of changes made to both the service of documents Regulation and the Brussels I Regulation.[110] These decisions in fact entail Denmark applying most of the EU Regulation on maintenance proceedings, except for the rules on applicable law and cooperation between central authorities, on the basis that the other provisions of this Regulation are simply amendments of provisions which were previously in the Brussels I Regulation.[111]

---

[105] [2009] OJ L 10/22 and [2009] OJ L 149/73. The UK also held discussions with the Council about possible changes to the Regulation on successions which would facilitate a decision to opt in after the adoption of that Regulation. But ultimately it decided not to do so.

[106] See II:8.9 below.   [107] For more on the Danish Title IV position, see II:2.2.5.2 above.

[108] For the signature and text of these treaties, see [2005] OJ L 299/61 and [2005] OJ L 300/53; for ratification by the EC, see [2006] OJ L 120/22 and 23. Both treaties entered into force on 1 July 2007: see [2007] OJ L 94/70. On the parallel treaty between the EU and Denmark concerning asylum responsibility, see I:5.2.5.

[109] Arts 3 and 4 of each agreement. Note that in accordance with the opt-out Protocols, Denmark does not have a vote within the Council on such amendments or a role regarding implementing measures.

[110] See [2008] OJ L 331/21, [2009] OJ L 149/80, and [2014] OJ L 240/1.

[111] On the substance of the maintenance Reg, see further II:8.6 below.

According to the two EU-Denmark treaties, international agreements based on the relevant EU legislation which the EU concludes are not binding on Denmark,[112] but Denmark must 'abstain' from ratifying treaties which may 'affect or alter the scope' of this EU legislation, unless it agrees this with the EU and reaches satisfactory arrangements as regards either EU-Denmark treaty and the other treaty in question.[113] There was initially no provision in the treaties or the Council decisions concluding them which sets out how the EU should adopt its position in such cases, but the Council Decisions were amended in 2009, in order to provide for such a procedure.[114] Also, the treaties provide that when negotiating international treaties in such circumstances, Denmark must coordinate its position with the EU and must 'abstain from any actions that would jeopardise the objectives of [an EU] position within its sphere of competence in such negotiations'.[115]

As for the Court of Justice, it has the same jurisdiction as regards the relevant EU legislation concerning preliminary rulings, requests for interpretation, and infringement proceedings in respect of Denmark as it does for other Member States.[116] The treaties provide that if the Court's jurisdiction is amended in respect of the relevant legislation, as occurred with the entry into force of the Treaty of Lisbon, Denmark again had an option whether or not to accept these changes. But again, if Denmark did not accept these changes within a deadline (in this case, sixty days from the entry into force of the changes, so by 30 January 2010), the agreement(s) would have been terminated, with no possibility for the parties to decide otherwise.[117] In practice, Denmark accepted the changes to the Court's jurisdiction, and the Court of Justice of the European Union (CJEU) has delivered judgment in one case concerning Denmark.[118] The treaties will also be terminated if Denmark terminates its opt-out from Title V of the TFEU, or if either party decides to denounce the treaty, following a six-month waiting period.[119]

Denmark's position would have changed if the public had voted, in a referendum held in December 2015, to move to a system of opting in to individual JHA measures. A group of political parties had agreed that if the public voted for a change to the opt-out, Denmark would opt in to measures on: insolvency; payment orders; small claims; the European Enforcement Order; mediation; the Rome Regulation (on conflicts of law concerning contract); the Rome II Regulation (on conflicts of law concerning non-contractual liability); external relations; protection orders; inheritance; maintenance

---

[112] Art 5(1) of each agreement.

[113] Art 5(2) of each agreement. The wording 'affect or alter their scope' reflects the case law concerning the existence of exclusive EU external competence, and now Art 3(2) TFEU (see II:8.9 below).

[114] [2009] OJ L 331/24 and 26. The Decisions require the Commission to give such authorization if the ratification of the relevant agreement by Denmark 'would not render the Agreement ineffective and would not undermine the proper functioning of the system established by its rules' (new Art 1a(1)). Note that Denmark has signed and ratified the revised Lugano Convention alongside the EU (see II:8.9 below). This compares in part to EU legislation which delegates competence to Member States to sign civil law treaties (Art 4(2)(b), Reg 662/2009 ([2009] OJ L 200/25): see II:8.9 below).

[115] Art 5(3) of each agreement.

[116] Arts 6 and 7 of each agreement. There is no explicit provision addressing the question of whether, and if so on what basis, Denmark could bring an annulment action against an amendment to the relevant legislation or a measure implementing it.

[117] Art 6(6) of each agreement.   [118] Case C-49/12 *Sunico* ECLI:EU:C:2013:545.

[119] Art 11, Brussels I agreement; Art 9, service of documents agreement.

proceedings; parental responsibility; and account preservation orders. On the other hand, in contrast, the parties had agreed *not* to opt in to the Directive on legal aid in cross-border proceedings, or to the Rome III Regulation on conflicts of law in divorce cases. Nor did they agree on whether to opt in to the pending proposals relating to jurisdiction and choice of law over marital property, and the property of civil partnerships, in the event of relationship breakdown. In the event, the Danish public voted against a change to the opt-out rules.

As for the new Member States joining the EU in 2004 and 2007, the legislation in this area applied immediately to them (where that legislation was already in force in the earlier Member States). However, because the Rome Convention on conflict of law in contracts was still an intergovernmental measure until it was replaced by a Regulation in 2008, it was necessary to agree an accession convention to this Convention in 2004, and for the Council to adopt a decision applying this Convention to Romania and Bulgaria in 2007.[120] Some of the legislation was changed automatically by the 2003 Treaty of Accession,[121] and in two cases existing measures were altered by subsequent special implementing measures pursuant to that Accession Treaty.[122] Also, some civil law legislation was amended to add technical references to Bulgaria, Romania, and Croatia when they joined the EU.[123]

A particular issue arises in the case of northern Cyprus, which is not subject to EU law as long as the legitimate Cypriot government does not exercise *de facto* control over the territory.[124] In the *Apostolides* reference to the Court of Justice,[125] the question was whether the EU rules on recognition of civil and commercial judgments applied nevertheless where a Cypriot court had issued a ruling regarding property situated in the northern part of Cyprus, and the Cypriot claimant had sought to enforce that judgment against the purported purchasers of that property in the English courts. In the Court's view, exceptions and derogations from EU law set out in accession treaties had to be interpreted narrowly (following long-established case law). Applying that rule to this case, the EU rules did apply because the issue was the recognition of a *judgment* given in the southern part of Cyprus, even though the subject-matter of that judgment was *property* located in northern Cyprus. The judgment therefore had to be recognized in the UK, even though it related to an area over which the court issuing the original judgment did not exercise *de facto* control and even though there might therefore be practical problems enforcing the judgment.

Finally, no non-EU countries are formally associated as such with the EU's civil law measures. Civil law relationships between the EU and non-EU States are instead regulated wholly by the exercise of the EU's external relations powers in specific cases, an issue considered further below.[126]

---

[120] [2007] OJ L 347/1.   [121] See II:2.2.5.3 above.

[122] Council Reg 2116/2004 ([2004] OJ L 367/1), amending the external relations provisions of Council Reg 44/2001 ([2001] OJ L 12/1), and Council Decision 2004/664 ([2004] OJ L 303/28), amending Council Decision 2004/246 authorizing Member States to sign an international treaty (see II:8.9 below).

[123] Regs 1791/2006 ([2006] OJ L 363/1) and 517/2013 ([2013] OJ L 158/1).

[124] On other issues regarding the application of JHA law to Cyprus, see I:2.2.5.3.

[125] Case C-420/07 *Apostolides* [2009] ECR I-3571.   [126] II:8.9.

8.3 Human Rights

8.3.1 The right to a fair trial

Civil law cooperation between States raises questions comparable to criminal law cooperation between States[127]: should a State recognize another State's judgment which was issued following an unfair trial, or facilitate what appears to be an unfair trial?[128] This issue was addressed by the European Court of Human Rights in the case of *Pellegrini v Italy*,[129] which involved a woman who argued that the Italian courts had violated the right to a fair trial set out in Article 6 of the European Convention on Human Rights (ECHR) by recognizing a judgment of the Vatican courts annulling her marriage which had not observed the standards set out in Article 6.[130] The Strasbourg Court, noting that the Vatican City had not ratified the ECHR, ruled that:

> The Court's task therefore consists not in examining whether the proceedings before the ecclesiastical courts complied with Article 6 of the Convention, but whether the Italian courts, before authorising enforcement of the decision annulling the marriage, duly satisfied themselves that the relevant proceedings fulfilled the guarantees of Article 6. A review of that kind is required where a decision in respect of which enforcement is requested emanates from the courts of a country which does not apply the Convention. Such a review is especially necessary where the implications of a declaration of enforceability are of capital importance for the parties.

Applying these principles to the facts, Article 6 had been violated by the Italian recognition of the foreign judgment. In subsequent judgments, the Human Rights Court clarified that as in criminal law cases, an obligation to refuse to recognize a foreign court judgment pursuant to Article 6 ECHR in civil cases would only apply where there was a 'flagrant denial of justice' in the State where the original judgment was decided.[131] This case law has so far only addressed the recognition of judgments issued by non-contracting States to the ECHR; it is not clear what standards, if any, govern recognition of judgments issued by a Contracting State.

As for the enforcement of judgments, in the case of *K. v Italy*,[132] the Court ruled that Italy was responsible for the failure to guarantee a trial within a reasonable time (therefore breaching Article 6) because it had not acted swiftly enough to enforce a judgment of the Polish courts concerning maintenance, which Italy had assumed the liability to enforce. The case law of the Strasbourg Courts also confirms that the right to access to a court applies to the process for the enforcement of judgments, including foreign judgments in particular.[133]

---

[127] See generally J Fawcett, 'The Impact of Article 6(1) of the ECHR on Private International Law' (2007) 56 ICLQ 1.

[128] As regards this issue in the context of criminal law, see generally II:3.3 above.

[129] Reports 2001-VIII.   [130] On the substance of Art 6, see further II:4.3 above.

[131] *Eskinazi and Chelouche v Turkey*, 6 Dec 2005, and *Maumousseau and Washington v France*, 6 Dec 2007. On the test applicable to criminal law cases, see II:3.3.1 above.

[132] Reports 2004-VIII.   [133] See *Vrbica v Croatia*, judgment of 1 Apr 2010.

Finally, cases concerning child abduction obviously raise issues concerning the right to family life, as regards both parents and the child. The Human Rights Court has made clear that such cases must be decided in the best interests of the child, taking account of the 1980 Hague Convention on Child Abduction and the Convention on the Rights of the Child.[134]

8.3.2 Application to EU law

The general principles of EU law recognize the right to a fair trial as well as the right to family and private life.[135] Both rights also expressly appear in the EU Charter,[136] as noted by the Court of Justice, and will be enforceable against the EU as a party to the ECHR if and when the EU accedes to the ECHR. The rights of the child are also recognized as part of the general principles and in the Charter.[137]

Applying these principles first of all to the recognition of judgments, the Court of Justice has ruled that the 'public policy' exception to the Brussels Convention could apply where the right to a fair trial had been breached as regards the judgment issued by another Member State's courts.[138] The same principles apply to the 'public policy' exception in the Brussels Regulation and the insolvency Regulation,[139] alongside specific rules providing for possible non-recognition of a judgment if the defendant was not notified of the proceedings in the first Member State. Presumably this interpretation applies to the equivalent provisions in other EU legislation concerning civil jurisdiction.[140] Furthermore, EU civil law legislation provides for the possible refusal to accept service of documents which have not been translated, and the Court of Justice has interpreted the relevant rules in light of the right to a fair trial, distinguishing the level of protection in civil cases from the express additional rights provided for in criminal cases.[141] The CJEU has also clarified when there is a right to legal aid in cross-border proceedings.[142]

---

[134] See *Eskinazi and Chelouche* and *Maumousseau and Washington* (n 131 above) and the summary of jurisprudence with references to further case law in the Grand Chamber judgment of 6 July 2010 in *Neulinger and Shuruk v Switzerland*. Both the Hague Convention and the Convention on the Rights of the Child have been ratified by all Member States.

[135] See respectively II:3.3 and II:4.3 above (right to a fair trial) and I:6.3.4 (right to family life).

[136] Arts 7 and 47 of the Charter ([2007] OJ C 303).

[137] See Case C-540/03 *EP v Council* [2006] ECR I-5769 (making express reference to the Convention on the Rights of the Child as a source of the general principles) and, as regards civil law in particular, Case C-403/09 PPU *Detiček* [2009] ECR I-12193. The CJEU case law on child abduction (see II:8.6 below) refers frequently to the Hague Convention on Child Abduction and to the rights of the child in Art 24 of the Charter.

[138] Case C-7/98 *Krombach* [2000] ECR I-1935. In this case, Art 6 ECHR had been breached in the underlying criminal proceedings, as confirmed by a subsequent Strasbourg judgment: see II:3.3.1 above. See subsequently Case C-394/07 *Gambazzi* [2009] ECR I-2563.

[139] For the Brussels Reg, see Cases: C-420/07 *Apostolides* [2009] ECR I-3571; C-619/10 *Trade Agency*, ECLI:EU:C:2012:531; C-327/10 *Lindner* [2011] ECR I-11543; and C-112/13 *Aliyev*, ECLI:EU:C:2014:207. For the insolvency Reg, see Case C-341/04 *Eurofoods* [2006] ECR I-3813, paras 60–8, followed in Case C-444/07 *MG Probud* [2010] ECR I-417, paras 30–4 (insolvency Reg). The *Lindner* case concerns human rights protection in *in absentia* trials in civil proceedings; for the criminal law equivalent, see II:4.6.5 above. See also on the Brussels Convention, Case C-283/05 *ASML* [2006] ECR I-12041.

[140] For the relevant legislation, see II.8.5.1 and II.8.6 below.

[141] Case C-14/07 *Weiss* [2008] ECR I-3367, referring, inter alia, to the Strasbourg case law on Art 6(3)(e) ECHR, on which see II:4.3 above. Note that in the criminal law context, the EU has adopted legislation on the translation of documents (see II:4.6.1 above).

[142] Case C-156/12 *GREP*, ECLI:EU:C:2012:342. See also the specific legislation on this issue (II:8.5.5 below). For the proposals on criminal law legal aid, see II.4.6.6 above.

However, as regards issues of jurisdiction, the Court of Justice has ruled that there is no exception to the rules in EU civil law legislation on *lis pendens* (ie the rules which apply if the same cause of action is litigated in more than one Member State simultaneously) on the grounds that the action was brought first in a Member State which arguably systematically fails to decide cases within a reasonable time, in breach of Article 6(1) ECHR.[143] The Court reasoned that there was no express rule to this effect in the Brussels Convention, and that there was a requirement of 'mutual trust' between Member States' national courts. However, with great respect, the first argument fails to take account of the primary law requirement of respect for human rights in EU law, and the second argument ignores the public policy exception set out in the Convention, which shows that Member States' mutual trust was not absolute. It is submitted that this case was decided wrongly, and that there is an implied rule requiring a waiver of the jurisdiction rules in EU legislation in exceptional cases where necessary to avoid a breach of human rights.

Finally, the Court of Justice has not yet had the opportunity to rule on whether 'public policy' exception in the Rome Convention or EU legislation on conflicts of law encompasses human rights issues.[144] It seems obvious that it should, by analogy with the case law on the public policy exception to the recognition of judgments.

8.4 Impact of Other EU Law

The relationship between EU civil law measures and other (non-JHA) EU law measures raises general issues of competence, which are considered further elsewhere.[145] Rather, this section examines more specifically first the interaction between EU civil law legislation and non-JHA EU law, and then the more general relationship between civil law and EU law. This analysis leaves aside the general requirement of a connection between the internal market and EU civil law legislation, which applied until the entry into force of the Treaty of Lisbon, and which has already been examined above.[146] However, it has been argued that the very existence of a body of EU civil law legislation makes it difficult in principle to argue that a seller established in one Member State will find it more difficult to sue a consumer established in another Member State,[147] and the CJEU has ruled that in light of the EU's civil cooperation measures, Member States cannot justify restricting the free movement of people in order to ensure the collection of a civil debt.[148]

---

[143] Case C-116/02 *Gasser* [2003] ECR I-14693. Since the *lis pendens* rules require the courts in all other Member States to stay their proceedings in the same cause of action until the first court seized has determined its jurisdiction, even if it is clear that the first court seized lacks jurisdiction and some other Member State's court should have jurisdiction, this strategy results in an effective denial of justice.

[144] On the relevant legislation, see II:8.5.3 and II:8.6 below.   [145] See II:2.4 and II:8.2.4 above.

[146] See the Opinions in Cases C-420/07 *Apostolides* [2009] ECR I-3571 and C-14/08 *Roda Golf* [2009] ECR I-5439, and generally II:8.2.2 and II:8.2.4 above.

[147] See the Opinion in Case C-205/07 *Gysbrechts* [2008] ECR I-9947, para 38.

[148] Case C-249/11 *Byankov*, ECLI:EU:C:2012:608.

First of all, as a general point, the EU's data protection Directive is applicable to its civil law measures, as confirmed by the preambles to several of the measures under discussion in this Chapter.[149]

Moving on to specific legislation, the rules in the Brussels I Convention, now found in the Brussels I Regulation, have been integrated into Community (now EU) acts on a number of occasions,[150] and referred to in EU legislation on a number of other occasions.[151] Also, on a number of occasions the Court of Justice has ruled on the relationship between the Brussels I Convention or Regulation and the EC Treaty (as it then was),[152] secondary EU law,[153] or the general principles of EU law.[154]

---

[149] See, for instance, Reg 1348/2000 ([2000] OJ L 160/37), Art 22(4) and recital 13 of the preamble; Reg 1206/2001 ([2001] OJ L 174/1), recital 18 of the preamble; Dir 2003/8 ([2003] OJ L 26/41), recital 27 of the preamble; Reg 1393/2007 ([2007] OJ L 324/79), Art 22(4) and recital 24 of the preamble; and Reg 4/2009 ([2009] OJ L 7/1), Art 68(4) and recital 34 of the preamble.

[150] Reg 40/94 on Community trade mark ([1994] OJ L 11/1); Reg 2100/94 on Community plant variety right ([1994] OJ L 227/1); Reg 2271/96 on EC response to US 'Helms-Burton' legislation ([1996] OJ L 309/1); Reg 6/2002 on Community design right ([2002] OJ L 3/1); and Dir 2005/14 on motor insurance ([2005] OJ L 149/14). References to the Brussels Convention must now be read as references to Reg 44/2001 (Art 68(2) of Reg 44/2001 ([2001] OJ L 12/1)), and subsequently Reg 1215/2012 ([2012] OJ L 351/1). The CJEU has examined in detail the link between the trademark Regulation and the Brussels Reg: Case C-360/12 *Coty Prestige Lancaster Group*, ECLI:EU:C:2014:485.

[151] See the preambles to: Reg 392/2009 on liability for maritime accidents ([2009] OJ L 131/24), recital 11; Dir 2008/112 on timeshares ([2009] OJ L 33/11), recital 18; Dir 2002/65 on distance selling of financial services ([2002] OJ L 271/16), recital 8; Dir 2004/35 on civil liability for environmental damage ([2004] OJ L 143/56), recital 10; and the EC company statute (Reg 2157/2001, [2001] OJ L 294/1), recital 25.

[152] See particularly Case C-388/92 *Mund and Fester* [1994] ECR I-467, discussed further below; Case C-172/91 *Sontag v Waidmann* [1993] ECR I-1963, where the Court transposed the 'public employment' exception from EU free movement law to the public law exclusion from the scope of the Convention; and Case C-38/98 *Renault* [2000] ECR I-2973, on the link between the 'public policy' exception to mutual recognition under the Brussels Convention and errors in interpreting EU law. On the latter point, see also the Opinion in Case C-115/08 *CEZ II* [2009] ECR I-660 and the judgment in Case C-681/13 *Diageo Brands*, ECLI:EU:C:2015:471.

[153] See: Case C-271/00 *Baten* [2002] ECR I-10489, where the Court interpreted EU law in order to define the 'social security' exclusion from the Convention; Case C-266/01 *Préservatrice Foncière Tiard* [2003] ECR I-4867, where the Court touched on interpretation of the TIR Convention, concluded on behalf of the EC (now EU) by Council Reg 2112/78 ([1978] OJ L 252/1), in order to determine the scope of the public law and customs exclusions from the Convention; Case C-347/08 *Vorarlberger* [2009] ECR I-8661, in which the Court looks at EU motor insurance Directives (Dirs 2005/14 (n 150 above) and 72/166, [1972] OJ L 103/1, since consolidated by Dir 2009/103, [2009] OJ L 263/11) in order to interpret Reg 44/2001; and Case C-204/08 *Rehder* [2009] ECR I-6073, where the application of the rules on jurisdiction in Reg 44/2001 turns upon the Court's prior case law on the relationship between EU legislation on liability for airline delays, etc. (Reg 261/2004 ([2004] OJ L 46/1)) and the Montreal Convention on the same subject, which has moreover been concluded by the EC, now the EU ([2001] OJ L 194/38; see Case C-344/04 *IATA and ELFAA* [2006] ECR I-403). There was also an overlap between the Convention or Reg 44/2001 and secondary EU law in Cases C-96/00 *Gabriel* [2002] ECR I-6367, C-27/02 *Engler* [2005] ECR I-481, and C-180/06 *Ilsinger* [2009] ECR I-3961 (as regards Dir 97/7 ([1997] OJ L 144/19) on distance selling) and C-167/00 *Henkel* [2002] ECR I-3111 (as regards Dir 93/13 ([1993] OJ L 95/29) on unfair contact terms), but the overlap was not material to the Court's judgments. See similarly the Opinion and judgment in Case C-73/04 *Klein and Klein* [2005] ECR I-8667: the Opinion mentions Dir 94/47 ([1994] OJ L 280/83) on timeshare arrangements in passing, while the judgment relies upon case law concerning Dir 85/577 on doorstep sales ([1985] OJ L 372/31) to determine the scope of a jurisdictional rule in the Convention. Joined Cases C-585/08 *Pammer* and C-144/09 *Hotel Alpenhof* [2010] ECR I-12527 link the Reg to the EU's package holidays legislation (at that time, Dir 90/314 ([1990] OJ L 158/59)), and Case C-352/13 *CDC Hydrogen Peroxide*, ECLI:EU:C:2015:335 links the Reg closely to enforcement of EU competition law. See more generally the Opinion in *Ilsinger*, above, which examines a number of EU consumer law Directives in order to define when a contract exists for the purpose of the Brussels I rules.

[154] See II:8.3.2 above.

Next, as for the conflict of law rules, the Rome I Regulation (on conflict of law in contract) refers frequently to other EU legislation as regards its scope and interpretation,[155] and is also subject to a general override (as was the Rome Convention) by other EU legislation.[156] This override has been applied expressly on several occasions,[157] and implicitly on some others.[158] The Rome II Regulation (on conflict of law as regards non-contractual liability) is also subject to a potential override by other EU legislation.[159]

As for other EU civil law measures, an opinion on the Regulation on the taking of evidence in civil cases discusses the overlap with EU legislation on the enforcement of intellectual property rights,[160] and a judgment has clarified links between the latter legislation and the Brussels Regulation.[161] An opinion on the insolvency Regulation has referred to it as part of a body of EU insolvency law, along with the specific internal market legislation governing insolvency within the financial services sector.[162] Another opinion on this Regulation suggested that EU tax legislation should be interpreted in light of it.[163] The Court of Justice has also applied the insolvency Regulation by analogy to determine the issue of applicable law when the Commission brought an action against an insolvent company within the framework of EU administrative law.[164] Furthermore, the EU legislation on mediation has been referred to when interpreting

---

[155] See recitals 18, 26, 27, 30, 31, 34, and 40 in the preamble, as well as Arts 1(2)(j), 4(1)(h), 6(4), 7(2), and 7(6) of Reg 593/2008 ([2008] OJ L 177/6).

[156] Art 23, Reg 593/2008 (ibid).

[157] See particularly recitals 7–11 in the preamble to Dir 96/71 on the posting of workers ([1997] OJ L 18/1), and the relevant case law: paras 10–12 of the Opinion in Case C-346/06 *Rüffert* [2008] ECR I-1989; para 35 of the Opinion in Case C-319/06 *Commission v Luxembourg* [2008] ECR I-4323; para 13 of the Opinion in Case C-341/05 *Laval* [2007] ECR I-11767; and Case C-396/13 *Sähköalojen ammattiliitto*, ECLI:EU:C:2015:86. See also Art 12 of Dir 2008/112 (n 151 above) and recital 17 in the preamble to that Directive.

[158] See Case C-70/03 *Commission v Spain* [2004] I-7999, which concerns the relationship between the Rome Convention and the national application of Dir 93/13, n 153 above. See also the Opinions in Cases C-484/08 *Caja de Ahorros y Monte de Piedad de Madrid* [2010] ECR I-4785, note 81 and C-515/08 *Palhota* [2010] ECR I-9133, note 25. On the relationship between the Convention or Reg and other EU legislation, see: Dir 2007/64 on payment services ([2007] OJ L 319/1), recital 51 in the preamble; Dir 2002/65 (n 151 above), recital 8 in the preamble; Dir 2011/83 on consumer rights ([2011] OJ L 304/64), recitals 10 and 58 in the preamble; *Pammer* and *Hotel Alpenhof* (n 153 above), on the link with the package holidays Directive; Joined Cases C-359/14 and C-475/14 *ERGO Insurance* and *Gjensidige Baltic*, pending, on the link between the Rome I Reg and road traffic law; and Case C-483/14, *KA Finanz*, pending, on the link between the Convention and Reg and company law. See also the judgment in Joined Cases C-509/09 *eDate Advertising* and C-161/10 *Martinez* [2011] ECR I-10269, on the link between conflict of laws rules and the e-commerce Directive (Dir 2000/31 ([2000] OJ L 178/1)).

[159] Art 27 of Reg 864/2007 ([2007] OJ L 199/40). See also the links to other EU law set out in recitals 22, 23, and 35 of the preamble. See Case C-191/15, *Verein für Konsumenteninformation*, pending, on the link between the Reg and consumer law and Case C-240/14 *Pruller-Frey*, ECLI:EU:C:2015:567, on the links between the Reg and EU passenger transport legislation.

[160] Opinion in Case C-175/06 *Tedesco* [2007] ECR I-7929, paras 49–52, referring back to Dir 2004/48 ([2004] OJ L 157/45).

[161] Case C-406/09 *RealChemie* [2011] ECR I-9773. See also *Diageo Brands*, n 152 above.

[162] Opinion in Case C-339/07 *Deko Marty Belgium* [2009] ECR I-767, para 59 and note 47, with further references.

[163] Opinion in Case C-73/06 *Planzer Luxembourg* [2007] ECR I-5655.

[164] Case C-294/02 *Commission v AMI Semiconductor Belgium* [2005] ECR I-2175.

non-JHA EU legislation,[165] and there is EU legislation on mediation on consumer disputes, adopted pursuant to the EU's internal market powers.[166]

It should be noted, though, that the principle of integration between EU civil law and other areas of EU law has its limits. In particular, the Court of Justice has refused to transpose concepts of 'habitual residence' from other areas of EU law into the family law Regulation, and also refused to transpose the definition of 'services' from other areas of EU law into the Brussels I Regulation.[167]

As regards the development of a common frame of reference for European contract law,[168] Advocates-General (but not yet the Court of Justice) have shown some willingness to interpret EU legislation in light of the draft common frame of reference (DCFR).[169]

Finally, on the question of the link between EU law and criminal law, there are sometimes civil law consequences for the criminal acts of individuals, with resulting overlaps between the EU rules applicable.[170] It is also necessary to distinguish between a civil claim and a financial penalty.[171] But in the context of liability for Europol activities, the Brussels I jurisdiction rules are applicable.[172] The EU has also adopted parallel measures on civil and criminal aspects of protection orders,[173] after a difficult dispute about the legal base of these measures. In light of the CJEU's insistence upon the distinction between the criminal and non-criminal aspects of exchanging information on drivers,[174] the adoption of two different civil protection measures is surely correct.

The second issue to be examined is the general relationship between civil law and the rest of EU law. On this point, first of all it should not be thought that civil cooperation issues are confined to Title V of the TFEU (formerly Title IV of the EC Treaty), and fall entirely outside the remainder of the Treaties. Civil procedural rules affecting references to the Court from national courts under Article 267 TFEU (ex-Article 234 EC) are within the scope of EU law,[175] and national rules affecting access to remedies

---

[165] Opinion in Joined Cases C-317/08 to C-320/08 *Alassini* [2010] ECR I-2213 (note 19) and in Case C-509/11 *ÖBB-Personenverkehr*, ECLI:EU:C:2013:167 (note 28).

[166] Dir 2003/11, [2013] OJ L 165/63, and Reg 524/2013, [2013] OJ L 165/1. See also the late payments Directive (Dir 2011/7, [2011] OJ L 48/1, recital 34 in the preamble).

[167] See respectively Cases C-523/07 *A* [2009] ECR I-2805 and C-533/07 *Falco* [2009] ECR I-3327. See also Case C-322/14 *El Majdoub*, ECLI:EU:C:2015:334, which distinguishes the Brussels Reg from Dir 97/7 on distance contracts (n 153 above) on some issues.

[168] See further II:8.7 below.

[169] See, for example, the Opinions in Cases: C-412/06 *Hamilton* [2007] ECR I-2383, para 24; C-445/06 *Danske Slagterier* [2009] ECR I-2119, note 57; *Ilsinger* (n 153 above), paras 49–52; C-275/07 *Commission v Italy* [2009] ECR I-2005, note 55; C-227/08 *Martin Martin* [2009] ECR I-11939, para 51; C-215/08 *Friz* [2010] ECR I-2947, notes 62, 65, and 72; and C-540/08 *Mediaprint Zeitungs- und Zeitschriftenverlag* [2010] ECR I-10909, note 7. However, see the Opinion in *Messner* (Case C-489/07 [2009] ECR I-7315), para 85, which specifically refuses to interpret EU legislation in light of the DCFR.

[170] See, for instance, Case C-7/98 *Krombach* [2000] ECR I-1935, discussed further in II:8.3.2 and II:3.2.4 above.

[171] See Art 1(b)(iv) of the Framework Decision on recognition of financial penalties ([2005] OJ L 76/16), the discussion of competence in II:6.2.4 above, and the case law on double jeopardy (II:6.8 above).

[172] See II:7.8.3 above.

[173] For details of the civil law measure, see II:8.5.1.2 below; for the criminal measure, see II:3.7.6 above.

[174] See II:5.4 above.

[175] Case C-312/93 *Peterbroek* [1995] ECR I-4599; Joined Cases C-430/93 and C-431/93 *Van Schijndel* [1995] ECR I-4705.

for breach of EU law are governed by the 'equal remedies' and 'effective remedies' rules created by the Court of Justice.[176]

One judgment of the Court of Justice has required recognition of the civil status documents of other Member States, where refusal to recognize the documents would prevent EU citizens from claiming social security rights they would be due under EU law.[177] A proposed Regulation would simplify the acceptance of public documents, to make free movement of persons easier in practice.[178] Similarly, in at least some cases, a refusal by a Member State to recognize children's names as registered in another Member State may breach EU free movement law.[179] More broadly, direct or indirect discrimination in civil procedural matters has been condemned several times by the Court of Justice.[180] These cases usually involve subjecting non-citizens or non-residents to different rules on security for costs or on seizure. Initially, the Court criticized discriminatory rules for breaching the Treaty rules on free movement of services.[181] Subsequently it based its judgments on the general rule concerning non-discrimination on grounds of nationality (now Article 18 TFEU),[182] first taken in conjunction with the Brussels Convention,[183] then taken in conjunction with any rule which relates to the exercise, directly or indirectly, of the fundamental freedoms guaranteed by the Treaty.[184]

This principle is extremely broad and its outer limits are still unknown. It means that Member States are likely prohibited from procedural discrimination in a wider field than that covered by Article 81 TFEU or measures adopted under it. For example, it is arguable that Article 18 TFEU requires Member States to treat nationals or residents of other Member States equally as regards priority in insolvency claims.[185]

Issues of inheritance, wills, and succession in cross-border cases are potentially closely linked with EU free movement law, as confirmed by the Court of Justice as regards inheritance tax.[186] It might be argued that other types of national rules (deriving for instance from property law) which restrict or complicate the movement of inheritances across borders breach the Treaty rules on free movement of capital, or alternatively Article 18 TFEU.

---

[176] See generally M Dougan, *National Remedies Before the Court of Justice: Issues of Harmonisation and Differentiation* (Hart, 2004).

[177] Case C-336/94 *Dafeki* [1997] ECR I-6761.

[178] COM (2013) 228, 24 April 2013. The Reg does not have a JHA legal base.

[179] See, for instance: Case C-148/02 *Garcia Avello* [2003] ECR I-11613; *Grunkin and Paul*, n 31 above; and Case C-208/09 *Sayn-Wittgenstein* [2010] ECR I-13693.

[180] On discrimination in criminal procedure, see II:3.4 above.

[181] Case C-20/92 *Hubbard v Hamburger* [1993] ECR I-3777.

[182] Previously Art 7 EEC until the TEU, then Art 6 EC until the Treaty of Amsterdam, then Art 12 EC until the Treaty of Lisbon.

[183] *Mund and Fester*, n 152 above.

[184] Cases: C-43/95 *Data Delecta* [1996] ECR I-4661; C-323/95 *Hayes* [1997] ECR I-1711; and C-122/96 *Saldanha* [1997] ECR I-5325.

[185] In its judgment in C-325/11 *Alder and Alder*, ECLI:EU:C:2012:824, the CJEU ruled that it was not necessary to answer questions about Art 18 TFEU, since the service of documents reg by itself (see II:8.5.2 below) was sufficient to settle the dispute.

[186] See, for instance, Cases: C-364/01 *Barbier* [2003] ECR I-15013: C-513/03 *Van Hilten-van der Heijden* [2006] ECR I-1957; C-464/05 *Geurts and Vogten* [2007] ECR I-9325; C-256/06 *Jager* [2008] ECR I-123; C-43/07 *Arens-Sikken* [2008] ECR I-6887; C-11/07 *Eckelkamp* [2008] ECR I-6845; and C-67/08 *Block* [2009] ECR I-883.

8.5 Overview of Legislation Adopted

This section provides an overview of the EU (previously EC) legislation adopted or proposed within the field of civil cooperation, with the exception of family law measures and the development of European contract law.[187] Following the structure of the Treaty, this section is subdivided by topic, largely in the order set out in Article 81(2) TFEU.

8.5.1 Mutual recognition, enforcement, and jurisdiction

The first topic set out in Article 81(2) TFEU is 'the mutual recognition and enforcement between Member States of judgments and of decisions in extrajudicial cases'.[188] This reflects the EU's focus on mutual recognition, originally a political principle established by the Tampere European Council in 1999, but later confirmed as a legal obligation by the Treaty of Lisbon.[189] Within the sphere of civil law (but not criminal law) the mutual recognition principle has always been directly linked to the third topic listed in Article 81(2) TFEU, namely the adoption of rules on jurisdiction.[190]

8.5.1.1 General rules

The most important measure in this field is the Brussels I Regulation. There have been two versions of the Regulation. First of all, Regulation 44/2001, which fully communautarized (with amendments) the long-standing Brussels Convention, applied for over a decade.[191] In 2009, the Commission released a report on the implementation of the Regulation and a Green Paper on possible amendments to it.[192] It followed up with a proposal to amend the Regulation, and Regulation 1215/2012 ('the 2012 Reg') was subsequently adopted, replacing Regulation 44/2001 as from 10 January 2015.[193] The 2012 Regulation has also been amended in turn, to add further provisions relating to the jurisdiction of courts common to multiple Member States (the Benelux Court and the planned Unified Patent Court).[194]

As noted above, the Brussels Convention was the subject of over a hundred judgments of the Court of Justice following references from national courts, and the Brussels Regulation has attracted dozens of references of its own. It should be noted that there is a principle of continuity of interpretation of the Convention and the Regulation, to the extent that they are identical.[195]

---

[187] See respectively II:8.6 and II:8.7 below.   [188] Art 81(2)(a) TFEU.

[189] Art 81(1) TFEU. On mutual recognition in criminal matters, see generally II:3.

[190] Art 81(2)(c) TFEU. On jurisdiction in criminal matters, see generally II:6.

[191] [2001] L 12/1. The 'comitology' procedures in this Reg were amended in 2008 by Reg 1103/2008, [2008] OJ L 304/80. On this issue, see further I:2.2.2.1.

[192] COM (2009) 174 and 175, 21 Apr 2009.

[193] [2012] L 351/1. All references in this sub-section are to Reg 44/2001, along with the corresponding provisions of the 2012 Reg, unless otherwise indicated.

[194] Reg 542/2014 ([2014] OJ L 163/1), also applicable from 10 Jan 2015.

[195] See recital 19 in the preamble, and in particular Case C-533/07 *Falco Privatstiftung* [2009] ECR I-3327.

The Brussels Regulation applies to civil and commercial cases, to the exclusion of revenue, customs, and administrative matters, and to state liability.[196] The Regulation also excludes from its scope: the status or legal capacity of natural persons, rights in property arising out of a matrimonial relationship, wills and succession;[197] bankruptcy and insolvency proceedings;[198] social security;[199] and arbitration.[200] A number of these issues have, however, been the subject of separate legislation, or plans or proposals for legislation.[201] In particular, the question of the relationship between the Brussels Regulation and the insolvency Regulation has arisen a number of times.[202] Moreover, jurisdiction over maintenance proceedings was initially subject to the Brussels Regulation,[203] but became subject to a separate Regulation on maintenance proceedings once the latter became applicable on 18 June 2011.[204]

The Regulation sets out a general rule that the court where the defendant is domiciled shall have jurisdiction.[205] But there are derogations from the general rule as regards: special jurisdiction rules (eg concerning contract[206] or tort disputes,[207] disputes based on criminal law,[208] or cases with multiple defendants[209]); insurance

---

[196] Art 1(1). On the definition of 'civil and commercial', see II:8.2.4 above. On the customs exclusion, see Case C-266/01 *Préservatrice Foncière Tiard* [2003] ECR I-4867.

[197] Art 1(2)(a) and (f), 2012 Reg. On the interpretation of the 'legal capacity' exception, see Case C-386/12 *Schneider*, ECLI:EU:C:2013:633. On the 'matrimonial relationship' exception, see Case C-4/14 *Bohez*, ECLI:EU:C:2015:563.

[198] Art 1(2)(b).

[199] Art 1(2)(c). On this exclusion, see most recently the judgment in Case C-271/00 *Baten* [2002] ECR I-10489.

[200] Art 1(2)(d). On this exclusion, see the judgments in Cases C-185/07 *Riunione Adriatica Di Sicurta v West Tankers* [2009] ECR I-663 and C-536/13 *Gazprom*, ECLI:EU:C:2015:316.

[201] On jurisdiction over divorce, parental responsibility, and matrimonial property, see II:8.6 below; on insolvency and wills and succession, see II:8.5.1.2 below.

[202] See initially Case 133/78 *Gourdain* [1979] ECR 733 and more recently the judgments in Cases: C-339/07 *Deko Marty Belgium* [2009] ECR I-767; C-111/08 *SCT Industri* [2009] ECR I-5655; C-292/08 *German Graphics Graphische Maschinen* [2009] ECR I-8421; C-213/10 *F-Tex*, ECLI:EU:C:2012:215; Case C-147/12 *OFAB*, ECLI:EU:C:2013:490; C-157/13 *Nickel & Goeldner Spedition*, ECLI:EU:C:2014:2145; and C-295/13 *H*, ECLI:EU:C:2014:2410.

[203] Art 5(2); see now Art 1(2)(e), 2012 Reg.   [204] See II:8.6 below.

[205] Art 2(1) (Art 4(1), 2012 Reg).

[206] Art 5(1) (Art 7(1), 2012 Reg); see the judgments in *Falco* (n 195 above) and Cases: C-386/05 *Color Drack* [2007] ECR I-3699; C-204/08 *Rehder* [2009] ECR I-6073; C-381/08 *Car Trim* [2010] ECR I-1255; C-19/09 *Wood Floor* [2010] ECR I-2121; C-87/10 *Electrosteel* [2011] ECR I-4987; C-419/11 *Ceská Sporitelňa*, ECLI:EU:C:2013:165; C-519/12 *OTP Bank*, ECLI:EU:C:2013:674; C-469/12 *Krejci Lager & Umschlagbetriebs*, ECLI:EU:C:2013:788; C-9/12 *Corman-Collins*, ECLI:EU:C:2013:860; C-548/12 *Brogsitter*, ECLI:EU:C:2014:148; and Case C-375/13 *Kolassa*, ECLI:EU:C:2015:37.

[207] Art 5(3) (Art 7(2), 2012 Reg); see the judgments in Cases: C-189/08 *Zuid-Chemie* [2009] ECR I-6917; C-509/09 *eDate Advertising* and C-161/10 *Martinez* [2011] ECR I-10269; C-523/10 *Wintersteiger*, ECLI:EU:C:2012:220; C-133/11 *Folien Fischer*, ECLI:EU:C:2012:664; C-228/11 *Melzer*, ECLI:EU:C:2013:305; *OFAB* (n 202 above); Case C-170/12 *Pinckney*, ECLI:EU:C:2012:635; C-45/13 *Kainz*, ECLI:EU:C:2014:7; Case C-387/12 *Hi Hotel HCF*, ECLI:EU:C:2014:215; Case C-360/12 *Coty Prestige Lancaster Group*, ECLI:EU:C:2014:485; Case C-441/13 *Hejduk*, ECLI:EU:C:2015:28; *Kolassa* (n 206 above); and Case C-352/13 *CDC Hydrogen Peroxide*, ECLI:EU:C:2015:335.

[208] Art 5(4) (Art 7(3), 2012 Reg); see Case C-7/08 *Krombach* [2000] ECR I-1935.

[209] Art 6(1) (Art 8(1), 2012 Reg); see the judgments in Cases C-103/05 *Reisch Montage* [2006] ECR I-6827; C-98/06 *Freeport* [2007] ECR I-8319; C-462/06 *Glaxo SmithKline* [2008] ECR I-3965; C-145/10 *Painer* [2011] ECR I-12533; C-606/12 *Solvay*, ECLI:EU:C:2012:445; Case C-645/11 *Sapir*, ECLI:EU:C:2012:228; and *CDC Hydrogen Peroxide* (n 207 above).

contracts;[210] consumer contracts;[211] employment contracts;[212] and cases of exclusive jurisdiction (eg relating to immovable properties,[213] companies,[214] or the validity or registration of intellectual property rights).[215] There are also related rules on issues such as *lis pendens* (related pending actions)[216] and provisional and protective measures.[217]

Next, the Regulation contains detailed rules on recognition and enforcement, in particular providing for exceptions for recognition of judgments on the grounds that they are manifestly contrary to public policy,[218] the defendant's procedural rights were breached,[219] the judgment is irreconcilable with a prior judgment, or the rules on exclusive jurisdiction or jurisdiction over consumer or insurance contracts were breached.[220]

8.5.1.2 Specific rules

The EU has addressed jurisdiction and recognition issues in relation to some matters excluded from the scope of the Brussels I Regulation. In the area of family law, it has regulated jurisdiction and recognition as regards judgments concerning divorce and parental responsibility, and the Commission has proposed Regulations concerning matrimonial property and the property of civil partnerships.[221]

In other areas, first of all, in 2000 the Council adopted a Regulation (the 'insolvency regulation') transposing the stalled Convention on insolvency proceedings into EU law.[222] The Regulation was then replaced in 2015, by a recast Regulation replacing it (see discussion below).[223]

---

[210] Arts 8–14 (Arts 10–16, 2012 Reg); see the judgments in Cases C-463/06 *FBTO Schadeverzekeringen* [2007] ECR I-11321 and C-347/08 *Vorarlberger* [2009] ECR I-8661.
[211] Arts 15–17 (Arts 17–19, 2012 Reg); see the judgments in Cases: C-180/06 *Ilsinger* [2009] ECR I-3961; C-585/08 *Pammer* and C-144/09 *Hotel Alpenhof* [2010] ECR I-12527; C-327/10 *Lindner* [2011] ECR I-11543; C-190/11 *Muhlleitner*, ECLI:EU:C:2012:542; C-218/12 *Emrek*, ECLI:EU:C:2013:666; C-478/12 *Maletic and Maletic*, ECLI:EU:C:2013:735; and *Kolassa* (n 206 above).
[212] Arts 18–21 (Arts 20–3, 2012 Reg); see the judgments in *Glaxo SmithKline* (n 209 above), C-154/11 *Mahamdia*, ECLI:EU:C:2012:491, and C-47/14 *Holterman*, ECLI:EU:C:2015:574.
[213] Art 22(1) (Art 24(1), 2012 Reg); see the judgments in Cases C-420/07 *Apostolides* [2009] ECR I-3571 and C-438/12 *Weber*, ECLI:EU:C:2014:212.
[214] Art 22(2) (Art 24(2), 2012 Reg); see the judgments in Cases: C-372/07 *Hassett* [2008] ECR I-7403; C-144/10 *Berliner Verkehrsbetriebe* [2011] ECR I-3961; and C-302/13 *flyLAL-Lithuanian Airlines*, ECLI:EU:C:2014:2319.
[215] Art 22(4) (Art 24(4), 2012 Reg); see Case C-4/03 *GAT* [2006] ECR I-6509 and *Solvay* (n 209 above).
[216] Arts 27–30 (Arts 29–34, 2012 Reg); see the judgments in Case C-1/13 *Cartier Parfums-Lunettes*, ECLI:EU:C:2014:109, *Weber* (n 213 above), and *flyLAL-Lithuanian Airlines* (n 214 above). On the same issue arising in criminal cases, see II:6.6 above.
[217] Art 31 (Art 35, 2012 Reg).
[218] Art 34(1) (Art 45(1)(a), 2012 Reg); see II:8.3.2 above. The CJEU has ruled that, due to the strong principle of mutual trust, even another Member State's judgment breaching EU law must usually be enforced under the Reg: Case C-681/13 *Diageo Brands*, ECLI:EU:C:2015:471.
[219] Art 34(2) (Art 45(1)(b), 2012 Reg); see ibid.
[220] Art 35(1) (Art 45(1)(c) to (e), 2012 Reg). See Case C-157/12 *Salzgitter Mannesmann Handel*, ECLI:EU:C:2013:597.
[221] See II:8.6 below.   [222] Council Reg 1346/2000 ([2000] OJ L 160/1), in force 31 May 2002.
[223] Council Reg 2015/848 ([2015] OJ L 141/19), applicable from 26 June 2017 (Art 92).

There have been a large number of references to the Court of Justice specifically on this Regulation,[224] and furthermore several cases have concerned the relationship between the Brussels Regulation and the insolvency Regulation.[225]

Financial services are excluded from the scope of the Regulation.[226] The basic rule is that jurisdiction to open insolvency proceedings rests with the courts of the Member State where the debtor's main interests are situated,[227] although it is possible to open secondary proceedings also in other Member States where the debtor was established; the secondary proceedings can only concern the assets of the debtor in the territory of that Member State.[228] The Regulation also contains rules on applicable law.[229] It provides in detail for the recognition of insolvency judgments,[230] permitting Member States not to recognize judgments which are manifestly contrary to public policy, 'in particular [a Member State's] fundamental principles or the constitutional rights and liberties of the individual', or not to recognize or enforce 'a judgment...which might result in a limitation of personal freedom or postal secrecy.'[231] Finally, the Regulation contains detailed rules on the opening of secondary proceedings, the position of creditors, and the relationship with other measures.[232]

A report from the Commission on the application of the Regulation in practice showed that in general it was working well, subject to some issues that needed to be clarified or amended.[233] As a consequence, the Commission proposed a number of amendments, and the EP and Council, as noted above, adopted a new version of the insolvency Regulation in 2015.[234] The new Regulation changed the rules as regards: extension of the Regulation to cover pre-insolvency and hybrid proceedings, as well as personal bankruptcies; last-minute moves of the debtor's centre of main interests just before proceedings get underway (such moves will not result in a change of jurisdiction); clarification of how to determine the centre of main interests, based on CJEU case law; detailed new rules on insolvency of groups of companies; clarification

---

[224] Decided cases: C-1/04 *Staubitz-Schreiber* [2006] ECR I-701; C-341/04 *Eurofoods* [2006] ECR I-3813; C-444/07 *MG Probud* [2010] ECR I-417; C-396/09 *Interedil* [2011] ECR I-9915; C-112/10 *Zaza Retail* [2011] ECR I-11525; C-191/10 *Rastelli Davide and C* [2011] ECR I-13209; C-527/10 *Erste Bank*, ECLI:EU:C:2012:417; C-116/11 *Handlowy*, ECLI:EU:C:2012:739; C-251/12 *Van Buggenhout*, ECLI:EU:C:2013:566; C-328/12 *Schmid*, ECLI:EU:C:2014:6; C-327/13 *Burgo Group*, ECLI:EU:C:2014:2158; C-557/13 *Lutz*, ECLI:EU:C:2015:227; C-649/13 *Nortel Networks*, ECLI:EU:C:2015:384; C-310/14 *Nike European Operations*, ECLI:EU:C:2015:690; and C-594/14 *Kornhaas*, ECLI:EU:C:2015:806. Pending cases: C-195/15 *Mullhaupt*; C-212/15, *ENEFI*; and C-353/15 *Leonmobili and Leone*.

[225] II:8.5.1.1 above. For other issues on the scope of the insolvency Regulation, see *Handlowy* (n 224 above) and C-461/11 *Radziejewski*, ECLI:EU:C:2012:215.

[226] Art 1(2), 2000 and 2015 Regs.

[227] Art 3(1). On the concept of the centre of the debtor's interest, and the application of the rules to parent companies and subsidiaries, see *Eurofoods*, *Interedil*, and *Rastelli*. If the debtor moves his or her main interests after requesting the opening of insolvency proceedings, jurisdiction does not transfer accordingly (*Staubitz-Schreiber*). On the question of links with third States, see *Schmid*.

[228] Art 3(2) to (5). For the definition of 'establishment', see Art 2(h) and the *Interedil* judgment. On secondary proceedings, see *Handlowy*, *Burgo Group*, and *Nortel Networks*. There is a more limited possibility to open secondary proceedings before the main proceedings open: see *Zaza Retail*.

[229] See II:8.5.3 below.   [230] Arts 16–26.

[231] Arts 26 and 25(2). On the public policy exception, see the *Eurofoods* and *MG Probud* judgments (n 224 above), as well as II:8.3.2 above.

[232] Respectively Arts 27–38, 39–42, and 44.   [233] COM (2012) 743, 12 Dec 2012.

[234] Council Reg 2015/848, n 223 above.

of the boundary between the Brussels Regulation and the insolvency Regulation, with a greater possibility to link parallel proceedings under both Regulations; the inclusion of procedural rights related to insolvency proceedings, along with improved rules on lodging claims; and greater transparency of the insolvency process.

Secondly, in 2012 the EU adopted a Regulation concerning the jurisdiction and enforcement of decisions relating to wills and succession.[235] This Regulation allocates jurisdiction, as a general rule, to the court of the Member State on whose territory the deceased was habitually resident at the time of death.[236] There are also subsidiary rules on recognition and enforcement of judgments,[237] as well as provisions on the conflicts of law.[238]

Finally, there is an EU Regulation on the mutual recognition of civil law protection orders,[239] which was also adopted using the legal bases relating to access to justice and civil procedure (Article 81(2)(e) and (f) TFEU). The Regulation relates closely to a Directive on the mutual recognition of *criminal* law protection orders.[240] It requires mutual recognition of a 'protection measure', which is essentially an order requiring one person to stay away from another person;[241] and so it is obviously mostly relevant in domestic violence cases. There is a straightforward definition of 'cross-border' cases,[242] and a simplified procedure for cross-border enforcement.[243] The person considered dangerous must be notified of the certificate which constitutes the protection order, but cannot be informed of the whereabouts of the protected person.[244] Recognition of a protection order can be refused on limited grounds, if it is manifestly contrary to public policy or there is an irreconcilable judgment issued in the Member State asked to recognize it.[245] But recognition cannot be refused simply because the latter Member State would not have issued a protection order on the same facts.[246]

8.5.1.3 Enforcement of judgments

Several EU measures concerning civil procedure aim to contribute to the enforcement of judgments in practice.[247] However, the main measure in this area is the Regulation on Account Preservation Orders, adopted in 2014,[248] which was also adopted on the legal bases relating to access to justice and civil procedure (Article 81(2)(e) and (f)).

---

[235] Reg 650/2012 ([2012] OJ L 201/107). Member States had to apply this Reg by 17 Aug 2015 (Art 84). See earlier the Green Paper on this issue (COM (2005) 65, 1 Mar 2005). On the related competence issues, see II:8.2.4 above. On the scope of succession issues as distinct from divorce issues, see C-404/14 *Matouskova*, ECLI:EU:C:2015:653.

[236] Art 4; see generally Arts 3–19 on jurisdiction rules.   [237] Arts 39–58.

[238] II:8.5.3 below.

[239] Reg 606/2013 ([2013] OJ L 181/4). Member States had to apply this Reg by 11 Jan 2015 (Art 22). The Reg does not contain rules on jurisdiction.

[240] Dir 2011/99 ([2011] L 338/2). Member States also had to apply this Directive by 11 Jan 2015. On the related competence issues, see II:8.2.4 above; on the substance of the Directive, see II:3.7.6 above.

[241] Art 3(1).   [242] Art 2(2).   [243] Art 4.   [244] Art 8.   [245] Art 13(1).

[246] Art 13(3).   [247] II:8.5.6 below.

[248] Reg 655/2014, [2014] OJ L 189/59. Member States have to apply this Reg by 18 Jan 2017 (Art 54). See also the previous Green Papers on attachment of bank accounts and the transparency of debtors' assets (respectively COM (2006) 618, 24 Oct 2006 and COM (2008) 128, 6 Mar 2008). For the comparable criminal law measures concerning freezing orders, see II:3.6.2 above.

The Regulation has a similar scope to the Brussels Regulation.[249] It defines a cross-border proceeding as a case where a bank account is in a different Member State than the Member State of the creditor or the court seized with the dispute.[250] The usual jurisdiction rules apply, except that jurisdiction as regards a debtor who is a consumer is allocated to that consumer's Member State, and jurisdiction is also allocated to a Member State where a court judgment or settlement or authentic instrument was already reached.[251] To obtain an Account Preservation Order, a creditor must show that the Order is necessary to preserve assets; if there has been no judgment, settlement, or authentic instrument yet, the creditor must also show that his or her claim is 'likely to succeed on the substance'.[252] There is a special rule on the law applicable to liability of the creditor,[253] and many special rules on service of documents.[254] An Account Preservation Order must be recognized without any exequatur procedure,[255] and there are a number of remedies available to debtors, creditors, and third parties.[256]

8.5.2 Service of documents

The subject-matter of the second EU civil law power, set out in Article 81(2)(b) TFEU, is the service of documents. First of all, the Council adopted a Regulation on the service of documents in 2000,[257] replacing a 1997 third pillar Convention that had not been ratified.[258] It should be noted that there is also a Hague Convention on the issue of service of documents, to which a large majority of Member States are parties.[259] A review of the practical operation of this Regulation in 2004 concluded that it resulted in speedier proceedings, although its operation was still limited in some respects due to ambiguities in its text and certain national divergences which it provides for.[260] The Regulation was therefore replaced by a revised text in 2007.[261] The original version of the Regulation was the subject of four references to the Court of Justice from national courts,[262] and the 2007 Regulation has been the subject of several references to the Court.[263] It should be noted that the Regulation on Account Preservation Orders has a number of specific rules on service of documents.[264]

---

[249] Art 2.   [250] Art 3.   [251] Art 6.   [252] Art 7.

[253] Art 13(4); this derogates from the Rome II Regulation (Art 48(f)).

[254] Art 48(a); compare to the general rules discussed in II:8.5.2 below.   [255] Art 22.

[256] Arts 33–9.   [257] Reg 1348/2000 ([2000] OJ L 160/37), in force 31 May 2001.

[258] [1997] OJ C 261/1.

[259] For the ratification status, see Appendix I. Both Regs prevail over this treaty, or other international treaties, between the Member States: see Art 20(1) of both Reg 1348/2000 and Reg 1393/2007; but see also Art 21 of both Regs, as regards legal aid provisions of prior treaties. The CJEU interpreted this Convention in Case C-292/10 G, ECLI:EU:C:2012:142.

[260] COM (2004) 603, 1 Oct 2004.

[261] Reg 1393/2007 ([2007] OJ L 324/79), applicable from 13 Nov 2008 (Art 26).

[262] Cases: C-443/03 *Leffler* [2005] ECR I-9611; C-473/04 *Plumex* [2006] ECR I-1417; C-14/07 *Weiss* [2008] ECR I-3367; C-14/08 *Roda Golf* [2009] ECR I-5439.

[263] Decided cases: C-325/11 *Alder and Alder*, ECLI:EU:C:2012:824; C-226/13, C-245/13, C-247/13, and C-578/13 *Fahnenbrock and others*, ECLI:EU:C:2015:383; C-519/13 *Alpha Bank Cyprus*, ECLI:EU:C:2015:603; and C-223/14 *Tecom Mican*, ECLI:EU:C:2015:744. Pending cases: C-384/14 *Alta Realitat*; C-70/15 *Lebek*; and C-354/15 *Henderson*.

[264] Reg 655/2014, [2014] OJ L 189/59, Art 48(a). In the absence of those specific rules, however, the service of documents Regulation applies to account preservation orders.

Both the 2000 and the 2007 Regulation apply to civil and commercial cases; the 2007 Regulation clarified that revenue, customs, and administrative matters, as well as the liability of the state for state actions, were excluded. But there are no other exclusions from its scope.[265] According to the CJEU, even if there is a case that documents relate to a case concerning state liability (or presumably one of the other exceptions), they must be served, unless the issue is manifestly outside the scope of the Regulation, having regard to its application at an early stage of the proceedings.[266] The Regulations only apply if the documents have to be served from one Member State to another; the CJEU has clarified that the only exclusions from this rule are where the address of the person concerned is not known, or where one party has appointed a representative in the territory of the Member State where the proceedings are taking place.[267]

Documents must usually be served through designated government agencies.[268] The requested agency must try to serve the document within one month of the request, and keep trying after that period if there is still a reasonable prospect of serving the document.[269]

The addressee may refuse to accept the document if the document was not drawn up either in a language which the addressee understands[270] or in the official language of the Member State addressed (or at least (one of) the official language(s) of the place of service in that Member State).[271] An applicant can subsequently transmit a translated copy of the document.[272] The date of service of the document is usually determined by the law of Member State of service, but in some cases can be determined by the Member State of transmission.[273] There are rules on certificates to be drawn up when service is effected, and on the costs of service.[274]

---

[265] Art 1(1) of both Regs. In C-233/08 *Kyrian* ([2010] ECR I-177) it was assumed that the Reg did not apply to cooperation between Member States' tax authorities (see further II:8.2.4 above).

[266] *Fahnenbrock and others*, n 263 above.

[267] See *Alder and Alder*, n 263 above. On the non-application of the Reg where a defendant's address is not known, see also G, n 259 above.

[268] Arts 4–6 of both Regs.

[269] Art 7 of both Regs; the requirement to keep trying to serve the document after the one-month period was added in the 2007 Reg (Art 7(2)(b)).

[270] Art 8(1)(b), 2007 Reg; the 2000 Reg (Art 8(1)(a)) had referred instead to a language *of the Member State of transmission* that the defendant understood. On the question of whether the defendant can be deemed to understand a language, see the *Weiss* judgment, n 262 above. On the method of determining whether the defendant understands a language, and the consequences if he or she understands but refuses service, see Case C-384/14 *Alta Realitat*, pending. The receiving agency must comply with the procedural requirements in the Reg, but if it does not, the document can still be served again at a later date, this time complying with those requirements (*Alpha Bank Cyprus*, n 263 above).

[271] Art 8(1) of both Regs. The 2007 Reg clarified the time period and mechanism for refusal. On the definition of a 'document' to be translated, in the case of instituting proceedings, see again the *Weiss* judgment (n 262 above), and the discussion in II:8.3.2 above.

[272] Art 8(3), added by the 2007 Reg but effectively transposing the Court of Justice ruling regarding the 2000 Reg in *Leffler* (n 262 above), also as regards the consequences for the date of service in this case.

[273] Art 9(1) and (2) of both Regs. Art 9(3) of the 2000 Reg, which permitted a derogation from these rules, was replaced by the 2007 Reg.

[274] Arts 10 and 11 of both Regs. The 2007 Reg clarifies the level of fees to be charged (Art 11(2), second sub-paragraph).

Alternative methods of service are possible: consular or diplomatic channels, 'in exceptional circumstances';[275] consular or diplomatic agents;[276] by post;[277] or directly through the competent officers of the Member State addressed.[278] There is no hierarchy between the different methods of service: one or another or both (or presumably more than two) can validly be used. In case of multiple forms of service which are validly effected, dates start to run from the time of the first service.[279] The rules on refusal to accept service and date of service apply equally to these alternate forms of service.[280] Finally, the Regulation also applies to the transmission of extrajudicial documents.[281]

The Commission issued a second report on the application of the service of documents rules in 2013.[282] According to the Commission, the wide variety of national rules on civil procedure might make it difficult in some cases for defendants to exercise the rights provided for in the Regulation, especially where the exequatur procedure has been abolished. In particular, the Commission asked whether it would be appropriate to apply the Regulation to cases where the person's address was unknown. The Commission also pointed to problems with the use of standard forms in the context of the right of refusal, the date and cost of service, and the interpretation of the rules on postal service and direct service. But on the whole, the speed of service had increased again as compared to the prior Regulation. The Commission did not commit itself to propose an amendment of the Regulation, but raised some broader questions about the possible adoption of minimum standards as regards national law on civil procedure.[283]

8.5.3　Conflict of laws

The conflict of laws is the subject-matter in part of Article 81(2)(c) TFEU.[284] The main EU rules in this area concern contract law and non-contractual obligations, although there are also some specialized rules. Each will be considered in turn; the EU choice of law rules in family matters are discussed below.[285]

---

[275]　Art 12 of both Regs.

[276]　Art 13 of both Regs. A Member State may refuse to permit this type of service (Art 13(2) of both Regs).

[277]　Art 14 of both Regs. The 2007 Reg removed the possibility for Member States to insist on conditions applicable to postal service (see Art 14(2), 2000 Reg), and instead provides for standard conditions for postal service.

[278]　Art 15 of both Regs; the law of the Member State addressed may refuse to permit this method of service.

[279]　See *Plumex*, n 262 above. A Member State may not provide for other methods of service, such as a notional service within the territory of the Member State of proceedings (see *Alder and Alder*, n 263 above). See also the judgment in *Tecom Mican* (n 263 above), paras 47–61.

[280]　Arts 8(4), 8(5), and 9(3), all added by the 2007 Reg. The Reg overturned a judgment of the Court of Justice (*Weiss*, n 262 above), which ruled that the rules on refusal to accept service did not apply to postal service.

[281]　For interpretation of this concept, see *Roda Golf* (n 262 above), which confirmed that the concept was an autonomous one, which also applied to notarial documents in the absence of judicial proceedings. In its judgment in *Tecom Mican* (n 263 above), the CJEU ruled (at para 46) that extrajudicial documents are 'not only documents drawn up or certified by a public authority or official but also private documents of which the formal transmission to an addressee residing abroad is necessary for the purposes of exercising, proving or safeguarding a right or a claim in civil or commercial law'.

[282]　COM (2013) 858, 4 Dec 2013.

[283]　See similarly the Commission's assessment of the Brussels II Regulation (II:8.6 below).

[284]　Art 81(2)(c) TFEU also concerns conflict of jurisdiction; this issue was examined in II:8.5.1 above.

[285]　II:8.6.

8.5.3.1 Contract law

As noted above,[286] the conflict of contract laws was initially addressed by the 1980 Rome Convention on this subject,[287] which was replaced in 2008 by an EC Regulation.[288] The Regulation applies to all contracts which were or will be concluded after 17 December 2009,[289] so the Convention therefore continues to be relevant to contracts concluded before that date. There have been several references to the Court of Justice on the Convention and the Regulation.[290]

The Regulation applies to civil and commercial matters, excluding revenue, customs, and administrative matters,[291] and also excluding other matters outside the scope of the Brussels I Regulation (the status and legal capacity of natural persons; matrimonial property; wills and succession; arbitration).[292] It also does not apply to obligations arising from family or comparable relationships, including maintenance obligations, or to certain commercial law issues: negotiable instruments; agreements on choice of court; company law disputes (including the winding up of companies); the law of agency; the law of trusts; pre-contractual relationships; and certain insurance disputes.[293] It applies also to the designation of the law of non-Member States.[294]

The starting point of the Regulation is freedom of contract, leaving the parties free in principle to designate the law applicable to their contract.[295] In the absence of choice, the Regulation sets out general rules to choose the applicable law,[296] subject to special rules for particular types of contract (contracts of carriage, consumer contracts, insurance contracts, and employment contracts).[297] The Regulation permits the application of the 'overriding mandatory provisions' of the law of the forum or of the place where the contractual obligations would be performed;[298] the applicable law under the

---

[286] II:8.2.2.2.   [287] [1998] OJ C 27/34

[288] Reg 593/2008 ([2008] OJ L 177/6). See the earlier Green Paper on replacing and modernizing the Convention (COM (2002) 654, 14 Jan 2003).

[289] Art 28 of the Reg (ibid). The pending Case C-135/15 *Nikiforidis* asks the CJEU to clarify what happens if a contract was initially concluded before this date but renewed after it.

[290] On the Convention, see Cases: C-133/08 *ICF* [2009] ECR I-9687; C-29/10 *Koelzsch* [2011] ECR I-1595; C-384/10 *Voogsgeerd* [2011] ECR I-3275; C-64/12 *Schlecker*, ECLI:EU:C:2013:551; C-184/12 *UNAMAR*, ECLI:EU:C:2013:663; C-305/13 *Haeger and Schmidt*, ECLI:EU:C:2014:2320; and Case C-397/15 *Raiffeisen Privatbank Liechtenstein*, pending. On the Regulation, see Cases: C-359/14 and C-475/14 *ERGO Insurance* and *Gjensidige Baltic*; *Nikiforidis* (n 289 above); and C-222/15 *Hoszig*, all pending. On both the Convention and the Regulation, see Case C-483/14, *KA Finanz*, also pending.

[291] Art 1(1) of the Reg.

[292] Art 1(2)(a) to (c) and (e). On consistency with the Brussels I Reg, see recital 7 in the preamble and *Koelzsch*, para 33. Note that the Rome I Reg does not apply to arbitration *agreements*, whereas the Brussels I Reg does not apply to arbitration; and the Rome I Reg also does not apply to property issues deriving from relationships *comparable* to marriage. The CJEU interpreted the Brussels and Rome Regs consistently in Joined Cases C-585/08 *Pammer* and C-144/09 *Hotel Alpenhof* [2010] ECR I-12527.

[293] Art 1(2)(d) and (f) to (j). Pre-contractual relations are covered by the Rome II Reg: see recital 10 in the preamble. On the company law exception, see *KA Finanz*, pending.

[294] Art 2.   [295] Art 3. On issues of consent, validity, and incapacity, see Arts 10, 11, and 13.

[296] Art 4. See Joined Cases: C-359/14 and C-475/14 *ERGO Insurance* and *Gjensidige Baltic*, pending.

[297] Arts 5–8. The *ICF* and *Haeger and Schmidt* cases concerned the contracts of carriage rules in the Rome Convention, while the *Koelzsch*, *Voogsgeerd*, and *Schlecker* cases concern employment contracts under the Convention.

[298] Art 9. The *UNAMAR* judgment concerns the equivalent provisions of the Convention.

rules may also be rejected if it is 'manifestly incompatible' with the public policy of the forum.[299] Also, the Regulation contains rules on the scope of applicable law, assignment and subrogation, multiple liability, set-off, the burden of proof, the definition of 'habitual residence', the exclusion of *renvoi* (ie a reference to another state's conflict rules), the position of states with multiple legal systems, and the relationship with other legal rules.[300]

8.5.3.2 Non-contractual obligations

Prior to the adoption of the Rome I Regulation, the Council and EP negotiated the Rome II Regulation, which governs the conflict of law in non-contractual matters.[301] There have been several references to the Court of Justice on the Regulation.[302]

Like the Rome I Regulation, the Rome II Regulation applies to civil and commercial matters, excluding revenue, customs, and administrative matters; the liability of the state for the exercise of public powers is also excluded.[303] The issues of matrimonial (or comparable) property and wills and succession are also excluded, as are family law matters, including maintenance.[304] Certain commercial law issues are excluded: negotiable instruments; company law disputes (including the winding up of companies); the law of trusts; nuclear damage; and violations of privacy and rights relating to personality, including defamation.[305] Like the Rome I Regulation, the Rome II Regulation applies also to the designation of the law of non-Member States.[306]

The main rule in the Regulation as regards liability for torts or delicts is that the law of the country where the damage occurred is applicable, but this rule can be set aside if the plaintiff and defendant are habitually resident in the same country, or it if appears 'that the tort/delict is manifestly more closely connected with' another country.[307] There are special rules for tort/delict as regards product liability, competition, environmental damage, intellectual property, and industrial action,[308] as well as particular rules for

---

[299] Art 21. On the human rights aspects of this rule, see II:8.3.2 above. See *Nikiforidis*, pending.

[300] Arts 12, 14–20, and 22–5. On the relationship with non-JHA EU law, see the pending *Gjensidige Baltic* and *KA Finanz* cases, and generally II:8.4 above.

[301] Reg 864/2007 ([2007] OJ L 199/40), applicable to damages which occurred after 11 Jan 2009 (Arts 31 and 32). On the temporal scope of the Reg, see Case C-412/10 *Homawoo* [2011] ECR I-11603. For the definition of non-contractual obligations, see Art 2 of the Reg. On the distinction with the Brussels Reg, see C-45/13 *Kainz*, ECLI:EU:C:2014:7.

[302] *Homawoo* (n 301 above); Case C-240/14 *Pruller-Frey*, ECLI:EU:C:2015:567; Case C-350/14 *Lazar*, ECLI:EU:C:2015:802, and pending cases: C-359/14 and C-475/14 *ERGO Insurance*; and *Gjensidige Baltic*; and C-191/15, *Verein für Konsumenteninformation*.

[303] Art 1(1) of the Reg.

[304] Art 1(2)(a) and (b). On consistency with the Brussels I and Rome I rules, see recital 7 in the preamble. Note that issues concerning arbitration or the status and legal capacity of natural persons are not excluded from the scope of the Rome II Reg.

[305] Art 1(2)(c) to (g). The latter two issues are not excluded from the scope of the Rome I Reg. Conversely, several issues excluded from the scope of the Rome I Reg are *not* excluded from the scope of the Rome II Reg: agreements on choice of court; the law of agency; pre-contractual relationships; and certain insurance disputes. The exclusions for the law of trusts are also worded differently (compare Art 1(2)(h) of the Rome I Reg to Art 1(2)(e) of the Rome II Reg).

[306] Art 3.

[307] Art 4. On the interpretation of this rule, see *Lazar* (n 302): 'damage' occurs in the country where a car accident occurs, not where bereaved relatives reside. For the definition of 'habitual residence', see Art 23.

[308] Arts 5–9.

other forms of non-contractual liability (unjust enrichment, *negotiorum gestio* (an act performed without authority in connection with another person's affairs), and *culpa in contrahendo* (pre-contractual relations).[309] It is possible for the parties to choose the law applicable.[310] The Regulation permits the application of the 'overriding mandatory provisions' of the law of the forum;[311] the applicable law under the rules may also be rejected if it is 'manifestly incompatible' with the public policy of the forum.[312] Also, the Regulation contains rules on the scope of applicable law, rules of safety and conduct, direct actions against insurers, subrogation, multiple liability, validity, the burden of proof, the exclusion of *renvoi*, the position of states with multiple legal systems, and the relationship with other legal rules.[313]

8.5.3.3 *Other EU rules on conflict of laws*

To some extent, the exclusions from the scope of the Rome I and II Regulations are covered by other EU measures. As regards family law, the EU rules on maintenance obligations include rules on conflict of laws, the Rome III Regulation sets out EU rules on choice of law as regards divorce, and the Commission has proposed rules regarding conflict of laws as regards matrimonial property and the property of civil partnerships.[314] In other areas, there are EU rules for the choice of law regarding wills and successions,[315] which provide that the basic rule (subject to exceptions) is to apply the law of the State of habitual residence of the deceased at time of death. There are also choice of law rules in the insolvency Regulation.[316]

8.5.4 Transmission of evidence

Article 81(2)(d) TFEU confers power on the EU as regards cooperation in the taking of evidence. This issue has been addressed by a Regulation adopted in 2001.[317] The Regulation has attracted four references from national courts to the Court of Justice.[318] Again there is also a Hague Convention on this issue, to which a large majority of Member States are parties.[319]

---

[309] Arts 10–12. However, the rules in Art 8 cover all forms of non-contractual liability relating to intellectual property infringements (Art 13).

[310] Art 14.   [311] Art 16.

[312] Art 26. Again, for the human rights implications, see II:8.3.2 above.

[313] Arts 15, 17–22, 24–5, and 27–8. On the relationship with other EU law, see further II:8.4 above. The CJEU has clarified the special provision on action against insurers (Art 18): *Pruller-Frey* (n 302).

[314] See II:8.6 below.

[315] Arts 20–38, Reg 650/2012 (OJ 2012 L 201/107). Member States had to apply this Reg by 17 Aug 2015 (Art 84).

[316] Arts 4 and 28, Reg 1346/2000 ([2000] OJ L 160/1); see also Arts 5–15 of that Reg. These rules were not amended by the revised insolvency Regulation (Reg 2015/848), discussed in II:8.5.1.2 above. Presumably the exclusion of winding up of companies from the Rome I and II Regs precludes any overlap between those Regs and the insolvency Regulation.

[317] Reg 1206/2001 ([2001] OJ L 174/1), applicable from 1 Jan 2004 (Art 24(2)). All references in this subsection are to this Reg unless otherwise indicated. The 'comitology' procedures in this Reg were amended in 2008 (Reg 1103/2008, [2008] OJ L 304/80).

[318] Cases: C-175/06 *Tedesco* [2007] ECR I-7929; C-283/09 *Werynski* [2011] ECR I-601; C-170/11 *Lippens*, ECLI:EU:C:2012:540; and C-332/11 *ProRail*, ECLI:EU:C:2013:87. The *Tedesco* case was withdrawn before judgment (but after a detailed Opinion of an Advocate-General was issued).

[319] For the ratification status, see Appendix I. The Reg prevails over the Convention, or other pre-existing treaties, in relations between the Member States: Art 21(1). The CJEU has interpreted the Reg in light of the Convention (*Werynski*).

The Regulation applies to all civil and commercial matters, without any clarification of this concept,[320] wherever one Member State's court requests another Member
State's court to obtain evidence,[321] or asks that the latter court permit the former court's
officials to enter the latter Member State and collect evidence there.[322] It effectively
establishes a mutual recognition regime, because the execution of requests can only
be refused on limited grounds (such as incompatibility with the requested State's law,
major practical difficulties, or the right of a person whose hearing is requested to refuse
to testify).[323]

In 2007 the Commission issued a report on the application of the Regulation in practice,[324] which concluded that: the time to process requests for evidence had speeded
up, but still often exceeded the deadlines in the Regulation; central bodies were used
too often to forward requests, instead of contact directly between courts; standard
forms are sometimes not filled in completely; communications technology was not
widely used to take evidence yet, and nor was the direct taking of evidence by a court
in another Member State; and there was confusion over the definition of 'evidence'. The
Commission concluded that there was no need to amend the Regulation, but rather
that its application should be promoted by means, inter alia, of the European Judicial
Network.

8.5.5 Access to justice

Article 81(2)(e) TFEU confers power on the EU as regards 'effective access to justice';
this power was expressly conferred for the first time by the Treaty of Lisbon. On this
topic, in 2003 the Council adopted a Directive governing legal aid in cross-border
cases.[325] Because this Directive was adopted before the entry into force of the Treaty of
Lisbon, the Community's competence to adopt it derived from its power to adopt legislation concerning compatibility of civil procedure rules to eliminate obstacles to the
good functioning of civil proceedings.[326] Any amendments to this Directive, or other
measures on the issue of access to justice, would now be adopted on the basis of Article
81(2)(e) TFEU. It should also be noted that the Regulation on Account Preservation
Orders, discussed above,[327] also has a legal base of Article 81(2)(e).[328]

The Commission has adopted measures to implement this Directive, which establish standard forms regarding legal aid applications and their transmission.[329] There

---

[320] Art 1(1). On the definition of 'civil and commercial', see II:8.2.4 above.

[321] On the definition of 'taking evidence', see the *Tedesco* Opinion.

[322] If the national court does not choose to use one of these two methods of obtaining evidence in
another Member State, it is free to use other means to attempt to summon a witness in another Member
State (*Lippens*). More generally, national courts are not obliged to use the Regulation at all (*ProRail*). The
requested court cannot ask the requesting court to refund a witness' travel costs (*Werynski*).

[323] Arts 10(2) and (3), 14, and 17. The list of grounds for refusal is exhaustive (*Werynski*); see also the
Tedesco Opinion. Compare with the Directive establishing a European Investigation Order (II:3.6 above).

[324] COM (2007) 769, 5 Dec 2007.

[325] Dir 2003/8 ([2003] OJ L 26/41); all references in this sub-section are to this Dir unless otherwise indicated. Member States had to transpose this Directive by 30 Nov 2004, except for Art 3(2)(a) on pre-judicial
assistance, which they had to transpose by 30 May 2006 (Art 21). See earlier the Green Paper on the issue
(COM (2000) 51, 9 Feb 2000). Compare with the proposed criminal law Directive on this issue (II:4:6.6 above).

[326] See recital 2 in the preamble.   [327] II:8.5.1.   [328] Reg 655/2014, [2014] OJ L 189/59.

[329] [2004] OJ L 365/27 and [2005] OJ L 225/23.

have been no references to the Court of Justice concerning the Directive. There is again a Hague Convention dealing with aspects of this issue, although barely half of the Member States have ratified it.[330] However, a large majority of Member States have ratified a Council of Europe Agreement on transmission of requests for legal aid.[331]

The Directive applies to all civil and commercial matters,[332] excluding only customs, revenue, and administrative matters.[333] It applies only to cross-border matters, with the standard definition of this concept.[334] The Directive confers a right to legal aid for pre-judicial assistance with a view to a settlement and legal assistance and representation in court, including the costs of proceedings, although Member States need not ensure legal aid for specialist tribunals where the parties can make their case effectively in person, or for persons who have sufficient financial resources to pay the relevant costs.[335] Member States must grant aid without discrimination to EU citizens and legally resident third-country nationals[336]—although the obligation as regards EU citizens derives in any event from the equal treatment rule of the EC Treaty, now the TFEU.[337] Member States can reject claims which appear to be manifestly unfounded and apparently also in certain other circumstances.[338] There are also provisions concerning: cross-border costs; allocation of costs between Member States; legal aid in relation to enforcement, appeals, extrajudicial procedures, or authentic instruments;[339] and the procedure for transmitting and processing legal aid applications.[340]

The Commission has reported on the application of this Directive in practice.[341] In its view, the Directive has been satisfactorily applied by Member States, although there is limited awareness of it or use of it in practice, and there are divergences between Member States on interpretation of some provisions, and a limited notion of 'cross-border' cases.

8.5.6 Civil procedure

Article 81(2)(f) TFEU, replacing the previous Article 65(c) EC, confers powers on the EU as regards 'the elimination of obstacles to the proper functioning of civil proceedings, if necessary by promoting the compatibility of the rules on civil procedure applicable in the Member States'. Before the entry into force of the Treaty of Lisbon, Article 65(c) EC was used expressly to adopt a Directive on legal aid and implicitly to adopt a Directive on mediation;[342] these two measures are considered separately, since the Treaty of Lisbon has now introduced separate legal bases on those two issues.[343]

Three other measures concerning civil procedure have been adopted, each of which aims to expedite further the recognition of judgments within the scope of the Brussels I Regulation, without amending that Regulation's rules on jurisdiction. Furthermore,

---

[330] For the ratification status, see Appendix I. Note that this Convention also addresses other issues relating to access to justice, such as security for costs.

[331] CETS 92 (1977); a Protocol to the Agreement, which has attracted far fewer ratifications, was agreed in 2001 (CETS 179). For ratification details, see Appendix I. The Directive takes precedence, as between Member States, over both of these measures, the Hague Convention, and any other international treaties: see Art 20.

[332] On the definition of this concept, see II:8.2.4 above.   [333] Art 1(2), Dir 2003/8.

[334] Art 2.   [335] Arts 3 and 5.   [336] Art 4.   [337] See II:8.4 above.   [338] Art 6.

[339] Arts 7–11.   [340] Arts 12–16.   [341] COM (2012) 71, 23 Feb 2012.

[342] Dirs 2003/8 ([2003] OJ L 26/41) and 2008/52 ([2008] OJ L 136/3).

[343] II:8.5.5 above and II:8.5.7 below.

the Regulation on Account Preservation Orders, discussed above,[344] also has a legal base of Article 81(2)(f).[345]

First of all, in 2004, the Council and EP adopted a Regulation establishing a European Enforcement Order for uncontested claims.[346] This Regulation does not make clear whether its legal basis is the recognition of judgments or the harmonization of civil procedure law. It has the same scope as the Brussels I Regulation,[347] and like that Regulation it has not been applicable to maintenance claims since the EU's maintenance Regulation became applicable.[348] There have been several references to the Court of Justice concerning this Regulation.[349]

The European Enforcement Order Regulation abolishes much of the procedural requirements to enforce a judgment in another Member State (in particular the requirement of an exequatur),[350] along with the grounds for refusal of recognition of a judgment except for the existence of a previous irreconcilable judgment,[351] provided that the claim is 'uncontested' as defined in the Regulation,[352] and that specific minimum procedural standards were complied with, in particular as regards the service of the documents concerned and the possibility of review of the judgment.[353]

Secondly, the Council and the EP adopted a Regulation establishing a European Payment Order in 2006.[354] It is based explicitly on Article 65(c) EC (now Article 81(2)(f) TFEU).[355] So far there have been several references to the Court of Justice concerning this Regulation.[356] The amendments to the small claims Regulation adopted in 2015 also made a number of changes to this Regulation.[357]

The scope of the payment orders Regulation is the same as the enforcement order Regulation, except that the payment orders Regulation does not apply to claims concerning non-contractual liability, and there is no exclusion of arbitration or maintenance

---

[344] II:8.5.1.3.   [345] Reg 655/2014 ([2014] OJ L 189/59).

[346] Reg 805/2004 ([2004] OJ L 143/15). The Reg applied from 21 Oct 2005 (Art 33). The following six footnotes refer to this Reg, unless otherwise indicated. The 'comitology' procedures in this Reg were amended in 2008 (Reg 1103/2008, [2008] OJ L 304/80).

[347] Compare Art 2, Reg 805/2004 to Art 1, Reg 1215/2012 ([2012] OJ L 351/1).

[348] See further II:8.6 below.

[349] Cases: C-292/10 *G*, ECLI:EU:C:2012:142; C-508/12 *Vapenik*, ECLI:EU:C:2013:290; and Cases C-300/14 *Imtech*, C-511/14 *Pebros Servizi*, and Case C-484/15 *Zulfikarpašić*, all pending.

[350] Art 5.

[351] See Art 21; it is not specified if the grounds for refusal listed here are exhaustive.

[352] For this definition, see Art 3. On the meaning of the term, see C-511/14 *Pebros Servizi*, pending. Also, the Reg only applies where the debtor is a consumer, and the creditor seeks to enforce a consumer claim against him or her (Art 6(1); see *Vapenik*).

[353] Chapter III (Arts 12–19). The service rules apply in conjunction with the general EU legislation on service of documents (recitals 21 and 28 of the preamble). On the review of the judgment, see Case C-300/14 *Imtech*, pending. The Reg cannot be applied where the address of the other party is unknown (*G*).

[354] Reg 1896/2006 ([2006] OJ L 399/1). The Reg was applicable from 12 Dec 2008 (Art 33). The following ten footnotes refer to this Reg, unless otherwise indicated. See earlier the Green Paper on payments orders and small claims (COM (2002) 742, 20 Dec 2002).

[355] See recital 2 in the preamble.

[356] Cases: C-215/11 *Szyrocka*, ECLI:EU:C:2012:794; C-324/12 *Novontech-Zala*, ECLI:EU:C:2013:205; C-144/12 *Goldbet Sportwetten*, ECLI:EU:C:2013:393; C-119/13 and C-120/13 *eco cosmetics*, ECLI:EU:C:2014:2144; C-488/13 *Parva Investitsionna Banka and Others*, ECLI:EU:C:2014:2191; C-245/14, *Thomas Cook Belgium*, ECLI:EU:C:2015:715; and C-94/14 *Flight Refund*, pending.

[357] Reg 2015/2421 ([2015] OJ L 241/1). The amendments will apply from 14 July 2017.

proceedings.[358] There is a specific definition of 'cross-border' cases.[359] The Regulation sets out the process by which a creditor can apply to a court for a European Payment Order for an overdue pecuniary claim.[360] If the court issues the payment order, there are detailed rules relating to service of the payment order on the defendant,[361] which are important because the defendant has thirty days from the date of service to lodge a statement of opposition to the payment order.[362] In the absence of such a statement, the order becomes enforceable—in other words, the consent of the defendant is presumed.[363] The effect of a statement of opposition is to force the plaintiff to use normal civil proceedings in order to collect the debt.[364] If the order becomes enforceable, there is no need for an exequatur and the only express ground for refusal of recognition is irreconcilability with a prior judgment.[365] However, the Regulation grants the possibility of an exceptional review of the order for payment in the Member State of origin even after the time period for lodging a statement of opposition has expired, in specified exceptional cases.[366]

The third measure addressing the issue of simplified recognition of judgments is a Regulation establishing a European small claims procedure, adopted in 2007.[367] Like the payment order Regulation, the small claims Regulation is based explicitly on Article 65(c) EC (now Article 81(2)(f) TFEU).[368] The Regulation excludes the same matters as the Brussels I Regulation; also, the issues of employment law, tenancies of immovable property (with the exception of actions on monetary claims), and violations of privacy and of rights relating to personality (including defamation) are excluded from its scope.[369] It applies to claims of €2000 or less at the time that the claim was received by the court or tribunal with jurisdiction, excluding interest, expenses, and disbursements.[370] There is a specific definition of 'cross-border' cases, which is identical to the rule set out in the payment order Regulation.[371] So far there are no references to the Court of Justice concerning this Regulation.

---

[358] Art 2. The CJEU has confirmed that the Reg does not apply to national insolvency proceedings: *Parva Investitsionna Banka and Others*.

[359] Art 3; see II:8.2.4 above.

[360] Arts 7–12. Art 7 sets out an exhaustive list of the requirements to apply for an order for payment; the plaintiff can request interest up until the payment of the principal; and national law can set the amount of court fees, subject to the principles of equivalence and effectiveness (*Szyrocka*).

[361] Arts 13–15.

[362] Art 16. If the minimum standards for service are not complied with, then the strict rules concerning opposition to or review of the order do not apply either (*eco cosmetics*).

[363] Art 18.

[364] Art 17. On the effect of a statement of opposition, see further *Goldbet Sportwetten*.

[365] Arts 19 and 22. Again it is not clear whether the grounds for refusal are exhaustive.

[366] Art 20. A failure to apply for a review in time due to human error is not an exceptional ground (*Novontech-Zala*). The ruling in *Thomas Cook* also takes a narrow view of this exception. See also *Flight Refund*, pending.

[367] Reg 861/2007 ([2007] OJ L 199/1). The Reg applied from 1 Jan 2009 (Art 29). The following nine footnotes refer to this Reg, unless otherwise indicated. See again the earlier Green Paper on payments orders and small claims, n 354 above.

[368] See recital 2 in the preamble.

[369] Art 2(2). In comparison with the payment orders Reg, there is no general exclusion of claims for non-contractual liability.

[370] Art 2(1).   [371] Art 3; see II:8.2.4 above.

The Regulation sets out the basic elements of the small claims procedure, specifying that the process is usually written, with discretion for the court to hold an oral hearing, and setting out deadlines of thirty days to respond to the claim and the counter-claim.[372] Within thirty days of receiving the response, the court shall either give a judgment or move to a further procedural stage, still subject to strict deadlines; if there has been no response by the deadline, the court must give judgment.[373] Unlike the payment orders Regulation, the defendant must contest the merits of the case immediately, as there is no prospect of lodging a statement of opposition in order to require the plaintiff to commence ordinary civil proceedings instead. It is up to each Member State to decide whether an appeal of a small claims judgment is possible,[374] but at least there must be the possibility of a review of the judgment on certain limited grounds.[375] Again, there is no exequatur process as regards the recognition of the judgment, and the only express ground to refuse recognition is irreconcilability with a prior judgment.[376]

In 2013, the Commission issued a report on the implementation of the Regulation, concluding that it was not widely used in practice but had an impact in reducing the length of litigation when it was used.[377] The Commission proposed in parallel a number of changes to the Regulation to increase its use and effectiveness.[378] The EP and Council agreed to make some amendments, and a Regulation to that effect was adopted in December 2015.[379]

These amendments: apply the Reg to claims of up to €5,000; provide for service via electronic means; create a limited obligation to hold oral hearings; vaguely limit the possible court fees; require Member States to allow fees to be paid from a distance; reduce the proportion of a judgment that has to be translated; and oblige Member States to provide more information on the dismissal of a claim, filling out forms, and the amount and payment of fees. The amendments to the Regulation seem likely to have only a modest effect on its use and effectiveness.

8.5.7 Alternative dispute resolution

Article 81(2)(g) TFEU confers competence on the EU as regards 'the development of alternative methods of dispute settlement'; this power was expressly conferred for the first time by the Treaty of Lisbon. Even before the entry into force of that Treaty, the issue of alternative dispute resolution was addressed by a Directive on mediation adopted in 2008.[380] Presumably the EC's competence to adopt the Directive at that time derived from its power to adopt legislation concerning compatibility of civil procedure rules to eliminate obstacles to the good functioning of civil proceedings, although this

---

[372] Art 5. The languages concerned are set out in Art 8, which is comparable to the languages provisions in the Regs on service of documents; on the interpretation of the latter rules, see II:8.5.2 above.

[373] Art 7; Arts 8–13 set out rules applicable to further procedural steps.   [374] Art 17.

[375] Art 18; compare to the wider possibility of review set out in Art 20 of the payment orders Reg.

[376] Arts 20 and 22. Again it is not clear whether the grounds for refusal are exhaustive.

[377] COM (2013) 795, 19 Nov 2013.   [378] COM (2013) 794, 19 Nov 2013.

[379] Reg 2015/2421 ([2015] OJ L 241/1). The amendments will apply from 14 July 2017.

[380] Dir 2008/52 ([2008] OJ L 136/3). Member States had to transpose this Directive by 21 May 2011 (Art 12). See earlier the Green Paper on alternative dispute settlement (COM (2002) 196, 19 Apr 2002).

was not made explicit in the Directive. Any amendments to the Directive, or other measures on this issue, would now be adopted on the basis of Article 81(2)(g) TFEU, although it should be noted that there are other EU measures addressing mediation, adopted on the basis of EU internal market powers.[381] The CJEU has been asked to rule on this Directive, but the questions proved to be hypothetical in the circumstances.[382]

The Directive applies to all civil and commercial matters,[383] except for matters not at the parties' disposal under the applicable law, with exclusions only for customs, revenue, and administrative matters and state liability for acts of state authority.[384] It applies only to cross-border matters, with the standard definition of this concept amended to clarify the applicable date at which to determine this issue.[385] The Directive requires Member States: to encourage quality control as regards mediation and training of mediators; to permit courts to invite the parties to mediate their dispute; to make mediation agreements enforceable, subject to certain conditions (note that the Directive does not address the issue of enforceability of the agreements in other Member States); to keep mediation confidential, subject to certain exceptions; to waive limitation or prescription periods as regards access to court and arbitration while mediation is underway, unless ruled out by international treaties; and to make information on mediation available to the public.[386]

8.5.8 Judicial training

Finally, the last competence conferred upon the EU by Article 81(2) TFEU is a power to adopt measures concerning 'support for the training of the judiciary and judicial staff', a new express power added by the Treaty of Lisbon (Article 81(2)(h) TFEU). Until now, the question of judicial training in the field of civil law has been addressed alongside the issue of judicial training in the field of criminal law,[387] and this link has been strengthened by the adoption of a law that applies to EU funding of both civil and criminal law matters.[388]

8.6 Family Law

There are a significant number of EU measures on the cross-border aspects of family law. Firstly, the EU adopted the Brussels II Regulation, which in its original form concerned jurisdiction over divorce proceedings and mutual recognition of divorce judgments, as well as parental responsibility proceedings which were linked to the divorce proceedings.[389] As noted above, this Regulation replaced the Brussels II Convention,[390]

---

[381] See II:8.2.4 above.   [382] Case C-492/11 *Di Donna*, ECLI:EU:C:2013:428.
[383] On the definition of this concept, see II:8.2.4 above.   [384] Art 1(2), Dir 2008/52.
[385] Art 2. See the discussion of the payment orders and small claims Regs (II:8.5.6 above).
[386] Arts 4–9.
[387] See further II:3.8 above. It should be noted that the TFEU provision regarding the training of criminal law judges (Art 82(1)(c)) is identical to the provision concerning training of civil law judges.
[388] See Art 3(e) of the 2007 funding decision ([2007] OJ L 257/16), now replaced by Reg 1382/2013 ([2013] OJ L 354/73).
[389] Reg 1347/2000 ([2000] OJ L 160/19), in force 1 Mar 2001.   [390] [1998] OJ C 221/1.

which had been signed in 1998 but which had not yet been ratified when the Treaty of Amsterdam entered into force. In 2003 this Regulation was itself replaced by an amended text (Regulation 2201/2003), which extended the rules to apply to all proceedings concerning parental responsibility, and also provided for simplified recognition of judgments concerning access to or return of a child.[391] The Brussels II Regulation has been the subject of many references to the Court of Justice from national courts.[392]

In 2006, the Commission suggested some amendments to the jurisdiction rules in the Brussels II Regulation, alongside provisions for conflict of law in divorce cases.[393] Since Member States could not agree on the latter set of rules, they were later adopted on the basis of 'enhanced cooperation', in the form of a separate Regulation which only some Member States participate in (see discussion below). The Commission subsequently withdrew its proposal to amend the Brussels II Regulation.[394]

However, the Commission's analysis of the application of the Regulation in practice has identified a number of provisions which could be amended.[395] As regards jurisdiction: there is still the possibility of a 'rush to court' between divorcing spouses as long as one of the Member States does not participate in the Rome III Regulation; the divorcing spouses do not have the option of agreeing on the competent court, unlike other some other EU measures; and there are no rules on 'residual jurisdiction' or declining jurisdiction as regards third states. On recognition and enforcement of judgments, there are complications because: the 'exequatur' procedure has been abolished for some types of proceedings, but not others; there are divergent applications of the 'public policy' exception, particularly as regards children's right to be heard; and there are different definitions of the concept of 'enforcement'. Cooperation between central authorities could be improved by making more provision for mediation, and there are problems collecting and exchanging information on the situation of children. As for the return of abducted children, Member States diverge on the application of the relevant safeguards. Furthermore, the Commission is dissatisfied with the existence of different enforcement procedures in Member States. Finally, the Commission believes that the provisions on placement of children could be improved. However, the Commission has not committed itself to propose amendments to the Regulation, and it remains to be seen if it will do so.

---

[391] [2003] OJ L 338/1; applicable from 1 Mar 2005 (Art 72).

[392] Cases: C-435/06 *C* [2007] ECR I-10141; C-68/07 *Sundelind Lopez* [2007] ECR I-10403; C-523/07 *A* [2009] ECR I-2805; C-168/08 *Hadadi* [2009] ECR I-6871; C-195/08 *Rinau* [2008] ECR I-5271; C-256/09 *Purrucker I* [2010] ECR I-7349; C-312/09 *Michalias* [2010] ECR I-82*; C-403/09 PPU *Detiček* [2009] ECR I-12193; C-211/10 PPU *Povse* [2010] ECR I-6669; C-400/10 PPU *McB* [2010] ECR I-8965; C-296/10 *Purrucker II* [2010] ECR I-11163; C-497/10 PPU *Mercredi* [2010] ECR I-14309; C-491/10 PPU *Aguirre Zarraga* [2010] ECR I-14247; C-92/12 PPU *Health and Safety Executive*, ECLI:EU:C:2012:255; C-436/13 *E*, ECLI:EU:C:2014:2246; C-376/14 PPU *C*, ECLI:EU:C:2014:2268; C-656/13 *L*, ECLI:EU:C:2014:2364; C-498/14 PPU *Bradbrooke*, ECLI:EU:C:2015:3; C-507/14 *P*, ECLI:EU:C:2015:512; C-4/14 *Bohez*, ECLI:EU:C:2015:563; C-404/14 *Matouskova*, ECLI:EU:C:2015:653; C-489/14 *A*, ECLI:EU:C:2015:654; C-215/15 *Gogova*, ECLI:EU:C:2015:710; and C-455/15 PPU *P*, ECLI:EU:C:2015:763. Pending: Cases C-294/15, *Mikolajczyk*; C-428/15 *CAFA*; C-492/15 *R*; and C-499/15 *W and V*.

[393] COM (2006) 499, 17 July 2006.   [394] COM (2012) 629, 23 Oct 2012.

[395] COM (2014) 225, 15 Apr 2014; see also the studies referred to in the Annex to this report.

Secondly, in 2008 the Council adopted a Regulation on jurisdiction, mutual recognition, and cooperation as regards maintenance proceedings,[396] which furthermore refers to an international treaty (the Protocol to the Convention on maintenance proceedings) agreed within the auspices of the Hague Convention as regards applicable law on maintenance.[397] The Regulation has applied since 18 June 2011, when the Protocol also became applicable in the EU.[398] Previously, jurisdiction over and recognition of judgments relating to maintenance was subject to the Brussels Regulation, but that Regulation ceased to apply to maintenance claims brought after the maintenance Regulation became applicable.[399] The Regulation establishing the European Enforcement Order also ceased to apply to maintenance proceedings, except as regards UK judgments.[400] On the other hand, the maintenance Regulation is 'without prejudice' to the legal aid Directive, 'subject to' the specific rules in the maintenance Regulation on legal aid;[401] the Decision establishing the Judicial Network in civil and commercial matters is also applicable.[402] Moreover, the Lugano Convention still continues to apply for those non-Member States which do not participate in the maintenance Regulation.[403] The CJEU has delivered two judgments to date on this Regulation.[404]

Thirdly, in 2010, the Council adopted the Rome III Regulation, which sets out standard rules on choice of law in divorce proceedings. Member States could not agree on the Commission's original proposal by means of a unanimous vote, even without the participation of the UK, Ireland, and Denmark in the negotiations.[405] However, a number of Member States nevertheless wanted to consider the adoption of this proposal pursuant to the rules on 'enhanced cooperation',[406] and made a formal request to the Commission to this end.[407] The Commission responded to this request in March 2010, by proposing that the Council authorize enhanced cooperation to enable ten Member States to go ahead and adopt EU legislation on this issue; at the same time, it proposed a new version of the legislation on this issue.[408] In June 2010, the Council agreed in principle to authorize enhanced cooperation, and also agreed guidelines as regards

---

[396] Reg 4/2009 ([2009] OJ L 7/1). See the earlier Green Paper on maintenance claims (COM (2004) 254, 15 Apr 2004).

[397] The EU has concluded the relevant Protocol, as well as the underlying Convention: see II:8.9 below. It should be recalled that the UK is not bound by the Protocol, with the consequence that the exequatur process is not abolished as regards recognition of UK judgments (see II:8.2.5 above).

[398] See Art 76, Reg 4/2009. The Council's decision to conclude the Protocol (ibid) made the Protocol provisionally applicable in the EU as of 18 June 2011, to ensure that the Reg became applicable on that date.

[399] See Arts 68(1) and 75, Reg 4/2009.   [400] Art 68(2), Reg 4/2009.

[401] Art 68(3), Reg 4/2009. See also recitals 36 and 37 in the preamble to the Reg.

[402] Arts 70 and 71, Reg 4/2009.   [403] See II:8.2.5 above.

[404] Joined Cases C-184/13 and C-408/13 *Sanders and Huber*, ECLI:EU:C:2014:2461, and Case C-184/14 A, ECLI:EU:C:2015:479, both concerning the jurisdiction rules. At para 23 of the first judgment, the CJEU confirms that the prior case law on this issue interpreting the Brussels Regulation on this issue remains relevant.

[405] COM (2006) 499, 17 July 2006. See the earlier Green Paper on conflict of law and jurisdiction in divorce matters (COM (2005) 82, 14 Mar 2005).

[406] The Council established that there was no prospect of attaining the objectives of this proposal within a reasonable period by using the provisions of the Treaties (press release of JHA Council, June 2008 and Council doc 9985/08, 29 May 2008); this is a legal requirement before establishing enhanced cooperation (Art 20(2) TEU)). See also press release of JHA Council, July 2008 and Council doc 11984/08, 18 July 2008.

[407] See Art 329(1) TFEU.

[408] COM (2010) 104 and 105, 24 Mar 2010. On the enhanced cooperation rules generally, see I:2.2.5.5.

the Rome III proposal itself.[409] The Rome III Regulation was then adopted later that year.[410] It initially applied to fourteen Member States,[411] and two more Member States opted in later on.[412] So far, there is one reference to the CJEU on its interpretation, asking whether it applies to Sharia law.[413]

Finally, in 2011 the Commission proposed two Regulations concerning conflict of law, jurisdiction over, and recognition of judgments concerning issues of matrimonial property, along with property issues deriving from registered partnerships and *de facto* unions. These proposals are still under discussion, and in light of continued disagreement it is possible that the 'enhanced cooperation' procedure will be invoked so that some Member States participate in their adoption.[414]

8.7 European Contract Law

The gradual development of a European contract law began with a detailed Commission communication on this topic in 2001.[415] The communication suggested consideration of four options to address contract law issues: to leave solutions to the market; to develop common principles of European contract law via research; to improve existing EU contract rules, which largely govern specified areas of consumer law; or to develop an EU instrument aimed at harmonizing the general part of contract law. In February 2003, a follow-up to the communication assessed the reaction to it and suggested an Action Plan. The Commission focused on improving the coherence of EU contract law, researching the prospect of a 'common frame of reference' (CFR) for EU contract law which could be used as a non-binding model law, gathering information regarding the possible development of EU-wide general contract terms and reflecting further on a possible EU instrument setting out standard contractual rules which contracting parties could opt for.[416]

A subsequent communication in autumn 2004 elaborated upon the Commission's plans,[417] in particular linking the development of the CFR to the simplification and standardization of EU consumer law, clarifying the Commission's intentions as regards EU-wide standard terms and conditions (the development of which is to be left to the private sector), and reflecting upon the potential usefulness of an optional instrument. The communication then set out in detail the Commission's plans to fund research into

---

[409] [2010] OJ L 189/12. See also the press release of the JHA Council, 3–4 June 2010.

[410] Reg 1259/2010 (OJ 2010 L 343/10). The participating Member States had to apply the Reg by 20 June 2012 (Art 21).

[411] Belgium, Bulgaria, Germany, Spain, France, Italy, Latvia, Luxembourg, Hungary, Malta, Austria, Portugal, Romania, and Slovenia.

[412] Lithuania ([2012] OJ L 323/18), as from 22 May 2014; and Greece ([2014] OJ L 23/41), as from 29 July 2015.

[413] Case C-281/15, *Sahyouni*.

[414] COM (2011) 126 and 127, 16 Mar 2011; see conclusions of the Dec 2015 JHA Council. See also the earlier Green Paper on these issues (COM (2006) 400, 17 July 2006), as well as the communication attached to the proposals (COM (2011) 125, 16 Mar 2011).

[415] COM (2001) 398, 11 July 2001; [2001] OJ C 255/1.

[416] COM (2003) 68, 12 Feb 2003. See the Council resolution in response ([2003] OJ C 246/1).

[417] COM (2004) 651, 11 Oct 2004.

the CFR, and suggested an outline for it. Two subsequent annual reports on the implementation of this programme detailed the Commission's work, which it focused on issues of consumer law.[418]

For its part, the Council defined a view on the development of the CFR. In a first set of conclusions, it argued that: the purpose of the CFR should be to serve as a 'toolbox' for EU law-makers; the content of the CFR should consist of rules and principles drawn from a variety of sources; its scope should encompass general contract law as well as consumer contract law; and its legal effect should be as a set of non-binding guidelines.[419] The Council subsequently adopted further conclusions on the structure and scope of the CFR, respect for differing national traditions, and the role of the EU institutions,[420] as well as guidelines on the content of the CFR.[421]

The academic work funded by the Commission ultimately culminated in an draft common frame of reference,[422] which attracted great controversy.[423] However, this has had limited impact to date in practice,[424] as there is no reference to the DCFR in the main consumer rights Directive,[425] and a 2011 proposal to establish a Common European Sales Law, as an optional set of rules for use in cross-border transactions, was not acceptable to the Council.[426] Presumably that was because (as set out in the Stockholm Programme) Member States only support the CFR as 'a non-binding set of fundamental principles, definitions and model rules to be used by the law-makers at Union level to ensure greater coherence and quality in the law-making process'.[427] In light of these objections, the Commission decided to withdraw its proposal and table instead a proposal for a Directive on certain aspects of the online sale of goods.[428]

8.8 Administrative Cooperation and EU Funding

The main developments in this area are the creation of a European Judicial Network in civil matters and successive EU funding programmes, which will be considered in turn.[429]

---

[418] COM (2005) 456, 23 Sep 2005 and COM (2007) 447, 25 July 2007.

[419] See Council doc 8286/08, 11 Apr 2008.   [420] See Council doc 15306/08, 7 Nov 2008.

[421] See Council conclusions (press release of the JHA Council, 4–5 June 2009).

[422] For the text, see: <http://ec.europa.eu/justice/policies/civil/docs/dcfr_outline_edition_en.pdf>.

[423] For example, see: S Whitaker, 'The Draft "Common Frame of Reference": An Assessment', online at: <http://www.justice.gov.uk/publications/docs/Draft_Common_Frame_of_Reference__an_assessment. pdf>; the report prepared for the Scottish government by L MacGregor, online at: <http://www.scotland. gov.uk/Resource/Doc/262952/0078639.pdf>; and the House of Lords Select Committee on the European Union, 12th report for 2008/9.

[424] However, as noted above the DCFR has had some influence on Advocates-General of the Court of Justice (see II:8.4 above). The Commission has also established an experts' group on this issue ([2010] OJ L 105/109).

[425] Dir 2011/83, [2011] OJ L 304/64. See the earlier Green Paper on this issue (COM (2006) 744, 8 Feb 2007).

[426] COM (2011) 365, 11 Oct 2011. See the earlier Green Paper on policy options for a European Contract Law (COM (2010) 348, 1 July 2010).

[427] [2010] OJ C 115, point 3.4.2.   [428] COM (2015) 635, 9 Dec 2015.

[429] See also the Resolution establishing a network for legislative cooperation ([2008] OJ C 326/1).

8.8.1 European Judicial Network

Following the example of the previously-established judicial network relating to criminal law,[430] the Council established a European Judicial Network in civil and commercial matters in 2001.[431] This Network was initially composed of national contact points,
central bodies or authorities provided for in EU or national instruments, criminal law
liaison magistrates who have civil law responsibilities,[432] and other appropriate judicial or administrative authorities.[433] According to the Commission, at the beginning of
2008 the Network had 437 members falling into four categories: 102 contact points, 140
central authorities, 12 liaison magistrates, and 181 other judicial authorities active in
judicial cooperation.[434] The main tasks of the Network are to facilitate judicial cooperation between Member States, to assist in the implementation of EU and international
rules, and to furnish information to the public.[435]

   The Commission released a report in 2006 on the operation of the Network,[436] which
concluded that the effectiveness of the Network depended on the resources available to
the contact points in each Member State, but that nevertheless the Network had helped
to facilitate the application of civil law instruments by speeding up the transmission
and processing of requests for assistance. Its website for the public was also helpful and
widely used.

   In order to enhance the effectiveness of the Network, the 2001 Decision was amended
in 2009.[437] The major changes are: the participation in the Network of organizations
representing legal practitioners; a requirement to ensure sufficient resources for the
contact points; the use of the Network to exchange information on foreign law, given
the adoption of EU measures on conflict of laws;[438] establishing time limits on the processing of requests for judicial cooperation; providing for the participation of observers
(from Denmark, accession and candidate countries, and States which are party to civil
law treaties concluded by the EU); and providing for relations with other networks and
international organizations. Time will tell whether it is considered necessary to develop
the Network into an EU agency, along the lines of developments within other areas of
EU JHA law.

8.8.2 EU funding

The first use of EU funds to support civil law measures was during the Maastricht
period, when the Council adopted the 'Grotius' Joint Action to establish a programme

---

[430] See II:3.8 above.

[431] Decision 2001/470 ([2001] OJ L 174/25), applicable from 1 Dec 2002.

[432] On the liaison magistrates, see II:3.8 above.   [433] Art 2, 2001 Decision.

[434] COM (2008) 380, 23 June 2008.

[435] Art 3, 2001 Decision. For the EJN website, see: <http://ec.europa.eu/civiljustice/index_en.htm>.

[436] COM (2006) 203, 16 May 2006. See also the Council conclusions on the EJN (press release of JHA
Council, 19–20 Apr 2007).

[437] [2009] OJ L 168/35, applicable from 1 Jan 2011 (Art 2). The amended Decision has not been codified.

[438] To the same end, note also that nearly every Member State has ratified the Council of Europe
Convention on information on foreign law and its additional Protocol (see Appendix I for ratification
details).

of incentives and exchanges for legal practitioners.[439] This five-year programme had a budget of €8.8 million,[440] and concerned both civil and criminal law. It funded 'training, exchange and work-experience programmes, organization of meetings, studies and research, and distribution of information' as defined in the Joint Action.[441] Following the entry into force of the Treaty of Amsterdam, the civil law part of the Grotius Joint Action was extended for one year (2001) by a Council Regulation.[442]

Subsequently, the Council adopted a longer-term programme, covering 2002–06.[443] This programme funded the same five types of projects,[444] but with more clearly specified objectives: promoting judicial cooperation in civil matters; ensuring mutual knowledge of national judicial systems; contributing to the application of EU legislation; and improving information to the public on relevant civil law matters.[445] An initial report on this programme indicated that it was too early to evaluate its outcome, but that the Commission had been focusing on enhancing public awareness of EU legislation and conducting research which would be useful in preparing further proposals for legislation.[446]

On the expiry of the 2002 Regulation, a new civil law funding programme was established, which ran from 2007 to 2013.[447] This programme had a budget of €109.3 million over seven years.[448] Compared to the previous programme, this programme also addressed issues of conflicts of jurisdiction, the evaluation of EU measures, training of legal practitioners; it also aimed to reinforce mutual confidence, as well as to facilitate the operation of the European Judicial Network in civil and commercial matters.[449] This programme has in turn been replaced by the 'Justice Programme', which merged support for civil and criminal justice issues and runs from 2014 to 2020.[450]

8.9 External Relations

The adoption of internal EU legislation gives rise to exclusive external powers for the EU to the extent that any treaty would affect the internal rules or alter their scope.[451] Applying these principles to civil cooperation, the Court of Justice has ruled that the main EU legislation regulating civil jurisdiction and recognition of judgments in civil and commercial matters creates an exclusive external competence for the EU as regards the revised version of the Lugano Convention, which extends the Brussels I Regulation rules on jurisdiction over and enforcement of civil and commercial judgments to selected non-EU countries.[452] Subsequently, the Court extended this reasoning to the

---

[439] [1996] OJ L 287/3. On criminal law funding measures, see II:3.8 above.
[440] Art 2, Joint Action.
[441] Art 1(3), Joint Action; see the definitions in Arts 2–7 of the Joint Action.
[442] Reg 290/2001 ([2001] OJ L 43/1). The budget for this year was €650,000 (Art 2(1)).
[443] Reg 743/2002 on a general framework for EC activity on civil law ([2002] OJ L 115/1).
[444] Art 5, Reg 743/2002 (ibid).   [445] Art 2, Reg 743/2002.
[446] COM (2005) 34, 9 Feb 2005.
[447] Decision establishing the 'Civil Justice' programme ([2007] OJ L 257/16).
[448] Art 13 of Decision (ibid).   [449] Art 3 of 2007 Decision.
[450] Reg 1382/2013 ([2013] OJ L 354/73). For the details, see II:3.8 above.
[451] See: Case 22/70 *Commission v Council (ERTA)* [1971] ECR 263; Art 3(2) TFEU; and generally II:2.7.1 above.
[452] *Opinion 1/03*, [2006] ECR I-1145.

Hague Convention on child abduction, because the subject-matter of that treaty was closely linked to some of the provisions of the Brussels II Regulation.[453] This exclusive competence even extended to the specific issue of extending that Convention to more third countries. In this case, there was a particular complication because only Member States could be parties to the Convention; it therefore followed that they could only act if the EU authorized them to do so.

The obvious implication of this case law is that any rules governing jurisdiction and enforcement of judgments which are part of any international treaties fall within the exclusive external competence of the EU, to the extent that they fall within the scope of that legislation. Furthermore, since the EU's choice of law legislation applies regardless of whether the law designated by the rules is that of a Member State or a third state,[454] then exclusive external competence is also conferred upon the Union whenever such legislation is adopted. However, the question of whether EU legislation on account preservation orders, service of documents, mediation, evidence, and legal aid confers exclusive or only shared external competence may be debatable. The answer is probably that EU competence is exclusive for any matters in the external which are closely related to EU legislation, although that test must be applied on a case-by-case basis.[455]

Although Declaration 36 in the Final Act of the Treaty of Lisbon 'confirms' that Member States have competence to 'negotiate and conclude agreements with third countries or international organisations' in this field, such competence exists only 'insofar as such agreements comply with Union law'. So the Declaration clarifies that Member States' external competence in this area is not completely extinguished, in that it still applies *where the EU has not yet acted*, but it does not restrain the existence or the intensity of the Union's competence.[456]

In light of its exclusive powers, in recent years the EU has negotiated to become party to a number of international treaties which either focus largely upon the issue of jurisdiction and choice of law, or address such matters as subsidiary to regulation of substantive legal issues. In the latter case, given that the treaties concerned also address substantive matters other than civil cooperation, the EU shared external competence with its Member States for the treaty as a whole—but nevertheless its powers over the specific provisions on civil cooperation remained exclusive, so the EU had to become a party in respect of those provisions of those treaties. Also, in some cases, where negotiations on international treaties were either concluded or well underway when the Treaty of Amsterdam came into force, it was too late for the EU to become a party to the relevant treaty in its own name; therefore it authorized the Member States to sign and/ or conclude the relevant treaties, as 'trustees' of the EU's competence. This also applies to pre-existing treaties like the Hague Convention on child abduction, where further

---

[453] *Opinion 1/13*, ECLI EU:C:2014:2303.

[454] See, for instance, Art 3 of Reg 864/2007 ([2007] OJ L 199/40) and Art 2 of Reg 593/2008 ([2008] OJ L 177/6).

[455] See particularly Case C-114/12 *Commission v Council*, ECLI EU:C:2014:2151, for the most recent restatement and development of these principles.

[456] Note that the CJEU did not interpret this Declaration in *Opinion 1/13*.

measures have to be taken by Member States, such as the acceptance of ratification by new third States.

The treaties which the EU has solely concluded, since they relate only to matters within the EU's exclusive external competence in this area, are: the Lugano Convention;[457] the treaties with Denmark which extend the Brussels I Regulation and the service of documents Regulation to that Member State, despite its opt-out from EU law in this field;[458] the Hague Convention on maintenance obligations;[459] the Protocol to that Convention, concerning choice of law;[460] and the Hague Convention on choice-of-court agreements.[461]

As for its shared competence, the EU has concluded the Unidroit Convention on international interests in mobile equipment and its protocols relating to aircraft equipment and railway rolling stock, as regards issues within the scope of the Brussels I Regulation, the insolvency Regulation, and the Rome I Regulation.[462] It has also concluded the Protocol to the Athens Convention 1974 on carriage of passengers and luggage by sea.[463]

For the reasons explained above, the Council has also adopted a number of Decisions authorizing Member States to sign or ratify treaties which fall partly or wholly within the scope of the EU's external competence. These decisions concern: authority to sign or ratify the Convention on civil liability for bunker oil pollution damage (Bunkers Convention);[464] authority to ratify the Convention on liability for damage caused by carrying hazardous and noxious substances by sea (HNS Convention);[465] authority to sign the Hague Convention on parental responsibility for children;[466] authority to sign a Protocol to the Paris Convention on liability in case of nuclear accident;[467]

---

[457] For the Decision on conclusion, see [2009] OJ L 147/1; for the Convention itself, see [2009] OJ L 147/5; for the explanatory memorandum on the Convention, see [2009] OJ C 319/1. The Convention, which was also signed by Denmark, Norway, Iceland, and Switzerland, entered into force for the EU, Denmark, and Norway as from 1 Jan 2010 ([2010] OJ L 140/1). It applied to Switzerland from 1 Jan 2011 and Iceland from 1 May 2011 ([2011] OJ L 138/1). For the earlier Council Decision on signature of the Convention, see [2007] OJ L 339/1. For the previous version of the Convention, to which the (then) Member States and Norway, Iceland, and Switzerland were parties, see [1988] OJ C 319/9.

[458] These treaties also include obligations for Denmark as regards the exercise of its own external competence for matters within the scope of the treaties. See further II.8.2.5 above.

[459] [2011] OJ L 192/39, amended by [2014] OJ L 113/1.

[460] [2009] OJ L 331/17. On the implications of concluding the Protocol, see II.8.6 above.

[461] [2014] OJ L 353/5 (signature in [2009] OJ L 133/1).

[462] [2009] OJ L 121/3 and [2014] OJ L 353/9. For the railway protocol, the declaration of EU competence also concerns some EU rail transport legislation.

[463] This took the form of two separate Decisions on conclusion ([2012] OJ L 8/1 and 13), concerning respectively EU maritime transport competence (in light of Reg 392/2009 ([2009] OJ L 131/24), recital 11 of the preamble) and the jurisdiction provisions of the Protocol, due to the Brussels I Regulation.

[464] [2002] OJ L 256/7. The preamble to the Decision specifies that exclusive competence applies to two Articles of this Convention concerning jurisdiction and enforcement of judgments, due to the Brussels I Regulation, but not to the rest of the Convention.

[465] [2002] OJ L 337/55. The preamble to the Decision specifies that exclusive competence applies to three Articles of this Convention concerning jurisdiction and enforcement of judgments, due to the Brussels I Regulation, but not to the rest of the Convention. The Commission has proposed a Decision permitting Member States to ratify a Protocol to this Convention: COM (2015) 305, 22 June 2015.

[466] [2003] OJ L 48/1.

[467] [2003] OJ L 338/30. The Decision does not apply to Ireland, Austria, and Luxembourg, since they are not parties to the Paris Convention. The preamble to the Decision specifies that exclusive competence applies to one Article of the main Convention (as amended by the Protocol) concerning jurisdiction, due to the Brussels I Regulation, but not to the rest of the Convention.

authority to sign and ratify a 2003 Protocol to a Convention on a fund for oil pollution damage;[468] authority to *ratify* the aforementioned Protocol to the Paris Convention on liability in case of nuclear accident;[469] authority for Slovenia, which joined the EU later, to ratify the same Protocol;[470] authority to *ratify* the Hague Convention on parental responsibility for children;[471] authority for Member States to accede to a Protocol to the Vienna Convention on nuclear liability;[472] and authority to extend the Hague Convention on child abduction to Andorra and Singapore,[473] and then to five further countries.[474]

There are also proposals to authorize Austria and Malta to accede to the Hague Convention on the service of documents;[475] and authorize Austria and Poland to accede to the Budapest Convention on carriage of goods.[476]

Next, the EU has obtained membership in its own name of the main negotiating forum for civil law treaties—the Hague Conference on private international law.[477] However, since EU competence in civil law is shared with Member States, all Member States have also retained their membership in the Hague Conference.

As for the jurisdiction of the Court of Justice over the civil law treaties concluded by the EU, and the legal effect of those treaties, so far neither issue has been addressed in the Court's case law, although the two civil law treaties with Denmark specifically give the Court jurisdiction in relation to Denmark, and the Court has ruled on a reference from the Danish courts.[478] It would be very odd, therefore, if the Court had no jurisdiction regarding those treaties in relation to the other Member States. In the case of other civil law treaties concluded by the EU, there seems no reason to doubt that the normal rules governing the Court's jurisdiction and the legal effect of international treaties in the EU legal order apply equally to civil law treaties.[479] Indeed, the Court has assumed as much in a judgment which briefly interpreted the Lugano Convention.[480]

---

[468] Decision 2004/246 ([2004] OJ L 78/22), amended following the 2003 Act of Accession (see II:8.2.5 above). The Decision does not apply to Ireland, Austria, and Luxembourg, since they are not parties to the Paris Convention. The preamble to the Decision specifies that exclusive competence applies to two Articles of the Protocol concerning jurisdiction, due to the Brussels I Regulation, but not to the rest of the Protocol. One judgment of the Court of Justice has touched on this Decision (Case C-188/07 *Commune de Mesquer* [2008] ECR I-4501), which was not relevant on the facts of that case.

[469] [2004] OJ L 97/53.   [470] [2007] OJ L 294/23.

[471] [2008] OJ L 151/36. The preamble to this decision asserts that the EU and Member States share competence as regards the subject-matter of the Convention. As matters stand, Member States' competence principally concerns the issue of choice of law on parental responsibility (Chapter III of the Convention), which has not (yet) been the subject of EU legislation.

[472] [2013] OJ L 220/1. The Decision only applies to the seven Member States which are parties to the Vienna Convention. The preamble to the Decision specifies that exclusive competence applies to two Articles of the Protocol concerning jurisdiction, due to the Brussels I Regulation, but not to the rest of the Protocol.

[473] [2015] OJ L 163/29 and 32. This issue was addressed in *Opinion 1/13*, discussed above.

[474] [2015] OJ L 331. The third States concerned are Seychelles, Russia, Albania, Morocco, and Armenia. A proposal to extend the Convention to Gabon is still under discussion (COM (2011) 904, 21 Dec 2011).

[475] COM (2013) 338, 6 June 2013.   [476] COM (2014) 721, 8 Dec 2014.

[477] [2006] OJ L 297.   [478] For more on these treaties, see II:8.2.5 above.

[479] For more on this issue, see II:2.7.1 above.

[480] Case C-295/13 *H*, ECLI:EU:C:2014:2410, which confirmed that the exception in the Lugano Convention for insolvency proceedings had to be interpreted the same way as the parallel exception in the Brussels Regulation (on that exception, see II:8.5.1.1 above).

Finally, one key issue for Member States in light of EU exclusive external competence over many civil law issues is the power to negotiate and sign treaties in their own name.[481] Most EU legislation does permit Member States to retain in force existing treaties which they ratified before the legislation was adopted, at least as regards relations with third states,[482] but this implicitly rules out the negotiation of *future* treaties by Member States dealing with the relevant subject-matter. Some Member States objected strongly to this restriction on their external competence, particularly after the Court of Justice's 2006 judgment in *Opinion 1/2003* had made clear the extent of the EU exclusive competence over civil law matters. So Member States made clear they would only agree to the adoption of new EU civil law legislation if they were still permitted some leeway to negotiate treaties in future.

The solution to this dispute was to adopt legislation in 2009 that delegates competence to the Member States to negotiate their own treaties, subject to strict substantive and procedural conditions.[483] Two separate Council Regulations authorize, on the one hand, the power to negotiate treaties relating to conflict of law matters,[484] and, on the other hand, maintenance and family law jurisdiction matters.[485] There is no EU legislation authorizing national treaty negotiations within the scope of the EU's other civil law legislation, but of course it remains possible to adopt legislation to that effect in future,[486] or for the Council to continue to authorize Member States to negotiate such treaties on a case-by-case basis. It is also still possible for the Council to authorize Member States to negotiate and conclude *multilateral* treaties within the scope of EU civil law legislation on a case-by-case basis, although in practice the Commission is unlikely to propose such authorization.

The Regulations apply either to bilateral agreements concluded between a Member State and a third country, or to a regional agreement between a 'limited' number of Member States and 'neighbouring' third states.[487] When a Member State intends to enter into negotiations for a new agreement (or to amend an existing agreement), it must inform the Commission 'at the earliest possible' time before opening negotiations, and make available to the Commission information on the planned treaties.[488] The Commission must then assess the Member State's plan to start negotiations, first

---

[481] It should be noted that the position regarding the capacity of Denmark to sign civil law treaties with third states is governed by the distinct rules on this issue in the two treaties with the EU by means of which Denmark has agreed to apply certain EU civil law regulations. See II:8.2.5 above.

[482] See also Art 351 TFEU, discussed further in II:2.7.1 above.

[483] See similarly the legislation on border traffic treaties (I.3.8) and Art 2(1) TFEU, discussed also in I.2.7.

[484] Reg 662/2009, [2009] OJ L 200/25, applicable to matters within the scope of the Rome I or Rome II Regulations (Art 1(2)). The Reg entered into force on 20 Aug 2009 (Art 15).

[485] Reg 664/2009, [2009] OJ L 200/46, applicable to matters within the scope of Regs 4/2009 or 2201/2003 (Art 1(2)). The Reg also entered into force on 20 Aug 2009 (Art 15).

[486] See recitals 5 and 21 of Regs 662/2009 and 664/2009. Some of the legislation adopted since 2009 contains specific rules on Member States' pre-existing treaties (Art 75, Reg 650/2012; Art 19, Rome III Reg; Arts 69–73, revised Brussels I Regulation; and Arts 71a to 71c of the latter Reg, as inserted by Reg 542/2014), but this does not amount to an authorization to sign any future treaties. There are no rules on Member States' treaties in the Regulations establishing a European Protection Order or Account Preservation Orders, and the revised insolvency Regulation does not provide for Member States to sign new treaties.

[487] Art 2, Reg 662/2009. Art 2 of Reg 664/2009 has a more specific definition of a regional agreement, by reference to the EU family law legislation concerned.

[488] Art 3, Regs 662/2009 and 664/2009.

of all examining whether a relevant negotiating mandate for a treaty between the EU and the country concerned is envisaged within the next two years, and then checking whether all of the following conditions are present: a 'specific interest' for the Member State to conclude the treaty 'due to economic, geographic, cultural, historical, social or political ties' with the third state concerned; the planned agreement 'appears not to render [EU] law ineffective and not to undermine the proper functioning of the system established by that law'; and the envisaged treaty 'would not undermine the object and purpose of the [EU's] external relations policy as decided by the [Union]'.[489]

If the planned treaty meets these conditions, the Commission must authorize negotiations within ninety days of the Member State's request; it 'may propose negotiating guidelines and may request the inclusion of particular clauses in the envisaged agreement.' The treaty must contain a form of priority clause in case the EU subsequently negotiates a treaty with the country concerned on the same subject.[490] If the Commission believes that the planned treaty does not meet the required conditions, it shall inform the Member State concerned within ninety days. If the Member State concerned wishes to argue the point, the Regulations provide for a procedure for discussions between the Member State and the Commission—but the Commission has the final say.[491] Presumably an aggrieved Member State could then have recourse to the EU courts to bring an annulment action against the Commission's decision.

Once negotiations (if authorized) begin, the Commission may participate as an observer.[492] When negotiations conclude, the Member State concerned then needs the approval of the Commission again to conclude the agreement, and the Commission must assess it in light of most of the same substantive criteria and procedural rules which were applicable to the earlier decision to authorize the start of the negotiations.[493] Finally, there is a 'sunset' clause for the Regulations: the Commission must review their operation by 13 July 2017 at the earliest and then recommend either that they expire or that they be replaced by a new Regulation (with a proposal for legislation to that effect); the Regulations will then expire three years after the date of this report.[494]

8.10 Conclusions

Civil law measures adopted within the framework of EU law have maintained a strong focus on mutual recognition, with their basic goal of ensuring that only one court system and one set of legal rules applies to a dispute and that a judgment issued in one Member State is recognized and enforced in another. The lack of accompanying harmonization of law has caused concern among those who argue for greater similarity in national civil procedural laws, but the EU has shied away from any significant steps in that direction.

As for human rights, while the EU's civil cooperation measures have not given rise to the same concerns over civil liberties and human rights protection as other issues

---

[489] Art 4, Regs 662/2009 and 664/2009.   [490] Art 5, Regs 662/2009 and 664/2009.
[491] Art 6, Regs 662/2009 and 664/2009.   [492] Art 7, Regs 662/2009 and 664/2009.
[493] Arts 8 and 9, Regs 662/2009 and 664/2009.
[494] Arts 13 and 14, Regs 662/2009 and 664/2009.

discussed in this book, all such matters fall within the scope of Article 6 ECHR. The case law of the Court of Justice has largely (but not entirely) struck the right balance between developing efficient rules on civil jurisdiction and mutual recognition of judgments, on the one hand, and the protection of human rights on the other. Furthermore, effective civil cooperation measures have the desirable result of assisting the Member States to fulfil their Article 6 ECHR obligation to guarantee a trial within a reasonable time and to ensure the execution of judgments, as regards civil proceedings with a cross-border element.

Ratification of Treaties

(as of 14 Dec 2015)

* An asterisk indicates that the treaty is not yet in force

EU/Member States' Treaties

Extradition (1995)*

Ratified by:	20 Member States: all the 'old' Member States except Italy, plus Cyprus, Poland, Estonia, Lithuania, Latvia, and Slovenia
Applied by:	14 Member States: the ratifying States except Greece, Ireland, Netherlands, Portugal, Cyprus, and Estonia
Report:	[1996] OJ C 375/4

Convention on Protection of EC Financial Interests (PIF) (1995)

Ratified by:	27 Member States: all except Croatia
Report:	[1997] OJ C 191/1

Extradition (1996)*

Ratified by:	20 Member States: all the 'old' Member States except Italy, plus Cyprus, Poland, Estonia, Lithuania, Latvia, and Slovenia
Applied by:	14 Member States: the ratifying States except Greece, Ireland, Netherlands, Cyprus, Estonia, and Latvia
Report:	[1997] OJ C 191/13

First Protocol to PIF Convention (1996)

Ratified by:	27 Member States: all except Croatia
Report:	[1998] OJ C 11/5

Court of Justice Protocol to PIF Convention (1996)

Ratified by:	26 Member States: all except Estonia and Croatia

Second Protocol to PIF Convention (1997)

Ratified by:	27 Member States: all except Croatia
Report:	[1999] OJ C 91/8

Convention on corruption (1997)

Ratified by:	26 Member States: all except Malta and Croatia
Report:	[1998] OJ C 391/1

Naples II Convention (1998)

Ratified by:	All Member States
Report:	[1998] OJ C 189/1

Driving Disqualification Convention (1998)*

Ratified by:	7 Member States: Bulgaria, Cyprus, Spain, UK, Ireland, Romania, and Slovakia
Applied by:	Ireland and UK
Report:	[1999] OJ C 211/1

Convention on mutual assistance (2000)

Ratified by: 24 Member States: all except Greece, Italy, Ireland, and Croatia
Report: [2000] OJ C 379/7

Protocol to Convention on mutual assistance (2001)

Ratified by: 23 Member States: all except Croatia, Greece, Italy, Ireland, and Luxembourg
Report: [2002] OJ C 257/1

Rome Convention accession treaty (2005)

Ratified by: 24 Member States: all except UK, Denmark, Croatia, and Ireland

European Political Cooperation

Abolition of legalization of documents (1987)*

Ratified by: 7 Member States: Belgium, Denmark, France, Italy, Ireland, Cyprus, and Latvia

Double jeopardy (1987)*

Ratified by: 9 Member States: Austria, Belgium, Germany, Denmark, France, Italy, Ireland, Netherlands, and Portugal
Signed by: 3 Member States: Luxembourg, Spain, and United Kingdom

Transfer of sentenced persons (1987)*

Ratified by: 6 Member States: Belgium, Denmark, Spain, Italy, Ireland, and Luxembourg

Faxing of extradition requests (1989)*

Ratified by: 9 Member States: Austria, Belgium, Germany, Spain, UK, Italy, Luxembourg, Netherlands, and Sweden

Transfer of criminal proceedings (1990)*

Ratified by: 2 Member States: France and Portugal
Signed by: 1 Member State: Luxembourg

Maintenance payments (1990)*

Ratified by: 5 Member States: Spain, United Kingdom, Greece, Italy, and Ireland
Signed by: 1 Member State: France

Enforcement of criminal sentences (1991)*

Ratified by: 5 Member States: Cyprus, Germany, Spain, Latvia, and Netherlands
Signed by: 1 Member State: Portugal
*Applied
provisionally by:* Germany, Latvia, and Netherlands

Council of Europe

ETS 24 *Extradition Convention (1957)*
Ratified by: All Member States

ETS 30 *Convention on mutual assistance (1959)*
Ratified by: All Member States

ETS 46 *Fourth Protocol to the ECHR (1963)*
Ratified by: 26 Member States: all except Greece and United Kingdom
Signed by: 1 Member State: United Kingdom

ETS 51	*Convention on the supervision of conditionally released or conditionally sentenced offenders (1964)*
Ratified by:	13 Member States: Austria, Belgium, Czech Republic, Estonia, France, Italy, Luxembourg, Netherlands, Portugal, Slovakia, Slovenia, Sweden, and Croatia
Signed by:	4 Member States: Denmark, Germany, Greece, and Malta
ETS 52	*Convention on road traffic offences (1964)*
Ratified by:	4 Member States: Cyprus, Denmark, France, and Sweden
Signed by:	8 Member States: Austria, Belgium, Germany, Greece, Italy, Luxembourg, Netherlands, and Portugal
ETS 62	*Convention on information on foreign law (1968)*
Ratified by:	27 Member States: all except Ireland
ETS 70	*Convention on the international validity of criminal judgments (1970)*
Ratified by:	12 Member States: Austria, Belgium, Bulgaria, Cyprus, Denmark, Estonia, Latvia, Lithuania, Netherlands, Romania, Spain, and Sweden
Signed by:	6 Member States: Germany, Greece, Italy, Luxembourg, Portugal, and Slovenia
ETS 73	*Convention on transfer of criminal proceedings (1972)*
Ratified by:	13 Member States: Austria, Bulgaria, Czech Republic, Cyprus, Denmark, Estonia, Latvia, Lithuania, Netherlands, Romania, Slovakia, Spain, and Sweden
Signed by:	8 Member States: Belgium, Greece, Hungary, Italy, Luxembourg, Portugal, Slovenia, and Croatia
ETS 86	*First Protocol, Extradition Convention (1975)*
Ratified by:	20 Member States: all except Austria, Finland, France, Germany, Greece, Ireland, Italy, and United Kingdom
Signed by:	1 Member State: Greece
ETS 90	*Convention on the suppression of terrorism (1977)*
Ratified by:	All Member States
ETS 92	*European Agreement on the transmission of applications for legal aid (1977)*
Ratified by:	22 Member States: all except Germany, Hungary, Malta, Slovenia, Slovakia, and Croatia
Signed by:	Germany
ETS 97	*Additional Protocol to the Convention on information on foreign law (1978)*
Ratified by:	25 Member States: all except Ireland, Slovenia, and Croatia
ETS 98	*Second Protocol, Extradition Convention (1978)*
Ratified by:	24 Member States: all except France, Greece, Ireland, and Luxembourg
Signed by:	1 Member State: Greece
ETS 99	*First Protocol to Convention on mutual assistance (1978)*
Ratified by:	All Member States
ETS 108	*Data protection Convention (1981)*
Ratified by:	All Member States
ETS 112	*Convention on the transfer of sentenced persons (1983)*
Ratified by:	All Member States

ETS 116	*Compensation for crime victims (1983)*
Ratified by:	19 Member States: Austria, Belgium, Cyprus, Czech Republic, Denmark, Estonia, Finland, France, Germany, Luxembourg, Netherlands, Portugal, Romania, Slovakia, Spain, Sweden, United Kingdom, Malta, and Croatia
Signed by:	3 Member States: Greece, Hungary, and Lithuania

ETS 117	*Seventh Protocol to the ECHR (1984)*
Ratified by:	25 Member States: all *except* Germany, Netherlands, and United Kingdom
Signed by:	2 Member States: Germany and Netherlands

ETS 141	*Convention on the proceeds of crime, etc.(1990)*
Ratified by:	All EU Member States

ETS 167	*Protocol to the Convention on the transfer of sentenced persons (1997)*
Ratified by:	24 Member States: all except Italy, Portugal, Spain, and Slovakia
Signed by:	3 Member States: Italy, Spain, and Portugal

ETS 173	*Criminal law Convention on corruption (1999)*
Ratified by:	27 Member States: all except Germany
Signed by:	1 Member State: Germany

ETS 179	*Protocol to Agreement on the transmission of applications for legal aid (2000)*
Ratified by:	8 Member States: Czech Republic, Denmark, Estonia, Finland, Latvia, Lithuania, Sweden, and Cyprus
Signed by:	9 Member States: Belgium, France, Ireland, Italy, Luxembourg, Poland, Portugal, Romania, and UK

ETS 181	*Protocol to the data protection Convention (2001)*
Ratified by:	23 Member States: all except Belgium, Greece, Italy, Malta, and United Kingdom
Signed by:	4 Member States: Belgium, Greece, Italy, and United Kingdom

ETS 182	*Second Protocol to Convention on mutual assistance (2001)*
Ratified by:	23 Member States: all except Hungary, Greece, Italy, Spain, and Luxembourg
Signed by:	5 Member States: Hungary, Greece, Italy, Spain, and Luxembourg

ETS 185	*Cyber-crime (2001)*
Ratified by:	25 Member States: all except Greece, Ireland, and Sweden
Signed by:	3 Member States: Greece, Ireland, and Sweden

ETS 189	*Protocol to Cyber-crime Convention (2003)*
Ratified by:	15 Member States: Cyprus, Denmark, France, Latvia, Lithuania, Portugal, Romania, Slovenia, Croatia, Czech Republic, Finland, Germany, Luxembourg, Poland, and Spain
Signed by:	8 Member States: Austria, Belgium, Estonia, Greece, Malta, Netherlands, Italy, and Sweden

ETS 190	*Protocol to Convention on the suppression of terrorism (2003)**
Ratified by:	19 Member States: Belgium, Bulgaria, Cyprus, Denmark, Estonia, Finland, France, Latvia, Lithuania, Luxembourg, Netherlands, Poland, Portugal, Romania, Slovakia, Slovenia, Croatia, Germany, and Spain
Signed by:	9 Member States: all other Member States

CETS 196	*Convention on the prevention of terrorism (2005)*
Ratified by:	20 Member States: Austria, Bulgaria, Cyprus, Denmark, Estonia, Finland, France, Latvia, Poland, Slovenia, Slovakia, Spain, Sweden, Croatia, Germany, Hungary, Lithuania, Luxembourg, Malta, and Portugal
Signed by:	7 Member States: all others except Czech Republic
CETS 197	*Convention on trafficking in persons (2005)*
Ratified by:	27 Member States: all except Czech Republic
CETS 198	*Convention on the proceeds of crime, etc. (2005)*
Ratified by:	17 Member States: Belgium, Bulgaria, Cyprus, France, Hungary, Latvia, Malta, Netherlands, Poland, Portugal, Romania, Slovakia, Slovenia, Spain, Sweden, Croatia, and UK
Signed by:	7 Member States: Austria, Finland, Estonia, Denmark, Greece, Italy, and Luxembourg
CETS 201	*Convention on the Protection of Children against Sexual Exploitation and Sexual Abuse (2007)*
Ratified by:	All except 5 Member States: Czech Republic, Estonia, Ireland, Slovakia, and UK
Signed by:	5 Member States: Czech Republic, Estonia, Ireland, Slovakia, and UK
CETS 209	*Third Protocol to Extradition Convention (2010)*
Ratified by:	8 Member States: Austria, Cyprus, Czech Republic, Latvia, Netherlands, Slovenia, Spain, and UK
Signed by:	13 Member States: Bulgaria, Croatia, Finland, Germany, Greece, Hungary, Italy, Lithuania, Luxembourg, Poland, Portugal, Romania, and Sweden
CETS 212	*Fourth Protocol to Extradition Convention (2012)*
Ratified by:	4 Member States: Latvia, Slovenia, Sweden, and UK
Signed by:	7 Member States: Austria, Hungary, Italy, Luxembourg, Poland, Portugal, and Romania
CETS 215	*Convention on the Manipulation of Sports Results (2014)**
Ratified by:	1 Member State: Portugal
Signed by:	11 Member States: Bulgaria, Germany, Finland, France, Denmark, Greece, Lithuania, Luxembourg, Netherlands, Poland, and Spain

United Nations

Convention on transnational organized crime	
Ratified by:	All Member States
Protocol on smuggling, Convention on transnational organized crime	
Ratified by:	27 Member States: all except Ireland
Signed by:	1 Member State: Ireland
Protocol on trafficking in persons, Convention on transnational organized crime	
Ratified by:	All Member States
Protocol on firearms, Convention on transnational organized crime	
Ratified by:	23 Member States: all except France, Germany, Luxembourg, UK, and Ireland
Signed by:	3 Member States: Germany, Luxembourg, and the UK

Convention on corruption

Ratified by: 25 Member States: all except Czech Republic, Germany, and Ireland
Signed by: 3 Member States: Czech Republic, Germany, and Ireland

Hague Conference

14.   *Service of documents (1969)*

Ratified by: 27 Member States: all except Austria

20.   *Evidence convention (1970)*

Ratified by: 25 Member States: all except Austria, Belgium, and Ireland

29.   *International access to justice (1980)*

Ratified by: 18 Member States: all except Austria, Belgium, Denmark, Germany, Greece,
                 Hungary, Ireland, Italy, Portugal, and UK
Signed by: 3 Member States: Germany, Greece, and Italy

OECD

Anti-bribery (corruption) convention (1997)

Ratified by: 26 Member States: all except Romania and Croatia

Pre-Treaty of Lisbon Third Pillar Measures Still in Force

*The following third pillar measures adopted before the entry into force of the Treaty of Lisbon were still in force (or could come into force in future) as of 15 December 2015. The provisions of the Schengen acquis which were **not** allocated to the third pillar are discussed in Appendix II to volume 1.*

1) Schengen *acquis* (integrated into EU legal order 1.5.1999) – [2000] OJ L 239

a) Schengen Convention:

Arts 39–45, 47–49, 51, 54–58, 71–72, 75–76, 126–30; also some provisions of Schengen accession treaties

Notes: Arts 39(1), (2), and (3) and 46 were repealed by the *Framework Decision on exchange of data between law enforcement services ([2006] OJ L 386/89)*, Art 12(1); Art 47(4) was repealed by a 2003 Decision ([2003] OJ L 67/27); Art 40(1) and (7) were amended by a 2003 Decision ([2003] OJ L 260/47)

Arts 49(a), 52, 53, and 73 were repealed by the 2000 EU mutual assistance Convention, Art 2(2); Art 50 was repealed by Art 8(3) of the 2001 protocol to that Convention (see below); but note that a few Member States have not ratified the Convention or the Protocol (see Appendix I); a treaty between the EU, Norway, and Iceland extends the Convention and Protocol to those States, but there is no such treaty with Switzerland and Liechtenstein

Arts 48–53 on mutual assistance will be replaced by the Directive on the European Investigation Order from May 2017, to the (unclear) extent that they correspond to that Directive; however, the Directive does not apply to Denmark, Ireland, or the Schengen associates

Arts 59–60, 62–66 (extradition) were repealed by the Framework Decision on the European Arrest Warrant ([2002] OJ L 190/1), Art 31(1)(e), but might still apply in a few cases where the effect of the EAW is restricted, and to Schengen associates

Articles 67–69 were repealed by the Framework Decision on transfer of prisoners (OJ 2008 L 327/27), Art 26(1), but they still apply to Schengen associates

b) Schengen Executive Committee Decisions/Declarations/Central Group acts:

SCH/Com-ex (93) 10 - 14.12.1993—Confirmation of the declarations by the Ministers and Secretaries of State of 19 June 1992 and 30 June 1993 on bringing into force

SCH/Com-ex (93) 14 - 14.12.1993—Improving practical cooperation between the judicial authorities to combat drug trafficking

– *the Commission has proposed to repeal this measure (COM (2014) 714)*

SCH/Com-ex (94) 28 Rev - 22.12.1994—Certificate provided for in Article 75 for the transportation of drugs and/or psychotropic substances

SCH/Com-ex (97) 2 Rev 2 - 25.4.1997—Awarding the tender for the SIS II preliminary study

SCH/Com-ex (97) 6 Rev 2 - 24.6.1997—Schengen Manual on police cooperation in the field of public order and security

SCH/Com-ex (97) 29 Rev 2 - 7.10.1997—Bringing into force the Convention implementing the Schengen Agreement in Greece

SCH/Com-ex (98) 29 Rev - 23.6.1998—Catch-all clause to cover the whole technical Schengen *acquis*

SCH/Com-ex (98) 37 def 2 - 16.9.1998—Action plan to combat illegal immigration

SCH/Com-ex (98) 43 Rev - 16.12.1998—Ad hoc Committee for Greece
SCH/Com-ex (98) 49 Rev 3 - 16.12.1998—Bringing the Convention implementing the Schengen Agreement into force in Greece
SCH/Com-ex (98) 52 - 16.12.1998—Handbook on cross-border police cooperation

– the Commission has proposed to repeal this measure (COM (2014) 714)

SCH/Com-ex (99) 3 - 28.4.1999—Help Desk budget for 1999
SCH/Com-ex (99) 6 - 28.4.1999—Telecomms situation
SCH/Com-ex (99) 7 Rev 2 - 28.4.1999—Liaison officers

– the Commission has proposed to repeal this measure (COM (2014) 713)

SCH/Com-ex (99) 8 Rev 2 - 28.4.1999—Payments to informers
SCH/Com-ex (99) 10 - 28.4.1999—Illegal trade in weapons
SCH/Com-ex (99) 11 Rev 2 - 28.4.1999—Agreement on cooperation in proceedings for road traffic offences
SCH/Com-ex (96) Decl 6 - Rev 2 - 26.6.1996—Declaration on extradition
SCH/Com-ex (97) Decl 13 - Rev 2 - 21.4.1998—Abduction of minors

– the Commission has proposed to repeal this measure (COM (2014) 714)

SCH/C (98) 117 - 27.10.1998—Action plan to combat illegal immigration
SCH/C (99) 25 - 22.3.1999—General principles for the remuneration of informants and infiltrators
SCH/Com-ex (93)14 and (98) 52, the Declaration of the Executive Committee SCH/Com-ex (97) decl. 13 rev 2 and the Council Decision 2008/173/EC are repealed.

2) Maastricht era (1 Nov 2003 to 1 May 1999)

a) Joint Actions

1. Council Joint Action 94/795/JHA on crossing internal borders by organised school groups ([1994] OJ L 327/1)
2. Joint Action 98/700/JHA on European Imaging Archive System ([1998] OJ L 333/4)
3. Joint Action 96/277/JHA on exchange of liaison magistrates ([1996] OJ L 105/1)
4. Joint Action 96/750/JHA on drug trafficking ([1996] OJ L 342/6)

Note: the Commission has proposed to repeal this (COM (2014) 715)

5. Joint Action 98/427/JHA on good practice in mutual legal assistance ([1998] OJ L 191/1)

Note: the Commission has proposed to repeal this (COM (2014) 715)

6. Joint Action 98/699/JHA on money laundering and confiscation of proceeds ([1998] OJ L 333/1)

Note: Framework Decision of 2001 amended and supplemented this Joint Action in part (see below); Directive 2014/41 repeals it as from 4 Oct 2016

7. Joint Action 96/610/JHA on directory of specialist counter-terrorist expertise ([1996] OJ L 273/1)

Note: the Commission has proposed to repeal this (COM (2014) 715)

8. Joint Action 96/698/JHA on customs and business cooperation in drug trafficking ([1996] OJ L 322/3)
9. Joint Action 96/699/JHA on exchange of information on chemical profiling of drugs ([1996] OJ L 322/5)

Note: the Commission has proposed to repeal this (COM (2014) 715)

10. Joint Action 96/747/JHA on directory of expertise on international organised crime ([1996] OJ L 342/2)

Note: the Commission has proposed to repeal this (COM (2014) 715)

11. Joint Action 97/339/JHA on cooperation in law and order ([1997] OJ L 147/1)

Note: the Commission has proposed to repeal this (COM (2014) 715)

12. Joint Action 97/372/JHA on targeting criteria for police ([1997] OJ L 159/1)

Note: the Commission has proposed to repeal this (COM (2014) 715)

13. Joint Action 97/827/JHA on evaluation ([1997] OJ L 344/7)
14. Joint Action 98/429/JHA on collective evaluation of application of acquis by applicant states ([1998] OJ L 191/8)
15. Joint Action 96/658/JHA on US Helms-Burton legislation ([1996] OJ L 309/7)

b) Conventions

1. Convention on simplified extradition ([1995] OJ C 78/1)

Note: not in force; provisionally applied by some Member States (see Appendix I)

2. Convention on fraud against EC budget ([1995] OJ C 316/48)
2a. First Protocol to Convention on fraud against EC budget ([1996] OJ C 313/1)
2b. ECJ Protocol to Convention on fraud against EC budget ([1997] OJ C 151/1)
2c. Second Protocol to Convention on fraud against EC budget ([1997] OJ C 221/12)

Note: a proposed Directive would repeal all the fraud measures, although they would still apply in Ireland and Denmark

3. Convention on extradition ([1996] OJ C 313/11)

Note: not in force; provisionally applied by some Member States (see Appendix I)

4. Convention on corruption ([1997] OJ C 195/1)
5. Driving Disqualification Convention ([1998] OJ C 216/1)

Note: not in force; provisionally applied by some Member States (see Appendix I)

6. Naples II Convention ([1998] OJ C 24/1)

3) Treaty of Amsterdam era—Title VI
EU Police and Criminal Law

a) Common Positions

1. Combatting terrorism ([2001] OJ L 344/90)

Note: also a CFSP measure

2. Application of specific measures to combat terrorism ([2001] OJ L 344/93)

Note: amended since the entry into force of the Treaty of Lisbon ([2009] OJ L 346/58)

3. Common Position on transfer of data to Interpol ([2005] OJ L 27/61)

b) Decisions

1. Exchange of information on counterfeit travel documents ([2000] OJ L 81/1)
2. Combatting child pornography on the Internet ([2000] OJ L 138/1)
3. Decision 2000/586/JHA: Procedure for amending Articles 40(4) and (5), 41(7) and 65(2) of Schengen Convention ([2000] OJ L 248/1)
4. Decision 2000/641/JHA: Joint Secretariat for third pillar data protection authorities ([2000] OJ L 271/1)
5. Decision 2000/642 concerning Member States' Financial intelligence units (FIUs) ([2000] OJ L 271/4)
6. Decision 2001/419/JHA on the transmission of samples of controlled substances ([2001] OJ L 150/1)
7. Decision 2001/887/JHA on protection of the euro against counterfeiting ([2001] OJ L 329/1)
8. Decision establishing Eurojust ([2002] OJ L 63/1)

Note: a proposed Reg would repeal this Decision

9. Decision 2002/348/JHA concerning security in connection with football matches with an international dimension ([2002] OJ L 121/1)
10. Decision 2002/494 on exchange of information and contact points concerning genocide, crimes against humanity and war crimes ([2002] OJ L 167/1)
11. Decision on network for protection of public figures ([2002] OJ L 333/1)
12. Decision on evaluating Member States' implementation of international commitments regarding terrorism ([2002] OJ L 349/1)
13. Decision 2003/169 designating which provisions of the 1995 and 1996 EU extradition Conventions are related to the Schengen *acquis* ([2003] OJ L 76/25)
14. Decision 2003/170 on joint use of liaison officers ([2003] OJ L 67/27)
15. Decision 2003/335 on investigation and prosecution of genocide, crimes against humanity and war crimes ([2003] OJ L 118/12)
16. Decision extending Convention on corruption to Gibraltar ([2003] OJ L 226/27)

Note: this was not a legislative act, but a *sui generis* decision

17. Decision amending Eurojust decision ([2003] OJ L 245/44)

Note: a proposed Reg would repeal this Decision

18. Decision amending Article 40, Schengen Convention to permit extended cross-border police surveillance ([2003] OJL 260/37)
19. Decision on vehicle crime ([2004] OJ L 389/28)
20. Decision on synthetic drugs ([2005] OJ L 127/32)

Note: a proposed Reg would repeal this Decision

21. Decision designating Europol as the central office for counterfeiting the euro ([2005] OJ L 185/35)
22. Decision on exchange of information on terrorism ([2005] OJ L 253/22)
23. Decision on European police college ([2005] OJ L 256/63)

Note: the Decision was amended by Reg 543/2014, and then fully repealed by Reg 2015/2219

24. Decision amending 2003 Decision on police liaison officers ([2006] OJ L 219/31)
25. Decision establishing SIS II (Criminal law/policing aspects) ([2007] OJ L 205/63)
26. Decision amending Decision on football hooligans ([2007] OJ L 155/76)
27. Decision establishing an asset recovery network ([2007] OJ L 332/103)
28. Decision on cross-border intervention teams ([2008] OJ L 210/73)
29. Decision on cross-border police cooperation (Prum Treaty Decision) ([2008] OJ L 210/1)
30. Decision on cross-border police cooperation (Prum Treaty Decision) ([2008] OJ L 210/12)
31. Decision on law enforcement access to VIS ([2008] OJ L 218/129)
32. Decision establishing an anti-corruption network ([2008] OJ L 301/38)
33. Decision on migration from SIS to SIS II ([2008] OJ L 299/43)

Note: amended by Reg 542/2010 ([2010] OJ L 155/23) after the entry into force of the Treaty of Lisbon; the Commission has proposed to repeal this measure (COM (2014) 714)

39. Decision amending Decision establishing Eurojust ([2009] OJ L 138/14)

Note: a proposed Reg would repeal this Decision

40. Decision on the European Judicial Network ([2008] OJ L 348/130)
41. Decision implementing the Framework Decision on the exchange of criminal records ([2009] OJ L 93/33)
42. Decision establishing Europol ([2009] OJ L 121/37)

Note: a Reg agreed in Dec 2015 will repeal this Decision

43. Decision amending the Decision establishing a network for the protection of public figures ([2009] OJ L 283/62)
44. Decision on a crime prevention network ([2009] OJ L 321/44)

45. Decision on Customs Information System ([2009] OJ L 323/20)
46. Decision extending US/EU extradition treaty to Aruba, etc ([2009] OJ L 325/4)

Note: this is not a legislative act, but a *sui generis* decision

c) Framework Decisions

1. Criminal sanctions for counterfeiting the euro ([2000] OJ L 140/1)

- *Repealed by Directive 2014/62, as from 23 May 2016*

2. Framework Decision 2001/413/JHA on payment card fraud and counterfeiting ([2001] OJ L 149/1)
3. Framework Decision 2001/500 on money laundering, the identification, tracing, freezing, seizing and confiscation of instrumentalities and the proceeds from crime ([2001] OJ L 182/1)

- *Amended by Directive 2014/42, as from 4 Oct 2016*

4. Framework Decision 2001/888/JHA on criminal records for counterfeiting the euro
5. Framework Decision on terrorism ([2002] OJ L 164/3)

- *would be repealed by proposed Directive*

6. Framework Decision on European arrest warrant ([2002] OJ L 190/1)
7. Framework Decision on joint investigation teams ([2002] OJ L 162/1)
8. Framework Decision on the penal framework to prevent the facilitation of illegal entry and residence ([2002] OJ L 328/1)
9. Framework Decision on the execution of orders freezing assets and evidence ([2003] OJ L 196/45)

- *Repealed in part by Directive 2014/41, as from May 2017*

10. Framework Decision on corruption in private sector ([2003] OJ L 192/54)
11. Framework Decision on illicit drug trafficking ([2004] OJ L 335/8)
12. Framework Decision on mutual recognition of financial penalties ([2005] OJ L 76/16)
13. Framework Decision on confiscation ([2005] OJ L 68/49)

- *Amended by Directive 2014/42, as from 4 Oct 2016*

14. Framework Decision on the execution of confiscation orders ([2006] OJ L 328/59)
15. Framework decision on exchange of data between law enforcement services ([2006] OJ L 386/89)
16. Framework decision on taking account of prior convictions in another Member State ([2008] OJ L 220/32)
17. Framework Decision on organised crime ([2008] OJ L 300/42)
18. Framework Decision on the transfer of custodial sentences ([2008] OJ L 327/27)
19. Framework Decision on data protection in the sphere of criminal law and policing ([2008] OJ L 350/60)

- *will be repealed by Directive agreed in Dec 2015*

20. Framework Decision on mutual recognition of alternative sanctions and suspended sentences ([2008] OJ L 337/102)
21. Framework Decision on racism and xenophobia ([2008] OJ L 328/55)
22. Framework Decision amending the framework decision on terrorism ([2008] OJ L 330/21)

- *would be repealed by proposed Directive*

23. Framework Decision on European evidence warrant ([2008] OJ L 350/72)

- *Repealed (except in Denmark and Ireland) by Directive on European Investigation Order, from May 2017*

24. Framework decision on criminal record exchange ([2009] OJ L 93/23)
25. Framework Decision on 'in absentia' trials ([2009] OJ L 81/24)
26. Framework decision on mutual recognition of pre-trial supervision orders ([2009] OJ L 294/20)

27. Framework decision on conflicts of jurisdiction ([2009] OJ L 328/42)
28. Framework decision on accreditation of forensic laboratory activities ([2009] OJ L 322/14)

d) Conventions

1. Mutual assistance on criminal matters ([2000] OJ C 197/1)
2. Protocol to May 2000 Mutual Assistance Convention ([2001] OJ C 326/1)
– *Repealed (except in Denmark and Ireland) by Directive on European Investigation Order, from May 2017, to the extent that it corresponds to them*

4) International treaties

in force:
1. Schengen association agreement with Norway and Iceland ([1999] OJ L 176)
2. Schengen association agreement with Switzerland ([2008] OJ L 53)
3. Treaties with US on mutual assistance and extradition ([2003] OJ L 181/25)

Bibliography

Alegre S and Leaf M, *European Arrest Warrant: A Solution Ahead of its Time?* (Justice, 2003)

Bassiouni M, *International Criminal Law, Vol. I: Sources, Subjects and Contents*, 3rd edn (Martinus Nijhoff, 2008)

Blextoon R, ed., *Handbook on the European Arrest Warrant* (Asser, 2005)

Breyer P, 'Telecommunications Data Retention and Human Rights: The Compatibility of Blanket Traffic Data Retention with the ECHR' (2005) 11 ELJ 373

Bunyan T, ed., *Key Texts on Justice and Home Affairs in the European Union* (Russell Press, 1997)

Carrera S and Geyer F, *The Reform Treaty and Justice and Home Affairs: Implications for the Common Area of Freedom, Security and Justice* (CEPS Policy Brief No. 141, Aug 2007)

Curtin D, 'The Constitutional Structure of the Union: A Europe of Bits and Pieces' (1993) 30 CMLRev 17

Denza E, *The Intergovernmental Pillars of the European Union* (OUP, 2002)

Denza E, 'The 2000 Convention on Mutual Assistance in Criminal Matters' (2003) 40 CMLRev 1047

Dougan M, *National Remedies Before the Court of Justice: Issues of Harmonisation and Differentiation* (Hart, 2004)

Fawcett J, 'The Impact of Article 6(1) of the ECHR on Private International Law' (2007) 56 ICLQ 1

Gilbert G, 'Crimes *Sans Frontieres*: Jurisdictional Problems in English Law' (1992) 63 BYIL 415

Grief N, 'EU Law and Security' (2007) 32 ELRev 752

Guild E and Marin L, *Still Not Resolved? Constitutional Issues of the European Arrest Warrant* (Wolf, 2009)

Herlin-Karnell E, 'Commission v Council: Some Reflections on Criminal Law in the First Pillar' (2007) 13 EPL 69

Hetzer W, 'Fight Against Fraud and Protection of Fundamental Rights in the European Union' (2006) 14 IJCCLCJ 1:20

Keijzer N and van Sliedregt E, eds., *The European Arrest Warrant in Practice* (Asser, 2009)

Lenaerts K and Corthaut T, 'Of Birds and Hedges: The Role of Primacy in Invoking Norms of EU Law' (2006) 31 ELRev 287

Lenaerts K, Arts D, and Maselis I, *Procedural Law of the European Union*, 2nd edn (Thomson, 2006)

Loof R, 'Shooting from the Hip: Proposed Minimum Rights in Criminal Proceedings Throughout the EU' (2006) 12 ELJ 421

McClean D, *International Cooperation in Civil and Criminal Matters*, 2nd edn (OUP, 2002)

McMahon R, 'Maastricht's Third Pillar: Load-Bearing or Purely Decorative?' (1995) 22 LIEI 1:51

Mitsilegas V, 'The New EU-USA Cooperation on Extradition, Mutual Legal Assistance and the Exchange of Police Data' (2003) 8 EFARev 515

Mitsilegas V, 'Trust-Building Measures in the European Judicial Area in Criminal Matters: Issues of Competence, Legitimacy and Institutional Balance' in Balzacq T and Carrera S, eds., *Security versus Freedom? A Challenge for Europe's Future* (Ashgate, 2006), 282

Muller-Graff P, 'The Legal Bases of the Third Pillar and its Position in the Framework of the Union Treaty' (1994) 29 CMLRev 493

Peers S, 'EU Responses to Terrorism' (2003) 52 ICLQ 227

Peers S, 'Mutual Recognition and Criminal Law in the European Union: Has the Council Got it Wrong?' (2004) 41 CMLRev 5

Peers S, 'Governance and the Third Pillar: The Accountability of Europol' in Curtin D and Wessel R, eds., *Good Governance and the European Union* (Intersentia, 2005), 253

Peers S, 'Double Jeopardy and EU Law: Time for a Change?' (2006) 8 EJLR 199

Peers S, 'Salvation outside the Church? The Development of the EU's Third Pillar' (2007) 44 CMLRev 883 at 919–20

Peers S, 'The Community's Criminal Law Competence: The Plot Thickens' (2008) 33 ELRev 399

Peers S, 'EU Criminal Law and the Treaty of Lisbon' (2008) 33 ELRev 507 at 522–29

Peers S, 'Finally "Fit for Purpose?" The Treaty of Lisbon and the End of the Third Pillar Legal Order' (2008) 27 YEL 47

Peers S, 'Mission Accomplished? EU Justice and Home Affairs Law and the Treaty of Lisbon' (2011) 48 CMLRev 661

Rijken C, 'Legal and Technical Aspects of Cooperation Between Europol, Third States and Interpol' in Kronenberger V, ed., *The European Union and the International Legal Order: Discord or Harmony?* (Asser, 2001), 577

Sharpston E and Maria Fernandez-Martin J, 'Some Reflections on Schengen Free Movement Rights and the Principle of *Ne Bis in Idem*' (2007–08) 10 CYELS 413

Trechsel S and Summers S, *Human Rights in Criminal Proceedings* (OUP, 2005)

van Dijk P and van Hoof G, *Theory and Practice of the European Convention on Human Rights*, 4th edn (Intersentia, 2006)

Weyembergh A, 'La reconnaissance mutuelle des decisions judiciaires en matiere penale entre les Etats Membres de l'Union europeenne: mise en perspective' in de Kerchove G and Weyembergh A, eds., *La reconnaissance mutuelle des decisions judiciaires penales dans l'Union europeenne* (Institut d'Etudes Europeennes, 2001), 25–63

White S, 'Harmonisation of Criminal Law under the First Pillar' (2006) 31 ELRev 81

Wouters J and Naert F, 'Of Arrest Warrants, Terrorist Offences and Extradition Deals: An Appraisal of the EU's Main Criminal Law Measures Against Terrorism After "11 September"' (2004) 41 CMLRev 909

Index